Crime and Punishment
in America

This bibliography was conceived and compiled from the periodicals database of the American Bibliographical Center by editors at ABC-Clio Information Services.

Lance Klass and Susan Kinnell, project coordinators

Robert de V. Brunkow
Jeffery B. Serena

Pamela R. Byrne
Gail Schlachter

Crime and Punishment in America

a historical bibliography

ABC-Clio Information Services

Santa Barbara, California
Oxford, England

Library of Congress Cataloging in Publication Data
Main entry under title:

Crime and punishment in America: a historical bibliography.

Includes index.
1. Crime and criminals—United States—Bibliography.
2. Violent crimes—United States—Bibliography.
3. Political crimes and offenses—United States. 4. Criminal
justice, Administration of—United States. 5. Punishment—
United States. I. ABC-Clio Information Services.
Z5703.5.U5C7 1983 [HV6789] 016.364'973 83-12248
ISBN 0-87436-363-2

ABC-Clio Information Services
2040 Alameda Padre Serra, Box 4397
Santa Barbara, California 93103

Clio Press Ltd.
55 St. Thomas Street
Oxford 0X1 1JG, England

Cover design and graphics by Lance Klass
Printed and bound in the United States of America

ABC-CLIO RESEARCH GUIDES

The ABC-Clio Research Guides are a new generation of annotated bibliographies that provide comprehensive control of the recent journal literature on high-interest topics in history and related social sciences. These publications are created by editor/historians and other subject specialists who examine every article entry in ABC-Clio Information Services' vast history database and select abstracts of all citations published during the past decade that relate to the particular topic of study.

Each entry selected from this database—the largest history database in the world—has been reedited to ensure consistency in treatment and completeness of coverage. The extensive subject profile index (ABC-SPIndex) accompanying each volume has also been reassessed, specifically in terms of the particular subject presented, to allow precise and rapid access to the entries.

The titles in this series are prepared to save researchers, students, and librarians the considerable time and expense usually associated with accessing materials manually or through online searching. ABC-Clio's Research Guides offer unmatched access to significant scholarly articles on the topics of most current interest to historians and social scientists.

ABC-CLIO RESEARCH GUIDES

Gail Schlachter, Editor
Pamela R. Byrne, Executive Editor

1.
World War II from an American Perspective
1982   LC 82-22823   ISBN 0-87436-035-8

5.
Corporate America
1983   LC 83-11232   ISBN 0-87436-362-4

2.
The Jewish Experience in America
1982   LC 82-24480   ISBN 0-87436-034-x

6.
Crime and Punishment in America
1983   LC 83-12248   ISBN 0-87436-363-2

3.
Nuclear America
1983   LC 83-12227   ISBN 0-87436-360-8

7.
The Democratic and Republican Parties
1983   LC 83-12230   ISBN 0-87436-364-0

4.
The Great Depression
1983   LC 83-12234   ISBN 0-87436-361-6

8.
The American Electorate
1983   LC 83-12229   ISBN 0-87436-372-1

CONTENTS

LIST OF ABBREVIATIONS

A.	Author-prepared Abstract	*Illus.*	Illustrated, Illustration
Acad.	Academy, Academie, Academia	*Inst.*	Institute, Institut-.
Agric.	Agriculture, Agricultural	*Int.*	International, Internacional,
AIA	Abstracts in Anthropology		Internationaal, Internationaux,
Akad.	Akademie		Internazionale
Am.	America, American	*J.*	Journal, Journal-prepared Abstract
Ann.	Annals, Annales, Annual, Annali	*Lib.*	Library, Libraries
Anthrop.	Anthropology, Anthropological	*Mag.*	Magazine
Arch.	Archives	*Mus.*	Museum, Musee, Museo
Archaeol.	Archaeology, Archaeological	*Nac.*	Nacional
Art.	Article	*Natl.*	National, Nationale
Assoc.	Association, Associate	*Naz.*	Nazionale
Biblio.	Bibliography, Bibliographical	*Phil.*	Philosophy, Philosophical
Biog.	Biography, Biographical	*Photo.*	Photograph
Bol.	Boletim, Boletin	*Pol.*	Politics, Political, Politique, Politico
Bull.	Bulletin	*Pr.*	Press
c.	century (in index)	*Pres.*	President
ca.	circa	*Pro.*	Proceedings
Can.	Canada, Canadian, Canadien	*Publ.*	Publishing, Publication
Cent.	Century	*Q.*	Quarterly
Coll.	College	*Rev.*	Review, Revue, Revista, Revised
Com.	Committee	*Riv.*	Rivista
Comm.	Commission	*Res.*	Research
Comp.	Compiler	*RSA*	Romanian Scientific Abstracts
DAI	Dissertation Abstracts International	*S.*	Staff-prepared Abstract
		Sci.	Science, Scientific
Dept.	Department	*Secy.*	Secretary
Dir.	Director, Direktor	*Soc.*	Society, Societe, Sociedad,
Econ.	Economy, Econom-.		Societa
Ed.	Editor, Edition	*Sociol.*	Sociology, Sociological
Educ.	Education, Educational	*Tr.*	Transactions
Geneal.	Genealogy, Genealogical, Genealogique	*Transl.*	Translator, Translation
		U.	University, Universi-.
Grad.	Graduate	*US*	United States
Hist.	History, Hist-.	*Vol.*	Volume
IHE	Indice Historico Espanol	*Y.*	Yearbook

INTRODUCTION

Few issues in American history have been so chronically troublesome, or so often subject to acrimonious debate, as the problem of crime. Although often treated as an essentially modern problem, crime in America is deeply imbedded in the country's social history. "Virtually every generation since the founding of the Nation and before," stated the Katzenbach Commission in 1966, "has felt itself threatened by the spectre of rising crime and violence."

The salience of crime as a political and social issue has given rise to an extraordinarily important body of modern scholarship that seeks to understand crime by examining its historical context. The explanatory power of this approach derives from its social-historical perspective; its political power derives from its increasing influence on public policy.

Crime and Punishment in America: A Historical Bibliography is designed to provide immediate and thorough access to the modern scholarship on crime and criminal justice in American history. It is a compendium of 1,396 abstracts of articles on crime in America published during 1973-82. The abstracts are drawn from the database of ABC-Clio Information Services—the largest history database in the world—which includes abstracts of articles from over 2,000 journals in 42 languages, published in 90 countries.

Access to the abstracts in this volume is provided by ABC-SPIndex, one of the most advanced and comprehensive indexing systems in the world. ABC-SPIndex links together the key subject terms and the chronology of each abstract to form a composite index entry that furnishes a complete subject profile of the journal article. Each set of index terms is rotated so that the complete profile appears in the index under every subject term. In this way, the number of access points is increased severalfold over conventional hierarchical indexes, and irrelevant works can be eliminated early in the search process.

Access to the abstracts is further enhanced by the organization of the bibliography into eight chapters. Each of these chapters focuses on a particular aspect of crime or criminal justice. Scholars concerned with specific issues or topics, such as the capital punishment debate, prison reform, or urban riots, can turn immediately to the relevant chapter to gain a broad insight into the scope, thrust, and basic issues of modern scholarship on these subjects.

Chapter 1, "Crime and Criminality in American Life," encompasses abstracts of both general articles on crime and articles on criminal organizations. Each of the following five chapters focuses on a particular kind of criminal activity. Chapter 2 comprises scholarship on crimes of violence; Chapter 3, crimes against property;

Chapter 4, riots, public disturbances, and civil disobedience; Chapter 5, political crimes and corruption; and Chapter 6, "victimless" crimes such as gambling, prostitution, and narcotics use. Chapter 7, "Law Enforcement, Criminal Law, and the Courts," focuses on the criminal justice system's role in the maintenance of order and the establishment of guilt. "Punishment, Rehabilitation, and the Prisons," the final chapter, includes studies of penal institutions and reform, the death penalty, punishments as rehabilitation or retribution, and the history of internment and prisoner-of-war camps in the United States.

The article abstracts were selected by the editors, who examined every abstract in the database for 1973-82. This careful selection process has provided very thorough coverage of the modern periodical literature on crime and justice in America. The result far exceeds in breadth of coverage what is obtainable through an online search of the database or even through an extensive manual search using the database's subject index. Great care has been taken to ensure consistency and clarity in the index terms. In addition, cross-references have been added to the subject index to facilitate rapid and accurate searching. These editorial labors have produced a bibliography that combines readability, easy accessibility, and thorough coverage of the modern scholarship on a complex and controversial aspect of American life.

1

CRIME AND CRIMINALITY
IN AMERICAN LIFE

1. Abbey, Sue Wilson. THE KU KLUX KLAN IN ARIZONA, 1921-1925. *J. of Arizona Hist. 1973 14(1): 10-30.* Established in Phoenix and Tucson in 1921, the Ku Klux Klan soon spread to smaller towns and the rural and mining areas. It campaigned for better law enforcement through prohibition and the closing of brothels and gambling halls. The Klan, alarmed at the growth of the Mexican American population and the spread of Catholicism, preached the return to "higher" moral standards and the doctrine of white supremacy. Defeated in the November 1924 elections, the Klan became a victim of its own intolerance when its violence and excesses were widely publicized. 2 illus., 86 notes.
D. L. Smith

2. Abbott, Edith. THE CIVIL WAR AND THE CRIME WAVE OF 1865-70. *Social Service Rev. 1977 51(1): 71-93.* Describes the effects of the American Civil War on the occurrence of crime during 1865-70.

3. Adams, Paul K. JAMES P. WICKERSHAM ON EDUCATION AND CRIME IN NINETEENTH-CENTURY PENNSYLVANIA. *Pennsylvania Mag. of Hist. and Biog. 1980 104(4): 422-433.* In his work on behalf of neglected children, in his writings, and in his legislative lobbying, School Superintendent James P. Wickersham revealed his faith in intellectual and moral education in the deterrence of crime. Covers ca. 1866-81. Based on official reports and secondary sources; 107 notes.
T. H. Wendel

4. Adler, Joyce. MELVILLE'S *BENITO CERENO*: SLAVERY AND VIO-LENCE IN THE AMERICAS. *Sci. and Soc. 1974 38(1): 19-48.*

5. Akins, Carl. POLITICAL ISSUES IN LABELLING: CRIMINALIZA-TION AND DECRIMINALIZATION. *Policy Studies J. 1974 3(1): 12-18.*

6. Alexander, Yonah. TERRORISM, THE MEDIA AND THE POLICE. *J. of Int. Affairs 1978 32(1): 101-113.* The communications purposes which revolutionary terror groups seek through the media are attention, recognition, and legitimacy; the law enforcement agencies, which now lack the legal authority and practical ability to control coverage of terrorist activities, in general look upon the media as a powerful force which should somehow be restrained, so that these aims of the terror groups could not be achieved. 43 notes.
V. Samaraweera

7.   Ashdown, Paul G.   WTVJ'S MIAMI CRIME WAR: A TELEVISION CRUSADE.   *Florida Hist. Q. 1980 58(4): 427-437.* Ralph Renick broadcast 65 consecutive weekday editorials against organized crime in Dade County in 1966. This was the first television editorial crusade in the nation and indicates that television could have impact through editorials. 55 notes.   N. A. Kuntz

8.   Atkins, Burton M. and Green, Justin J.   CONSENSUS ON THE UNITED STATES COURTS OF APPEALS: ILLUSION OR REALITY?   *Am. J. of Pol. Sci. 1976 20(4): 735-748.* Despite major advances in the study of judicial behavior, one problem that still affects much research concerns the dependence upon the nonunanimous decision as the unit of analysis, and the resultant effect of this upon the inferences drawn from such studies. Often, the expression of conflict on collegial courts is dependent upon the decisionmaking rules used. One such example is the United States Courts of Appeals. The dissent rate on these courts is approximately six percent. By utilizing research strategies that gear themselves to the manner in which dissensus is manifested on these courts, it is possible to tap the mine of data represented by the other ninety-four percent. Focusing on criminal appeals, this study examines dissensus that exists in unanimous decisions but which is usually masked by the three-member rotating panel system.   J

9.   Barnett, Harold.   THE POLITICAL ECONOMY OF RAPE AND PROSTITUTION.   *Rev. of Radical Pol. Econ. 1976 8(1): 59-68.* Social and legal precedents concerning rape and prostitution reinforce attitudes toward women as property of men.

10.   Bartel, Ann P.   WOMEN AND CRIME: AN ECONOMIC ANALYSIS. *Econ. Inquiry 1979 17(1): 29-51.* Examines women's employment and marriage status and presents a model to analyze why female crime in the United States rose during 1960-74.

11.   Bassiouni, M. Cherif.   MEDIA COVERAGE OF TERRORISM: THE LAW AND THE PUBLIC.   *J. of Communication 1982 32(2): 128-143.* Because media coverage of events often interrupts or impedes law enforcement-terrorist negotiations, and because media can exacerbate problems with crowd control, conflicts between the two groups arise; suggests measures that might control media coverage of terrorist activities in spite of government protection of free speech; 1968-78.

12.   Bazelon, David L.   CRIMINALS ARE THE FINAL RESULT OF "OUR FAILING SOCIAL JUSTICE SYSTEM."   *Center Mag. 1977 10(4): 28-32.* Discusses alternatives to rehabilitation for dealing with crime.

13.   Belknap, Michal R.   PICKING "STRANGE FRUIT."   *Rev. in Am. Hist. 1981 9(2): 239-243.* Review essay of Robert L. Zangrando's *The NAACP Crusade Against Lynching, 1909-1950* (1980).

14.   Benson, H. W.   GROWTH OF REFORM AMONG THE TEAMSTERS. *Dissent 1979 26(2): 153-157.* Describes two reform groups that have recently arisen in the Teamsters Union to fight against corruption within the Union, and gives examples from several books published in the 1970's on the Teamsters.

15. Berk, Richard A.; Lenihan, Kenneth J.; and Rossi, Peter H. CRIME AND POVERTY: SOME EXPERIMENTAL EVIDENCE FROM EX-OFFENDERS. *Am. Sociol. Rev. 1980 45(5): 766-786.* Building on perspectives from sociology, criminology, and economics, this article reports findings from a randomized experiment undertaken with over 2,000 ex-offenders in the states of Texas and Georgia in which unemployment benefits were extended to individuals immediately upon release from prison. The analysis focuses on the endogenous relationships (over a one-year follow-up period) between these "transfer payments," unemployment, arrests for property and nonproperty crimes, and the resulting time spent in jail or prison. By and large, the hypotheses derived from a priori theory are supported by the data.   J

16. Best, Joel. KEEPING THE PEACE IN ST. PAUL: CRIME, VICE, AND POLICE WORK, 1869-1874. *Minnesota Hist. 1981 47(6):. 240-248.* Unlike some growing eastern cities during the 1870's, the policing of the burgeoning St. Paul was mostly a matter of combating simple disruptions of the peace, prostitution, and gambling. Despite limited resources, the police managed to preserve order. Despite occasional complaints, they walked a middle ground between eradication and regulation of prostitution. They paid less attention to gambling. Most arrests were of the young, unmarried males for being drunk or disorderly; immigrants and blacks were arrested more often. 25 notes, 6 illus., table.   C. M. Hough

17. Betten, Neil. NATIVISM AND THE KLAN IN TOWN AND CITY: VALPARAISO AND GARY, INDIANA. *Studies in Hist. and Soc. 1973 4(2): 3-16.* A study of the Ku Klux Klan during the 1920's in two urban centers. Indicates that "The Klan grew in Gary and Valparaiso by fashioning its appeal to the concerns of its white Protestant citizens . . ." and focused on such "myriad enemies" as corrupt politicians, bootleggers, prostitutes, imagined radicals, and immigrants who would not or could not instantly assimilate.   J. O. Baylen

18. Billi, Mirella. QUEL DOPPIO GIOCO DI DASHIELL HAMMETT [Dashiell Hammett's double game]. *Ponte [Italy] 1981 37(7-8): 710-716.* It is almost impossible to classify Hammett's work or the man, who was a workman, private investigator, author of police novels and screen plays, bohemian, Hollywood luminary, and political suspect.

19. Binder, Arnold and Geis, Gilbert. EDITORS' INTRODUCTION. *Am. Behavioral Scientist 1979 22(6): 613-620.* Outlines the development of the study of criminology in the United States to introduce a special issue on progress and prospects of US criminal justice.

20. Blake, Nelson Manfred. WAS NAT TURNER RIGHT? VIOLENCE IN AMERICAN HISTORY. Hague, John A., ed. *American Character and Culture in a Changing World: Some Twentieth-Century Perspectives* (Westport, Conn.: Greenwood Pr., 1979): 185-195. Violence is a perennial theme of physical and literary life in America. Anarchists and political activists, not only impatient but pessimistic about passive resistance and orderly protest, underestimate human rights claims based on the Declaration of Independence. Such claims have respectability and credibility in American society; courts, for example, respect legal arguments. Nat Turner's hanging in 1831 dubiously served the cause of

black slaves. Neither political assassination nor police brutality deserves heroic status. 19 notes, biblio.   P. M. Cohen

21. Bodenhamer, David J.   LAW AND DISORDER ON THE EARLY FRONTIER: MARION COUNTY, INDIANA, 1823-1850. *Western Hist. Q. 1979 10(3): 323-336.* Disputes the close identification between the American frontier environment and the strain of violence which runs through the nation's history. Among other things, scholars have neglected to examine the best evidence of criminal activity—local court records—to measure crime and to analyze community response to disorder. The environment of frontier Marion County, also seat of Indiana's capital, did not invite violence. Although the public feared a rising crime rate, Marion County was part of "a remarkably peaceful frontier." 3 tables, 3 graphs, 38 notes.   D. L. Smith

22. Boland, Barbara and Wilson, James Q.   AGE, CRIME, AND PUNISHMENT. *Public Interest 1978 (51): 22-34.* The best evidence now available indicates that juvenile offenders commit a far larger proportion of serious crimes than was previously realized. The rate at which juveniles commit these crimes decreases as they get older, but the chances of their being arrested, convicted, and incarcerated are higher when they are older and less active. Youthful criminals are less likely to be punished than older ones because of the different values accorded by judges to retribution and because of missing or incomplete prior arrest records. The two-track justice system—one for juveniles, one for adults—is weak in both fairness and crime control. It deals the heaviest punishment to offenders at the end of their careers when their criminal activities are decreasing rather than earlier when it is rising. Consequently, adult prisoners find the criminal justice system unjust, while young offenders find it irrelevant. Significant punishment must be dealt to all offenders, especially young ones who commit serious crimes. Perhaps there should be a two-track system, but it should be defined by the nature of the crime rather than by the age of the criminal. 2 tables.   S. Harrow

23. Bowker, Lee H.   THE INCIDENCE OF FEMALE CRIME AND DELINQUENCY: A COMPARISON OF OFFICIAL AND SELF-REPORT STATISTICS. *Int. J. of Women's Studies [Canada] 1978 1(2): 178-192.* A comparison of statistics from the FBI Uniform Crime Report with social science studies since 1972 indicates that there has been a rise in female property crimes and delinquency, but that female violent crimes have remained steady.

24. Braithwaite, John.   *THE MYTH OF SOCIAL CLASS AND CRIMINALITY* RECONSIDERED. *Am. Sociol. Rev. 1981 46(1): 36-57.* Class is one of the few correlates of criminality which can be taken, on balance, as persuasively supported by a large body of empirical evidence. Self-report studies, however, fail to provide consistent support for a class-crime relationship. Yet even here more studies show significant class differences than would be expected on the basis of chance. Studies of official records consistently show notable class differences in criminality. A considerable literature has failed to demonstrate widespread class biases in official records, but neglected evidence suggests that self-reports exaggerate the proportion of delinquency committed by the middle class.   J/S

25. Brede, Richard M. COMPLAINANTS AND KIDS: THE ROLE OF CITIZEN COMPLAINANTS IN THE SOCIAL PRODUCTION OF JUVENILE CASES. Hawes, Joseph M., ed. *Law and Order in American History* (Port Washington, N.Y.: Kennikat Pr., 1979): 77-100. Using data collected over an 18-month period by the Policing of Juveniles Project in three of Chicago's 21 police districts, discusses citizen complaints involving juveniles, specifically, "Who are the complainants in juvenile cases; what conditions, acts or incidents do they report to the police; and what legally substantive or moral interests of complainants are served by the police when they take a juvenile into custody"; 1968-69.

26. Britt, David W. and Tittle, Charles R. CRIME RATES AND POLICE BEHAVIOR—A TEST OF TWO HYPOTHESES. *Social Forces 1975 54(2): 441-451.* Two hypotheses concerning the relationship between arrest rates for major and minor offenses are tested using 1971 and 1972 arrest data from Florida municipalities. The results of a regression analysis using lagged variables in a system of difference equations support a dragnet interpretation of police behavior and discount a displacement hypothesis. The data further suggest that the relationship between arrest rates for major and minor offenses achieves stability over time.   J

27. Brooks, James. COMPENSATING VICTIMS OF CRIME: THE RECOMMENDATIONS OF PROGRAM ADMINISTRATORS. *Law & Soc. R. 1973 7(3): 445-472.* Senators Mike Mansfield and John McClellan have introduced national legislation for crime compensation programs in both houses of Congress, but only the Senate has taken action. A few states with such programs offer guidelines for future national legislation. Among the recommendations are a crime compensation board with a permanent staff, quick reporting of crimes, and established compensation procedures.   H. R. Mahood

28. Brown, Marilyn A. MODELLING THE SPATIAL DISTRIBUTION OF SUBURBAN CRIME. *Econ. Geog. 1982 58(3): 247-261.* Describes the spatial distribution of crime among Chicago's 126 suburbs, using information gathered between 1969 and 1973; shows how suburban crime has increased steadily.

29. Brun-Rovet, Jeanine. "MAFIA OR NOT MAFIA?": NEW YORK ET SES GANGSTERS ["Mafia or not Mafia?": New York and its gangsters]. *Histoire [France] 1981 (39): 80-82.* Analyzes organized crime in the United States, and more specifically in New York, suggesting that most views of the power of the Mafia have been exaggerated and need clarification; focuses on the involvement of ethnic groups other than Italian Americans in corruption and organized crime. French.

30. Bryant, Pat. JUSTICE VS. THE MOVEMENT. *Radical Am. 1980 14(6): 7-22.* Events after the November 1979 Klan shooting of Communist Workers Party members in Greensboro, North Carolina, bring the work of the federal government's Community Relations Service into question. From its founding in 1964 to 1966 (when transferred from the Commerce to the Justice Department) it served its legislated purpose to assist the civil rights movement. Since then, and increasingly in the 1970's, it has played a role akin to intelligence collection for

the FBI and divided and distracted the local and national civil rights groups from concerted action in communities throughout the nation. Based primarily on interviews in communities like Greensboro and with Community Relations Service representatives; 5 illus. C. M. Hough

31. Buckwalter, Doyle W. THE AMERICAN DILEMMA. *Social Studies 1973 64(1): 3-10.* America is now facing one of the greatest dilemmas since the Civil War because of crime, poverty, race relations, pollution, and resource abuse. America needs to reexamine the nature of democracy and to reassert democratic principles to ever-changing societal conditions. 4 notes. L. R. Raife

32. Burris, Carol. THE WOMAN'S LOBBY. *Public Welfare 1978 36(1): 28-31.* The Woman's Lobby in Washington, D.C., is pursuing national health insurance, pregnancy disability, divorced spouses' civil service pensions, full employment, jobs for displaced homemakers, permanent part-time employment, tax reform, Social Security, welfare reform, and help for battered wives and for rape victims.

33. Burrows, Jack. JOHN RINGO: THE STORY OF A WESTERN MYTH. *Montana 1980 30(4): 2-15.* Gunfighter John Ringo (1850-82) had an outlaw career in Texas and Arizona which has been the subject of much study, but which has produced much myth. His relationships with Doc Holliday and Wyatt Earp and his reputation as a killer have been exaggerated. It is probable that he did not kill a single man. He committed suicide near Tombstone, Arizona, and is buried on the spot. Based on secondary works and contemporary newspapers; 5 illus., 69 notes. R. C. Myers

34. Cadbury, Henry J. THE KING'S MISSIVE. *Quaker Hist. 1974 63(2): 117-123.* Reproduces Charles I's 9 September 1661 mandamus to stop corporal punishment and execution of "vagabond Quakers" in Massachusetts Bay Colony. Also reproduces Samuel Shattuck's letter reporting its delivery and reception. Discusses the May 1661 law by which four were hanged and some 30 jailed, evidence of compliance with the King's order, and the master whose ship brought the letter. 6 notes. T. D. S. Bassett

35. Caldeira, Greg A. and Cowart, Andrew T. BUDGETS, INSTITUTIONS, AND CHANGE: CRIMINAL JUSTICE POLICY IN AMERICA. *Am. J. of Pol. Sci. 1980 24(3): 413-438.* This paper assesses the budgetary responsiveness of American governmental and political institutions to the growth of crime over the last four decades. Several linear decision models are developed which posit that changes in budgetary requests and appropriations for seven criminal justice agencies are functions of changes in the level of criminal activity and of partisan control of the presidency. Tests of these decision models confirm a substantial degree of budgetary responsiveness to growth in the observed crime rate. A significant degree of that responsiveness occurs at the request-formulation stage. While in the short run Congress has actually treated the proposed budgets of the more responsive agencies more severely, it has nonetheless allowed appropriations for criminal justice agencies to grow over the long run in a pattern quite consistent with changes in the crime rate. Virtually all of that responsiveness has occurred, however, under Republican presidents. The statistical performance of the models is quite good—with, typically, over half of the variance accounted for,

statistically significant longitudinal regression coefficients, and trivial levels of serial correlation. J

36. Capeci, Dominic J. AL CAPONE: SYMBOL OF A BALLYHOO SOCIETY. *J. of Ethnic Studies 1975 2(4): 33-46.* In the late 1920's Al Capone, the "King of the gangsters, . . . Dictator of Chicago's underworld," was a folk hero and symbol for a multitude of Americans. His "public image was purified," just as those of Western heroes, to make it "acceptable to societal values . . . allowing many to identify with it." His image, bolstered by many sympathetic journalists and some writers, projected power, wealth, and infallibility, interwoven with the prestige these produced. Capone was seen to be an Horatio Alger protagonist, a defender of 100% American ideals, a family man, a philanthropist. Editorialists viewed him as a product of circumstances, an effect of prohibition, an historic necessity of sorts; thus the public could rationalize its own violations of the Volstead Law. Finally, his exciting and dangerous life-style became the "surrogate self for thousands . . . providing the change and excitement they desired but were unable to achieve themselves." As Lindbergh was the actualization of the "spirit of America," so too, in a different vein, was Capone. Based on primary and secondary sources; 90 notes. G. J. Bobango

37. Cary, Lorin Lee. THE BUREAU OF INVESTIGATION AND RADICALISM IN TOLEDO, OHIO: 1918-1920. *Labor Hist. 1980 21(3): 430-440.* A series of US Bureau of Investigation reports on the activities of the Industrial Workers of the World and other radical groups in Toledo, Ohio, between 1918-20, illustrates the importance of the Bureau's files for future studies of early 20th-century radicalism in Toledo and elsewhere. 14 notes. L. F. Velicer

38. Cawelti, John G. MYTHS OF VIOLENCE IN AMERICAN POPULAR CULTURE. *Critical Inquiry 1975 1(3): 521-541.* Public concern about the portrayal of violence in the mass media has been cyclical. Agitation usually peaks during social upheaval and then gradually subsides. American culture since the end of the 17th century has reflected a large public demand for violence, but the fundamental belief in America's role as a harbinger of peace has persisted. The paradox is largely explained by the American belief in the moral necessity of violence. This theme is explored with special reference to the western, the detective story, the gangster saga, and the police melodrama. American stories of violence justify the culminating acts of violence by emphasizing one or more of the following myths: crime does not pay, the vigilante, equality through violence, the hard-boiled hero and his code, and regeneration through violence. Secondary sources; 25 notes. R. G. Neville

39. Chadwick, Bruce; Strauss, Joseph; Bahr, Howard M.; and Halverson, Lowell K. CONFRONTATION WITH THE LAW: THE CASE OF THE AMERICAN INDIANS IN SEATTLE. *Phylon 1976 37(2): 163-171.* A serious adjustment for American Indians migrating to cities is learning how to conform to metropolitan legal norms. For the nation as a whole Indians are arrested at a rate three times higher than blacks and 10 times higher than whites. Few Indian migrants "have the sophistication to obtain assistance from helping agencies." Proposes "an intensive informational campaign designed to acquaint the urban Indian population with the existing opportunities for legal assistance." Based on a survey of Indians in Seattle; 4 tables, 6 notes. E. P. Stickney

40.   Chalmers, David.   RULE BY TERROR.   *Am. Hist. Illus. 1980 14(9): 8-9, 44-48, (10): 28-37.* Part I. Traces the history of the Ku Klux Klan from its formation in 1868 by a group of ex-Confederate soldiers in Pulaski, Tennessee, who named their social club after the Greek kyklos, meaning circle, until 1880. Part II. Conclusion discussing the revival of the Ku Klux Klan from the release of D. W. Griffith's film, *The Birth of a Nation* in 1915 to the 1920's.

41.   Chambliss, William J.   THE BUSINESS OF CRIME.   *Working Papers for a New Soc. 1978 6(5): 59-67.* Examines organized crime in Seattle, Washington, 1960-78.

42.   Clemente, Frank and Kleiman, Michael B.   FEAR OF CRIME IN THE UNITED STATES: A MULTIVARIATE ANALYSIS.   *Social Forces 1977 56(2): 519-531.* Fear of crime in the United States has become a problem as serious as crime itself. Many commentators have pointed out that fear is greatly out of proportion to the objective probability of being victimized. But to date, few multivariate analyses of fear of crime have been undertaken. The present research moves in this direction by combining and analyzing two national samples from 1973 and 1974 in regard to fear *(n = 2,700).* We employed five variables central to the victimization literature—sex, race, age, socioeconomic status, and community size. Multivariate Nominal Scale Analysis (MNA) was employed to assess the independent ability of each variable to predict respondents who indicated a fear of crime (42%) and those who did not (58%). Findings indicated that sex and city size are strong predictors of fear. Age and race were somewhat less important than has generally been supposed and the socioeconomic variables, income and education, had small effects. Merely on the basis of this system of explanatory variables, however, it was possible to classify correctly almost 72 percent of the entire sample in regard to fear. Implications of this high explanatory power as well as limitations of the analysis are presented and discussed.
J

43.   Cohen, Lawrence E.; Felson, Marcus; and Land, Kenneth C.   PROPERTY CRIME RATES IN THE UNITED STATES: A MACRODYNAMIC ANALYSIS, 1947-1977; WITH EX ANTE FORECASTS FOR THE MID-1980S.   *Am. J. of Sociol. 1980 86(1): 90-118.* Trends in robbery, burglary, and automobile theft, 1947-77, adjusted regionally for population density, age structure, unemployment rate, total consumer expenditures and automobiles per capita, indicate that decrease in population in areas that are normally sites of primary groups leads to increase in crime.

44.   Cohen, Shari.   A COMPARISON OF CRIME COVERAGE IN DETROIT AND ATLANTA NEWSPAPERS.   *Journalism Q. 1975 52(4): 726-730.* Compares the crime coverage of Detroit and Atlanta newspapers to determine if such coverage is a factor in Detroit's poor image. Atlanta newspapers devoted more coverage to crime in proportion to the incidence of crime, and gave crime articles more prominent coverage. However, Detroit newspapers used banner headlines and more photographs and specific details. Such coverage is not the only reason for Detroit's negative image. The study was done by the organization New Detroit; it was based on content analysis of the major newspapers in Detroit and Atlanta for a two-week period. Based on primary sources; table, 5 notes.
K. J. Puffer

45. Coleman, Evans. THE JURY STRIKE OF SOLOMONVILLE. *J. of Arizona Hist. 1975 16(4): 323-334.* Discusses the events of the murder trial of Otis McIntosh in 1902 in Solomonville, Arizona; though McIntosh was clearly guilty, he was acquitted by a jury of his friends, aided by the fallacious report of a smallpox epidemic in the jail which forced early adjournment of the case. Edited from notes of Evans Coleman (1874-1954). 2 photos.

46. Coleman, Evans. NESTERS, RUSTLERS AND OUTLAWS. *J. of Arizona Hist. 1973 14(3): 177-184.* Anecdotes of "nesters" who stole Mormon cattle and sold the beef, a fatal shootout over a horse race, a gang raid on the county treasury, and a gun fight over a poker game prize cow. From an essay by the author on desperadoes in Arizona in the 1880's and 1890's. 2 illus.
D. L. Smith

47. Cook, Fay Lomax and Cook, Thomas D.. EVALUATING THE RHETORIC OF CRISIS: A CASE STUDY OF CRIMINAL VICTIMIZATION OF THE ELDERLY. *Social Service Rev. 1976 50(4): 632-646.* Claims that victimization of the elderly has reached crisis proportions are exaggerated rhetoric for the purpose of mobilizing public attention; the real victimization of the aged is a problem of fear rather than of actual street crime.

48. Cook, Thomas J. and Scioli, Frank P., Jr. PUBLIC PARTICIPATION IN THE CRIMINAL JUSTICE SYSTEM: VOLUNTEERS IN POLICE, COURTS, AND CORRECTIONAL AGENCIES. *Policy Studies J. 1974 3(1): 44-48.*

49. Corman, Hope. CRIMINAL DETERRENCE IN NEW YORK: THE RELATIONSHIP BETWEEN COURT ACTIVITIES AND CRIME. *Econ. Inquiry 1981 19(3): 476-487.* Provides new evidence on the deterrent effects of criminal justice sanctions, using 1970 cross-sectional data for the 62 counties in New York State, including the length of time needed to dispose of a case and the severity of conviction charge as well as the expected prison sentence.

51. Croyle, James L. THE CRIMINAL JUSTICE SYSTEM IN AMERI-CAN CITIES. *Urban Affairs Q. 1977 12(4): 545-554.* Criminal justice research has been influenced by the cost effective, deterrent Crime Control Model and the expensive civil liberties oriented Due Process Model. Isaac D. Balbus' book *The Dialectics of Legal Repression: Black Rebels Before the American Criminal Courts,* (Russell Sage Foundation, 1973) argues that while the formal neutrality of due process enables the strong to oppress the weak, it can thwart crime control. Martin A. Levin's *Urban Politics and the Criminal Courts* (Chicago: Univ. of Chicago Pr., 1977) argues that pre-judicial careers determine sentencing behavior. The political regime indirectly influences sentencing behavior by judicial selection. James Eisenstein and Herbert Jacob, in *Felony Justice: An Organizational Analysis of Criminal Courts* (Boston: Little, Brown, 1977), argue that

sentencing variation is determined by working group cohesion and stability in the court system. Lynn M. Mather's book, *Plea Bargaining or Trial: The Dynamics of Criminal Case Disposition* (Lexington, Mass.: Lexington Books, 1977), concludes that the disposition of cases is significantly influenced by the substantive effects of conviction. It also identifies the defendant as an independent actor in the disposition of cases. Secondary sources; biblio.   L. N. Beecher

52.   Crump, Nancy Carter.   HOPEWELL DURING WORLD WAR I: "THE TOUGHEST TOWN NORTH OF HELL."   *Virginia Cavalcade 1981 31(1): 38-47.* The boomtown of Hopewell from 1915, when a new Du Pont powder plant provided jobs for 20,000 workers, to Armistice Day in 1918 was characterized by lawlessness, crowded living conditions, an inept police department, prostitution, and corruption.

53.   Culley, Margaret.   DOROTHY DIX: THE THIRTEENTH JUROR. *Int. J. of Women's Studies [Canada] 1979 2(4): 349-357.* Traces the career of Dorothy Dix (Elizabeth Gilmer, 1870-1951), a crime reporter for the New York *Journal;* although best known for her syndicated advice column, she first gained fame reporting on crimes involving women, 1901-16.

54.   Darley, Roger G.   LAW, DISCIPLINE, AND JUSTICE.   *US Naval Inst. Pro. 1973 99(9): 36-45.* While the American military justice system works well as a system of criminal justice, it has serious problems as a system of discipline because of limits placed on the power of commanders to punish unacceptable behavior. Many of these problems can be resolved, however, if commanders impose military discipline through corrective measures used in conjunction with or instead of punishment. 2 illus.   J. K. Ohl

55.   Davis, John A.   BLACKS, CRIME, AND AMERICAN CULTURE. *Ann. of the Am. Acad. of Pol. and Social Sci. 1976 (423): 89-98.* Attempts to understand crime patterns among blacks in the United States have systematically failed to consider the impact of slavery and resultant racist policies on black self-esteem. This paper explores the thesis that cultural domination was fundamentally more damaging than economic domination to black self-esteem. The ruthless attacks on blacks and black culture, usually justified by legal interpretations by whites, destroyed their faith that justice could be secured in this society. Data is presented which indicates that social inequalities have been perpetuated under the law and blacks were aware of this. Indeed, the law appears as a major instrument of racial oppression and, historically, many blacks have resisted oppression through illegal acts. Economic oppression of blacks *under the law* and their resistance created the condition in which the connection between crime and punishment lost the power to constrain antisocial acts. Blacks often secretly admired resistance, particularly those who felt oppressed, while whites developed extreme paranoia that blacks were out to take their lives and property. The euphemism "crime in the streets" is the perpetuation of this paranoia. The records show that blacks mainly victimize blacks. Chances are far greater for a white to be victimized by another white than by a black. The predominant crime pattern among blacks is against property, and the rate is not significantly higher

than for whites. In crime against persons, black rates are higher than white rates.

J

56.   Decker, Raymond G.   THE SECULARIZATION OF ANGLO-AMERI-
CAN LAW, 1800-1970.   *Thought 1974 49(194): 280-298.* Anglo-American constitutional, family, and criminal law have absorbed from the Christian tradition,
especially in its Protestant form, metaphysical constructs, moral standards, and
linguistic forms. In a pluralistic society a value consensus is lacking. In order to
protect individual freedom under these circumstances, the religious elements in
the law are being removed.   J. C. English

57.   Dibble, Ursula.   SOCIALLY SHARED DEPRIVATION AND THE
APPROVAL OF VIOLENCE: ANOTHER LOOK AT THE EXPERIENCE
OF AMERICAN BLACKS DURING THE 1960s.   *Ethnicity 1981 8(2): 149-
168.* Personally experienced discrimination tends to make blacks more likely to
approve of political violence. This effect is especially pronounced when it is
shared with others and when it is considered to be a salient matter. 7 tables, 16
notes, biblio.   T. W. Smith

58.   Dominick, Joseph R.   CRIME AND LAW ENFORCEMENT ON
PRIME-TIME TELEVISION.   *Public Opinion Q. 1973 37(2): 241-250.* Analyzes crime on prime-time television programs in one week (22-29 February 1972)
in New York City. The characteristics of television's crimes, criminals, victims,
frequency, locales, and law enforcement officials were inaccurate when compared
with data from the files of the Federal Bureau of Investigation. 4 tables, 9 notes.
V. L. Human

59.   Douglass, Wayne J.   THE CRIMINAL PSYCHOPATH AS HOLLY-
WOOD HERO.   *J. of Popular Film and Television 1981 8(4): 30-39.* The
appearance of criminal psychopaths as hero-figures in films during 1947-76 is an
expression of a prevalent antipathy in American culture toward modern bureaucratic society; three writings deal with this phenomenon: Robert Warshow, "The
Gangster as Tragic Hero," in *The Immediate Experience* (1971), Norman Mailer,
Advertisements for Myself (1959), and Alan Harrington, *Psychopaths* (1972).

60.   Dudley, J. Wayne.   "HATE" ORGANIZATIONS OF THE 1940S: THE
COLUMBIANS, INC.   *Phylon 1981 42(3): 262-274.* A wave of racial violence
followed World War II. A number of racist organizations emerged to promote
patriotism, faith, and the white community. In 1946, several white men chartered
the Columbians in Atlanta, Georgia. To join, one had to hate Negroes and Jews
and have three dollars. While the Columbians stirred up Atlanta for several
months, the city and state governments, local politicians, and the city's newspapers attacked the group until it was legally disbanded, June 1947.
A. G. Belles

61.   Eckhardt, Bob.   TWO HUNDRED YEARS OF SOCIAL AND ECO-
NOMIC CHANGE HAVE SHAPED OUR CRIME PROBLEM.   *Center
Mag. 1977 10(4): 33-38.* Because the causes of the current crime problem are not
recent, recommends a study of the changing social and economic conditions
which cause social problems, to arrive at effective public policy for the criminal
justice system.

62.   Edwards, John C.   SLAVE JUSTICE IN FOUR MIDDLE GEORGIA COUNTIES. *Georgia Hist. Q. 1973 57(2): 265-273.* Surveys accounts of 10 slave trials in the Inferior Court records of DeKalb, Hancock, Lincoln, and Putnam counties in Georgia, 1819-58. Indictment was not tantamount to conviction, and all slaves did receive jury trials. The defendant might be summarily executed if found guilty of a capital offense, but sometimes the court tempered the cutting edge of the slave code for reasons not disclosed in the records. 6 notes.

D. L. Smith

63.   Edwards, John Carver.   PLAYING THE PATRIOT GAME: THE STORY OF THE AMERICAN DEFENSE SOCIETY, 1915-1932. *Studies in Hist. and Society 1976 1(1): 54-72.* The American Defense Society (ADS) began as a basically Republican organization to discredit President Wilson and advocate preparedness for World War I. Discusses the activities of the ADS and the less-partisan National Security League. Both advocated US military preparedness, but the ADS blatantly harangued the government. A fund-raising scandal resulted from the activities of ADS trustee George Baxter in 1916, and another scandal in Boston led to an investigation of the Society's finances in 1918. Amateur spy-catching, universal military training, and a large standing army were campaigns that the ADS worked on; the formation of the Vigilantes in 1916 brought together 60 writers whose articles denouncing US neutrality were sold to newspapers and magazines across the nation. In 1917 Vigilante leader Cleveland Langston Moffett organized disturbances of pacifist rallies. The Society lasted until 1932, reacting against real or imagined threats to US security. 69 notes.

64.   Ehrlich, Isaac.   PARTICIPATION IN ILLEGITIMATE ACTIVITIES: A THEORETICAL AND EMPIRICAL INVESTIGATION. *J. of Pol. Econ. 1973 81(3): 521-565.* "A theory of participation in illegitimate activities is developed and tested against data on variations in index crimes across states in the United States. Theorems and behavioral implications are derived using the state preference approach to behavior under uncertainty. The investigation deals directly with the interaction between offense and defense: crime and collective law enforcement. It indicates the existence of a deterrent effect of law-enforcement activity on all crimes and a strong positive correlation between income inequality and crimes against property. The empirical results also provide some tentative estimates of the effectiveness of law enforcement in reducing crime and the resulting social losses."

J

65.   Ellerin, Milton.   KU KLUX KLAN REVIVAL. *Patterns of Prejudice [Great Britain] 1979 13(4): 17-19.* Discusses the current tactics, image, and violence of the southern Ku Klux Klan and the various factors related to their recent upsurge.

66.   England, Ralph W.   CRIMINAL JUSTICE IN THE AMERICAN DEMOCRACY. *Current Hist. 1976 70(417): 241-244, 277.* Emphasizes the treatment of crime and criminals in the 1970's, in the federal, state, county, and municipal systems, and notes the 18th-20th-century development of criminal law, courts, the police, and prisons.

67. Erskine, Hazel. THE POLLS: CONTROL OF VIOLENCE AND CRIME. *Public Opinion Q. 1974 38(3): 490-502.* "When Americans are given a choice between authoritarianism vs. amelioration of social situations, they overwhelmingly choose a constructive approach to a crackdown. Most notably characteristic of this collection of questions on crime control is the disarray of research efforts, absence of continuity in the collective findings, and consequent ambivalence of conclusions. . . . In 1967, 56 percent did not consider present methods of treatment a deterrent to crime as compared with 69 percent in 1973. Thus, one of the few solid conclusions is that Americans increasingly agree that present methods of law enforcement are ineffective and not making perceptible progress." 4 notes.　　　　　　　　　　　　　　　　　　　　　　　D. D. Cameron

68. Etchison, J. C. THE SETTING OF CRIMINAL JUSTICE DECISION-MAKING. *Policy Studies J. 1974 3(1): 7-12.* Examines various theories of crime causation to establish a basis for further study of criminal justice reforms.　　　　　　　　　　　　　　　　　　　　　　　　　　　　　　　　　　　　S

69. Faber, Eli. PURITAN CRIMINALS: THE ECONOMIC, SOCIAL, AND INTELLECTUAL BACKGROUND TO CRIME IN SEVENTEENTH-CENTURY MASSACHUSETTS. *Perspectives in Am. Hist. 1977-78 11: 81-144.* Analysis of 315 convicted criminals in 17th-century Middlesex County, Massachusetts, shows that offenders were equally represented in all classes. The percentage of convictions for sexual offenses was highest among the lower classes. Convictions for religious offenses, alcoholic abuse, and defiance of authority were highest among the upper classes. Further analysis shows that Puritans tended to reaccept offenders as contributing members of society after a reasonable period.　　　　　　　　　　　　　　　　　　　　　　　　　　　W. A. Wiegand

70. Feeley, Malcolm M. TWO MODELS OF THE CRIMINAL JUSTICE SYSTEM: AN ORGANIZATIONAL PERSPECTIVE. *Law & Soc. R. 1973 7(3): 407-425.* Systematic studies of the administration of justice in the United States have stressed either the rational-goal model or the functional-systems model. The former model emphasizes problems with the justice system's formal rules of operation and appears to be the dominant view of appellate judges, lawyers, and law students, while the latter model is concerned with the identification and adaptation of action to the environment and the interests of action within the system.　　　　　　　　　　　　　　　　　　　　　　　　　　　　H. R. Mahood

71. Fellman, Michael. VIOLENCE AND CRIME IN NINETEENTH-CENTURY AMERICA. *Can. Rev. of Am. Studies [Canada] 1981 12(3): 323-330.* Reviews Dickson D. Bruce, Jr.'s *Violence and Culture in the Antebellum South* (1979), David R. Johnson's *Policing the Urban Underworld: The Impact of Crime on the Development of the American Police, 1800-1887* (1979), and Roger Lane's *Violent Death in the City: Suicide, Accident and Murder in Nineteenth-Century Philadelphia* (1979). Besides treating 19th-century crime and violence in certain localities, these monographs contain useful hypotheses for syntheses of crime and violence in American society.　　　　　　　　　H. T. Lovin

72. Fine, David M. JAMES M. CAIN AND THE LOS ANGELES NOVEL. *Am. Studies 1979 20(1): 25-34.* Surveys James M. Cain's Los Angeles novels of the 1930's and 1940's, which have now been revived amid the rediscovery of

thirties Los Angeles in text and film. The gangster and the tough guy pervade these works, reflecting the fantasies and nightmares of the depression years. Cain presented us with the major metaphors for the literary identity of Los Angeles —the road, the landscape, and the commonplace. Primary and secondary sources; 11 notes.					J. A. Andrew

73. Fishman, Mark. CRIME WAVES AS IDEOLOGY. *Social Problems 1978 25(5): 531-543.* Studies the late 1976 crime wave against elderly people in New York City to show how crime waves are constructed in the media and how they contribute to an ideological concept of crime. Crime waves are "things of the mind" but have real consequences. News organizations construct crime waves and the media seems to respond to that construction. This crime wave did not really exist, but it still affected public issues and events. Other accepted political realities, such as Watergate and the Bert Lance affair, may have been produced by the same ideological machinery that underlies crime waves. Primary and secondary sources; 10 notes; refs.					A. M. Osur

74. Fitzpatrick, John W. PSYCHOANALYSIS AND CRIME: A CRITICAL SURVEY OF SALIENT TRENDS IN THE LITERATURE. *Ann. of the Am. Acad. of Pol. and Social Sci. 1976 (423): 67-74.* Psychoanalytic studies of criminal motivation generally have followed the salient trends within the historical development of psychoanalytic theory. The first trend, initiated by Sigmund Freud in an essay entitled "Criminals from a Sense of Guilt" (1916), highlighted the motivational priority of unconscious psychosexual conflict. Social and economic factors were minimized. Psychoanalytic ego psychologists subsequently have questioned the explanatory adequacy of the libido theory and have modified the theoretical orientation of psychoanalysis. This theoretical reorientation has been reflected in recent psychoanalytic studies of crime, which not only seek to account for the contextual diversity of antisocial behavior but also emphasize the etiological significance of character development, the adaptational functions of the ego, and the important role played by the environment in the criminal's life.					J

75. Flaherty, David H. CRIME AND SOCIAL CONTROL IN PROVINCIAL MASSACHUSETTS. *Hist. J. [Great Britain] 1981 24(2): 339-360.* Studies incidents of criminal behavior and the system of social control in provincial Massachusetts in the 18th century. The scale of deviant behavior was low, a common feature of rural life in North America and Western Europe during the period. Social control was exerted by and through the church and family and was aided by conscious efforts to preserve a homogeneous community and an effective law-enforcement apparatus. Based on records of the Superior Court of Judicature in Boston and secondary sources; 5 tables, 70 notes, appendix.					G. M. Alexander

76. Flanigan, Daniel J. CRIMINAL PROCEDURE IN SLAVE TRIALS IN THE ANTEBELLUM SOUTH. *J. of Southern Hist. 1974 40(4): 537-564.* The slaves' personality was nearly completely suppressed in antebellum civil law, but in criminal law it was another matter. Slaves could not own horses, but they could steal them. The law demanded more of the slave than of his master, since he was often more severely punished for an identical offense. Contends that southern legislatures and courts were, nevertheless, very concerned about the procedural

rights of slaves in criminal cases. For example, the high courts of the South recognized the power of private authority in extracting forced confessions. Southerners even used procedural fairness to sustain the pro-slavery argument, and during the Civil War, southern courts continued to insist upon procedural fairness. Southern legislators and judges at times granted rights to slaves which were not granted to whites in an effort to reconcile fairness and a degree of equality with slavery. Based on manuscripts and published primary and secondary sources; 92 notes.

T. D. Schoonover

77. Fletcher, Tyler. THE CRIMINAL JUSTICE SYSTEM AND THE ROLE OF EDUCATION. *Southern Q. 1975 13(2): 119-130.* Examines federal and state criminal justice systems and public attitudes toward them. Includes an evaluation of present educational programs concerned with criminal justice and recommendations for modification and improvement. New directions in criminal justice education are analyzed. 13 notes.

R. W. Dubay

78. Flynn, Edith Elisabeth. CRIME AND VIOLENCE IN AMERICAN SOCIETY: AN OVERVIEW. *Am. Behavioral Scientist 1980 23(5): 637-652.* Surveys the extent and nature of crime and violence in America since the 1940's and discusses the other articles in this issue which deal with the subjects.

79. Frease, Dean E. DELINQUENCY, SOCIAL CLASS, AND THE SCHOOLS. *Sociol. and Social Res. 1973 57(4): 443-459.* "The study reports findings showing no relationship between social class and juvenile delinquency, using three different dimensions of juvenile misconduct: 1) over-all delinquency, 2) seriousness of offense, and 3) recidivism. A tentative explanation is put forth which argues specifically that the questionable relevance of school for youngsters not going to college could act as a source of rebellious behavior."

J

80. French, Laurence and Hornbuckle, Jim. AN ANALYSIS OF INDIAN VIOLENCE: THE CHEROKEE EXAMPLE. *Am. Indian Q.: A J. of Anthrop., Hist., and Literature 1977-78 3(4): 335-356.* Cultural frustration in the form of anomie and internal conflict, and a no longer viable "informal subculture control structure," provides reasons for seemingly excessive violence among Eastern Cherokee Indians in Appalachia. Some members of the group adhere to traditional culture, and some have joined "majority society," but most are "marginal Indians" without benefit of membership in either group. Deterioration of traditional mechanisms of aggression release and the imposition of oppressive formal controls of the reservation system result in sporadic eruptions of violence. Based on crime records of the Eastern Cherokee Tribe, secondary sources, and includes 12 case histories.

G. L. Olson

81. Fried, Albert. THE SAGA OF MEYER LANSKY: JUST ANOTHER RETIRED SENIOR CITIZEN. *Present Tense 1980 7(3): 32-35.* Reviews the professional life of Meyer Lansky, a gangster who is the product of New York City's Lower East Side and who worked his way up to the top of his field.

82. Friedrichs, David O. VIOLENCE AND THE POLITICS OF CRIME. *Social Res. 1981 48(1): 135-156.* Discusses the various ways that criminologists especially in the 1970's have viewed violence.

83. Frost, J. William. QUAKER VERSUS BAPTIST: A RELIGIOUS AND POLITICAL SQUABBLE IN RHODE ISLAND THREE HUNDRED YEARS AGO. *Quaker Hist. 1974 63(1): 39-52.* George Fox visited Rhode Island three weeks after the May 1672 election put Quakers in power for five years. Quakers had won by taking credit for repeal of sedition, confiscation, and other unpopular laws, thus identifying themselves with popular liberties. Fox's farewell sermon at Newport and the Baptist minister Thomas Olney, Jr.'s reply of a year later continued the Fox-Williams debates of 1672. Fox urged keeping weekly markets and vital records, and warned Friends to use their new power righteously. Olney's much longer polemic called government by inspiration oppressive and generally argued from different assumptions. These tracts illustrated rather than changed Rhode Island politics. Manuscripts preserved in the Rhode Island Historical Soceity and here published and edited.   T. D. S. Bassett

84. Fugate, Francis L. and Fugate, Roberta B. ERLE STANLEY GARDNER. *Am. West 1981 18(3): 34-37.* After reading in law offices, Erle Stanley Gardner passed the California bar examination in 1910 at age 21 and began practice. He soon became well-known because of his knack at defending Chinese clients. He reveled in the courtroom aspect of law, but hated the tedium of preparation for trials. Deciding that only writers could be completely independent, he settled down in 1923 to learn to write. He produced prodigious quantities of traditional and contemporary western stories and adventure, western, and detective yarns set against primarily western backgrounds. Gardner's production of the Perry Mason-Della Street accounts alone numbered 82 novels and three novelettes. 4 illus.   D. L. Smith

85. Gibbs, Jack P. and Erickson, Maynard L. CRIME RATES OF AMERICAN CITIES IN AN ECOLOGICAL CONTEXT. *Am. J. of Sociol. 1976 82(3): 605-620.* Given a city that contains only a small proportion of the residents in the larger ecological community, the conventional crime rate for that city could be high merely because the denominator of the rate underestimates the potential number of victims or offenders. Accordingly, there is a basis for anticipating a direct relationship among cities between (1) community/city population size ratios and (2) rates for particular types of crimes. The relationship does hold for many American cities when Urbanized Areas (UAs) or Standard Metropolitan Statistical Areas (SMSAs) are taken as approximations of communities; but it holds only for singular cities, each of which is the only central city in a SMSA. The argument of this paper is that singular cities are much more homogeneous as regards dominance within the community than are other types of cities, and that dominance determines the extent to which a city will attract nonresident participants in crimes. In any case, the findings cast doubts on the use of conventional crime rates for cities in testing theories.   J

86. Giffin, Frederick C. THE RUDOWITZ EXTRADITION CASE. *J. of the Illinois State Hist. Soc. 1982 75(1): 61-72.* In October 1908, Ernest von Schilling, the Russian consul in Chicago, demanded the extradition of Christian Ansoff Rudowitz, a refugee who had participated in the Revolution of 1905. Upon the arrest of Rudowitz, massive public agitation for his release centered in Chicago among radicals, but quickly spread throughout the nation as attention focused on American relations with the government of Tsar Nicholas II and the establishment of a precedent abolishing political asylum in the United States. On

7 December, Commissioner Mark A. Foote ordered the extradition but he was overruled on 26 January 1909 by Secretary of State Elihu Root, who noted the political nature of Rudowitz's offenses. 6 illus., 35 notes.   A. W. Novitsky

87. Giordano, Peggy C. and Cernkovich, Stephen A. ON COMPLICATING THE RELATIONSHIP BETWEEN LIBERATION AND DELINQUENCY. *Social Problems 1979 26(4): 467-481.* Data from three US urban high schools and two state institutions show little or no association between liberated attitudes among women and self-reported delinquency, though at the level of the criminal act itself, particularly in mixed-sex groups, women are apt to take a more active role, thus departing from passive female stereotypes and resembling, rather, male delinquents.

88. Glaser, Daniel. ECONOMIC AND SOCIOCULTURAL VARIABLES AFFECTING RATES OF YOUTH UNEMPLOYMENT, DELINQUENCY, AND CRIME. *Youth and Soc. 1979 11(1): 53-82.* A review of research shows that there is little difference between true rates of crime between the poor and the middle class, although more violent crime occurs in poor areas. Unemployment does seem to correlate with youthful crime, but interacts with other factors. Modern youth crime is influenced by the separation of youth from adults, the lack of success of some students in school and extracurricular organizations, and futile criminalization of drug use. Biblio.   J. H. Sweetland

89. Glasrud, Bruce A. ENFORCING WHITE SUPREMACY IN TEXAS, 1900-1910. *Red River Valley Hist. Rev. 1979 4(4): 65-74.* White supremacists used terror and violence to restrict blacks, to force them out of lucrative employment, and to remove them from politics.

90. Goldberg, Robert A. THE KU KLUX KLAN IN MADISON, 1922-1929. *Wisconsin Mag. of Hist. 1974 58(1): 31-44.* The stereotype of the Ku Klux Klan as violence-prone bigots who attacked blacks, Catholics, Jews, and immigrants is inaccurate for Madison Klansmen and for most Klans in the 1920's. Members were, instead, "ordinary men bewildered by changes that threatened to disrupt their lives and their city." Klan activity, aside from its similarity to other fraternal social organizations, concentrated on a law and order campaign and a drive to reassert American patriotism by stripping school textbooks of any negative remarks about American history or society. Internal dissension and the reform efforts of Dane County District Attorney Philip La Follette hastened their rapid decline. 7 illus., 58 notes.   N. C. Burckel

91. Golden, Daniel. THE AGE DEMANDED AN IMAGE: THE GANGSTER AS AMERICAN. *Can. Rev. of Am. Studies [Canada] 1979 10(1): 71-75.* According to Jack Shadoian in *Dreams and Dead Ends: The American Gangster/Crime Film* (Cambridge: MIT Pr., 1977), gangster and other crime films mirror US "culture's psyche." These films exploded self-made man myths long before most Americans questioned such notions. 2 notes.   H. T. Lovin

92. Graber, Doris A. IS CRIME NEWS COVERAGE EXCESSIVE? *J. of Communication 1979 29(3): 81-92.* Television and newspaper coverage of crime news is exaggerated but crime news does not displace other news coverage as statistics indicate from a 1976 study of news content of the Chicago Tribune, three national, and two local Chicago television news broadcasts.

93.   Granger, Frank.   REACTION TO CHANGE: THE KU KLUX KLAN
IN SHREVEPORT, 1920-1929.   *North Louisiana Hist. Assoc. J. 1978 9(4):
219-227.* The new morality following World War I shook the foundations of
moral standards. The revival of the Ku Klux Klan during 1915-44 appealed to
those elements who desired to salvage them. The Klan revival was based not so
much on racism and nativism as on moral authoritarianism: the preservation of
premarital chastity, marital fidelity, respect for parental authority, obedience to
state and national prohibition laws and the fight against crime and dishonest
politicians. Shreveport was a boom town, rampant with bootlegging and prostitution, making it a good locale for Klan revival and growth. At first, the Klan
attracted a large membership; but after two men were murdered allegedly by
Klansmen in 1922, the Klan was accused of taking the law into its own hands,
and its membership and influence began to wane. Assesses the moral contributions of the Klan and describes its gradual demise. Based on contemporary
accounts in the *Shreveport Journal;* 54 notes.   H. M. Parker, Jr.

94.   Green, Justin J.   JUDICIAL POLICY-MAKING, 1973-1974.   *Western
Pol. Q. 1975 28(1): 167-191.* The 1973-74 term of the US Supreme Court was
characterized by major decisions in the areas of Federal Court jurisdiction, school
desegregation, search and seizure law, and the rights of prisoners. Substantially
reaffirmed were existing precedents which encouraged governmental regulation
of pornography, weakened the *Miranda* rule, expanded access to the ballot, and
accepted a balancing approach to the right of a free press. The Court often divided
along ideological lines in civil liberties cases. The Court seems to have passed
through a period of hesitation following the Nixon appointments and now appears to be under the control of a conservative coalition. Documentation comes
from published court opinions. 7 notes.   G. B. McKinney

95.   Greenberg, Douglas.   PATTERNS OF CRIMINAL PROSECUTION IN
EIGHTEENTH-CENTURY NEW YORK.   *New York Hist. 1975 56(2): 133-
153.* Discusses patterns of criminal prosecution among women, blacks, and descendants of original Dutch settlers living in 18th-century New York. Based on
computer-assisted analysis of 5,300 criminal cases reported in court records
during 1691-1776; 3 illus., 34 notes.   R. N. Lokken

96.   Grenander, M. E.   THE HERITAGE OF CAIN: CRIME IN AMERI-
CAN FICTION.   *Ann. of the Am. Acad. of Pol. and Social Sci. 1976 (423):
47-66.* For almost two centuries American fiction has featured crime, but its
treatment in popular literature, which strokes the norms of a mass audience, has
been quite different from that in high art, which examines critically the assumptions and values of our society. A study of serious fiction can, therefore, probe
fundamental issues for us: How does literature define crime? Why does this
definition differ occasionally from the statutory one? What crimes has fiction
taken most seriously? How does fiction assess the criminal's circumstances and
motivation? What is the literary attitude to criminal responsibility? What is the
victim's role in crime? How is the criminal apprehended? How does the trial
contribute to equity? How are legal professionals, the jury, and the insanity
defense portrayed? How does literature rank criminal punishments? We can
postulate tentative answers to these rather open-ended questions, but in a larger
sense their value is heuristic, forcing us to reconsider some hypotheses we may
have taken for granted.   J

97. Grindstaff, Carl G. PUBLIC ATTITUDES AND COURT DISPOSI-
TIONS: A COMPARATIVE ANALYSIS. *Sociol. and Social Res. 1974 58(4):*
417-426. "Public attitudes on sanctions for criminal offenses are compared with
court sentences for: 1) Personal Crimes, 2) Property Crimes, and 3) Crimes
Without Victims. On the whole, the findings support the interest group rather
than value consensus perspectives on the relationship between law and society in
that the public give more severe sanctions for crimes than are presently prescribed
by the courts." J

98. Guillot, Ellen Elizabeth. WHAT'S OLD, WHAT'S NEW IN THE JAIL
REGISTERS OF SAN JOAQUIN COUNTY, CALIFORNIA. *Pacific Hist.*
1979 23(2): 53-68. Reports and compares the findings of the offenses which were
charged at booking at the San Joaquin County jail for the years 1890 and 1970.
Also presents patterns of offenses for which individuals were booked in both years
and explains the differences as reflections of the conditions and values of the
times. The registers give a flavor of the times indicative of the society in which
the crimes were committed. 2 photos, 2 tables, 5 notes. H. M. Parker, Jr.

99. Hagan, John. CRIMINAL JUSTICE IN RURAL AND URBAN COM-
MUNITIES: A STUDY OF THE BUREAUCRATIZATION OF JUSTICE.
Social Forces 1977 55(3): 597-612. This paper inquires into the effects of urbanization and bureaucratization on one type of institutionalized decision-making:
judicial sentencing. Theoretical and empirical links between urbanization, bureaucratization, and sentencing are reviewed. Then, two data sets from a Canadian province (Alberta) are analyzed: (1) 507 questionnaires based on
pre-sentence reports completed in all provincial probation departments, and (2)
974 offenders admitted to the five major provincial prisons. The analysis is built
on comparisons of sentencing patterns for North American Indians and whites
in urban and rural communities. The results reveal that probation officers in rural
jurisdictions, as contrasted with those in urban communities, sentence Indians
severely, without the justification of correlated legal variables. In addition, Indians are more likely to be sent to jail in default of fine payments in rural, than in
urban communities. The implications of these findings for an understanding of
the bureaucratization of criminal justice are discussed. J

100. Hagan, John. THE LEGISLATION OF CRIME AND DELIN-
QUENCY: A REVIEW OF THEORY, METHOD, AND RESEARCH.
Law & Soc. Rev. 1980 14(3): 603-628. This essay reviews a number of North
American case studies in an attempt to clarify the theoretical and methodological
limitations, prospects, and findings of the literature on criminal lawmaking. I
introduce this review by contrasting the two principal theoretical perspectives
that guide such studies. I then discuss problems of evidence related to these rival
theories, using an analysis of the origins of theft laws as my example. Following
this, I review a large number of empirical studies concerned with the origin of
laws that I have grouped into three categories: 1) delinquency and probation;
2) alcohol and drug abuse; and 3) prostitution and sexual psychopathy. Finally,
I examine the implications of these and other legislative studies for future work
in this important area of research. A

101. Hall, Roger Allan. FRONTIER DRAMATIZATIONS: THE JAMES GANG. *Theatre Survey 1980 21(2): 117-128.* Analyzes some aspects of the dramatizations of the exploits of the Jesse James gang, popular during the late 19th century, the reasons for their emotional appeal in spite of aesthetic shortcomings, to what extent the plays relied on factual material, the impact of the use of actual participants and paraphernalia of the events, special features, and adaptation of elements of the James legend.

102. Halperin, Morton H. FURTHER ADVENTURES OF A TAPPEE. *Civil Liberties R. 1974 1(2): 131-133.* The author relates the experience of having his telephone wiretapped while a member of the National Security Council during 1969-71, and his subsequent lawsuit against agents of the Federal Bureau of Investigation and various government officials.

103. Halperin, Morton H. NATIONAL SECURITY AND CIVIL LIBERTIES. *Foreign Policy 1975 (21): 125-167.* Contradicts prowiretappers who claim that such surveillance helps national security. Bugging and similar activities undermine constitutional rights, particularly those guaranteed by the First and Fourth Amendments. Wiretapping has a chilling effect on free speech, and the Fourth Amendment prohibits unreasonable searches and seizures. From the viewpoint of gathering information of value to national security, generally wiretapped information has had limited value. For dubious values, intelligence agencies are destroying constitutional rights.   R. F. Kugler

104. Handberg, Roger. THE MOSAIC OF DISCRETION: CRIMINAL JUSTICE POLICY. *Policy Studies J. 1980 8(5): 785-788.* Review article prompted by Martin A. Levin's *Urban Politics and the Criminal Courts* (Chicago: U. of Chicago Pr., 1977), Lynn M. Mather's *Plea Bargaining or Trial?* (Lexington, Mass.: Lexington Books, 1979), Ralph A. Rossum's *The Politics of the Criminal Justice Process* (New York: Marcel Dekker, 1978), and Thomas M. Uhlman's *Racial Justice* (Lexington, Mass.: Lexington Books, 1979) which discuss the US system of criminal justice and judicial administration, 1960's-70's.

105. Harper, Mary Jill Robinson. COURTS, DOCTORS, AND DELINQUENTS: AN INQUIRY INTO THE USES OF PSYCHIATRY IN YOUTH CORRECTIONS. *Smith Coll. Studies in Social Work 1974 44(3): 158-178.*

106. Harris, W. Stuart. ROWDYISM, PUBLIC DRUNKENNESS, AND BLOODY ENCOUNTERS IN EARLY PERRY COUNTY. *Alabama Rev. 1980 33(1): 15-24.* Perry County, Alabama, during 1820-32, passed through a frontier period when rowdyism, public drunkenness, and bloody encounters were commonplace. This article describes many events of this nature during this era. Primary sources; 28 notes.   J. Powell

107. Hill, Gary D. and Harris, Anthony R. CHANGES IN THE GENDER PATTERNING OF CRIME, 1953-77: OPPORTUNITY VS. IDENTITY. *Social Sci. Q. 1981 62(4): 658-671.* The evidence for 1953-77 does not support the theory that the participation of women in crime increases as female participation in the labor force grows and traditional gender stereotyping erodes.

108.   Hindelang, Michael J.   RACE AND INVOLVEMENT IN COMMON
LAW PERSONAL CRIMES.   *Am. Sociol. Rev. 1978 43(1): 93-109.* Most
contemporary sociological theories of crime predict that blacks will be overrepresented among arrestees in common law personal crimes. These theories differ,
however, in the extent to which this overrepresentation is attributed to disproportionate involvement in criminal offenses vs. criminal justice system selection
biases. Studies that have relied upon official data have generally supported the
differential involvement hypothesis, whereas studies relying on self-report techniques generally have supported the differential selection hypothesis. National
victimization survey data on victims' reports of racial characteristics of offenders
are introduced as a third measurement technique in order to shed additional light
on this controversy. These data for rape, robbery, and assault, are generally
consistent with official data on arrestees and support the differential involvement
hypothesis. Some evidence of differential selection for criminal justice processing
is found; however, most of the racial disproportionality in arrest data is shown
by victimization survey data to be attributable to the substantially greater involvement of blacks in the common law personal crimes of rape, robbery, and assault.
These results suggest that traditional admonitions against using arrest data as an
index of involvement in these crimes may be overly cautious. In fact, the results
imply that more caution should attend the use of self-report data in this vein and
that more attention should be given to sampling and instrument concerns in
self-report techniques. As *currently* used, the method may not be adequate for
assessing the correlates of serious illegal conduct. The results also suggest that
research emphasis be placed on those theories, such as the subcultural and
differential opportunity perspectives, which attempt to explain differential racial
involvement in these common law personal crimes.   J

109.   Hindelang, Michael J.   SEX DIFFERENCES IN CRIMINAL ACTIV-
ITY.   *Social Problems 1979 27(2): 143-156.* Data gathered between 1972 and
1976 show that involvement in common-law crimes in the United States was
higher among men than among women, thus drawing a strong correlation between sex and criminal and delinquent behavior.

110.   Hindelang, Michael J.   VARIATION IN SEX-RACE-AGE-SPECIFIC
INCIDENCE RATES OF OFFENDING.   *Am. Sociol. Rev. 1981 46(4): 461-
474.* Studies rates of offending in personal crimes (rape, robbery, assault, and
personal larceny) using data from the National Crime Survey (NCS) for 1973-77.
Victims' reports of offenders' sex, race, and age are strongly related to incidence
rates of offending. The highest incidence rate in personal crimes is for male, black,
18 to 20 year olds. Arrest data at the national level for robbery yield comparable
results. Household crimes (burglary, household larceny, and vehicle theft) in
which the victims saw and were able to report offenders' sex, race, and age
constituted about 5% of all household crimes. The patterns in incidence rates of
offending in these household crimes closely parallel those for personal crimes.
                                                                           J/S

111.   Hindus, Michael S.   BLACK JUSTICE UNDER WHITE LAW: CRIM-
INAL PROSECUTIONS OF BLACKS IN ANTEBELLUM SOUTH
CAROLINA.   *J. of Am. Hist. 1976 63(3): 575-599.* Justice for blacks in South
Carolina depended upon informal arrangements that could not be subject to
public scrutiny. Separate penal codes for blacks supplemented the private planta-

tion justice administered to slaves. Despite its haphazard forms black justice invariably supported white dominance. Trial records show that courts responded to the race crisis of the 1850's by increasing conviction rates and the severity of punishments. "Black justice may have served some bureaucratic need for certification, while . . . soothing some slaveholders' consciences, but it was never intended to be just." Primary and secondary sources; 11 tables, 80 notes.

W. R. Hively

112. Hirschi, Travis and Rudisill, David. THE GREAT AMERICAN SEARCH: CAUSES OF CRIME 1876-1976. *Ann. of the Am. Acad. of Pol. and Social Sci. 1976 (423): 14-22.* Biology, psychology, and sociology have successively dominated American criminology over the last 100 years. Given that the biological and psychological approaches were both oriented toward the characteristics of the offender, they were easy to test in principle, and their eventual decline is now interpreted as a consequence of their failure to survive empirical tests. With the rise of the sociological view, there was a corresponding decline in testability, especially with reference to the characteristics of the offender, and there followed a lengthy period of theoretical development virtually independent of research. The sociological theories prominent during this period stressed the multiplicity of cultures in American life, on the one hand, and the differential distribution of opportunity to achieve common goals, on the other. With the rise of large-scale research conducted by sociologists, these theories were themselves subject to test, and theories more closely grounded on the results of research became possible. At the moment, sociological theorizing focuses on the effects of the processing of offenders by agencies of social control.   J

113. Hoffer, Peter C. COUNTING CRIME IN PREMODERN ENGLAND AND AMERICA: A REVIEW ESSAY. *Hist. Methods 1981 14(4): 187-193.* Reviews *An Ungovernable People: The English and their Law in the Seventeenth and Eighteenth Centuries* (1980), edited by John Brewer and John Styles, Barbara A. Hanawalt's *Crime and Conflict in English Communities, 1300-1348* (1979), Lyle Koehler's *A Search for Power: The Weaker Sex In Seventeenth-Century New England* (1980), and Michael S. Hindus's *Prisons and Plantation: Crime, Justice, and Authority in Massachusetts and South Carolina, 1767-1878* (1980). Their uses of quantification are of an uneven quality. Unfortunately the methodology used in these books generally does not fully develop the available records. Explanation, therefore, is not complete. 13 notes.   D. K. Pickens

114. Homer, Frederic and Caputo, David A. CONCEPTUAL AND OPERATIONAL PROBLEMS OF STUDYING ORGANIZED CRIME. *Soc. and Culture [India] 1973 4(2): 163-178.* Reviews the literature about organized crime in the United States over the past generation. The authors consider the problem of definition of organized crime and suggest that defective definitions do more harm than good in opening up inquiry. They suggest a viable alternative definition which will broaden the researcher's perspective, claiming that recent writers have failed to consider organized crime in a systematic and comprehensive manner. Writers tend to be too concerned with personality traits and class or ethnicity and to assume the existence of a nationwide, monolithic syndicate of organized crime. The authors believe these concerns and assumptions lead to narrow perspectives and poor questions. They suggest three areas which need attention: the comparative aspects of organized crime, the latent functions of organized crime, and the behavioral aspects of organized crime. Based on secondary sources; biblio.

115. Horowitz, Irving Louis. POLITICAL TERRORISM AND THE STATE. *J. of Pol. and Military Sociol. 1973 1(1): 147-158.* "Attempts to locate the problem of political terrorism within the larger context of the current blending and fusion of radical political practice and social deviance generally. Beyond that, it attempts to develop a profile of the terrorist that distinguishes the terrorist from the guerrilla or the national revolutionary. It also seeks to show how the problem of terrorism manifests particular concern within the Marxist tradition, where this issue of the use of terror remains a viable theoretical and pragmatic consideration—unlike the older western democratic political traditions. Finally, the paper offers some brief remarks on the control of terror and the limits of such control within a democratic society." J

116. Hoskins, Richard J. A COMPARATIVE ANALYSIS OF CONSPIRACY IN GERMANY, FRANCE, AND THE UNITED STATES. *New York U. J. of Internat. Law and Pol. 1973 6(2): 245-270.* Analyzes the crime of conspiracy in the penal codes of the United States, West Germany, and France. The approach may vary, but all of the countries "express the judgment that punishment for agreements to commit crimes is a necessary element of a criminal code." Based on primary sources; 100 notes. M. L. Frey

117. Humphries, Drew and Wallace, Don. CAPITALIST ACCUMULATION AND URBAN CRIME, 1950-1971. *Social Problems 1980 28(2): 179-193.* The Marxist preoccupation with unemployment and underemployment as causes of increased crime rates in American capitalist society overlooks another possible cause, that economic expansion generates crime; examines the impact of such expansion on urban variations in the US crime rate from 1950 to 1971.

118. Hux, Roger K. THE KU KLUX KLAN IN MACON 1919-1925. *Georgia Hist. Q. 1978 62(2): 155-168.* The Macon, Georgia, Ku Klux Klan of the 1920's, led by dentist C. A. Yarbrough, administered floggings primarily to punish moral offenders rather than to combat racial or foreign influences. Condemnation of violence, several trials of Klansmen, and political defeat brought about Klan decline. Newspapers and secondary sources; 30 notes.
G. R. Schroeder

119. Ianni, Francis A. J. NEW MAFIA: BLACK, HISPANIC AND ITALIAN STYLES. *Society 1974 11(3): 26-39.* Discusses the entrance of blacks and Puerto Ricans into organized crime. S

120. Iorizzo, Luciano and Mondello, Salvatore. ORIGINS OF ITALIAN-AMERICAN CRIMINALITY: FROM NEW ORLEANS THROUGH PROHIBITION. *Italian Americana 1975 1(2): 217-236.* Discusses "the hostile, fanciful stereotypes" of Italian Americans as predisposed to crime and suggests ways in which the activities of the Mafia in the United States, particularly during the late 19th and early 20th centuries, has contributed to this false image. S

121. Jacobson, Alvin L. CRIME TRENDS IN SOUTHERN AND NON-SOUTHERN CITIES: A TWENTY-YEAR PERSPECTIVE. *Social Forces 1975 54(1): 226-242.* Using annual data from 1951-70, for 467 U.S. cities, this study reexamines the extent to which reported crime offenses between the South

and non-South continue to manifest regional differences. Alternative structuralist and normative hypotheses are evaluated with respect to both property and personal crimes. The data generally support a structural interpretation of converging crime trends with some lag among selected person crime categories. The effects of census regions and states are also examined, and here the data tentatively indicate a small but potentially increasing state effect.   J

122.   Jensen, Gary F.; Stauss, Joseph H.; and Harris, V. William.   CRIME, DELINQUENCY, AND THE AMERICAN INDIAN.   *Human Organization 1977 36(3): 252-257.* Examines the disproportionately high arrest rate for Indians as compared to blacks and whites in urban and nonurban situations; discusses tribal variation in rule-breaking and how this is reflected in three different boarding schools among Navajo, Apache, and Hopi, 1976.

123.   Jordan, Philip D.   THE CAPITAL OF CRIME.   *Civil War Times Illus. 1975 13(10): 4-9, 44-47.* Crime and police activity in Washington, D. C., during the Civil War.   S

124.   Katz, William Loren.   THE PEOPLE VS. THE KLAN IN MASS COMBAT.   *Freedomways 1980 20(2): 96-100.* Surveys the activities of the Ku Klux Klan and reactions to them since Reconstruction and argues that there has always been forcible resistance to their efforts.

125.   Katzman, Martin T.   THE CONTRIBUTION OF CRIME TO URBAN DECLINE.   *Urban Studies [Great Britain] 1980 17(3): 277-286.* The fact that crime is higher in the larger urban centers and in the central cities of metropolitan areas suggests that crime has contributed to suburbanization. Previous studies have been unable to extricate crime from other causes of suburbanization and central city decline. The present study of residential mobility isolates the effect of property crime from other neighborhood characteristics, such as accessibility to workplace and social composition. In Dallas it is found that the repelling effects of crime for potential movers is greater for families with children than without and for more affluent families, white and black.   J

126.   Keeny, Susan.   THE STORY OF A BAD GIRL.   *Washington Monthly 1977 9(5/6): 31-39.* Recounts work with a volunteer probation agency for juvenile delinquents in Arlington, Virginia, 1976.

127.   Kelly, William R. and Snyder, David.   RACIAL VIOLENCE AND SOCIOECONOMIC CHANGES AMONG BLACKS IN THE UNITED STATES.   *Social Forces 1980 58(3): 739-760.* This paper reports an inquiry into the relationship between racial violence and the socioeconomic gains among blacks that occurred in the United States during the 1960's. The few previous studies of the effects of racial disorders are limited in scope and are marred by methodological problems. We take the resource management framework, which conceptualizes violence as a potential political resource for its users, as a substantive warrant to examine this relationship. We also locate the analysis in the general (though largely neglected) arena of violence and social change. We argue that the effects of violence are likely conditional on other factors, and develop hypotheses concerning the differential influence of racial disorders according to the political structure of American cities and the public versus private sector location of socioeconomic changes. We analyze the effects of racial violence

frequency and severity on changes between 1960 and 1970 in three socioeconomic variables: nonwhite income, unemployment rates, and the racial composition of selected occupations. These analyses are estimated separately for cities in the South and those in other regions. Our results consistently indicate no relationship between racial violence and black socioeconomic gains *at the local level.* These findings suggest that earlier evidence of reform responses to disorder in some cities may have reflected attempts to cool out black protest but did not result in substantive changes. Our conclusions on the effects of racial violence therefore parallel those on its causes: *if* there were socioeconomic consequences, they must have operated at the national level and affected blacks uniformly across local communities. 3 tables, 23 notes, biblio.   J

128. Kennedy, Edward M.   CRIME REFORM OR SOCIAL REFORM IS THE WRONG QUESTION; WE NEED BOTH.   *Center Mag. 1977 10(4): 22-28.* Discusses sources of current crime; the solution is to deal with underlying social causes and develop a modern, comprehensive federal criminal code.

129. Klein, Malcolm W.   LABELING, DETERRENCE, AND RECIDIVISM: A STUDY OF POLICE DISPOSITIONS OF JUVENILE OFFENDERS.   *Social Problems 1974 22(2): 292-303.* Analyzes 49 police agencies in Los Angeles County to determine the ratio of arrested juveniles that are released to those handled through the juvenile justice system. The data provide only partial support for the assumption that the stigma of police labeling leads to an increase in the offender's criminal behavior. Notes, bibliography.   A. M. Osur

130. Klein, Milton M.   CORRUPTION IN COLONIAL AMERICA.   *South Atlantic Q. 1979 78(1): 57-72.* Corruption was imported with the first settlers, flourished in its new environment, took on slightly new forms, but never reached the level of Europe. Colonial corruption expressed itself in three forms: landed, commercial, and political. Colonial Americans developed a hostility to corruption which mitigated its extent and intensity without eliminating it. By 1776 the theme of European corruption and American virtue was one of the most powerful ideological impulses propelling the colonists toward revolution. Secondary monographs; 30 notes.   H. M. Parker, Jr.

131. Kubicek, Earl C.   THE LINCOLN CORPUS CAPER.   *Lincoln Herald 1980 82(3): 474-480.* Biography of Terrance Mullen (b. 1849), one of the men charged and found guilty of an attempt to steal the body of Abraham Lincoln in Springfield, Illinois, in exchange for the release from prison of counterfeiter Ben Boyd on the night of the presidential election in 1876.

132. Lack, Paul D.   SLAVERY AND VIGILANTISM IN AUSTIN, TEXAS, 1840-1860.   *Southwestern Hist. Q. 1981 85(1): 1-20.* During the 1840's and 1850's, the citizens of Austin, Texas, periodically feared slave rebellions abetted by Mexican residents. In 1854 and 1856, they responded to those dangers by forming vigilante committees to preserve social order. Although the vigilantes succeeded in driving away the Mexicans supposedly helping slaves escape, they did not oppress the slave community. Furthermore, the committees never challenged the legitimate government and law enforcement agencies. When the threat of slave insurrections passed, the vigilante committees quickly disbanded. 33 notes.   R. D. Hurt

133. Lalli, Michael and Savitz, Leonard D. THE FEAR OF CRIME IN THE
SCHOOL ENTERPRISE AND ITS CONSEQUENCES. *Educ. and Urban
Soc. 1976 8(4): 401-416.* Summarizes a multiyear study begun in 1970 among a
large cohort of young Philadelphia males and their mothers. In the study group
a significant number of truancies and dropouts may be explained by actual fear
of physical danger in the school setting. Four tables, 3 notes, biblio.
C. A. D'Aniello

134. Landes, William M. AN ECONOMIC STUDY OF U.S. AIRCRAFT
HIJACKING, 1961-1976. *J. of Law and Econ. 1978 21(1): 1-31.* Increases in
the probability of apprehension and punishment have significantly reduced domestic hijacking; foreign hijacking is not much affected. The cost of screening
passengers just offsets the expected hijacking losses. Primary and secondary
sources; 10 tables, 56 notes.   C. B. Fitzgerald

135. Landon, Brooks. "NOT SOLVE IT BUT BE IN IT": GERTRUDE
STEIN'S DETECTIVE STORIES AND THE MYSTERY OF CREATIVITY.
Am. Literature 1981 53(3): 487-498. Blood On the Dining-Room Floor (1933),
the result of Gertrude Stein's long interest in detective stories, marked the beginning of an important phase in her literary career. She was attempting to reconcile
the conflict in her writing between human nature and the human mind. Stein was
then struggling to adjust to her new-found literary success and to redefine her role
as a writer. 28 notes.   T. P. Linkfield

136. Lane, Roger. CRIME AND THE INDUSTRIAL REVOLUTION:
BRITISH AND AMERICAN VIEWS. *J. of Social Hist. [Great Britain] 1974
7(3): 287-303.* Explores the British and American approaches to the relation
between crime and the Industrial Revolution in the late 18th and 19th centuries.
The British have accepted and explored the implications of such a relationship;
American social scientists have not. The fact that the urban and the industrial
revolutions have largely coincided in time in the United States has prevented
Americans from identifying their separate effects. 73 notes.   R. V. Ritter

137. Lane, Roger. CRIMINAL VIOLENCE IN AMERICA: THE FIRST
HUNDRED YEARS. *Ann. of the Am. Acad. of Pol. and Social Sci. 1976 (423):
1-13.* America has long been notorious for its violence, but illegitimate criminal
violence has received relatively little attention. *Vigilantism* is the best known of
the specifically American forms of social violence. Woven deeply into our history,
bound up in the westward movement, the gun culture, and slavery, vigilantism
in its wider sense was an important form of political expression. Mob violence
reached its apogee in the North before the Civil War, but continued to flourish
in the South and West through 1876 and gave the whole nation a heritage of direct
action in the name of justice. *Gunfighting* has been less important in our actual
history, but very significant in our national imagination. The gunfighting mys-
tique, and our fascination with it, has contributed heavily to our tradition of
violence. *Urban riot and crime* are new fields of study, drawing heavily on
interdisciplinary methods. Recent work on the city of Philadelphia, for example,
may be used in several ways. The nature of collective violence reveals something
about the city's own polity and, in connection with other studies of individual
violence, something about social and economic stages of development. In brief,
all sorts of street violence decreased with the Industrial Revolution, and the
Centennial City was quieter than any earlier.   J

138. Langum, David J. PIONEER JUSTICE ON THE OVERLAND TRAILS. *Western Hist. Q. 1974 5(4): 421-439.* The prevailing historical wisdom is that wagon traveling pioneers bound for the West exercised a spontaneous judicial skill in dealing with crimes and disorders they encountered on the trail. Jesse Applegate's widely-published article, "A Day with the Cow Column," (*Oregon Hist. Soc. Q.* 1900 1: 371-383) is the basis for this view. Hard evidence of diaries, letters, and other documents, however, do not support Applegate's "romantic reminiscence." Rather, many of the trials were like informal courts-martial; frequent simple expulsion of the presumed offender obviated the necessity of forming courts and indulging in any judicial process; and when trials were conducted they were frequently diversions from the monotony of travel. Calm judicial deliberation and punishment, usually in cases of deliberate murder, were the principle exceptions to these generalizations. 54 notes.   D. L. Smith

139. Ledeen, Michael. HISS, OSWALD, THE KGB AND US. *Commentary 1978 65(5): 30-36.* Discusses information from Allen Weinstein's *Perjury: The Hiss-Chambers Case* and Edward J. Epstein's *Legend: The Secret World of Lee Harvey Oswald.* In both instances, experts were extremely unwilling to accept evidence of KGB espionage. Indeed, a mood of anti-anti-Communism has developed, which may only now be yielding to a more realistic appraisal of the KGB's intelligence ability and the lack of American expertise in counterintelligence.   J. Tull

140. Lee, Carol F. DISCRETIONARY JUSTICE IN EARLY MASSACHUSETTS. *Essex Inst. Hist. Collections 1976 112(2): 120-139.* At the outset of Puritan rule in Massachusetts magistrates and courts had the authority to enforce order and morality by making judgments and punishments. Only the Bible, their background in English local and common law, and their individual sense of justice guided them in defining criminal activity and in passing sentence on criminal offenders. Justice was administered by personal discretion until 1648 when written law culminated in a comprehensive codification known as the "Laws and Liberties of Massachusetts." Despite traditional beliefs that Puritans were harsh, the magistrates usually handed out mild sentences, and these frequently were softened when there was evidence of true repentance. Discretion in sentencing usually was based on the offender's past history, social status, marital status and ability to make restitution as well as the gravity of the offense. The decision to abandon discretionary justice was a political one. Based on primary sources of the Colony of Massachusetts, records of the Governor, and records of Essex County, Massachusetts; 49 notes.   H. M. Parker, Jr.

141. Leont'ev, Iu. B. PRESTUPNOST' MOLODEZHI V S.SH.A. [Juvenile crime in the USA]. *Sovetskoe Gusodarstvo i Pravo [USSR] 1978 (10): 139-143.* Gives American percentages for murder, robbery, abduction, etc., committed during 1960-75.

142. Lernack, Paul. PEACE BONDS AND CRIMINAL JUSTICE IN COLONIAL PHILADELPHIA. *Pennsylvania Mag. of Hist. and Biog. 1976 100(2): 173-190.* In reaction to persecution at the hands of English authorities, the Pennsylvania Quakers established a mild criminal code. The peace bond, a legal device aimed at diverting troublemakers from the criminal justice system, was one manifestation of this lenient code. The peace bond was a form of civil

or criminal bail which judges could order without criminally charging the accused. In the close-knit Quaker community, the peace bond was a flexible alternative to criminal prosecution, but by 1780, the growing anonymity of city dwellers and the inflation of the cash value of the bail nullified its flexibility and thereafter it was used infrequently. Based on primary and secondary sources; 64 notes.

E. W. Carp

143. LeSueur, Marc.   THE PRIVATE EYE: SECOND "GOLDEN AGE." *J. of Popular Film and Television 1979 7(2): 181-189.* Discusses the recently renewed interest in American films of the private eye genre and gives a brief history of detective films during 1940's-79.

144. Levesque, George A.   BLACK CRIME AND CRIME STATISTICS IN ANTE-BELLUM BOSTON.   *Australian J. of Pol. and Hist. [Australia] 1979 25(2): 216-227.* Discusses the pathology (crime, disease, mortality) of black life in Boston in the 1830's-60's. Considers the roles of urbanization, upbringing, drink, and poverty as causes of crime, and discusses the ratio of black to white prisoners. In 1821, the ratio of black convicts was one in 146.5, while the white ratio was one in 2,140. In 1843, when the statewide black population was 9,000, there were 364 black inmates; the proportion was one in 24 for blacks and one in 120 for whites. Provides case studies of convictions. Based on newspapers and jail returns; 23 notes.   W. D. McIntyre

145. Levin, Martin A. and Dornbusch, Horst D.   PURE AND POLICY SOCIAL SCIENCE: EVALUATION OF POLICIES IN CRIMINAL JUSTICE AND EDUCATION.   *Public Policy 1973 21(3): 383-424.*

146. Levine, James P.   THE INEFFECTIVENESS OF ADDING POLICE TO PREVENT CRIME.   *Public Policy 1975 23(4): 523-545.* A survey of 10 American cities reveals that increasing the size of police forces neither reduces nor prevents crime; rather crimes often increase proportionately. The unwillingness of courts to imprison arrested criminals is the main cause of crime. A criminal is not deterred by additional police if he knows he is unlikely to be imprisoned even if arrested. Other causes of crime are intolerable conditions in the cities and the large number of young people whose lives are without hope. Until these conditions are corrected, adding police will not reduce crime. 4 tables, fig., 50 notes.   V. L. Human

147. Lewit, David.   SOCIAL PSYCHOLOGY AND CRIME CONTROL. *J. of Social Issues 1975 31(1): 193-210.* Considering the limitations of individual, interpersonal, and other partial approaches, open-system theory of organizational psychology is proposed as a framework for effective crime control. Social psychological principles of diversity, cohesiveness, power base, voluntarism, option communication, and modular leadership are presented as functional essentials within the open-system framework. Innovations in evaluation and action research, utilizing public participation and permitting deviation from ideal experimental control, are outlined. Three-way bargaining is seen as a means of achieving constructive social accommodation among potentially criminal groups and others, utilizing coalitions to extend perception and induce cooperation while reducing administrator conflicts.   J

148. Lizotte, Alan J. and Bordua, David J. FIREARMS OWNERSHIP FOR SPORT AND PROTECTION: TWO DIVERGENT MODELS. *Am. Sociol. Rev. 1980 45(2): 229-244.* A rationale for investigating subcultures of firearms ownership is developed. Two gun-owning populations are investigated by using survey data for the State of Illinois, those who own guns for sport and those who own guns for protection. Models of individual level gun ownership for sport and for protection are constructed and tested. Sporting gun ownership appears to be subcultural. Sporting gun ownership can be predicted by using family socialization variables and indicators of contact among members of the subculture, independent of situational variables. Protective ownership has none of the trappings of a subculture. It does not respond to family socialization and indicators of contact with other people who own guns for protection. Further, there is no indication of a subculture of violence among protective gun owners. Violent attitudes and behavior do not predict protective gun ownership. In fact, a situational variable (county violent crime) was the only predictor of gun ownership for protection. Further, gun ownership for protection and gun ownership for sport were found to be independent events, with no joint probability of occurrence. This suggests that the impetus for a subculture of protective ownership could not be a logical extension of a subculture of firearms ownership for sport. 5 tables, 2 fig., biblio. J

149. Loftin, Colin and McDowall, David. THE POLICE, CRIME, AND ECONOMIC THEORY: AN ASSESSMENT. *Am. Sociol. Rev. 1982 47(3): 393-401.* Although several economic theories of crime postulate that crime rates and police strength are simultaneously determined, empirical research on the issue has produced highly divergent results. Describes a statistical technique which permits a more flexible approach to temporal analysis and applies it to data on crime and police strength in Detroit. Finds no evidence for the systematic relationships envisioned in economic theory, and attributes this to important organizational and political variables which are omitted from these theories. J/S

150. Louthan, William C. RELATIONSHIPS AMONG POLICE, COURTS, AND CORRECTIONAL AGENCIES. *Policy Studies J. 1974 3(1): 30-37.*

151. Lovritch, Nicholas P., Jr. REDUCING CRIME THROUGH POLICE-COMMUNITY RELATIONS: EVIDENCE OF THE EFFECTIVENESS OF POLICE-COMMUNITY RELATIONS TRAINING FROM A STUDY OF 161 CITIES. *Policy Studies J. 1978 7(special issue): 505-511.* Cities with greatest commitment have a lower crime rate and a higher reportage of crime, 1960-75.

152. MacNamara, Donald E. J. and Sullivan, John J. MAKING THE VICTIM WHOLE. *Urban R. 1973 6(3): 21-25.* Examines methods of restitution for victims of crimes. S

153. Magaddino, Joseph P. CRIME, VICTIM COMPENSATION, AND THE SUPPLY OF OFFENSES. *Public Policy 1973 21(3): 437-440.*

154. Mal'kov, V. L. TOM MUNI: UZNIK SAN-KVENTINA [Tom Mooney: prisoner of San Quentin]. *Novaia i Noveishaia Istoriia [USSR] 1975 (2): 101-115, (4): 81-94, (5): 93-103.* Part I. Gives an account of the trial of Tom

Mooney following an explosion in San Francisco in 1916. Describes Mooney's life against the background of socialist activities and the labor movement in the United States. He was elected a delegate at the California Socialist Party Conference and in 1910 attended the Copenhagen Congress of the Second International. Mooney became increasingly involved in the intrigues of repression and violence which characterized industrial unrest in the 1910's. The anti-war mood made the summer of 1916 particularly tense. Secondary sources; 64 notes. Part II. Discusses hypotheses concerning the explosion in San Francisco in 1916 of which Mooney was accused and sentenced to death. After widespread protests in the United States and Russia the sentence was commuted. Describes the many unsuccessful political and legal attempts in the 1920's to free Mooney. Secondary sources; 54 notes. Part III. Stresses the heroism of Mooney in the horrific conditions of San Quentin Prison and the constant support of the International Workers' Movement until his release in 1939, interpreting his saga as the typical plight of fighters for the working class in the West. Based on letters, first-hand accounts and newspapers; 44 notes.   E. R. Sicher/V. A. Packer

155. Marks, Judith A. and Traugott, Michael W.   DATA RESOURCES AND SERVICES FROM THE CRIMINAL JUSTICE ARCHIVE AND INFORMATION NETWORK.   Raben, Joseph and Marks, Gregory, ed. *Data Bases in the Humanities and Social Sciences* (Amsterdam: North-Holland Publ., 1980): 27-30. Availability of computer-readable data has made the study of crime and the criminal justice system more cost-effective, 1980.

156. Martin, Michael J. and Smith, Glenn H.   VICE AND VIOLENCE IN WARD COUNTY, NORTH DAKOTA, 1905-1920.   *North Dakota Hist. 1980 47(2): 10-21.* Minot and its surrounding area were wide open throughout 1905-20. Population grew rapidly due to railroad construction and availability of unclaimed land. Nearly complete court records of Ward County and Minot document the prevalence and different types of criminal activity, and offer strong support for the dubious title of "crime capitol of North Dakota." Based on court records and newspapers; 5 illus., 3 tables, 77 notes.   G. L. Olson

157. May, Philip A.   CONTEMPORARY CRIME AND THE AMERICAN INDIAN: A SURVEY AND ANALYSIS OF THE LITERATURE.   *Plains Anthrop. 1982 27(97): 225-238.* Studies of contemporary Indian crime and criminal justice are reviewed and analyzed. Each study is presented according to its major thrust, description, or inference. In addition, the studies are described regarding the specific methods used and significant findings. Eight principal themes of explanation found in this literature are named and described: adjustment/acculturation, social disorganization, traditional social organization, overt criminality, discrimination, over-surveillance, under-utilization of legal resources, and recidivism.   J/S

158. Mazur, Allan.   BOMB THREATS AND THE MASS MEDIA: EVIDENCE FOR A THEORY OF SUGGESTION.   *Am. Sociol. Rev. 1982 47(3): 407-411.* Suicides that are publicized in the newspaper are known to trigger additional, imitative suicides. Examines data on bomb threats against nuclear energy facilities, finding that threat incidence closely follows fluctuations in mass media coverage of nuclear power issues. Bomb threats, like suicides, are clearly influenced by the mass media.   J/S

159. McAleer, John. THE GAME'S AFOOT: DETECTIVE FICTION IN THE PRESENT DAY. *Kansas Q. 1978 10(4): 21-40.* Extended bibliographical essay on research and critical works dealing with detective fiction, 1840's-1970's.

160. McCormick, Albert E., Jr. RULE ENFORCEMENT AND MORAL INDIGNATION: SOME OBSERVATIONS ON THE EFFECTS OF CRIMINAL ANTITRUST CONVICTIONS UPON SOCIETAL REACTION PROCESSES. *Social Problems 1977 25(1): 30-39.* History of antitrust legislation and enforcement, 1890's-1970's. Originally antitrust activities caused moral indignation within the public sector, but nonenforcement of laws has led to a neutralization of the indignation through redefinition of antitrust.

161. McDade, Thomas M. AFTER THE FACT OR THE MURDEROUS CAREER OF LOUIS CLARK JONES. *New York Folklore Q. 1975 1(1/2): 15-19.* Notes the large number of murder cases studied in the writing of New York State Historical Association leader Louis C. Jones, ca. 1899-1924.

162. McKenna, Jeremiah B. CRIME IN THE SCHOOLS. *New York Affairs 1974 1(3): 3-13.* "The police last year arrested 219 school age children for murder, 353 for rape, 8056 for robbery and 252 for arson. Many of these children were back in class after only a month, effectively transforming the city's schools into sanctuaries for criminals who prey upon their fellow students." J

163. McKinney, Gordon B., ed. THE KLAN IN THE SOUTHERN MOUNTAINS: THE LUSK-SHOTWELL CONTROVERSY. *Appalachian J. 1981 8(2): 89-104.* Reproduces the account provided in 1923 by Virgil Lusk of his violent encounter in 1869 with Randolph Shotwell in Asheville, North Carolina, which grew out of these men's political and personal differences over Republican Party policies during Reconstruction and out of Lusk's opposition to and Shotwell's support of Ku Klux Klan terrorism.

164. McLoughlin, William G. PARSON BLACKBURN'S WHISKEY AND THE CHEROKEE INDIAN SCHOOLS, 1809-1810. *J. of Presbyterian Hist. 1979 57(4): 427-445.* Relates an incident involving the Reverend Gideon Blackburn's whiskey still and trade with the demise of the first Presbyterian mission among the Cherokee Indians in the Old Southwest. Although the documentary evidence appears to exonerate Blackburn from the charge of trying to sell whiskey to the Indians, nevertheless his being caught in the act of transporting whiskey across Indian lands weakened his credibility and was responsible for closing down Presbyterian schools among the Cherokees. Based largely on Records of the Bureau of Indian Affairs, M-221; illus., 27 notes. H. M. Parker, Jr.

165. Mechling, Elizabeth Walker. PATRICIA HEARST: MYTH AMERICA 1974, 1975, 1976. *Western J. of Speech Communication 1979 43(3): 168-179.* Investigates, via content analysis, the rhetorical presence of a specific myth in the mass media coverage of the Patricia Hearst story, hypothesizing that media coverage tapped into a preexisting captivity myth basic to American culture, that metaphors growing out of that myth were used to "make sense" of the event, and that these metaphors were used to create an outline that was filled in by believers of the myth.

166. Melching, Richard. THE ACTIVITIES OF THE KU KLUX KLAN
IN ANAHEIM, CALIFORNIA, 1923-1925. *Southern California Q. 1974*
56(2): 175-196. The Ku Klux Klan in Anaheim was unlike the national organization in several respects; violence was at a minimum, Klan supporters endorsed
prohibition, and their opponents were accused of favoring vice and gambling, thus
presenting the Klan and their candidates as reformers. For a time, the Klan
captured most of Anaheim's city offices, but a major blow against them occurred
when the klavern's membership list was made public, revealing that the claimed
membership of 1,400 did not match the reality of less than 300. Without its
secrecy and with its true size revealed, the Klan went into decline, with the
February, 1925 city election bringing about its complete defeat. For months
afterwards resignations and firings purged the Klan from city hall, and despite
a few subsequent attempts to resurrect it, the organization never regained its
earlier power. Based chiefly on accounts in the Anaheim newspaper; 88 notes.
                                                                    A. Hoffman

167. Mellman, Harry G. CRIMINAL JUSTICE IN THE U.S.: RESTRUC-
TURING A NON-SYSTEM. *Natl. Civic R. 1973 62(5): 240-247.* "A 'system'
of justice does not exist in the United States; i.e., we have municipal ordinances,
state statutes, national legislation, constitutions, opinions of attorneys general and
city counselors, court decisions, as well as law enforcement officials and officers,
and correctional facilities, with all their problems."   J

168. Mennel, Robert M. JUVENILE DELINQUENCY IN PERSPECTIVE.
Hist. of Educ. Q. 1973 13(3): 275-287. Reviews Sanford J. Fox's "Juvenile Justice
Reform: An Historical Perspective" *Stanford Law Review* 22 (June 1970): 1187-
1239, Robert S. Pickett's *House of Refuge: Origins of Juvenile Reform in New
York State, 1815-1857* (Syracuse: Syracuse U. Pr., 1969), and Anthony M. Platt's
The Child Savers: The Invention of Delinquency (Chicago: U. of Chicago Pr.,
1969).

169. Meyer, Richard E. THE OUTLAW: A DISTINCTIVE AMERICAN
FOLKTYPE. *J. of the Folklore Inst. 1980 17(2-3): 94-124.* A study of American folk ballads and legends which focus on four famous outlaws indicates that
12 basic narrative elements are regularly repeated. These characteristics, as applied to Jesse James (1847-82), Sam Bass (1851-78), Billy the Kid (1859-81), and
Charles Arthur "Pretty Boy" Floyd (1901-34), demonstrate that a significant
distinction must be drawn between the terms "outlaw" and "criminal" in American folklore. These four, and others like them, are more properly categorized as
"outlaw-heroes" whose exploits tend to be popular among some groups because
they seemingly strike a blow against repression. Their fame is spread even farther
among the urbanized masses via television, pulp literature, and other vehicles of
popular culture. 107 notes.   C. D. Geist

170. Michalowski, Raymond J. and Bohlander, Edward W. REPRESSION
AND CRIMINAL JUSTICE IN CAPITALIST AMERICA. *Sociological Inquiry [Canada] 1976 46(2): 95-106.* Discusses sociological constructs making
difficult the incorporation of repressive functions for the purpose of social control; examines legal ramifications of social control.

171.   Mirande, Alfredo.   THE CHICANO AND THE LAW: AN ANALYSIS OF COMMUNITY-POLICE CONFLICT IN AN URBAN BARRIO.   *Pacific Sociol. Rev. 1981 24(1): 65-86.* A case study of a southern California barrio in 1975 suggests that a rising crime rate increases support for police power, limiting civil liberties, while fear of police reduces support of police power and increases support for civil guarantees.

172.   Mirande, Alfredo.   FEAR OF CRIME AND FEAR OF THE POLICE IN A CHICANO COMMUNITY.   *Sociol. and Social Res. 1980 64(4): 528-541.* Compares the attitudes of Mexican Americans in a southern California barrio toward crime, the police, and civil liberties with the attitudes on these issues of Negroes and white respondents from a previous survey. Among the groups, fear of crime leads to support for augmenting police power, and, conversely, fear of the police increases support for civil liberties. Fear of the police similarly was associated with a desire to curtail police power. Whites reported receiving better treatment from the police and were less fearful of crime than Chicanos who, in turn, appeared less fearful than blacks. Though Chicanos seemed to have less fear of crime than blacks, they have had more fear of the police. Chicanos were also most supportive of civil liberties, and anglos least supportive.   J

173.   Mitchell, John G.   SAID CHICAGO'S AL CAPONE: "I GIVE THE PUBLIC WHAT THE PUBLIC WANTS . . . "   *Am. Heritage 1979 30(2): 82-93.* Al Capone, who considered himself a pleasurable benefactor, arrived in Chicago in 1919 and gained control of most of that city's underworld prior to his demise in 1931 when found guilty of tax evasion. After eight years in prison, Capone was released. Syphilis had nearly destroyed his nervous system and he died in Miami in 1947. 18 illus.   J. F. Paul

174.   Monahan, John and Geis, Gilbert.   CONTROLLING "DANGEROUS" PEOPLE.   *Ann. of the Am. Acad. of Pol. and Social Sci. 1976 (423): 142-151.* The label "dangerous" often has been applied in America to persons whose major threat lay in the fact that they offended the moral or esthetic sensibilities of those holding power. In the America of the Revolutionary period, there was comparatively little violent crime, but by today's standards, punishments tended to be harsh and/or humiliating. The mentally aberrant were seen as especially dangerous, since their condition was traced to a devilish infestation, and they were handled with great brutality. Blacks, too, often restive under slavery, were regarded as dangerous persons. Today, similar kinds of ascriptions as "dangerous" are applied to criminals, mental patients, and minorities—with similarly unconvincing evidence to justify the treatment such persons often receive. Danger ought to be determined on a social basis, not by theological or medical dictation, and the category ought to include all (but only) forms of human and group action which represent real threats.   J

175.   Monkkonen, Eric H.   BLOOD AND SPACE: MORE STUDIES OF NINETEENTH-CENTURY CRIME AND JUSTICE.   *J. of Urban Hist. 1981 7(2): 239-245.* Reviews two recent books on 19th-century violence: John C. Schneider's *Detroit and the Problem of Order, 1830-1880* and Roger Lane's *Violent Death in the City.* Both books add much useful data to a very new and understudied field. While their perspectives are greatly different, Schneider's geographical and Lane's sociopsychological, they show that various interdisciplinary perspectives add greatly to the interpretation of historical data. 2 notes.   T. W. Smith

176.   Monkkonen, Erik H.   A DISORDERLY PEOPLE? URBAN ORDER IN THE NINETEENTH AND TWENTIETH CENTURIES. *J. of Am. Hist. 1981 68(3): 539-559.* Uses arrest rates for public drunk and disorderly conduct to analyze general public order in cities from 1860 to 1980. The overall trend during this period (with notable exceptions in some urban areas) was a decrease in both public order offenses and public disorder. More extensive city-level research is necessary, however, since many local exceptions seem to contradict the national trend. Based on FBI crime reports, local police records, and several editions of the *American Digest;* 2 fig., 3 tables, 33 notes, appendix.

T. P. Linkfield

177.   Moore, William Howard.   THE KEFAUVER COMMITTEE AND OR-GANIZED CRIME.   Hawes, Joseph M., ed. *Law and Order in American History* (Port Washington, N.Y.: Kennikat Pr., 1979): 136-147. Disputes the findings of Senator Estes Kefauver's (D-Tenn.) Senate Special Committee to Investigate Interstate Crime in 1950-51 that a nationwide Italian American syndicate called the Mafia held a monopoly on US organized crime. The Committee perpetuated the myth that organized crime existed "outside the social, political, and economic structure of American life". Also gives a history of US organized crime since the 1890's.

178.   Moore, William Howard.   WAS ESTES KEFAUVER "BLACK-MAILED" DURING THE CHICAGO CRIME HEARINGS?: A HISTORIAN'S PERSPECTIVE.   *Public Hist. 1982 4(1): 4-28.* Narrates Seymour Hersh and Jeff Gerth's questionable 1976 *New York Times* exposé, which claimed that in 1950 Chicago labor lawyer Sidney R. Korshak, assisted by underworld acquaintances, blackmailed Senator Estes Kefauver, head of the Senate committee investigating organized crime, in an attempt to end the investigation.

179.   Morris, H. H.   THE USS "SOMERS" AFFAIR.   *Am. Hist. Illus. 1974 9(5): 24-31.* In 1841 Commander Alexander Slidell MacKenzie, in charge of the brig *USS Somers,* suspected a mutiny among his crew and hanged three men; for this he stood court-martial in 1843 and was subsequently found innocent.

180.   Morris, Norval.   REORDERING PRIORITIES WOULD FREE PO-LICE AND CRIMINAL COURTS TO DEAL WITH PREDATORY CRIMES.   *Center Mag. 1977 10(4): 39-42.* Reforming the criminal justice system will not change the deep social, cultural, and political causes of crime, but a reordering of priorities in crime control would make agencies more effective.

181.   Morris, Thomas D.   "AS IF THE INJURY WAS EFFECTED BY THE NATURAL ELEMENTS OF AIR, OR FIRE": SLAVE WRONGS AND THE LIABILITY OF MASTERS.   *Law & Soc. Rev. 1981-82 16(4): 569-599.* Discusses slavery, law, and the liability of masters for the damage that resulted from the wrongs of slaves. Legal traditions, styles of reasoning, and, above all, social relationships and perceptions (including those between slaveholders and non-slaveholders) help unravel the policy choices of Southerners made in the years before the Civil War.

J/S

182.   Morsberger, Robert E. and Morsberger, Katharine M.   AFTER AN-DERSONVILLE: THE FIRST WAR CRIMES TRIAL.   *Civil War Times Illus. 1974 13(4): 30-41.*

183. Mossman, Keith. PRESCRIPTION FOR CRIMINAL JUSTICE: THE STANDARDS GO TO THE PEOPLE. *Judicature 1973 57(5): 204-210.* In implementing its Criminal Justice Standards, the American Bar Association has met with favorable citizen and expert response.   S

184. Mugleston, William F. JULIAN HARRIS, THE GEORGIA PRESS, AND THE KU KLUX KLAN. *Georgia Hist. Q. 1975 59(3): 284-295.* Chronicles a 1920's anti-Ku Klux Klan campaign waged by Columbus, Georgia, *Enquirer-Sun* editor Julian LaRose Harris in a traditionally pro-Klan area.

185. Munson, Naomi. THE CASE OF JANET COOKE. *Commentary 1981 72(2): 46-50.* Recapitulates the events surrounding Janet Cooke's winning of a Pulitzer Prize for a story she invented; criticizes explanations for this lapse in journalistic professionalism provided by apologists for the *Washington Post;* and asserts that the latitude given to Cooke in her reportorial duties stemmed from her being black and female.

186. Mysak, Joe and Giner, Juan Antonio. EL CASO DEL PULITZER PARA JANET COOKE: POR QUIEN DOBLAN LAS CAMPANAS? [The case of the Pulitzer for Janet Cooke: for whom do the bells toll?]. *Nuestro Tiempo [Spain] 1981 56(325-326): 96-114.* Janet Cooke's winning of the Pulitzer Prize in 1980 for an invented story is described in detail, including the mechanism of prize awarding; while she returned the prize and the money and left the *Washington Post,* great damage resulted to journalism, especially investigative reporting, at a time when public respect for the press is already at an all-time low.

187. Nagin, Daniel. CRIME RATES, SANCTION LEVELS, AND CONSTRAINTS ON PRISON POPULATION. *Law and Soc. Rev. 1978 12(3): 341-366.* In recent years there has been an accumulation of analyses showing a negative association between crime rates and various measures of criminal sanctions, which have been widely interpreted as evidence of the deterrent effect of sanctions (see Tullock, 1974; Tittle, 1973; van den Haag, 1975). In this paper, results are presented that are in conflict with such an interpretation. For the sanction of imprisonment (time served in prison and the risk of imprisonment given commission of a crime), the analysis indicates that the negative association is more readily interpreted as a negative effect of crime rates on sanction levels rather than its reverse—a deterrent effect.   J

188. Neier, Aryeh. FBI FILES: MODUS INOPERANDI. *Civil Liberties R. 1974 1(3): 50-58.* "How can we hope to reduce crime if we disseminate records which make it impossible for people to stop being criminals?"   J

189. Nickerson, Edward A. "REALISTIC" CRIME FICTION: AN ANATOMY OF EVIL. *Centennial Rev. 1981 25(2): 101-132.* Analyzes the villains in the crime fiction of Dashiell Hammett, Raymond Chandler, and Ross Macdonald of the "California" school of realism as opposed to the Golden Age mystery writing of such authors as Dorothy Sayers, Agatha Christie, and Ellery Queen. A disproportionate number of primary villains in the stories by Hammett, Macdonald, and especially Chandler are women, a statistic that contrasts with the actual number of murders committed by women. Methods, however, are more realistic than those employed by Golden Age authors: shooting, stabbing, and other violent methods are far more common than poisoning or exotic inventions.

Motives are similar in both schools of writing: greed, jealousy, fear of exposure, and the amateur status of the villain. The California school, by viewing the milieu of its villains as corrupt, fake, and illegitimate, indicts America for these short-comings and holds a pessimistic view of society. Secondary sources; 35 notes.

A. Hoffman

190.   O'Brien, Robert M.; Shichor, David S.; and Decker, David L.   AN EM-PIRICAL COMPARISON OF THE VALIDITY OF UCR AND NCS CRIME RATES. *Sociol. Q. 1980 21(3): 391-401.* The Uniform Crime Reports (UCR) have been criticized since their inception in the early 1930's, and these criticisms led to the initiation of the National Crime Surveys (NCS); a study assessing the validity of these two indicators of the crime rate for six different crimes—robbery, burglary, rape, aggravated assault, personal larceny, and motor vehicle theft—found convergent validity low for rape, aggravated assault, and personal larceny, and suggested that the nomological validity of the NCS rates is somewhat supe-rior to that of the UCR rates.

191.   Pantaleone, Michele.   MAFIA E VIOLENZA   [The Mafia and vio-lence]. *Problemi di Ulisse [Italy] 1978 14(86): 96-112.* Traces the Mafia from its roots in rural Sicily, through its suppression under the Fascist regime in Italy, to its spread to the United States, and today, to Europe, the Middle East, and other areas; blames it for the assassinations of John and Robert Kennedy, as well as Martin Luther King.

192.   Pao-Min, Chang.   HEALTH AND CRIME AMONG CHINESE-AMERICANS: RECENT TRENDS.   *Phylon 1981 42(4): 356-368.* Since the adoption of a new immigration law in 1965, the total number of Chinese-Ameri-cans has nearly doubled. At the same time, the socioeconomic status has im-proved, resulting in improved health conditions, but the trends of crime have worsened. Feelings of powerlessness, frustration, congestion, and the waning role of the traditional Chinese family have caused this problem.   A. G. Belles

193.   Pate, J'Nell.   INDIANS ON TRIAL IN A WHITE MAN'S COURT. *Great Plains J. 1974 14(1): 56-71.* In 1871 a band of Kiowas attacked a wagon train in Texas, killing and torturing several of the teamsters. Under General William Tecumseh Sherman's orders the Kiowa chiefs Satank, Santanta, and Big Tree were arrested at Fort Sill, Oklahoma, and taken to Texas to stand trial in a civil court. Satank committed suicide on the way, but Satanta and Big Tree were sentenced to death. Following public outcry in the East the sentence was changed to life imprisonment. By 1873 disagreements over the Indians' legal status led to their release. Big Tree adapted to white culture, but Satanta, following further Kiowa attacks, was arrested in 1874 and committed suicide in prison in 1878. In 1963 Satanta's body was returned to Oklahoma and buried with honor.

O. H. Zabel/S

194.   Pearl, Arthur.   PUBLIC POLICY OR CRIME: WHICH IS WORSE? *Social Policy 1977 7(4): 47-54.* Examines the penal system, crime, youth, and the need for more comprehensive rehabilitation programs and for the redefinition of crime; extensively examines the criminal justice system.

195. Pepinsky, Harold E. THE GROWTH OF CRIME IN THE UNITED STATES. *Ann. of the Am. Acad. of Pol. and Social Sci. 1976 (423): 23-30.* The growth of crime in the United States has been viewed as a social problem since the founding of the Republic. From at least the middle of the nineteenth century, this growth can be explained as an outcome of the development of crime measurement technology. American crime measurement specialists have consistently operated under a pair of assumptions: that crime is underreported rather than overreported in crime statistics and that rates of crime generally increase. These assumptions have become the foundation of a self-fulfilling prophecy. Efforts have been devoted to detecting larger rates of crime by using each measure that has been developed, and new measures have continued to be created to supplement the old. Recently, for instance, police departments "refined" their procedures for compiling offense reports, so rates of offenses known to the police climbed dramatically. And the victim survey was developed to supplement police data, with the victim data interpreted as indicating that crime rates are increasing far faster than we had previously imagined. It is proposed that those engaged in crime measurement be given incentives to report fewer offenses. Otherwise, regardless of change in the level of interpersonal conflict in American society, the prophecy of American crime measurement specialists can be expected to continue to fulfill itself, with an unabated growth of crime.   J

196. Pepitone, Albert. SOCIAL PSYCHOLOGICAL PERSPECTIVES ON CRIME AND PUNISHMENT. *J. of Social Issues 1975 31(4): 197-216.* This article addresses itself to the psychological basis of the legal system. The author examines attitudes toward crime and punishment and analyzes the psychological and cultural processes underlying them, with particular attention to the nonlegal or lay person (the observer). Questions of blame and causal responsibility, victim involvement, perceived seriousness of a violation, victim/offender relations, and motivations for punishment are considered. It is proposed that proto-legal moral and ethical values function in normative fashion to determine the person's judgments of violations and reactions to offenders, and that the existence of these value sets has important implications for the legal system.   J

197. Peterson, Russell W. THE CHANGING CRIMINAL JUSTICE SYSTEM. *Natl. Civic R. 1974 63(3): 123-127.* "It is urgent that we develop a rational approach to the problem of crime and delinquency, define it and root out its causes if we are to improve the quality of life in the U. S. The recommendations of the National Advisory Commission on Criminal Justice Standards and Goals constitute such an approach."   J

198. Phillips, David P. THE IMPACT OF FICTIONAL TELEVISION STORIES ON U.S. ADULT FATALITIES: NEW EVIDENCE ON THE EFFECT OF THE MASS MEDIA ON VIOLENCE. *Am. J. of Sociol. 1982 87(6): 1340-1359.* Presents statistics showing that television violence triggers actual violence, particularly imitative suicides, vehicle deaths, and non-fatal accidents; 1977.

199. Platt, Anthony. THE TRIUMPH OF BENEVOLENCE: THE ORIGINS OF THE JUVENILE JUSTICE SYSTEM IN THE UNITED STATES. Hawes, Joseph M., ed. *Law and Order in American History* (Port Washington, N.Y.: Kennikat Pr., 1979): 53-76. Traces the origins of the Ameri-

can juvenile justice system to the child-saving movement of the Progressive Era in the late 19th century, concluding that the juvenile justice system then, as today, failed to be humanitarian and reformist; rather it served as a means of control by the middle class with support from philanthropic industrialists.

200.   Powers, Richard Gid.   [CRIME STORIES].   *J. of Popular Culture 1975 9(3): 743-747.* Reviews *Stories of Great Crimes and Trials* (New York: American Heritage, 1973), Richard Hammer's *Playboy's Illustrated History of Organized Crime* (Chicago: Playboy Press, 1975), Jay Robert Nash's *Bloodletters and Badmen* (New York: M. Evans, 1973), and *Detective World* (Montreal: Fax Publishing, Inc., bimonthly). Suggests possible beginnings for the nonfiction crime stories the author calls anatomies of crime, which fall into two categories, genteel and vulgar.   J. D. Falk

201.   Powers, Richard Gid.   ONE G-MAN'S FAMILY: POPULAR ENTERTAINMENT FORMULAS AND J. EDGAR HOOVER'S F. B. I.   *Am. Q. 1978 30(4): 471-492.* Discusses the public relations efforts and image creation methods employed by J. Edgar Hoover during 1930's-60's. The emphasis in early years via every medium of the entertainment industry was of the tough cop, sophisticated, and uncorruptible who always got his man, achieving justice as living proof that crime did not pay and that the Federal Bureau of Investigation was effective protection for the American public from its "public enemies." A shift to moralism and an overlay of domesticity as an important part of the public relations pitch made the operatives especially vulnerable whenever one made a misstep. 42 notes.   R. V. Ritter

202.   Quen, Jacques M.   ANGLO-AMERICAN CRIMINAL INSANITY: AN HISTORICAL PERSPECTIVE.   *J. of the Hist. of the Behavioral Sci. 1974 10(3): 313-323.* Reviews the history of Anglo-American attitudes regarding the criminal responsibility of the insane.

203.   Ravitz, Justin C. and Gaylin, Willard.   "THE CRIMINAL JUSTICE SYSTEM IS AMERICA'S ONLY WORKING RAILROAD."   *Civil Liberties R. 1974 1(4): 62-76.* "In November 1972, a 32-year-old, jeans-clad, boot-shod Marxist lawyer, Justin C. Ravitz, was elected to a ten-year term as judge of the Detroit Recorder's (Criminal) Court." Interview excerpted from Gaylin's *Partial Justice: A Study of Bias in Sentencing* (New York: Alfred A. Knopf, 1974).
                                                                                    S

204.   Rediker, Marcus.   "UNDER THE BANNER OF KING DEATH": THE SOCIAL WORLD OF ANGLO-AMERICAN PIRATES, 1716 TO 1726. *William and Mary Q. 1981 38(2): 203-227.* Examines the social order of pirates, with emphasis on the non-legal aspects. From a background as merchant seamen, navy sailors, and privateers, the men who were the pirates had experienced brutality. Rules and customs were relatively uniform aboard private ships. Contractual agreements and the organizational and operating structures are discussed. Connections among crews helped to transmit and preserve customs and maintain a social structure. Discusses problems of discipline. A crackdown by authorities, with 400-600 executions, along with the wide dispersal of pirates brought about their downfall. In many ways pirate life represents responses that might be expected of destitute poor thrown into communities of their own mak-

ing. Based on archival records, newspapers, and secondary studies; chart, 99 notes. H. M. Ward

205. Reuter, Peter and Rubinstein, Jonathan B. FACT, FANCY, AND OR-GANIZED CRIME. *Public Interest 1978 (53): 45-67.* Reports the results of a systematic analysis of data obtained from police and law enforcement agencies on the operation of the gambling rackets in metropolitan New York since 1965. The facts sharply conflict with the standard account that gambling provides the main financial base for crimes such as narcotics traffic, prostitution, and hijacking. Examination of the activities of "sheetwriters," bookmaking, and the numbers business reveals that accurate information is almost impossible to obtain. As a result the campaign against organized crime, a topic for facile rhetoric by politicians, too often has been based on myths and misinterpretations.
R. V. Ritter

206. Rhodes, Robert P. POLITICAL THEORY, POLICY ANALYSIS, AND THE INSOLUBLE PROBLEMS OF CRIMINAL JUSTICE. *Policy Studies J. 1974 3(1): 83-89.*

207. Richards, Pamela and Tittle, Charles R. GENDER AND PERCEIVED CHANCES OF ARREST. *Social Forces 1981 59(4): 1182-1199.* Examines gender differences in perceived chances of arrest for six familiar types of lawbreaking. Most crime theories predict that women should give higher arrest estimates than men; five common explanations for this prediction are noted. Survey data from a sample of adults show that women perceive systematically higher chances of arrest than do men, and that differential visibility and differential stakes in conformity seem to be the most promising accounts for these differences. At the same time, these variables are only modest predictors of overall individual patterns in perceived arrest risks. Covers 1972.
J/S

208. Richardson, Richard J. PUBLIC ATTITUDES TOWARD THE CRIMINAL JUSTICE SYSTEM. *Policy Studies J. 1974 3(1): 37-44.*

209. Riley, Sam G. and Wiessler, Joel M. PRIVACY: THE REPORTER AND TELEPHONE AND TAPE RECORDER. *Journalism Q. 1974 51(3): 511-514.* Focuses on a Pennsylvania case wherein Gregory P. Walter, an investigative reporter, was found guilty of wiretapping in 1972 and reviews the relevant law.
S

210. Rinaldi, Matthew. THE DISTURBING CASE OF FEODOR FEDO-RENKO. *Radical Am. 1979 13(5): 37-47.* Feodor Fedorenko, a former armed guard at the Treblinka concentration camp was allowed to keep his US citizenship in 1978; this is a significant ruling for other Nazi war criminals residing in the United States.

211. Robbins, Thomas and Anthony, Dick. NEW RELIGIONS, FAMILIES AND BRAINWASHING. *Society 1978 15(4): 77-83.* Discusses the forced deprogramming of religious cult converts, and its effectiveness and morality, 1970's.

212.   Roberts, John W.   "RAILROAD BILL" AND THE AMERICAN OUTLAW TRADITION. *Western Folklore 1981 40(4): 315-328.* Analyzes the "connotative meanings" of images in "Railroad Bill," an Afro-American ballad, and compares those meanings with those in Anglo-American outlaw ballads. The author examines the distinctions in form and meaning in Afro-American and Anglo-American ballads, distinctions which reveal a "level of meaning common to both" and distinct cultural differences in style and form. Based on variations of the ballad, "Railroad Bill"; 49 notes.   S. L. Myres

213.   Rodino, Peter W.   THE SYSTEM'S TASK: TO PROTECT LIVES AND PROPERTY, BUT ALSO CONSTITUTIONAL FREEDOM. *Center Mag. 1977 10(4): 16-22.* The political system encounters problems in finding a single, coherent policy for crime prevention; suggests initial areas in which to search for answers.

214.   Roncek, Dennis W.   DANGEROUS PLACES: CRIME AND RESI-DENTIAL ENVIRONMENT. *Social Forces 1981 60(1): 74-96.* Investigates how the characteristics of residential areas in the city affect where crimes occur, using data for city blocks in Cleveland and San Diego. A substantial portion of the variance in crime depends on the opportunities provided by the social and physical differentiation of the city.   J/S

215.   Roncek, Dennis W.; Bell, Ralph; and Francik, Jeffrey M. A.   HOUSING PROJECTS AND CRIME: TESTING A PROXIMITY HYPOTHESIS. *Social Problems 1981 29(2): 151-166.* Examines the relationship of proximity to public housing for families in adjacent neighborhoods, focusing on statistics gathered in Cleveland, Ohio.

216.   Rosso, Martha.   PHILADELPHIA'S GREAT DROOD TRIAL. *Pennsylvania Mag. of Hist. and Biog. 1981 105(1): 99-104.* Charles Dickens died before completing *The Mystery of Edwin Drood.* Philadelphia's leading citizens put on a mock trial of the unfinished novel's leading suspect, John Jasper. The "trial," staged by the Dickens Fellowship of Philadelphia, was held before a packed house in the Academy of Music. Based on newspapers and secondary works; 15 notes.   T. H. Wendel

217.   Russell, Diana E. H.   REPORT ON THE INTERNATIONAL TRIBU-NAL ON CRIMES AGAINST WOMEN. *Frontiers 1977 2(1): 1-6.* Describes the proceedings at the Tribunal in Brussels, 4-8 March 1976, tracing its potential to mobilize women; discusses particularly the topics chosen for discussion by the US committee.

218.   Russell, Evlyn Belz.   AN OVERVIEW OF THE CRIMINAL JUSTICE SYSTEM OF HAMPSHIRE COUNTY, 1677-1728. *Hist. J. of Western Massa-chusetts 1977 5(2): 13-20.* Surveys the types of cases heard before Hampshire County's Courts of Quarter Sessions and how various offenses were punished. Illus., 19 notes.   W. H. Mulligan, Jr.

219.   Saari, David J.   THE CRIMINAL JURY FACES FUTURE SHOCK. *Judicature 1973 57(1): 12-17.* Opposes recent changes in the size and decision-making procedure of juries.   S

220. Sanders, Clinton R. CAUGHT IN THE CON-GAME: THE YOUNG, WHITE DRUG USER'S CONTACT WITH THE LEGAL SYSTEM. *Law and Soc. R. 1975 9(2): 197-217.* An in-depth focus on the experiences of young, white drug users in their first serious involvement with the legal system. The study is presented through a series of interactions between users, law enforcement, and court personnel, including narcotics officers, judges, and defense lawyers. Users' overall assessments of the fairness of the legal system tend to be negative because of a general dissatisfaction with society and its institutions.
H. R. Mahood

221. Saunders, Robert M. CRIME AND PUNISHMENT IN EARLY NATIONAL AMERICA: RICHMOND, VIRGINIA, 1784-1820. *Virginia Mag. of Hist. and Biog. 1978 86(1): 33-44.* Analysis of early 19th-century court records in Richmond, Virginia, reveals not only that the city was already a comparatively violent community, but also that whites used the courts to help perpetuate slavery. Based on City of Richmond Hustings Court Order Books and Minute Books; 30 notes.
R. F. Oaks

222. Schlossman, Steven L. JUVENILE JUSTICE IN THE AGE OF JACKSON. *Teachers Coll. Record 1974 76(1): 119-133.* A study of the organization of the New York House of Refuge in 1825, one of the earliest reformatories, and one which brought together several theories of reform. Examines the motives and actions of the founders, and places the entire episode in the context of 19th-century literature on children and education. Notes.
W. H. Mulligan, Jr.

223. Schrag, Peter and Divoky, Diane. THE NEW JUVENILE JUSTICE AT WORK. *Civil Liberties R. 1975 2(3): 57-75.* The technology is changing rapidly, the ideology hardly at all, and the consumers have yet to organize.
A

224. Schwarz, Philip J. GABRIEL'S CHALLENGE: SLAVES AND CRIME IN LATE EIGHTEENTH CENTURY VIRGINIA. *Virginia Mag. of Hist. and Biog. 1982 90(3): 283-309.* In October 1799, an altercation occurred between a Virginia tenant farmer and three slaves. The following year, the same slaves were named and subsequently executed in the Gabriel's Plot incident. Both events illuminate a basic dilemma faced by Americans after the Revolutionary War: a war had been fought to gain freedom for the nation, but not for its slaves. The slaves vowed rebellion against the society, a commitment largely ignored by the planters. The whites' failure to recognize the nature of the 1799 incident contributed to the slaves' continued pursuit of freedom through violence. Based on records of Henrico County, Virginia, records of the State of Virginia, census records, contemporary newspapers and travel accounts, and secondary sources; 3 tables, 60 notes.
D. J. Cimbala

225. Scitovsky, Tibor. THE DESIRE FOR EXCITEMENT IN MODERN SOCIETY. *Kyklos [Switzerland] 1981 34(1): 3-13.* Modern man has become increasingly tolerant of violence in a search for the excitement and stimulation formerly provided by the everyday struggle for existence and the necessities of life, which has been eased by technological progress; from this perspective examines the rise in dangerous sports, violence, and crime.

226.   Sebastian, Richard J.; Parke, Ross D.; Berkowitz, Leonard; and West, Stephen G.   FILM VIOLENCE AND VERBAL AGGRESSION: A NATU-RALISTIC STUDY.   *J. of Communication 1978 28(3): 164-171.*   Research on boys at a minimum security penal institution for juvenile offenders was consistent with earlier laboratory-setting findings that movie portrayals of film violence increase verbal aggression in the observer.

227.   Seidman, David and Couzens, Michael.   GETTING THE CRIME RATE DOWN: POLITICAL PRESSURE AND CRIME REPORTING. *Law & Soc. R. 1974 8(3): 457-493.* Analyzes the impact during 1965-73 of political pressures on the Federal Bureau of Investigation's Uniform Crime Reporting Program and crime statistics reported by city police departments.   S

228.   Seidman, David.   PUBLIC SAFETY: CRIME IS UP, BUT WHAT ABOUT PUNISHMENT?   *Ann. of the Am. Acad. of Pol. and Social Sci. 1978 (435): 248-267.* Reported crime rates have risen, and arrest rates have too, particularly among the young. Men have higher victimization rates than women, and blacks have higher victimization rates for crimes of violence than whites. *Social Indicators, 1976* tells us this and a bit more about crime and responses to it, but overall the picture presented is at once insufficiently informative and inappropriately precise. The shortcomings of major data sources are acknowledged, but questionable findings are presented as near certain. Uniform Crime Reports trends for 1960-75 are presented without the important context of earlier trends. Important data from the National Crime Survey are presented without mention of probable artifacts. Data on system response to crime could have been presented so as to provide insight into the probable cause of the increases shown in trends in reported offenses. Important data, particularly those showing a declining rate of imprisonment, have been omitted, and the interrelations of crime and response have not been highlighted. The major shortcomings of the chapter seem to result not from inadequacies in execution of the design, but rather from limitations in available data and from the apparent assumption that data presented in chart form speak for themselves.   J

229.   Seretan, L. Glen.   THE "NEW" WORKING CLASS AND SOCIAL BANDITRY IN DEPRESSION AMERICA.   *Mid-America 1981 63(2): 107-117.* The US working class did not suffer the depression without engaging in criminal activity. Admiration for and cooperation with bank robbers, kidnappers, and shooters of public officials, encouraged by the mass media, was a form of striking at an oppressive society. The phenomenon withered with New Deal era reforms of federal police operations, and with the attack on those social problems that had led to identification with Robin Hood-like criminals.   21 notes.
P. J. Woehrmann

230.   Shankman, Arnold.   JULIAN HARRIS AND THE KU KLUX KLAN. *Mississippi Q. 1975 28(2): 147-169.* Chronicles the efforts of Julian LaRose Harris, editor of the *Enquirer-Sun*, to expose the bigotry and racism of the Ku Klux Klan in Columbus, Georgia, during the 1920's.   S

231.   Sharp, Elaine B.   SOURCES OF AND REACTIONS TO THE FEAR OF CRIME.   *Urban Affairs Q. 1982 17(4): 519-524.* Reviews Wesley G. Skogan and Michael G. Maxfield's *Coping with Crime: Individual and Neighborhood*

Reactions (1981), and Sally Engle Merry's *Urban Danger: Life in a Neighbor-hood of Strangers* (1981). Both works attempt to synthesize methodologically diverse research on the fear of crime among urban residents, including sources of fear and reactions to fear. Note, ref.   J. Powell

232.   Sheley, Joseph F. and Ashkins, Cindy D.   CRIME, CRIME NEWS, AND CRIME VIEWS.   *Public Opinion Q. 1981 45(4): 492-506.* Compares police, newspaper, television, and public images of crime trends for the seven Federal Bureau of Investigation index crimes over time, the relative frequency of occurrence of these offenses, and the characteristics of persons committing them. Media presentations of crime trends generally are unrelated to trends in police statistics. Newspaper presentation of the relative distribution of crimes approxi-mates police figures more closely than does the television presentation. Public views of the relative distribution of crimes, but not of crime trends, more closely approximate media presentations than police presentations. Television's impact on public views of crime is apparently minor. Reasons for these findings and their implications for crime news reporting are discussed.   J/S

233.   Shellow, James.   "DOCUMENTARY" INCRIMINATION.   *Center Mag. 1982 15(5): 41-45.* Discusses how people involuntarily incriminate them-selves because of the records they are required to keep, such as income tax records and bank statements, and how fear of surveillance and other invasions of privacy by the government or the media changes people's behavior.

234.   Shingleton, Royce Gordon.   THE TRIAL AND PUNISHMENT OF SLAVES IN BALDWIN COUNTY, GEORGIA 1812-1826.   *Southern Hu-manities R. 1974 8(1): 67-73.*

235.   Shinnar, Reuel and Shinnar, Shlomo.   THE EFFECTS OF THE CRIMI-NAL JUSTICE SYSTEM ON THE CONTROL OF CRIME: A QUANTITA-TIVE APPROACH.   *Law and Soc. R. 1975 9(4): 581-611.* Describes the development of a mathematical model on available crime statistics as they apply to New York State. Through use of their model, the authors are able to identify certain statistical relationships not generally appreciated through more tradi-tional studies. Increased crimes, for example, correlate strongly with recent judi-cial changes that reduce both the chances of conviction and the length of incapacitation. Based on the model data, uniform prison sentencing could reduce crime frequency.   H. R. Mahood

236.   Shofner, Jerrell H.   CUSTOM, LAW, AND HISTORY: THE ENDUR-ING INFLUENCE OF FLORIDA'S "BLACK CODE."   *Florida Hist. Q. 1977 55(3): 277-298.* The black codes and Jim Crow laws of the late 19th century gave legal sanction to segregation and white supremacy attitudes which already existed in social custom. The legal justification of segregation eventually crumbled. Ra-cial prejudice still exists but Floridians, for the most part, have rejected the violent repressive segregationist practices of the past. With time, racial equality may be not only the law, but the social custom. Based on government documents, news-papers, and secondary sources; 52 notes.   P. A. Beaber

237.   Short, James F., Jr. and Meier, Robert F.   CRIMINOLOGY AND THE STUDY OF DEVIANCE.   *Am. Behavioral Scientist 1981 24(3): 462-478.* Ana-lyzes the major shift in theoretical focus and the expansion of the empirical

database relating to the fields of criminology and deviance research from 1949 to 1980, when sociologists' interest shifted from the causes of criminal or deviant behavior to the social meaning of such behavior.

238.   Simon, Rita J.   AMERICAN WOMEN AND CRIME. *Ann. of the Am. Acad. of Pol. and Social Sci. 1976 (423): 31-46.* The topic of women and crime is currently enjoying a vogue, because women, in general, and research related to many aspects of women's lives are now popular topics for research. This article analyzes the relationship between the contemporary woman's movement, the role of women in crime, and the changing socioeconomic and political statuses of American women. Statistics on female arrest patterns for different types of offenses going back four decades are presented. The changes in women's propensities for committing different types of crimes are discussed and explanations about why these changes have occurred are offered. Statistics describing American women are compared with female crime data available for some 25 different countries. The extent to which women are victims of various types of offenses is also discussed. In its conclusion, the article offers some prognosis for the short-run future on how American women are likely to participate in criminal activities.
                                                                                                  J

239.   Sinicropi, Giovanni.   THE SAGA OF THE CORLEONES: PUZO, COPPOLA AND *THE GODFATHER*. *Italian Americana 1975 2(1): 79-90.* Writer Mario Puzo and moviemaker Francis Ford Coppola have hardly told the full story on Italian-American life and crime in their *Godfather* I and II of the 1970's.

240.   Skogan, Wesley G.   THE CHANGING DISTRIBUTION OF BIG CITY CRIME: A MULTI-CITY TIME SERIES ANALYSIS. *Urban Affairs Q. 1977 13(1): 33-48.* Analyzes the nation's 32 largest cities' crime statistics during 1946-70. Louis Wirth's 1938 model of urbanism predicted positive correlations for 1) density and crime, 2) size and crime, and 3) racial heterogeneity and crime. It is accurate for the 1970 data, but not for the 1946 data. However, the orderly changes in the time series data in a positive direction probably reflect fundamental change in the urban system. Suburbanization is the most likely causative systemic change, and is most advanced around high-crime cities. Biblio., 8 notes.   L. Beecher

241.   Skogan, Wesley G.   THE VALIDITY OF OFFICIAL CRIME STATISTICS: AN EMPIRICAL INVESTIGATION. *Social Sci. Q. 1974 55(1): 25-38.* "Comparison of official FBI 'crimes known' totals with sample survey estimates of city crime rates reveals considerable overlap between the two. He also finds that both measures are related in similar fashion to independent and dependent variables commonly used in quantitative studies. Concludes that if we make careful and modest demands of the data, official crime statistics may be valid indicators of inter-city variations in crime."   J

242.   Slotkin, Richard.   NARRATIVES OF NEGRO CRIME IN NEW ENGLAND, 1675-1800. *Am. Q. 1973 25(1): 3-31.* The published execution sermons of New England enjoyed considerable circulation. They stereotyped Negroes as oversexed, brutish, and ungrateful rogues conspiring against the permissive paternalism of their masters. These narratives distorted Negro crime

by overemphasizing murder, and, in the 18th century, rape as well as the threat of revolution. Primary and secondary sources; 75 notes, biblio.

W. D. Piersen

243.   Smith, Baxter.   THE RESURGENCE OF THE KKK.   *Black Scholar 1981 12(1): 25-30.* Describes activities of the Ku Klux Klan since the 1960's, its increasing violence since 1979, its infiltration into politics and industry, and the fight of labor leaders in 1980 against Klan racism.

244.   Smith, David.   THE PUBLIC EYE OF RAYMOND CHANDLER. *J. of Am. Studies [Great Britain] 1980 14(3): 423-441.* Raymond Chandler (b. 1888) came to Los Angeles, California, in 1919 and observed the rapid transformation of the area into a sprawling metropolis during the next several decades. An oil executive who became a writer of detective fiction in the 1930's, Chandler interpreted this new westward movement, focusing on the frustrations of migrants who, expecting a western utopia, helped to fashion a society contrary to their ideals. Chandler's earliest novels included *The Big Sleep* (1939), *Farewell, My Lovely* (1940), and *The High Window* (1943). Based on Chandler's writings; 65 notes.

H. T. Lovin

245.   Smith, Douglas A. and Visher, Christy A.   SEX AND INVOLVEMENT IN DEVIANCE/CRIME: A QUANTITATIVE REVIEW OF THE EMPIRI-CAL LITERATURE.   *Am. Sociol. Rev. 1980 45(4): 691-701.* Forty-four studies reporting data on the relationship between sex and indicators of deviance/criminality are reduced to a single data base. Contingency tables (1,118) are generated from the extant empirical literature on sex and deviance and comparable statistics are calculated, using instances where the sex-deviance relationship was reported for specific categories of class position, age, data type, year of study, level of family intactness, race, place of residence, and type of offense. The findings from 1,118 instances are summarized, and patterns are discussed. The overall results indicate that the magnitude of the relationship between sex and deviance is contingent on the year the data were gathered, the type of data used, the percentage classified as deviant in a particular table, whether the indicator of deviance is a single behavior or composite index, race, and the specific offense. Moreover, analysis demonstrates that trends in the sex-deviance relationship over time vary by type of data and by population group.   J

246.   Smith, Dwight C., Jr. and Alba, Richard D.   ORGANIZED CRIME AND AMERICAN LIFE.   *Society 1979 16(3): 32-38.* Provides a brief history of organized crime in America since the early 1900's, and examines the social organization, strength, and domain of organized crime in American business and politics.

247.   Sohn, Ardyth Broadrick.   DETERMINING GUILT OR INNOCENCE OF ACCUSED FROM PRETRIAL NEWS STORIES.   *Journalism Q. 1976 53(1): 100-105.* To examine how newspaper readers relate guilt or innocence to crime story elements, 24 subjects sorted news stories by guilt or innocence of the accused. Some subjects found those accused of felonies most guilty and those accused of misdemeanors most innocent. The name of the accused and the severity of penalty upon conviction did not affect perceptions of guilt or innocence. Based on primary sources; 2 tables, 18 notes.   K. J. Puffer

248.   Stafford, Mark C. and Gibbs, Jack P.   CRIME RATES IN AN ECO-LOGICAL CONTEXT: EXTENSION OF A PROPOSITION. *Social Sci. Q. 1980 61(3-4): 653-665.* City crime rates are a function of the population ratio (SMSA/city) and the dominance of cities in metropolitan areas. Reviews the consistency of the Gibbs-Erickson proposition that the relationship of crime rates may be understood within community-city population ratio as well as between SMSAs and urbanized areas. To test the Gibbs-Erickson proposition, 368 US cities with populations of at least 50,000 were surveyed. The findings modify the theory. Ecological correlations are introduced to suggest that crime rates in those 368 cities are partially a function of its SMSA/city population ratio and city dominance. US Bureau of Census data, and other sources; 2 tables, 19 notes.
M. Mtewa

249.   Stagg, J. C. A.   THE PROBLEM OF KLAN VIOLENCE: THE SOUTH CAROLINA UP-COUNTRY, 1868-1871.   *J. of Am. Studies [Great Britain] 1974 8(3): 303-318.* Analyzes several reasons for the pervasive racism which developed in up-country South Carolina after the Civil War. Political motivations, economic considerations, and common social attitudes produced solid anti-Negro alliances between professionals, the planter elite, and the poorer whites. Hence, the Klan enjoyed the support of virtually the entire "white community" for the widespread violence it perpetrated upon Negro Carolinians. Based on newspaper and secondary sources; 51 notes.   H. T. Lovin

250.   Staples, Robert.   WHITE RACISM, BLACK CRIME, AND AMERICAN JUSTICE: AN APPLICATION OF THE COLONIAL MODEL TO EXPLAIN CRIME AND RACE.   *Phylon 1975 36(1): 14-22.* Examines and explains the relationship between race and crime in the United States by applying a colonial model similar to that developed by Frantz Fanon in *The Wretched of the Earth,* and Robert Blauner in "Internal Colonialism and Ghetto Revolt," among others. The black community in the United States is an underdeveloped colony whose economics and politics are controlled by the dominant white group. Negroes find themselves caught by, and believe in the fact that the laws are discriminatory, the system of justice biased against them, and that they often are incarcerated in prison because they are political liabilities to the general public, thus becoming political prisoners. Remedies for the difficulty of alleviating colonialism in the relationship between race and crime include community control of the police and trial by one's actual peers. Based on primary and secondary sources; 35 notes.   B. A. Glasrud

251.   Steffensmeier, Darrell J. and Jordan, Charlene.   CHANGING PATTERNS OF FEMALE CRIME IN RURAL AMERICA, 1962-75.   *Rural Sociol. 1978 43(1): 87-100.* Compares the trends of female crime in rural and urban areas, finding that violent and property crimes are increasing among rural females; assesses the impact of the women's movement on crime and women, 1962-75.

252.   Steffensmeier, Darrell J.   SEX DIFFERENCES IN PATTERNS OF ADULT CRIME, 1965-77: A REVIEW AND ASSESSMENT.   *Social Forces 1980 58(4): 1080-1108.* This report examines current conceptions of sex differences in adult crime trends and assesses continued differences in female relative to male criminality. Our analysis relies mainly on national arrest statistics of the

Uniform Crime Reports, but our treatment of these statistics goes considerably beyond that of previous analysts. Our interpretation of the national data is supplemented by a variety of localized studies of police and court statistics as well as by autobiographical and case history studies of thieves. In contrast to popular and scientific claims, we question whether female crime is rising and whether women are catching up with males in the commission of masculine, violent, serious, male-dominated and white-collar types of crime. The arrest gains of females are in the category of vagrancy and in the petty-property crime categories of larceny, fraud, and forgery. Alternative views concerning female crime and the forces shaping it are suggested. It is proposed that the factors shaping sex differences in arrest patterns are changes in reporting procedures and law enforcement practices, economic factors, the maintenance of traditional conceptions of female roles, limited access to illegitimate opportunities due to restricted participation in the legitimate labor market, and the absence of viable female criminal subcultures or of access to male criminal subcultures. 3 tables, 10 notes, 96 ref.   J

253. Steffensmeier, Darrell J. and Kramer, John H.   SEX-BASED DIFFER-ENCES IN THE SENTENCING OF ADULT CRIMINAL DEFENDANTS: AN EMPIRICAL TEST AND THEORETICAL OVERVIEW.   *Sociol. and Social Res. 1982 66(3): 289-304.* Examines sex-based differences in the sentencing of adult criminal defendants. Provides a theoretical overview of the factors that are likely to influence differential sentencing of male and female defendants and speculates on the potential effects of the contemporary women's movement on sentencing patterns.   J

254. Stein, Harry H.   AMERICAN MUCKRAKERS AND MUCK-RAKING: THE 50-YEAR SCHOLARSHIP.   *Journalism Q. 1979 56(1): 9-17.* Surveys scholarly commentary on the investigative, muckraking literature that has appeared in magazines, newspapers, and novels in the United States since the late 19th century. The study of muckraking has dwelt on the content, rather than the influence, of muckrakers' writings, and it has been motivated primarily by scholars' own concerns over social progress. Furthermore, this scholarship, plagued by conceptual weakness, has generated few debates over the findings or approaches to the study. 23 notes.   R. P. Sindermann, Jr.

255. Stern, Madeleine B.   MATHEW B. BRADY AND *THE RATIONALE OF CRIME:* A DISCOVERY IN DAGUERREOTYPES.   *Q. J. of the Lib. of Congress 1974 31(3): 127-135.* The American edition of *The Rationale of Crime* by Marmaduke B. Simpson (1846) contained 19 engravings from among Brady's earliest daguerreotypes; the book was devoted to the phrenological analysis of criminals. Long overlooked, it is now seen as perhaps the first printed work containing a series of engravings from the daguerreotypes by Mathew Brady, famous for his pictures of the Civil War. Illus., 22 notes.   E. P. Stickney

256. Swallow, Craig A.   THE KU KLUX KLAN IN NEVADA DURING THE 1920S.   *Nevada Hist. Soc. Q. 1981 24(3): 202-220.* During the 1920's, the Ku Klux Klan, using rhetoric against Orientals, attracted sympathizers in north-ern Nevada. It had limited influence, however, and functioned primarily as a social and fraternal organization. Conversely, the Klan prospered in southern Nevada. Its larger membership remained stable, participating in municipal poli-tics and vigilantism. Based on newspaper sources and interviews; photo, 58 notes.   H. T. Lovin

257. Swan, Bradford F. FRONTIER JUSTICE IN NEWPORT—1652. *Rhode Island Hist. 1974 33(1): 3-7.* Suggests that the illegal trial and execution of Captain Alexander Partridge may have delayed the union of the mainland towns (Providence and Warwick) with the island towns (Newport and Portsmouth) to form the colony of Rhode Island. Based on published documents, papers, and secondary accounts.   P. J. Coleman

258. Swan, Marshall W. S. THE BEDEVILMENT OF CAPE ANN (1692). *Essex Inst. Hist. Collections 1981 117(3): 153-177.* Historical attention paid to the Salem witches has overshadowed the 11 or 12 witches from Cape Ann. A detailed examination of the surviving fragmentary records provides an important footnote to the witchcraft hysteria of this period. The author discusses each case, including participants, charges, and resolutions. Primary sources; 42 notes.
R. S. Sliwoski

259. Taylor, Edmond. THE TERRORISTS. *Horizon 1973 15(3): 58-65.* Terrorism began with The Terror during the French Revolution. Terrorists are seldom loyal to a state or a group; often they are easily converted, providing that they can continue to practice terrorism for their new group. They need not be revolutionaries; many have been safely ensconced in government offices. Terrorism may be an individual or a group activity. Terrorism is becoming increasingly prevalent. It will not disappear until injustice disappears, but measures must be taken to lessen its prevalence and impact in the modern world. Based on secondary sources; 6 photos.   V. L. Human

260. Taylor, Morris F. THE COE GANG: RUSTLERS OF "ROBBER'S ROOST." *Colorado 1974 51(3): 199-215.* Uses the post-Civil War Coe Gang of rustlers in the southeastern Colorado-northeastern New Mexico area to illustrate "that some of the classical features of outlaw stories are rooted in fact." The background of William Coe is in doubt, but he was in the area by 1867. Robber's Roost, the rustlers' hideout, was on the Cimarron River. Coe was captured and escaped several times, but in 1868 he was hung by vigilantes. Primary and secondary sources; map, 59 notes.   O. H. Zabel

261. Teodori, Massimo. VIOLENZA DIFFUSA E VIOLENZA ISTITU-ZIONALIZZATA IN AMERICA [Diffused violence and institutionalized violence in America]. *Problemi di Ulisse [Italy] 1978 14(86): 88-95.* Discusses the violence of criminals and revolutionaries since 1960 in the United States and its relationship to the violations of civil rights by the police and the Federal Bureau of Investigation, especially during the Nixon Administration.

262. Toby, Jackson. CRIME IN AMERICAN PUBLIC SCHOOLS. *Public Interest 1980 (58): 18-42.* Analyzes the study, *Violent Schools-Safe Schools,* published in 1978 by the National Institute of Education and reported to Congress. It found considerable crime in schools and that students, not intruders from the community, were responsible for thefts, assaults, robberies, and vandalism. Student criminals could not be identified by specific racial, ethnic, or socioeconomic background, but they often were having academic difficulty, in trouble in the community, and from troubled homes. Most attacks and robberies of students occurred outside of classrooms, between or after classes. The principal victims were younger students and the least experienced teachers. Male students

and teachers were most likely to be robbed or attacked. Minority students and teachers were more likely to be victimized, because their schools were most often urban schools with high crime rates. The causes of school crime were not studied. There was considerable violence in schools with above-average proportion of poor children and in high-crime urban neighborhood schools, however, causality was not ascertained. School principals suggested tightened security and improved discipline might effectively reduce crime. Traces events possibly contributing to erosion of schools' authority over students. Argues against the thesis that arbitrary school rules that violate "due process" encourage student rebellion and crime. Proposes solutions including increased disciplinary control by school officials. 2 notes. J. M. Herrick

263. Tracy, Charles Abbot, III. POLICE FUNCTION IN PORTLAND, 1851-1874. *Oregon Hist. Q. 1979 80(1): 5-29, (2): 134-169, (3): 287-322.* Part I. Shortly after incorporation, Portland's city council elected Hiram Wilbur as the city's first marshall. Wilbur's function, however, was limited to the execution of judicial and administrative actions of the mayor, in whom all authority was vested. The city charter of 1853 stripped the mayor of judicial authority, distributed police power between the mayor and city council, and provided for election of the marshall by a vote of the populace. In October 1857 a resolution was passed requiring voters to 'think" about supporting a permanent police force. Nothing came of the resolution; however, passage of the resolution marked the first official consideration of such a force. Based on documents in the Portland City Archives, newspaper accounts, and published secondary sources; 6 illus., 2 maps, 79 notes. Part II. The election of James H. Lappeus as city marshall in April 1859 marked the beginning of a sense of stability for the Portland police. Each year Portland's mayor called for the organization of a permanent police force and each year the city council failed to take any action on the matter. The city charter of 1864 made the city council responsible, once again, for election of the marshall. Two deputy marshalls were officially appointed in November 1864, thereby increasing the police force to a total of three full time employees. In early 1867 the city council passed two ordinances, one establishing a day police and the other establishing a night police. However, it was not until September 1870 that Portland's police department was officially established. Fall of 1870, however, saw passage in the state legislature of a bill which would establish a Portland Board of Police Commissioners whose members would be appointed by the governor. Based on documents in the Portland City Archives, newspaper accounts, and published secondary sources; 10 illus., map, 195 notes. Part III. The board abolished local control over the police, but by 1874 a new law provided for the public election of board commissioners, thus returning the police to local control. 13 illus., 285 notes. D. R. McDonald

264. Ulmer, Gregory L. CRIME, VIOLENCE, AND THE POPULAR ARTS. *Southern Humanities Rev. 1975 9(3): 277-287.* Examines the apparent dichotomy of distaste for violence compounded with society's concern with law and order and the apparent glorification of violence in art forms such as television and films, during the 20th century; examines both European and American contemporary thought on the subject.

265. van den Haag, Ernest. NO EXCUSE FOR CRIME. *Ann. of the Am. Acad. of Pol. and Social Sci. 1976 (423): 133-141.* Criminologists often regard offenders as victims of conditions beyond their control or as "political prisoners," punished for "the inevitable consequences" of their socioeconomic status (S. I. Shuman). However, offenders do not become "political prisoners" unless their offenses were addressed to the sociopolitical system. Nor do crimes "inevitably" arise from poverty any more than corruption inevitably arises from power. Therefore, neither poverty nor power are legal excuses. Criminal law always is meant to perpetuate the existing order, although Richard Quinney objects because the burden of legal restraint falls most heavily on the disadvantaged who are most tempted to disrupt the legal order. Yet the criminal law is meant to restrain those tempted to violate it. Quinney's view that socialism will solve "the crime problem" appears bereft of evidence. The comparative crime rates of blacks and whites are analyzed and the punitive and social reform approaches compared. They are found to be not alternative but cumulative.   J

266. VanWest, Carroll. PERPETUATING THE MYTH OF AMERICA: SCOTTSBORO AND ITS INTERPRETERS. *South Atlantic Q. 1981 80(1): 36-48.* In the telling of their Scottsboro stories, whether offered at the time or in retrospect, the guardians of the myth of America have said much more about the manner in which American society views itself and its relationship to the past than they have about the true meaning of that sad series of events in depression-ridden northeastern Alabama. Discusses the various myths which have arisen out of the 1931 Alabama incident. 26 notes.   H. M. Parker, Jr.

267. Villmoare, Adelaide H. NORMAL & ABNORMAL JUSTICE IN AMERICA: REFLECTIONS ON THE RULE OF LAW & AMERICAN POLITICS. *Polity 1980 13(2): 300-311.* The seven books reviewed here present diverse but to some extent complementary perspectives on the interaction of the rule of law and politics, but together they suggest that, since the 1940's, the rule of law has become the exception rather than the norm of governmental action: the four social scientists—Herman Goldstein, Steven R. Schlesinger, George F. Cole, and Richard Quinney—discuss the relation between rule of law and politics in the criminal justice system and how best to adjust that relation; the journalists —David Caute, David Wise, and the team of Richard Ben-Veniste and George Frampton, Jr.—portray events and activities, such as McCarthyism, the CIA, and Watergate, that reflect weaknesses in American liberal democracy.

268. Warr, Mark. THE ACCURACY OF PUBLIC BELIEFS ABOUT CRIME. *Social Forces 1980 59(2): 456-470.* Studies of public beliefs about crime often assert a marked discrepancy between public beliefs about crime and objective conditions. Data from four independent sample surveys of the adult residents of a major Southwestern metropolitan area indicate that any general statement about the accuracy of public beliefs about crime may be premature. Although there is systematic distortion in the survey responses, the overall degree of accuracy is remarkable. Alternative explanations of that accuracy are examined, and an explanation based on additional evidence is proposed.   J/S

269. Weis, Kurt and Milakovich, Michael E. POLITICAL MISUSES OF CRIME RATES. *Society 1974 11(5): 27-33.* Studies the war on crime, the failings of the federal Law Enforcement Assistance Administration (LEAA), and the bureaucratic interests of criminal justice agencies.   S

270. Wexman, Virginia Wright. KINESICS AND FILM ACTING: HUMPHREY BOGART IN *THE MALTESE FALCON* AND *THE BIG SLEEP.* *J. of Popular Film and Television 1978 7(1): 42-55.* Applies kinesics to the study of the acting style of Humphrey Bogart in *The Big Sleep* (1946) and *The Maltese Falcon* (1941).

271. Weyl, Nathaniel. RACE, NATIONALITY AND CRIME. *Mankind Q. [Great Britain] 1973 14(1): 41-48.* Explores the hypothesis that criminality of races and subraces tends to vary inversely with their intelligence, excluding certain offenses which are differentially attractive to people of above-average intelligence. Further discusses crime and American Negroes. Concludes that criminality seems to be greatest among the least intelligent and least creative races. Based on US and European statistics and secondary sources; 17 notes.

K. Halil

272. Wilentz, Sean. CRIME, POVERTY AND THE STREETS OF NEW YORK CITY: THE DIARY OF WILLIAM H. BELL (1850-51). *Hist. Workshop J. [Great Britain] 1979 7(6): 126-131.* Provides an annotated selection of entries from the diary of the New York policeman, William H. Bell, preceded by an introduction describing the nature of Bell's work and characterizing the locale of his employment, within the context of contemporary crime in New York City. While mapping the New York City underworld of crime, poverty and politics, the diary also gives insights into the culture, mentality, and daily lives of the poorer classes in the city. It is in the manuscript collection of the New York Historical Society. 3 illus., 90 notes.

A. Fenn

273. Wilkins, Leslie T. CRIME AND CRIMINAL JUSTICE AT THE TURN OF THE CENTURY. *Ann. of the Am. Acad. of Pol. and Social Sci. 1973 408:13-29.* "The probability that the criminal justice system will suffer a complete breakdown before the year 2000 should not be discounted. If law and social control systems are to accommodate change in their environment at the necessary rate, a new philosophy, as well as quite different operating procedures, must be worked out. The present strategy of law enforcement agencies to develop more-of-the-same can only ensure breakdown. Pressures for control will increase, and with each new pressure on criminals, more side-effects of these pressures will have an impact upon all citizens. The best moral standard which can be expected to guide policy in the intervening years is enlightened self-interest; this may suffice to ensure survival. The quality of that survival may be improved by the development of a new class of moral philosophers out of the ranks of scientists and technicians. No great new moral leadership is expected from organized religions. Politics will mix dangerous sentimentality and nostalgia with more than a small modicum of fear. Much of that fear will be focused on the criminal. Millions of dollars will continue to be wasted on research. If we wish for a better kind of future for criminal justice, we must start to invent it now. However, there is no indication that we are ready to consider the necessary issues."

J

274. Wilson, James Q. CRIME AND THE CRIMINOLOGISTS. *Commentary 1974 58(1): 47-53.*

275.   Wilson, James Q.   THINKING ABOUT *THINKING ABOUT CRIME.* *Society 1977 14(3): 10-11, 19-21.* Discusses criminologist Lynn A. Curtis' disagreement with the author regarding the causes of crime, its relationship with unemployment, and deterrents, 1970's.

276.   Winick, Charles and Winick, Mariann Pezzella.   COURTROOM DRAMA ON TELEVISION.   *J. of Communications 1974 24(4): 67-73.* Discusses misleading stereotypes of trials and the criminal justice system created by television shows from 1949-73, emphasizing the shows "Perry Mason" and "The Defenders."

277.   Winkle, John W., III.   INTERGOVERNMENTAL RELATIONS IN CRIMINAL JUSTICE.   *Policy Studies J. 1974 3(1): 25-29.*

278.   Winks, Robin W.   AMERICAN DETECTIVE FICTION.   *Am. Studies Int. 1980 19(1): 3-16.* Few studies take detective fiction seriously, though it deserves study as a mirror of national paranoia and a means for understanding national aspirations and myth. Through it we can trace "the changing preoccupations, the fears, the sexual mores, of a vast American public." Spy fiction also is a mirror to a culture, though dealing more with "collectively sordid truths" than with individual cases. 2 photos, 18 notes, biblio.   R. E. Noble

279.   Wolfgang, Marvin E.   CRIME IN A BIRTH COHORT.   *Pro. of the Am. Phil. Soc. 1973 117(5): 404-411.* In 1964 the National Institute of Mental Health sponsored a study to determine the probability of Philadelphia youth becoming officially recorded as juvenile delinquents. The sample, called a birth cohort, chose boys born in 1945 who lived in the city from age 10 to 18. Nearly 10,000 were traced through school, police, and Selective Service files, with 35% being classed as delinquents. Discusses weaknesses in methodology and progress of a follow-up study begun in 1968 with the same birth cohort from ages 18 to 26 years. 3 tables, 2 figs., 11 notes.   C. W. Olson

280.   Woolsey, Ronald C.   CRIME AND PUNISHMENT: LOS ANGELES COUNTY, 1850-1856.   *Southern California Q. 1979 61(1): 79-98.* Describes the administration of justice in Los Angeles city and county at the beginning of the American period. Southern California experienced rapid growth, a high rate of transiency, and an increasing number of violent crimes. Indians were generally believed to be the cause of crime and were immediately suspected when a crime was committed. It soon became obvious that crime in Los Angeles was due to more complex factors. Local elected officials often lacked training to enforce proper legal procedure. To reduce crime the Board of Supervisors created a force of Los Angeles Rangers which often failed to observe the letter of the law. Failure to create nighttime law enforcement, belief in Indian culpability, and frustration at the failure of the legal system led citizens to endorse violent extra-legal action, including vigilantism and lynching. Los Angeles provided opportunity for all immigrants, but the criminal element overwhelmed the legal system in the years immediately following statehood. Primary and secondary sources; 86 notes.   A. Hoffman

281.   Wynne, Edward A.   WHAT ARE THE COURTS DOING TO OUR CHILDREN?   *Public Interest 1981 (64): 3-18.* Self-destructive and criminal behavior among white children is occurring at unprecedented rates. The chil-

dren's rights movement and the courts may have weakened schools' ability to provide the discipline necessary to maintain order and an atmosphere conducive to education. Since 1955, numbers of suicides, homicides, out-of-wedlock births, and crimes committed by young people have risen sharply. The children's rights movement has weakened the sense of community that is necessary for schools and other social institutions to provide structure and authority for young people. Graph.   J. M. Herrick

282. Yin, Peter P. FEAR OF CRIME AMONG THE ELDERLY: SOME ISSUES AND SUGGESTIONS. *Social Problems 1980 27(4): 492-504.* Provides a review of the literature on fear of crime among elderly Americans since 1970 and its determinants, and a conceptual framework within which to locate the strengths and weaknesses of these works.

283. Younger, Irving. WAS ALGER HISS GUILTY? *Commentary 1975 60(2): 23-37.* Reexamines the circumstances, issues, evidence, and personalities surrounding the Alger Hiss case of the late 1940's and early 1950's.   S

284. —. [THE BLACK SCHOLAR FORUM ON REPRESSION]. *Black Scholar 1981 12(1): 58-71.*
Boyd, Herb. BLACKS AND THE POLICE STATE: A CASE STUDY OF DETROIT, *pp. 58-61.* Describes police brutality in Detroit since 1971, the efforts by Mayor Coleman Alexander Young to end such violence, and the recent resurgence in Detroit of Ku Klux Klan and Nazi activity.
Payton, Brenda. POLICE USE OF DEADLY FORCE IN OAKLAND, *pp. 62-64.* Describes police killings of blacks in Oakland during 1979-80, and the power struggle between the city's black mayor and its predominantly white police department.
YaSalaam, Kalamu. IN THE FACE OF OPPRESSION: A CASE STUDY OF NEW ORLEANS, *pp. 65-67.* Describes murders of blacks in New Orleans in 1980, subsequent conferences held to discuss police brutality, and movements to effect political change.
Damu, Jean. ECONOMIC REPRESSION: THE SAN FRANCISCO HOTEL WORKERS STRIKE, *pp. 68-71.* Describes the hotel workers' strike of 1980, marking the first time in 40 years that laborers in the city's hotel industry marched in order to fight for better pay and working conditions.

285. —. COMMENTS [IN A SPECIAL SECTION ON CRIMINAL JUSTICE]. *Center Mag. 1977 10(4): 43-47.* Presents comments by 15 experts on the problems inherent in the criminal justice system and recommendations for new policies and alternative programs.

286. —. [CRIMINOLOGY SYMPOSIUM]. *Sociol. Q. 1974 15(4): 591-598.*
Mugford, Stephen K. MARXISM AND CRIMINOLOGY: A COMMENT ON THE SYMPOSIUM REVIEW ON "THE NEW CRIMINOLOGY," *pp. 591-596.* Following the publication of Taylor, Walton and Young's *New Criminology* (London: Routledge and Kegan Paul, 1972 and New York: Harper Torch Books, 1974), the *Quarterly* asked Anthony Platt, Richard Quinney and Paul Rock to write review essays which were subsequently published in the *Quarterly* in the Autumn 1973 issue [(see abstract 12A:3423)]. These reviews elicited the following response by Stephen Mug-

ford. It was circulated to the authors of the *New Criminology* who declined to comment, choosing to formulate a general response to the many review comments the book has generated. Mugford's comment was also sent to the original reviewers, and Paul Rock's reply follows.
Rock, Paul. COMMENT ON MUGFORD, *pp. 597-598.*   J

287. —. [CROWDING AND URBAN CRIME RATES]. *Urban Affairs Q. 1975 11(3): 291-322.*
Booth, Alan; Welch, Susan; and Johnson, David Richard. CROWDING AND URBAN CRIME RATES, *pp. 291-308.* Attempts to establish connections between city crime and crowding. 4 tables, notes, biblio.
Higgins, Paul C.; Richards, Pamela; and Swan, James H. CROWDING AND URBAN CRIME RATES: A COMMENT, *pp. 309-316.* Questions the research, mainly on methodological grounds. Table, notes, biblio.
Booth, Alan; Welch, Susan; and Johnson, David Richard. A REPLY TO HIGGINS, RICHARDS, AND SWAN, *pp. 317-322.* The criticism is insignificant and irrelevant. Note, biblio.   P. J. Woehrmann

288. —. [THE JOAN LITTLE CASE]. *Southern Exposure 1978 6(1): 30-47.*
Reston, James, Jr. THE INNOCENCE OF JOAN LITTLE, *pp. 30-38.*
Braden, Anne. AN OPEN LETTER: JERRY PAUL ON TRIAL, *p. 38.*
Pinsky, Mark. THE INNOCENCE OF JAMES RESTON, JR., *pp. 39-41.*
Little, Joan and Ranson, Rebecca, ed. I AM JOAN, *pp. 42-47.*
The Joan Little case, involving the killing by a black female prisoner of a white male jailer allegedly making a sexual attack, attracted much media coverage in 1974 and later, giving civil rights and feminist overtones to the case. The case revolved around the credibility of Sheriff Ottis (Red) Davis of Beaufort County, North Carolina, and of Joan Little, and the courtroom and extra-courtroom behavior of defense attorney Jerry Paul. Paul achieved notoriety through his calculated appeal to outside pressure groups and his attacks on the North Carolina legal system and its operations. He faces disbarment proceedings brought by the North Carolina Bar Association. Joan Little grew up in a segregated environment in Washington, North Carolina, and reacted against a repressive behavior situation exerted by her mother. Based on personal observations, oral interviews, and autobiographical statements.   N. Lederer

289. —. MARK OF THE BEAST. *Southern Exposure 1980 8(2): 49-100.*
Bryant, Pat. MARK OF THE BEAST, *p. 49.*
Loggins, Kirk and Thomas, Susan. THE MENACE RETURNS, *pp. 50-54.*
—. KLAN KASH & KARRY: "NO COMMENT," *pp. 54-55.*
Braden, Anne. LESSONS FROM A HISTORY OF STRUGGLE, *pp. 56-61.*
—. 111 YEARS OF KKKRONOLOGY, *pp. 58-59.*
Kennedy, Stetson. KKK VS. LABOR: A SAMPLER, *p. 61.*
—. 1872: VISITOR FROM HELL, *pp. 62-63.*
Ingalls, Robert. THE MURDER OF JOSEPH SHOEMAKER, *pp. 64-68.*
—. THE POLICE JUST LAUGHED, *p. 69.*
Williams, Robert. 1957: THE SWIMMING POOL SHOWDOWN, *pp. 70-72.*

Marx, Andrew and Tuthill, Tom.   MISSISSIPPI ORGANIZES: RESISTING THE KLAN,   *pp. 73-76.*
Gallman, Vanessa.   KLAN CONFRONTATIONS: OFFENSIVE DEFENSIVE TACTICS,   *pp. 76-78.*
Bryant, Pat.   JUSTICE VS. THE MOVEMENT,   *pp. 79-87.*
Riccio, Bill and Wilkinson, Bill.   THE KLAN SPEAKS,   *pp. 88-90.*
Warnecke, Nancy; Loggins, Kirk; and Thomas, Susan.   KLAN YOUTH CORPS: JUST LIKE THE SCOUTS,   *pp. 91-92.*
Salim, Yusuf and Roaf, Marilyn, interviewer.   SET A POSITIVE EXAMPLE, *pp. 92-94.*
Ellis, C. P. and Terkel, Studs, interviewer.   WHY I QUIT THE KLAN, *pp. 95-100.*
Campbell, Will.   CLEAN UP THE BOTULISM,   *p. 99.*
Short articles focusing on the history of the Ku Klux Klan (founded in 1866), how it raises money and starts new chapters, its history of racism and violence, its words and actions, and how to fight its menace.

290.   —.   WOMEN AND CRIME.   *Social Sci. Q. 1976 56(4): 650-663.*
Noblit, George W. and Burcart, Janie M.   WOMEN AND CRIME: 1960-1970, *pp. 650-657.* Presents data which suggest both changes in crime rates among women and some changes in the patterns of their crimes.
Simon, Rita J.   WOMEN AND CRIME REVISITED,   *pp. 658-663.* Elaborates on—and disputes some of—Noblit and Burcart's findings and interpretations by presenting data from her recent monograph, *The Contemporary Woman and Crime.*   J

2

CRIMES OF VIOLENCE

291. Abel, Mary Bilderback. MASSACRE AT GNADENHUTTEN: RE-CREATED VILLAGE MARKS THE SITE WHERE PENNSYLVANIA BACKWOODSMEN MURDERED NINETY-SIX CHRISTIAN INDIANS IN 1782. *Am. Hist. Illus. 1981 16(8): 28-31.* Account of the massacre of Moravian Indians at the village of Gnadenhutten, Ohio, on 7-8 March 1782, by backwoods militiamen from Pennsylvania under the command of Colonel David Williamson, who accused the Indians of aiding warriors who terrorized white Americans and of raiding Pennsylvania border settlements.

292. Allen, H. David and Bankston, William B. ANOTHER LOOK AT THE SOUTHERN CULTURE OF VIOLENCE HYPOTHESIS: THE CASE OF LOUISIANA. *Southern Studies 1981 20(1): 55-66.* A high rate of homicide, a culture of violence, is associated with the South. Various studies have shown this to be either a product of cultural tradition or of the socioeconomic structure. This study finds that in Louisiana the socioeconomic factor has greater influence; Catholic and Protestant areas do not differ significantly. Structural poverty is an indicator, although not necessarily a significant one, in explaining violence. No single factor offers a full explanation; further research is needed on an unproven assumption of southern violence. Based on federal, state, and special statistical studies; 2 tables, 2 notes, biblio.   J. J. Buschen

293. Alviti, John V. and Haller, Mark H. LOANSHARKING IN AMERICAN CITIES: HISTORICAL ANALYSIS OF A MARGINAL ENTERPRISE. *Am. J. of Legal Hist. 1977 21(2): 125-156.* Loansharking involves both salary lending through a legitimate business operation with only the threat of law as means of collection, and a racketeer loanshark who relies on physical force and violence. The discussion of the first form takes the 1870's to the turn of the century as its formative period. The examples come largely from New York City and Chicago, and the loans were generally of small amounts, with the lenders comprising old stock American families who made their profits from a large-volume business. The racketeer variety developed during the 1930's-50's, especially in New York in the 1930's, and in Chicago in the 1950's. Based largely on newspaper reports; 61 notes.   L. A. Knafla

294. Archer, Dane and Gartner, Rosemary. VIOLENT ACTS AND VIOLENT TIMES: A COMPARATIVE APPROACH TO POSTWAR HOMICIDE RATES. *Am. Sociol. Rev. 1976 41(6): 937-963.* The idea that waging war might increase the level of domestic violence in warring societies has occurred

to many researchers. Discussions of this possibility have been limited to a very small number of case studies—often as limited as the experience of a single nation in a single war. A major obstacle to the general investigation of this question has been the unavailability of comparative data on homicide rates. Over a three-year period, a Comparative Crime Data File was assembled. The file includes time-series rates of homicide for roughly 110 nations beginning in about 1900. Postwar rather than wartime homicide rates were analyzed, since postwar data appear much less problematic and are likely to be affected by artifacts in only a conservative direction. The homicide data were analyzed to: 1) determine if postwar increases did occur and 2) identify which of seven competing theoretical models appeared to offer the most adequate explanation. The homicide rate changes after 50 "nation-wars" were compared with the changes experienced by 30 control nations. The major finding of the study was that most of the nation-wars in the study did experience substantial postwar increases in their rates of homicide. These increases were pervasive, and occurred after large wars and smaller wars, with several types of homicide rate indicators, in victorious as well as defeated nations, in nations with both improved and worsened postwar economies, among both men and women offenders and among offenders of several age groups. Homicide rate increases occurred with particular consistency among nations with large numbers of combat deaths. Using homicide and other data, it was possible to disconfirm or demonstrate the insufficiency of six of the seven explanatory models.   J

295.   Bankston, William B. and Allen, H. David.   RURAL SOCIAL AREAS AND PATTERNS OF HOMICIDE: AN ANALYSIS OF LETHAL VIOLENCE IN LOUISIANA.   *Rural Sociol. 1980 45(2): 223-237.* Studies lethal violence in Louisiana, based on research of the structural and cultural factors in 10 rural Louisiana counties; concludes that both cultural and sociodemographic structure affect patterns of lethal violence, but that it is unknown whether all or some Southerners operate under a value system "associated with the possession and carrying of lethal weapons, and, especially, the willingness to use them," that is different from the rest of the United States; 19th century-1979.

296.   Bell, Pearl K.   MAILER: SETTLING FOR LESS.   *Commentary 1980 69(2): 65-68.* Criticizes Norman Mailer's *Executioner's Song,* a novel about convicted murderer Gary Gilmore; 1970's.

297.   Belshaw, Michael.   THE DUNN-HOWLAND KILLINGS: A RECONSTRUCTION.   *J. of Arizona Hist. 1979 20(4): 409-422.* The author and three others tried to retrace the probable route of William Dunn, Seneca Howland, and Oramel Gass Howland when they left the first Grand Canyon expedition in an attempt to reach the Mormon settlements north of the confluence of the Colorado and Virgin Rivers. Log Spring is probably where the men were killed by Shivwits Paiute Indians. It is reasonable to assume that on the last of August or first part of September 1869, the Howland brothers and Dunn had reached the base of Mount Dellenbaugh. Near the summit is an inscription, "Water," placed by Dunn. 5 photos, 2 maps, notes.   K. E. Gilmont

298.   Blau, Judith R. and Blau, Peter M.   THE COST OF INEQUALITY: METROPOLITAN STRUCTURE AND VIOLENT CRIME.   *Am. Sociol. Rev. 1982 47(1): 114-129.* Tests the hypothesis that variations in rates of urban

criminal violence largely result from differences in racial inequality in socioeconomic conditions. Socioeconomic inequality between races, as well as economic inequality generally, increases rates of criminal violence, but once economic inequalities are controlled, poverty no longer influences these rates, neither does Southern location, and the proportion of blacks in the population hardly does. If there is a culture of violence, its roots are pronounced economic inequalities, especially if associated with ascribed position.   J/S

299. Blight, David W. THE MARTYRDOM OF ELIJAH P. LOVEJOY. *Am. Hist. Illus. 1977 12(7): 20-27.* The murder of abolitionist newspaper editor Lovejoy 7 November 1837 by a pro-slavery, anti-free press mob in Alton, Illinois, culminated several antiabolitionist incidents in the Alton, Illinois-St. Louis, Missouri, area. In 1835 two whites were lashed for aiding five runaway slaves who were recaptured in Illinois. In 1836 a St. Louis mob burned to death free Negro Francis McIntosh for killing a white man. Judge Luke E. Lawless blamed Lovejoy's St. Louis *Observer*'s abolitionist sentiments for the murder. The *Observer* moved to Alton after several destructive attacks and damage to the press. In Alton four presses were destroyed and Lovejoy was attacked twice. Illinois attorney-general Usher F. Linder and the pro-slavery St. Louis *Missouri Republican* newspaper appealed to the mob to stop Lovejoy. Elijah P. Lovejoy was buried 8 November 1837, his 35th birthday. His murder provoked discussion of the abolition movement, and led to the acceptance of an antislavery ideology by John Brown, William Herndon (Lincoln's law partner), and Wendell Phillips. Primary and secondary sources; 8 illus.   D. Dodd

300. Bonnet, Frédéric. LES FRÈRES JAMES: HÉROS OU BANDITS? [The James brothers: Heroes or bandits?]. *Écrits de Paris [France] 1979 (383): 76-82.* Discusses family background and aspects that made the James brothers, Jesse (1847-82) and Frank (1843-1915), "well-loved" bandits.

301. Bork, A. W. and Boyer, Glenn G., eds. THE O.K. CORRAL FIGHT AT TOMBSTONE: A FOOTNOTE BY KATE ELDER. *Arizona and the West 1977 19(1): 65-84.* Adds additional information about the Earp-Clanton feud and the 1881 gunfight near the O.K. Corral in Tombstone, Arizona. Glenn W. Boyer describes his interest in Mary Katherine Horony (Haroney), alias Kate Elder or Big-Nosed Kate, who was the paramour of Doc Holliday and later became Mrs. Mary Cummings. He also discusses his contacts with Kate's family and with A. W. Bork. Also included are Bork's recollections of Kate Elder and Kate's memoir of her experiences in Tombstone. 7 illus., map, 6 unnumbered notes, 55 notes.   D. L. Smith

302. Botein, Barbara. THE HENNESSY CASE: AN EPISODE IN ANTI-ITALIAN NATIVISM. *Louisiana Hist. 1979 20(3): 261-279.* By 1890, Italians constituted the largest segment of the foreign-born population in New Orleans. In October, after investigating "Dagoes" involved in organized crime, police chief David Hennessy was assassinated. Police immediately arrested 45 people, mainly Sicilian immigrants. In March 1891, following shady tactics used by both prosecution and defense in the *State of Louisiana* v. *Natali et al.* (1891), the nine Italians tried for Hennessy's murder were acquitted. This enraged many New Orleanians. A huge mob led by the cream of society stormed the jail and killed 11 Italian prisoners. No vigilantes were even indicted; in fact, they became heroes.

This incident exemplified the deep-seated nativist sentiment which existed throughout the nation in 1890, generated more anti-Italian feelings, and popularized the word "Mafia." Based on contemporary newspapers; 66 notes.

D. B. Touchstone

303. Braden, Anne. A SECOND OPEN LETTER TO SOUTHERN WHITE WOMEN. *Southern Exposure 1977 4(4): 50-53.* The issue of rape must not be regarded outside of its societal context. The women's movement must face the fact that there can be no security for males or females in American society without basic changes. Stringent measures must be taken to prevent the racist use of the rape charge as a device to oppress black men. Evidence indicates that the political Left of the past 40 years has approached the issue of rape of white women by black men through an analysis of the exploitative nature of the economic system and by stressing that white women as well as black men are victims of the system.

N. Lederer

304. Brazil, John R. MURDER TRIALS, MURDER, AND TWENTIES AMERICA. *Am. Q. 1981 33(2): 163-184.* The intense interest in murder in the 1920's stemmed from confusion about individualism. Public preoccupation with murder was largely an outgrowth of journalism's ability to familiarize readers with the personalities involved and build on the element of suspense during trials. At the same time, the *Black Mask* magazine infused the detective murder mystery with an interest in character conflict, and Zane Grey transformed the western with his creation of the gunslinger. In serious literature, murder became a theme in novels by Fitzgerald and Dreiser, while in the academic world, social scientists hotly debated its possible causes. Based on the Theodore Dreiser Papers; 47 notes.

D. K. Lambert

305. Cann, Arnie; Calhoun, Lawrence G.; Selby, James W.; and King, H. Elizabeth. RAPE: A CONTEMPORARY OVERVIEW AND ANALYSIS. *J. of Social Issues 1981 37(4): 1-4.* Introduces this issue devoted to the problem of rape. Though rape has a long history, societal attention to it is recent. The emergence of the women's movement and increased attention to rape are not just coincidental. In a male-oriented society rape occupies a position somewhere between accepted practice and unacceptable crime. The result is a system in which the roles of victim and criminal are often confused. There is a lack of knowledge concerning the psychological effects of rape and its frequency, and the effect that fear of rape has on women in general. Ref.

J. V. Coutinho

306. Castel, Albert. THE DAY THE MARSHAL TRIED TO ROB THE BANK. *Am. Hist. Illus. 1980 15(5): 14-22.* Story of the attempted robbery of the Medicine Valley Bank, 50 miles northwest of Caldwell, Kansas, in 1884, by the marshal of Caldwell, Henry Brown, and three others, and their subsequent lynching for the attempted robbery and the murder of two bankers; also discusses lawlessness in Caldwell from 1881 which Brown got under control when he was named marshal.

307. Chegwidden, Paula; Felt, Lawrence F.; and Miller, Anne. BATTERED WOMEN: MYTHS, REALITIES AND NEW DIRECTIONS FOR FUTURE RESEARCH. *Atlantis [Canada] 1981 6(2): 186-193.* Intrafamilial violence is thought to occur in 16% to 50% of American families, scarcely relating to such

factors as social class, alcoholism, or alleged female masochism. Most victims are female. Revision of a paper presented to the Atlantic Association of Anthropologists and Sociologists, Halifax, March 1979. Photo, 25 notes.

C. G. P. Gillespie

308. Chesson, Michael B. "EDITORS INDULGING IN DOUBLE-LEADED MATTER": THE SHOOT-OUT AT THE CAPITOL IN 1866. *Virginia Cavalcade 1980 30(3): 100-109.* Account of the 1866 shoot-out in the Rotunda of the Virginia Capitol involving Henry Rives Pollard, editor of the *Richmond Examiner,* and William D. Coleman and Nathaniel Tyler, editors of the *Daily Richmond Enquirer,* following Pollard's editorial attack over the naming of the public printer by the General Assembly.

309. Childress, William. LULA'S BUTCH. *Westways 1976 68(4): 18-21, 76.* Interview with Lula Parker Betenson, sister of Butch Cassidy (Robert Leroy Parker) in which she discusses her book *Butch Cassidy, My Brother* (Provo, Utah: Brigham Young University Press, 1975) and her vague reminiscences of her outlaw brother, who, she claims, survived and lived incognito in the United States until 1925.

310. Chobanian, Peter. THE SACCO-VANZETTI CASE: AN ANNOTATED BIBLIOGRAPHY. *Bull. of Biblio. 1982 39(2): 59-62.* The bibliography on the trial, imprisonment, and execution of Nicola Sacco and Bartolomeo Vanzetti, 1920-27, appears in two parts, organized according to whether the treatment is factual or fictional.

311. Christian, Garna L. RIO GRANDE CITY: PRELUDE TO THE BROWNSVILLE RAID. *West Texas Hist. Assoc. Year Book 1981 57: 118-132.* Describes several incidents of violence between Anglo and Hispanic civilians and black soldiers along the Texas-Mexican border during 1899-1900, and focuses on one incident at Rio Grande City in November 1899 when, after discrimination and police harassment, black soldiers of Troop D of the 9th Cavalry fired on the town.

312. Clark, Andrienne G. WHO MURDERED MARCUS LYON? *New-England Galaxy 1977 19(2): 15-21.* In strongly anti-Catholic, anti-Irish, and anti-immigrant Northampton, Massachusetts, Irish immigrants Dominic Daley and James Halligan were convicted with little defense and on doubtful evidence in April 1806, and hanged in June, for the murder of Marcus Lyon in November 1805. Father (later Cardinal) Jean Louis Lefebvre de Cheverus, in an eloquent sermon to Protestants waiting for the hanging, attempted to diminish their prejudice.

D. J. Engler

313. Cook, Philip J. THE EFFECT OF GUN AVAILABILITY ON VIOLENT CRIME PATTERNS. *Ann. of the Am. Acad. of Pol. and Social Sci. 1981 (455): 63-79.* The distribution of violent crimes among different types of victims is governed in part by the "vulnerability pattern" in weapon choice. The seriousness of robbery and assault incidents is influenced by weapon type, as indicated by the objective dangerousness and instrumental violence pattern.

J/S

314. Cooper, Eileen M. WHISKEY RUN: WHERE COAL DUST MIXED WITH MURDER. *Pennyslvania Heritage 1980 6(2): 15-19.* The almost exclusively Italian community of Whiskey Run began as a coal town in 1906, and had a reputation for violence, particularly revenge killings, until 1941.

315. Crudele, Juanita W. A LYNCHING BEE: BUTLER COUNTY STYLE. *Alabama Hist. Q. 1980 42(1-2): 59-71.* The majority of lynchings in the United States at the end of the 19th century took place in the lower South. Most of the victims were black. A study of one such lynching in Butler County, Alabama, reveals the public outrage surrounding such an incident. Although an outcry was made through the press, no response was made to a reward offered for the apprehension of the lynchers. Primary sources; 49 notes.
A. Drysdale

316. Daniel, Mike. THE ARREST AND TRIAL OF RYLAND RANDOLPH: APRIL-MAY, 1868. *Alabama Hist. Q. 1978 40(3-4): 127-143.* White supremacist Ryland Randolph, editor of the Tuscaloosa *Independent Monitor* and supporter of the Ku Klux Klan, opposed Reconstruction and Radical Republican rule in Alabama. Intervening in a racially mixed fight on 28 March 1868, he stabbed a black man in self-defense. For this he was illegally tried before a military court in Selma. Civil, military, and federal authorities involved themselves in the case. For still disputed reasons, on 13 May the military acquitted Randolph. Based on contemporary newspaper articles; 67 notes.
E. E. Eminhizer

317. Daniell, Elizabeth Otto. THE ASHBURN MURDER CASE IN GEORGIA RECONSTRUCTION, 1868. *Georgia Hist. Q. 1975 59(3): 296-312.* Chronicles the political career of George W. Ashburn, and the events of the military trial of his murderers, 1868; examines his murder at the hands of anti-Radical supporters as a reflection of anti-Radical feelings in Georgia.

318. d'Assac, Jacques Ploncard. POLANSKI, MANSON OU LA RUPTURE DE L'ORDRE [Polanski, Manson or the rupture of order]. *Écrits de Paris [France] 1977 (373): 73-76.* Assesses the moral and political implications of the murder of Sharon Tate, wife of filmmaker Roman Polanski, by Charles Manson and his "family" in 1969.

319. Davis, Angela Y. RACISM AND CONTEMPORARY LITERATURE ON RAPE. *Freedomways 1976 16(1). 25-33.* Discusses rape in the context of the black male and the negative and wholly racist images which are conjured in Susan Brownmiller's *Against Our Will: Men, Women, and Rape* (New York: Simon and Schuster, 1975).

320. Davis, Angela Y. RAPE, RACISM AND THE CAPITALIST SETTING. *Black Scholar 1978 9(7): 24-30.* Calls rape a symptom of ever-increasing frustration within capitalism; asserts the virtual nonexistence of rape in Communist countries.

321. Deming, Mary Beard and Eppy, Ali. THE SOCIOLOGY OF RAPE. *Sociol. and Social Res. 1981 65(4): 357-380.* Rape research is organized to illustrate the contributions and the potential of sociological theory and methods. The first half of the review deals with social structural determinants of rape. Support

is found for feminist, conflict, ecological and subcultural theories, but not for theories of sexual access. The second half of the review focuses on social reactions to rape, as indicated in studies of attribution and criminal justice processing. The disparate studies reviewed in the article are integrated with a common focus on theoretical perspectives, on those aspects of rape that distinguish it from other crimes of violence, and on methodological issues.　　　　　　　　　　　　J

322.　Dershowitz, Alan M.; Silverglate, Harvey A.; and Baker, Jeanne. THE JDL MURDER CASE: "THE INFORMER WAS OUR OWN CLIENT." *Civil Liberties R. 1976 3(1): 43-60.* Civil rights questions were raised by the trial of Sheldon Seigel. Seigel, along with other members of the Jewish Defense League, was indicted for murder in the bombing of Sol Hurok's office in New York City. The authors, Seigel's lawyers, learned that Seigel was a government informer after they accepted his case. Subsequently, their focus on the 1972-73 case changed to investigating the legal and moral limits "of governmental intervention to prevent and prosecute the most serious kinds of crime," and to protecting the civil rights of informers.　　　　　　　　　　　　　　　　　　　　S

323.　Dobyns, Henry F. and Euler, Robert C. THE DUNN-HOWARD KILLINGS: ADDITIONAL INSIGHTS. *J. of Arizona Hist. 1980 21(1): 87-95.* Challenges the conclusion of Michael Belshaw (see abstract 297) that robbery was the motive for the killing of William Dunn and O. G. and Seneca Howland by Shivwits Paiute Indians in 1869. The authors present circumstantial evidence for their opinion that the ambush "may have constituted the final native American offensive" of the Walapai War. Secondary and archival sources; map, 29 notes.
　　　　　　　　　　　　　　　　　　　　　　　　　　　G. O. Gagnon

324.　Earl, Philip I. THE LYNCHING OF ADAM UBER. *Nevada Hist. Soc. Q. 1973 16(1): 2-19.* On 25 November 1897 Adam Uber shot Hans Anderson in Douglas County, Nevada. An angry mob in turn lynched Uber on 7 December. The lynching sparked protest in Nevada and elsewhere. Many accused county officials of less than diligent efforts to prosecute the lynchers. A grand jury declined to indict the lynchers. Based primarily on newspaper sources; 3 illus., photo, 59 notes.　　　　　　　　　　　　　　　　　　　　H. T. Lovin

325.　Edgerton, Samuel Y., Jr. THE MURDER OF JANE MCCREA. *Early Am. Life 1977 8(3): 28-30.* Despite being a Tory sympathizer and en route to meet her lover, an officer with the British, when she was murdered and scalped by British-hired mercenary Indians in New York in 1777, Jane McCrea became a symbol of anti-British sentiment and a legend in painting and poetry, 1777-1850's.

326.　Ellsworth, Paul D. MOBOCRACY AND THE RULE OF LAW: AMERICAN PRESS REACTION TO THE MURDER OF JOSEPH SMITH. *Brigham Young U. Studies 1979 20(1): 71-82.* Reviews the attitude of the national press to news of the murder in 1844 of Joseph Smith, founder of the Church of Jesus Christ of Latter-day Saints. Newspapers in the vicinity of the murder generally justified it, but the remainder of the nation's press clearly did not. Most of them saw more in the act than the simple murder of a man by a mob; the era was one of considerable rioting and violence, causing many thoughtful persons to speculate that an age of anarchy was at hand. Smith's murder was viewed as another horrifying evidence of the trend.　　　　　　　　　　　V. L. Human

327.   Erickson, Rosemary J. and Crow, Wayman J.   VIOLENCE IN BUSI-
NESS SETTINGS.   *Am. Behavioral Scientist 1980 23(5): 717-743.* Analyzes the
nature and components of violent crime in the 1970's and their implications for
the business community and its efforts to deter it.

328.   Erlanger, Howard S.   ESTRANGEMENT, MACHISMO AND GANG
VIOLENCE.   *Social Sci. Q. 1979 60(2): 235-248.* Examines the nature and
causes of gang violence in the Chicano barrios of East Los Angeles, California.
Not falling back on socioeconomic causes and consequences of violence, the
author argues that values inherent within the group, and perhaps the community,
are the root cause. The concept of *machismo,* the idea that masculinity is synony-
mous with violence, is very much a supreme value among barrio youths. But of
itself, *machismo* is not enough, nor is violence; conditions also must exist which
reward the disciple of the value, and this structural support is indeed present in
the East Los Angeles community. Hence, the value achievement brings the
promised reward. Note, ref.   V. L. Human

329.   Feuerlicht, Roberta Strauss.   VANZETTI'S FIRST TRIAL: AN ITAL-
IAN GETS PURITAN JUSTICE.   *Civil Liberties Rev. 1977 4(3): 53-67.* Excerpts a chapter from Roberta Strauss Feuerlicht's book *Justice Crucified: The
Story of Sacco and Vanzetti* examining a trial in which Bartolomeo Vanzetti was
convicted of a murder in 1920.

330.   Fischer, Claude S.   THE SPREAD OF VIOLENT CRIME FROM
CITY TO COUNTRYSIDE, 1955 TO 1975.   *Rural Sociol. 1980 45(3): 416-434.*
Discusses whether cultural differences among communities of varying degrees of
urbanism are declining, taking as a case in point acts of violent crime, using
material compiled by the Federal Bureau of Investigation during 1955-75 and
data for California from sources within the state.

331.   Galant, Debbie.   ALONG FOR THE RIDE.   *Southern Exposure 1980
8(4): 84-86.* Story of Connie Lynn Kyles, 20, now serving the third year of her
40-50 year sentence for second-degree murder; 1977-80.

332.   Gass, W. Conard.   THE MISFORTUNE OF A HIGH MINDED AND
HONORABLE GENTLEMAN: W. W. AVERY AND THE SOUTHERN
CODE OF HONOR.   *North Carolina Hist. Rev. 1979 56(3): 278-297.* On
Tuesday, 11 November 1851, William Waightstill Avery (1816-64), a lawyer, shot
and killed Samuel Flemming (b. 1812), a businessman and politician, in the Burke
County courthouse at Morganton, North Carolina. Three weeks earlier Flemming had cowhided and beaten an unarmed and surprised Avery on the main
street of Marion, North Carolina, culminating their several years of political,
legal, and personal disputes. Avery, of an upper class North Carolina family, felt
he had to kill Flemming to retain his standing according to the southern gentleman's code of honor. Tried immediately after the killing, Avery was acquitted
by a jury which believed so firmly in that code that it was willing to overlook
outright murder to uphold it. Based on newspaper accounts, published and
unpublished family papers, and court minutes; 9 illus., 65 notes.
                                                              T. L. Savitt

333.   Gerlach, Larry R.   OGDEN'S "HORRIBLE TRAGEDY": THE LYNCHING OF GEORGE SEGAL.   *Utah Hist. Q. 1981 49(2): 157-172.* When George Segal shot Mrs. Mary Gudgell outside the Gem Restaurant over what references have indicated as back pay due to his recent dismissal or a rejected love, he was apprehended and taken to the city jail. Almost immediately, a masked mob appeared, broke into the jail, dragged Segal out, and lynched him. A grand jury, assembled by Judge P. H. Emerson, acquitted all accused men. Mayor David Perry seems to have been negligent in not protecting Segal from mob violence. Photo, map.   K. E. Gilmont

334.   Gleason, Kathy and Devereux, Sean.   RAPE LAW: A CASE STUDY. *Southern Exposure 1977 4(4): 55-57.* With the convening of the Research Committee on Sexual Assault on 15 October 1975, work began in North Carolina to investigate sexual assault on both men and women. The goal was to make legislative recommendations for reform. The resultant bill proposal has the approval of the State Supreme Court, provides for degrees of punishment based on various forms of sexual assault, and seeks the abolition of capital punishment as a penalty for rape. The bill also encompasses a definition of consent in sexual assault cases and the formulation of a new rule regarding the admissibility of evidence of the victim's previous sexual conduct.   N. Lederer

335.   Goldring, Philip.   WHISKY, HORSES AND DEATH: THE CYPRESS HILLS MASSACRE AND ITS SEQUEL.   *Can. Hist. Sites [Canada] 1979 (21): 41-70.* For about three years before the establishment of Fort Walsh in 1875, the Cypress Hills had been a haven for whisky traders. Their activities are chiefly remembered for the slaughter inflicted in 1873 on a band of Assiniboine by some of the traders and a passing band of white men from Montana. The immediate cause of the massacre was the supposed theft of a trader's horse, but the case gave rise to wide controversy about the value and application of the law to native peoples on the frontier of white trade and settlement. Based on archival and published documents; notes, biblio., appendixes.   J

336.   Goodwin, D. W.   ALCOHOL IN SUICIDE AND HOMICIDE. *Q. J. of Studies on Alcohol 1973 34(1A): 144-156.* "The literature [58 items] on the association between suicide and alcoholism and between homicide and drinking is reviewed. While suicide is substantially more frequent among alcoholics than in the general population, alcoholism is more common among attempters than among suicides; men outnumber women alcoholics among both suicides and attempters. Suicide rates are lower among Black than among White alcoholics, and risk of suicide declines in all alcoholics after age 50. Suicide in alcoholics seems to be a response to loss of status, occupational role and relationships and occurs relatively early. The low suicide rate among Black alcoholics may be due to the early onset of problem drinking among them which may produce enough brain damage by middle age to dull the sufferings of alcoholics, and to the fact that few Black alcoholics have had much wealth or status to lose. Suicide and alcoholism can be considered as expressions of the same self-destructive instinct or of the same predisposition to depression. Although about one-quarter of all suicide victims (alcoholics and nonalcoholics) drink immediately before death, little is known concerning the role of intoxication in suicide. In homicide, both killer and victim commonly have been drinking, often to intoxication, immediately before the event, but few murderers are alcoholics. Most murderers appar-

ently do not respond to drinking in a pathological way, and drinking does not seem to produce aggressive behavior except in certain social situations." J

337. Grimsted, David. MAKING VIOLENCE RELEVANT. *Rev. in Am. Hist. 1976 4(3): 331-338.* Review article prompted by Richard Maxwell Brown's *Strain of Violence: Historical Studies of American Violence and Vigilantism* (New York: Oxford U. Pr., 1975).

338. Gross, Mary J. H. THE MEDICAL MURDER: AN ALMOST SUCCESSFULLY SILENT SUPPRESSION. *Papers of the Biblio. Soc. of Am. 1978 72(2): 259-260.* Discusses the deletion of the story of Sam Sheppard from a 1966 American edition of a 1957 British book, *The Medical Murderer* (dealing with homicidal physicians) due to the reopening of the case and the acquittal of Sheppard.

339. Hankerson, Henry E. CHILDREN IN CRISIS IN THE UNITED STATES: CHILD ABUSE AND NEGLECT—A CONTINUING PROBLEM. *J. of Negro Educ. 1979 48(3): 396-407.* Provides a brief history of child abuse from Biblical times, defines child abuse, and reports on the current status of the problem. Cases of child abuse and neglect are estimated at over one million per year in the United States. The typically abusive parent has been characterized as below 30 years of age, with a family income of less than $6,000 per year, residing in the Midwest, having a high school diploma, and belonging to a minority religion or race. However, the more affluent inflict psychological harm, which may be more damaging than physical harm. Children under 4 years of age constitute 62% of abused children. Boys are abused more than girls. There are four broad categories of public policy comprising the child welfare system: criminal law, juvenile court acts, child abuse reporting laws, and legislatively established protective services. Primary sources; 43 notes. J. Powell

340. Harris, Trudier. CEREMONIAL FAGOTS: LYNCHING AND BURNING RITUALS IN BLACK LITERATURE. *Southern Humanities Rev. 1976 10(3): 235-247.* Provides examples in black literature published between 1853 and the 1960's, of the threat and practice of the hanging and burning of blacks in the United States (which occurred especially frequently between 1882 and 1903).

341. Henig, Gerald S. "HE DID NOT HAVE A FAIR TRIAL": CALIFORNIA PROGRESSIVES REACT TO THE LEO FRANK CASE. *California History 1979 58(2): 166-178.* Analyzes the reaction of California progressives to the Leo Frank case, 1913-15. Frank, a Jew, was convicted of the murder of a 13-year-old factory girl in Georgia in 1913. Evident violations of due process of law provoked criticism of the verdict, especially in California where progressives actively protested. Progressive newspapers and spokesmen commented on aspects of social injustice involved in the affair. On the other hand, except for California Jewish leaders, few progressives discussed the problems of capital punishment and anti-Semitism evoked by the trial. When the death sentence was commuted to life imprisonment in 1915, Californians praised the courage of Georgia's governor. Soon after, however, Frank was lynched by a mob. Progressives and conservatives alike united in condemning that act. California stood as a leader in the fight for justice for Frank, though its leadership failed to confront the deeper issues brought forth by the Frank case. Photo, 91 notes. A. Hoffman

342. Higgins, Renelda. BRUTAL LYNCH/MURDER IN ALABAMA. *Crisis 1981 88(5): 226-231, 257-258.* On the night of 21 March 1981, 19-year-old Michael Lee Donal of Mobile, Alabama, was murdered and lynched while walking to the grocery store. The next night, three whites were arrested for the crime. Later they were all released. Against the background of Mobile's history, this stands as a classic unresolved case of racial violence.   A. G. Belles

343. Hilen, Andrew. MURDER ON SHAW ISLAND. *Pacific Northwest Q. 1978 69(3): 97-106.* In 1872 Hugh Park homesteaded the lightly inhabited Shaw Island on the border between Washington and British Columbia. His mental health gradually deteriorated and he became combative toward his neighbors. The mysterious death of James Baker in 1885 was traced to Park who resisted arrest and was killed by a posse. Park's property was subsequently auctioned off by the court. Primary sources; 3 photos, map, 26 notes.
M. L. Tate

344. Hinds, Margery. MINA. *Beaver [Canada] 1976 307(3): 20-24.* Mina was an Eskimo woman living on an island in Hudson's Bay. In February 1941, based on celestial changes and reading the Bible, she caused the death of 10 reluctant Eskimos in an effort "to meet Jesus." After a trial at Moose Factory, she was judged mildly insane, but authorities felt that she would best survive if returned to a familiar environment. She was sent to Port Harrison (now Inoucd-jouac, Quebec), where she spent the rest of her days as a household helper and cook. She adjusted well, was proud of her earlier messiah role, was usually in good spirits, and proved to be an effective, reliable worker. Mina worked for the author, a teacher at Port Harrison. 3 illus.   D. Chaput

345. Hindus, Michael Stephen. INEVITABLE ACQUITTAL, TRIAL BY JURY, AND TRIAL BY HISTORY. *Rev. in Am. Hist. 1976 4(3): 397-402.* Review article prompted by Dallin H. Oaks and Marvin S. Hill's *Carthage Conspiracy: The Trial of the Accused Assassins of Joseph Smith* (Urbana: U. of Illinois Pr., 1975) discusses the concepts of frontier justice, Mormon history, and the history of law in the 1844 murder trial.

346. Hockings, Paul. ALBERT STAUB: THE STORY OF A WAYWARD IMMIGRANT. *Swiss Am. Hist. Soc. Newsletter 1978 14(3): 17-21.* Details the short criminal life of Albert Staub, a 19-year-old Swiss immigrant to America, who committed theft and murder in Blue Island, a village south of Chicago, in 1857 and was hanged in Chicago in 1858.

347. Holmes, William F. WHITECAPPING IN GEORGIA: CARROLL AND HOUSTON COUNTIES, 1893. *Georgia Hist. Q. 1980 64(4): 388-404.* Whitecapping flourished in rural areas around the United States from about 1887-1920. It consisted of violent attacks by disguised night riders on victims who somehow threatened the community. Discusses two incidents in 1893 in Carroll and Houston counties, Georgia, their causes, and their aftermath. Based on newspapers, court records and secondary sources; 43 notes.
G. R. Schroeder

348. Hortsman, Ronald L. THE GRAND NATIONAL BANK ROBBERY. *Missouri Hist. Soc. Bull. 1980 36(3): 168-173.* On 25 May 1930, the largest bank robbery ever perpetrated in St. Louis happened as a consequence of the transfer

of the Grand National Bank's vault to another location. The crime triggered a serious bank-run and, more importantly, the ensuing investigations of the robbery uncovered the efforts of a syndicate, the Vandeventer Securities Company, to take control of the bank. Based on *St. Louis Globe-Democrat* accounts; 4 photos.

H. T. Lovin

349. Howard, Barbara and Braby, Junia. THE HODGES HANGING. *Palimpsest 1979 60(2): 48-58.* Members of the Danite sect of the Mormon Church, William and Stephen Hodges were indicted and hanged for the murder of two Iowa farmers whose home they broke into intending to rob, 1845.

350. Hudelston, Jesse. *THE BALLAD OF THE BRASWELL BOYS:* A PUTNAM COUNTY INCIDENT. *Tennessee Folklore Soc. Bull. 1980 46(1): 25-30.* The Ballad of the Braswell Boys, from the Upper Cumberland region and still sung today, tells of the execution by hanging of George (Teak) and Joe Braswell on 27 March 1878 for the murder of Russell and John Allison on 29 November 1875.

351. Inciardi, James A. THE CHANGING LIFE OF MICKEY FINN: SOME NOTES ON CHLORAL HYDRATE DOWN THROUGH THE AGES. *J. of Popular Culture 1977 11(3): 591-596.* Explores several versions of the nature, origins, and myths surrounding the illegal use of "knockout drops," or the "Mickey Finn." The evidence suggests that the widespread use of the "Mickey" may be more popular myth than reality, but also that its notoriety was coincident with the emergence of urban vice areas about the middle of the 19th century and their decline during the early years of the 20th century. Primary and secondary sources; 24 notes.

D. G. Nielson

352. Ingalls, Robert P. ANTIRACIAL VIOLENCE IN BIRMINGHAM DURING THE 1930S. *J. of Southern Hist. 1981 47(4): 521-544.* An analysis of the causes and consequences of domestic violence in Birmingham, Alabama. Focuses on the case of Joseph Gelders, who was surreptitiously and severely beaten after publicly supporting radical labor leaders. Covers the public, media, and court history of his case, which resulted in no action being taken. The sudden cessation of antilabor and antiracial vigilante action immediately thereafter suggests that the entire campaign was not spontaneous, but carefully planned. The actual goal was the prevention of labor unions; violence ended when a new labor contract was signed. 113 notes.

V. L. Human

353. Ingalls, Robert P. THE FLOGGING OF JOSEPH GELDERS: A POLICEMAN'S VIEW. *Labor Hist. 1979 20(4): 576-578.* Reprints a letter (20 October 1936) from G. C. Giles, Chief of Detectives of Birmingham, Alabama, to Governor Bibb Graves. Giles expressed doubts about the possibility of convicting the known floggers of pro-Communist agitator Joseph Gelders, saying that the people opposed agitation because the United States Steel Corporation was planning to expand its Tennessee Coal and Iron facilities in the area. Based on the Graves papers; 6 notes.

L. L. Athey

354. Institute for Southern Studies. THE THIRD OF NOVEMBER. *Southern Exposure 1981 9(3): 55-67.* Reviews the televised murders of five Communist Workers Party demonstrators in Greensboro, North Carolina, on 3 November 1979 by members of the Ku Klux Klan and Nazi Party and the acquittal one year later of the six men charged with the crime.

355.   Jacob, Kathryn Allamong.   SHE COULDN'T HAVE DONE IT, EVEN
IF SHE DID: WHY LIZZIE BORDEN WENT FREE.   *Am. Heritage 1978
29(2): 42-53.* In 1893, Lizzie Borden was tried in Massachusetts for the ax
murders of her father and stepmother. Her attorneys made use of the prevailing
myths that a genteel young woman could not commit such a crime, either
physically or psychologically. Though her testimony was full of discrepancies, the
all male jury found her not guilty. Living the rest of her life in seclusion, she died
in 1927. 11 illus.   J. F. Paul

356.   Johnson, Allan Griswold.   ON THE PREVALENCE OF RAPE IN
THE UNITED STATES.   *Signs 1980 6(1): 136-146.* According to Edward
Shorter (see abstract 412), the chances of being raped are minimal. Actually,
sexual violence is widespread in the United States, and Shorter's statistics are
incorrect and misleading. Using data supplied by the Federal Bureau of Investigation (FBI) and the Law Enforcement Assistance Administration (LEAA), a
conservative estimate under current conditions would predict that 20% to 30%
of all girls now 12 years old will suffer violent sexual attack during their lives.
Based on demographic statistics and life expectancy tables and secondary sources;
4 tables, 17 notes.   S. P. Conner

357.   Jones, Ann.   SHE HAD TO DIE!   *Am. Heritage 1980 31(6): 20-31.* On
12 January 1928, Ruth Snyder and her lover, Judd Gray, were executed in New
York for the murder of Snyder's husband. Public outrage led to a widespread
desire that Snyder be put to death. Women's morality was stressed in news
accounts of the trial and execution. 22 illus.   J. F. Paul

358.   Kallison, Frances Rosenthal.   WAS IT A DUEL OR A MURDER: A
STUDY IN TEXAS ASSIMILATION.   *Am. Jewish Hist. Q. 1973 62(3): 314-
320.* In 1857, the merchant Siegmund Feinberg died after a quarrel with Benedict
Schwartz, a Jewish immigrant from Russia. Whether he was murdered by
Schwartz or was shot accidentally has never been established. A Hebrew poem
on his tombstone implies that he was murdered. Schwartz was killed in his
pawnshop in 1882. The incident indicates the rapidity with which immigrant Jews
assimilated to the surrounding society. 20 notes.   F. Rosenthal

359.   Katz, Maude White, ed.   LEARNING FROM HISTORY: THE IN-
GRAM CASE OF THE 1940'S.   *Freedomways 1979 19(2): 82-86.* Reprints a
petition by W. E. B. Du Bois submitted in 1949 to the UN, requesting its
intercession in the case of a black Georgian, Rosa Lee Ingram, serving (with two
of her sons) a life sentence for the 1947 death of her neighbor, John Stratford,
who, after severely beating her, was clubbed over the head by her 16-year-old son.

360.   Keller, Allan.   "THE BABY IS FOUND . . . DEAD!"   *Am. Hist. Illus.
1975 10(2): 10-21.* Discusses the investigation of the kidnapping of Charles A.
Lindbergh's son, Charles, Jr., in New Jersey in 1932 which led to the execution
of Bruno Richard Hauptmann in 1936.

361.   Kennedy, Edward M.   THE NEED FOR GUN CONTROL LEGISLA-
TION.   *Current Hist. 1976 71(418): 26-28, 31.* Counters common arguments
against gun control, including the 2nd Amendment, and cites international gun
murder rates, 1970's.

362. Klotter, James C. FEUDS IN APPALACHIA: AN OVERVIEW. *Filson Club Hist. Q. 1982 56(3): 290-317.* Presents a detailed overview and analysis of the 19th-century family wars in Kentucky and West Virginia. Prominent among these vendettas were the Hatfield-McCoy feud, the Hargis-Marcum-Cockrell-Callahan feud, and the Rowan County war. Examines a variety of explanations for this violence including those of Henry D. Shapiro, John A. Williams, and Gordon B. McKinney. Finds all previous explanations not comprehensive enough and suggests that the breakdown of the legal system was the primary cause of the family murders. Based on contemporary newspaper accounts. G. B. McKinney

363. Kritzer, Herbert M. and Uhlman, Thomas M. SISTERHOOD IN THE COURTROOM: SEX OF JUDGE AND DEFENDANT IN CRIMINAL CASE DISPOSITION. *Social Sci. J. 1977 14(2): 77-88.* Examines the behavioral differences in male and female judges, addressing the problems of rape and how it is dealt with, the amount of compassion comparatively displayed by both sexes, and the effects which the sex of the judge and the sex of the defendant have on the trial outcome; 4 tables (information collected in 1968), 20 notes.

364. Kubicek, Earl C. THE CASE OF THE MAD HATTER. *Lincoln Herald 1981 83(3): 708-719.* Biography of Thomas H. "Boston" Corbett, a hat finisher who claimed to have shot John Wilkes Booth while part of the detail that participated in the search for Booth after the assassination of President Abraham Lincoln; Corbett disappeared in 1908.

365. LaBastille, Anne. AN AMERICAN TRAGEDY, REVISITED. *Adirondack Life 1973 4(3): 46-51.* Indicates the changes in Big Moose Lake and the western Adirondacks during the 67 years since Chester Gillette presumably murdered the pregnant Grace Brown in 1906 and dumped her body in the lake. 9 illus. D. R. Jamieson

366. Labowitz-Starus, Leslie and Lacy, Suzanne. "IN MOURNING AND IN RAGE . . . ." *Frontiers 1978 3(1): 52-55.* Ten rape-stranglings in Los Angeles during 1977 prompted a mass media presentation by members of Los Angeles women's groups protesting violence against women; includes the script of protest presented at the event and the purpose of the group.

367. LaFantasie, Glenn W. MURDER OF AN INDIAN, 1638. *Rhode Island Hist. 1979 38(3): 67-77.* In 1638 four fugitive indentured servants from Plymouth Colony murdered a friendly Narragansett Indian. Three of the four were eventually captured, tried, and hanged. This was the first instance in which whites were punished by colonial authorities for a serious crime against an Indian. The executions temporarily eased tensions on the New England frontier, but did not set a precedent for dealing with white criminals. Based on published documents and secondary accounts; 4 illus., map, 37 notes. P. J. Coleman

368. Lanier, Robert A. THE CARMACK MURDER CASE. *Tennessee Hist. Q. 1981 40(3): 272-285.* On 9 November 1908, the editor of the *Nashville Tennessean,* former congressman Edward Ward Carmack, was fatally shot near the Capitol in Nashville. Although the incident was triggered by the approach of Duncan J. Cooper to Carmack, the fatal shots were fired by Cooper's son, Robin J. The altercation was the result of a long-standing antagonism between

the former friends. In the well-publicized trial, the Coopers were found guilty. However, the governor, Malcolm Patterson, immediately pardoned the elder Cooper and charges were dropped against the son. The case raised numerous questions concerning murder and self-defense and probably ended the career of Governor Patterson. Also, since Patterson was proalcohol and Carmack favored prohibition, the episode no doubt contributed to the state's decision to adopt prohibition in 1909. Mostly court records and newspaper accounts; 85 notes.

C. L. Grant

369.   Levy, Jerrold E.; Kunitz, Stephen J.; and Everett, Michael.   NAVAJO CRIMINAL HOMICIDE.   *Southwestern J. of Anthrop. 1969 25(2): 124-152.* Examines homicide among the Navajo Indians and its relationship with alcoholism and acculturation, based on data on reported Navajo homicides, 1956-65.

370.   Littlefield, Daniel F. and Underhill, Lonnie E.   NED CHRISTIE AND HIS ONE-MAN FIGHT WITH THE UNITED STATES MARSHALS. *J. of Ethnic Studies 1974 1(4): 3-15.* In 1888, Ned Christie, a Cherokee, was charged with murder of a United States marshal in May 1884. Professing innocence, Christie refused to either surrender or flee. He remained with his family on his homestead and for four years frustrated all attempts at capture. In November 1892, a force of 18 marshals armed with dynamite succeeded in destroying his stronghold and killing Christie. Christie's fight symbolizes the struggle between the Indian concept of justice and the white officials' notions of law and order. Based on primary sources; 61 notes.   T. W. Smith

371.   Marable, Manning.   THE QUESTION OF GENOCIDE.   *J. of Intergroup Relations 1982 10(3): 19-29.* Discusses genocide as evidenced by the continuing violence against Negroes in the South, especially of young men and children in Atlanta; surveys some of the literature dealing with the problem.

372.   Margarita, Mona.   KILLING THE POLICE: MYTHS AND MOTIVES.   *Ann. of the Am. Acad. of Pol. and Social Sci. 1980 (452): 63-71.* Analyzes the motives of assailants who murdered on-duty police in New York City. Police have not often been killed during domestic disturbances, nor have they been the victims of madmen or lunatics. New York police were more likely to be killed by rational robbers fleeing the scene of a crime, who routinely used potentially lethal weapons as tools of the trade.   J/S

373.   Marr, Warren.   JUSTICE, AT LAST, FOR "SCOTTSBORO BOY?" *Crisis 1976 83(9): 310-312.* Clarence Norris is seeking a pardon for a crime that he insists the "Scottsboro Boys" never committed. On 18 October 1976, the NAACP joined Norris in asking George Wallace, governor of Alabama, to issue a pardon. In 1931 when Norris was 19, he and eight other black youths were accused of raping two white women on a freight train. Investigations have repeatedly demonstrated that the boys were not guilty. He awaits the governor's action.

A. G. Belles

374.   Martin, Charles H.   OKLAHOMA'S "SCOTTSBORO" AFFAIR: THE JESS HOLLINS RAPE CASE, 1931-1936.   *South Atlantic Q. 1980 79(2): 175-188.* The Jess Hollins rape case in Oklahoma, sometimes compared to Alabama's notorious Scottsboro rape case, attracted fleeting national interest. Although it never received the notoriety of Scottsboro, it did raise briefly a number of issues

important in Afro-American, southern, and US history—the specters of black rape and interracial sex, the fairness of the southern judicial system, the exclusion of blacks from juries, and the conflicting and competing tactics practiced by the National Association for the Advancement of Colored People (NAACP) and its archrival, the Communist-influenced International Labor Defense. Based largely on the NAACP Papers, Library of Congress, the *Oklahoma City Black Dispatch,* other newspaper accounts, and secondary sources; 30 notes.

H. M. Parker, Jr.

375. Matthews, Janet Snyder. HE HAS CARRIED HIS LIFE IN HIS HANDS: THE SARASOTA ASSASSINATION SOCIETY OF 1884. *Florida Hist. Q. 1979 58(1): 1-21.* Charles E. Abbe was murdered on 27 December 1884 by the Sara Sota Vigilance Committee. Karl H. Grismer's *The Story of Sarasota* (1946) pictured Abbe as a land-grabber and the vigilantes as righteous avengers. Abbe's murder was a dastardly crime and the guilty parties were punished. Based on court records and other primary sources; 2 illus., 68 notes. N. A. Kuntz

376. Matthews, Nancy Torrance. THE DUEL IN NINETEENTH CEN- TURY SOUTH CAROLINA: CUSTOM OVER WRITTEN LAW. *Pro. of the South Carolina Hist. Assoc. 1979: 78-84.* Despite strong antidueling laws in South Carolina, duels continued until 1880 because respectable members of soci- ety approved of them as means of redressing personal insults. The Cash-Shannon duel in 1880 was the culmination of a gradual shift away from support of the duel since the Civil War. The tremendous displacement in the society, politics, and economics of the state after the Civil War contributed to the decline of dueling. Published works; 60 notes. J. W. Thacker, Jr.

377. McDonald, Greg. JOHNNY HARRIS: THE HIGH PRICE OF JUS- TICE. *Southern Exposure 1978 6(4): 80-83.* Harris, a black man, is on death row in Alabama owing to a conviction of being involved in a 1974 prison riot in which a white guard was killed. Harris was imprisoned at an early age for minor crimes and later received five lifeterms in prison for rape and four counts of robbery. His conviction had racial overtones in that it occurred following the movement of his family into a previously white neighborhood in Birmingham, Alabama. At his trial Harris, although pleading innocence, accepted a plea bar- gain which was subsequently not supported by the prosecution. In prison Harris became an activist in openly protesting prison conditions. His stance appears to have been a major factor in his receiving the death penalty. Based mainly on interviews with Harris. N. Lederer

378. Meurer, Emil M., Jr. VIOLENT CRIME LOSSES: THEIR IMPACT ON THE VICTIM AND SOCIETY. *Ann. of the Am. Acad. of Pol. and Social Sci. 1979 (443): 54-62.* Crimes of violence have increased rapidly since 1950. In the face of increasing crime, the rights of the criminal have been protected and increased. At the same time, the rights of the victim of crime have remained relatively unchanged. The traditional rights of the victim have proven largely ineffective in providing compensation for losses suffered as a result of violent crimes. Against this setting, a number of states have seen fit to enact victim compensation programs. The existing state programs indemnify only losses which result from medical expenses and loss of earnings. They do not cover intangible personal losses or property losses. While far from a perfect solution, these laws

emphasize the changing attitude of society toward the victims of violent crime.

J

379. Millbrook, Minnie Dubbs. THE JORDAN MASSACRE. *Kansas Hist. 1979 2(4): 218-230.* Richard Jordan and his wife Mary Smith Jordan lived at Parks Fort (now Wakeeney) where he had a buffalo hide business. On 1 August 1872 the couple, George Jordan, and hired hand Fred Nelson went hunting. When they failed to return and a hunter reported finding broken equipment on the prairie, a rescue party was sent from Fort Hays. Eventually the soldiers found the bodies of the three men; Mary was believed to have been carried off by the Indians. The Army and Indian Bureau made a long but unsuccessful effort to find Mrs. Jordan and to discover the guilty Indians. The numerous versions of this incident are woven together and enriched with records of the army, Department of War, and Bureau of Indian Affairs in the National Archives. Illus., map, 41 notes.   W. F. Zornow

380. Miller, Isabel Winner. THE SENSATIONAL STUMP MURDERS. *Daughters of the Am. Revolution Mag. 1978 112(4): 278-282.* On 10 January 1768 Frederick Stump massacred 10 Indians, for mysterious reasons, in Cumberland County, Pennsylvania.

381. Miller, Kathleen Atkinson. THE LADIES AND THE LYNCHERS: A LOOK AT THE ASSOCIATION OF SOUTHERN WOMEN FOR THE PREVENTION OF LYNCHING. *Southern Studies 1978 17(3): 221-240.* In 1930 Jessie Daniel Ames (b. 1893), Director of Woman's Work for the Commission on Interracial Cooperation (CIC), helped found the Association of Southern Women for the Prevention of Lynching (ASWPL). Until 1942 this association of Southern white women, working through church and civic groups, attempted to curb lynchings by educating the public and officials and by eliciting and publicizing commitments against lynching by prominent citizens, public officials, and newspapers. The basic reasons for the increased lynchings during the Depression were economic rivalry and racial antipathy. Based on papers of ASWPL at Atlanta U., primary and secondary sources; 72 notes.   J. Buschen

382. Miller, M. Sammy. LEGEND OF A KIDNAPPER. *Crisis 1975 82(4): 118-120.* One sad chapter of American history is of kidnappers who spirited away unsuspecting free blacks and had them sold to slave trading operators in the lower South. Kidnappers usually avoided slaves because the risk of tampering with someone else's property was too high. Patty Cannon was a Delaware kidnapper and notorious murderess. She confessed to 11 murders of her own and was accessory to more than a dozen others.   A. G. Belles

383. Mitchell, Elaine Allen. FREDERICK HOUSE MASSACRE. *Beaver [Canada] 1973 303(4): 30-33.* In the winter of 1812-13, three traders and at least nine Indians were killed at Frederick House, the Hudson's Bay Company post in Ontario. Evidence pointed to an Abitibi Indian named Capascoos, but he was never apprehended and his motives in the crime were unclear. He had apparently been at the post all winter, waylaying all who came to trade. The post, never very productive, was not reopened. Illus., map.   D. Chaput

384. Mitchell, Louis D. ANOTHER REDEMPTION: BAXLEY IN BIR-MINGHAM. *Crisis 1978 85(9): 311-317.* On Sunday, 15 September 1963, a gigantic explosion roared into the basement of the Sixteenth Street Baptist Church in Birmingham, Alabama, killing four young black girls. William Baxley, then a second-year law student at the Tuscaloosa campus of the University of Alabama, resolved to do something about it. In 1970, Baxley was elected Attorney General of Alabama. He reopened the case. In 1975, a grand jury returned an indictment against Robert Chambliss for the bombing. In November 1977, Chambliss was convicted, symbolizing the redemption of a human tragedy.

A. G. Belles

385. Mondale, Walter. CHILD ABUSE: ISSUES AND ANSWERS. *Public Welfare 1974 32(2): 9-11.* Outlines the issues and legislative history of child abuse laws on federal and local levels.

S

386. Montgomery, James W. HARRY ORCHARD, SINNER OR SAINT? KIN OF IDAHO KILLER'S LAST VICTIM CONVERTED HIM. *Pacific Northwesterner 1975 19(4): 49-56.* After 20 or more murders, 1899-1906, Idaho killer Harry Orchard was converted to Christianity by the widow and son of his final victim.

387. Moore, Kathryn McDaniel. THE DILEMMA OF CORPORAL PUN-ISHMENT AT HARVARD COLLEGE. *Hist. of Educ. Q. 1974 14(3): 335-346.* The trial and conviction in 1638 of Harvard College's first executive officer, Nathaniel Eaton, for undue and excessive use of corporal punishment was an excellent demonstration of the administration of Puritan justice and served to establish Harvard's precedent of the use of reason rather than physical punishment in student corrections.

388. Moseley, Charlton and Brogdon, Frederick. A LYNCHING AT STATESBORO: THE STORY OF PAUL REED AND WILL CATO. *Georgia Hist. Q. 1981 65(2): 104-118.* When the Henry Hodges family was murdered and their home in rural Bulloch County, Georgia, burned on 28 July 1904, evidence pointed toward the involvement of two Negroes, Paul Reed and Will Cato. Though the evidence was never conclusive, they were convicted of the murders and burned alive by an angry mob on 16 August 1904. Based on newspapers, court records, and an interview; 33 notes.

G. R. Schroeder

389. Muller, Howard W. HORROR ABOARD A DOWNEASTER. *New-England Galaxy 1978 20(2): 3-11.* Details the murder of the second mate and the captain and his wife aboard the *Herbert Fuller,* a barkentine "downeaster," so-called because it was built in Harrington, Maine; in the trial that followed, the first mate was convicted of murder; late 19th century.

390. Northwood, Lawrence K.; Westgard, Richard; and Barb, Charles E., Jr. LAW-ABIDING ONE-MAN ARMIES. *Society 1978 16(1): 69-74.* Examines the characteristics of civilians who apply for permits to carry concealed weapons, based on data collected in 1972 in Seattle, Washington. This data confirms that weapon availability and homicides are on the rise.

391. Ogle, Gary. THE MYSTERIOUS DEATH OF MRS. LELAND STANFORD. *Pacific Hist. 1981 25(1): 1-7.* On 28 February 1905, in Honolulu's Moama Hotel, Jane Stanford, widow of California's Senator Leland Stanford, died in her hotel room, presumably of strychnine poisoning. After the autopsy, controversy over the cause of death broke out. She was officially declared the victim of poisoning, but the murderer was never discovered. Based on primary sources.   J. Powell

392. Parenti, Michael and Kazdin, Carolyn. THE UNTOLD STORY OF THE GREENSBORO MASSACRE. *Monthly Rev. 1981 33(6): 42-50.* Examines the role played by agents of the law in the murder of five Communist Workers' Party leaders in 1979 in Greensboro, North Carolina, and in the acquittals in 1980 of the Klansmen and American Nazis charged with the murders; singles out Bernard Butkovitch, an agent of the Bureau of Alcohol, Tobacco, and Firearms, Edward Dawson, a former FBI informant, Detective Cooper of the Greensboro police, and District Attorney Michael Schlosser as partly responsible for the killings and acquittal.

393. Parker, Everett C. THE SCANDAL OF THE WILMINGTON TEN. *Crisis 1977 84(1): 29-32.* New evidence uncovered in August 1976 should convince impartial observers that nine young black men and a white woman have been railroaded into prison by the North Carolina criminal justice system. The case grew out of a 1971 school desegregation situation in Wilmington. Black students and parents were faced with opposition from the Ku Klux Klan and the Rights of White People. Crowds and protests accompanied the formal grievance procedures. A white man was shot near a black church that had been the constant target of night-riding fire-starters. The Wilmington Ten were arrested for attempted murder and arson. So much evidence has been suppressed that a new trial seems justified.   A. G. Belles

394. Parker, Grant. DISASTER IN BATH. *Michigan Hist. 1981 65(3): 12-17.* Recreates, with meticulous detail, Michigan's worst mass murder when, in 1927, a discontented school board treasurer named Andrew Kehoe dynamited the Bath Consolidated School and killed 45 persons. Kehoe also killed his wife and blew up his truck, killing himself and four other people. Excerpts from the author's *Mayday;* 6 illus.   L. E. Ziewacz

395. Parkin, Andrew. THE HOMICIDAL NATION: AN INVESTIGATION INTO VIOLENCE IN THE UNITED STATES. *Politics [Australia] 1977 12(1): 78-88.* Seeks to identify the root of an American "penchant" for violent crime, homicide in particular, and sketches political implications. An opportunity model, stressing reaction to social immobility in a society with pervasive achievement-oriented symbols, suggests a probable cause. However, it fails to explain the regional violence characterizing the South. Institutional factors, notably the weakness in a fragmented, locally-controlled system of law enforcement within a nonparliamentary democracy, also contributes to this American problem. While liberals in Congress emphasize the need to combat poverty and social injustice in the cities and conservatives call for increased funding for police forces and the reversal of Supreme Court rulings, the American Dream continues to carry with it, on its shadowy individualistic extremities, a violent nightmare. Secondary sources; table, 64 notes   A. W. Howell

396. Pateman, Carole. WOMEN AND CONSENT. *Pol. Theory 1980 8(2): 149-168.* Criticizes democratic consent theorists by presenting empirical evidence on legal and judicial actions concerning women, their implied consent to domination in marriage, and the difficulty of proving lack of consent in rape.

397. Pernicone, Nunzio. CARLO TRESCA AND THE SACCO-VAN-ZETTI CASE. *J. of Am. Hist. 1979 66(3): 535-547.* Reviews and analyzes a critical piece of evidence that has figured prominently in historian Francis Russell's revisionist interpretation of the Sacco-Vanzetti case. Russell posited the interpretation of Nicola Sacco's guilt and Bartolomeo Vanzetti's innocence based on declarations to that effect by Carlo Tresca, the prominent Italian anarchist and contemporary of Sacco and Vanzetti, 1941-43. Although Tresca definitely made such remarks, it is doubtful whether they shed new light on the South Braintree robbery and murder of 15 April 1920. 49 notes.   T. P. Linkfield

398. Peters, Steve. POSTMORTEM OF AN ASSASSINATION: PARSON TOLBY AND THE MAXWELL LAND GRANT FIGHT. *Texana 1973 11(4): 328-361.* Gives the historical background of and decribes, the events surrounding the Colfax County War, from the 1875 assassination of Methodist minister Thomas Colby, to 1900; in dispute was the territory in New Mexico known as the Maxwell Grant.

399. Pettey, Weston A. THE SEMINOLE INCIDENT AND TOM ROSS. *West Texas Hist. Assoc. Year Book 1980 56: 133-142.* Cattle rustlers Milt Good and Tom Ross, who murdered two cattle inspectors of the Texas and Southwestern Cattle Raisers Association in the lobby of the Gaines Hotel in Seminole, Texas, in 1923, were imprisoned, but escaped after about a year; Good was captured about three months later, and Ross committed suicide in 1929 after another murder.

400. Pittman, Walter E., Jr. THE MEL CHEATHAM AFFAIR: INTER-RACIAL MURDER IN MISSISSIPPI IN 1889. *J. of Mississippi Hist. 1981 43(2): 127-133.* On 19 March 1890, Mel Cheatham of Grenada County became the first white man to be executed for killing a black man in postbellum Mississippi. In addition to Cheatham, another white and three blacks were arrested and charged with the murder of the black, James Tillman, who had testified before the Grand Jury of the Circuit Court of the County concerning gambling in his neighborhood. The author describes the reaction of the local populace to Tillman's murder on 13 July 1889, and the trial, which ended with a unanimous vote for the conviction of Cheatham. One of the black men was released in return for his testimony, and the other conspirators were given lengthy sentences in the state penitentiary at Parchman. The author maintains that incidents such as this show that occasionally racial barriers in the South became meaningless when whites and blacks found a common purpose more important than their differences. Based on newspapers, Grenada Circuit Court Records, Minutes of the Board of Supervisors, Grenada County, and Governor J. M. Stone Papers; 15 notes.
M. S. Legan

401. Quinn, Bernard. THE GENERAL'S DAUGHTER. *New-England Galaxy 1977 18(4): 54-59.* Describes the 1778 murder of Joshua Spooner by three men as he returned from Cooley's Tavern in Brookfield Township, Massachusetts. His wife, Bathsheba, was implicated in the plot, convicted, and hanged.
P. C. Marshall

402.   Reid, Herbert O.   TASK FORCE ON VIOLENT CRIME REPORT MISSES MARK.   *Crisis 1982 89(1): 13-15.* Like all presidents since the 1960's, Ronald Reagan created a Task Force on Violent Crime. He gave the group 120 days to bring back recommendations for legislative proposals and administrative actions that could combat violent crime. The final report emphasized one point of view, the need for more incarcerations in prison. The task force did not deal with the causes of crime. The recommendations included preventive detention, use of all evidence, elimination of bail, requiring fixed sentences, and certain mandatory sentences.   A. G. Belles

403.   Rogers, William Warren, Jr.   RUBE BURROW, "KING OF OUT-LAWS," AND HIS FLORIDA ADVENTURES.   *Florida Hist. Q. 1980 59(2): 182-198.* Reuben Huston Burrow gained fame as a train robber. The Southern Express Company hired detective Thomas Jackson to track Burrow. For two years Jackson trailed Burrow in and out of Florida. He was killed in a shoot-out in October 1890. Based on newspaper accounts; 2 fig., 39 notes.
                                                                            N. A. Kuntz

404.   Rowell, George S.   A MAINE LYNCHING: THE VIOLENT DEATH OF JAMES CULLEN AT MAPLETON, 1873.   *Maine Hist. Soc. Q. 1980 19(4): 207-225.* The author (1846-1933) describes some of his memories of 19th-century Aroostook County, Maine, focusing on a double murder by James Cullen. The murderer's attitude and his killing a popular man so enraged the local people that they gathered in two separate mobs to lynch him. The authorities could take no action and the lynching was generally approved. This paper was read to the Maine Historical Society in 1909 and is here published for the first time.   C. A. Watson

405.   Rushing, Fred J., III.   THE ASSASSINATION OF JUDGE T. S. CRAWFORD, BITTER FRUIT OF THE TRAGIC ERA.   *North Louisiana Hist. Assoc. J. 1976 7(4): 131-134.* On 8 September 1873, Thomas S. Caldwell, the then Ouachita-Caldwell District Judge, and A. H. Harris, the district attorney, "were murdered in cold blood on the road between Columbia and Winnsboro in Franklin Parish." No one was ever convicted of the murders, and while the murders "had possible non-political motives, the political motives far exceed them." Based on newspaper accounts of the time. 18 notes.   A. N. Garland

406.   Saalberg, Harvey.   DON MELLETT, EDITOR OF THE CANTON "NEWS," WAS SLAIN WHILE EXPOSING UNDERWORLD.   *Journalism Q. 1976 53(1): 88-93.* Donald Ring Mellett (1856-1926) was shot after half a year of fighting corruption in Canton, Ohio, as editor of the Canton *Daily News.* His many enemies included the police department. Public good and increased circulation of his paper motivated him. His campaign and death had little effect on the corruption. Based on primary and secondary sources; 42 notes.
                                                                            K. J. Puffer

407.   Scarpitti, Frank R. and Scarpitti, Ellen C.   VICTIMS OF RAPE. *Society 1977 14(5): 29-32.* Examines societal, attitudinal, and legal changes surrounding the psychology and criminality of rape, 1970's.

408. Schooley, Harry B., III. THE LATTIMER MASSACRE AND TRIAL. *Slovakia 1977 27(50): 62-79.* Discusses a trial which led to the acquittal of Sheriff James Martin and his deputies for the murder of two dozen Slovak American coal miners during a strike in the Lattimer area of Pennsylvania, 1897.

409. Schrink, Jeffrey and Schrink, Frances. HANGMAN'S CROSSING. *Indiana Folklore 1978 11(1): 87-97.* Hangman's Crossing, a railroad crossing located outside of Seymour, Indiana, received its name when it served as the site of the vigilante hanging of six members of the Reno brothers gang in 1868, following a series of daring railroad robberies.

410. Sessions, Gene A. MYTH, MORMONISM, AND MURDER IN THE SOUTH. *South Atlantic Q. 1976 75(2): 212-225.* Examines inhumane acts directed against members of the Church of Jesus Christ of Latter-day Saints from the post-Reconstruction period to the early 20th century for the purpose of understanding the broader question of violence in Southern history. Sociological and psychological explanations are analyzed in accounting for such mistreatment. Tennessee, Georgia and Alabama receive primary focus. 29 notes.

R. W. Dubay

411. Shofner, Jerrell H. JUDGE HERBERT RIDER AND THE LYNCH-ING AT LABELLE. *Florida Hist. Q. 1981 59(3): 292-306.* Judge Herbert A. Rider witnessed the torture and lynching of Henry Patterson, a black construction worker, in LaBelle in 1926. He and a handful of others attempted, without success, to bring the mob to justice. Judge Rider lost all support and community standing. Based on newspaper reports, personal correspondence, and other sources; 41 notes.

N. A. Kuntz

412. Shorter, Edward. ON WRITING THE HISTORY OF RAPE. *Signs: J. of Women in Culture and Soc. 1977 3(2): 471-482.* Susan Brownmiller's thesis, in *Against Our Will,* that rape is a "political" crime, ignores two specific areas: the nature of rape in times past and an apparent decrease in the incidence of rape over the past century. In the three or four centuries before the French Revolution sexual frustration, not politics, seems to be the primary explanation of rape. Brutality has been the norm for most sexual encounters. The recent increase of rape in Anglo-Saxon countries, following a period of decline until the 1960's, is probably caused by the new mobilization of women for political action. Thus, the politicizing of rape is a new development. Based on secondary works, especially the author's; 2 tables, 18 notes.

J. K. Gammage

413. Showalter, Elaine. RETHINKING THE SEVENTIES: WOMEN WRITERS AND VIOLENCE. *Antioch Rev. 1981 39(2): 156-170.* Reviews the work of feminist novelists of the 1970's dealing with violence against women, especially rape, which stems at least partly from the loosening of traditional female roles and the recent feminist will toward greater self-autonomy.

414. Sifuentes, Roberto. APROXIMACIONES AL "CORRIDO DE LOS HERMANOS HERNANDEZ EJECUTADOS EN LA CAMARA DE GAS DE LA PENITENCIARIA DE FLORENCE, ARIZONA EL DIA 6 DE JULIO DE 1934" [Approaches to the "Corrido de los Hermanos Hernández Ejecutados en la Cámara de Gas de la Penitenciaría de Florence, Arizona, el día 6 de Julio de 1934"]. *Aztlán 1982 13(1-2): 95-109.* Analyzes the content of the

ballad of the Hernández brothers by Epifanio Alonso, based on a true incident. Federico and Manuel Hernández were convicted of murdering an old miner in the Arizona desert in 1934. Originally sentenced to die by hanging, the brothers were chosen to be the first to test the state's new gas chamber. The ballad places the Hernández brothers and the state of Arizona in opposition, symbolizing the conflict between the Mexican minority in the United States and Anglo dominance of that minority. Ballad text and secondary sources; 3 notes. Spanish.

A. Hoffman

415. Silvestrini dePacheco, Blanca. LA VIOLENCIA CRIMINAL EN PUERTO RICO, DE 1940 A 1973: ¿CAMBIO EN EL TIEMPO? [Criminal violence in Puerto Rico from 1940 to 1973: a new phenomenon?]. *Rev. Interamericana [Puerto Rico] 1978 8(1): 65-84.* Part II. Continued from a previous article (see abstract 16A:8294). Crime in Puerto Rico has increased in the decades since 1940, but the most significant increase is not the number of criminal acts; it is the fact that a much higher percentage of the victims of criminal activities do not know personally their aggressors. Crime has become impersonal. 6 tables, 6 graphs, 41 notes.

J. Lewis

416. Simon, Dorothy. FEMINISTS AND HISTORY: A NEW VIEW OF RAPE. *Mankind 1976 5(8): 20-22, 46-49.* A discussion of Susan Brownmiller's *Against Our Will: Men, Women and Rape* was engaged in by 12 men and women, including lawyers, police officers, a historian, a rape victim, and women active in the feminist movement. Includes portions of the book as well as excerpts from an interview with Brownmiller. Seven issues were explored, including the author's method of history, the relationship of prostitution and pornography to rape, rape as a political crime, the laws on rape, jail as a deterrent, female self-defense, and women in positions of authority.

N. Lederer

417. Smith, M. Dwayne and Parker, Robert Nash. TYPE OF HOMICIDE AND VARIATION IN REGIONAL RATES. *Social Forces 1980 59(1): 136-147.* A reanalysis of regional differences in homicide rates is conducted for two types of homicide, derived from the victim-offender relationship. A social-structural, as opposed to subcultural, explanation is supported, but is found to have limitations. Social-structural variables, particularly poverty, are shown to be important predictors of differences in primary homicide rates (generally involving family members or friends), but are less important in explaining variations in nonprimary rates (those generally involving strangers).

J

418. Smith, Thomas S. A MARTYR FOR PROHIBITION: THE MURDER OF REVEREND GEORGE C. HADDOCK. *Palimpsest 1981 62(6): 186-193.* With a brief background describing prohibitionist sentiment in Iowa beginning in 1855, focuses on the murder of Methodist minister and vigorous prohibitionist George C. Haddock in Sioux City on 3 August 1886 by an unidentified person; 1855-1915.

419. Somkin, Fred. HOW VANZETTI SAID GOODBYE. *J. of Am. Hist. 1981 68(2): 298-312.* Reviews the controversy surrounding Philip Duffield Strong's sympathetic interview and subsequent articles on Bartolomeo Vanzetti in 1927—whether the prose style was actually Vanzetti's and whether Strong took considerable literary license in transcribing the interview into articles for the *New*

York World. Based on Vanzetti's letters, contemporary newspaper and journal articles, and Strong's original interview of 13 May 1927; 46 notes.

T. P. Linkfield

420. Spatz, Marshall. CHILD ABUSE IN THE NINETEENTH CENTURY. *New York Affairs 1977 4(2): 80-90.* Discusses child abuse in New York City 1820's-80's and the establishment of the Society for the Prevention of Cruelty to Children.

421. Steffens, Pete. FRANKLIN'S EARLY ATTACK ON RACISM: AN ESSAY AGAINST A MASSACRE OF INDIANS. *Journalism Hist. 1978 5(1): 8-12, 31.* Benjamin Franklin's 1764 pamphlet, "A Narrative of the late Massacres in Lancaster County, or a Number of Indians, Friends of this Province, by Persons Unknown," in which he urged coexistence with the Indians, may have helped prevent repetitions of the Paxton Boys' massacre of 20 friendly Christian Indians.

422. Steiner, Stan. ON THE TRAIL OF JOAQUIN MURIETA. *Am. West 1981 18(1): 54-57, 66.* When the forty-niners reached the California gold fields, Sonorans were already exploiting the best claims. These "foreigners" were soon subjected to brutal treatment and run off their claims. In response, some of the Mexicans became outlaws. After Joaquin Murieta was beaten and his wife raped and murdered, Murieta bacame leader of a gang of highwaymen. His style and bravado catapulted him into legend. He was credited with simultaneous robberies and murders over hundreds of miles. His band of outlaws were soon called revolutionaries who were bent on ousting the Yankees. The California Rangers collected a reward for Murieta's head; but the Mexican Indians insisted it was the wrong head and that Murieta lived on. He is remembered as a patriot in California barrios and Sonora to this day. Hard evidence and vital statistics are fragmentary at best. 2 illus., biblio.

D. L. Smith

423. Stern, Norton B. A "MURDER" TO BE FORGOTTEN. *Western States Jewish Hist. Q. 1977 9(2): 176-185.* On 20 May 1875 in the settlement of Rincon, California, in today's Riverside County, Simon Goldsmith fatally shot his business partner George Kallman. The dispute concerned Goldsmith's handling of a large sum of the firm's money. A popular and respected man in his community and in Los Angeles, Goldsmith was tried and found innocent. The general feeling in the community was that the universal practice of carrying concealed weapons was a large cause of the tragedy. Goldsmith continued to operate his store in Rincon until 1883 when he joined his brothers in a general merchandise business in Santa Ana, and later retired to San Francisco in 1902 or 1903. The reaction of the Jewish community was to repress the memory of the killing to the extent that none of the direct or collateral descendants has ever heard of it. Based on newspaper reports, court records, interviews and published sources; 2 photos, 40 notes.

B. S. Porter

424. Stern, Norton B. and Kramer, William M. THE PHOSPHORESCENT JEWISH BRIDE: SAN FRANCISCO'S FAMOUS MURDER CASE. *Western States Jewish Hist. Q. 1980 13(1): 63-72.* Cecilia Benhayon Levy, wife of Dr. J. Milton Bowers, died at the age of 29 in 1885. As she was the third of Dr. Bowers's young wives to sicken and die, and her life insurance was considerable,

an autopsy was performed. Evidence of phosphorous poisoning convicted Bowers of murder. After lengthy appeals, the charges were dropped and Bowers returned to medical practice. The case is significant because the victims and witnesses were Jews; the accused had converted to Judaism. Based on newspaper articles and other primary sources; 33 notes.   B. S. Porter

425.   Sutton, E. S.   THE TRIAL AND DEATH OF WILLIAM H. (HANK) DODGE, 1875-1876.   *Nebraska Hist. 1982 63(3): 412-437.* William H. Dodge, convicted of murdering James McGuire, was shot and fatally wounded by assassins who broke into the Nebraska City jail on the night of 10 July 1876. Reviews the facts pertaining to McGuire's murder in 1874 and to the subsequent events leading to Dodge's trial and death.   Based on newspapers and court records primarily.   R. Lowitt

426.   Swigert, Victoria Lynn and Farrell, Ronald A.   CORPORATE HOMICIDE: DEFINITIONAL PROCESSES IN THE CREATION OF DEVIANCE.   *Law & Soc. Rev. 1980-81 15(1): 161-182.* Focuses on the history of events surrounding the indictment of Ford Motor Company on the charge of reckless homicide. Using information from media accounts, suggests that the expansion of legal parameters to include formerly exempt behavior was preceded by the development of a vocabulary of deviance, personalization of harm, and attributions of nonrepentance to the offender.   J/S

427.   Taylor, Jerome G., Jr.   UPPER CLASS VIOLENCE IN NINE- TEENTH CENTURY TENNESSEE.   *West Tennessee Hist. Soc. Papers 1980 (34): 28-52.* Three members of Tennessee's upper class in the 19th century committed a total of four criminal assaults and three homicides: Sam Houston, Nathan Bedford Forrest, and Joseph A. Mabry. They were men of strong, aggressive personalities, not habitually violent; yet violence seems to have played a larger role in their lives than in the lives of others. The causes of their violence were related generally to their professions. After 1850 Tennessee society as a whole became more critical of this type of behavior, requiring that to be successful, politicians had to be responsive to public opinion. Biographical, newspaper, and other secondary studies; 109 notes.   H. M. Parker, Jr.

428.   Thompson, Tommy R.   THE GREAT OMAHA TRAIN ROBBERY OF 1909.   *Nebraska Hist. 1982 63(2): 216-231.* On the night of 22 May 1909, a small band of outlaws stopped the Union Pacific Overland Limited passenger train just outside the Omaha city limits and relieved the mail car of several sacks of mail. The article discusses the robbery, the apprehension of the bandits, and their trial, and conviction. Examines the controversy over the distribution of the reward offered by the railroad and federal government. Based on official documents, including court and prison records, and newspapers; 62 notes.
                                                              R. Lowitt

429.   Tierney, Kathleen J.   THE BATTERED WOMEN MOVEMENT AND THE CREATION OF THE WIFE BEATING PROBLEM.   *Social Problems 1982 29(3): 207-220.* Wife beating has become the object of media attention and government policy, not because of an increase in its frequency, nor because the public has become more concerned, but because a social movement developed in the 1970's to help battered women.

430. Trafzer, Clifford E. FRONTIER MARSHAL OF THE 1920'S: SAM DAY AND THE MURDER OF FRANK DUGAN. *Pacific Historian 1974 18(2): 13-20.* Describes the Frank Dugan murder case of 1922 in St. Michael's, Arizona, and the attempts of US deputy marshal Samuel Edward Day, Jr. to bring the Navajo Indian suspects to trial. C. W. Olson

431. Turner, George A. THE LATTIMER MASSACRE AND ITS SOURCES. *Slovakia 1977 27(50): 9-43.* Chronicles antecedents of a massacre of two dozen Slovak American coal miners in the Lattimer area of Pennsylvania, 1897; hiring discrimination, low wages, and exclusionary practices toward Slovak Americans led to a strike and the massacre.

432. Voigt, Barton R. THE LIGHTNING CREEK FIGHT. *Ann. of Wyoming 1977 49(1): 5-21.* Recounts an October 1903 fight between Oglala Sioux Indians and a white posse from Weston County, Wyoming. Though the Indians had passes to be in the area, whites concluded that they were illegally hunting and should be driven away. Several participants on both sides were killed and the Indian survivors faced murder charges. Testimony produced conflicting accounts and no convictions, but a definite anti-Indian bias emerged. Based on government reports and archival sources; 2 photos, 46 notes. M. L. Tate

433. Wachs, Eleanor. "WITH MY HEART IN MY THROAT AND MY WHISTLE IN MY HAND": WOMEN'S CRIME-VICTIM NARRATIVES FROM THE URBAN SETTING. *New York Folklore 1980 6(1-2): 11-26.* Describes crime-victim narratives as "verbal reiterations of high-anxiety life and death confrontations which are honed and structured into personal experience accounts which discuss criminogenic circumstances, such as mugging, murder, rape, burglary or robbery"; discusses "how narrative strategies and strategies within narratives are available as options for the reporting of crime-victim events," based on a description of the Third Annual Irene Adler High Tea of Sherlock Holmes Adventuresses in New York City in 1978.

434. Walker, Lenore E. WHO ARE THE BATTERED WOMEN? *Frontiers 1977 2(1): 52-57.* Analyzes violence against women in and out of marriage, finding that it is more common than previously assumed (possibly one of every two women); suggests refuge centers for battered wives once they can psychologically break from the victimization of the battery situation.

435. Ward, Francis B. DE MAU MAU: MYTH AND REALITY. *Black Scholar 1973 5(2): 28-33.* Describes the case surrounding the murders of eight suburban Chicago whites who were allegedly killed by six black Vietnam veterans, all members of the fraternal organization De Mau Mau, which was formed in Vietnam by blacks to combat psychologically and physically the pressure of war. M. T. Wilson

436. Wasserman, Ira M. RELIGIOUS AFFILIATIONS AND HOMICIDE: HISTORICAL RESULTS FROM THE RURAL SOUTH. *J. for the Sci. Study of Religion 1978 17(4): 415-418.* Examines the relationship of religious affiliation to murder, comparing whites and blacks; based on information from a 1916 census department study and the 1920 murder rates in the rural South.

437. White, Richard. OUTLAW GANGS OF THE MIDDLE BORDER: AMERICAN SOCIAL BANDITS. *Western Hist. Q. 1981 12(4): 387-408.* The James-Younger gang of western Missouri and its lineal successors under Jesse James, ca. 1866-82, the Dalton gang of Oklahoma Territory, 1890-92, and the Doolin-Dalton gang of Oklahoma Territory, 1892-96, are the most famous representatives of the western social bandit tradition. "Social bandits are almost by definition creations of their supporters": kinship networks, active supporters, passive sympathizers. Peculiar social conditions allowed them to emerge as "variants of the widespread extralegal organizations already common." Respect for strong men who could protect and avenge themselves was at the heart of their appeal. Confined to small areas with extreme conditions, their actual social impact was minor. They did, nevertheless, become national cultural symbols in legend, folksongs, and movies. 81 notes.   D. L. Smith

438. Wilbanks, William. A TEST OF VERKKO'S STATIC AND DYNAMIC "LAWS" OF SEX AND HOMICIDE. *Int. J. of Women's Studies [Canada] 1981 4(2): 173-180.* Veli Verkko's study, published in Copenhagen in 1951, was the first to test the common assumption that women's crime rates are stable both across and within countries over time; however, a further study of murder rates by sex for 28 countries from 1965-79 failed to support either Verkko's theory or that of F. Adler, published in 1975, that homicide by and against women was increasing as the result of the women's movement.

439. Williams, Lynora. VIOLENCE AGAINST WOMEN. *Black Scholar 1981 12(1): 18-24.* Describes instances of rape, wife beating, and sterilization of black women since 1975, the scapegoating of the black man as a threat to white women, and struggles by Third World feminists to reverse stereotypical roles of whites and blacks.

440. Wilson, Benjamin C. KENTUCKY KIDNAPPERS, FUGITIVES, AND ABOLITIONISTS IN ANTEBELLUM CASS COUNTY MICHIGAN. *Michigan Hist. 1976 60(4): 339-358.* In the years after 1840, the black population of Cass County, located in southwestern Michigan, increased dramatically. Attracted by white defiance of discriminatory laws, by numerous Quakers, and by low-priced land, free and runaway blacks found the county an ideal haven. The situation quickly attracted the attention of southern slaveholders. In 1847 and 1849, planters from Bourbon and Boone Counties in northern Kentucky led ultimately unsuccessful raids into Cass County. On the national level, the raids helped bring about passage of the Fugitive Slave Act of 1850. Primary and secondary sources; 2 illus., 3 photos, map, 72 notes.   D. W. Johnson

441. Wilson, Walter. THE MERIDIAN MASSACRE OF 1871. *Crisis 1974 81(2): 49-52.* Discusses murders, rapes, and other crimes of the Ku Klux Klan in Mississippi during Reconstruction, emphasizing 1871 as Meridian's "worst year of terror."   S

442. Wise, Leah. THE ELAINE MASSACRE. *Southern Exposure 1974 1(3/4): 9-10.* In 1919 black sharecroppers and tenant farmers in Arkansas organized themselves to protest for equitable wages. Racial tensions were already heightened by race riots in Washington, D. C., Chicago, and East St. Louis during the summer. When the black community armed itself, whites assumed they would

be attacked. The violence was started when a drunken white terrorized the black community, resulting in state and federal troops being called in to quell the violence. Based on published accounts and oral interviews.   G. A. Bolton

443. Workman, Mark E. SON OF SAM: AS INTERPRETED BY CRIME REPORTERS AND AS A POSSIBLE SOURCE OF FOLKLORE. *Indiana Folklore 1978 11(2): 151-159.* Discusses the multiple murders committed by David Berkowitz in New York City in 1977.

444. Wright, Barton. QUEJO: THE LAST RENEGADE INDIAN. Dodd, Horace L. and Long, Robert W., ed. *People of the Far West* (Brand Book no. 6; San Diego: Corral of the Westerners, 1979): 37-43. Perhaps unjustly, Quejo, a half-Indian, was accused of murdering several whites in Nevada during 1909-19. He was never caught and for years was accused of stealing horses. The discovery of his partly mummified body in his cave rekindled interest in him in the 1970's.

445. Wyatt-Brown, Bertram. JEFFERSON'S NEPHEWS AND OTHER MURDERERS: THOUGHTS ON SOUTHERN VIOLENCE. *Rev. in Am. Hist. 1977 5(2): 203-210.* Review article prompted by Boynton Merrill, Jr.'s *Jefferson's Nephews: A Frontier Tragedy* (Princeton: Princeton U. Pr., 1976).

446. Young, Mary. REFLECTIONS ON VIOLENCE. *Rev. in Am. Hist. 1975 3(1): 8-12.* Review article prompted by W. Eugene Hollon's *Frontier Violence: Another Look* (New York: Oxford U. Pr., 1974) and Richard Slotkin's *Regeneration through Violence: The Mythology of the American Frontier, 1600-1860* (Middletown, Conn.: Wesleyan U. Pr., 1973).

447. Zanger, Martin. CONFLICTING CONCEPTS OF JUSTICE: A WINNEBAGO MURDER TRIAL ON THE ILLINOIS FRONTIER. *J. of the Illinois State Hist. Soc. 1980 73(4): 263-276.* The Winnebago Indians near Fort Armstrong, Illinois, had a system of justice based on kinship. When in 1820 three men of that tribe killed two American soldiers in retribution for the death of family members, they were brought to trial. The Indians submitted to the Anglo-American legal system, but the Americans also gave gifts to the families of the Indians who were tried and executed, thus bowing to Indian custom. This article shows how the two legal systems conflicted. Primary sources; 52 notes.
                                                                              J. Powell

448. Zarbin, Earl. THE WHOLE WAS DONE SO QUIETLY: THE PHOENIX LYNCHINGS OF 1879. *J. of Arizona Hist. 1980 21(4): 353-362.* Relates the circumstances surrounding the August, 1879, lynching of two alleged murderers by a group of Phoenix, Arizona's leading citizens. Contemporary newspapers; 38 notes.   G. O. Gagnon

449. Zellner, Richard. STAND WATIE AND THE KILLING OF JAMES FOREMAN. *Chronicles of Oklahoma 1981 59(2): 167-178.* The Cherokee Indians had been badly factionalized since the Removal Era of the 1830's. The factions of "Cherokee West," which had agreed to early removal from Georgia, and "Cherokee East," which had fought removal to the end, continued their rivalries in Indian Territory. Stand Watie represented the former group and his May 1842 murder of James Foreman from the latter faction created the possibility of bloody reprisals. An Arkansas court found Watie innocent by reason of

self-defense. Fortunately, Cherokee Agent Pierce M. Butler cooled tempers and prevented further bloodshed. Based on the John Ross Papers and *Letters Received by the Office of Indian Affairs;* 47 notes.   M. L. Tate

450. Zenor, B. J.   IOWA GOTHIC: THE VILLISCA AX MURDERS. *Palimpsest 1977 58(5): 130-143.* Chronologues the unsolved murders of eight residents of Villisca, Iowa, in June 1912. Discusses the search for the killer, the efforts of detective J. N. Wilkerson to indict prominent Villisca businessman F. F. Jones, and the ultimate acquittal of the chief suspect, Reverend George J. Kelly, in November 1917. Illus., 11 photos, note on sources.   D. W. Johnson

451. —.   CHILD ABUSE AND NEGLECT IN THE AMERICAN SOCIETY. *Center Mag. 1978 11(2): 70-77.* Discussion among 14 specialists on family violence and child abuse; discusses current workshops, shelters, and counseling services available to affected persons.

452. —.   COMMENTS ON INVERARITY (ASR APRIL, 1976).   *Am. Sociol. Rev. 1977 42(2): 355-368.*
Bagozzi, Richard P.   POPULISM AND LYNCHING IN LOUISIANA, *pp. 355-358.* Critiques James M. Inverarity, "Populism and Lynching in Louisiana" (see abstract 14A:8510), which tested Kai T. Erickson's theory on community solidarity and repressive justice. There are a number of methodological and conceptual problems, yet it is "a highly original operationalization and test of mechanical solidarity." A portion of the reanalysis indicates that "the data support the theory to a greater extent than reported in certain instances." Ref., 2 fig.
Wasserman, Ira M.   SOUTHERN VIOLENCE AND THE POLITICAL PROCESS, *pp. 359-362.* The Inverarity article illustrates how social investigators might employ limited historical data to test social theories. It is questionable, however, to assume that "Populism was related to increases in the lynching incident rate in Louisiana in the 1890s," nor is it appropriate to use the "boundary crisis" model. "In its place, a model which defines lynching as a form of collective violence and related change in this variable to political changes has been proposed." Ref., 2 tables.
Pope, Whitney and Ragin, Charles.   MECHANICAL SOLIDARITY, REPRESSIVE JUSTICE, AND LYNCHINGS IN LOUISIANA, *pp. 363-368.* Inverarity erroneously treats white society in Louisiana as an instance of mechanical solidarity and lynchings as an example of repressive justice. He "does not show how the relationship between Populism and lynching in Louisiana can be explained in terms of boundary crisis, mechanical solidarity, and repressive justice." Ref., fig.   R. V. Ritter

453. —.   RESOURCE LIST: BATTERED WOMEN.   *Frontiers 1977 2(1): 58-63.* A bibliography created collectively to provide sources for the study of battered women in the United States.

454. —.   WHY DID THEY DIE? A DOCUMENT OF BLACK FEMINISM.   *Radical Am. 1979 13(6): 40-49.* Reprint of a pamphlet prepared by the Combahee River Collective, a group of black feminists in Boston, which successfully taught women about self-defense, responding to the murders of 13 women, including one white, in early 1979; gives racial, sexual, and political reasons for the murders.

3

CRIMES AGAINST PROPERTY

455. Arndt, Karl J. R. DID FREDERICK RAPP CHEAT ROBERT OWEN? *Western Pennsylvania Hist. Mag. 1978 61(4): 358-365.* Questions the accusation that Harmonist Frederick Rapp cheated Robert Owen in the sale of New Harmony to Owen in 1825.

456. Barrett, Glen. BANKS, BANKERS AND BANK ROBBERS. *Idaho Yesterdays 1975 19(3): 8-13.* Most early Western bankers began as freighters and merchants and gradually evolved into their communities' bankers as the need arose. They were town leaders, involved in many projects, interested in civic development, and usually had little formal education. Gives details of several bank robberies. 2 illus., 9 notes. B. J. Paul

457. Bell, Robert G. THE U.S. RESPONSE TO TERRORISM AGAINST INTERNATIONAL CIVIL AVIATION. *Orbis 1976 19(4): 1326-1343.* In recent years, aviation has been "a natural target for terrorist attack." Between 1960 and 1975, for example, "there were 439 hijacking attempts on American and foreign aircraft." Because it has "the most comprehensive aviation network in the world . . . the United States assumed leadership of the international response to aerial terrorism." The US effort "was in no way perfect," but all in all its effort worked. Still, "unless the broad and fundamental causes of terrorism themselves are addressed, governments will remain one step behind the terrorists." 45 notes. A. N. Garland

458. Berthrong, Donald J. LEGACIES OF THE DAWES ACT: BUREAU-CRATS AND LAND THIEVES AT THE CHEYENNE-ARAPAHO AGEN-CIES OF OKLAHOMA. *Arizona and the West 1979 21(4): 335-354.* Many Indians who received allotments under the Dawes Act (US, 1887) leased their land to farmers and ranchers for substantial sums. Work-ethic-imbued reformers reasoned that if the Indians owned less land they would be forced to earn a living as farmers. Selling the allotted land would buy farm machinery, build houses, and help the Indians to begin farming. Congressional legislation, 1902-10, permitted sale of all allotted lands. Poor administration of these statutes created opportuni-ties for fraud. The alienation of Cheyenne-Arapaho lands on their Oklahoma reservation in the 1910's is a vivid illustration of the national disgrace that reduced half of the Indians under the Dawes Act to a landless, rival, and econom-ically devastated condition. 4 illus., map, 35 notes. D. L. Smith

459. Brandenburg, Kurt. THE GREAT MILITARY ANTIQUE SWINDLE. *Civil War Times Illus. 1976 14(10): 22-28.* Fraudulent military antiques are sold to unsuspecting customers by less-than-scrupulous dealers, 1970-76; shows antiques and frauds.

460. Coase, R. H. PAYOLA IN RADIO AND TELEVISION BROADCASTING. *J. of Law and Econ. 1979 22(2): 269-328.* Discusses undisclosed payments (payola) in the music industry and how that system made its way into broadcasting, focusing on the reasons for payola and the possible effects of federal regulation.

461. Cohen, Lawrence E.; Cantor, David; and Kluegel, James R. ROBBERY VICTIMIZATION IN THE UNITED STATES: AN ANALYSIS OF A NON-RANDOM EVENT. *Social Sci. Q. 1981 62(4): 644-657.* Examines the combined effects of sociodemographic and lifestyle characteristics on the risk of being robbed using the independent and joint effects of age, race, income, number of individuals in the household, and employment status as analysis criteria.

462. Davis, Perry. CORRUPTION IN JEWISH LIFE. *Present Tense 1978 5(2): 19-24.* Investigates the growth of "white-collar" crime within the Jewish community, and opposition to such crimes, 1969-78.

463. Ellis, Bruce T. FRAUD WITHOUT SCANDAL: THE ROQUE LOVATO GRANT AND GASPAR ORTIZ Y ALARID. *New Mexico Hist. Rev. 1982 57(1): 43-62.* The Roque Lovato Grant claim of 1871 is an example of a fraudulent land grant claim in New Mexico. Chronicles an attempt to acquire land in the public domain, a socially acceptable practice at the time, and provides a biography of the perpetrator. Based on the US Bureau of Land Management, Surveyor General's Reports, records of the Archives of the Archdiocese of Santa Fe, and other primary sources; illus., 40 notes. A. C. Dempsey

464. Feiner, Joel S. and Klein, Stephan Marc. GRAFFITI TALKS. *Social Policy 1982 12(3): 47-53.* Presents a psychosocial approach to why adolescents write graffiti in public places, particularly in New York City's subways, focusing on graffiti's style, visual aspects and content, and its function as a rite of passage and support system; 1969-82.

465. Ferguson, Henry N. DOUBLE DEAL AT DIAMOND MESA. *Am. Hist. Illus. 1982 17(5): 35-39.* Describes the Great Diamond Fraud of 1872 during which prospectors Philip Arnold and John Slack convinced William Chapman Ralston, head of the Bank of California, and his friends of the existence of a diamond, ruby, sapphire, and emerald mine in Utah; the site had been salted by the miners to swindle Ralston and his investors.

466. Fitzgerald, Randy. GAMBLING ON TRUTH. *Reason 1981 13(6): 42-47.* Joan Bowden's attempts in late 1980 and early 1981 to reform corrupt and unethical practices in Atlantic County, New Jersey's, Comprehensive Employment and Training Act program (CETA) for potential casino employees led to her firing on blatantly spurious charges.

467. Friedman, Lawrence M. LENDERS AND BORROWERS. *Rev. in Am. Hist. 1975 3(1): 42-46.* Review article prompted by Peter J. Coleman's *Debtors and Creditors in America: Insolvency, Imprisonment for Debt, and Bankruptcy, 1607-1900* (Madison: State Hist. Soc. of Wisconsin, 1974).

468. Gastwirt, Zvi. KASHRUT AND THE LAW IN NEW YORK CITY. *Michael: On the Hist. of the Jews in the Diaspora [Israel] 1975 3: 281-301.* Reproduces and analyses a document found among the personal papers of Lewis J. Gribetz, legal counsel to the Kashruth Association of Greater New York in its struggle to control *kashrut* supervision in New York City's kosher poultry industry during the 1930's. Scandals revealed in the *shohatim* (slaughterers) union prompted New York Jews to encourage Mayor James J. Walker to investigate the kosher poultry industry. The document represents the report issued in 1931 by Walker's committee. Despite the report's recommendations, the Department of Markets retained responsibility for the enforcement of New York State's 1915 "Kosher Bill" and licensing was never implemented. Primary and secondary sources; 31 notes. T. Sassoon

469. Gerlach, Don R. BLACK ARSON IN ALBANY, NEW YORK: NOVEMBER 1793. *J. of Black Studies 1977 7(3): 301-312.* A 1793 arson incident in Albany, New York, suggests that the slave rebelliousness of this period was spontaneous and involved only a few slaves. The three slaves involved, however, did not act out of a grudge against their master and perhaps were hired by white men to set the fire. A period of uneasiness followed the fire. Restrictions on slaves were tightened, but the reaction was mild, although the perpetrators were speedily arrested, tried, convicted, and hanged. Whether or not this incident influenced the state legislature's position on slavery can only be conjectured. Primary and secondary sources; 9 notes, biblio. D. C. Neal

470. Glazer, Nathan. ON SUBWAY GRAFFITI IN NEW YORK. *Public Interest 1979 54: 3-11.* On the outside of New York City subway cars, graffiti makers spray paint large representations of their names, while inside they obscure maps, signs, and windows. To the subway rider the graffiti is part of the story of "crime in the subways," and it contributes to the feeling that New York City is menacing and uncontrollable. At any given time there are about 500 graffiti makers, ranging in age from around 11 to 16. Various means of stopping them, from arrest to attempts to get them to paint on canvas, have failed. A new approach that might succeed involves education and therapy programs for the offenders run by youth workers and social agencies. S. Harrow

471. Hagan, John; Nagel, Ilene H.; and Albonetti, Celesta. THE DIFFERENTIAL SENTENCING OF WHITE-COLLAR OFFENDERS IN TEN FEDERAL DISTRICT COURTS. *Am. Sociol. Rev. 1980 45(5): 802-820.* Discusses the relationship between the status characteristics of criminal offenders and the sentences they receive, examining data from 10 federal district courts whose statutes and resources provide potential for the prosecution of the white-collar crimes of higher status offenders. There may be an inverse relationship between the volume of white-collar prosecutions and the severity with which they are sentenced. J/S

472.   Hay, George A. and Kelley, Daniel.   AN EMPIRICAL SURVEY OF THE PRICE FIXING CONSPIRACIES.   *J. of Law and Econ. 1974 17(1): 13-38.* Survey of the Department of Justice Antitrust Division cases of price fixing, 1963-73, finds that competition conspiracies correlate with situations where companies are few, concentration high, and the product homogeneous.

473.   Helms, Andrea R. C. and Mangusso, Mary Childers.   THE NOME GOLD CONSPIRACY.   *Pacific Northwest Q. 1982 73(1): 10-19.* The 1898 discovery of gold near Nome, Alaska, created tension when late arrivals found that the choice sites already had been taken. Frustration led to nativist agitation against the "foreign" claim holders. Amid this hostility, Alexander McKenzie conspired to invalidate all alien claims and to establish his ownership over some of the property. McKenzie used political influence in Washington, DC to have his friends named to key territorial offices. The scheme failed and McKenzie was convicted of contempt of court.   6 photos, 51 notes.   M. L. Tate

474.   Hilliard, Celia.   THE THOMAS WISE FORGERIES: THE CASE OF THE WRENN LIBRARY.   *Chicago Hist. 1980-81 9(4): 212-218.* Describes the fraudulent activities of Thomas Wise, who published bogus first editions of books, many of which were purchased, beginning in the 1890's, by Chicagoan John Wrenn for his library.

475.   Jacobs, David.   INEQUALITY AND ECONOMIC CRIME.   *Sociol. and Social Res. 1981 66(1): 12-28.* Tests the assumption that crime for economic gain results from contrasts in economic resources. With other causes of theft controlled, the measure of economic inequality received the strongest coefficient when burglary and grand larceny rates were analyzed. Its relationship to robbery was not as strong although it also was in the predicted direction.   J/S

476.   Johnson, Victor L.   FAIR TRADERS AND SMUGGLERS IN PHILA-DELPHIA, 1754-1763.   *Pennsylvania Mag. of Hist. and Biog. 1959 83(2): 125-149.* Discusses the impact of the French and Indian War on marine trading patterns, especially smuggling, in the Atlantic colonies and in the West Indies; and suggests that British trade policies to America during the war contributed to colonial hostility toward Great Britain; 1754-63.

477.   Kruse, Horst H.   MYTH IN THE MAKING: THE JAMES BROTH-ERS, THE BANK ROBBERY AT NORTHFIELD, MINN., AND THE DIME NOVEL.   *J. of Popular Culture 1976 10(2): 315-325.* Case study of the role of the dime novel in the myth-making process. Asserts that analysis of *The James Boys in Minnesota* (1882), by D. W. Stevens (John Roy Musick), and the kinds of parallels to popular classics (e.g., by Sir Walter Scott) employed, may indicate a reassessment of the conventional interpretation is needed. Primary and secondary sources; 26 notes.   D. G. Nielson

478.   Libecap, Gary D. and Johnson, Ronald N.   PROPERTY RIGHTS, NINETEENTH-CENTURY FEDERAL TIMBER POLICY, AND THE CONSERVATION MOVEMENT.   *J. of Econ. Hist. 1979 39(1): 129-142.* In campaigning for the establishment of the National Forests in the late 19th century, conservationists pointed to fraud and timber theft in the Pacific Northwest. In this paper we argue that the conservationists were misdirected; that it was a costly Federal land policy that encouraged fraud and theft. In the face of restric-

tive land laws, fraud was necessary if lumber companies were to acquire large tracts of land to take advantage of economies of scale in logging. Since fraud used real resources, it raised the actual cost of acquiring land and thus delayed the establishment of property rights. Such delays led to theft. The paper examines the public land laws, explains their selection by claimants, and calculates the added transaction costs or rent dissipation that resulted from circumventing the law.

J

479. Moore, James Tice. GUNFIRE ON THE CHESAPEAKE: GOVERNOR CAMERON AND THE OYSTER PIRATES, 1882-1885. *Virginia Mag. of Hist. and Biog. 1982 90(3): 367-377.* Virginia Governor William Evelyn Cameron, candidate for the reformist Readjuster Party, was elected in 1881. A major problem facing his administration was the oyster piracy off Virginia's Eastern Shore. Authorities feared exhaustion of the oyster supply was imminent, but licensing and seasonal regulations were ignored by fishermen. Governor Cameron led two raids against the oyster pirates, during 1882-83. The first was successful; the governor's popularity increased substantially. But the 1883 expedition failed miserably, encouraging the press and the opposition Funder Party to ridicule the venture. The oyster wars were ultimately successful, providing the catalyst for effective fishery regulation. Based on federal and Virginia records, newspaper accounts, the William Mahone Papers, Duke University, the Susie Cameron Whitfield Papers, Florida State University, and secondary sources; 36 notes.

D. J. Cimbala

480. Moorhead, Max L. THE PRESIDIO SUPPLY PROBLEM OF NEW MEXICO IN THE EIGHTEENTH CENTURY. *New Mexico Hist. Rev. 1961 36(3): 210-229.* Discusses various attempts to compensate the troops serving at the Presidial Company of Sante Fe with enough income to cover their expenses in the remote outpost, and to prosecute the officers who cheated the troops by overcharging and double charging them for supplies; 18th century.

481. Morris, James O. THE ACQUISITIVE SPIRIT OF JOHN MITCHELL, UMW PRESIDENT (1899-1908). *Labor Hist. 1979 20(1): 5-43.* Documents the "acquisitive spirit" of John Mitchell who used his position for personal profit, squeezed the miners, and joined coal operators in business and financial deals which constituted conflicts of interest. Five specific ventures where Mitchell profited directly from miners are detailed, and his financial benefits from the National Civic Federation are delineated. Mitchell was bothered by these activities; a conscience-ridden man, he may have turned to alcohol as a result of his dilemma of wanting to move farther and faster financially than his position would allow. Based upon the Mitchell papers; table, 76 notes.

L. L. Athey

482. Nelson, Daniel. FIFTH COLUMN AT CANANEA: A STOCKHOLDER CIRCUMVENTS COLONEL W. C. GREENE. *J. of Arizona Hist. 1979 20(1): 47-64.* Describes economist-financier Frederick Winslow Taylor's efforts to penetrate the financial operations of Colonel William Cornell Greene's Greene Consolidated Copper, located in Cananea, Sonora, Mexico. Greene, in New York City, met with Taylor, a highly established financial consultant. From his investigation of the market, Taylor began buying large blocks of Greene Consolidated Copper stock, eventually placing Atherton B. Wadleigh, a mechanical engineer, in a financial position in the Cananea operations in Mexico. Wad-

leigh gave private reports to Taylor who used the information, which often differed from that released by Greene. The efforts of Taylor and Greene to operate the works independently of the rival Amalgamated Copper Company were relatively short-lived, because, in 1907, Thomas F. Cole from Amalgamated negotiated a merger which saw the demise of Greene's holdings. Greene fell from notoriety, but Taylor later became known as the promoter of scientific management. 4 photos, 35 notes.   K. E. Gilmont

483. Nikiforov, A. S. BELOVOROTNICHKOVAIA PRESTUPNOST' V S.SH.A. [White-collar crime in the USA]. *Sovetskoe Gosudarstvo i Pravo [USSR] 1979 (3): 118-124.* Examines the growth of crime among American white-collar workers in the 1970's, resulting from increasing economic monopolies, with quotations from H. Mannheim and E. Sutherland.

484. Patterson, Richard. TRAIN ROBBERY: THE BIRTH, FLOWERING, AND DECLINE OF A NOTORIOUS WESTERN ENTERPRISE. *Am. West 1977 14(2): 48-53.* The first train robbery, in southern Indiana in 1866, was "ridiculously easy." The Reno brothers pulled off several more in the vicinity in the following months. The idea did not catch on in the West until the 1870's. In that decade the James gang, the Youngers, and Sam Bass systematically robbed easy target express cars. Express companies and railroads belatedly took defensive measures, and the robbers refined their methods. In the 1880's such names as Fred Whitrock (alias Jim Cummings), Chris Evans, John Sontag, and the Rube Burrows gang made newspaper headlines. By the 1890's the frequency of train robberies inspired a show-stopping, climax scene in Buffalo Bill's Wild West Show and the plot for America's first motion picture. The last train robbery occurred in California in 1932. 5 illus.   D. L. Smith

485. Richter, William L. THE BRENHAM FIRE OF 1866: A TEXAS RECONSTRUCTION ATROCITY. *Louisiana Studies 1975 14(3): 287-314.* In September of 1866 a group of US soldiers who were stationed nearby burned a section of the Brenham, Texas, business district to the ground, and the incident quickly became a *cause celebre*. Subsequently, numerous myths emerged regarding the fire. Reexamines the background, issues, local conditions, individuals, and specific events of the Brenham fire. Eventually three investigations of the incident were undertaken, each with its own, and often conflicting, accounts: 1) a report by Lt. Colonel E. C. Mason, the acting commander of the 17th Infantry Regiment, 2) another by a Texas legislative committee, and 3) one by a Washington-organized military board of inquiry. Summarizes the conclusions of these reports, portrays the strong northern versus southern viewpoints, and points out that the fire led to two specific results—a reshuffling of the Texas military command, and a belief by General Philip Sheridan that Texas needed drastic renovation through Reconstruction. Based on primary and secondary sources; 108 notes.
         B. A. Glasrud

486. Robertson, Deane and Robertson, Peggy. THE PLOT TO STEAL LINCOLN'S BODY. *Am. Heritage 1982 33(3): 76-83.* In an effort to win the release from prison of his best counterfeit-bill engraver, James Kinealy plotted in 1876 to steal the body of Abraham Lincoln and exchange it for the freedom of Ben Boyd and some cash. A Secret Service agent foiled the plot. Two of the would-be thieves were arrested and imprisoned by Illinois officials. 6 illus.
         J. F. Paul

487.   Robinson, Robert L.   THE U.S. NAVY VS. CATTLE RUSTLERS: THE U.S.S. RIO BRAVO ON THE RIO GRANDE, 1875-1879.   *Military Hist. of Texas and the Southwest 1979 15(2): 43-52.* Conflict between Americans and Mexicans along the Texas-Mexico border began in the 1840's and reached a peak in 1875, over cattle rustling; the US Navy patrolled the Rio Grande in the USS *Rio Bravo* to prevent cattle rustling.

488.   Rubenstein, Bruce A.   JUSTICE DENIED: INDIAN LAND FRAUDS IN MICHIGAN, 1855-1900.   *Old Northwest 1976 2(2): 131-140.* Since by a 1872 federal law Michigan Indians were awarded land in severalty with immediate powers to alienate, they were subject to fraudulent loss of the same land. Unscrupulous speculators, lumbermen, land office officials, and even church officers united to cheat the Indians. Their tools were fraudulent loans, illegal *ex parti* hearings, false abandonment advertising, perjury, misrepresentation, alcohol, violence, and political pressure on protecting Indian agents. When a Michigan Indian agent supported by the Grover Cleveland administration attempted to prosecute fraud, the lumber lobby persuaded Congress to close the agency. Based on statutes, correspondence and petitions in the National Archives, and Indian Commissioner reports; 15 notes.   J

489.   Schleimer, Joseph D.   THE DAY THEY BLEW UP SAN ONOFRE. *Bull. of the Atomic Scientists 1974 30(8): 24-27.* A scenario for sabotaging atomic power plants, including possible sources of nuclear materials, entrance to plant facilities, and results of destruction of the plant for surrounding urban areas; examines the threat of nuclear power in the hands of terrorist groups.

490.   Shaw, Robert B.   GREAT SCHUYLER STOCK FRAUD.   *Railroad Hist. 1979 (141): 5-18.* Discusses the first large-scale stock swindle, perpetrated in 1854 by Robert Schuyler, president of the New York & New Haven Railroad; covers 1844-1902.

491.   Shergold, Peter R.   THE LOAN SHARK: THE SMALL LOAN BUSINESS IN EARLY TWENTIETH-CENTURY PITTSBURGH.   *Pennsylvania Hist. 1978 45(3): 195-223.* Between 24 and 53 money lenders provided credit at very high interest to Pittsburgh laborers during 1900-13. The charges reformers leveled at these "sharks" were only partly valid, and reform legislation drove many legitimate lenders from the field and made possible the entry of criminal elements into the small loan business. 3 tables, 96 notes.   D. C. Swift

492.   Shindle, Richard D.   LANCASTER'S INFAMOUS COUNTERFEITERS.   *J. of the Lancaster County Hist. Soc. 1979 83(4): 198-211.* Discusses the counterfeiting of revenue stamps from 1896 to 1899 by Lancaster, Pennsylvania, cigar manufacturer William M. Jacobs and his employee, William L. Kendig, and their attempt to have $10 million in counterfeit currency circulated.

493.   Simms, Adam.   WATCHING AND WAITING ON LONG ISLAND. *Present Tense 1981 8(4): 19-22.* Describes anti-Semitic vandalism in 1980 by white male juveniles and the Jewish Defense League response of sending armed patrols to protect the area and the programs formed in local schools to address prejudice and vandalism.

494. Steffensmeier, Darrell J.   CRIME AND THE CONTEMPORARY WOMAN: AN ANALYSIS OF CHANGING LEVELS OF FEMALE PROPERTY CRIME, 1960-75.   *Social Forces 1978 57(2): 566-584.* This report examines female property crime trends since 1960. Previous research on this issue has suffered because of a failure to specify the major questions on female property crime and because of inappropriate use of UCR arrest statistics. In this study, the central questions about female property crime are clarified and arrest rates are computed to determine the extent of change in female property crime since 1960. The effects of the women's movement on female property crime are also examined. I conclude that female levels of property crime are rising. But it is only for the offenses of larceny—theft and fraud/embezzlement—that female levels are increasing at a faster pace than male levels. Moreover, absolute differences still exist and have generally increased so that female property crime levels continue to lag far behind those of males. The pattern of the data also suggests that the upward trend in female property crime is not due to the women's movement; that women are still typically nonviolent, petty property offenders; and that the "new female criminal" is more of a social invention than an empirical reality.   J

495. Story, Ronald D.   "THAT DAMNED PACK OF SHARPERS": SAVINGS BANKS AND AMERICAN SOCIETY IN THE NINETEENTH CENTURY.   *Rev. in Am. Hist. 1977 5(3): 335-341.* Review article prompted by Alan L. Olmstead's *New York City Mutual Savings Bank, 1819-1861* (Chapel Hill: U. of North Carolina Pr., 1976) and Carl R. Osthaus's *Freedmen, Philanthropy, and Fraud: A History of the Freedman's Savings Bank* (Urbana: U. of Illinois Pr., 1976).

496. Stotland, Ezra.   WHITE COLLAR CRIMINALS.   *J. of Social Issues 1977 33(4): 179-196.* White collar crime, which is a generic term for all forms of criminal misuse of trust, creates great problems of economic, political, and moral damage to all segments of American society, and helps to sustain common or street crime. It takes an ever increasing variety of forms, ranging from consumer fraud to complex business thefts. White collar criminals appear to be motivated by money, avoidance of threats to goal attainment, sense of superiority, mastery, the admiration of others, conformity pressures, etc. Psychological restraints on their criminal behavior are weakened by their jungle view of society, the perception of the moral ambiguity of white collar crime, the lightness of punishment, the view of victims as being morally culpable, the size of some organizational victims, and a belief in their own beneficence. An appeal is made to psychologists to participate in the growing national effort to fight white collar crime.   J

497. Strum, Harvey.   SMUGGLING IN THE WAR OF 1812.   *Hist. Today [Great Britain] 1979 29(8): 532-537.* Despite an embargo on trade with the British, merchants in Vermont and New York carried on a lively smuggling trade with Canada, 1807-14.

498. Taylor, John M.   AN ACCOMPLISHED VILLAIN.   *Am. Hist. Illus. 1979 13(9): 4-9, 47-49.* Though never convicted in three inquiries into his behavior, James Wilkinson was a known scoundrel who played upon his political associations and polished disreputability to better himself financially, 1787-1813, in pseudodiplomatic and economic relations between Great Britain, France, Spain, and the United States.

499. Upton, Richard. ART THEFT: NATIONAL STOLEN PROPERTY ACT APPLIED TO NATIONALIZED MEXICAN PRE-COLUMBIAN ARTIFACTS: UNITED STATES VS. MCCLAIN. *New York U. J. of Int. Law and Pol. 1978 10(3): 569-611.* Chronicles the events of *United States* v. *McClain* (US, 1973) dealing with the possession and sale of art pieces (in this case, pre-Columbian artifacts from Mexico) and the applicability of the National Stolen Property Act (US, 1976); further, discusses Mexican law pertaining to nationalized art pieces.

500. Walker, Henry P. ARIZONA LAND FRAUD: MODEL 1880, THE TOMBSTONE TOWNSITE COMPANY. *Arizona and the West 1979 21(1): 5-36.* The Tombstone Townsite Company was formed in 1879 to promote a settlement near promising silver-mining claims in the southeastern corner of Arizona Territory. Tents, frame shacks, and adobe structures soon appeared. Although the company had only filed a claim without taking further steps to secure the patent it was soon engaged in a lively real estate business. Uncertainty concerning the legality of titles to town lots bred tension and violence by citizens prepared to defend their investments against claim jumpers. Further trouble was assured when it was discovered that there was some overlay of townsites and mineral claims. Legal entanglements, rumor, political intrigue, territorial and national government involvement, and fraud combined to create a situation that still clouds the title of unsold lots in the Tombstone townsite. 3 illus., 2 maps, 86 notes. D. L. Smith

501. Walters, Jonathan. ARSON: A HERITAGE IN FLAMES. *Hist. Preservation 1981 33(2): 10-17.* Discusses the severe problem of arson in the United States from 1975 to 1981 with respect to historic buildings, the motives of arsonists in such instances, and preventive suggestions.

502. Warner, Fred B. THE *HANGING JUDGE* ONCE MORE BEFORE THE BAR. *Papers of the Biblio. Soc. of Am. 1976 70(1): 89-96.* Presents evidence indicating that Edmund Gosse and T. J. Wise collaborated on an unauthorized edition of Robert Louis Stevenson's play *The Hanging Judge* in 1914 in order to falsely sell it as the only printed edition of the play.

503. Watkins, T. H. THE PURLOINED PAST. *Am. Heritage 1978 29(5): 48-49.* Theft of historical documents and photographs from archives is widespread, sometimes unreported and even unnoticed, extremely difficult to prevent, and harmful to the field of history. Illus. D. J. Engler

504. Wert, Jeffry D. THE GREAT CIVIL WAR GOLD HOAX. *Am. Hist. Illus. 1980 15(1): 20-24.* Discusses the sensational scheme fabricated by Joseph Howard, city editor of the Brooklyn *Eagle*, in 1864 to raise the price of gold on the New York Stock Exchange; after speculating on the gold market, he published a statement that he falsely attributed to President Abraham Lincoln on the sad state of the Union.

505. Wohlenberg, Ernest H. THE "GEOGRAPHY OF CIVILITY" REVISITED: NEW YORK BLACKOUT LOOTING, 1977. *Econ. Geog. 1982 58(1): 29-44.* Examines the geographical distribution of looting during the 1977 electrical power blackout in New York City as the basis to assess the correlation between looting sites and poor residential areas and discusses data problems connected with the incident.

506.   —.   RAT SHEETS.   *Am. Heritage 1979 30(3): 34-37.* Summary and illustrations of "rat sheets" posted by circus promoters attacking the integrity of their competitors, ca. 1870-1910. 7 illus.   J. F. Paul

4

RIOTS, DISTURBANCES,
AND CIVIL DISOBEDIENCE

507. Alberts, William E. THE WHITE MAGIC OF SYSTEMIC RACISM. *Crisis 1978 85(9): 295-308.* The cause of racial violence in Boston, 1976, is covert, subtle, pervasive, sophisticated, and traditional systemic racism. Problems are redefined to mask the real issues. White magic transforms segregated neighborhoods, discriminatory election laws, unemployment, poverty, and low self-esteem into arguments about busing. Rhetoric about equality replaces analysis of racism. Institutionalized religion provides a ritualistic cathartic cop-out replacing folded hands for action. White magic is based on white persons, politically powerful and rich, who use their office and institution and the influence of their affluence to perpetuate their power, profit, and privilege at the expense of the common good. Mayor Kevin H. White and his "Committee for Boston" are excellent examples of the practitioners of white magic.   A. G. Belles

508. Alderson, Stanley. WHEN IS CIVIL DISOBEDIENCE JUSTIFIED? *Pol. Q. [Great Britain] 1974 45(2): 206-215.* Considers occasions when civil disobedience in a democracy is justified, showing that it need not be anti-democratic and when it "is anti-democratic it may still be good." Discusses civil disobedience against 1) nuclear arms, 2) a government abusing its mandate, 3) a government ignoring an arbiter's decision, 4) democratic imperfections, and 5) civil wrongs. 5 notes.   L. Brown

509. Allen, Frederick Lewis. SPAIMA ROŞIE [The Red Scare]. *Magazin Istoric [Romania] 1979 13(6): 56-59.* Extracts translated from *Only Yesterday* (New York, 1931) describing violent repression of workers' movements in the United States from 1919 to 1922.

510. Allen, James B. "GOOD GUYS" VS. "GOOD GUYS": RUDGER CLAWSON, JOHN SHARP, AND CIVIL DISOBEDIENCE IN NINETEENTH-CENTURY UTAH. *Utah Hist. Q. 1980 48(2): 148-174.* When the federal government outlawed polygamy in 1862, Mormons faced a moral dilemma of obeying a law that violated their religious convictions or disregarding the law of the land, which it was their religious duty to obey. Rudger Clawson went to prison advocating civil disobedience. Bishop John Sharp despised the law but conformed to it, and was ostracized by Mormons. Based on LDS Archives; 9 illus., 65 notes.   J. L. Hazelton

511.   Anderson, Ken.   THE ROLE OF ABRAHAM LINCOLN AND MEM-
BERS OF HIS FAMILY IN THE CHARLESTON RIOTS DURING THE
CIVIL WAR.   *Lincoln Herald 1977 79(2): 53-60.* On 28 March 1864 a serious
riot occurred in Charleston, Illinois between Unionist Republicans and local
Copperheads. Even though several Union soldiers were either killed or wounded,
this was not a draft riot. Lincoln had practiced law in the area and had several
relatives living there, two of whom were arrested for participating in the riot.
Fifteen Copperhead civilians were shipped to Delaware for military trial, but
Lincoln transferred them back to the civil authorities in Illinois. Dennis Hanks,
Lincoln's second cousin, claimed credit for obtaining their release. 4 photos,
biblio.   T. P. Linkfield

512.   Beeler, Dorothy.   RACE RIOT IN COLUMBIA, TENNESSEE: FEB-
RUARY 25-27, 1946.   *Tennessee Hist. Q. 1980 39(1): 49-61.* The February 1946
race riot in Columbia, Tennessee, mobilized many civil rights organizations to use
increasing black political power to force President Harry S. Truman into a
stronger civil rights stance. The incident and reaction to it, major events of the
period, helped create a base from which black organizations gained strength for
the civil rights push of the 1950's and 1960's. Civil rights had become a national
issue. Based on *Journal, Headquarters, Second Infantry Brigade, Nashville, Tennessee and Second Brigade Task Force, Columbia, Tennessee,* contemporary
newspaper accounts, and secondary sources; 39 notes.   H. M. Parker, Jr.

513.   Blaser, Kent.   NORTH CAROLINA AND JOHN BROWN'S RAID.
Civil War Hist. 1978 24(3): 197-212. In October 1859 initial reaction to John
Brown's Harpers Ferry raid in North Carolina revealed attitudes on slavery
between moderation and complacency. Playing on Southern insecurity, pro-slavery extremists manufactured a Northern conspiracy; moderates retreated on
issues like patrols and vigilance systems. Hysterical fear of strangers aided the
main radical objective of a statewide militia system. By early 1860 even moderates
were affected, and the state was armed. Relatively untouched by the Southern
"Great Reaction" in the 1830's, North Carolina for the first time isolated itself
from the North. Newspapers, primary family and secondary sources; 58 notes.
                                                                        R. E. Stack

514.   Brown, Ira V.   RACISM AND SEXISM: THE CASE OF PENNSYL-
VANIA HALL.   *Phylon 1976 37(2): 126-136.* The Garrisonian abolitionists
stood wholeheartedly for racial integration and woman's liberation. The Pennsylvania State Anti-Slavery Society, formed in 1833, built a handsome new building
in 1837. It was destroyed by a mob a year later when a large assembly of the
Anti-Slavery Convention of American Women, organized in New York City in
1837, met in Pennsylvania Hall. The mixed company, including men and women,
black and white, provoked the mob. "Not even Pennsylvania was ready for racial
integration ... Southerners actually rejoiced in the burning of Pennsylvania
Hall." However, the burning and other violence resulted in many previously
hostile persons taking a view more sympathetic to the abolition movement. 53
notes.   E. P. Stickney

515.   Brown, Lisle G.   WEST VIRGINIA AND MORMONISM'S RAREST
BOOK.   *West Virginia Hist. 1978 39(2-3): 195-199.* The first printing of Joseph
Smith's *Book of Commandments* was disrupted by an anti-Mormon mob that

wrecked the printing office in Independence, Missouri, in 1833. A few copies of the book were saved, printed on paper furnished by William Lambdin of Wheeling, West Virginia. By 1968 a copy of the book brought $4500. Primary and secondary sources; illus., 16 notes. J. H. Broussard

516. Burran, James A. LABOR CONFLICT IN URBAN APPALACHIA: THE KNOXVILLE STREETCAR STRIKE OF 1919. *Tennessee Hist. Q. 1979 38(1): 62-78.* In the period of demobilization and search for normalcy following World War I, a streetcar strike occurred in October 1919 in conservative, typically Republican, Knoxville, Tennessee. It was part of a larger movement of the American Federation of Labor which was aimed at organizing, among others, the Knoxville police. When violence broke out after strike breakers were hired, the governor called in Federal troops. The presence of troops broke the strike. Primary and secondary sources; 35 notes. M. B. Lucas

517. Casciato, Arthur D. and West, James L. W., III. WILLIAM STYRON AND *THE SOUTHAMPTON INSURRECTION. Am. Literature 1981 52(4): 564-577.* William Styron was faithful to the historical record in his attempt to reconstruct past events for his novel *The Confessions of Nat Turner* (1967), which covered Nat Turner's slave insurrection in Southampton, Virginia, in 1831. Styron relied heavily upon two secondary works for realistic details: William S. Drewry's *The Southampton Insurrection* (1900) and Frederick Law Olmsted's *A Journey in the Seaboard Slave States* (1856). 14 notes, 2 fig.
T. P. Linkfield

518. Cramer, James A. and Champion, Dean J. FACTORS ASSOCIATED WITH THE INTENTION OF NATIONAL GUARDSMEN TO PARTICIPATE IN THE CONTROL OF CIVIL DISORDER. *J. of Pol. and Military Sociol. 1975 3(1): 43-56.*

519. Crow, Jeffrey J. SLAVE REBELLIOUSNESS AND SOCIAL CONFLICT IN NORTH CAROLINA, 1775 TO 1802. *William and Mary Q. 1980 37(1): 79-102.* Follows three lines of inquiry on race relations in North Carolina: Afro-American contribution to social upheaval; white response to the realization that independence affected the institution of slavery and slave behavior; and conflict in perception of blacks and whites that led to the slave insurrection hysteria of 1800-02. The war produced a variety of slave protest actions; many blacks ran away, some joining the British. After the war, collective resistance of blacks mounted. There was greater repression by whites. Fear of slave revolts increased. In 1802, plans for Negro insurgency were discovered in several counties, which resulted in wide-scale executions. The insurrection scare of 1802 provided the opportunity for whites to gain greater social control. Uses newspapers and colony and local archives; 66 notes. H. M. Ward

520. Crowe, Charles. SOUTHERN REPRESSION AND BLACK RESISTANCE: 1900, 1917 AND 1932. *Rev. in Am. Hist. 1977 5(3): 379-390.* Review article prompted by William Ivy Hair's *Carnival of Fury: Robert Charles and the New Orleans Race Riot of 1900* (Baton Rouge: Louisiana State U. Pr., 1976), Robert V. Haynes's *A Night of Violence: The Houston Riot of 1917* (Baton Rouge: Louisiana State U. Pr., 1976), and Charles H. Martin's *The Angelo Herndon Case and Southern Justice* (Baton Rouge: Louisiana State U. Pr., 1976).

521.   Curvin, Robert and Porter, Bruce.   BLACKOUT LOOTING!   *Society*
1979 16(4): 68-76. The looting during the blackout of New York City, 13 July
1977, resulted from declining legitimacy, criminality, material aspirations ac-
cented by the media, and ghetto poverty, but not from the social upheavals of the
1960's.

522.   Daniel, Cletus E.   IN DEFENSE OF THE WHEATLAND WOB-
BLIES: A CRITICAL ANALYSIS OF THE IWW IN CALIFORNIA.
Labor Hist. 1978 19(4): 485-509. Analyzes the "hop pickers riot" in Wheatland,
California, in August 1913. IWW action in Wheatland reinforced ideological and
tactical deficiencies among California Wobblies and increased their powerlessness. The incident occurred in spite of IWW organizational policies and produced
many more failures than successes. Based on newspapers; 50 notes.
                                                                    L. L. Athey

523.   Dart, Dennis M.   SACRAMENTO SQUATTER RIOT OF AUGUST
14, 1850.   *Pacific Hist. 1980 24(2): 159-167.* Describes antecedents of the violent
clash on 14 August 1850 between squatters and owners of land covered by
Spanish-Mexican land grants. The latter claimed title to the land under John
Augustus Sutter's original grant; the former claimed that his grant was illegal.
Sutter and his sons had also sold and bought land back and forth, so no one really
knew who owned which parcel of land. The squatters lost the court battle.
Violence erupted. Both sides had the original land grant translated and interpreted. The courts, again, ruled against the squatters. A demonstration turned
into a riot and many were killed. The militia came to protect the city of Sacramento. The squatters moved on. Sutter's claim to the land of the Spanish-
Mexican land grant finally was validated in 1866. Based on local newspaper
accounts, county records, and court records; 52 notes.   G. L. Lake

524.   Daugherty, Robert L.   PROBLEMS IN PEACEKEEPING: THE 1924
NILES RIOT.   *Ohio Hist. 1976 85(4): 280-292.* A riot on 1 November 1924 in
Niles, Ohio, involved the Ohio Knights of the Ku Klux Klan and the Knights
of the Flaming Circle. The riot, terminated by the Ohio National Guard, was a
prime example of a state government's hesitation to become involved in local law
enforcement problems. Based on archival, MS., contemporary comments, and
secondary sources; 5 illus., 31 notes.   N. Summers

525.   David, Pam and Helmbold, Lois.   SAN FRANCISCO: COURTS AND
COPS VS. GAYS.   *Radical Am. 1979 13(4): 27-32.* The riot in San Francisco
on 21 May 1979 in protest of the voluntary manslaughter conviction given to
Daniel White, the slayer of Mayor George Moscone and City Supervisor Harvey
Milk, was a reflection, in part, of the growing tension and apprehension in the
city's gay community over a growing trend among the city's police and government toward conservatism and repression of homosexuals as well as a reaction
to national trends. Along with being on the defensive, the homosexual community
in the city is divided along male and female, conservative and radical, and class
lines; gay businesspeople exploit the labor of nonunionized gay employees. The
gay community is opposed by working class persons living in neighborhoods
being rehabilitated by gays with resulting high rents for the renovated areas.
Based on participant observation by members of Lesbians against Police Violence.
                                                                N. Lederer

526. Decter, Midge. LOOTING AND LIBERAL RACISM. *Commentary 1977 64(3): 48-54.* Liberal spokesmen explained the looting during the July 1977 New York City blackout as another manifestation of minority youth's rage and desperation over the failure of society to respond to the needs of socially and economically disadvantaged individuals. This familiar line overlooks the billions of dollars spent on aid for the urban poor, and fails to recognize that the liberal consensus had, ironically, sanctioned the looting. Liberal racism, which refuses to hold certain individuals morally responsible for their actions and thus encourages social deviance, does the disadvantaged no favor. D. W. Johnson

527. DeWitt, Howard A. THE WATSONVILLE ANTI-FILIPINO RIOT OF 1930: A CASE STUDY OF THE GREAT DEPRESSION AND ETHNIC CONFLICT IN CALIFORNIA. *Southern California Q. 1979 61(3): 291-302.* Examines the anti-Filipino riot in Watsonville, California, 19-23 January 1930. Hostility to Filipino Americans, most of whom lived in California, had been building for several years in the Watsonville area. Filipinos were victims of discrimination, exploitation, and stereotyping. Politicians and newspapers issued overtly racist statements concerning alleged Filipino threats in health, social relations, and vice. Following public anti-Filipino pronouncements by local political and business leaders, mobs of young men prowled Watsonville streets looking for Filipinos to beat up. One Filipino was shot dead. After five days the riots subsided as the public reacted negatively to the excessive violence. Police and sheriff's deputies acted impartially in protecting Filipinos but arrested few rioters. The California Filipino community failed to unite against the assault, its leaders divided on how to approach the problem. Onset of the Great Depression thus culminated years of anti-Filipino sentiment in the Watsonville riot. 33 notes. A. Hoffman

528. Dickson, Paul. THE GREAT RAILROAD WAR OF 1877. *Am. Heritage 1978 29(2): 56-61.* The railroad strike of 1877 resulted from wage cuts made by the railroads during the Depression of 1873. Though most of the nation was affected, Pittsburgh was hit hardest. Before it ended, federal troops had been sent in and more than 100 persons had been killed. The strike failed primarily because of its lack of organization. 14 illus. J. F. Paul

529. Dorsey, George. THE BAYONNE REFINERY STRIKE OF 1915-1916. *Polish Am. Studies 1976 33(2): 19-30.* This strike started on 15 July 1915 at "Jersey Standard's great refinery in Bayonne" when about 100 still cleaners demanded a 15% pay increase justified by a work speedup and publicly announced anticipated company profits. When other workers joined in, the company answered by hiring armed guards from P. J. Berghoff, a New York City "industrial service." The strike, of unorganized workers, spread to other companies. In confrontations, one Pole was killed and four others were wounded. The strike ended by the end of July after promises of pay increases, a change of a foreman, and an appeal to wartime patriotism. Fifteen months later, another strike erupted to improve upon the two dollars-per-day wages. Though not apparent in 1915 and 1916, a new industrialism, one of concern for the worker, was beginning to play a recognizable role in the American economic world. Based primarily on newspaper accounts; 27 notes. S. R. Pliska

530. Eastland, Terry. THE COMMUNISTS AND THE KLAN. *Commentary 1980 69(5): 65-67.* The confrontation between the Ku Klux Klan and the Communist Workers' Party (then the Workers' Viewpoint Organization) in November 1979 in Greensboro, North Carolina, proceeded from the class relations of industrial North Carolina and from the deliberate ideological intentions of the Communists.

531. Eaves, Jehu and Lutz, Chris. MIAMI REBELLION. *Southern Exposure 1981 9(1): 104-109.* Discusses blacks' ongoing battle against police brutality in Liberty City, an unincorporated section of Dade County, Florida since 1970, focusing on both the rioting after a black man was beaten to death by policemen in December, 1979, and the summer riots of 1980.

532. Eggert, Gerald G. GUNFIRE AND BRICKBATS: THE GREAT RAILWAY STRIKES OF 1877. *Am. Hist. Illus. 1981 16(2): 16-25.* Tells of the bloody railway strike that began in West Virginia in July 1877 and spread to rail centers in all parts of the country leading to disorders that "produced the first near-national emergency strike in the country's history, led to massive governmental intervention in a labor dispute, established important precedents for dealing with later strikes, and opened a new epoch in American labor history."

533. Eklund, Monica. MASSACRE AT LUDLOW. *Southwest Econ. and Soc. 1978 4(1): 21-30.* A strike of coal miners in 1913-14 in Ludlow, Colorado (against the Colorado Fuel and Iron Company), elicited attempted strike-breaking; mine guards, detectives, and the National Guard attacked and burned the strikers' tent city and at least 13 women and children died.

534. Fairweather, Gordon L. et al. CIVIL VIOLENCE AND CIVIL RIGHTS: A COMPARATIVE APPROACH TO LAW, ORDER, AND REFORM. *Am. Soc. of Int. Law Pro. 1974 68: 156-169.* Discusses the sources of violence in the US, Canada, and Mexico since the 18th century and the general problem of legally curbing violence while protecting civil rights.

535. Fickle, James E. RACE, CLASS, AND RADICALISM: THE WOBBLIES IN THE SOUTHERN LUMBER INDUSTRY, 1900-1916. Conlin, Joseph R., ed. *At the Point of Production: The Local History of the I.W.W.* (Westport, Conn.: Greenwood Pr., 1981): 97-113. Details the conflict between lumber workers and mill operators in eastern Texas and western Louisiana, especially from 1911 to 1912. Central to the conflict was Arthur L. Emerson, who formed his first local union at Carson in western Louisiana in 1910, leading to the founding of the Brotherhood of Timber Workers in 1911. The conflict with the mill operators reached violent proportions, as the BTW was backed by the Industrial Workers of the World and other organizations. On 7 July 1912, a gun battle erupted at an Emerson speech. Emerson and other unionists were jailed, and the operators were successful in breaking the financial and psychological strength of the union. By 1914 the BTW was practically destroyed. Mainly secondary sources; 70 notes. Portions of this chapter previously appeared in *Louisiana History* in 1975 (see entry 14A:5386).   J. Powell

536. Foner, Philip S. ZUR ROLLE DER WORKINGEMEN'S PARTY OF THE U.S.A. IM EISENBAHNERSTREIK VON 1877 [On the role of the Workingmen's Party of the U.S.A. in the railroad strike of 1877]. *Zeitschrift für*

Geschichtswissenschaft [East Germany] 1978 26(4): 325-335. The 1877 railroad strike, coming near the end of the depression which followed the 1873 panic, was a true workers' revolt, similar in many ways to the 1871 Paris Commune. The US Workingmen's Party, a federation founded in Philadelphia in 1876, fused the nation's growing Marxist elements. Initially the Party was divided over support for the strike, but when workers were repeatedly attacked by army and national guard troops, it moved to support the striking railroad workers. It fought to gain decent working and living conditions for the oppressed workers and to gain reasonable wages and job security for workers continually threatened with unemployment. 73 notes. G. H. Libbey

537. Forman, James. FREEDOM RIDES. *Southern Exposure 1981 9(1): 34-39.* Brief description of the Freedom Rides of 1961, when blacks and whites took buses from Washington D.C., to the South to integrate Greyhound and Trailways buses and terminals, followed by recollections culled from a 1980 speech by a founder of the Congress of Racial Equality (CORE), James Farmer, and from Lucretia Collins, a Nashville student and Freedom Rider, whose 1961 account appears in James Forman's *The Making of Black Revolutionaries.*

538. Fowler, James H., II. CREATING AN ATMOSPHERE OF SUP-PRESSION, 1914-1917. *Chronicles of Oklahoma 1981 59(2): 202-223.* Although the United States endorsed a policy of neutrality toward World War I, Americans increasingly developed an intolerance toward Germany and toward unpatriotic persons. The level of intolerance boiled over in Oklahoma as both vigilantes and respected newspapers harangued pacifists, labor union organizers, and political leftists. President Woodrow Wilson's frequent outbursts against the same groups seemingly gave legitimacy to local vigilante groups such as the Oklahoma State Council of Defense. Freedom of speech evaporated in this poisoned atmosphere. Based on Oklahoma newspapers; 3 illus., 85 notes. M. L. Tate

539. Franklin, Vincent P. THE PHILADELPHIA RACE RIOT OF 1918. *Pennsylvania Mag. of Hist. and Biog. 1975 99(3): 336-350.* During 1910-20 there was a 58% increase in the Negro population of Philadelphia, resulting in racial tension and riots in 1918. The city police were ineffectual in curbing the violence and the black community accused some policemen of joining the mob. The Colored Protective Association was formed to look after black interests. This and other citizens' committees "were well aware of the connection between the overt brutality of the mob, and the more subtle discriminations to which blacks were subjected in the schools, theaters, and other public places. And though many of the committees and associations were short-lived, they did have the effect of pushing the lethargic N.A.A.C.P. branch in Philadelphia into action on behalf of civil rights for blacks." 48 notes. C. W. Olson

540. Gilje, Paul A. "THE MOB BEGIN TO THINK AND REASON": RECENT TRENDS IN STUDIES OF AMERICAN POPULAR DISORDER, 1700-1850. *Maryland Hist. 1981 12(1): 25-36.* An interpretive bibliographic essay describing the strengths, weaknesses, and missions of research on the role of the mob in American history. Provides analysis of periodicals and monographs. Secondary sources, 44 notes. G. O. Gagnon

541.   Grable, Stephen W.   RACIAL VIOLENCE WITHIN THE CONTEXT
OF COMMUNITY HISTORY.   *Phylon 1981 42(3): 275-283.* The history of
violence between the races in United States history can best be understood by
investigating local history. Each riot has its own particular configuration of
causes. Very few can fit into large generalizations based on national history. Riots
and protests arise from local problems as illustrated by looking at the Vesey plot
(1822), the Blackburn riot (1833), the Philadelphia riots (1829-49), the Atlanta
riot (1906), and the Chicago riot (1919).   A. G. Belles

542.   Graham, Hugh Davis.   ON RIOTS AND RIOT COMMISSIONS:
CIVIL DISORDERS IN THE 1960'S.   *Public Hist. 1980 2(4): 7-27.* Surveys
the literature—especially its theoretical debates—that deals with the civil disorders of the 1960's and complains that its largely social scientific approach rooted
in behaviorism was deficient because it was both ahistorical and noncross-cul-
tural.

543.   Graves, Carl R.   THE RIGHT TO BE SERVED: OKLAHOMA CITY'S
LUNCH COUNTER SIT-INS, 1958-1964.   *Chronicles of Oklahoma 1981
59(2): 152-166.* Six years of struggle to integrate the lunch counters of downtown
Oklahoma City began in August 1958 when Clara Luper and 13 black children
sat down at Katz Drugstore and requested food service. Continued sit-ins compelled other restaurants to end their segregationalist practices, and those that
refused were met by a fairly unified black boycott. Although confrontationist in
nature, the NAACP-directed sit-ins achieved beneficial results without violence.
The discipline and youth of the demonstrators helped win respect from many
whites and minimized the possibility of bloodshed. Based on Oklahoma City
newspapers; 4 photos, 48 notes.   M. L. Tate

544.   Gregory, Rick.   ROBERTSON COUNTY AND THE BLACK PATCH
WAR, 1904-1909.   *Tennessee Hist. Q. 1980 39(3): 341-358.* The tobacco farmers
of the Black Patch region of Kentucky and Tennessee organized to gain higher
prices for their special dark-fired burley tobacco. The farmers of Robertson
County, Tennessee, played a dominant role. Overproduction and the formation
of the American Tobacco Company in the late 1890's had led to a change from
auction sales to noncompetitive "barn-buying" and consequent lower prices.
Sharecroppers formed the Dark Tobacco District Planters Protective Association
of Kentucky and Tennessee to improve farming techniques while calling for
reduced crops and lower federal tobacco taxes. Individuals who resisted organization were branded "hillbillies" by the association and treated violently. By 1909
the association had won higher prices and so disbanded. Primary sources; 56
notes.   W. D. Piersen

545.   Greiert, Steven G.   THE EARL OF HALIFAX AND THE LAND
RIOTS IN NEW JERSEY, 1748-1753.   *New Jersey Hist. 1981 99(1-2): 13-31.*
Land riots broke out in New Jersey during the mid-18th century between the
colony's proprietors and the residents who had purchased their land directly from
the Indians. Governor Jonathan Belcher advocated a lax policy in punishing the
residents for their action, while George Montagu Dunk, the Earl of Halifax,
president of the Board of Trade, hoped to put the rioters down with overwhelming force. Robert Hunter Morris appeared before the board and reinforced the
proprietors' stringent measures. In its final report, however, the board recom-

mended a lenient, threefold approach: a commission should investigate the cause of the riots, the colonial government should be reprimanded, and amnesty should be granted to those who deserved it. Based on colonial documents and correspondence and secondary sources; 3 photos, map, 57 notes.   E. R. McKinstry

546. Hampshire, Annette P. THE TRIUMPH OF MOBOCRACY IN HANCOCK COUNTY 1844-1846. *Western Illinois Regional Studies 1982 5(1): 17-37.* Anti-Mormonism in Hancock County, Illinois, which culminated in the jail murders of Joseph Smith and his brother Hyrum Smith led to "the temporary supremacy of the mob": state authority lost all credibility with the anti-Mormons and the Mormons; state agents were unable to control the situation; the anti-Mormons' power waxed; and state agents began to accept the anti-Mormons' version of events.

547. Haynes, Robert V. THE HOUSTON MUTINY AND RIOT OF 1917. *Southwestern Hist. Q. 1973 76(4): 418-439.* A black infantry battalion was sent to Houston, Texas, in July 1917 to assume guard duty at a new training cantonment. The fighting soldiers were not happy at this reduction to guard detail, and Texas was a rigidly segregated state with a reputation of violence against non-whites. Black troopers and white civilians anticipated trouble—which soon came. A series of physical assaults on blacks by the Houston police escalated into a sizable mutiny and riot, 23 August. The largest court-martial in American military history sentenced several soldiers to death and more to life in prison. 79 notes.   D. L. Smith

548. Hazen, Lester B. WITHOUT MUCH BLOOD. *Military Rev. 1982 62(9): 57-66.* John Brown's Harpers Ferry raid in 1859 is an example of terrorism and government response. Brown employed terrorist methods to achieve political objectives, and the government response was immediate and efficient. Map, 6 pictures, 14 notes.   D. H. Cline

549. Hennessey, Melinda Meek. RACE AND VIOLENCE IN RECONSTRUCTION NEW ORLEANS: THE 1868 RIOT. *Louisiana Hist. 1979 20(1): 77-92.* The New Orleans race riot, September-October 1868, grew out of efforts by white Democrats to reduce the Republican vote in New Orleans in the upcoming presidential election and to emasculate the recently created Metropolitan Police Force, one-third of whom were black. The worst phase of the violence began on the evening of 24 October 1868 in a clash between white Democratic and black Republican marching clubs, during their processions on Canal Street. During the next few nights Negroes indiscriminately attacked whites on the streets, and whites retaliated by ransacking the homes and businesses of black political leaders and relieving black citizens of their registration certificates. The crisis was defused when General Jame Steedman agreed to assume command of the Metropolitan Police Force. The result was 6-7 white deaths, at least 13 black deaths, and an overwhelming Democratic majority in the November election. Primary and secondary sources; 43 notes.   L. N. Powell

550. Hennessey, Melinda Meek. POLITICAL TERRORISM IN THE BLACK BELT: THE EUTAW RIOT. *Alabama Rev. 1980 33(1): 35-48.* During Reconstruction, Southern blacks were subjected to racial riots. One of the most violent was the 1870 riot in Eutaw, Alabama, where 79% of the population

was black. The area was plagued by nightrider activities. Terrorists destroyed black schools and murdered two prominent Republican leaders, Alexander Boyd and Jim Martin. The riot took place at a Republican rally on 25 October. Several blacks were wounded. The Republicans claimed that the Democrats caused the riot. Primary sources; 48 notes.   J. Powell

551.   Hewitt, John H.   THE SACKING OF ST. PHILIP'S CHURCH, NEW YORK.   *Hist. Mag. of the Protestant Episcopal Church 1980 49(1): 7-20.* On the night of 11 July 1834 the black Episcopal St. Philip's Church, New York City, was sacked by an antiblack, antiabolition mob. The black rector of the church was Peter Williams, Jr., who would later emerge as a leader in the abolition movement. The mob had been excited by the yellow journalism of the New York newspapers. Reveals the Jim Crow status of New York at this time, with Williams himself not being equal to the white priests in the diocese. His bishop even required him to resign offices he held in abolition societies. Nor was St. Philip's entitled to representation in the Diocesan Convention. Based largely on newspaper accounts of the incident and secondary sources; 78 notes.

H. M. Parker, Jr.

552.   Holmes, William F.   MOONSHINING AND COLLECTIVE VIOLENCE: GEORGIA, 1889-1895.   *J. of Am. Hist. 1980 67(3): 589-611.* Analyzes an outbreak of collective whitecap violence in a five-county region of northern Georgia from 1889 to 1895. The violence was a response by poor whites attempting to maintain control over their way of life and geographical area in light of perceived threats from a powerful federal government and a changing economic order. Although immoral whites and free blacks were occasionally targets of terrorism, revenue informers were the main targets of violence by white secret societies. This violence was representative of a type of collective protest that became widespread in America in the late 19th and early 20th centuries. It proved futile as a protest against the forces that transformed the nation after the Civil War. 5 tables, 73 notes.   T. P. Linkfield

553.   Hopkins, Jerry.   VIOLENCE IN CHICAGO: AN APPRAISAL OF SOURCES ON THE VIOLENCE RELATED TO THE 1968 DEMOCRATIC CONVENTION.   *Fides et Hist. 1979 12(1): 7-28.* Examines the diverse opinions about the causes of the violence at the Democratic National Convention in Chicago during August 1968. Among those expressing views were the representatives of the mass media at the convention, who some felt were at least partly responsible for the trouble. This is a clear example of the enormous power wielded by the mass media in their ability to shape and mold public opinion. Christian historians should note such incidents carefully, because they are bound at all times to seek the truth. In so doing, they must use, but must simultaneously treat with skepticism, sources emanating from the mass media, which report often with manipulative intent. Printed primary sources; 43 notes.   J. A. Kicklighter

554.   Howard, Victor B.   JOHN BROWN'S RAID AT HARPERS FERRY AND THE SECTIONAL CRISIS IN NORTH CAROLINA.   *North Carolina Hist. Rev. 1978 55(4): 396-420.* John Brown's Harpers Ferry raid greatly frightened North Carolinians owing to its proximity of their state. During 1840-57 North Carolinians engaged in sporadic activities such as intercepting antislavery mail and harrassing known abolitionists. Publication of *The Impending Crisis* by

fellow state resident Hinton Rowan Helper embarrassed North Carolinians and caused an intensification of these antiabolitionist efforts. John Brown's raid brought home the threat of a change of status for blacks. Reaction was especially strong in the Piedmont, though suspicion and harrassment of blacks and antislavery whites was present throughout the state. In addition, Democrats used the raid to discredit Whigs. Contemporary newspaper accounts, unpublished correspondence, published state and local records and personal papers, and secondary sources; 8 illus., map, 88 notes. T. L. Savitt

555. Hutchinson, Thomas. THE BOSTON PRESS GANG RIOT OF 1747. Karsten, Peter, ed. *The Military in America: From the Colonial Era to the Present* (New York: Free Pr., 1980): 15-17. Discusses the riot of 17-19 November 1747 in Boston, Massachusetts, which occurred when British naval officers sent representatives ashore from their ship to draft personnel by kidnapping them.

556. Isacsson, Alfred. A STUDY OF LOUIS J. WEICHMANN. *Lincoln Herald 1978 80(1): 25-38.* Louis J. Weichmann, a principal witness in the conspiracy trial of 1865, suffered from a mental disorder in an advanced stage when he wrote his *A True History of the Assassination of Abraham Lincoln and of the Conspiracy of 1865* 30 years after Abraham Lincoln's death. Weichmann's advanced paranoia prevented him from placing the events of 1865 in their proper perspective; consequently he created his own reality in his book. Obsessed with the delusion that he possessed truth and virtue, Weichmann distorted the facts, events, and people surrounding the assassination to fit his predetermined thesis. Photo, 80 notes. T. P. Linkfield

557. Jervey, Edward D. and Huber, C. Harold. THE *CREOLE* AFFAIR. *J. of Negro Hist. 1980 65(3): 196-211.* In November 1841, a black slave, Madison Washington, led a slave mutiny against the white crew of the brig *Creole.* The ship, en route from Richmond to New Orleans, was taken by the 19 mutineers to Nassau in the Bahamas, where the British authorities assumed control. Ignoring the white protests, the British set free all of the black slaves except the 19 mutineers, who were detained for questioning about the deaths during the revolt. Eventually, they were released. This episode raised the question of the British taking property from US citizens. By 1841, the British did not accept black persons as property. A. G. Belles

558. Johnstone, John W. C. YOUTH GANGS AND BLACK SUBURBS. *Pacific Sociol. Rev. 1981 24(3): 355-375.* Focuses on gang activity among young Negroes living in the suburbs and suburban fringe communities of the Chicago metropolitan area since 1970, thus altering the long-held notion of the American suburb as a bastion of tranquillity and prosperity, since several of these suburban areas differ little in economic character from inner-city slums.

559. Jones, Daniel P. FROM MILITARY TO CIVILIAN TECHNOLOGY: THE INTRODUCTION OF TEAR GAS FOR CIVIL RIOT CONTROL. *Technology and Culture 1978 19(2): 151-168.* Although tear gas was developed during World War I, for three years after the war the War Department forbade the Chemical Warfare Section (CWS) to make it available to civil police for riot control. Then in the summer of 1921, private suppliers, mostly former officers of the CWS, began to manufacture tear gas, and by 1923 had supplied it to over

600 cities. Tear gas was far more humane than bullets; yet it also meant a "dramatic increase in the power of police" to put down any mass challenge to established order. Based on War Department papers; 81 notes.   C. O. Smith

560.   Juhnke, James C.   MOB VIOLENCE AND KANSAS MENNONITES IN 1918.   *Kansas Hist. Q. 1977 43(3): 334-350.* Discusses mob violence in central Kansas during 1918 against certain local Mennonites, some of them German-speaking, who refused on account of their pacifist convictions to buy Liberty bonds and to otherwise support the World War I effort. No legal action was ever taken against the vigilantes. Based on archival materials, interviews, contemporary newspaper accounts, and secondary sources; 5 illus., 56 notes.
L. W. Van Wyk

561.   Kapsis, Robert E.   CONTINUITY IN DELINQUENCY AND RIOT PATTERNS IN BLACK RESIDENTIAL AREAS.   *Social Problems 1976 23(5): 567-580.* Explores patterns of violence during a race riot in 1968 in Richmond and North Richmond, California.

562.   Keller, Allan.   JOHN BROWN'S RAID.   *Am. Hist. Illus. 1976 11(5): 34-45.* Discusses the events of John Brown's raid at Harpers Ferry, 1859.

563.   Kenneally, James J.   THE BURNING OF THE URSULINE CONVENT: A DIFFERENT VIEW.   *Records of the Am. Catholic Hist. Soc. of Philadelphia 1979 90(1-4): 15-22.* The Superior of the Ursuline Convent in Charlestown, Massachusetts, Sister Mary Edmond St. George (born Anne Moffet in 1793), was self-assured to the point of arrogance and exacerbated suspicions by her "unladylike" conduct. Were she more of a 19th-century traditionalist in her behavior, her manner more in tune with societal perceptions of proper female conduct, things might have taken a different course in 1834. Based on materials in the Archives of the Archdiocese of Boston and contemporary newspapers; 29 notes.   J. M. McCarthy

564.   Kenner, Charles L.   THE GREAT NEW MEXICO CATTLE RAID: 1872.   *New Mexico Hist. Rev. 1962 37(4): 243-259.* Provides a description of, and background to, the raid led by John Hittson in 1872 against the Comancheros (Hispanic traders) to restore cattle stolen by Indians: an event which increased racial antagonism between Hispanic New Mexicans and Texas ranchers.

565.   King, Gerald M.   MAN VS. STATE: A FATAL SHOWDOWN WITH COMPULSORY SCHOOLING.   *Reason 1979 11(3): 24-28, 40.* On 18 January 1979, in Summit County, Utah, sheriff's deputies shot to death John Singer, 47, for refusing to surrender himself and his children, whom Singer declined to send to the public schools, choosing instead to educate them at home; there is some public feeling that Singer was killed because of his fierce independence, rejection of authority, and polygamy.

566.   King, Martin Luther, Jr.   LETTER FROM A BIRMINGHAM JAIL. *Southern Exposure 1981 9(1): 50-54.* Reprints King's letter written 16 April 1963 in response to an open letter written to him by eight Alabama clergymen who criticized civil rights demonstrations in Birmingham.

567. Klaassen, Walter. MENNONITES AND WAR TAXES. *Pennsylvania Mennonite Heritage 1978 1(2): 17-22.* Traces traditional views of government and taxation held by Anabaptists in Switzerland and Germany during the 16th century; examines Anabaptists' refusal to pay taxes connected with war in the United States from the American Revolution to the Vietnam War.

568. Koroleva, A. P. MARTIN LIUTER KING I REBUSY AMERIKANSKOI DEMOKRATII [Martin Luther King and abuses of American democracy]. *Voprosy Istorii [USSR] 1978 (10): 122-140.* The Reverend Martin Luther King, Jr. (1929-68), was noted for his criticism of the US social and legal system and for advocating civil rights. His utopian ideas drew hatred from white racists and from black nationalists. During 1955-68, King's marches and sit-in strikes provoked clashes with racists. Shadowed by the FBI, and the target of smear campaigns, King was finally murdered in mysterious circumstances. 74 notes.
A. P. Oxley

569. Koroleva, A. P. NEGRITIANSKIE VYSTUPLENIIA 1960-KH GODOV V SSHA [The Negro disturbances of the 1960's in the United States]. *Voprosy Istorii [USSR] 1973 (12): 123-138.* Surveys the unrest and disturbances in black urban districts of American cities during the summers of the 1960's. Chronicles various disturbances, describes the development and organization of black movements, the reaction of business to the turmoil, the government's response at various levels, and the position of the American Communist Party in the crisis. Based on news reports; 85 notes.
S

570. Kritzer, Herbert M. POLITICAL PROTEST AND POLITICAL VIOLENCE: A NONRECURSIVE CAUSAL MODEL. *Social Forces 1977 55(3): 630-640.* This paper presents a nonrecursive causal model of violence at protest demonstrations; it seeks to account for violence by both the police and the protestors. The model is tested using data on 126 protest events in the United States. The results of the analysis suggest strongly that the outbreak of violence at protest demonstrations is the result of a dynamic process resulting from the interaction of police and protestors; exogenous variables are found to have little predictive power when the reciprocal causal link between protestor violence and police violence is included in the model.
J

571. Lapsansky, Emma Jones. SINCE THEY GOT THOSE SEPARATE CHURCHES: AFRO-AMERICANS AND RACISM IN JACKSONIAN PHILADELPHIA. *Am. Q. 1980 32(1): 54-78.* White rioters involved in the August 1834 attack on Philadelphia blacks directed their anger against the visibly well-to-do black middle and upper class and its institutions. This black community was to some extent well off, was relatively large, had formed its own religious and social organizations due to white racism, and consciously aspired to respectability. Lower class whites, frustrated by unemployment, saw blacks as "uppity" and correctly guessed that violence against the black community would not be actively prosecuted. Each of the five major riots in Philadelphia against blacks during 1834-49 followed this pattern. 4 illus., map, 61 notes. D. K. Lambert

572. Launitz-Schurer, Leopold S., Jr. SLAVE RESISTANCE IN COLONIAL NEW YORK: AN INTERPRETATION OF DANIEL HORSMANDEN'S NEW YORK CONSPIRACY. *Phylon 1980 41(2): 137-151.* The chief

source of information on aspects of the historical experience of Afro-Americans in New York in the 1740's is Daniel Horsmanden's *Journal,* which recounts the Negro plot of 1741. 53 notes.

N. G. Sapper

573. Lieske, Joel A. THE CONDITIONS OF RACIAL VIOLENCE IN AMERICAN CITIES: A DEVELOPMENTAL SYNTHESIS. *Am. Pol. Sci. Rev. 1978 72(4): 1324-1340.* This article analyzes the social and political conditions associated with the incidence of racial violence in a sample of 119 American cities. Data on the incidence of racial disorders are drawn from newspaper accounts compiled by the Lemberg Center for the Study of Violence during the period 1967-1969. A total of 334 disorders are analyzed. Two alternative hypotheses are examined. The first assumes that the causes of the black urban riots are rooted largely in the disorganized environment of socially marginal individuals. The second attempts to locate the outbreak of rioting primarily within a closed and unresponsive political system. Paradoxically, the results tend to provide empirical support for both theoretical perspectives. At the same time, the data suggest the need to reformulate and revise conventional interpretations of the black urban riots. This is done by synthesizing and testing a developmental model which implies a curvilinear relationship between the incidence of racial violence on the one hand, and black political development on the other. J

574. Lovett, Bobby L. MEMPHIS RIOTS: WHITE REACTION TO BLACKS IN MEMPHIS, MAY 1865-JULY 1866. *Tennessee Hist. Q. 1979 38(1): 9-33.* The bloody racial riots in Memphis, Tennessee, on 1-2 May 1866, were the result of demographic changes caused by the influx of large numbers of black refugees, thus creating an urban black community and new race relationships. The claim that the presence of black troops caused the riots is a myth. The results of the riot were the opposite of what the white instigators desired since the riot helped convince national and state Republicans to pass protective civil rights legislation for blacks. Primary and secondary sources; 2 illus., 49 notes.

M. B. Lucas

575. Mannard, Joseph G. THE 1839 BALTIMORE NUNNERY RIOT: AN EPISODE IN JACKSONIAN NATIVISM AND SOCIAL VIOLENCE. *Maryland Hist. 1980 11(1): 13-23.* Utilizes the 1839 Baltimore Nunnery Riot to explain the complex motivations underlying nativism in antebellum America. The riot was triggered by anti-Catholic propaganda but was motivated by values concerning individual freedom, antiauthoritarianism, the need of women for protection, and dislike of secrecy. Nativism's impact varied with time, conditions and setting. 75 notes.

G. O. Gagnon

576. Marable, Manning. THE FIRE THIS TIME: THE MIAMI REBELLION, MAY, 1980. *Black Scholar 1980 11(6): 2-18.* Examines the May 1980 riots in Miami's black neighborhoods, emphasizing the social, economic, and racial tensions that caused them, and what they may presage.

577. Mehler, Gregory S. CIVIL DISOBEDIENCE OF DEMOCRATIC SOCIETY: THE CASE OF [THE] UNITED STATES. *Pol. Sci. Rev. [India] 1976 15(2-4): 40-61.* Develops a theory of civil disobedience and analyzes a number of cases in the United States. Suggests that civil disobedience, as opposed to revolutionary behavior or criminal disobedience, must include the following char-

acteristics: the act must be nonviolent, a public violation of the law, a breaking of a special policy, an act expressing a sense of justice, taken as a last resort, for the purpose of changing the law, and done with the intention of accepting the penalty which the law imposes. Reviews the Montgomery bus boycott led by Martin Luther King, Jr. in 1956, the Lamar, South Carolina school bus attacks of 1970, the burning of selective service records by the Berrigan brothers, and the publication of the Pentagon Papers by Dr. Benjamin Spock and Senator Mike Gravel. Secondary sources; 65 notes.   S. H. Frank

578. Midlarsky, Manus I.   ANALYZING DIFFUSION AND CONTA-GION EFFECTS: THE URBAN DISORDERS OF THE 1960'S.   *Am. Pol. Sci. Rev. 1978 72(3): 996-1008.* This study concerns the analysis of diffusion and contagion processes using a lognormal model of overdispersion phenomena. The urban disorders of the past decade are examined and two processes are found to exist in the 1966-67 period. One is a classic diffusion effect in which disorders are precipitated by events which are independent of each other, but lead to outcomes such as numbers of arrests which are proportional to previous disorders. The second process is a contagious one in which disturbances occur as a consequence of smaller cities imitating the behavior of large ones experiencing a disorder. It was found that the explanatory power of the interaction effect between police and black city residents tended to increase as city size increased. Concomitantly, the effects of environmental variables tended to decrease in explanatory power as city size decreased.   J

579. Monti, Daniel J.   INTERGROUP CONFLICT AND COLLECTIVE VIOLENCE: THE CASE OF NEW YORK CITY, 1960-JULY 1964.   *J. of Pol. and Military Sociol. 1978 6(2): 147-162.* Data on racial controversies involving New York's black and Puerto Rican population between 1960 and July, 1964 were obtained from an analysis of *New York Times* articles. These data deal with "events" or exchanges between representatives of the city's minority populations and public officials or non-minority actors. Rifts among minority and government actors appear to have grown more than among non-minority actors before the outbreak of rioting in July, 1964. Government representatives made some small effort to realign themselves with non-minority actors as racial controversies intensified, but the latter did not respond in that fashion. The role of non-minority and moderate minority actors as potential allies or antagonists of civil rights activists and government parties helps to clarify why violence occurred when it did, and it is suggested on the strength of these findings that such conflicts may be a necessary precondition for violent outbursts.   J

580. Monti, Daniel J.   THE RELATION BETWEEN TERRORISM AND DOMESTIC CIVIL DISORDERS.   *Terrorism 1980 4(1-4): 123-141.* Examines 300 years of civil disturbances in New York City, pointing out the essentially conservative nature of collective violence and the conditions which might change it into political terrorism.

581. Monti, Daniel J.   VIOLENCE AS SOCIAL INTERVENTION.   *J. of Intergroup Relations 1981 9(2): 31-45.* Discusses rioting in American cities between 1960 and 1980 against a background of urban violence in America since the 1690's, focusing on the labor and black riots of the late 19th and 20th centuries.

582. Moore, John Hammond. THE NORFOLK RIOT: 16 APRIL 1866. *Virginia Mag. of Hist. and Biog. 1982 90(2): 155-164.* Racial unrest grew in Norfolk, Virginia, during the spring of 1866. The national political climate was also tense as Congress overrode President Andrew Johnson's veto of the civil rights bill. On 16 April a riot broke out during a parade organized by Norfolk's black leaders to celebrate the passage of the bill. Although the riot was not the worst of its kind, the aftermath was a disappointing example of the abuse of justice in Reconstruction Virginia. Based on records in the National Archives and contemporary newspaper accounts; 11 notes, illus.   D. J. Cimbala

583. Morrison, Howard Alexander. GENTLEMEN OF PROPER UNDER-STANDING: A CLOSER LOOK AT UTICA'S ANTI-ABOLITIONIST MOB. *New York Hist. 1981 62(1): 61-82.* The antiabolitionist riot in Utica, New York on 21 October 1835 was politically motivated. Democratic politicians seeking reelection and other Democratic Party leaders led the riot in order to identify themselves and their party with the antiabolitionist majority. The Utica riot, moreover, was orchestrated by a Democratic political machine in order to strengthen the presidential candidacy of Martin Van Buren. Based on the Martin Van Buren Papers, James Watson Williams Papers, and contemporary newspapers and books; 6 illus., 52 notes.   R. N. Lokken

584. Newbill, James G. YAKIMA AND THE WOBBLIES, 1910-1936. Conlin, Joseph R., ed. *At the Point of Production: The Local History of the I.W.W.* (Westport Conn.: Greenwood Pr., 1981): 167-190. Describes confrontations between the Industrial Workers of the World and ranchers and farmers in Yakima before 1933, the combination of depression economics and racism which led to mass meetings and eventual violence, fruit rancher-laborer difficulties in July and August 1933, and the "Congdon orchards battle" of 24 August 1933, and its aftermath. The major confrontation at Congdon resulted from a distorted image the IWW held of their own strength, and the fear of the farming community of the union. The confrontation and legal actions against the union in 1933 resulted in the collapse of the union's power in the Yakima Valley. Based on newspaper, journal, and personal accounts; 53 notes.   J. Powell

585. Newhall, David W. CIVIL DISOBEDIENCE AND DEMOCRACY. *Social Studies 1973 64(7): 307-312.* Civil disobedience is sanctioned under the qualified conditions of nonviolence and "orderly procedure" because democratic processes, as now understood, are often too slow and ineffective in bringing about proper reforms in social institutions.   L. R. Raife

586. Norman, Liane Ellison. COMPANIONS AGAINST THE STORM. *Center Mag. 1981 14(6): 2-6.* Interviews the family of nuclear activist Molly Rush, a member of the Plowshares Eight, who demonstrated against General Electric's King of Prussia, Pennsylvania, plant in 1980 and was subsequently jailed.

587. Ortiz, Roxanne Dunbar. WOUNDED KNEE 1890 TO WOUNDED KNEE 1973: A STUDY IN UNITED STATES COLONIALISM. *J. of Ethnic Studies 1980 8(2): 1-15.* Provides an eyewitness description of the occupation of Wounded Knee, South Dakota, 27 February-8 May 1973, by Agnes LaMonte, whose son was killed there by federal marshals, and summarizes historical ante-

cedents of the infamous 1890 Wounded Knee massacre of Sioux Indians. The flourishing field of western history should be analyzed in the framework of the American colonization process of the continent, and Indian resistance should be viewed as the main cause of Indian survival, as opposed to the assumption that Indians exist today largely as the result of white benevolence. Moreover, Indian resistance may have been a vital force in curbing US imperialism, by keeping the US military intensely occupied for a generation in the second half of the 19th century. 2 notes, 31 ref.   G. J. Bobango

588. Osborne, James D. PATERSON: IMMIGRANT STRIKERS AND THE WAR OF 1913. Conlin, Joseph R., ed. *At the Point of Production: The Local History of the I.W.W.* (Westport, Conn.: Greenwood Pr., 1981) 61-78. Details the history of the textile strike of 1913 in Paterson. Police, city government, and the local judiciary combined to back local manufacturers against strikers. Almost 2,000 mill hands were arrested, picket lines broken up, and workers' processions dispersed. Even strike headquarters were closed down. The Industrial Workers of the World attracted attention to the strike, bringing it before a national audience, and for a time seemed near to prompting federal intervention and a favorable settlement. The central incident of the strike was the death of Valentino Modestino, an Italian metal worker who lived in Paterson's Riverside section. The strike resulted in the partial emigration of the industry, the changed ethnic composition of the workforce, and the reform of local government, particularly the police department. Based on US Bureau of Census data, journal articles; 60 notes.   J. Powell

589. Osur, Alan M. THE ROLE OF THE COLORADO NATIONAL GUARD IN CIVIL DISTURBANCES. *Military Affairs 1982 46(1): 19-24.* Analysis of the role of the Colorado National Guard in a civil disturbance role: strike duty within the state. The guard developed out of the insecurity of the mining frontier of the early 1860's and was utilized when law and order had collapsed and the governor recognized that its reestablishment was beyond the power of local officials. Its involvement ran the gamut from peaceful occupation to hazardous involvement, and the guard saw action in such places as Leadville, Lake City, Cripple Creek, the southern coalfields, and the University of Denver. Its main difficulties were that it was not prepared for a civil disturbance role and that it often did not act in an impartial manner. Based on Colorado and other primary sources; 30 notes.   A

590. Parman, Donald L. THE "BIG STICK" IN INDIAN AFFAIRS: THE BAI-A-LIL-LE INCIDENT IN 1909. *Arizona and the West 1978 20(4): 343-360.* Disagreements developed in 1907 between federal officials and a band of Navajo Indians in southeastern Utah who refused to send their children to boarding school. The Indians, whose leader was Bai-a-lil-le, a medicine man, were seized by federal troops and sent to Fort Huachuca, Arizona, where they were tried without the customary legal procedures. The Indian Rights Association took court action. Bai-a-lil-le and his followers were finally released in 1909. The incident demonstrates the nature of Indian affairs in the early years of the century, provides an insight into Indian reform organization effectiveness, and reveals much about racial attitudes. 2 illus., map, 41 notes.   D. L. Smith

591.   Pfaff, Eugene.   GREENSBORO SIT-INS.   *Southern Exposure 1981 9(1): 23-28.* Interviews four people involved behind the scenes in the 1960 sit-in by black students at a segregated lunch counter in Greensboro, North Carolina, and in the second wave of protests in 1962: William A. Thomas, Jr., a high school student; Dr. Elizabeth "Lizzie" Laizner, a teacher at Bennett College, a black women's college in Greensboro; Clarence C. "Buddy" Malone, Jr., Movement lawyer; and Dr. Willa B. Player, president of Bennett College.

592.   Poteet, James M.   UNREST IN THE "LAND OF STEADY HABITS": THE HARTFORD RIOT OF 1722.   *Pro. of the Am. Phil. Soc. 1975 119(3): 223-232.* Details the event that led up to the Hartford riot of 1722. A mob of his tenants freed Jeremiah Fitch from jail on 22 October 1722. Fitch had refused to vacate disputed lands awarded by the courts to Major John Clark. Fitch and the mob held their lands through purchase from the Indians, while Clark had received his from the colonial government. The government was hard pressed to restore order after this riot. For Connecticut, it was a period of social change. Population growth, disagreement on the validity of land sales by Indians, and an impotent legislature torn between a rigid governor and a populistic lower house caused such examples of social instability. Based on primary and secondary sources; 85 notes.   W. L. Olbrich

593.   Prioli, Carmine A.   THE URSULINE OUTRAGE.   *Am. Heritage 1982 33(2): 100-105.* Anti-Catholicism led, in 1834, to the burning of Mount Benedict school for girls, an Ursuline order school established in 1820 in Charlestown, Massachusetts. The men accused of the crime were tried and acquitted, and the state legislature failed several times to vote indemnification to the school. 5 illus.
                                                      J. F. Paul

594.   Raphalides, Samuel J.   THE PRESIDENT'S USE OF TROOPS IN CIVIL DISORDER.   *Presidential Studies Q. 1978 8(2): 180-187.* Examines the President's constitutional and statutory authority to use federal troops during civil disorders. Articles I and IV of the Constitution plus various statutes passed since 1789 and surviving in sections 331-333 of Title 10 of the United States Code provide for federal intervention with or without a state's request. Semantical inconsistencies have given the President broad discretionary powers in determining what constitutes "domestic violence." Historic examples of federal intervention are discussed including the Whisky Rebellion, the Pullman Strike of 1894, and the civil rights disorders of the 1960's. Despite the reluctance of Presidents to exercise these extensive powers, there is concern about possible abuses. The National Emergencies Act (US, 1976) addresses this concern, but more should be done to define the circumstances where intervention may be employed. 43 notes, biblio.   S. C. Strom

595.   Rothenberg, Irene Fraser.   CHICANOS, THE PANAMA CANAL ISSUES AND THE REAGAN CAMPAIGN: REFLECTIONS FROM 1976 AND PROJECTIONS FOR 1980.   *J. of Ethnic Studies 1980 7(4): 37-49.* Mexican Americans, like many US ethnic groups before them, are beginning to see themselves as a domestic lobby for policies favoring the homeland, as evidenced by the unanimity and intensity of the Mexican American and Spanish-language press opposition to Ronald Reagan's Panama Canal treaties position in the spring of 1976. Content analysis of all available issues of 12 newspapers published

between 1 April and 8 June 1976 showed them to be bitterly against Reagan. Any efforts by the ex-governor to revive the issue against the Carter administration in 1980 is certain to provoke a dramatic Chicano response. This group indeed has a better reason than most minorities to look beyond US boundaries in seeking an ethnic identity, living as it does in "conquered Mexico." Contemporary ethnic press, secondary works; 36 notes.   G. J. Bobango

596. Rudwick, Elliott. A TALE OF TWO RIOTS. *J. of Urban Hist. 1978 4(2): 239-246.* Compares William I. Hair's *Carnival of Fury: Robert Charles and the New Orleans Race Riot of 1900* with Robert V. Haynes's *A Night of Violence: The Houston Riot of 1900.* Hair's monograph is more of a biography than a case study of the New Orleans riot, and not fully successful at either endeavor. Haynes's work is a good example of the type of research that is needed on interracial violence.   T. W. Smith

597. Rutherford, Philip. THE GREAT GAINESVILLE HANGING. *Civil War Times Illus. 1978 17(1): 12-20.* Gainesville, in Cook County, north Texas, was a seat of a Unionist secret organization. By use of informers, members were identified. Confederate troops and militia poured into the area, and 150 were arrested. Martial law was declared. A people's court was constituted, and prisoners testified against each other. At first few were condemned and hanged, but there was a brief respite with two-thirds of a jury vote replacing majority vote for condemnation. The mob intervened, and the hysteria was revived. The hangings, over several weeks, included: 26 hanged by the peoples court, 15 by the mob, two shot, and three hanged by the military. The roles of certain individuals are discussed.   H. M. Ward

598. Ryan, James Gilbert. THE MEMPHIS RIOTS OF 1866: TERROR IN A BLACK COMMUNITY DURING RECONSTRUCTION. *J. of Negro Hist. 1977 62(3): 243-257.* During 1-3 May 1866, race rioting in downtown Memphis resulted in nearly 50 deaths, mostly of Negroes, and widespread destruction of property, mostly Negroes'. Earlier accounts blamed black ex-soldiers but ignored the responsibility of white policemen for the onset of the rioting. Previous historical treatment also failed to examine the aggravation of the rioting by white civilian politicians and the refusal of federal General George Stoneman to declare martial law until 3 May when the black community had been ravaged. Primary and secondary materials; 95 notes.   N. G. Sapper/S

599. Sadler, Lynn Veach. DR. STEPHEN GRAHAM'S NARRATION OF THE "DUPLIN INSURRECTION": ADDITIONAL EVIDENCE OF THE IMPACT OF NAT TURNER. *J. of Am. Studies [Great Britain] 1978 12(3): 359-367.* Describes a journal kept by Stephen Graham (1786-1834) of Kenansville, North Carolina, and reprints a portion in which Graham recorded in detail the suppression of slave rebellions in Duplin County, North Carolina, in 1831. 17 notes.   H. T. Lovin

600. Schafer, Judith Kelleher. THE IMMEDIATE IMPACT OF NAT TURNER'S INSURRECTION ON NEW ORLEANS. *Louisiana Hist. 1980 21(4): 361-376.* In the aftermath of Nat Turner's rebellion in August 1831, Louisiana and New Orleans in particular enacted laws and ordinances to control the black population. Few doubted that a revolt could occur in Louisiana. News-

papers violated their own policies by writing about slave revolts, and from these editorials we see that they blamed abolitionists and black preachers for encouraging servile revolutions. In Louisiana, Nat Turner's rebellion produced new laws to control slaves and free Negroes and efforts by writers to defend slavery as a beneficial system for the slaves. Based on newspapers, letters, and journals of official proceedings of the Louisiana state government; 73 notes.

R. H. Tomlinson

601.   Schneirov, Richard.   CHICAGO'S GREAT UPHEAVAL OF 1877. *Chicago Hist. 1980 9(1): 2-17.* During the national railroad strike of 1877, unskilled laborers (mainly Irish, German, Bohemian, and Polish) in Chicago during 23-26 July went on strike, went about in crowds to enlist other workers, and fought bloody battles with the police and the state militia; many workers won restoration of their recently cut wages.

602.   Schwantes, Carlos A.   LAW AND DISORDER: THE SUPPRESSION OF COXEY'S ARMY IN IDAHO.   *Idaho Yesterdays 1981 25(2): 10-26.* The Coxeyite army that tried to move across southern Idaho in May of 1894 was arrested for commandeering Union Pacific rolling stock. After a trial, federal judge James H. Beatty sentenced 184 men to prison for 30 to 60 days. A special compound was built, and the army helped guard it. Based on letters and newspaper accounts; 6 photos, 51 notes.   B. J. Paul

603.   Vandal, Gilles.   LE ROLE JOUE PAR LE PARTI REPUBLICAIN LOUISIANAIS DANS L'EMEUTE DE LA NOUVELLE-ORLEANS DE 1866   [The role played by the Louisiana Republican Party in the New Orleans Riot of 1866]. *Louisiana Rev. 1981 10(1): 51-75.* Analyzes the events leading to the New Orleans Riot of 1866; contrary to the generally accepted interpretation, it had not been initiated by the Radical Republicans. French.

604.   Vandal, Gilles.   THE ORIGINS OF THE NEW ORLEANS RIOT OF 1866, REVISITED.   *Louisiana Hist. 1981 22(2): 135-165.* Examines the immediate causes of the New Orleans racial riot of 30 July 1866, in which 40 to 50 were killed and 150 to 300 were wounded. The riot was caused by the social tension surrounding the movement to reconvene the 1864 convention, the application of the new federal Civil Rights Act to two controversial cases in New Orleans in July, and the emotions aroused by speeches given at a preliminary meeting of the conventionists on 27 July. Primary sources; 5 tables, 102 notes.

J. Powell

605.   Vandal, Gilles.   VIOLENCE ET RELATIONS RACIALES A LA NOUVELLE-ORLEANS PENDANT LA GUERRE CIVILE: UN PRELUDE A L'EMEUTE DU 30 JUILLET 1866   [Violence in racial relations in New Orleans during the Civil War: a prelude to the riot of 30 July 1866]. *Can. Rev. of Am. Studies [Canada] 1982 13(1): 15-38.* After federal forces occupied New Orleans during the Civil War, the social and demographic character of the city changed with the influx of many blacks. Lincoln's Reconstruction policies raised the newcomers' social expectations but ran counter to the wishes of many in the city's economic and political elites. Political struggles over federal policies generated bitterness and tension, which finally produced a major riot on 30 July 1866. Based on National Archives materials, newspapers, and other primary and secondary sources; 105 notes. French.   H. T. Lovin

606. Williams, William J. BLOODY SUNDAY REVISITED. *Pacific Northwest Q. 1980 71(2): 50-62.* On 5 November 1916, the steamship *Verona* carried approximately 250 members of the Industrial Workers of the World (IWW) from Seattle to a rally at Everett, Washington. A large number of Everett's deputized citizens attempted to stop the landing and gunshots were fired by unidentified assailants. Seven people were killed and 47 wounded in the "Everett Massacre" before the *Verona* could escape and return to Seattle. Documents recently uncovered at the Seattle Federal Archives and Records Center offer new eyewitness testimony about the event, but fail to answer the ultimate question of who fired the initial shots. 5 photos, map, 13 notes. M. L. Tate

607. Woodward, Isaiah A. JOHN BROWN'S RAID AT HARPERS FERRY AND GOVERNOR HENRY ALEXANDER WISE'S LETTER TO PRESIDENT JAMES BUCHANAN CONCERNING THE INVASION. *West Virginia Hist. 1981 42(3-4): 307-313.* Discusses the letter from Governor Henry Alexander Wise to President James Buchanan with regard to John Brown's Harpers Ferry raid in 1859. Based on the correspondence and journal articles. J. D. Neville

608. Zellick, Anna. PATRIOTS ON THE RAMPAGE: MOB ACTION IN LEWISTOWN, 1917-1918. *Montana 1981 31(1): 30-43.* Patriotism in Lewistown, Montana, reached hysterical proportions during World War I, exacerbated by a large ethnic population, coupled with suspicion of the Industrial Workers of the World and the Nonpartisan League activities in the area. This hysteria produced numerous violations of civil liberties and culminated in a spontaneous demonstration on 27 March 1918, an anti-German book burning, and possible arson of the Fergus County Free High School. Based on contemporary newspapers; 9 illus., 75 notes. R. C. Myers

609. —. THE MISSISSIPPI MOVEMENT. *Southern Exposure 1981 9(1): 40-42, 45-48.* Background to the Mississippi Movement, first noticed nationwide when three civil rights workers were murdered during summer 1964, followed by interviews with Ella Jo Baker on the decision to invite students from around the country for an organizing project in Mississippi under the sponsorship of the Council of Federated Organizations (COFO), an umbrella group for NAACP, CORE, SNCC, etc., and Fannie Lou Hamer on her role in the Mississippi Freedom Democratic Party's delegation to the Democratic National Convention in 1964.

610. —. THE NASHVILLE SIT-INS: NONVIOLENCE EMERGES. *Southern Exposure 1981 9(1): 30-32.* Provides a brief background to black college students' sit-ins in Nashville, Tennessee, during winter, 1960, and interviews Marion Barry and John Lewis, participants who provided leadership for Civil Rights Organizations for several years after 1960.

5

POLITICAL CRIMES AND CORRUPTION

611. Alexander, Milnor. POLITICAL REPRESSION IN THE USA. *Can. Dimension 1976 11(6): 16-22.* Discusses 1946-50's repression of political radicals, the Communist Party, and ordinary citizens by the House Committee on Un-American Activities, by Congress in such legislation as the International Security Act of 1950 (the McCarran Act) and the McCarran-Walter Immigration Act of 1952, and by state loyalty oaths.

612. Alexander, Thomas G. TEAPOT DOME REVISITED: REED SMOOT AND CONSERVATION IN THE 1920S. *Utah Hist. Q. 1977 45(4): 352-368.* In the Teapot Dome scandal investigation of the early 1920's, Utah Senator Reed Smoot (1862-1941) was consistent with his previous conservation activity. He was a business-minded conservationist who favored combined private, state, and federal control, preservation, and development of natural resources. He saw the need to recover and store oil for future naval use. The transfer and drilling were matters of administrative discretion. Primary and secondary sources; 3 illus., 41 notes.
J. L. Hazelton

613. Anders, Roger M. THE ROSENBERG CASE REVISITED: THE GREENGLASS TESTIMONY AND THE PROTECTION OF ATOMIC SECRETS. *Am. Hist. Rev. 1978 83(2): 388-400.* This article examines how the U.S. Atomic Energy Commission solved the security problem raised by David Greenglass' testimony against the Rosenbergs. It discusses how the Commission verified the technological data in the Greenglass testimony and how it took measures to protect other closely related technological secrets. Using documents recently declassified it shows that Greenglass tried to tell the truth about the technology of the atomic bomb. Refers to earlier article by Michael Parrish (see abstract 1131).
A

614. Anderson, Jack and Boyd, James. THE REPUBLICANS' FALL FROM POWER. *Washington Monthly 1979 11(2): 12-26.* Discusses the role of the press in exposing House corruption in relation to an investigation by a subcommittee of the House Commerce Committee, 1957-58.

615. Aragonnès, Claude. LINCOLN ASSASSINÉ: UN DRAME SHAKE-SPEARIEN [Lincoln assassinated: a Shakespearian drama]. *Miroir de l'Hist. [France] 1959 (120): 1574-1584.* Describes the last days of President Abraham Lincoln, 8-14 April 1865, and his assassination in a theater, by an actor, John Wilkes Booth.

616. Archdeacon, Thomas J. THE ERIE CANAL RING, SAMUEL J. TILDEN, AND THE DEMOCRATIC PARTY. *New York Hist. 1978 59(4): 409-429.* The economic decline of New York State's Erie and Oswego Canals culminated in post-Civil War allegations of corruption by contractors and politicians who had a common interest in profiting from canal repairs—the Erie Canal Ring. Samuel J. Tilden, elected governor in 1874, appointed an independent commission to investigate canal repairs since 1868 and the Ring's operations. Few convictions resulted from the commission's findings, but canal management was reformed. The Canal Ring investigation enchanced Tilden's popularity on the eve of the 1876 presidential race. Suggests that Tilden was a timid reformer motivated by political ambition. 6 illus., 35 notes.   R. N. Lokken

617. Banner, James M., Jr. HISTORIANS AND THE IMPEACHMENT INQUIRY: A BRIEF HISTORY AND PROSPECTUS. *Rev. in Am. Hist. 1976 4(2): 139-149.* Review article prompted by C. Vann Woodward, ed., *Responses of the Presidents to Charges of Misconduct* (New York: Dell, 1974); discusses the role of historians in 1974 in compiling evidence for the Impeachment Inquiry of the House Judiciary Committee.

618. Barnes, Merritt. "FOUNTAINHEAD OF CORRUPTION": PETER P. MCDONOUGH, BOSS OF SAN FRANCISCO'S UNDERWORLD. *California History 1979 58(2): 142-153.* For more than 25 years Peter P. McDonough and his brother Tom controlled San Francisco's vice operations. Outwardly a successful businessman, having established the first bail bonds business in the United States in 1896, McDonough became a millionaire through his connections to gambling, prostitution, graft, bootlegging, and political contacts. Without his approval, vice operations could not operate. For almost three decades San Franciscans tolerated the situation. McDonough's control of vice prevented the gang wars that occurred in other cities during this period. McDonough's fall from power is attributed to a change in public attitude caused by the Great Depression. People objected to the millions gained by vice when their own economic prospects were dim. When the Atherton Investigation of 1935 uncovered clear evidence of police graft, politicians abandoned McDonough. He lost his bail bond license in 1937. Despite repeated efforts, he never regained the license or his power. Photos, 70 notes.   A. Hoffman

619. Barros, James. ALGER HISS AND HARRY DEXTER WHITE: THE CANADIAN CONNECTION. *Orbis 1977 21(3): 593-606.* The contents of a personal diary kept by Canadian Prime Minister William Lyon Mackenzie King give further information on the espionage activities of Alger Hiss and Harry Dexter White as related to King (and thence to Harry S. Truman) by Igor Gouzenko, a defector from the USSR to Canada, 1945.

620. Bates, J. Leonard. WATERGATE AND TEAPOT DOME. *South Atlantic Q. 1974 73(2): 145-159.* In both the Teapot Dome Scandal and the Watergate Scandal the executive branch attempted to withhold evidence which Congress tried to discover. Compares the roles of Senators Thomas J. Walsh and Samuel J. Ervin. In the earlier period the scandals occurred because Secretary of the Interior Albert B. Fall and others took payoffs; the men around Nixon were not interested in personal gain. "The methods by which Fall exploited both the Navy Department and the marines are reminiscent of the later manipulations of

the Federal Bureau of Investigation, the Central Intelligence Agency, the Internal Revenue Service, and other agencies." 4 notes.   E. P. Stickney

621.   Becker, Lee B.   TWO TESTS OF MEDIA GRATIFICATIONS: WATERGATE AND THE 1974 ELECTION.   *Journalism Q. 1976 53(1): 28-33, 87.* Describes two studies in which the level of knowledge about Senate Committee hearings on the Watergate scandal and the congressional elections of 1974 was measured to test the effect of motives for using or avoiding political news. Reasons tested for using news were voting guidance, keeping up with events, entertainment, and information for future discussions. Motives for avoidance were alienation, partisanship, and lack of interest. Results of the two studies varied. Based on primary sources; 2 tables, 16 notes.   K. J. Puffer

622.   Beloff, Max.   AMERICA AFTER WATERGATE: THE DANGERS OF CONSTITUTIONAL UTOPIANISM.   *Round Table [Great Britain] 1975 (257): 29-36.* Examines the impact of the Watergate scandal on American politics. Many Americans believe that their institutions successfully resolved the immediate constitutional crisis. There are two kinds of constitutional utopianism. The first holds that the Constitution works most effectively when presidential leadership can be exercised honestly. The second attaches greater importance to what can be done by legislation within the present structure.   C. Anstey

623.   Bensman, Joseph.   WATERGATE: IN THE CORPORATE STYLE. *Dissent 1973 20(3): 279-280.*

624.   Benson, George C. S.   CAUSES AND CURSES OF POLITICAL CORRUPTION.   *West Georgia Coll. Studies in the Social Sci. 1975 14: 1-19.* Discusses economic, legal, social class, and ethical aspects of the historiography of political corruption in federal, state, and local government from the 1870's-1970's.

625.   Berger, Raoul.   EXECUTIVE PRIVILEGE IN LIGHT OF UNITED STATES V. NIXON.   *Maryland Historian 1975 6(2): 67-78.* Traces the history of executive privilege which was recognized in *United States* v. *Nixon* (US, 1974). Contends that no basis for executive privilege exists in the constitution nor is intent to establish executive privilege evidenced in the commentary of the framers of the constitution. Based on primary and secondary constitutional law sources; 70 notes.   G. O. Gagnon

626.   Berwanger, Eugene H.   ROSS AND THE IMPEACHMENT: A NEW LOOK AT A CRITICAL VOTE.   *Kansas Hist. 1978 1(4): 235-242.* Edmund Ross (1826-1907) was one of seven Republicans who voted to acquit President Andrew Johnson (1808-75). His vote had less to do with idealism than it did with a belief that an attempt was being made to destroy his political career. He intimated that the trial had degenerated into a scheme by certain Republicans to retain control of the government through patronage. Letters to President Johnson reveal the degree to which Ross believed this to be true. A letter from Henry C. Whitney (1831-1905) to the editor of the Burlington *Kansas Patriot* on 13 June 1868 reveals the degree to which Ross feared Kansas Senator Samuel C. Pomeroy (1816-91) and Representative Sidney Clarke (1831-1909) were conspiring to turn out all of Ross's friends after the conviction of Johnson. Illus., 35 notes.
                    W. F. Zornow

627. Bethell, Tom. WAS SIRHAN SIRHAN ON THE GRASSY KNOLL? *Washington Monthly 1975 7(1): 31-39.* A former associate of Jim Garrison, head of the Kennedy assassination investigation, analyzes the common elements among believers in conspiracies as the "answer" to political crimes.   S

628. Bickel, Alexander M. WATERGATE AND THE LEGAL ORDER. *Commentary 1974 57(1): 19-25.* Discusses ideological motivation in relation to the Watergate Scandal.   S

629. Blakey, George T. CALLING A BOSS A BOSS: DID ROOSEVELT LIBEL BARNES IN 1915? *New York Hist. 1979 60(2): 195-216.* Theodore Roosevelt, defendant in a $50,000 libel suit brought against him by William Barnes, Jr., used the courtroom as a forum for his attack on political bossism and corruption, defense of democratic principles against political machine rule, and an attempt to restore his political prestige. Barnes, long influential in New York Republican politics, sued Roosevelt for having publicly called him a corrupt political boss. The trial revealed the contrasting political styles and philosophies of the principals. Based on the New York State Supreme Court trial records. 10 illus., 45 notes.   R. N. Lokken

630. Bloom, Richard. SILAS DEANE: PATRIOT OR RENEGADE? *Am. Hist. Illus. 1978 13(7): 32-42.* Silas Deane (1737-89), a Connecticut politician initially chosen to secure financial and military aid from France during the American Revolution, was accused by subsequent diplomat to France, Arthur Lee, of having personally profitted from his negotiations. Deane kept poor records and thus was vulnerable but he further alienated Congress by defending his position and attacking Lee in the press. When the French he dealt with did not assist him, Deane began an exile in England and Holland. After the publication of private letters allegedly written by Deane and urging a US-British conciliation short of US independence, Deane was branded a traitor. Deane may have mixed profit and patriotism, as other colonials had done, but he did secure large quantities of needed supplies for the colonial cause.   D. Dodd

631. Bone, Beverly. EDWIN STANTON IN THE WAKE OF THE LINCOLN ASSASSINATION. *Lincoln Herald 1980 82(4): 508-521.* Reassesses some accepted historical views on the actions and involvement of Secretary of War Edwin M. Stanton during the capturing, imprisonment, and trials of the people involved in the assassination of President Abraham Lincoln.

632. Boyd, Marjorie. IS THE PRESIDENT A PERJURER? *Washington Monthly 1975 7(8): 32-38.* Explores allegations that Gerald R. Ford perjured himself during his confirmation hearings for the vice presidency when he denied sidetracking House investigations of the Watergate Scandal at the order of President Nixon.   S

633. Brodie, Fawn M. "I THINK HISS IS LYING." *Am. Heritage 1981 32(5): 4-21.* Excerpts from Fawn M. Brodie's *Richard Nixon: The Shaping of His Character* (1981) in which Richard M. Nixon's role in the trial and conviction (for perjury) of Alger Hiss is retraced, and similarities between the character of Hiss and Nixon are noted. 9 illus.   J. F. Paul

634.   Brooks, John.   THE BUSINESSMAN AND THE GOVERNMENT: CORRUPTION, YESTERDAY AND TODAY.   *Am. Heritage 1977 28(4): 66-73.* Graft and corruption were present in the colonial period and during the American Revolution. The "golden age of graft" came in the years after the Civil War. In the 1890's, bribery was involved in getting overseas contracts for American businesses. After reform efforts of the Progressive period and the New Deal, the post-World War II era became the first in which government had more financial favors to confer on business than vice versa. 7 illus.   J. F. Paul

635.   Brownfeld, Allan C.   POLITICAL CORRUPTION: ONE RESULT OF ALL-POWERFUL GOVERNMENT AND CENTRALIZED POWER. *Freeman 1973 23(11): 643-647.*

636.   Bruns, Roger.   ASSASSINATION ATTEMPT OF PRESIDENT ANDREW JACKSON.   *West Tennessee Hist. Soc. Papers 1977 31: 33-43.* On 30 January 1835, on the steps of the US Capitol, Richard Lawrence attempted to kill President Andrew Jackson. This was the first attempt on the life of a President. The attacker was wrestled to the ground by the crowd and Jackson. Jackson's friends endeavored to find conspiracy as a motive, but the later investigation ruled this out. Lawrence suffered from the delusion that he was King of England and was found not guilty by means of insanity. Based on proceedings of the trial in congressional documents and newspaper accounts; 3 pictures, 30 notes.
H. M. Parker, Jr.

637.   Bukowski, Douglas.   JUDGE EDMUND K. JARECKI: A RATHER REGULAR INDEPENDENT.   *Chicago Hist. 1979-80 8(4): 206-218.* Judge Edmund Kasper Jarecki of Cook County, Illinois (1879-1966), was the Democrat-backed judge in charge of Chicago's elections from 1922-54 who fought corruption and misconduct to clean up the elections.

638.   Bulman, Raymond F.   LOVE, POWER, AND THE JUSTICE OF THE U.S. PRESIDENTIAL PARDONS.   *J. of Church and State 1979 21(1): 23-38.* Focuses on the legal and ethical issues surrounding Gerald R. Ford's unconditional pardon of Richard M. Nixon and conditional amnesty for Vietnam War resisters and deserters. The Nixon pardon was possibly illegal because it frustrated the completion of the judicial process by pardoning a man before he was convicted. It was unethical because it applied a double standard of justice. Based on the works of Paul Tillich and secondary sources; 27 notes.   S

639.   Burton, William L.   DOES CORRUPTION PAY?   *Midwest Q. 1976 18(1): 53-63.* Discusses the effect of corruption on political parties. Watergate provides a model indicating that when corruption in a national party is exposed that party suffers in the next election. Earlier examples do not bear out this theory. Corruption was a public issue during the administrations of Presidents Ulysses S. Grant and Warren Harding, yet the party in power during the scandals maintained its political position in the following election. Corruption is rarely the only election issue. Voters often are more concerned with other issues. Historically, the exposure of corruption has not been a serious handicap to a national party. Biblio.   S. J. Quinlan

640. Bushnell, Eleanor. THE IMPEACHMENT AND TRIAL OF JAMES H. PECK. *Missouri Hist. Rev. 1980 74(2): 137-165.* James Hawkins Peck was defendant in the fourth federal impeachment and trial in the nation's history. He was named district judge in Missouri at a time when the new state was torn by political strife and beset with many questionable land claims. Peck in 1825 invalidated a claim held by Antoine Soulard because there was no definite proof of ownership. Luke Lawless, one of Soulard's attorneys, was held in contempt for publishing a letter critical of the decision. The letter and Judge Peck's reaction were at the center of the impeachment. Lawless decided that impeachment was the only way to keep Peck from hearing more land cases. Efforts to impeach Peck began in the House in 1826, but they were not crowned with success until 1830. In 1831 the Senate acquitted Peck. The impeachment was unique: it was initiated and directed by just one complainant, and it is the only impeachment in which just a single charge of misconduct was levied. Based on Arthur Stansbury's *Report of the Trial of James H. Peck,* and on recollections and articles; illus., 62 notes.   W. F. Zornow

641. Butler, Broadus N. FOUNDER'S DREAM AND AMERICAN RE-ALITY. *Crisis 1977 84(2): 71-79.* The Watergate Scandal was a crisis of moral integrity and leadership. There is a need for intellectual and spiritual leadership as we enter our third century.   A. G. Belles

642. Candeloro, Dominic. LOUIS F. POST AND THE RED SCARE OF 1920. *Prologue 1979 11(1): 41-55.* In 1920 as Assistant Secretary of Labor, 71-year-old Louis F. Post successfully thwarted the arbitrary and capricious enforcement of the Alien Anarchist Act (US, 1918), by which scores of foreign-born radicals were deported under the aegis of Attorney General Mitchell Palmer and his assistant J. Edgar Hoover. Post, a long-time sympathizer with left-wing causes and a public admirer of the Russian Revolution, came under intensive Congressional scrutiny for his stand and an effort was made to remove him from office through impeachment proceedings. The effort failed, owing in large part to Post's own inspired defense of his position before Congressional committees. Post's insistence that due process and a rigid adherence to law mark governmental operations against foreign-born radicals did a great deal to stem the tide of wanton and arbitrary deportation of dissenters resident in the United States. Based mainly on research in the National Archives.   N. Lederer

643. Caraley, Demetrios, et al. AMERICAN POLITICAL INSTITUTIONS AFTER WATERGATE—A DISCUSSION. *Pol. Sci. Q. 1974/75 89(4): 713-750.* States " . . . first impressions about the long-term impact of the Watergate events on American political institutions."   J

644. Caraley, Demetrios and Greissman, Edythe, eds. SEPARATION OF POWERS AND EXECUTIVE PRIVILEGE: THE WATERGATE BRIEFS. *Pol. Sci. Q. 1973 88(4): 582-654.* "The editors reprint the original legal briefs filed in the historic lawsuit to obtain for grand jury use the tape recordings of presidential conversations concerning the Watergate break-in. While President Nixon's attorneys argue in their brief that if disclosure of the tapes can be compelled by the courts 'the damage to the institution of the Presidency will be severe and irreparable,' the brief of the Special Watergate Prosecutor contends that 'even the highest executive officials are subject to the rule of law' and 'there is no exception

for the President from the guiding principle that the public, in pursuit of justice, has a right to every man's evidence.' "   J

645.   Chan, Ying Kwong and Starck, Kenneth.   THE NEW YORK *TIMES'* STANCE ON NIXON AND PUBLIC OPINION.   *Journalism Q. 1976 53(4): 723-727.* Concerning the resignation and proposed impeachment of Richard M. Nixon, *The New York Times* seems to have preceded the formulation of public opinion in 1973 by proposing an impeachment process before the majority agreed with it and urging the President to resign before a consensus was formed.

646.   Cherne, Leo and Drummond, Roscoe.   THE CHALLENGE OF WATERGATE: TWO OFFICERS OF FREEDOM HOUSE DISCUSS THE REINFORCING OF CONSTITUTIONAL GOVERNMENT.   *Freedom At Issue 1973 (20): 2-5.* President Nixon must eliminate the scandal in his administration or suffer paralysis of his foreign policy.   S

647.   Clark, Janet M.   MORAL PREREQUISITES OF POLITICAL SUPPORT: BUSINESS REACTIONS TO THE WATERGATE SCANDAL. *J. of Pol. Sci. 1979 7(1): 40-61.* A case study of the impact of Watergate on political support indicates a strong relationship between diffuse and specific support. Without sufficient diffuse support, due to the scandal, President Richard M. Nixon was without a solid political base for taking desired actions for improving the economy; it appears that his economic failures rather than his moral shortcomings were of primary concern. Based on editorials and feature articles in major business publications, and on other published materials; 12 tables, 40 notes, 3 appendixes.   T. P. Richardson

648.   Clarke, James W.   AMERICAN ASSASSINS: AN ALTERNATIVE TYPOLOGY.   *British J. of Pol. Sci. [Great Britain] 1981 11(1): 81-104.* Attempts a psychological classification of assassins and would-be assassins in the United States from Richard Lawrence in 1835 to Sara Jane Moore in 1975.

649.   Cochran, Hamilton.   BOOTH'S OTHER PISTOL.   *Civil War Times Illus. 1975 13(9): 20-24.* A discussion of the possibility that John Wilkes Booth had an auxiliary weapon besides the derringer he used to shoot Abraham Lincoln.
                                                                           S

650.   Cohen, Robert A.   UNITED STATES EXCLUSION AND DEPORTATIONS OF NAZI WAR CRIMINALS: THE ACT OF OCTOBER 30, 1978. *New York U. J. of Int. Law and Pol. 1980 13(1): 101-133.* Discusses the workability and constitutionality of recent changes in the Immigration and Nationality Act (US, 1952; amended 1978), designed to exclude and deport former Nazi war criminals.

651.   Combs, Bert T.   WILLIAM GOEBEL (BOONE DAY ADDRESS, 1978).   *Register of the Kentucky Hist. Soc. 1978 76(4): 307-313.* Recounts the life and career of William Justus Goebel (1856-99), the only American governor who was assassinated while in office. Elected in a disputed election in 1899 Goebel was shot on 30 January and died on 3 February, shortly after being sworn into office. Three men were tried and convicted for the murder, although trial errors resulted in appeals, retrials, and eventual pardons for two of the three. One of those convicted, Caleb Powers, ran for Congress after being pardoned and served from 1910-20.   J. F. Paul

652. Conner, Cliff. THE LEFT AND WATERGATE. *Internat. Socialist R. 1973 34(11): 12-17, 41-42.*

653. Conyers, John, Jr. WHY NIXON SHOULD BE IMPEACHED. *Black Scholar 1974 6(2): 2-8.* As a member of the House Judiciary Committee, the author maintains that Nixon should have been impeached because of his extension of the Vietnam War and authorization and concealment of Cambodian bombing.

654. Cooney, Charles F., ed. AT THE TRIAL OF THE LINCOLN CON-SPIRATORS: THE REMINISCENCES OF GENERAL AUGUST V. KAUTZ. *Civil War Times Illus. 1973 12(5): 22-31.*

655. Cooney, Charles F. TREASON OR TYRANNY? THE GREAT SEN-ATE PURGE OF '62. *Civil War Times Illus. 1979 18(4): 30-31.* By vote of the US Senate on 5 February 1862, Jesse D. Bright (1812-75) of Indiana gained "the singular distinction of being the only senator from a non-slave state to be expelled from the Senate during the Civil War for treason"; on 1 March 1861 he had written a letter of introduction to Jefferson Davis for a friend who had "an improvement in firearms."

656. Cooper, Melvin G. ADMINISTERING ETHICS LAWS: THE ALA-BAMA EXPERIENCE. *Natl. Civic Rev. 1979 68(2): 77-81.* The reason 40 or more states have passed ethics laws during the past few years is the undermining of the trust of the citizens by corrupt behavior on the part of a few officials at every level of government. Discusses not outright bribery or thievery, but rather a total lack of ethical standards where a separation of public responsibilities and private business interests are involved. The amendments of 1975 weakened the law, but the "removal of many of the overkill provisions made it far easier to administer and implement." Chief Justice Warren said in 1962 "that such laws cannot be effective unless there is law behind the law, i.e., an ethical concept on the part of all those who accept public responsibilities." E. P. Stickney

657. Davenport, John F. SKINNING THE TIGER: CARMINE DE SAPIO AND THE END OF THE TAMMANY ERA. *New York Affairs 1975 3(1): 72-93.* Discusses the career of Carmine DeSapio, the last of the Tammany Hall bosses, emphasizing his activities during the 1950's and 60's. S

658. Davis, Kenneth S. INCIDENT IN MIAMI. *Am. Heritage 1980 32(1): 86-95.* An account of the attempted assassination of Franklin D. Roosevelt by Giuseppe Zangara in Miami, Florida, on 15 February 1933. Zangara wounded several persons, including Chicago's Mayor Anton Cermak who died on 6 March. Zangara was tried and executed. Roosevelt refused to let the incident unnerve him. 12 illus. J. F. Paul

659. Decter, Midge. NOTES FROM THE AMERICAN UNDER-GROUND. *Commentary 1982 73(1): 27-33.* Key members of the Weather Underground, the Black Liberation Army, and other fugitive groups involved in terrorist activities in the late 1960's and early 1970's, including Kathy Boudin, were captured in October 1981, and only recently has the Left disassociated itself from these terrorist groups, whose revolutionary activity was previously viewed as innocent idealism or insanity.

660.   Demos, John.   JOHN GODFREY AND HIS NEIGHBORS: WITCH-CRAFT AND THE SOCIAL WEB IN COLONIAL MASSACHUSETTS. *William and Mary Q. 1976 33(2): 242-265.* John Godfrey, unlike other men accused of witchcraft, was a bachelor. Details Godfrey's life from the time of his arrival in New England, about 1634, until his death in 1675. Godfrey was involved in numerous litigations. He brought suit for slander for being called a witch in 1659, resulting in a trial for witchcraft which ended in acquittal. Tried again in 1666, he was barely acquitted. Afterward he was convicted of various minor crimes. Lists six reasons in the sociocultural context for Godfrey's prosecution as a witch. The problems of Godfrey represent the collective life of the community versus the individual. Based on court and other local records. 64 notes.   H. M. Ward

661.   Deutsch, Kenneth L.   EXISTENTIALISM AND LIBERAL DEMO-CRATIC VALUES: REFLECTIONS ON INDIVIDUALISM AND COR-RUPTION IN AMERICAN POLITICS.   *West Georgia Coll. Studies in the Social Sci. 1975 14: 67-90.* Discusses the effect of political corruption on existential and fatalistic attitudes of intellectuals toward liberalism, individualism, and democratic values in the 20th century.

662.   Domer, Thomas.   THE ROLE OF GEORGE S. BOUTWELL IN THE IMPEACHMENT AND TRIAL OF ANDREW JOHNSON.   *New England Q. 1976 49(4): 596-617.* A combination of party animosity, concern for Negro suffrage in the South, and a genuine fear that Andrew Johnson was conspiring to seat, by force if necessary, a Congress controlled by Democrats and representatives from the southern states as well as to seize control of the government, prompted Congressman George S. Boutwell of Massachusetts to lead the drive to impeach the president. Based on congressional records and newspapers; 51 notes.   J. C. Bradford

663.   Dunham, Roger G. and Mauss, Armand L.   WAVES FROM WATER-GATE: EVIDENCE CONCERNING THE IMPACT OF THE WATER-GATE SCANDAL UPON POLITICAL LEGITIMACY AND SOCIAL CONTROL.   *Pacific Sociol. Rev. 1976 19(4): 469-490.* Discusses the impact of the Watergate scandal on public opinion toward the Nixon administration, political leadership, and the US political system in general in 1973-74.

664.   Dunlay, Thomas W.   GENERAL CROOK AND THE WHITE MAN PROBLEM.   *J. of the West 1979 18(2): 3-10.* General George Crook recognized that corrupt government Indian agents, and the expansion of white settlement, did much to provoke Indian violence. Crook publicly advocated citizenship for Indians and recognition of their legal rights in courts of law. Reformers, including Crook, were overly optimistic about the Indians' ability to adapt to a settled, agricultural life. In reaction to the gross abuses of Indian agents, military men frequently suggested that Indian affairs become a function of the War Department. Crook was one of the most outspoken critics of white greed, which, as he saw it, caused most of the Indian troubles. Published sources and some government records; 4 photos, 57 notes.   B. S. Porter

665. Elsmere, Jane Shaffer. THE TRIALS OF JOHN FRIES. *Pennsylvania Mag. of Hist. and Biog. 1979 103(4): 432-445.* Samuel Chase's instructions to the jury in the second Fries treason case (1800) were later (1804-05) utilized in the bill of impeachment against the judge. Fries's arrest and first trial, in 1799, resulted from his rescue of Pennsylvanians who had been confined by a US marshal on an insurrection charge after they had resisted federal excise officers. Based on newspapers, official records, and secondary sources; 31 notes.

T. H. Wendel/S

666. Emerson, Thomas I. SOUTHERN JUSTICE IN THE THIRTIES. *Civil Liberties Rev. 1977 4(1): 70-74.* Uses Charles H. Martin's *The Angelo Herndon Case and Southern Justice* (Baton Rouge: Louisiana State U. Pr., 1976) to chronicle the 1932 Atlanta, Georgia case against a young black Communist who organized a protest regarding depletion of county relief funds, was arrested and convicted under the Georgia Insurrection Law, was defended by the largely Communist International Labor Defense of New York, and was freed from an 18-to-20-year sentence by the US Supreme Court in 1937.

667. Epstein, Edward Jay. DID THE PRESS UNCOVER WATERGATE? *Commentary 1974 58(1): 21-24.* Discounts the thesis of Carl Bernstein and Bob Woodward's *All the President's Men* (New York: Simon & Schuster, 1974).

S

668. Erskine, Hazel. THE POLLS: CORRUPTION IN GOVERNMENT. *Public Opinion Q. 1973/74 37(4): 628-644.* Traces the public opinion polls on corruption perceived in government during the course of six presidential administrations. The Harris Poll reported that the 46% who agreed in 1967 that "most politicians are in politics to make money for themselves" had expanded to 63% by late 1973. Utilizes published findings of 10 research organizations.

E. P. Stickney

669. Evans, Les. WATERGATE AND THE WHITE HOUSE: FROM KENNEDY TO NIXON AND BEYOND. *Internat. Socialist R. 1973 34(11): 4-11, 25-40.* Consistent accumulation of presidential power, especially in the Nixon administration, culminated in the Watergate Scandal. S

670. Fairlie, Henry. THE LESSONS OF WATERGATE—ON THE POSSIBILITY OF MORALITY IN POLITICS. *Encounter [Great Britain] 1974 43(4): 8-27.* Discusses the ramifications of the break-in escapade, 1972-74, in which President Nixon gradually became enmeshed, and through which the corruption of his entire administration was sanctioned, showing that in general public opinion the Watergate scandal was viewed as normal politics.

671. Felt, Jeremy P. VICE REFORM AS A POLITICAL TECHNIQUE: THE COMMITTEE OF FIFTEEN IN NEW YORK, 1900-1901. *New York Hist. 1973 54(1): 24-51.* History of the Committee of Fifteen, an upper-middle-class reform organization dedicated to the eradication of police-protected vice and gambling in New York City. To committee members, the antivice crusade was the most effective tactic in the political war against Tammany Hall. Defeat of Tammany, rather than moral reform, was their primary objective. Primary and secondary sources; 11 illus., 36 notes.

G. Kurland

672.   Ferguson, E. James and Nuxoll, Elizabeth Miles.   INVESTIGATION OF GOVERNMENT CORRUPTION DURING THE AMERICAN REVOLUTION.   *Congressional Studies 1981 8(2): 13-35.* Discusses Congressional investigations into political corruption during the American Revolution, focusing on Robert Morris, Silas Deane, Arthur Lee, Benedict Arnold, and James Mease.

673.   Flaccus, Elmer W.   ARIZONA'S LAST GREAT INDIAN WAR: THE SAGA OF PIA MACHITA.   *J. of Arizona Hist. 1981 22(1): 1-22.* Chronicles the consternation and excessive reaction of Bureau of Indian Affairs bureaucrats, federal marshals, and paranoid Arizonans to the intransigent resistance of Pia Machita, a Papago leader in 1940-41. He refused to allow draft registration for his band, and, after a series of comic attempts to force the octogenarian to capitulate, he was imprisoned for 16 months. Based on contemporary records and reminiscences; 4 illus., 52 notes.   G. O. Gagnon

674.   Flatto, Elie.   THE IMPEACHMENT OF A PRESIDENT: REFLECTIONS ON WATERGATE.   *Contemporary Rev. [Great Britain] 1973 223(1292): 129-131.* Discusses the Watergate hearings of 1973 as a televised public trial, making the impeachment of President Richard M. Nixon seem academic.

675.   Flatto, Elie.   THE IMPEACHMENT OF RICHARD M. NIXON. *Contemporary Rev. [Great Britain] 1975 226(1310): 146-148.* Reflections on the "trial by television" of President Nixon in 1973-74 and the possible effects of his resignation.

676.   Frazer, Catherine S.   THE TRAGEDY OF WATERGATE.   *Midwest Q. 1973 15(1): 8-15.*

677.   Frome, Michael.   BLOWING THE WHISTLE.   *Center Mag. 1978 11(6): 50-58.* Offers six case histories of civil servants who reported substandard service, inefficiency, or political corruption, and were fired.

678.   Fry, Brian R. and Stolarek, John S.   THE IMPEACHMENT PROCESS: PREDISPOSITIONS AND VOTES.   *J. of Pol. 1980 42(4): 1118-1134.* The House Judiciary Committee voted three of five bills of impeachment against President Richard M. Nixon in 1974. Members of the committee confronted a problem of information overload and those predisposed to support Nixon may have experienced cognitive dissonance. The attitude of each member on each bill of impeachment could be predicted by: liberal or conservative ideology, party membership, and district's vote for Nixon during the 1972 presidential election. Of 190 votes, 165 were successfully predicted by these criteria. While politics did not determine Nixon's fate, it did condition the interpretation of the Watergate affair. 2 tables, 38 notes.   A. W. Novitsky

679.   Gallagher, Robert S.   "I WAS ARRESTED, OF COURSE."   *Am. Heritage 1974 25(2): 16-24, 92-94.* Interview with Alice Paul (b. 1885) on her role in the women's suffrage movement, the ratification of the 21st amendment, and the early beginnings of the Equal Rights Amendment.   S

680. Galvin, John T. THE DARK AGES OF BOSTON POLITICS. *Massachusetts Hist. Soc. Pro. 1977 89: 88-111.* During the 1880's women emerged as a political force, questions of corruption emerged, the park system developed, the parochial school system was debated, and Irish Americans became a force in local politics. Many of these issues' effects are still felt. Primary and secondary sources; 109 notes. G. W. R. Ward

681. George, Joseph, Jr. NATURE'S FIRST LAW: LOUIS J. WEICH- MANN AND MRS. SURRATT. *Civil War Hist. 1982 28(2): 101-127.* Louis J. Weichmann, one of Mrs. Mary Surratt's boarders, was the government's star witness on the guilt of Mrs. Surratt in her trial for complicity in the assassination of Abraham Lincoln. Fear for his own life caused Weichmann to change his testimony and not tell the truth in a number of instances. Based on papers relating to the assassination of Lincoln; 89 notes. G. R. Schroeder

682. Giddens, Paul H. THE NAVAL OIL RESERVE, TEAPOT DOME AND THE CONTINENTAL TRADING COMPANY. *Ann. of Wyoming 1981 53(1): 14-27.* Traces the Teapot Dome Scandal beginning in 1921 when Secretary of the Interior Albert Fall received control over the naval oil leases from the secretary of the navy. Despite immediate complaints from Senator Robert LaFollette, Congress was slow to investigate the questionable transfer, and President Calvin Coolidge offered little help when the question was again raised in 1923. Senator Thomas Walsh kept the issue before a congressional committee and in 1924 uncovered the financial connection between Fall and oil magnates Edward Doheny and Harry Sinclair. Amid the unraveling of the scandal, three cabinet officers resigned and Fall went to prison. Based on congressional studies of naval oil leases; 4 photos, 84 notes. M. L. Tate

683. Gienapp, William E. THE CRIME AGAINST SUMNER: THE CAN- ING OF CHARLES SUMNER AND THE RISE OF THE REPUBLICAN PARTY. *Civil War Hist. 1979 25(3): 218-245.* South Carolina Democratic Congressman Preston S. Brooks's caning of Massachusetts Republican Senator Charles Sumner on the Senate floor on 22 May 1856, after Sumner had made scathing personal attacks on Brooks's relative, South Carolina Democratic Senator Andrew P. Butler, created even more support for the fledgling Republican Party than did the repeal of the Missouri Compromise and the troubles in the Kansas Territory. Describes the instant, rampant, and deep-seated indignation in the North, protest meetings, Republican themes, the destruction of Millard Fillmore's chances in the 1856 election, and John Frémont's good showing in that election. The caning caused such political and sectional animosity that it "was a major landmark on the road to civil war." 97 notes. S

684. Gouran, Dennis S. THE WATERGATE COVER-UP: ITS DYNAM- ICS AND ITS IMPLICATIONS. *Communication Monographs 1976 43(3): 176-186.* Discusses the group dynamics of the Watergate scandal of 1972, examining its background, four aspects of the group dynamic process, and the implications of the "group-think" process for American politics.

685. Grant, Marilyn. JUDGE LEVI HUBBELL: A MAN IMPEACHED. *Wisconsin Mag. of Hist. 1980 64(1): 28-39.* Levi Hubbell, judge of the second circuit court, associate justice, and chief justice of Wisconsin's first supreme

court, was first active as a Whig in New York, then as a Democrat and finally a Republican in Wisconsin. Charged on multiple counts of bribery, prejudice, improper judicial behavior, and several other articles, Hubbell was prosecuted before the Senate by his arch-Democratic foe, Edward G. Ryan. Although acquitted, Hubbell was the only judge in Wisconsin ever to be impeached, and that stigma effectively ended his influence in the state and shortened his judicial career. Covers 1827-76. 10 illus., note.   N. C. Burckel

686. Grigulevich, I. R.   DELO SUPRUGOV ROZENBERG   [The Rosenbergs]. *Voprosy Istorii [USSR] 1980 (11): 87-96.* An account of the case, trial, and execution of Soviet atomic spies Julius and Ethel Rosenberg, 1951-53. The arrest of the Rosenbergs was seen as a move to strengthen the Cold War and to frighten progressive elements within the United States. 38 notes.

S. J. Talalay

687. Guggenheim, Colette.   L'AFFAIRE HISS, UNE AFFAIRE DREYFUS AMÉRICAINE?   [The Hiss affair, an American Dreyfus affair?]. *Esprit [France] 1975 (1): 106-112.* In the wake of the resignation of Richard Nixon, the case of Alger Hiss has received renewed attention. A review of the facts in the Hiss case supports the need to reexamine whether or not Hiss received justice. Compares the Hiss case with that of Alfred Dreyfus, who was eventually vindicated, and suggests the possible vindication of Hiss. 6 notes.

G. F. Jewsbury

688. Häggman, Bertil.   THE VULNERABLE MODERN INDUSTRIAL SOCIETY.   *Jerusalem J. of Int. Relations [Israel] 1978 3(4): 1-18.* Because of increased technological development in the United States, Western Europe, particularly Sweden, and Japan, modern industrial society is seen as being vulnerable to threats of political terrorism.

689. Hanchett, William.   BOOTH'S DIARY.   *J. of the Illinois State Hist. Soc. 1979 72(1): 39-56.* Reviews the evidence presented in a book and film, *The Lincoln Conspiracy* (1977), to the effect that a gigantic conspiracy was responsible for the assassination of President Abraham Lincoln, and that John Wilkes Booth was set up for the blame. The case rests on missing pages in Booth's diary, which the men behind the movie claim have been recovered, although they have failed to produce them. Covers evidence that contradicts such a view, and closes with the argument that Secretary of War Edwin M. Stanton suppressed the diary for the purpose of preventing ex-rebels and sympathizers from making a martyr of Booth. 10 illus., 40 notes.   V. L. Human

690. Hanchett, William.   THE WAR DEPARTMENT AND BOOTH'S ABDUCTION PLOT.   *Lincoln Herald 1980 82(4): 499-508.* Reevaluates sources that led Otto Eisenschiml and researchers influenced by him to the conclusion that the War Department knew about a conspiracy, conceived by John Wilkes Booth, to kidnap President Abraham Lincoln in the spring of 1865.

691. Handlin, Oscar.   WATERGATE: REFLECTIONS FROM AFAR. *Freedom At Issue 1973 (21): 11-13.*

692. Harrington, Michael. WATERGATE: ON POLITICS AND MONEY. *Dissent 1973 20(3): 278-279.*

693. Harris, Charles H., III and Sadler, Louis R. THE 1911 REYES CONSPIRACY: THE TEXAS SIDE. *Southwestern Hist. Q. 1980 83(4): 325-348.* Views the Mexican Revolution from a Texan perspective. General Bernardo Reyes tried to overthrow Mexican President Francisco I. Madero in 1911 with support from Mexican American politicians in Texas, and the benevolent neutrality of state officials. But when the plot fell apart under pressure from the US government, Texas Governor Oscar B. Colquitt claimed credit. Reyes's associates, Amador Sanchez and Francisco A. Chapa, were defended by leading Texas lawyers and received light sentences and friendly treatment from federal judge Waller T. Burns. Primary sources; 78 notes. J. H. Broussard

694. Harrison, Lowell H. THE AARON BURR CONSPIRACY. *Am. Hist. Illus. 1978 13(3): 16-25.* Aaron Burr (1756-1836) was born in Newark, New Jersey, graduated from Princeton, and was state attorney-general and US Senator before becoming Vice-President in 1800. He challenged Alexander Hamilton for the top legal position in New York City in 1783; that rivalry ended in an infamous duel years later. Faced by indictments in New York and New Jersey, Burr purchased 350,000 acres on the Washita River and organized an expedition to settle it. Covertly, he considered taking Spanish-held Baton Rouge and New Orleans, possibly to use the latter as a base for a sea invasion of Mexico. Betrayed by a coconspirator, James Wilkinson, Burr was arrested and taken to Richmond for trial. Thomas Jefferson pushed the prosecution, but Wilkinson proved a poor witness as his involvement with Burr became apparent. Presiding Judge John Marshall's interpretation of treason as requiring an overt act (rather than just advising treason) made possible the exclusion of most collateral testimony, and Burr's acquittal followed. Primary and secondary sources; 12 illus. D. Dodd

695. Harrison, Robert. THE HORNET'S NEST AT HARRISBURG: A STUDY OF THE PENNSYLVANIA LEGISLATURE IN THE LATE 1870'S. *Pennsylvania Mag. of Hist. and Biog. 1979 103(3): 334-355.* Inexperience, lack of party discipline, corruption, logrolling, and constituent disinterest all influenced the legislature, which was characterized by untidy procedures and importuned by conflicting interests. Based on Randall Papers, University of Pennsylvania, official records, newspapers, and secondary sources; 88 notes. T. H. Wendel

696. Havens, Murray Clark and McNeil, Dixie Mercer. PRESIDENTS, IMPEACHMENT, AND POLITICAL ACCOUNTABILITY. *Presidential Studies Q. 1978 8(1): 5-18.* The Watergate experience has highlighted the inadequacy of present restraints on the chief executive. The quasi-legal impeachment procedure, the election process, and the party system have not prevented presidential incompetence or malfeasance. Impeachment is viewed as a time consuming, paralyzing process to determine the personal guilt or innocence of an office holder. The feasibility of alternative methods of removal is discussed. Impeachment based on the concept of the collective executive is the only realistic solution. Congress must abandon its parochial concerns and assume a watchdog function by refusing to pass legislation, appropriate funds, or confirm nominations, by casting censure votes, and finally by impeaching the president for poor performance by any member of the administration. 32 notes. S. C. Strom

697.   Head, Constance.   INSIGHTS ON JOHN WILKES BOOTH FROM HIS SISTER ASIA'S CORRESPONDENCE.   *Lincoln Herald 1980 82(4): 540-544.* Conveys a portrait of John Wilkes Booth, depicted by his sister Asia Booth Clarke in 45 letters written between 1852 and 1874 to her childhood friend Jean Anderson.

698.   Head, Constance.   J. W. B.: HIS INITIALS IN INDIA INK.   *Virginia Mag. of Hist. and Biog. 1982 90(3): 359-366.* Discusses the unresolved controversy over the presence (or absence) and description of the self-inflicted tattoo John Wilkes Booth bore on his hand. Witnesses' and friends' accounts of the tattoo's location, size, and appearance differ greatly. This uncertainty contributes to speculation about the identity of the man shot at Garrett's farm near Bowling Green, Virginia, following the Lincoln assassination. Based on records at the National Archives and Records Service, and secondary sources.
D. J. Cimbala

699.   Head, Constance.   JOHN WILKES BOOTH IN AMERICAN FICTION.   *Lincoln Herald 1980 82(3): 454-462.* Discusses approaches to the assassin of President Abraham Lincoln, actor John Wilkes Booth, as tragic hero and as villain in American fiction since the first piece appeared for sale in 1865—by Ned Buntline (Edward Zane Carroll Judson).

700.   Helfand, Barry.   LABOR AND THE COURTS: THE COMMON-LAW DOCTRINE OF CRIMINAL CONSPIRACY AND ITS APPLICATION IN THE BUCK'S STOVE CASE.   *Labor Hist. 1977 18(1): 91-114.* Details the origins and development of the legal fight between the Buck's Stove and Range Co. and the American Federation of Labor during 1907-11. The decision continued the anti-labor tendency of the courts and utilized the common-law doctrine of criminal conspiracy to refute labor's defense of freedom of speech. Based upon legal records and court reports; 66 notes.
L. L. Athey

701.   Hoffer, Peter C. and Hull, N. E. H.   THE FIRST AMERICAN IMPEACHMENTS.   *William and Mary Q. 1978 35(4): 653-667.* Discusses the impeachments of Governor John Harvey of Virginia (1635), Councillor John Morecroft, Captain Thomas Trueman, sheriff Charles James, and Indian agent Jacob Young in Maryland (1669-83), and Chief Justice Nicholas More in Pennsylvania (1685). The English background for impeachment by the House of Commons dated to the 14th century. The early American impeachments, although conducted with some knowledge of English precedents, were experimental. None involved criminal penalties. Notes similarities and differences of these six cases and their influence on subsequent impeachment doctrine. Based largely on the colonial archives; 24 notes.
H. M. Ward

702.   Hoffer, Peter C. and Hull, N. E. H.   POWER AND PRECEDENT IN THE CREATION OF AN AMERICAN IMPEACHMENT TRADITION: THE EIGHTEENTH-CENTURY COLONIAL RECORD.   *William and Mary Q. 1979 36(1): 51-77.* Searches the American past before the Constitution for precedents for impeachment. Six celebrated cases are detailed: Captain Samuel Vetch, Massachusetts, 1706; James Logan, provincial agent for Pennsylvania, 1703; Chief Justice Nicholas Trott, South Carolina, 1719; Chief Justice William Smith, North Carolina, 1739; county Judge William Moore, Pennsylvania, 1758-

59; and Chief Justice Peter Olivers, Massachusetts, 1773. Some discussion also on English 17th- and 18th-century precedents. Contemporary sources; 49 notes.

H. M. Ward

703. Hoffman, Daniel. CONTEMPT OF THE UNITED STATES: THE POLITICAL CRIME THAT WASN'T. *Am. J. of Legal Hist. 1981 25(4): 343-360.* An analysis of how the founders of the United States understood the First Amendment ramifications of government secrecy. The author assesses the early criminal prosecutions during 1794-98, focusing on events involving freedom of the press and political libel: the Cobbett Case (1797), Bache's Case (1798), Duane's Case (1800), and the Sedition Act of 1798. The founders believed fervently that the First Amendment protected the people in their right to know what the government did, and that the disclosure of government secrets was not a criminal offense as long as the facts were true. Based on court records, government documents, and newspapers; 50 notes.

L. A. Knafla

704. Hogan, Neil. A LOYALIST EXECUTION. *New-England Galaxy 1978 20(2): 52-60.* Describes the events surrounding the execution of Moses Dunbar of Waterbury, Connecticut, in 1777, he was hanged in Hartford after being convicted of treason for enlisting with the British Army and for encouraging others to enlist during the American Revolution.

705. Hollinger, David A. THE CONFIDENCE MAN. *Rev. in Am. Hist. 1979 7(1): 134-141.* Review article prompted by Allen Weinstein's *Perjury: The Hiss-Chambers Case* (New York: Alfred A. Knopf, 1978).

706. Hoogenboom,Ari and Hoogenboom,Olive. WAS BOSS TWEED REALLY SNOW WHITE? *Rev. in Am. Hist. 1977 5(3): 360-366.* Review article prompted by Leo Hershkowitz's *Tweed's New York: Another Look* (Garden City, N.Y.: Anchor Pr., 1977), which argues William Tweed's innocence of corruption in the control of public works in New York City from 1869 to 1871.

707. Hook, Sidney. AN AUTOBIOGRAPHICAL FRAGMENT: THE STRANGE CASE OF WHITTAKER CHAMBERS. *Encounter [Great Britain] 1976 46(1): 78-89.* Discusses the role of Whittaker Chambers as a witness in the 1949 trial which convicted Alger Hiss of perjury concerning espionage on behalf of the Communist Party.

708. Hook, Sidney. THE CASE OF ALGER HISS. *Encounter [Great Britain] 1978 51(2): 48-55.* Analyzes research by Allen Weinstein in *Perjury: The Hiss-Chambers Case* (New York: Alfred A. Knopf); due to the evidence Weinstein changed his mind and concluded that, without a doubt, Alger Hiss was guilty of espionage and treason despite his persistent denials.

709. Hook, Sidney. DAVID CAUTE'S FABLE OF "FEAR & TERROR": ON "REVERSE MCCARTHYISM." *Encounter [Great Britain] 1979 52(1): 56-64.* In British author David Caute's fantasy *The Great Fear: The Anti-Communist Purge under Truman and Eisenhower* (New York: Simon and Schuster) liberal US anti-Communists emerge as the major villains. He calls Communist Party members mere "Leftists," refuses to admit Soviet control over the Communist Party, USA, thinks Communist Party membership not a legitimate issue in security risk and espionage cases, treats facts and quotations cava-

lierly and selectively, and ignores not only the arguments of the anti-Communist liberals he criticizes but also the Korean War, the danger of war with the USSR, and the genuine Fifth Column activity of the CPUSA. 5 notes.

D. J. Engler

710.   Howe, Irving.   WATERGATE: THE Z CONNECTION.   *Dissent 1973 20(3): 275-277.*

711.   Hurst, James Willard.   WATERGATE: SOME BASIC ISSUES. *Center Mag. 1974 7(1): 11-25.* Views the work of the Senate's "Watergate Committee" against the background of Congressional investigative functions and of separation-of-powers issues.   S

712.   Iakovlev, N. N.   IZ ISTORII KLANA KENNEDI   [From the history of the Kennedy clan]. *Voprosy Istorii [USSR] 1970 (9): 113-128.* Discusses the circumstances surrounding the assassination of President John F. Kennedy. Emphasizes the apparent incompetence displayed by the police holding the alleged assassin Lee Harvey Oswald and by the investigatory committee set up by President Johnson. The report produced by this committee was criticized both from the political right and left but the most cogent criticism came from Mark Lane in his book *Rush to Judgement* (New York: 1966). Describes the agreement made between the Kennedy family and W. Manchester about the latter's exclusive right of access to material concerning Kennedy and criticizes the chase for profits in which many other writers engaged. Mentions Robert Kennedy's ambitions and gives a brief analysis of his character. Article to be continued. Published sources; 45 notes.   S

713.   Ingram, Timothy H.   ITT AND WATERGATE: THE COLSON CONNECTION.   *Washington Monthly 1973 5(9): 32-37.*

714.   Ives, C. P.   SCHOOLING FOR WATERGATE.   *Modern Age 1977 21(3): 289-294.* Because bright young Nixon lawyers had been schooled by left-leaning Yale (and other) professors, they were prepared to try new methods rather than work through old channels; so—just as leftward expostulations in the 40's and 50's based on the philosophies of New Dealers in the 30's caused McCarthyist radicalism—liberal teachers of the 60's caused the Watergate scandal.

715.   Ives, C. P.   WATERGATE: TWO PARABLES AND A PROPOSITION.   *Modern Age 1976 20(2): 141-153.* Parable I concerns a young Public Man and a drive from a cottage party. Parable II concerns a government worker who publicized classified materials. They lead to the proposition that the total phenomenon of the Watergate scandal happened because present security laws are unreasonable. Based on primary court documents and secondary sources; 21 notes.   M. L. Lifka

716.   James, Judson Lehman and James, Dorothy Buckton.   LESSONS OF WATERGATE: THE NIXON CAMPAIGNS.   *Current Hist. 1974 67(395): 30-33, 38.* Discusses the impact of the Watergate scandal on political parties and analyzes Nixon's campaigns of 1968 and 1972. One of seven articles in this issue on the two-party system.   S

717. Jeffreys-Jones, Rhodri. REVIEW ESSAY: WEINSTEIN ON HISS. *J. of Am. Studies [Great Britain] 1979 13(1): 115-126.* Review article prompted by Allen Weinstein's *Perjury: The Hiss-Chambers Case* (London: Hutchinson, 1978), a work in which the author attempted to prove that Alger Hiss perjured himself (and thereupon was sentenced to five years' imprisonment in 1950). Weinstein's book, although favorably reviewed elsewhere and based on substantial new evidentiary material, may not be "definitive." Moreover, Weinstein failed to "deflate the cult of martyrdom" in which Hiss's partisans have enshrouded him. 21 notes. H. T. Lovin

718. Johnson, James P. THE ASSASSINATION IN DALLAS: A SEARCH FOR MEANING. *J. of Psychohistory 1979 7(1): 105-121.* Reviews the following books on Lee Harvey Oswald and the assassination of John F. Kennedy: Edward J. Epstein's *Legend: The Secret World of Lee Harvey Oswald* (New York: Reader's Digest Pr. and McGraw-Hill Book Co., 1978) and Priscilla Johnson McMillan's *Marina and Lee* (New York: Harper and Row, 1977). Epstein emphasizes elements of the assassination drama indicating a conspiracy directed by the KGB. McMillan focuses on Lee Harvey Oswald's childhood, and the trauma responsible for his solitary, violent acts. 36 notes. M. R. Strausbaugh

719. Johnson, Ralph H. and Altman, Michael. COMMUNISTS IN THE PRESS: A SENATE WITCH-HUNT OF THE 1950S REVISITED. *Journalism Q. 1978 55(3): 487-493.* In the mid-1950's the US Senate Internal Security Subcommittee conducted investigative hearings on the alleged influence of Communists in the press. Although the hearings were without legislative purpose, they raised issues regarding the rights of congressional witnesses. During the period, the US Supreme Court ruled on those rights, especially in *Watkins* v. *United States* (US, 1957) and *Barenblatt* v. *United States* (US, 1959), and usually decided against persons accused of being Communists. Newspaper publishers often fired employees for associating with Communists and in general were slow to recognize and debate the threat to constitutional rights posed by the hearings and court decisions. 38 notes. R. P. Sindermann, Jr.

720. Kaiser, Frederick M. PRESIDENTIAL ASSASSINATIONS AND ASSAULTS: CHARACTERISTICS AND IMPACT ON PROTECTIVE PROCEDURES. *Presidential Studies Q. 1981 11(4): 545-558.* Since 1804, attacks on presidents have been occurring with more frequency, forcing the Secret Service to almost continually reexamine its procedures. The service has responded by increasing its cooperation with the Federal Bureau of Investigation and the National Security Agency, and by greatly increasing its protective activities of different individuals. From its origins as an anticounterfeiting organization in the 1890's, the Secret Service has expanded and continually modified its methods. But, it is still an agency with limited law enforcement authority, and thus it remains restricted. Table, 62 notes. D. H. Cline

721. Kelly, Alfred H. HISTORY AS THEATER. *Rev. in Am. Hist. 1976 4(1): 132-137.* Review article prompted by Theodore H. White's *Breach of Faith: The Fall of Richard Nixon* (New York: Atheneum, 1975) which documents the personal character of Nixon and the involvement in political corruption which led to his political demise.

722. Kilar, Jeremy W. "THE BLOOD-RUGGED ISSUE IS IMPEACH-MENT OR ANARCHY": MICHIGAN AND THE IMPEACHMENT AND TRIAL OF ANDREW JOHNSON. *Old Northwest 1980 6(3): 245-269.* Examines the process in Michigan between 1865 and 1868, which created the eventual consensus for the impeachment of President Andrew Johnson. Johnson's intransigence against congressional Reconstruction policies was used by politicians and the press to persuade the people to support impeachment. The study of the impeachment campaign in Michigan demonstrates the depth and diversity of the antipathy displayed against Johnson by the populace. It also provides an insight into the process by which consensus may be developed within the body politic. Based on the Blair Papers in the Burton Historical Collection at the Detroit Public Library and other primary sources; 67 notes.   P. L. McLaughlin

723. King, Duane H. and Evans, E. Raymond. THE DEATH OF JOHN WALKER, JR: POLITICAL ASSASSINATION OR PERSONAL VEN-GEANCE? *J. of Cherokee Studies 1976 1(1): 4-16.* Concludes that John Walker, Jr., was assassinated by James Foreman for political rather than private motivations. Walker was a proremoval Cherokee leader during the 1820's-30's. Although there were personal animosities between Walker and Foreman because of Foreman's bootlegging of whiskey into Cherokee lands, Foreman had never acted on them. Foreman also was implicated in other politically motivated killings. John Ross may have been involved. Primary and secondary sources; 2 photos, map, 66 notes.   J. M. Lee

724. Kirk, Russell. THE PERSISTENCE OF POLITICAL CORRUPTION. *Center Mag. 1974 7(1): 2-7.* Discussion of political corruption from the time of ancient Greeks to the Watergate Scandal.   S

725. Kramer, Rita. "WELL, WHAT ARE YOU GOING TO DO ABOUT IT?" *Am. Heritage 1973 24(2): 17-21, 94-97.* Richard Croker (1843?-1922), better known as "Boss Croker," became the leader of Tammany Hall and usually dominated politics in New York City 1886-1901. He seemed immune to bitter satirical attacks against the graft and corruption of his reign, and his typical response to muckrakers' detailed charges of police corruption was, "Well, what are you going to do about it?" He lost bids to get control of the state and national Democratic Party mechanisms, and he retired to the splendor of his English, Irish, and Florida estates. 7 illus.   D. L. Smith

726. Kurtz, Henry I. THE IMPEACHMENT OF ANDREW JOHNSON. *Hist. Today [Great Britain] 1974 24(5): 299-306, (6): 396-405.*

727. Kurtz, Michael L. LEE HARVEY OSWALD IN NEW ORLEANS: A REAPPRAISAL. *Louisiana Hist. 1980 21(1): 7-22.* Outlines Lee Harvey Oswald's arcane life (1939-63) and demonstrates that many intriguing questions about his five-month stay in New Orleans (April-September 1963) remain unanswered. Returning to his native city in these months shortly before the 22 November assassination of President John F. Kennedy in Dallas, Oswald quickly developed close ties with pro- and anti-Castro groups. Although the Federal Bureau of Investigation and the Central Intelligence Agency had him under close surveillance at this time, significant information on Oswald's Cuban connections is missing from the FBI's John F. Kennedy Assassination Files which were

released in December 1977 and January 1978. Based on FBI and CIA files and several confidential interviews; 38 notes.   D. B. Touchstone

728. Lamb, Blaine P. "A MANY CHECKERED TOGA": ARIZONA SENATOR RALPH H. CAMERON, 1921-1927. *Arizona and the West 1977 19(1): 47-64.* Ralph Henry Cameron (1863-1953) was the first Republican Senator from Arizona. His single term, 1921-27, was controversial. He did not hesitate to castigate the federal bureaucracy and to seek federal aid at the same time. He was charged with personal impropriety and political corruption. He alienated many of his colleagues and constituents and lost his bid for reelection. 2 illus.; 43 notes.
D. L. Smith

729. Lasky, Melvin J. JOHN REED & ALGER HISS: TWO CASES IN IDEOLOGY. *Encounter [Great Britain] 1982 59(2): 86-93.* Compares the careers of 20th-century Communists John Reed and Alger Hiss and reviews two film accounts of their activities: Warren Beatty's *Reds* and a British Broadcasting Corporation documentary on Hiss.

730. Lee, David L. THE ATTEMPT TO IMPEACH GOVERNOR HORTON. *Tennessee Hist. Q. 1975 34(2): 188-201.* The close relationship between Governor Henry Horton and Rogers Caldwell led to an investigation of Caldwell's financial activities involving state funds upon the collapse of his empire in 1930. An investigation led by Horton's political opponent, E. H. Crump, soon implicated the Tennessee governor in negligent, if not fraudulent, handling of state money. In 1931, to avoid impeachment, Horton and his allies began making blatant political deals with Democrats and Republicans, a controversial policy which proved successful in the end. 37 notes.   M. B. Lucas

731. Lemmey, William. BOSS KENNY OF JERSEY CITY, 1949-1972. *New Jersey Hist. 1980 98(1-2): 9-28.* John V. Kenny, a Hague ward healer for many years, was in power in Jersey City for 23 years both as an officeholder and power broker. He offered the poor, elderly, and displaced city resident hope and turned political defeats into victories by manipulating circumstances to his advantage and by rebuilding his organization on the ashes of his former opponent. Kenny, in short, would do business with anyone. A scandal having to do with the extortion of money from contractors used by Jersey City put an end to Kenny's reign; a conviction for income tax evasion sent him to jail. Based on newspaper accounts, interviews, court records, and secondary sources; 5 illus., 3 tables, 31 notes.   E. R. McKinstry

732. Levin, David. IN THE COURT OF HISTORICAL CRITICISM: ALGER HISS'S NARRATIVE. *Virginia Q. R. 1976 52(1): 41-78.* Comparing Alger Hiss's *In the Court of Public Opinion* (1972), Whittaker Chambers's *Witness* (1968) and Richard M. Nixon's *Six Crises* (1962), the author concludes not only that Hiss is innocent, but that the legal principle which presumes the accused innocent until proven guilty was reversed both by the House Committee on Un-American Activities and the court. He marshals evidence to demonstrate "the value of historical criticism in both the understanding of factual books and the evaluation of a baffling case."   O. H. Zabel

733.   Levine, Arthur.   THE MAN WHO NAILED GORDON LIDDY. *Washington Monthly 1974 6(10): 38-48.* Exposes the political ethics of Henry Petersen, a public official whose reputation emerged largely unscathed despite the Watergate Scandal.   S

734.   Maness, Lonnie E. and Chesteen, Richard D.   THE FIRST ATTEMPT AT PRESIDENTIAL IMPEACHMENT: PARTISAN POLITICS AND IN-TRA-PARTY CONFLICT AT LOOSE.   *Presidential Studies Q. 1980 10(1): 51-62.* Studies the role of impeachment in the American constitutional system. Sixty-six impeachment attempts reached the investigative stage; many others never advanced beyond their introduction. Some involved presidents; the first (1843) was against President John Tyler, the second and third were against President Herbert C. Hoover in 1932 and 1933. Already in 1787, voices were warning that impeachment power could be abused for partisan reason. 65 notes.
                                                                    G. E. Pergl

735.   Marbury, William L.   THE HISS-CHAMBERS LIBEL SUIT.   *Maryland Hist. Mag. 1981 76(1): 70-92.* The author was counsel for and life-long friend of Alger Hiss, accompanying the accused man in his initial response to the Communist espionage accusations of Whittaker Chambers before the House Committee on Un-American Activities. Reviews Hiss's life and relates the background and facts of the filing of Hiss's $50,000 libel suit against Chambers on 27 September 1948 in Maryland's US District Court. Discusses the author's subsequent interrogations of Chambers, and the problem of recovered State Department memoranda and the Hiss typewriter which helped produce Hiss's indictment in New York in December 1948, his trials, his conviction for perjury, and his imprisonment, which brought a dismissal with prejudice of the libel suit in April 1951. Based on Marbury's own notes and recall.   G. J. Bobango/S

736.   Marina, William.   SHOOTING DOWN THE CONSPIRACY THE-ORY.   *Reason 1979 11(1): 18-24.* While admitting that the Warren Commission made errors of judgment in its study of President Kennedy's assassination, concludes that alternative theories—especially those suggesting conspiracy—are implausible, and that the Warren Commission's conclusions are basically correct.

737.   Markowitz, Arthur M., ed.   TRAGEDY OF AN AGE: AN EYEWIT-NESS ACCOUNT OF LINCOLN'S ASSASSINATION.   *J. of the Illinois State Hist. Soc. 1973 66(2): 205-211.* Reprints an overlooked account of Abraham Lincoln's assassination, that of Roeliff Brinkerhoff (1828-1911), a general in the Quartermaster Corps. Brinkerhoff's seat gave him a view of the president's theater box and thus of the assassination. The account also describes the capture of John Wilkes Booth at Richard H. Garrett's farm and Sergeant Boston Corbett's shooting of Booth. Based on Brinkerhoff's autobiography; illus., 11 notes.
                                                                    A. C. Aimone

738.   Markowitz, Gerald E. and Meeropol, Michael.   THE "CRIME OF THE CENTURY" REVISITED: DAVID GREENGLASS' SCIENTIFIC EVI-DENCE IN THE ROSENBERG CASE.   *Sci. & Soc. 1980 44(1): 1-26.* The US government perpetrated a fraud in the trial that led to the execution of Julius and Ethel Rosenberg in 1953 for allegedly passing on to the USSR the secret to the atomic bomb. The Atomic Energy Commission and the Federal Bureau of Inves-

tigation knew that the material passed from David Greenglass to the Rosenbergs was (even if true) insignificant, worthless, and full of gross errors. The testimony of such important scientists as Philip Morrison, Henry Linshitz, Harold Urey, J. Robert Oppenheimer, George Kistiakowsky, and Victor Weiskoff verifies the worthlessness of Greenglass's information. Based on documents won from the US government in a Freedom of Information Act lawsuit; 62 notes.   L. V. Eid

739.   Martin, Charles H.   COMMUNISTS AND BLACKS: THE ILD AND THE ANGELO HERNDON CASE.   *J. of Negro Hist. 1979 64(2): 131-141.* The International Labor Defense, a Communist-supported legal defense organization, secured the freedom of Angelo Herndon, an Atlanta, Georgia, black arrested on that state's outmoded anti-insurrection laws, but failed to gain the continued support of Atlanta blacks due to contradictory actions in other similar cases, 1932-37.

740.   Mayer, Joseph.   WATERGATE FLIMFLAM.   *Social Sci. 1974 49(2): 99-103.* Discusses the Watergate scandal, glancing "at factors not generally emphasized in the continuing nationwide ballyhoo . . . with a minimum of speculation about the gaps."   E. P. Stickney

741.   Mayer, Milton.   AN AMERICAN BANALITY.   *Center Mag. 1975 8(3): 2-5.* Discusses the tragic aspects of Richard M. Nixon and the Watergate scandal.   S

742.   McFadyen, Richard E.   THE FDA'S REGULATION AND CONTROL OF ANTIBIOTICS IN THE 1950S: THE HENRY WELCH SCANDAL, FÉLIX MARTÍ-IBÁÑEZ, AND CHARLES PFIZER & CO.   *Bull. of the Hist. of Medicine 1979 53(2): 159-169.* In late 1959, Dr. Henry Welch, a high official of the Food and Drug Administration, was charged with conflict of interest involving the federal regulation of antibiotics. The scandal indicated that it was dangerous for the agency to be closely intertwined with the industry it was supposed to regulate. Welch, who was chief regulator of the antibiotics industry, was chief editor of scientific papers sponsored by drug companies and which appeared in periodicals supported by the drug companies' own advertising and purchases of reprints. This went on from 1953 to 1960. The Kefauver investigation revealed the degree to which Welch was indebted to the drug industry, and Welch resigned and received a federal disability pension. In 1962, amendments to the Food and Drug law revised the status of the agency and revitalized its regulation of drugs. 44 notes.   M. Kaufman

743.   McGinnis, Patrick J.   A CASE OF JUDICIAL MISCONDUCT: THE IMPEACHMENT AND TRIAL OF ROBERT W. ARCHBALD.   *Pennsylvania Mag. of Hist. and Biog. 1977 101(4): 506-520.* The House voted 13 impeachment articles against US Commerce Court Judge Robert Wodrow Archbald involving conflict of interest in the judge's coal and railroad dealings in eastern Pennsylvania. Before the Senate, Archbald admitted the charges, pled no criminal intent, and was found guilty on five counts and removed from office. Based on official records, other published and secondary sources; 66 notes.
T. H. Wendel

744.   Miller, Ernest C.   JOHN WILKES BOOTH AND THE LAND OF OIL. *Pennsylvania Heritage 1981 7(3): 9-12.* Biography of Abraham Lincoln's assassin John Wilkes Booth (1838-65), focusing on his interest in the oil region of northwestern Pennsylvania, particularly his investments in land there that he eventually sold because of a low volume of oil.

745.   Morton, Michael.   NO TIME TO QUIBBLE: THE JONES FAMILY CONSPIRACY TRIAL OF 1917.   *Chronicles of Oklahoma 1981 59(2): 224-236.* During the summer of 1917 a group of farmers from central Oklahoma were arrested on charges of sedition. Dubbed the "Green Corn Rebellion," this insurrection resulted from the desperate economic plight of tenant farmers who had been inflamed by leftist spokesmen within the Working Class Union (WCU). The superpatriotism of World War I created an intolerant climate toward these "antiwar radicals," and resulted in a kangaroo court for the seven men arrested in Cleveland and Pottawatomie counties. Collectively known as the Jones Family, the seven were convicted on flimsy evidence. Based on Oklahoma newspapers; photo, 42 notes.   M. L. Tate

746.   Murray, Richard K.   THE PRESIDENT UNDER FIRE.   *Am. Hist. Illus. 1974 9(5): 32-40.* The Teapot Dome Scandal in the administration of President Warren G. Harding, 1923-24, shook up the Justice Department, engendered hearings, and eventually ended in the untimely death of Harding.

747.   Newcomb, Wellington.   ANNE HUTCHINSON VERSUS MASSA-CHUSETTS.   *Am. Heritage 1974 25(4): 12-15, 78-81.* Anne Hutchinson's criminal trial in Puritan Boston for her role in the Antinomian controversy.   S

748.   Nocera, Joseph.   BARRY IN AFRICA: HOW WASHINGTON'S MAYOR GOT A FREE RIDE.   *Washington Monthly 1979 11(9): 12-23.* Washington, D.C., mayor Marion Barry and his wife Effi, an assistant vice president of marketing for Pacific Consulting (a company with many Agency for International Development contracts) spent two weeks in Africa at taxpayers' expense in July 1979; meanwhile, the city's budget bill was bogged down in Congress. The *Washington Post* (including its well-known investigative reporter Bob Woodward), contrary to its customary attitude toward political junkets, did not question the propriety of Barry's trip, his accepting (and not accounting for) official gifts, his promises of assistance to African countries, his apparent decision to act as head of an 'Africa lobby" in Washington, and his wife's conducting business while a member of the mayor's entourage. All of this suggests a dereliction of journalistic duties because the mayor is black and the *Washington Post* does not wish to antagonize the black readership of Washington, D.C.   C. Moody

749.   Nuechterlein, James A.   WATERGATE: TOWARD A REVISIONIST VIEW.   *Commentary 1979 68(2): 38-45.* Discusses the historical inaccuracies and injustices caused by hysteria during and after the Watergate trials, especially as revealed indirectly in *The Terrors of Justice: The Untold Side of Watergate* by Maurice H. Stans, and *To Set the Record Straight: The Break-in, the Tapes, the Conspirators, the Pardon* by John J. Sirica.

750. Paletz, David L. TELEVISION DRAMA: THE APPEALS OF THE SENATE WATERGATE HEARINGS (1976). *Midwest Q. 1979 21(1): 63-70.* First published in *Midwest Quarterly* in 1976, accounts for the continuing, broad appeal of the Watergate hearings. With many elements characteristic of traditional television drama, hardly the political norm, they revealed conflict, power in decline, clashes and suspense. Missing was a denouement typical of television drama, in which the problem is resolved by confession or otherwise; on television the guilty are convicted. President Ford spoiled it with his pardon. Select bibliography.   R. V. Ritter

751. Perman, Michael. A PRESIDENT AND HIS IMPEACHMENT. *R. in Am. Hist. 1975 3(4): 462-466.* Hans L. Trefousse in *Impeachment of a President: Andrew Johnson, the Blacks, and Reconstruction* (Knoxville: U. of Tennessee Pr., 1975) feels that Andrew Johnson was "not simply a forceful and aggressive politician but a skillful one too" in pursuing his conservative brand of Reconstruction, 1865-68.

752. Peskin, Allan. CHARLES GUITEAU OF ILLINOIS: PRESIDENT GARFIELD'S ASSASSIN. *J. of the Illinois State Hist. Soc. 1977 70(2): 130-139.* Portrayal of Charles Guiteau (1841-82) as a "disappointed office-seeker" is inaccurate. Court records and Guiteau's published autobiography show that James Garfield's assassin had a long history of recognized mental instability and that he was never a candidate for a patronage job. 6 illus., 52 notes.   J/S

753. Peters, Charles. SENATOR BAKER AND THE BUREAU CHIEF: WHY THEY'RE WRONG ABOUT WATERGATE. *Washington Monthly 1973 5(7): 22-24.*

754. Peters, John G. and Welch, Susan. THE EFFECTS OF CHARGES OF CORRUPTION ON VOTING BEHAVIOR IN CONGRESSIONAL ELECTIONS. *Am. Pol. Sci. Rev. 1980 74(3): 697-708.* Assesses the electoral impact of charges of corruption on candidates in contests for the US House of Representatives in five elections from 1968 to 1978. While most candidates accused of corruption are reelected, overall they appear to suffer a loss of 6%-11% from their expected vote. The type of corruption charge is an important determinant of vote loss. Allegations of corruption appear to have little effect on the net turnout.   J/S

755. Peters, John G. and Welch, Susan. POLITICAL CORRUPTION IN AMERICA: A SEARCH FOR DEFINITIONS AND A THEORY, OR IF POLITICAL CORRUPTION IS IN THE MAINSTREAM OF AMERICAN POLITICS WHY IS IT NOT IN THE MAINSTREAM OF AMERICAN POLITICS RESEARCH? *Am. Pol. Sci. Rev. 1978 72(3): 974-984.* Lack of a clear definition of political corruption has limited its systematic study by analysts of American politics. This article offers a conceptual framework with which to view corruption. A corrupt act is categorized by its four components: the donor, the favor, the public official and the payoff. For each component, propositions about perceived corrupt and noncorrupt elements can be formulated and tested. The usefulness of this scheme in analyzing attitudes about corruption is demonstrated with data from state legislators. Finally, the article suggests some future research possibilities using this scheme to compare elites and public or other groupings in the political system.   J

756. Pincus, Ann. WATERGATE: TWO WHO GOT AWAY. *Washington Monthly 1976 8(9): 43-47.* Because they were influential Washington lawyers, William Bittman and Paul O'Brien escaped prosecution even though they passed along information to the White House to aid in the Watergate cover-up.

757. Planck, Gary R. LINCOLN ASSASSINATION: THE "FORGOT-TEN" LITIGATION: *SHUEY V. UNITED STATES* (1875). *Lincoln Herald 1973 75(3): 86-92.* William Shuey, the executor of Henry Beaumont de Sainte-Marie's estate, sued the United States for Sainte-Marie's reward money and expenses for informing General Rufus King, the American Minister to the Pope, that John H. Surratt was a palace Swiss guard. In the Shuey decision, the court held that the revocation of the reward had been official. Based on U.S. executive orders, joint resolutions, and acts; 47 notes. A. C. Aimone

758. Planck, Gary R. LINCOLN ASSASSINATION: THE "FORGOT-TEN" INVESTIGATION: A. C. RICHARDS, SUPERINTENDENT OF THE METROPOLITAN POLICE. *Lincoln Herald 1980 82(4): 521-539.* Utilizes overlooked sources to examine the role of A. C. Richards, superintendent of Washington, D.C.'s metropolitan police force, in the investigation and trial of the conspirators involved in the murder of President Lincoln.

759. Planck, Gary R. LINCOLN'S ASSASSINATION: MORE "FORGOT-TEN" LITIGATION—EX PARTE MUDD (1868). *Lincoln Herald 1974 76(2): 86-90.* Dr. Samuel A. Mudd, sentenced to hard labor for life at Fort Jefferson, Dry Tortugas Island, for his involvement in Abraham Lincoln's assassination, fought a legal battle for his release. Mudd had hoped to gain his freedom either by the Supreme Court case of *Ex parte Miligan* or by presidential proclamations of amnesty. Neither appeal worked, although Dr. Mudd's medical service rendered during a yellow fever epidemic gained his release through President Andrew Johnson. Based on secondary works; illus., 21 notes. A. C. Aimone

760. Pyle, Christopher H. THE INVASION OF PRIVACY. *Pro. of the Acad. of Pol. Sci. 1982 34(4): 131-142.* Discusses the state of informational privacy since 1890. The worst abuses associated recently with privacy invasion included the Federal Bureau of Investigation's secret program of covert action against political dissidents and those cases in which agents used information stored in private file cabinets. Primary sources; 6 notes. T. P. Richardson

761. Rable, George C. FORCES OF DARKNESS, FORCES OF LIGHT: THE IMPEACHMENT OF ANDREW JOHNSON AND THE PARANOID STYLE. *Southern Studies 1978 17(2): 151-173.* The impeachment of President Andrew Johnson (1808-75) began over implementation of Congress' Reconstruction orders. Partisan passion overshadowed constitutional issues, and the two sides in the controversy came to see one another as morally evil and engaged in dark conspiracies to subvert liberty. Charges were made that Johnson was involved in Lincoln's assassination and was attempting to rule dictatorially. Johnson saw himself as a martyr for freedom, fighting against unconstitutional Congressional activities. The removal of Secretary of War Edwin M. Stanton (1814-69) was based on highly ambiguous wording. Legally Johnson was right. Primary and secondary sources; table, 61 notes. J. Buschen

762. Read, Harry. "A HAND TO HOLD WHILE DYING": DR. CHARLES A. LEALE AT LINCOLN'S SIDE. *Lincoln Herald 1977 79(1): 21-26.* US Army Assistant Surgeon Charles Augustus Leale, who regarded Abraham Lincoln as the "Savior of his Country," was the first doctor to enter the presidential box at Ford's Theater on 14 April 1865. His subsequent diagnosis and treatment of the President remained the model, even though other doctors were also in attendance. After leaving the army in 1866, Dr. Leale pursued a distinguished career in civilian medicine. He died in 1932 at the age of 90. 2 photos. T. P. Linkfield

763. Reynolds, John. "THE SILENT DOLLAR": VOTE BUYING IN NEW JERSEY. *New Jersey Hist. 1980 98(3-4): 191-211.* Vote buying in New Jersey was common by 1877. Republican newspapers accused the foreign born of accepting the illegal money, while Democratic papers singled out the state's small black population. The two parties had ample funds to distribute since campaign expenses were modest. Reformers had difficulty because the general population tolerated the practice. During Woodrow Wilson's term as governor vote buying generally stopped due to a change in the concept of politics from a party-oriented to a candidate-oriented system. Based on newspaper stories and other secondary sources; 7 illus., 2 tables, 51 notes. E. R. McKinstry

764. Rieselbach, Leroy N. IN THE WAKE OF WATERGATE: CONGRESSIONAL REFORM? *R. of Pol. 1974 36(3): 371-393.*

765. Rietveld, Ronald D., ed. AN EYEWITNESS ACCOUNT OF ABRAHAM LINCOLN'S ASSASSINATION. *Civil War Hist. 1976 22(1): 60-69.* Provides a previously unpublished memoir of an eyewitness, Frederick A. Sawyer, to President Abraham Lincoln's assassination, on 14 April 1865, in Ford's Theater. The brief note was written a few hours after the attack was made. Sawyer was sitting in the orchestra seats just beneath the presidential box, heard the fatal shot, and saw John Wilkes Booth leap to the stage although at the time he did not know it was Booth. He describes the panic in the theater and the mood of gloom which quickly seized the District of Columbia. Sawyer did not hear Booth shout "Sic Semper Tyrannis," although he records that someone else heard such a cry. E. C. Murdock

766. Robbins, Peggy. "I AM ASHAMED OF MY CONDUCT": DR. SAMUEL MUDD'S ATTEMPT TO ESCAPE FROM FORT JEFFERSON. *Civil War Times Illus. 1978 16(10): 10-16.* Confined to the Dry Tortugas under sentence of life imprisonment for his alleged role in the Lincoln assassination conspiracy, Dr. Samuel Mudd suffered in many ways. In late 1865, he made an unsuccessful attempt to escape Fort Jefferson by hiding under some planks in the lower hold of a ship. Several years later he helped to stem the yellow fever epidemic in the prison, and was pardoned by President Johnson in February 1869, returning home to his Maryland farm, where he died in 1883. Some comment on Abraham Lincoln's assassination. H. M. Ward

767. Robitscher, Jonas. STIGMATIZATION AND STONEWALLING: THE ORDEAL OF MARTHA MITCHELL. *J. of Psychohistory 1979 6(3): 393-408.* Chronicles the events surrounding Martha Mitchell (wife of John Mitchell, US Attorney General in the Nixon Administration) during and after

the break-in at the Democratic National Headquarters (Watergate), focusing on the efforts of the Nixon administration to stigmatize Martha Mitchell as mentally ill in order to discredit her with the press. Based on newspaper accounts and secondary sources; 37 notes.   R. E. Butchart

768. Rohrs, Richard C. PARTISAN POLITICS AND THE ATTEMPTED ASSASSINATION OF ANDREW JACKSON. *J. of the Early Republic 1981 1(2): 149-163.* In January 1835, an unemployed housepainter, Richard Lawrence, attempted to kill President Andrew Jackson, but both of his pistols misfired. Despite early evidence that Lawrence was insane, partisan attempts to link this attack to Jackson's political foes led to a Senate committee investigation into Jackson's accusations, later dismissed, against Mississippi Senator George Poindexter. The opposition press used the incident to call attention to incompetence and corruption in Jackson's administration, even suggesting Jacksonian Democrats had staged the attack. The clamor died down in the aftermath of Lawrence's April 1835 acquittal by reason of insanity. Based on contemporary newspaper accounts, correspondence, and Senate records; 45 notes.   C. B. Schulz

769. Rosenberg, Harold. THUGS ADRIFT. *Partisan R. 1973 40(3): 341-348.* Reviews Watergate-related events and personalities and analyzes Richard Milhous Nixon's policy as the politics of cover-up. After citing several literary associations with the Watergate caper, the author concludes that "the Nixon collaboraters were moved by an essence beyond speech . . . . I know of nothing more offensive to the sensibility of a free individual than the Hollywood-style metaphysics by which Nixon has glamorized his corrupt invention of a Presidency that exists independently of the President."   D. K. Pickens

770. Rosenberg, Leonard B. LUCK OR DESIGN: THE FALL OF RICHARD M. NIXON. *Politico [Italy] 1975 40(4): 706-709.* The political system itself caused Richard M. Nixon's fall from power because the certainty of impeachment and probability of conviction forced him to resign. The behavior of the military, the media, and business prove the stability of the American political system. The orderly transition of power from Nixon to Gerald Ford is another example. However, the potential for the abuse of power remains.
                                                           M. T. Wilson

771. Ross, Irwin. FIFTEEN SECONDS OF TERROR. *Am. Hist. Illus. 1975 10(4): 10-13.* Discusses Giuseppi Zangara's attempted assassination of President-elect Franklin D. Roosevelt in Miami, Florida, in 1933.

772. Royster, Charles. "THE NATURE OF TREASON": REVOLUTIONARY VIRTUE AND AMERICAN REACTIONS TO BENEDICT ARNOLD. *William and Mary Q. 1979 36(2): 163-193.* Americans enthusiastically supported the American Revolution at its start, but after 1776 they grew war weary and became disillusioned when they saw public virtue corrupted by war profiteering and the like. In 1780, defeats at Charleston and Camden and Arnold's betrayal caused shock that led to revival of interest in the war and in recovering public virtue. Examines the change of attitudes toward the war effort. Cites the reactions to Arnold's treason, and relates it to the movement for stronger government. Based on contemporary documents and letters; 110 notes.   H. M. Ward

773. Royster, Vermont. THE PUBLIC MORALITY: AFTERTHOUGHTS ON WATERGATE. *Am. Scholar 1974 43(2): 249-259.* The Watergate Scandal was "an attempt to use governmental power to subvert the political process in the broadest sense of that term." Relates this to the separate indictment of Vice President Spiro T. Agnew. There was nothing original in either crime: kickbacks, bribes, income tax evasion, and a myriad of political dirty tricks and campaign spying. Watergate was unusual in that no money was stolen despite the millions available. Attempts to explain the reasons for this political behavior and countless other forms of political acts as a "lawlessness in pursuit of virtue." The chief concern is that the morality of high government officials reflects the public morality.
C. W. Olson

774. Salmond, John A. "THE GREAT SOUTHERN COMMIE HUNT": AUBREY WILLIAMS, THE SOUTHERN CONFERENCE EDUCA-TIONAL FUND, AND THE INTERNAL SECURITY SUBCOMMITTEE. *South Atlantic Q. 1978 77(4): 433-452.* A detailed account of the Senate Internal Security Subcommittee, headed by Eastland of Mississippi, and the hearings held in New Orleans in March 1954 at which time Aubrey W. Williams, president of the Southern Conference Educational Fund Inc., was queried and harassed re-garding Communists in the SCEF. The hearing emphasized that in the McCarthy era the pursuit of subversion too easily turned into the harassment of domestic dissenters; in this instance it was the uncompromising advocates of integration in a region girding itself for the battle against what would be the most serious challenge yet to its social structure, the anticipated Supreme Court decision outlawing public school segregation. Suggests that Eastland had very much in his mind the need to destroy the credibility of those white southerners who opposed the prevailing system. Based on two collections of Aubrey Williams's papers— one in the Roosevelt Library, the other in the possession of Mrs. Anita Williams— contemporary newspaper accounts and interviews; 43 notes.
H. M. Parker, Jr.

775. Schuetz, Janice. COMMUNICATIVE COMPETENCE AND THE BARGAINING OF WATERGATE. *Western J. of Speech Communication 1978 42(2): 105-115.* Assesses the bargaining behavior and ability of Richard M. Nixon, H. R. Haldeman, and John Erlichman on 17 April 1973 after John Dean resigned.

776. Seraile, William. THE ASSASSINATION OF MALCOLM X: THE VIEW FROM HOME AND ABROAD. *Afro-Americans in New York Life and Hist. 1981 5(1): 43-58.* Presents US and foreign attitudes and political commentary in four categories about Malcolm X at the time of his assassination in 1965: "1) Malcolm as a budding integrationist; 2) Malcolm as the victim of violence; 3) Malcolm as the confused racist with the wasted talent; 4) Malcolm as a revolutionary martyr."

777. Seraile, William. BEN FLETCHER, I.W.W. ORGANIZER. *Pennsyl-vania Hist. 1979 46(3): 213-232.* Benjamin Harrison Fletcher (1890-1949) was an extraordinarily successful organizer of dockworkers for the Industrial Workers of the World in Philadelphia, Baltimore, and Boston. He was particularly effec-tive in appealing to fellow blacks who were dockworkers. Sentenced to prison in 1918 with other IWW leaders for alleged violations of the Selective Service Act

and Espionage Act of 1917, he was released in 1922 with a conditional commutation of his sentence. In 1933, President Franklin D. Roosevelt granted him a full pardon. Based upon Pardon Attorney files, Haywood et al. vs. U.S., and other sources; illus., 24 notes.   D. C. Swift

778.   Shankman, Arnold.   DRAFT RESISTANCE IN CIVIL WAR PENN-SYLVANIA. *Pennsylvania Mag. of Hist. and Biog. 1977 101(2): 190-204.* Discusses the widespread draft resistance in Civil War Pennsylvania. Democrats were the major resisting force. They had no desire to fight for Negro emancipation, and their party was identified with the South. Draft officers were attacked, pelted, beaten, and frequently murdered. The government responded by sending troops to arrest violators of the law, but legal convictions were rare. This state of affairs continued throughout the war, and the draft did more harm than good. 33 notes.   V. L. Human

779.   Shattuck, Petra T.   LAW AS POLITICS. *Comparative Pol. 1974 7(1): 127-154.* Reviews works by Isaac D. Balbus, Theodore L. Becker, Charles Goodell, and Heinrich and Elisabeth Hannover dealing with political prisoners in modern America and in Weimar Germany.

780.   Socarides, Charles W.   WHY SIRHAN KILLED KENNEDY: PSY-CHOANALYTIC SPECULATIONS ON AN ASSASSINATION. *J. of Psychohistory 1979 6(4): 447-460.* Sirhan B. Sirhan was born in Jerusalem to a brutal father. Their life was disrupted by the Arab-Israeli War of 1948-49; the family finally settled in California. His failure to achieve academic excellence and, later, a career as a jockey damaged his concept of self. Sirhan idealized Robert F. Kennedy as an omnipotent father figure capable of doing great good, but when Kennedy made pro-Israeli statements, Sirhan's love turned to hate. All of his frustrations were displaced on Kennedy and released by assassinating him. Biblio.
                                                                                    S

781.   Spoehr, Luther.   MUCKRAKING AND MUDSLINGING: LOUIS FILLER VERSUS RECENT AMERICAN HISTORY. *Rev. in Am. Hist. 1977 5(3): 391-396.* Review article prompted by Louis Filler's *The Muckrakers,* a new and enlarged edition of *Crusaders for American Liberalism* (University Park: Pennsylvania State U. Pr., 1976) and Filler's *Appointment at Armageddon: Muckraking and Progressivism in the American Tradition,* Contributions in American Studies no. 20 (Westport, Conn.: Greenwood Pr., 1976); compares Filler's traditional historical interpretation of Progressivism and the recent reassessment of muckrakers and Progressivism.

782.   Spragens, William C.   POLITICAL IMPACT OF PRESIDENTIAL ASSASSINATIONS AND ATTEMPTED ASSASSINATIONS. *Presidential Studies Q. 1980 10(3): 336-347.* Violence against political elites such as presidents is not new, but massive media attention to it has created more problems. A presidential assassination is not just a cataclysmic event for the American public; it can also cause profound political change. John F. Kennedy's assassination helped Lyndon B. Johnson get social legislation passed more easily, but it may have also greatly changed American strategy toward Vietnam. 20 notes.
                                                                              D. H. Cline

783. Stein, Howard F. THE SILENT COMPLICITY AT WATERGATE. *Am. Scholar 1973/74 43(1): 21-37.* Suggests that Americans are blinded to the wider context of the Watergate Scandal by focusing attention on the individual guilt of those involved. Examines the political campaign of 1972 as background and believes that Richard M. Nixon's power was very broadly based. Voters were repelled by the "apocalyptic arrogance of the new Left" and got "what was sought and what was preserved through this election, . . . a stern veneer and a corrupt core, so that one can get away with as much as possible, while righteously punishing those who get away with too much too openly." One social concern emerging from the election was the desire of many Americans for a Hitler to restore social order. Watergate intensified the "fundamental polarity of values that has been a dialectic of American history . . . lineal authority versus individualism." C. W. Olson

784. Stepanova, O. L. IMPICHMENT [Impeachment]. *Voprosy Istorii [USSR] 1974 (11): 217-220.* Impeachment, in Great Britain and the United States, means the misuse of power by a serving member of the lower ranks of Parliament or Congress and the judgment given by members of the higher ranks. Examines the case of President Andrew Johnson's impeachment in the United States after the simultaneous end of the Civil War and the death of President Lincoln in 1865. Describes the case and considers its significance at the time and its relevance to present-day politics, with reference to work on the subject by John F. Kennedy. Based on US secondary works on subject; 16 notes. L. Smith

785. Stumpf, Stuart O., ed. THE ARREST OF AARON BURR: A DOCU-MENTARY RECORD. *Alabama Hist. Q. 1980 42(3-4): 113-123.* Presents a detailed account of the events surrounding the arrest of Aaron Burr for treason in Alabama in 1807. The statement was given by Nicholas Perkins, one of Burr's captors. Primary sources; 19 notes. A. Drysdale

786. Sully, Langdon. THE INDIAN AGENT: A STUDY IN CORRUP-TION AND AVARICE. *Am. West 1973 10(2): 4-9.* Before 1861, Indian agents were generally honorable and respectable. Perhaps the agent who best epitomized this tradition was Lawrence Taliaferro at Fort Snelling, Minnesota, 1819-39. Within six months of the appointment of Dr. Walter M. Burleigh in 1861, complaints began to flow into the Bureau of Indian Affairs. During the Civil War most of the agents were unscrupulous, vacillating, and lacking in judgment. President Ulysses Simpson Grant tried to reverse the situation by establishing a Board of Indian Commissioners. The board did bring some order to the government's relations with the Indians, but never quite restored the honor that had once existed. 8 illus. D. L. Smith

787. Swindler, William. HIGH COURT OF CONGRESS: IMPEACH-MENT TRIALS, 1797-1936. *Am. Bar Assoc. J. 1974 60(4): 420-428.* History shows that impeachment trials have moved from barely disguised political vendettas to quasi-judicial proceedings. J

788. Swindler, William F. VICTIM OR VILLAIN?: THE TRIALS OF AARON BURR. *Supreme Court Hist. Soc. Y. 1978: 18-24.* Briefly traces the life of Aaron Burr, focusing on his schemes in the Old Southwest and the resulting treason trial.

789.   Taylor, John M.   ASSASSIN ON TRIAL.   *Am. Heritage 1981 32(4):*
30-39. Discusses the trial of Charles Guiteau, the assassin of President James A.
Garfield, a trial in which the defense claimed insanity. The national atmosphere
and the case presented by the prosecution combined to produce a guilty verdict.
At his execution, Guiteau convinced some of the legitimacy of his insanity plea.
10 illus.   J. F. Paul

790.   Toinet, Marie-France.   LES ÉTATS-UNIS APRÈS WATERGATE: LE
RÈGNE DE L'AMBIGUÏTÉ   [The United States after Watergate: The reign
of ambiguity]. *Études [France] 1975 342: 63-82.* Studies the residual problems,
contradictions, and the indecisiveness which characterize the long-range psychological effect of Richard M. Nixon's resignation on the American people, 1974-
75, and on the congressional elections of 1974.

791.   Tucker, Edward L., ed.   THE ATTEMPTED ASSASSINATION OF
PRESIDENT JACKSON: A LETTER BY RICHARD HENRY WILDE.
Georgia Hist. Q. 1974 58(Supplement): 193-199. Reprints a letter from Richard
Henry Wilde, a member of the House of Representatives, to his brother, John
Walker Wilde, describing the attempted assassination of Andrew Jackson. The
letter reflects the conflicting opinions current at the time concerning the details
of the assassination attempt. Richard Lawrence, the would-be assassin, was mentally deranged. His attempt on Jackson's life was foiled by two guns which
misfired. Lawrence was then rescued from Jackson and the crowd who attempted
to kill him, was placed on trial, and spent the remainder of his life in various
mental hospitals. Based on primary sources; 7 notes.   M. R. Gillam

792.   Turner, Thomas R.   DID WEICHMANN TURN STATE'S EVI-
DENCE TO SAVE HIMSELF?: A CRITIQUE OF A TRUE HISTORY OF
THE ASSASSINATION OF ABRAHAM LINCOLN.   *Lincoln Herald 1979
81(4): 265-267.* Review of Floyd Risvold, ed., *A True History of the Assassination of Abraham Lincoln and of the Conspiracy of 1865 by Louis J. Weichmann*
(New York: Knopf, 1975), a manuscript by one of the witnesses at the Lincoln
assassins' trial.

793.   Turner, Thomas R.   PUBLIC OPINION AND THE ASSASSINATION
OF ABRAHAM LINCOLN.   *Lincoln Herald 1976 78(1): 17-24, (2): 66-76.*
Part I. Many modern writers discussing the Lincoln assassination have tried to
develop a theory of a conspiracy among Northern leaders and have ignored the
reactions of contemporaries who felt Secretary of War Edwin M. Stanton handled
the post-assassination crises adequately. The "sensational dime press" and the
clergy both contributed to stirring up public opinion against the South. Many of
the supposedly suppressed facets of the assassination and subsequent investigations appeared in the press. Primary and secondary sources; 32 notes. Part II. The
historians' sympathy for those conspiring to assassinate Abraham Lincoln was
not shared by contemporaries. Five members of the military commission signed
a clemency plea in the case of Mrs. Mary E. Surratt but Judge Holt withheld this
information from President Andrew Johnson when he signed the sentence. It is
doubtful that Johnson would have acted differently had he known about the plea.
Public opinion favored the sentence. During the civil trial of John Surratt public
opinion shifted from belief in his guilt to confusion and doubt after the defense
made its case. Primary and secondary sources; 83 notes.   B. J. LaBue

794. Unsigned. WATERGATE: ITS IMPLICATIONS FOR RESPONSI-
BLE GOVERNMENT. *Administration and Society 1974 6(2): 155-170.*

795. Uyeda, Clifford I. THE PARDONING OF "TOKYO ROSE": A RE-
PORT ON THE RESTORATION OF AMERICAN CITIZENSHIP TO IVA
IKUKO TOGURI. *Amerasia J. 1978 5(2): 69-93.* The 1977 presidential pardon
of Iva Ikuko Toguri d'Aquino, who, as "Tokyo Rose," had been convicted of
treason after World War II, was the result of the work of many people, institutions, and organizations. A committee formed by John Hada and the author
coordinated the massive campaign to reeducate the public about the facts of the
case, the garnering of support from widespread sources, and the mechanics of
filing the petition for pardon. The Japanese American Citizens League had done
little or nothing for Toguri prior to the work of the committee and did not order
the formation of the committee, but it tried to claim credit for the pardon.
T. L. Powers

796. Viehe, Fred W. THE RECALL OF MAYOR FRANK L. SHAW: A
REVISION. *California History 1980-81 59(4): 290-305.* Frank L. Shaw, mayor
of Los Angeles 1933-37, was not so dishonest as history has portrayed him; nor
were the reformers who ousted him so pure of motive. Shaw was a friend of
organized labor, efficient rather than bungling, and only sometimes supported by
the *Los Angeles Times.* The reformers, led by Clifford Clinton and Fletcher
Bowron, represented a coalition of conservative businessmen and liberal reformers who expressed racist views, opposed organized labor, and condemned the New
Deal. They accused Shaw of tolerating vice and gambling, and publicized the
trials of several Shaw commissioners during the 1937 recall campaign. After
Shaw's defeat, the ex-mayor successfully sued *Liberty* magazine for libel, and the
three people in Shaw's administration convicted of criminal offenses were never
actually linked to Shaw. Photos, 107 notes. A. Hoffman

797. Vollrath, Ernst. KORRUPTION IN DER POLITIK UND KORRUP-
TION DER POLITIK [Corruption in politics and corruption of politics].
Zeitschrift für Politik [West Germany] 1977 24(4): 333-341. Political corruption
is a specific vice of republican government and liberal constitutional societies as
has been shown in the Greek *polis,* the Roman republics, the Italian republics
in the Renaissance, the United States, and West Germany.

798. Wainer, Howard. PREDICTING THE OUTCOME OF THE SENATE
TRIAL OF RICHARD M. NIXON. *Behavioral Sci. 1974 19(6): 404-406.*
Predicts the outcome of the Senate vote on the impeachment of Richard M. Nixon
by using a three-mode factor analysis model. S

799. Waldo, Dwight. REFLECTIONS ON PUBLIC MORALITY. *Administration and Soc. 1974 6(3): 267-282.* Attempts "to see Watergate in the
perspective of Western history and to discern how it relates to the deepest, most
significant forces shaping the future." S

800. Walzer, Michael. WATERGATE WITHOUT THE PRESIDENT.
Dissent 1974 21(1): 5-7. The Watergate scandal extends past the President to
corporations and the mass media. S

801. Weinstein, Edwin A. PRESIDENTIAL ASSASSINATION: AN AMERICAN PROBLEM. *Psychiatry 1976 39(3): 291-293.* Discusses psychological, sociopathological, and political aspects of assassination and assassination attempts on presidents, 1950's-70's, including public opinion toward the presidency and gun control.

802. Werlin, Herbert H. THE CONSEQUENCES OF CORRUPTION: THE GHANAIAN EXPERIENCE. *Pol. Sci. Q. 1973 88(1): 71-85.* Political corruption in America in the past has not retarded economic development. In view of the American experience, some scholars have minimized the extent to which corruption might retard the development of emerging nations. The case of Ghana, however, suggests that political corruption functions differently in the United States than it does in developing nations. In the United States, illegally gained money generally goes back into internal production, while corrupt profits in Ghana are usually invested abroad or spent on wasteful imports. Further, incentive for profitmaking under US capitalism may induce corruption, but it also facilitates the performance of work, while in socialist Ghana corrupt practices often result in the loss of goods and services. Finally, while US political machines might be corrupt, they still serve a political function and are based on the legitimacy of the American political system—popular consensus was necessary, so that the machine had to follow the rules of the government process—while in Ghana, corruption undermined the very legitimacy of Kwame Nkrumah's regime, and undermined the ideological commitment consistent with the betterment of the public welfare under socialism. Based on primary and secondary sources; 42 notes.   B. C. Tharaud

803. Wesser, Robert F. THE IMPEACHMENT OF A GOVERNOR: WILLIAM SULZER AND THE POLITICS OF EXCESS. *New York Hist. 1979 60(4): 407-438.* New York Democratic Governor William Sulzer's investigation of graft in state government, gubernatorial appointments, promotion of the direct primary, and intemperate attacks on members of the state legislature resulted in the legislature's investigation of the Sulzer administration. Sulzer was subsequently impeached and removed from office for violation of the New York Corrupt Practices Act. Originally a Tammany Hall Democrat, Sulzer saw his anti-Tammany stance as governor contribute to his downfall. Covers 1912-13. 5 illus., 80 notes.   R. N. Lokken

804. Wiener, Jon. TOCQUEVILLE, MARX, WEBER, NIXON: WATERGATE IN THEORY. *Dissent 1976 23(2): 171-180.* Analyzes the political crimes associated with the 1972 Watergate Scandal and Richard M. Nixon in reference to the political theories of Alexis de Tocqueville—an attack on pluralism; Max Weber—the growth of bureaucratic power and the failure of charisma; and Karl Marx—a split in the capitalist ruling class between the Yankees (the eastern old money elite) and the Cowboys (the new money of the "Southern rim").

805. Williams, Robert J. POLITICAL CORRUPTION IN THE UNITED STATES. *Pol. Studies [Great Britain] 1981 29(1): 126-129.* The Watergate affair has revived academic interest in political corruption in the United States. Students should take more note of the massive growth in governmental activity and should examine more closely the relationship of so-called victimless crime to

the form and incidence of corruption. The decline of urban machine politics has not led to a diminution of corruption; today it is predominantly middle-class and white-collar and the rewards have changed to meet the needs of the affluent. 15 notes. D. J. Nicholls

806. Withington, Anne Fairfax and Schwartz, Jack. THE POLITICAL TRIAL OF ANNE HUTCHINSON. *New England Q. 1978 51(2): 226-240.* Anne Hutchinson's (1591-1643) trial in 1637 was not to determine guilt or innocence, but a power struggle to solve the political problem of maintaining the social order, and must be judged in these terms. During the first part of the trial she outmaneuvered her accusers. Historians have explained her announcement that she had received divine revelation as a mistake which lost her the case, but the authors conclude that it was no error, but a conscious affirmation of the triviality of all men's endeavors, including both her own and the court's. She knew that she was certain to be found guilty from the beginning of her trial, and decided to make the statement as an act of conscience. Based on trial records and secondary works; 26 notes. J. C. Bradford

807. —. AN EXCHANGE ON WATERGATE. *Partisan R. 1974 41(4): 645-648.*
Chomsky, Noam. TEA PARTY, pp. 645-647. Argues that government repression during the 1960's was more extreme than under Richard M. Nixon, but because it was directed against the Socialist Workers Party, Black Panthers, Student Nonviolent Coordinating Committee, and the New Left in general, it was accepted. In the Watergate scandal, "Nixon's crime was not the choice of means but the choice of enemies"— the liberal establishment, the political and ideological center.
Phillips, William. TRAUMA, pp. 648. Dissents from Chomsky's interpretation. D. K. Pickens / S

808. —. [MORMONS AND WATERGATE]. *Dialogue 1974 9(2): 9-24.*
England, Eugene. HANGING BY A THREAD: MORMONS AND WATERGATE, *pp. 9-18.* Mormon theology posits natural laws of political justice and liberty which are described and guaranteed by the Declaration of Independence and the Constitution. Mormons were wrong to have given unquestioning loyalty to Nixon.
Rushforth, Brent N. WATERGATE: A PERSONAL EXPERIENCE, *pp. 19-24.* In contributing to the Committee to Re-elect the President in illegal ways, the business community revealed moral laxity. The author, in helping to prosecute the Northrop case, rediscovered the value of the gospels in shaping ethics. D. L. Rowe

809. —. [PUBLIC OPINION ON IMPEACHMENT]. *Pol. Sci. Q. 1974 89(2): 289-304.*
McGeever, Patrick J. "GUILTY, YES; IMPEACHMENT, NO": SOME EMPIRICAL FINDINGS, pp. 289-300. "Reports and analyzes another opinion survey that reveals a seeming contradiction in adult public opinion: Although some two-thirds of McGeever's sample believed President Nixon seriously culpable in the Watergate affair, about one-half of those who hold the President guilty nevertheless did not call for his removal from office through impeachment or resignation."

Finch, Gerald B.   IMPEACHMENT AND THE DYNAMICS OF PUBLIC
     OPINION: A COMMENT ON "GUILTY, YES; IMPEACHMENT,
     NO," pp. 301-304.   "In a commentary on the McGeever data, speculates
     that the size of the inconsistent 'Guilty, Yes; Impeachment, No' spectrum
     of opinion will shrink over time. Finch also predicts that the public's reaction
     to Watergate is unlikely to produce any permanent shifts in party loyalties
     among many Americans."   J

6

VICTIMLESS CRIMES

810. Aaron, William S.; Alger, Norman; and Gonzales, Ricardo T. CHICA-NOIZING DRUG ABUSE PROGRAMS. *Human Organization 1974 33(4): 388-390.* Examines drug addicts in a Mexican American population in Oxnard, California to establish what cultural values could be adapted for use in drug abuse treatment.   S

811. Aaronson, David E.; Dienes, C. Thomas; and Musheno, Michael C. CHANGING THE PUBLIC DRUNKENNESS LAWS: THE IMPACT OF DECRIMINALIZATION. *Law and Soc. Rev. 1978 12(3): 405-436.* Laws that decriminalize public drunkenness continue to use the police as the major intake agent for public inebriates under the "new" public health model of detoxification and treatment. Assuming that decriminalization introduces many disincentives to police intervention using legally sanctioned procedures, we hypothesize that it will be followed by a statistically significant decline in the number of public inebriates formally handled by the police in the manner designated by the "law in the books." Using an "interrupted time-series quasi-experiment" based on a "stratified multiple-group single-I design," we confirm this hypothesis for Washington, D.C., and Minneapolis, Minnesota. However, through intensive "microanalysis" of these two jurisdictions, we show that Minneapolis, in responding to strong business pressure, developed several alternative means of keeping the streets clear of transient public inebriates while Washington, D.C., treated decriminalization as an opportunity to shift police priorities and relied on informal "safe zones" to handle the inebriate population.   J

812. Allen, Ruby. MOONSHINING AS A FINE ART ON A KENTUCKY CREEK. *Kentucky Folklore Record 1975 21(2): 34-40.* Describes creekside locations of moonshining stills, with methods and recipes for various forms of liquor.   S

813. Allman, James. HAITIAN MIGRATION: 30 YEARS ASSESSED. *Migration Today 1982 10(1): 6-12.* Traces Haitian immigration during 1950-80; the countries receiving the most Haitians were the United States, the Dominican Republic, Canada, and the Bahamas; despite efforts to stop them, Haitians continue to enter Florida and the Dominican Republic illegally because of political and social reasons.

814. Anderson, Eric. PROSTITUTION AND SOCIAL JUSTICE: CHICAGO, 1910-15. *Social Service R. 1974 48(2): 203-228.*

815. Bach, Robert L. MEXICAN IMMIGRATION AND THE AMERICAN STATE. *Int. Migration Rev. 1978 12(4): 536-558.* Discusses illegal aliens during 1867-1977, in reference to the economic needs and strengths of organized labor in the United States.

816. Bair, Jo Ann W. and Jensen, Richard L. PROSECUTION OF THE MORMONS IN ARIZONA TERRITORY IN THE 1880'S. *Arizona and the West 1977 19(1): 25-46.* The federal Edmunds Law of 1882 prohibited both polygamy and cohabitation with more than one woman. Expansive Mormon colonization in the Southwest, particularly in Arizona, was regarded as a threat to the status quo. Polygamy became the rallying point for anti-Mormon crusades which usually occurred within the legal system. The legal battles were for control of the land and local government. Once objectives were largely achieved, the anti-Mormon antagonism subsided dramatically during the late 1880's. 6 illus.; 46 notes.   D. L. Smith

817. Barkan, Steven E. POLITICAL TRIALS AND THE *PRO SE* DEFENDANT IN THE ADVERSARY SYSTEM. *Social Problems 1977 24(3): 324-336.* Discusses pro se defendants in court trials involving politics, morals, and social issues, 1960's-70's.

818. Bashore, Melvin L. LIFE BEHIND BARS: MORMON COHABS OF THE 1880S. *Utah Hist. Q. 1979 47(1): 22-41.* More than 1,300 Mormon men and a few women were jailed for polygamy or unlawful cohabitation under the Edmunds Act (US, 1882). So many church, community, and business leaders were jailed that a prison sentence became a mark of honor. Prison diaries reveal problems with bedbugs, lice, poor food, oppressive heat, and overcrowded cells. Tedium was relieved by crafts, glee clubs, bands, sports, speeches, and visiting days. The presence of Mormons exerted a powerful restraining influence on criminals. 7 illus., 37 notes.   J. L. Hazelton

819. Bayer, Ronald. HEROIN DECRIMINALIZATION AND *IDEOLOGY OF TOLERANCE:* A CRITICAL VIEW. *Law and Soc. Rev. 1978 12(2): 301-318.* Analyzes conflicting views on decriminalization of narcotics and on drug abuse in American society. Pointing to repressive methods operating with respect to drug use, the so-called "drug store" approach is offered as a way of allowing a freedom of choice for drug users. 34 notes.   H. R. Mahood

820. Bernstein, Arnold and Lennard, Henry. DRUGS, DOCTORS AND JUNKIES. *Society 1973 10(4): 14-16, 18, 20, 22-25.* Explores issues of legal and illegal drug use.   S

821. Blackburn, George M. and Ricards, Sherman L. THE PROSTITUTES AND GAMBLERS OF VIRGINIA CITY, NEVADA: 1870. *Pacific Hist. Rev. 1979 48(2): 239-258.* Of the prostitutes, 71 were Chinese, 63 white, and 4 black; all were female. There were 45 white gamblers and 43 Chinese; all were male. Gambling was legal and socially accepted. Prostitution was illegal but accepted. Both prostitutes and gamblers were interested in making money, but only a few attained economic success. Based on an examination of federal census

manuscripts, a diary by Virginia City newspaperman Alfred Doten, and the Virginia City *Territorial Enterprise;* 58 notes.   R. N. Lokken

822. Bosmajian, Haig. RESTRICTING *STANLEY* AND FREEDOM OF SPEECH. *Midwest Q. 1979 20(3): 228-240.* Provides the background of the US Supreme Court's *Stanley* v. *Georgia* (US, 1969), in which Robert Stanley's 1968 obscenity conviction for private possession of three films was reversed; discusses the significance of the Stanley case in 1979.

823. Bourne, Peter G. IT IS TIME TO REEXAMINE OUR NATIONAL NARCOTICS POLICY. *Urban and Social Change Rev. 1976 9(2): 2-5.* Examines the apparent failure of the war on drug abuse initiated by Richard M. Nixon in 1971, and suggests consideration of revision of US drug policy.

824. Briggs, Vernon M., Jr. ILLEGAL ALIENS: THE NEED FOR A MORE RESTRICTIVE BORDER POLICY. *Social Sci. Q. 1975 56(3): 477-484.* Uses what many would regard as conventional economic arguments.   J

825. Briggs, Vernon M., Jr. ILLEGAL IMMIGRATION AND THE AMERICAN LABOR FORCE: THE USE OF "SOFT" DATA FOR ANALY-SIS. *Am. Behavioral Scientist 1976 19(3): 351-363.* Examines the knowledge crisis surrounding the issue of illegal immigration into the United States, focusing on the critical social issues which are influenced by the type of data used for analysis.

826. Brown, Bertram S. DRUGS AND PUBLIC HEALTH: ISSUES AND ANSWERS. *Ann. of the Am. Acad. of Pol. and Social Sci. 1975 417: 110-119.* "Since shortly after the turn of the century, drug abuse in the United States has been defined and treated, at least in part, as a public health issue requiring the intervention and services of the federal government. Thus, over the years the government has developed a broad spectrum of specialized agencies and activities to deal with the drug problem. These range from the creation of a 'Narcotics Farm' in 1935 to the establishment of the National Institute on Drug Abuse in 1973; from the study of marihuana use and its effects to the sponsorship of narcotic antagonist research; from the training of professional and paraprofessional treatment and rehabilitation personnel to the conduct of multi-modality field trials of heroin addict rehabilitation programs. Clearly, the principal weakness in the national public health approach to narcotic addiction and drug abuse lies in the area of primary prevention, particularly as it is directed to high risk adolescents. The intent of this paper is to highlight some of the drug abuse activities and accomplishments of the National Institute of Mental Health within the Public Health Service of the Department of Health, Education and Welfare; to examine some of the significant issues and demands of the national drug program in recent years; and to indicate the directions that have been pursued in an effort to find solutions to drug abuse problems."   J

827. Bruce-Briggs, B. SHOULD HEROIN BE LEGALIZED? *New York Affairs 1974 2(1): 32-45.* "The argument that legalization would solve the worst problem of heroin addiction—the crime and corruption it generates—is superficially simple and persuasive. But there are serious difficulties, practical and moral, with this seemingly attractive solution."   J

828.   Burran, James A.   PROHIBITION IN NEW MEXICO, 1917.   *New Mexico Hist. R. 1973 48(2): 133-149.* The Anti-Saloon League became active in New Mexico in 1910, two years before statehood. The prohibitionists were successful in 1917 because they argued that prohibition would save food, and because state leaders elected in 1916 favored prohibition.   J. H. Krenkel

829.   Butler, Anne M.   MILITARY MYOPIA: PROSTITUTION ON THE FRONTIER.   *Prologue 1981 13(4): 233-250.* Discusses the phenomenon of prostitution on frontier garrisons focusing on the possible institutionalized relationship between the army and the prostitute. In the *Idahoe* case, Captain John Newcombe brought suit against the army in 1865 because of alleged financial losses resulting from a military order directing him to transport prostitutes. Prostitution was a persistent theme of frontier military life and while the military did not officially sanction it, there is evidence that officers at all levels were aware of its existence. Military policies regulating sutlers' stores and laundresses, and permitting Mexicans to set up markets on garrison grounds unofficially fostered and encouraged prostitution, while the official military stance was to denounce it. Based on US General Accounting Office Accounts & Claims Records, Adjutant General's Office Records, US Department of War Office of the Surgeon General Records; 2 illus., 8 photos, 52 notes.   M. A. Kascus

830.   Carmichael, Carl W.   DRUG ABUSE IN AMERICA: THE GREAT COMMUNICATIONS FAILURE.   *J. of Popular Culture 1974 8(3): 653-657.* Examines problems of drug abuse (including the use of marijuana and tobacco), attempts to define "drugs" and "abuse," examines the mythology of drugs, and suggests a plan for initiating drug abuse education.

831.   Carter, Paul A.   PROHIBITION AND DEMOCRACY: THE NOBLE EXPERIMENT REASSESSED.   *Wisconsin Mag. of Hist. 1973 56(3): 189-201.* Challenges the traditional view of prohibition as a battle of liberal wets fighting for democratic principles against a conservative and well organized fanatic minority that imposed the 18th Amendment on an unsuspecting public. Examines prohibitionists' literature, leaders, and opponents, and argues that the prohibition movement used many of the arguments of future New Dealers and radicals. Explores the role of women's organizations in the prohibition controversy. 8 illus., 45 notes.   N. C. Burckel

832.   Castillo, Leonel J.   DEALING WITH THE UNDOCUMENTED ALIEN: AN INTERIM APPROACH.   *INS Reporter 1978 27(1): 1-6.* Discusses the Immigration and Naturalization Service Commissioner's proposal on illegal aliens, pending Senate approval of President Jimmy Carter's 1977 immigration program.

833.   Chartock, Alan.   NARCOTICS ADDICTION: THE POLITICS OF FRUSTRATION.   *Pro. of the Acad. of Pol. Sci. 1974 31(3): 239-249.* Examines New York's attempts to conquer drug addiction and the frustration met by social workers, law enforcement officials, and legislators alike.   S

834.   Christian, Garna L.   NEWTON BAKER'S WAR ON EL PASO VICE. *Red River Valley Hist. Rev. 1980 5(2): 55-67.* Secretary of War Newton D. Baker opposed liquor and prostitution in El Paso, Texas, in 1917 and 1918 during World War I, and halted the War Department's planned training cantonment there.

835.   Clark, Leroy D.   ON DRUGS AND ON LIBERTY.   *Civil Liberties R. 1974 1(2): 117-124.* Discusses an individual's right to use or abuse drugs, based on both contemporary and past definitions of liberty.

836.   Clayton, James L.   THE SUPREME COURT, POLYGAMY AND THE ENFORCEMENT OF MORALS IN NINETEENTH CENTURY AMERICA: AN ANALYSIS OF *REYNOLDS V. UNITED STATES. Dialogue 1979 12(4): 46-61.* The 1879 Supreme Court decision on the case of Mormon George Reynolds upheld the constitutionality of the antipolygamy act passed by Congress in 1862. The Mormons held that polygamy was protected under the First Amendment guarantee of the free exercise of religion. The Court held that religious belief could not be used to justify an overt act made criminal by the law of the land. The significant basis for the Court's decision, however, was that deviant sexual behavior which offended majority sentiment could not be tolerated. In light of changed public attitudes, the Court's decision could soon be modified. Based on Utah District Court and US Supreme Court records and on secondary sources; 66 notes.   R. D. Rahmes

837.   Cofer, Richard.   BOOTLEGGERS IN THE BACKWOODS: PROHI-BITION AND THE DEPRESSION IN HERNANDO COUNTY.   *Tampa Bay Hist. 1979 1(1): 17-23.* Illegal manufacture of alcohol (moonshining) and rum-running were common in Hernando County, Florida, with the sanction of (or at least unchallenged by) local law enforcement because of the lucrative nature of the business; 1929-33.

838.   Colburn, Deborah and Colburn, Kenneth.   INTEGRITY HOUSE: THE ADDICT AS A TOTAL INSTITUTION.   *Society 1973 10(4): 39-45.*

839.   Cuskey, Walter R. and Krasner, William.   THE NEEDLE AND THE BOOT: HEROIN MAINTENANCE.   *Society 1973 10(4): 45-52.*

840.   Cuthbert, Richard W. and Stevens, Joe B.   THE NET ECONOMIC INCENTIVE FOR ILLEGAL MEXICAN MIGRATION: A CASE STUDY. *Int. Migration Rev. 1981 15(3): 543-550.* Studies Mexican farm workers in the Hood River Valley in Oregon during the fall apple harvest to determine the "net earnings differential" between wages earned in the United States and those earned in Mexico; net earnings in the United States were three times those in Mexico, less than usually stated by researchers.

841.   Dammann, Grace and Soler, Esta.   PRESCRIPTION DRUG ABUSE: A SAN FRANCISCO STUDY.   *Frontiers 1979 4(2): 5-10.* Details the findings of the 1973-77 San Francisco Polydrug Project, a study done on the extent of prescription drug abuse and treatment, which revealed women as the primary abusers, largely neglected by the drug treatment industry.

842.   Dannenbaum, Jed.   THE CRUSADE AGAINST DRINK.   *Rev. in Am. Hist. 1981 9(4): 497-502.* Reviews *Alcohol, Reform and Society: The Liquor Issue in Social Context* (1979) edited by Jack S. Blocker, Jr., Ruth Bordin's *Woman and Temperance: The Quest for Power and Liberty, 1873-1900* (1981), Barbara Leslie Epstein's *The Politics of Domesticity: Women, Evangelism, and Temperance in Nineteenth-Century America* (1981), and Ian R. Tyrrell's *Sobering Up: From Temperance to Prohibition in Antebellum America, 1800-1860* (1979).

843.   Davis, Robert.   SUICIDE AMONG YOUNG BLACKS: TRENDS AND PERSPECTIVES.   *Phylon 1980 41(3): 223-229.* The current increase in suicide among young black people is due to the weakening of communal or family ties as a result of the illusion of widespread social acceptance and opportunities. 2 tables, 16 notes.   N. G. Sapper

844.   deConde, Eulalia D.   HAITIAN REFUGEES: A DILEMMA FOR THE UNITED STATES.   *SAIS Rev. 1981 (2): 71-79.* The repressive regime of Jean Claude Duvalier has caused many Haitians to flee to the United States for economic and political asylum; Congress should not delay granting these refugees special immigrant-entrant status.

845.   Diamond, Irene.   PORNOGRAPHY AND REPRESSION: A RECON-SIDERATION.   *Signs 1980 5(4): 686-701.* Liberals traditionally have viewed pornography as a sign of progress, as sexuality in the open. However, feminists protest the lack of government concern about the increase in pornography. To feminists, pornography is not solely sexual; it represents violence which spawns actual violence against women. Reports of the liberal male-dominated President's Commission on Obscenity and Pornography gave pornography a rating of harmless, although the Commission on Violence came to an opposite conclusion regarding violence alone. Survey instruments and samples show serious fallacies which may reflect the general backlash against women's liberation and which may do a serious disservice to women in general. Based on Technical Reports of the Commission on Obscenity and Pornography and on secondary sources; 53 notes.   S. P. Conner

846.   Dielman, T. E.   GAMBLING: A SOCIAL PROBLEM?   *J. of Social Issues 1979 35(3): 36-42.* This paper reports the results from a national survey of gambling behavior, social problems, and attitudes toward the legalization of gambling. Non-bettors perceived more negative consequences and fewer positive consequences associated with the legalization of gambling than did bettors. One negative consequence perceived by a majority of both groups was an increase in political corruption. The level of gambling activity was positively associated with several social problems such as divorce, absenteeism, and frequency of alcohol consumption. Respondents who were classified as probable compulsive gamblers reported more family problems.   J

847.   Drachman, Mose.   THE TUCSON GAMBLERS.   *J. of Arizona Hist. 1973 14(1): 1-9.* As a young man in his uncle's cigar store in Tucson in the 1880's and 1890's, the author became acquainted with the gamblers who frequented the saloons and gambling halls. He recalls some of the leading gamblers, the saloon singers, gambling terminology, and how gambling was outlawed. 2 illus.
                                                           D. L. Smith

848.   Dworkin, A. Gary and Stephens, Richard C.   MEXICAN-AMERICAN ADOLESCENT INHALANT ABUSE: A PROPOSED MODEL.   *Youth & Soc. 1980 11(4): 493-506.* Solvents, spray paints, and other inhalants are popular in the barrio due to the cultural tradition in Mexico of inhalant use for medicinal purposes, poverty, and the cheapness of these drugs. Fig., 4 notes, biblio.
                                                       J. H. Sweetland

849. Earl, Philip I. THE LEGALIZATION OF GAMBLING IN NEVADA, 1931. *Nevada Hist. Soc. Q. 1981 24(1): 39-50.* Nevada legislators restored legalized gambling to Nevada in 1931 after its absence there for two decades. Some Nevadans expected renewed gambling to have little impact; others believed it wise to garner the revenues from legalized gambling; and many volubly expressed their approval when gambling establishments opened for business. Clergymen and their allies were the principal critics of gambling, and Reno Mayor E. E. Roberts its defender. Based on newspaper sources; 2 photos, 33 notes. H. T. Lovin

850. Eberhard, Kenneth D. HEROIN: AN EXAMINATION OF THE AMERICAN MYTHS. *Religion in Life 1974 42(4): 456-465.* Discusses the findings of the National Commission on Marijuana and Drug Abuse, and discusses the myths generally associated with drug abuse. S

851. Englemann, Larry. RUM-RUNNING GAVE DETROIT DIM VIEW OF PROHIBITION YEARS. *Smithsonian 1979 10(3): 113-125.* Describes rum-running from Ontario to Detroit on the Detroit River during the 1920's.

852. Epstein, Edward Jay. METHADONE: THE FORLORN HOPE. *Public Interest 1974 (36): 3-24.* The development of methadone treatment programs since World War II has failed to curb heroin addiction and crime. S

853. Fallows, James. DEATH ON THE ROAD: GOING BEYOND NADER AND THE *READER'S DIGEST. Washington Monthly 1973 5(10): 7-21.* Alternatives to preventive detention for drunks and teenagers. S

854. Feldman, Harvey. STREET STATUS AND DRUG USERS. *Society 1973 10(4): 32-38.*

855. Fishbein, Leslie. HARLOT OR HEROINE: CHANGING VIEWS OF PROSTITUTION, 1870-1920. *Historian 1980 43(1): 23-35.* Reformers in the 19th century believed that through republican institutions and economic opportunity they could cure social problems in the United States, especially the persistence of prostitution. In attacking prostitution, they were torn between containing it through regulation or eradicating it entirely. The abolitionists, however, misinterpreted prostitution. Their campaign was based on the assumption that the behavior of individuals and society could be regulated and on belief in human and social perfectibility. 53 notes. R. S. Sliwoski

856. Fragomen, Austin T., Jr. REGULATING THE ILLEGAL ALIENS. *Internat. Migration R. 1974 8(4): 567-572.* Analyzes Senate Bill S.3827 introduced by Senator Edward M. Kennedy (D-Mass), which would regularize the status of certain aliens and impose sanctions on employers.

857. Frisbie, Parker. ILLEGAL MIGRATION FROM MEXICO TO THE UNITED STATES: A LONGITUDINAL ANALYSIS. *Internat. Migration R. 1975 9(1): 3-13.* Analyzes illegal migration from Mexico to the United States, 1946-65, focusing on economic causes of migration.

858. Fujii, Edwin T. PUBLIC INVESTMENT IN THE REHABILITATION OF HEROIN ADDICTS. *Social Sci. Q. 1974 55(1): 39-51.* "Presents a methodology for evaluating the relative effectiveness of heroin addiction control

programs. . . . Applies welfare economics to the externalities generated by addiction, derives a ranking of alternatives, and offers some implications for public policies." J

859. George, Paul S. BOOTLEGGERS, PROHIBITIONISTS AND POLICE: THE TEMPERANCE MOVEMENT IN MIAMI, 1896-1920. *Tequesta 1979 39: 34-41.* Surveys attempts to enforce local and state prohibition laws in Miami, Florida, before national prohibition. Based on contemporary local newspaper articles; 34 notes. H. S. Marks

860. Graham, Otis L., Jr. THE PROBLEM THAT WILL NOT GO AWAY: ILLEGAL IMMIGRATION. *Center Mag. 1977 10(4): 56-66.* Each year, 60-90 percent of the million illegal immigrants to the United States are Mexicans; examines the causes and implications of this situation.

861. Greenberg, Andrea. DRUGGED AND SEDUCED: A CONTEMPORARY LEGEND. *New York Folklore Q. 1973 29(2): 131-158.* Folktales about the drugging and seduction of college women are a form of social control on morals. S

862. Griffin, Dick. OPIUM ADDICTION IN CHICAGO: "THE NOBLEST AND THE BEST BROUGHT LOW." *Chicago Hist. 1977 6(2): 107-116.* Opium addiction, at its worst during the 1800's-1910 in Chicago, resulted largely from nonprescription patent medicines.

863. Halvonik, Paul N. HOPE AND AFFECTION IN MILWAUKEE. *Civil Liberties R. 1974 1(4): 132-137.* Discusses issues raised at the 1974 American Civil Liberties Union Biennial Conference in Milwaukee, Wisconsin, particularly those involving victimless crimes. S

864. Hannah, Timothy H. THE BENEFITS AND COSTS OF METHADONE MAINTENANCE. *Public Policy 1976 24(2): 197-226.* Application of benefit-cost techniques to methadone maintenance treatment programs, focusing on the largest methadone program in the nation, New York City's. Analyzes direct benefits resulting from the changed behavior of treatment recipients. Methadone treatment reduces crime, thus effecting savings for potential crime victims as well as for taxpayers and methadone patients themselves. The benefits of methadone programs exceed their costs. Draws policy implications. Based on original research and secondary materials; 40 notes, biblio. J. M. Herrick

865. Hanneman, Gerhard J. COMMUNICATING DRUG-ABUSE INFORMATION AMONG COLLEGE STUDENTS. *Public Opinion Q. 1973 37(2): 171-191.* "For information on sensitive subjects, segments of the public may prefer to bypass the mass media for other sources of information that are considered especially trustworthy or informative. Information about drug use and abuse is one such subject. College students tend to utilize a variety of sources, especially personal informants, for most of their information about how and whether to sample particular drugs." J

866. Hansen, James E., II. MOONSHINE AND MURDER: PROHIBITION IN DENVER. *Colorado Mag. 1973 50(1): 1-23.* Studies the prohibition experience of Denver, Colorado, in relation to the report of the Wickersham Committee of 1931. The Denver situation exemplified the committee's conclu-

sions that prohibition was not living up to expectations. There was general resistance in the city; "undermanned, poorly organized and sometimes corrupt law enforcement; congested courts; conflicts between temperance and civil liberties; and failure to educate the public to the reform's merits." 7 illus., 85 notes.

O. H. Zabel

867. Hardaway, Roger D. PROHIBITING INTERRACIAL MARRIAGE: MISCEGENATION LAWS IN WYOMING. *Ann. of Wyoming 1980 52(1): 55-60.* In 1869, the Wyoming Territorial Legislature overwhelmingly passed a bill making illegal marriage or cohabitation between whites and other races. Some opposition to the bill materialized in white-owned newspapers, but a majority of people favored the concept. Governor John A. Campbell refused to sign the bill because it omitted Indians from the list, but it was passed over his veto. The original law was repealed in 1882, but a second miscegenation law was enacted in 1913 and lived an uneventful life until its repeal in 1965. Based on newspapers and primary sources; 58 notes.

M. L. Tate

868. Harper, John Paull. BE FRUITFUL AND MULTIPLY: ORIGINS OF LEGAL RESTRICTIONS ON PLANNED PARENTHOOD IN NINE-TEENTH-CENTURY AMERICA. Berkin, Carol Ruth and Norton, Mary Beth, ed. *Women of America: A History* (Boston: Houghton Mifflin Co., 1979): 245-269. Describes US 19th-century legal policy to suppress demands for birth control and trade in birth control devices. Some historians have claimed that this was an act to oppress women, but there is an indication that political leaders were afraid America would be underpopulated. Robert Dale Owen was a radical espouser of planned parenthood who believed birth control would improve the lot of the individual in society. Examines the place of abortion and the effect of Comstock laws. Primary sources; 10 notes.

K. Talley

869. Harrison, David and Seelig, Gus. POT BUSTS IN VERMONT. *Civil Liberties Rev. 1976 3(3): 60-64.* Paul Lawrence, an undercover narcotics officer in St. Albans, made more than 600 drug-related arrests (many of them false arrests) in eight years before his arrest and conviction in 1974 for perjury and use of police money under false pretenses.

870. Herman, Judith and Hirschman, Lisa. FATHER-DAUGHTER IN-CEST. *Signs 1977 2(4): 735-756.* Assesses current literature on incest, places it within the paradigm of patriarchal society, and reviews the psychotherapy history of 15 father-daughter incest victims, 1970's.

871. Herzog, Harold and Cheek, Pauline B. GRIT AND STEEL: THE ANATOMY OF COCKFIGHTING. *Southern Exposure 1979 7(3): 36-40.* Cockfighting enjoys its greatest popularity in rural communities in the United States ranging from Virginia to New Mexico. Although illegal in most areas, the sport enjoys a great deal of audience interest and flourishes owing to lax law enforcement and low visibility to the general public. The most common type of organized cockfighting match held today is the "derby" in which cocks fight in a round robin with the winner taking the pot. Cockfights end when a handler concedes the fight, when a cock does not adhere to the second's count in forms of attack called "pittings," or when a cock dies. Cockfights attract blacks and whites, men and women. Generally considerable gambling takes place around the pit. Based largely on interviews and personal observation.

N. Lederer

872. Hewlett, Sylvia Ann. COPING WITH ILLEGAL IMMIGRANTS. *Foreign Affairs 1981-82 60(2): 358-378.* Examines the influx of illegal aliens and efforts of the Carter and Reagan administrations to control it; 1977-81.

873. Hirata, Lucie Cheng. FREE, INDENTURED, ENSLAVED: CHINESE PROSTITUTES IN NINETEENTH-CENTURY AMERICA. *Signs 1979 5(1): 3-29.* When Chinese prostitution developed in 19th-century America, it provided a double economic benefit. Cheap labor in California was guaranteed, while economic benefits were transmitted to China. Families of the laborers in China were supported, and the problem of an over-abundance of nonproductive women was remedied. The Chinese patriarchal system supported prostitution because daughters had no choice except to submit. In America, conditions ranged from concubinage to ruthless slavery. A period of competition during 1849-54 was followed by the creation of a rigorous and corrupt trade network, which lasted until 1925, although prostitution had begun to decline by 1880. Based on California and US census records and secondary sources; 4 tables, 126 notes.
S. P. Conner

874. Holdsworth, William K. ADULTERY OR WITCHCRAFT? A NEW NOTE ON AN OLD CASE IN CONNECTICUT. *New England Q. 1975 48(3): 394-409.* Elizabeth Johnson of Hartford, Connecticut, was convicted of a capital crime in 1650. Historians have mistakenly thought that the crime was witchcraft, but new evidence and reexamination of existing evidence indicate that Johnson was convicted, along with Thomas Newton, of adultery. Reviews the history of the case, including Newton's subsequent escape to New York, Johnson's release, and the history of adultery as a capital crime in Connecticut and New England. Based on primary and secondary sources; 45 notes.
B. C. Tharaud

875. Hopkins, Jerry. COCAINE CONSCIOUSNESS: THE GOURMET TRIP. *J. of Popular Culture 1975 9(2): 305-314.* Reviews the history of the use of cocaine and its popularity and status in the early 1970's.

876. Hori, Joan. JAPANESE PROSTITUTION IN HAWAII DURING THE IMMIGRATION PERIOD. *Hawaiian J. of Hist. 1980 15: 113-124.* At the turn of the century, a considerable number of young Japanese women earned their livelihoods as prostitutes. Japanese males profited from the transport of prostitutes to the islands; in addition, wife selling became both common and lucrative. Japanese "picture" brides were sometimes coerced or blackmailed into prostitution by their husbands. Japanese gangsters controlled the majority of island prostitutes, housing them in shacks in Honolulu's Chinatown and Iwilei districts. Concerned citizens and missionary and church groups mounted campaigns and protests to stamp out the trade in the Iwilei district, but to no avail. After 1914, the number of prostitutes in Iwilei dwindled somewhat following wholesale arrests by immigration officials, however, the fate of the majority of Japanese prostitutes remains a mystery. Primary sources; 41 notes.
G. A. Glovins

877. Humm, Andrew. THE PERSONAL POLITICS OF LESBIAN AND GAY LIBERATION. *Social Policy 1980 11(2): 40-45.* Discusses "liberation from confining sex roles in relationships and in the larger social scheme," briefly

traces antihomosexual attitudes and actions, and focuses on the gay movement since the 1969 Stonewall riots in New York.

878. Hunsaker, David M. UPSETTING THE PORNOGRAPHER'S AP-PLECART: A CRITICAL REVIEW OF *MILLER V. CALIFORNIA*. *Rendezvous 1973-74 8(2): 39-50.* After *Miller* v. *California* (US, 1973), the question of what makes something obscene remains unresolved. At best, the decision maintains the status quo by reaffirming *Roth* (US, 1957). At worst, the decision regresses to a pluralistic concept of the meaning of obscenity with as many different community standards as there are juries applying them, and a concept which, due to the mass media and the increasing mobility of the population, is even less tenable than a decade ago when *Jacobellis* (US, 1964) was decided.   P. Travis

879. Hybels, Judith H. THE IMPACT OF LEGALIZATION ON ILLE-GAL GAMBLING PARTICIPATION. *J. of Social Issues 1979 35(3): 27-35.* This paper examines the effects of legalization on illegal gambling participation using a multivariate analysis to adjust for the influence of demographic variables. In addition, the incidence of illegal gambling in a nationwide sample was compared with the incidence reported by Nevada residents. Games with similar structures and psychological characteristics appear to be complementary. That is, people who participate in one tend to participate in the other as well, regardless of their legal status. Dissimilar games operate as substitutes for each other. [Covers 1974].   J

880. Jackson, Charles O. BEFORE THE DRUG CULTURE: BARBITU-RATE/AMPHETAMINE ABUSE IN AMERICAN SOCIETY. *Clio Medica [Netherlands] 1976 11(1): 47-58.* In 1903 American industry introduced to the public barbital (Veronae), an effective hypnotic. It was readily available and quickly abused. Amphetamines, developed to relieve nasal congestion, appeared in 1932. Within a few years students and truck drivers were using them to ward off sleep, and doctors were prescribing them for cases of obesity and depression. Some people combined the use of the two for the "ping-pong" effect. The 1965 Drug Abuse Control Amendment helped check the source from bootleggers, druggists, and physicians. Police action can only limit the supply but not eradicate the problem. 50 notes.   A. J. Papalas

881. Johnson, Bruce D. SENSE AND NONSENSE IN THE "SCIEN-TIFIC" STUDY OF DRUGS: AN ANTI-COMMISSION REPORT. *Society 1973 10(4): 53-58.* Critiques methods and conclusions of the National Commission on Marijuana and Drug Abuse (Schafer Commission), 1972.   S

882. Johnson, Claudia D. THAT GUILTY THIRD TIER: PROSTITU-TION IN NINETEENTH-CENTURY AMERICAN THEATERS. *Am. Q. 1975 27(5): 575-584.* The assignment of prostitutes to the third tier in 19th-century theaters was a serious problem to those working for the survival of the theatrical institution. Not only was the issue one of continual controversy between moralists and artists, but it also had an impact on theater design, theatrical economics, and the acceptance and support of the theater in American life. The theater gradually achieved respectability only through a dissociation from prostitution. Based on primary and secondary sources.   N. Lederer

883.   Jones, Richard C.   CHANNELIZATION OF UNDOCUMENTED MEXICAN MIGRANTS TO THE U.S.   *Econ. Geog. 1982 58(2): 156-176.* Based on the work of social geographers, discusses whether the migration of undocumented Mexicans to the United States is beneficial or detrimental, examines the migration in numbers, and focuses on the origins of migrants, their destinations, and flow patterns, particularly what is called "channelization" or "a disproportionately large flow of migrants between a specific origin and a specific destination"; 1975-82.

884.   Joyce, Kathleen M.   PUBLIC OPINION AND THE POLITICS OF GAMBLING.   *J. of Social Issues 1979 35(3): 144-165.* Examines the relation between the attitudes of the public toward gambling and recent changes in gambling laws. The nineteenth century wave of antigambling sentiment found expression in many state constitutions. Consequently, legalization or decriminalization of gambling became unusually difficult among that class of activities often referred to as "victimless crimes." Renewed interest in gambling as a revenue source, in the last few decades, has produced a number of surveys dealing with attitudes toward gambling and has required statewide votes on some 45 separate gambling items. Public attitudes are compared, along several dimensions, for results of a national survey and results of voting on particular gambling proposals. Attitudes are consistent between survey data and voting data, particularly as they pertain to administrative and regulatory form. Also, in one state, demographic variables discriminating favorability in the survey data predict voting outcome on a lottery proposal.   J

885.   Kallick-Kaufmann, Maureen.   THE MICRO AND MACRO DIMENSIONS OF GAMBLING IN THE UNITED STATES.   *J. of Social Issues 1979 35(3): 7-26.* A national probability sample of the 1736 respondents and a Nevada State probability sample of 296 respondents were surveyed during the summer of 1975 to determine the extent of gambling activity in the United States, to estimate the amount of government revenue that could result from various changes in the gambling laws, and to predict the social consequences of these changes. While there were large variations among regions and demographic groups, a majority of all adult Americans gamble. Wagers on commercial games amounted to $22.4 billion in 1974 of which $17 billion was wagered legally and approximately $5 billion illegally.   J

886.   Kandel, Denise.   INTER- AND INTRAGENERATIONAL INFLUENCES ON ADOLESCENT MARIJUANA USE.   *J. of Social Issues 1974 30(2): 107-135.* "To investigate inter- and intragenerational influences in adolescent marijuana use, a survey was undertaken on a representative sample of public secondary school students in New York State. Independent data were obtained from adolescents, their parents, and their best school-friends. These relational data document the crucial role which members of the same generation play in adolescent illegal drug use. Involvement with other drug-using adolescents is a more important correlate of adolescent marijuana use than is parental use of psychoactive drugs or alcohol (which provides a small influence). Inter- and intragenerational influences are synergistic, however. The highest rates of marijuana usage are observed among adolescents whose parents and best friends are drug users. Interactional generational factors influence levels of intragenerational influences. Implications of these data for parental and peer influence, the generation gap, and social change are discussed."   J

887. Kinder, Douglas Clark. BUREAUCRATIC COLD WARRIOR: HARRY J. ANSLINGER AND ILLICIT NARCOTICS TRAFFIC. *Pacific Hist. Rev. 1981 50(2): 169-191.* Federal Narcotics Commissioner Harry J. Anslinger exploited the passions of the Cold War to further the interests of his bureaucratic agency. He attributed the drug problem in the United States to an Italian-American "Mafia" conspiracy with international linkage, Communist China dumping of narcotics on the free world during the Korean War, and Castro's Cuban agents smuggling cocaine into the United States. Anslinger enlisted the support of anti-Communists, and impugned the integrity of the bureau's critics. Anslinger's charge against Communist China was inaccurate, because evidence proves that after 1949 Communist China cracked down on the drug traffic. Drug trafficking in Cuba preceded the Castro regime. Based on the Harry J. Anslinger Papers, Bureau of Narcotics circular letters, and other primary sources; 34 notes.   R. N. Lokken

888. Klotter, James C. SEX, SCANDAL, AND SUFFRAGE IN THE GILDED AGE. *Historian 1980 42(2): 225-243.* W. C. P. Breckinridge's affair with student Madeline Pollard began in 1884 and ended in a political scandal during 1893-94. Breckinridge, a Democrat in the House of Representatives since 1881, was known natioally as the "silver tongued orator of Kentucky." His scandal is indicative of the views of sex, morality, and politics during this period. The Gilded Age's morality has traditionally incorporated two images—that of a low state of public morals and strict Victorian outlook. In retrospect, "if sexual transgression could be quantified, the known examples of public officials would very probably fall beneath the general public's Gilded Age average." Primary sources; 61 notes.   R. S. Sliwoski

889. Kupperstein, Lenore R. ASSESSING THE NATURE AND DIMENSIONS OF THE DRUG PROBLEM. *Ann. of the Am. Acad. of Pol. and Social Sci. 1975 417: 76-85.* "Over the years, various attempts have been made to define, describe and measure the nature and dimensions of psychoactive drug use in the United States. The purpose of this article is to address the problems of definition associated with the traditional concept of 'drug abuse'; to examine the various formulations of 'the drug problem'; to assess the efficacy of the survey method and other research techniques currently utilized to estimate the nature and extent of drug use; and to report on some of the efforts made by the National Commission on Marihuana and Drug Abuse to provide guidance and direction in this area to researchers and policy makers alike."   J

890. Kushner, Howard I. THE SUICIDE OF MERIWETHER LEWIS: A PSYCHOANALYTIC INQUIRY. *William and Mary Q. 1981 38(3): 464-481.* Historians have been divided over the cause of Meriwether Lewis's death, 10 October 1809, at age 35. Using psychoanalysis, the author decides that the explorer's death was a suicide. Everything was a letdown after the famous western expedition. Lewis had an authoritarian manner as governor of Upper Louisiana Territory. He experienced extreme depression, and contemporaries noticed that his alcoholism produced states of mental derangement. The actions of Lewis during his last day, including his stay at the inn at Grinder's Stand, along the Natchez Trace, are closely detailed. Events of Lewis's childhood, such as the death of his father when Lewis was five, his abortive courtships, and his destructive recklessness during his career are factors contributing to Lewis's frame of mind.   H. M. Ward

891.   Lafree, Gary.   OFFICIAL REACTIONS TO SOCIAL PROBLEMS: POLICE DECISIONS IN SEXUAL ASSAULT CASES.   *Social Problems 1981 28(5): 582-594.* Provides data from 905 sexual-assault complaints to police in a large, midwestern town during 1970-75, and describes the creation of a special sex offense unit as a direct link with the perception of rape as a growing social problem.

892.   Lane, Roger.   SUICIDE AND THE CITY.   *Society 1980 17(2): 74-82.* Examines suicide rates in American cities, noting the social background of victims and methods employed.

893.   Leader, Jeanne P.   THE POTTAWATOMIES AND ALCOHOL: AN ILLUSTRATION OF THE ILLEGAL TRADE.   *Kansas Hist. 1979 2(3): 157-165.* The Potawatomi Indians lived near Council Bluffs, Iowa, from 1837 until 1847, when they were moved to Kansas. Already exposed to excessive drinking in their ancestral home in Indiana, Illinois, and Michigan, the Indians were now exposed to the white renegades' liquor trade along the Missouri River. Regulatory laws were ineffective, because they were violated with impunity by the agents sworn to carry them out. The military failed to curb the trade, and the government won only a modest court victory over a principal supplier, the American Fur Company. Increasing alcoholism among Indians demonstrated the detrimental quality of some of the "civilized" ways the Indians were being asked to follow. Based on books, articles, manuscripts in the National Archives and Kansas State Historical Society; illus., map, 30 notes.   W. F. Zornow

894.   Leonard, Carol and Wallimann, Isidor.   PROSTITUTION AND CHANGING MORALITY IN THE FRONTIER CATTLE TOWNS OF KANSAS.   *Kansas Hist. 1979 2(1): 34-53.* Prostitution was illegal in the cattle towns of Abilene, Ellsworth, Wichita, Dodge City, and Caldwell, but no effort was made to suppress it when most of the inhabitants were young, single, transient men engaged in the cattle trade. Prostitutes were arrested and fined on schedule to raise funds for the local government. There was no moral indignation about prostitution until the residents became permanent settlers who wished to establish families. The changes were not the same in every town but depended on the type and number of new settlers. Covers ca. 1868-85. Based on newspapers, police court records, and city council records; illus., map, graph, 95 notes.
                                                                                      W. F. Zornow

895.   Light, Ivan.   THE ETHNIC VICE INDUSTRY, 1880-1944.   *Am. Sociol. Rev. 1977 42(3): 464-479.* Sociologists have explained the association of ethnic minorities and illegal enterprise in terms of structural blockages and opportunities, emphatically denying any ethnic contribution. A comparison of blacks and Chinese in the vice industry, 1880-1940, confirms the guiding role of American society which rewarded ethnics' participation in prostitution but restricted legal earning opportunities. Nonetheless, divergent demographic and cultural characteristics of Chinese and blacks differentially affected the internal organization of each group's vice industry as well as the process of industrial succession. This finding supports a view of illegal enterprise as a synthesis of illegal work that consumers want to buy and what disadvantaged ethnics have to offer. In general, socio-cultural characteristics of provider subgroups define the manner in which they respond to consumer demand for illegal products and services.   J

896. Light, Ivan. FROM RACKETEERS TO RESTAURANTEURS. *Mankind 1976 5(10): 8-10, 52-53.* Between 1865 and 1920 American Chinatowns were centers of gambling, prostitution, and narcotics, attracting many whites as well as Chinese, especially to houses of prostitution. After 1890 middle-class white tourists began to discover Chinatown and sought vicarious pleasures through touring dens of vice. The result was that vice waned and the tourist business began to flourish in these areas.　　　　　　　　　　　N. Lederer

897. Lipton, Douglas S. and Marel, Rozanne. THE WHITE ADOLESCENT'S DRUG ODYSSEY. *Youth & Soc. 1980 11(4): 397-413.* A typical white, middle-class male high school student proceeds from early experiments with marijuana to heavy use. His story is interspersed with extracts from professional literature. Biblio.　　　　　　　　　　　J. H. Sweetland

898. Little, Joseph W. AN EMPIRICAL DESCRIPTION OF ADMINISTRATION OF JUSTICE IN DRUNK DRIVING CASES. *Law & Soc. R. 1973 7(3): 473-492.* An in-depth analysis (1969-73) of the disposition of drunk driving cases in Vermont as a way of increasing law enforcement and reducing the number of drunk driving cases throughout the country. There was a high conviction rate of DWI (Driving While Intoxicated) drivers in Vermont, although evidence shows that as time lag increases between the offense and disposition, a lesser punishment is obtained. Offers recommendations for administering DWI programs in all states.　　　　　　　　　　　H. R. Mahood

899. Maibaum, Matthew and López, Genevieve. DRUG ABUSE IN THE EAST LOS ANGELES HEALTH DISTRICT. *Aztlán 1981 12(1): 139-155.* A statistical analysis of drug abuse, drug abuse treatment, and drug abuse arrests in Los Angeles County in the 1970's. The data indicate that a serious drug abuse problem exists in the East Los Angeles Health District: while arrests for drug abuse are higher than in the rest of the county, drug abuse treatment facilities are lacking. 7 tables, 29 notes.　　　　　　　　　　　A. Hoffman

900. Marcum, Jess and Rowen, Henry. HOW MANY GAMES IN TOWN? —THE PROS AND CONS OF LEGALIZED GAMBLING. *Public Interest 1974 (36): 25-52.* Discusses the effects of widespread legalization of gambling on government revenues, crime, and other social issues.　　　　　　　　　　　S

901. Marshall, James R. POLITICAL INTEGRATION AND THE EFFECT OF WAR ON SUICIDE: UNITED STATES, 1933-76. *Social Forces 1981 59(3): 771-785.* The effect of war on the suicide rate and the need to disentangle the effects of economic and political integration in the relation of the suicide rate to war are discussed. Most explanations ignore economic conditions; they imply that the direct effect of a great national war on the suicide rate is a result of the war's generation of political integration and political integration's subsequent depressing of suicidal tendencies. An examination of suicide rate trends among white US adults does not show this, even with economic conditions held constant.　　　　　　　　　　　J

902. May, Philip A. ARRESTS, ALCOHOL, AND ALCOHOL LEGALIZATION AMONG AN AMERICAN INDIAN TRIBE. *Plains Anthropologist 1975 20(68): 129-134.* In the entire history of the contact between American Indians and Western culture, alcohol has been a source of friction and contro-

versy. This paper attempts to define the contemporary and historical relationship between alcohol, arrests and the Indians of a large tribe on the Great Plains. The situation on and off the Reservation is explored during periods of prohibition and also during one short legalization period. Some questions are raised regarding the relationships between Native American drinking patterns and the unique legal status which alcohol has had in relation to most tribal groups.   J

903. Mazón, Mauricio. ILLEGAL ALIEN SURROGATES: A PSYCHOHISTORICAL INTERPRETATION OF GROUP STEREOTYPING IN TIME OF ECONOMIC STRESS. *Aztlán 1976 6(2): 305-321.* Illegal Mexican immigrants historically have served as scapegoats for the irrational and aggressive impulses of the majority, especially during times of economic depression. Various psychological mechanisms of projection, condensation, reaction formation, and substitution have generated justifications for the oppression of the Mexican immigrant in American society. No one has yet dealt with the problem in a rational way. Based on newspapers, congressional records, and secondary sources; 58 notes.   R. Griswold del Castillo

904. McCaghy, Charles H. and Neal, Arthur G. THE FRATERNITY OF COCKFIGHTERS: ETHNICAL EMBELLISHMENTS OF AN ILLEGAL SPORT. *J. of Popular Culture 1974 8(3): 557-569.* Gives the history of cockfighting, 3000 BC-1975 and centers on the ethnic groups which are most frequently associated with the illegal sport, principally in the United States.

905. McCormick, John S. RED LIGHTS IN ZION: SALT LAKE CITY'S STOCKADE, 1908-11. *Utah Hist. Q. 1982 50(2): 168-181.* Prostitution in Salt Lake City centered around Commercial Street from the late 1870's until the second decade of the 20th century. Led by Police Chief Thomas D. Pitt (1907) and Mayor John Bransford, plans were made to relocate prostitutes into a series of cribs, which were small apartments facing each other in two parallel rows within a stockade. The new location was away from the central city area. Led by prominent madam Belle London, Police Chief Samuel Barlow, May Bransford, and Councilman Martin E. Mulvey, the stockade closed its doors for all business. Prostitution continues but not in the stockade or in any established business area. 7 photos, 43 notes.   K. E. Gilmont

906. Miles, Dwight E. THE GROWTH OF SUICIDE AMONG BLACK AMERICANS. *Crisis 1979 86(10): 430-433.* Recent statistics demonstrate a rapid increase in suicides among young urban blacks, especially women. Experts believe that suicide occurs as a result of some personal loss: actual, imagined, threatened, or potential, but to the person, real. Economic and political oppression are real. Belief in a myth that black matriarchy produces mental health problems may contribute to suicide, especially since the decline of the church as a support system.   A. G. Belles

907. Monkkonen, Eric. TOWARD AN UNDERSTANDING OF URBANIZATION: DRUNK ARRESTS IN LOS ANGELES. *Pacific Hist. Rev. 1981 50(2): 234-244.* Studies of Los Angeles have not resulted in a broad conceptual scheme for understanding that city and its history. An analysis of time series data provides a foundation for developing a conceptual frame that fits Los Angeles into a changing network of cities. An analysis of arrest cases for public drunken-

ness in Los Angeles since 1898, compared with the same offense data in 12 other major American cities, reveals an erratic trend in Los Angeles, running counter to the national trend during most of the period. The Los Angeles experience, however, was similar to Pittsburgh's. Based on annual reports of the Los Angeles Police Department and secondary sources; graph, 12 notes.   R. N. Lokken

908. Monson, Michael C.   THE DIRTY LITTLE SECRET BEHIND OUR DRUG LAWS.   *Reason 1980 12(7): 48-52.* Links the original prohibition of drugs to antipathy directed toward specific groups or minorities associated with drug use; before the antidrug laws no drug problem, syndicates, other criminal involvements, or "dope fiends" existed; covers ca. 1875-1980.

909. Mushkin, Selma.   POLITICS AND ECONOMICS OF GOVERN-MENT RESPONSE TO DRUG ABUSE.   *Ann. of the Am. Acad. of Pol. and Social Sci. 1975 417: 27-40.* "Relative numbers of relative costs define the type and size of political response to drug abuse in the United States. Those who are damaged by the crime originating in drug abuse outnumber the abusers. While the total costs of crime attributed to drug abuse is high and exceeds efforts of control, intractability of the problem stands in the way of effective action. This paper presents an alternative to the 'get-tough' policies represented by action recently taken in New York and the priorities of the federal 1975 budget. It is a second chance of self-help in a new life. Analysis of this proposal is a next step. Its potential adoption, given the relative numbers, is not favorable, and the preferred approach is likely to be incremental. But there is reason to expect that incremental solutions are not sufficient."   J

910. Neier, Aryeh.   PUBLIC BOOZERS AND PRIVATE SMOKERS. *Civil Liberties R. 1975 2(4): 41-56.* Despite the apparent differences between the victimless crimes of public drunkenness and marijuana use, the laws against them have served an identical purpose. They have served as weapons against those in our society who are despised.   J

911. Oaks, Bert F.   "THINGS FEARFUL TO NAME": SODOMY AND BUGGERY IN SEVENTEENTH-CENTURY NEW ENGLAND.   *J. of Social Hist. 1978 12(2): 268-281.* In recent years historians have begun to study human sexuality, but in recent demographic studies of 17th-century New England, there is almost no consideration of variant sexual activities such as homosexuality and bestiality. Corrects this absence with an examination of variant sexual activities documented principally in the court records. Discusses the confusion over terminology, punishments for the various offenses, and the attitudes of the colonials to variant sexual activity. Concludes that nothing is more symbolic of the failure of the city upon a hill than the history of variant sexual activity in 17th-century New England. Primary and secondary sources; 58 notes.
R. S. Sliwoski

912. Page, J. Bryan.   THE CHILDREN OF EXILE: RELATIONSHIPS BE-TWEEN THE ACCULTURATION PROCESS AND DRUG USE AMONG CUBAN YOUTH.   *Youth & Soc. 1980 11(4): 431-447.* Immigrant males from Cuba, more than any other ethnic or racial youth group, show a high level of drug abuse. They favor marijuana, quaaludes, and cocaine. This use is based in Cuban cultural patterns, especially those emphasizing alertness and macho strength.

Based on the records of the Dade County (Florida) Comprehensive Drug Program files, secondary sources; 3 tables, biblio.   J. H. Sweetland

913. Peck, Dennis L. and Bharadwaj, Lakshmi K.   PERSONAL STRESS AND FATALISM AS FACTORS IN COLLEGE SUICIDE. *Social Sci. 1980 55(1): 19-24.* The rise in the incidence of suicide among college students has been particularly dramatic and now ranks as the second most frequent cause of death within this group. Each year about 10,000 college students in the United States attempt suicide; about 1,000 are successful. Some believe that the higher suicide rate among college students than that recorded for nonstudents of comparable age-specific categories is due to the strain and frustration encountered by students. Yet, despite recent evidence which suggests a significant incidence of fatalistic suicide among youthful members of our society, the evaluation of the impact of fatalism on suicide has been largely neglected. This paper analyzes the college suicide problem by focusing on personal stress and fatalism as factors in college suicide. Evaluation of the contemporary educational system is presented and some suggestions are made for coping with the college suicide problem. Note, ref.   J

914. Petrik, Paula.   CAPITALISTS WITH ROOMS: PROSTITUTION IN HELENA, MONTANA, 1865-1900. *Montana 1981 31(2): 28-41.* Between 1865 and 1900, prostitution in Helena, Montana, constituted the largest single women's employment outside the home. Feminine entrepreneurs built a business "empire" in Helena, becoming leading (although socially unacceptable) capitalists and property owners, demonstrating upward and outward social mobility for women. Changing economic conditions brought about by the Panic of 1893, and changing social values curtailed the profitability of these business ventures by 1900 and circumscribed a more traditional role for women. Based on Helena city records, Lewis and Clark County property records and other legal documents, contemporary newspapers, and secondary sources; 3 illus., 4 maps, table, 58 notes.   R. C. Myers

915. Phillips, David P.   THE INFLUENCE OF SUGGESTION ON SUICIDE: SUBSTANTIVE AND THEORETICAL IMPLICATIONS OF THE WERTHER EFFECT. *Am. Sociol. Rev. 1974 39(3): 340-354.* Data collected 1947-68 in Great Britain and the United States indicate that suicides increase following public disclosure of a suicide.

916. Piore, Michael.   THE "ILLEGAL ALIENS" DEBATE MISSES THE BOAT. *Working Papers for a New Soc. 1978 6(2): 60-69.* Asserts that immigration policy should be responsible to the economic conditions in the United States and not to the whims of Congress, 1978.

917. Pivar, David J.   CLEANSING THE NATION: THE WAR ON PROSTITUTION, 1917-21. *Prologue 1980 12(1): 29-40.* The World War I effort prompted social engineering leading to a partnership (known as the American Plan) between social hygienists in voluntary associations and their counterparts in federal government. Under section 2 of the Army Appropriation Act (US, 1916), Congress established the Council of National Defense to provide for cooperation on social hygiene between volunteer agencies and government. The Chamberlain-Kahn Act (US, 1918) created a division of venereal disease within

the US Public Health Service. On 9 July 1918, an Interdepartmental Board of Social Hygiene was created by law. The new social policy was to control venereal disease and to eliminate prostitution in order to protect servicemen and keep them healthy. Based on correspondence and newspapers; 6 illus., 42 notes.

M. A. Kascus

918. Portes, Alejandro. ILLEGAL IMMIGRATION AND THE INTER-NATIONAL SYSTEM: LESSONS FROM RECENT LEGAL MEXICAN IM-MIGRANTS TO THE UNITED STATES. *Social Problems 1979 26(4): 425-438.* Data from case studies of illegal Mexican immigrants conducted during 1972-73 indicate that not all came from backward areas; several came from urbanized areas with comparatively high levels of education and headed for US cities and urban occupations, thus supporting the idea that such immigration is an outgrowth of the accelerating contradictions effected by capitalist development in Mexico and in other nations on the US periphery.

919. Power, Jonathan. THE GREAT DEBATE ON ILLEGAL IMMIGRA-TION: EUROPE AND THE USA COMPARED. *J. of Int. Affairs 1979 33(2): 239-248.* Compares European and US attempts to control illegal immigration from 1947 to 1978.

920. Preston, William. HOW WE BECAME ADDICTED TO DRUG CON-TROL. *Civil Liberties Rev. 1977 4(2): 68-71.* Discusses drug control legislation and police activities, 1914-76; sane attitudes toward discrimination and social acceptance will come only through medical and scientific research.

921. Preston, William, Jr. FEAR AND LOATHING IN ADDICTED AMERICA. *Rev. in Am. Hist. 1975 3(1): 123-128.* Review article prompted by Richard J. Bonnie and Charles H. Whitebread II's *The Marihuana Conviction: A History of Marihuana Prohibition in the United States* (Charlottesville: U. Pr. of Virginia, 1974) and David F. Musto's *The American Disease: Origins of Narcotic Control* (New Haven, Conn.: Yale U. Pr., 1973), which trace the origins of drug abuse, and subsequent law enforcement, in the United States from the Civil War.

922. Ragsdale, J. Donald. LAST TANGO IN PARIS, ET AL. V. THE SUPREME COURT: THE CURRENT STATE OF OBSCENITY LAW. *Q. J. of Speech 1975 61(3): 279-289.* The Supreme Court has so far failed to define obscenity and pornography and to let pass laws that would lead to censorship of X-rated films (1970's).

923. Randall, Richard S. OBSCENITY: DENATIONALIZATION AND THE CONFLICT OF COSMOPOLITAN AND LOCAL-POPULAR VAL-UES. *Policy Studies J. 1975 4(2): 151-156.* Discusses the Supreme Court's decision in *Miller v. California* (US, 1973) that erotica may be judged obscene by the application of state or local standards as opposed to national ones.

924. Robbins, Peggy. LOUISIANA LOTTERY SO BIG IT DIDN'T HAVE TO BE RIGGED. *Smithsonian 1980 10(10): 113-125.* Clever carpetbaggers easily milked wealth from the country after the Civil War. With a minimal pledge of $40,000 per year to state charities, John Morris and Charley Howard manipulated a corrupt legislature and obtained a 25-year lottery charter. Immensely

successful in Louisiana, the operation was extended throughout the United States and beyond, with an annual profit of up to $500 million. Opposition on moral grounds developed countrywide until finally the "Golden Octopus" was doomed by Congress, which made it a crime to send lottery material through the federal postal system. 10 illus.   H. F. Thomson

925. Robertson, Leon S.; Rich, Robert F.; and Ross, H. Laurence. JAIL SENTENCES FOR DRIVING WHILE INTOXICATED IN CHICAGO: A JUDICIAL POLICY THAT FAILED. *Law and Soc. R. 1973 8(1): 55-67.* Sentencing motorists to seven-day jail terms for drunken driving failed to lower motor-vehicle-related fatality rates in Chicago in 1971.   S

926. Robinson, Gerald L. and Miller, Stephen T. DRUG ABUSE AND THE COLLEGE CAMPUS. *Ann. of the Am. Acad. of Pol. and Social Sci. 1975 417: 101-109.* "Traditionally, American society has entrusted to its colleges and universities the authority to govern broad aspects of student life on campus; it has expected in return the mental, physical and moral well-being of the students in their charge. By the late 1960's, however, both the concept and practice of *in loco parentis* by educational institutions had come under increasing attack, with challenges most frequently being directed to the right of colleges and universities to control nonacademic aspects of student life and conduct, including the use of psychoactive drugs. Despite the concern voiced by parents and educators over the escalating use of psychoactive drugs by young people and the waves of drug use reaching the college campus, college administrators, with virtually no experience in this area, generally found themselves unprepared to cope with the problem. The intent of this paper is to examine the responses of college and university administrators to student drug use, to explore the manner in which drug policies have been formulated and implmeneted in response to the perceived problem, and to reflect on the impact and effectiveness of the policies which have emerged and which are currently in force at institutions of higher learning throughout the country."   J

927. Robles, Rafaela R.; Martinez, Ruth E.; and Moscoso, Margarita R. PREDICTORS OF ADOLESCENT DRUG BEHAVIOR: THE CASE OF PUERTO RICO. *Youth & Soc. 1980 11(4): 415-430.* Drug use among youths in Puerto Rico surprisingly resembles patterns in the United States. Parental control has little effect on the decision to use drugs, while peer group pressure has major effects. In general, the heaviest drug use is by males in private high schools. Girls tend to be heavier users of cigarettes and alcohol. Based on a stratified random sample of Puerto Rican high school students in 1975-76, and on other works; 10 tables, biblio.   J. H. Sweetland

928. Rodgers, Harrell R., Jr. CENSORSHIP CAMPAIGNS IN EIGHTEEN CITIES: AN IMPACT ANALYSIS. *Am. Pol. Q. 1974 2(4): 371-392.* Primarily examines the impact of urban censorship campaigns during 1967-68 on the effectiveness of US Supreme Court decisions on obscenity laws which protected the "right of newsdealers to sell and the public to buy certain types of publications."   S

929. Rollin, Roger B. TRIPLE-X: EROTIC MOVIES AND THEIR AUDI-ENCES. *J. of Popular Film and Television 1982 10(1): 2-21.* Attendance at hard-core erotic films challenges legal codes and religious and ethical standards; movie attendance usually has been a social ritual that unites all attendees "into a kind of community"; attendance at "Triple-X" films, a subversive and solitary experience usually socially frowned upon, fulfills the same function as other films.

930. Roucek, Joseph S. LOS PROBLEMAS DE LOS INMIGRANTES MEJICANOS EN LOS ESTADOS UNIDOS [Problems of Mexican immigrants in the United States]. *R. de Pol. Social [Spain] 1974 (103): 85-99.* Discusses the impact of the population explosion on illegal Mexican immigration into the United States since the 1950's, especially in southern California and in Texas, focusing on "Operation Wetback" and its effect on legal and illegal immigration; also notes the exploitation of Mexican workers by lawyers.

931. Roucek, Joseph S. PORNOGRAPHY, OBSCENITY AND CENSOR-SHIP IN THE U.S. *Rev. del Inst. de Ciencias Sociales [Spain] 1975 (25/26): 335-359.* Defines and discusses pornography and obscenity in contemporary US society, including the various media and effects on children and adolescents, and cites the recommendations and conclusions of the President's Commission on Obscenity and Pornography (1970), most of which were later disowned by President Nixon.

932. Sandos, James A. PROSTITUTION AND DRUGS: THE UNITED STATES ARMY ON THE MEXICAN-AMERICAN BORDER, 1916-1917. *Pacific Hist. Rev. 1980 49(4): 621-645.* General John J. Pershing, commander of the US Punitive Expedition into Mexico, reduced the number of venereal disease cases among his men at Columbus, New Mexico, and in Mexico by regulating prostitution to maintain troop morale and prevent infection. The venereal disease rate in his command was lower than elsewhere in the United States Army where War Department policy of abolishing prostitution in the vicinity of army camps was practiced. The ban on drugs worked better in Pershing's command than elsewhere, because Pershing isolated his men from towns and civilians, provided other diversions, and regulated prostitution. Based on the John J. Pershing Papers, reports of the Punitive Expedition in the National Archives, and other primary sources; 103 notes. R. N. Lokken

933. Serebnick, Judith. THE 1973 COURT RULINGS ON OBSCENITY: HAVE THEY MADE A DIFFERENCE? *Wilson Lib. Bull. 1975 50(4): 304-310.* Relative unconcern of the public and mild or nonexistent censorship in libraries followed the 1973 US Supreme Court rulings on obscenity.

934. Sexton, Robert F. THE CRUSADE AGAINST PARI-MUTUEL GAMBLING IN KENTUCKY: A STUDY OF SOUTHERN PROGRESSIV-ISM IN THE 1920'S. *Filson Club Hist. Q. 1976 50(1): 47-57.* Documents a continued Progressive movement in Kentucky in the 1920's. The anti-gambling crusade sprang from the religious attack on machine politics led by Helm Bruce and the Louisville Churchmen's Federation. The reformers had their greatest support in rural Kentucky, with support from the Ku Klux Klan and fundamentalist clergymen. Alben Barkley became the political spokesman of the anti-gambling group and nearly secured the Democratic gubernatorial nomination in

1923; four years later, former governor J. C. W. Beckham won the party's nomination as the anti-gambling candidate. Urban Democrats deserted Beckham, however, and Republican Slem Sampson was elected. Beckham's defeat marked the end of the Progressive movement in Kentucky. Documented from newspapers and the Barkley Papers at the University of Kentucky; 34 notes.

G. B. McKinney

935. Shore, James H.   AMERICAN INDIAN SUICIDE—FACT AND FANTASY. *Psychiatry 1975 38(1): 86-91.* An epidemiology report on suicide patterns of American Indians in the Pacific Northwest.   S

936. Shumsky, Neil Larry and Springer, Larry M.   SAN FRANCISCO'S ZONE OF PROSTITUTION, 1880-1934.   *J. of Hist. Geography 1981 7(1): 71-89.* External forces, notably selective law enforcement, provided the stimuli for spatial changes in the red-light district. Utilizing the labelling theory, social reaction to deviance is seen as a prime force in determining the prostitution zone. Immediate causal factors include the city's commercial expansion and social attitudes, which ranged from toleration to segregation and finally to abolition. Based on municipal and other sources; 7 maps, 3 tables, 40 notes.

A. J. Larson

937. Shumsky, Neil Larry.   VICE RESPONDS TO REFORM: SAN FRANCISCO, 1910-1914.   *J. of Urban Hist. 1980 7(1): 31-47.* Control of prostitution was one of the prominent urban reforms of the late Progressive Era (1910-20). In the case of San Francisco, criminal elements with ties to city officials tried to subvert the reform movement to protect their own interests. They did this by bankrolling reformers who supported regimentation and by organizing petition drives through front organizations. 35 notes.   T. W. Smith

938. Siegel, Adrienne.   BROTHELS, BETS, AND BARS: POPULAR LITERATURE AS GUIDEBOOK TO THE URBAN UNDERGROUND, 1840-1870.   *North Dakota Q. 1976 44(2): 4-22.*

939. Siegel, Paul.   PROTECTING POLITICAL SPEECH: *BRANDENBURG VS. OHIO* UPDATED.   *Q. J. of Speech 1981 67(1): 69-80.* Discerns what patterns emerge in the courts' interpretation of *Brandenburg* v. *Ohio,* and concludes that: a) the courts have taken the "imminence" requirement fairly seriously; b) it is less clear whether the speaker's intention is part of the Brandenburg test; c) courts seem to treat advocacy of victimless, nonviolent crime in the same way as they do advocacy of violent illegality; and d) rights under Brandenburg can be significantly curtailed.   J/S

940. Silbert, Mimi H. and Pines, Ayala M.   ENTRANCE INTO PROSTITUTION.   *Youth & Soc. 1982 13(4): 471-500.* Studies San Francisco Bay area prostitutes, noting their family backgrounds, educations, economic situations, relationships with parents and peers, family violence and sexual abuse as children; most entered prostitution for the money, although they almost all remained poor because they had no other means of income after they ran away from home at young ages.

941. Smardz, Zofia J. THE GREAT ILLEGAL ALIEN DEBATE. *Worldview 1976 19(5): 15-20.* Discusses the dearth of reliable statistics on the growing number of illegal aliens in the United States in the last decade, and the traumatic effects of the Immigration and Naturalization Service policies on aliens trying to avoid detection.

942. Stanmeyer, William A. "VICTIMLESS CRIMES" AND PUBLIC MORALITY. *Modern Age 1974 18(4): 369-380.* To make "victimless crimes" legal directly contradicts most secular imperatives essential to a free, humane, virtuous, and lasting social order. Secondary sources; 12 notes. M. L. Lifka

943. Stevens, Kenneth R. UNITED STATES V. 31 PHOTOGRAPHS: DR. ALFRED C. KINSEY AND OBSCENITY LAW. *Indiana Mag. of Hist. 1975 71(4): 299-318.* As head of Indiana University's Institute for Sex Research, Professor Alfred C. Kinsey was involved in a lengthy legal dispute with US Customs Bureau officials over the importation of erotic materials for scientific research. The controversy began in 1947 when Kinsey asked the Customs Bureau for an exception, under section 305 of the tariff law of 1930, to the ban on erotic materials. The government contended that the tariff law prohibited anyone from importing obscene materials. Kinsey and his associates argued that the principle of academic freedom guaranteed the scholar access to erotic materials necessary for scientific research. The case was finally resolved in 1957, a year after Kinsey's death, by a US District Court (156 F. Supp. 350) which ruled that the definition of obscenity as applied to the average person could not similarly be applied to scholars engaged in scientific research, and established a definition based on the variable identity of the receiving group. 76 notes. K. F. Svengalis

944. Stewart, Omer C. THE HISTORY OF PEYOTISM IN NEVADA. *Nevada Hist. Soc. Q. 1982 25(3): 197-209.* Peyote religious practices among Nevada Indians have attracted a minority of Indians in the 20th century. Because of prosecutions, imprisonments, and less overt discouragement from the Bureau of Indian Affairs since 1886, peyotism has languished. But scattered instances of the practices persisted as late as 1972, with the religion's remaining practitioners employing somewhat dissimilar rites. In Nevada, these recent devotees of peyotism also adhered to their Christian faiths with equal devotion. Based on the author's observations and anthropological fieldwork; 3 photos. H. T. Lovin

945. Stopp, G. Harry, Jr. THE DISTRIBUTION OF MASSAGE PARLORS IN THE NATION'S CAPITAL. *J. of Popular Culture 1978 11(4): 989-997.* Massage parlors in Washington, D.C., have become an accepted part of the business community; if proper licensing channels are followed, these parlors receive little harassment from local law enforcement even though generally they remain centers of prostitution.

946. Suits, Daniel B. ECONOMIC BACKGROUND FOR GAMBLING POLICY. *J. of Social Issues 1979 35(3): 43-61.* Legalized gambling as a revenue source is evaluated on the basis of data derived from a nationwide survey. The major findings include: 1) gambling is essentially a consumer commodity which people purchase because they enjoy it, rather than because they expect to make money; 2) maximum revenue potential depends on consumer responsiveness to the price of a given game; 3) high takeout rates encourage gamblers to participate

in illegal substitutes; 4) state receipts from gambling, regardless of the details of the way they are collected, are economically identical to any other form of excise tax; 5) although gambling outlays tend to increase with income, the amount of increase is disproportionate to the amount of income, and therefore gambling tends to be a highly regressive form of taxation; and 6) the maximum revenue which states could expect to collect as the result of legalizing gambling is about a 4 percent addition to total receipts from other sources of revenue.   J

947. Susman, Ralph M.   DRUG ABUSE, CONGRESS AND THE FACT-FINDING PROCESS.   *Ann. of the Am. Acad. of Pol. and Social Sci. 1975 417: 16-26.* "This article concerns Congress, its fact-finding process and its legislative efforts designed to deal with problems related to narcotic and drug abuse. In essence, it examines the perspective within which Congress has defined and has attempted to solve the 'drug problem' and traces the manner in which the law enforcement and criminal justice bureaucracy gradually came to be the principal architects and purveyors of drug control legislation. It also addresses the matter of public accountability and bureaucratic and congressional performance relative to fact-finding and the policy formulation process. Lastly, it provides an assessment of what is required of Congress if it is to undertake more rational and responsible action in reference to the problems of drug use and abuse."   J

948. Symanski, Richard.   PROSTITUTION IN NEVADA.   *Ann. of the Assoc. of Am. Geographers 1974 64(3): 357-377.* "Thirty-three brothels in rural and small-town Nevada, which contain between 225 and 250 prostitutes, are legal or openly tolerated and strictly controlled by state statute, city and county ordinances, and local rules. Twenty-two of the brothels are in places with populations between 500 and 8,000, and the remaining eleven are in rural areas. The legal and quasi-legal restrictions placed on prostitutes severely limit their activities outside brothels. These restrictions in conjunction with historical inertia, perceived benefits of crime and venereal disease control, and the good image of madams contribute to widespread positive local attitudes toward brothel prostitution. Interactions between clients and prostitutes in brothel parlors are also restricted and limited to a few basic types which are largely determined by entrepreneurial philosophy."   J

949. Szasz, Thomas.   DRUG PROHIBITION: ILL-CONCEIVED LAWS HAVE CREATED TODAY'S DRUG PROBLEM.   *Reason 1978 9(9): 14-18.* Federal regulation of drugs and chemical additives interferes with civil rights, and the individual, not government, has the right to determine what foreign substance he may take.

950. Tansey, Richard.   PROSTITUTION AND POLITICS IN ANTEBELLUM NEW ORLEANS.   *Southern Studies 1979 18(4): 449-479.* During the antebellum period, prostitution was a major industry in New Orleans. It brought economic profits to landlords, retail storeowners, lawyers, off-duty policemen, and ballroom owners. During the 1850's, merchants led two unsuccessful reform drives to eliminate prostitution in favor of other economic activities such as expanded railway facilities and greater economic diversification. The Third Municipality Reform of 1851 and the Know-Nothing Party reforms of 1854-58 were unsuccessful because most voters of the middle and working class preferred economic security and low taxes to the reformers' costly expansionist ideas. Based

on New Orleans newspaper accounts and Third District Court cases; 9 tables, 67 notes. J. J. Buschen

951. Tec, Nechama. PARENTAL EDUCATIONAL PRESSURE, ADOLESCENT CONFORMITY AND MARIJUANA USE. *Youth and Soc. 1973 4(3): 291-312.* Examines the relationship between parental educational pressures and students' rebellious attitudes and behavior. S

952. Terrell, Karen A. EXPOSURE OF PROSTITUTION IN WESTERN MASSACHUSETTS: 1911. *Hist. J. of Massachusetts 1980 8(2): 3-11.* Focuses on the attempt by the *Chicopee News* to expose prostitution in Westfield, Massachuetts. The articles led to arrests of newspaper employees for selling obscene material. The paper quickly abandoned its crusade. Local newspapers, contemporary and secondary sources; 30 notes. W. H. Mulligan Jr.

953. Thompson, David. THE HIDDEN WINE AND THE SHERIFF. *Pacific Hist. 1979 23(1): 28-42.* A first-person vignette of winemaking in 1930 in the California Prohibition era. 4 photos. H. M. Parker, Jr.

954. Thornton, William E. MARIJUANA USE AND DELINQUENCY: A REEXAMINATION. *Youth & Soc. 1981 13(1): 23-37.* Examines the relationship of self-reported marijuana use to other types of self-reported delinquency. The exploratory 1978 findings suggest that there is no significant relationship between marijuana use and selected social and aggressive delinquencies. A significant relationship is found, however, between marijuana use and the commission of property offenses. J/S

955. Tinklenberg, Jared R. ASSESSING THE EFFECTS OF DRUG USE ON ANTISOCIAL BEHAVIOR. *Ann. of the Am. Acad. of Pol. and Social Sci. 1975 417: 66-75.* "Nonmedical drug taking and antisocial behavior are both complex, dynamic processes; consequently, the impact of these behaviors on each other is difficult to assess. Among the multiple factors to be considered are the pharmacological properties of the drug, the psychological characteristics of the individual, the social environment, and the various categories of antisocial behavior. Many methodological problems are inherent in research that attempts to define relationships between illicit drug use and antisocial behavior. Sampling problems are common since deviant individuals are generally not used in controlled laboratory studies, whereas field studies often are confined to inherently deviant populations such as prison inmates. Field studies are limited to lack of information about pharmacological variables as well as the difficulty in obtaining adequate control groups. The extreme forms of antisocial behavior are not amenable to laboratory study. Thus, research on illicit drug use and assaultive or sexual crimes is usually restricted to retrospective field studies which often indicate both forms of deviance present in the same individual. A cause and effect relationship cannot be inferred from retrospective studies; both behaviors often appear to be covariants of the same developmental process." J

956. Toy, Eckard V. THE CONSERVATIVE CONNECTION: THE CHAIRMAN OF THE BOARD TOOK LSD BEFORE TIMOTHY LEARY. *Am. Studies 1980 21(2): 65-77.* Reevaluates the American experience with LSD in light of Defense Department and CIA experiments during the 1950's and 60's. Aldous Huxley, Henry Fitz Gerald Heard, and other intellectuals in Great Brit-

ain and California experimented with LSD from the 1930's to the 1950's. Surveys their writings and their experiences with hallucinogenic drugs. William C. Mullendore, Chairman of the Board of Southern California Edison Company, was one early convert to hallucinogens to cure depression. Based largely on the William C. Mullendore Papers and the James Ingebretren papers at the University of Oregon; 26 notes.   J. A. Andrew

957. Vázquez, Mario F.   THE ELECTION DAY IMMIGRATION RAID AT LILLI DIAMOND ORIGINALS AND THE RESPONSE OF THE ILGWU.   Mora, Magdalena and DelCastillo, Adelaida R., ed. *Mexican Women in the United States: Struggles Past and Present* (Los Angeles: U. of California Chicano Studies Res. Center, 1980): 145-148. Documents the conflict between management and labor at the Lilli Diamond Originals garment plant in Los Angeles, California. On 26 October 1976, the Western States Region Organizing Department of the International Ladies' Garment Workers' Union was informed that workers at the plant wanted to unionize. On election day, 14 January 1977, immigration officials arrested some of the strike supporters who were illegal aliens.   J. Powell

958. Vyhnanek, Louis.   "MUGGLES," "INCHY," AND "MUD": ILLEGAL DRUGS IN NEW ORLEANS DURING THE 1920S.   *Louisiana Hist. 1981 22(3): 253-279.* New Orleans was one of the two leading drug smuggling centers in the United States and a key distribution point for the South. Morphine, opium, and cocaine dominated the traffic; marijuana and heroin played lesser roles. Three principal drug rings operated in the city: a Jewish, a Spanish, and an Italian ring; Chinese involvement was much less. Federal legislation, as interpreted by the courts, did not recognize addiction as a disease. A drug clinic was closed owing to the hostility of narcotics authorities. Convicted addicts were sent to prison. Smuggling and use remained serious problems throughout the decade. Based on government documents, newspapers, and secondary sources; 68 notes.
                                                          R. E. Noble

959. Wagner, Michael K.   THE ALIENATION OF AMERICAN LABOR: THE NATIONAL LABOR RELATIONS ACT AND THE REGULATION OF ILLEGAL ALIENS.   *New York U. J. of Int. Law and Pol. 1981 13(4): 961-991.* Examines issues raised by the National Labor Relations Board's treatment of undocumented aliens by: 1) examining the case law precedents *NLRB* v. *Sure-Tan, Inc.* (US, 1978) and *NLRB* v. *Apollo Tire Co.* (US, 1979); 2) recounting the development of immigration law and its underlying purposes; 3) reviewing the purposes of the NLRA and its intended coverage; and 4) considering the standards of the judicial review and applying them to the decisions rendered in the *Sure-Tan* and *Apollo Tire* cases.

960. Walkowitz, Judith R.   THE POLITICS OF PROSTITUTION.   *Signs 1980 6(1): 123-135.* Reviews works on prostitution that show contradictions in women's attitudes in late 19th-century Great Britain and America: Edward Bristow's *Vice and Vigilance: Purity Movement in Britain since 1700* (Dublin: Gill and Macmillan, 1977), Mark Connelly's *The Response to Prostitution in the Progressive Era* (Chapel Hill: U. of North Carolina, 1980), *The Maimie Papers,* edited by Ruth Rosen and Sue Davidson (Old Westbury, N.Y.: Feminist Pr., 1977), and Deborah Gorham's "The 'Maiden Tribute of Modern Babylon' Reexamined," *Victorian Studies* 1978. 15 notes.   S. P. Conner

961. Webb, Robert. THE MOST FAMOUS RUM-RUNNER OF THEM ALL. *Nova Scotia Hist. Rev. [Canada] 1982 2(1): 30-43.* The schooner *I'm Alone* was purchased from the shipbuilders in Lunenburg by a consortium of American bootleggers. During 1924-29 the vessel carried contraband liquor to waiting motor boats in international waters; the smaller boats completed the trip to the mainland. The ship was sunk by the US Coast Guard in 1929. The incident assumed international proportions and involved Canada, Great Britain, and France. The controversy was not settled until 1935. 33 notes.   H. M. Evans

962. West, Elliott. SCARLET WEST: THE OLDEST PROFESSION IN THE TRANS-MISSISSIPPI WEST. *Montana 1981 31(2): 16-27.* The history of prostitution in the 19th-century trans-Mississippi West is obscured by two factors: it involves social attitudes about sex; and contemporary writers viewed prostitution from an eastern Victorian perspective. In the West, prostitution was a common social phenomenon; a business enterprise often linked with saloon and dance halls; an occupation which drew women for numerous reasons. There is no "typical" prostitute when specific examples are studied. Based on contemporary newspapers and secondary sources; 6 illus., 36 notes.   R. C. Myers

963. Whitaker, F. M. OHIO WCTU AND THE PROHIBITION AMENDMENT CAMPAIGN OF 1883. *Ohio Hist. 1974 83(2): 84-102.* Describes the founding of the Woman's Christian Temperance Union of Ohio in 1874 and its activities through the prohibition amendment campaign of 1883. In its first years the Union struggled with the liquor licensing issue and tried to avoid partisan politics. After a few years of reduced activity, the Union joined the prohibition campaign, which ended in defeat of the amendment. After the campaign of 1883 the Union became more closely associated with the Prohibition Party, and its independent influence declined. Based on minutes of the Ohio WCTU meetings, newspapers, the author's dissertation, and secondary works; 3 photos, 70 notes.
J. B. Street

964. Whiteside, Henry O. THE DRUG HABIT IN NINETEENTH-CENTURY COLORADO. *Colorado Mag. 1978 55(1): 46-68.* About the time of Colorado statehood (1867) psychotropic drugs appeared in "unprecedented array" upon pharmacists' shelves. Discusses the "evolving perception by Coloradoans of a social menace in the non-medical use of drugs ... " Concern with "dope" and the dangers of addiction and being poisoned were known. Use of opium became involved with anti-Chinese feelings. Discusses the largley ineffective state and local legislation to control drugs, and various remedies and cures widely advocated. The "ample evidence of relative public and official indifference to drugs" was a result not of ignorance of the effects of drugs but of "the absence of a perception of a singular social menace from their expanding use and "the absence of the conviction that law was the proper response to any social ill." Based mainly on primary sources; 10 illus., 58 notes.   O. H. Zabel

965. Wilson, James Q. THE RETURN OF HEROIN. *Commentary 1975 59(4): 46-50.* Discusses the upsurge in heroin use since 1973 and urges that drug abuse be placed "higher on the national political agenda."   S

966. Winfree, L. Thomas, Jr.; Theis, Harold E.; and Griffiths, Curt T. DRUG USE IN RURAL AMERICA: A CROSS-CULTURAL EXAMINATION OF COMPLEMENTARY SOCIAL DEVIANCE THEORIES. *Youth & Soc. 1981 12(4): 465-489.* Biographical data, legal criticism, and parental and peer support mechanisms all contribute to the understanding of adolescent drug use. However, there are also observed anomalies by type of drug (marijuana versus alcohol) and cultural background (native Americans versus Caucasians). Covers 1972-79.   J/S

967. Wunsch, James. THE SOCIAL EVIL ORDINANCE. *Am. Heritage 1982 33(2): 50-55.* In 1870, the St. Louis city council passed the "social evil law," an ordinance that attempted to license and regulate brothels. Although 1274 prostitutes were registered by the police during the first eight months of the ordinance, the law soon proved more than the city could handle. After nearly 10 years, several attempts to change the law, and much public outcry, St. Louis joined most other American cities in prohibiting brothels in 1879. 5 illus.
                                                                         J. F. Paul

968. Yoder, R. D. and Moore, R. A. CHARACTERISTICS OF CONVICTED DRUNKEN DRIVERS. *Q. J. of Studies on Alcohol 1973 34(3-Part A): 927-936.* "Demographic data were obtained from 310 persons (206 first and 104 repeat offenders, 56 women) consecutively convicted in El Cajon, California, of driving while under the influence of alcohol. Ages ranged from under 20 to over 60 and 93% were between 20 and 59 years old; 86% were "Anglos," 10% Mexican Americans, 3% American Indians; 55% were married and 11% single; 65% had 12 or more years of schooling; 85% were employed; all were enrolled in a course on drinking and driving as a condition of probation. Prior to being arrested, 52% of the 140 probationers who submitted narratives had been drinking at bars or pool halls and 22% at friends' homes, parties or picnics; 46% had been drinking beer, 16% mixed drinks, 14% beer and mixed drinks, 10% other combinations. Fatigue (21%), stress (17%) and concurrent use of other drugs (5%) were also involved. No attempt had been made to prevent 92% from driving. Denial or projection of guilt were noted in 31% of the narratives. The Michigan Alcoholism Screening Test (MAST) was given to 269 of these (201 first and 68 repeat offenders, 35 men and 5 women, respectively). Repeat offenders had significantly higher MAST scores (indicating likelihood of alcoholism) than first offenders (p [is less than] .01); among first offenders, men had higher mean MAST scores than women (9.4 vs. 5.9) but the proportion of men with scores indicating alcoholism (71%) was not significantly different from that of women (63%). There was no correlation between age and MAST scores. Blood alcohol concentrations (BAC) were obtained from 346 men and 78 women first offenders and from 131 men and 16 women repeat offenders. A significant difference between BACs of repeat offenders of both sexes and first offenders (mean 0.22 vs. 0.19%, p [is less than] .01) was found, but not between those of men and women."   J

969. Younger, Eric E. SENTENCED TO SERVICE. *Westways 1976 68(6): 57-60.* A Los Angeles judge discusses drunken driving cases in which he sentences the guilty party to minimum jail sentences, but also to do community work through the Voluntary Action Centers of Los Angeles and Orange counties.

970. Zentner, Joseph L. OPIATE USE IN AMERICA DURING THE EIGHTEENTH AND NINETEENTH CENTURIES: THE ORIGINS OF A MODERN SCOURGE. *Studies in Hist. and Soc. 1974 5(2): 40-54.* A review of the origins and development of opium use in the United States. Opium was used during the colonial period as a medical pain killer. The Civil War, invention of the hypodermic syringe, the rise of morphine, continuing medical use, opiates in patent medicines, and the immigration of Chinese users continued and increased the practice during the 19th century. The 20th-century interpretation of opium addiction as a crime has exacerbated the problems of drug-connected crime and law enforcement. 58 notes.   V. L. Human

971. —. [ADDICTION AND CRIMINAL RESPONSIBILITY]. *Center Mag. 1976 9(6): 46-58.*
Fingarette, Herbert. WHAT IS AFFLICTION?, *pp. 47-50.* Brief outline of legal responses to the question of criminal responsibility in the case of narcotic addiction, pointing out that the legal philosophy treats an addict as one afflicted by a disease.
Coleman, James; Morris, Herbert; and Scheff, Thomas. DISCUSSION, *pp. 51-58.* Discusses Fingarette's presentation and deals with the addict as a mental incompetent and continues with moral, ethical, and social repercussions of legal status for the addict, 1960's-70's.

972. —. [THE ECONOMICS OF HEROIN ADDICTION]. *Am. Econ. R. 1973 63(2): 257-279.*
Fernandez, Raul A. THE PROBLEM OF HEROIN ADDICTION AND RADICAL POLITICAL ECONOMY, *pp. 257-262.*
Clague, Christopher. LEGAL STRATEGIES FOR DEALING WITH HEROIN ADDICTION, *pp. 263-269.*
Moore, Mark H. POLICIES TO ACHIEVE DISCRIMINATION ON THE EFFECTIVE PRICE OF HEROIN, *pp. 270-277.*
Seagraves, James A. DISCUSSION, *pp. 278-279.*
Discusses economic issues associated with heroin addiction and public policy responses to the problem in 1972.

973. —. [ILLEGAL IMMIGRATION]. *Center Mag. 1979 12(3): 54-64.*
Graham, Otis L., Jr. ILLEGAL IMMIGRATION AND THE NEW RESTRICTIONISM, *pp. 54-64.* Discusses the magnitude of the problems and frustrations surrounding the issue of illegal immigration of Mexicans in the 1970's.
Villalpando, Vic. MR. GRAHAM'S LOYALTY TEST FOR CHICANOS, *pp. 63-64.* Criticizes Graham's perspective on the issue.

7

LAW ENFORCEMENT, CRIMINAL LAW, AND THE COURTS

974.   Ahern, James F.   WE DON'T KNOW WHAT WE WANT FROM THE POLICE.   *Center Mag. 1973 6(4): 32-35.*

975.   Alonzo, Frank O.   THE HISTORY OF THE MISSISSIPPI YOUTH COURT SYSTEM.   *J. of Mississippi Hist. 1977 39(2): 133-153.* Describes the development of the Mississippi juvenile justice system during 1916-75. Focuses on legislation and major court cases. Describes the Industrial and Training School Act (1916), the establishment of special juvenile courts in 1940, the Youth Court Act (1946), and the establishment of a separate family court in 1964. 89 notes.
J. W. Hillje

976.   Alschuler, Albert W.   PLEA BARGAINING AND ITS HISTORY. *Law and Soc. Rev. 1979 13(2): 211-245.* For most of the history of the common law, Anglo-American courts did not encourage guilty pleas but actively discouraged them. Plea bargaining emerged as a significant practice only after the American Civil War, and it generally met with strong disapproval on the part of appellate courts. This practice nevertheless became a dominant method of resolving criminal cases at the end of the 19th century and beginning of the 20th, and it attracted significant attention and criticism as a result of crime commission studies in the 1920's. In recent years, American criminal courts have become even more dependent on the guilty plea, but the good press that plea bargaining currently enjoys in legal and social science circles is a very recent development. Explores changes in guilty plea practices and in attitudes toward the guilty plea from the Middle Ages to the present. 36 notes, biblio.
J

977.   Arkes, Hadley.   PHILOSOPHY: MORALITY AND THE LAW. *Wilson Q. 1981 5(2): 100-111.* The contemporary view that the law ought to be limited to the relief of material injury, a view that would lead to the legalization of vices such as drugs, pornography, prostitution, and gambling, rests on a failure to understand what Aristotle and Abraham Lincoln understood: a government concerned only with categorical wrongs would impose fewer restrictions, and would never confuse moralism with morality as the prohibitionists did.

978.   Arons, Stephen and Katsch, Ethan.   RECLAIMING THE FOURTH AMENDMENT IN MASSACHUSETTS.   *Civil Liberties Rev. 1975 2(1): 82-89.* Legislative action in Massachusetts countermanded a US Supreme Court

decision to allow police searches without warrants, opting instead in favor of the individual's right to privacy, 1974.

979. Ashbrook, John M.   AGAINST COMPREHENSIVE GUN CONTROL.   *Current Hist. 1976 71(418): 23-25, 31.* Cites the 2nd Amendment right of the people to keep and bear arms and argues that gun control has no relation to crime control, 1975.

980. Baldwin, Fred D.   SMEDLEY D. BUTLER AND PROHIBITION ENFORCEMENT IN PHILADELPHIA, 1924-1925.   *Pennsylvania Mag. of Hist. and Biog. 1960 84(3): 352-368.* The two-year career of General Smedley D. Butler as director of public safety in Philadelphia accomplished more for the "suppression of vice and crime than in any period of like duration" in that city.

981. Ball, Larry D.   PIONEER LAWMAN: CRAWLEY P. DAKE AND LAW ENFORCEMENT ON THE SOUTHWESTERN FRONTIER.   *J. of Arizona Hist. 1973 14(3): 243-256.* The reputation of Dake, U.S. marshal for Arizona, has suffered irreparably from the famous fight in 1881 at the O.K. Corral, the "Tombstone Affair" involving his deputies Wyatt and Virgil Earp. This does not nullify the constructive leadership and contributions of Dake's first years in office. Before his appointment in 1878, lawlessness prevailed in the international boundary area of southern Arizona. Dake asserted authority and promoted cooperation between Mexican and American officers. He made the marshalcy independent of the Army, put good men to work, introduced new techniques, and at least once supported his staff with private funds. 2 illus., 45 notes.   D. L. Smith

982. Baum, Lawrence.   POLICE RESPONSE TO APPELLATE COURT DECISION: MAPP AND MIRANDA.   *Policy Studies J. 1978 7(Special issue): 425-430.* Police response to Supreme Court decisions, particularly *Mapp* v. *Ohio* (US, 1961) and *Miranda* v. *Arizona* (US, 1966), which placed substantial procedural requirements on police in evidence gathering, tends generally toward minimization of such requirements while retaining admissability of evidence, but overall response is still too negligible to detect trends in appellate courts's abilities to shape police behavior, 1961-78.

983. Bayley, David H.   IRONICS OF AMERICAN LAW ENFORCEMENT.   *Public Interest 1980 (59): 45-56.* The police, who may have the least status and training, are given wide discretionary authority within the criminal justice system; yet in a society preoccupied with law and order, the police are called upon most often to perform nonlaw-related services such as traffic control or domestic counseling. Police encounter victims, courts, and suspects, leading to police criticism of the judicial system. The criminal justice system fails because its task is impossible given the looseness of a social structure based on individualism. By contrast, China maintains considerable social control through informal socialization procedures. Our penchant for individual freedom, ironically, leaves only formal mechanisms for insuring law and order for resolving social problems.
                                                                                    J. M. Herrick

984. Beecher, Janice A.; Lineberry, Robert J.; and Rich, Michael J.   POLITICAL POWER, THE URBAN AGENDA, AND CRIME POLICIES.   *Social Sci. Q. 1981 62(4): 630-643.* Determines how police policy was made in 10 cities

during 1948-78, examining the connection between politics and policymaking.

985.   Belenchia, Joanne M.   COWBOYS AND ALIENS: HOW THE INS
OPERATES IN LATINO COMMUNITIES.   *Peace and Change 1980 6(3):
10-19.* Provides a brief background of the Immigration and Naturalization Service, focusing on INS operations involving Latinos in the Southwest and Midwest, particularly Illinois, Mexican migrants' destination choice after California
and Texas; ca 1973-76.

986.   Berens, John F.   THE FBI AND CIVIL LIBERTIES FROM FRANK-
LIN ROOSEVELT TO JIMMY CARTER: AN HISTORICAL OVERVIEW.
Michigan Academician 1980 13(2): 131-144. The history of the Federal Bureau
of Investigation since the presidency of Franklin D. Roosevelt, whose mandates
in 1936 and 1939 "opened the door to massive FBI surveillance of Americans who
deviated from the established and normal politics of the day," has adequately
shown the dangers to individual civil liberties of the FBI's programs.

987.   Bethell, Tom.   FREEING THE GUILTY.   *Washington Monthly 1977
8(11): 29-35.* Examines the events and legal conundrums of the *United States* v.
Willie Decoster, Jr. (1975), following an on-going 10-year deliberation, 1965-75.

988.   Bethune, Beverly M.   A CASE OF OVERKILL: THE FBI AND THE
NEW YORK CITY PHOTO LEAGUE.   *Journalism Hist. 1980 7(3-4): 87-91,
108.* Using information supplied by Angela Calomiris, during the 1940's the
Federal Bureau of Investigation probed the New York City Photo League, committed to social documentary, 1930-51, and sponsored by the Workers International Relief, an international Communist welfare and cultural agency.

989.   Billings, Warren M.   PLEADING, PROCEDURE, AND PRACTICE:
THE MEANING OF DUE PROCESS OF LAW IN SEVENTEENTH-CEN-
TURY VIRGINIA.   *J. of Southern Hist. 1981 47(4): 569-584.* An analysis of
the development of modern due process of law in 17th-century Virginia. The
term, as well as the practice, arrived from England, where it referred merely to
the processes of getting the accused through court procedures. Both term and
practice lacked flexibility, but the colonists were not content to let matters stand
there. Covers the development and origins of such modern ideas as the right to
jury trial, defense for the accused, right of the defendant to subpoena witnesses,
and the rapid clearing of court dockets. By century's end, Virginia had endorsed
the processes of change in legal practice, thus opening the door for a tradition
that has not yet come to an end. 39 notes.   V. L. Human

990.   Binder, Arnold.   THE JUVENILE JUSTICE SYSTEM: WHERE PRE-
TENSE AND REALITY CLASH.   *Am. Behavioral Scientist 1979 22(6): 621-
652.* Discusses the rise of the juvenile court in the 19th century, the tendency to
restore adult treatment and procedural protection to juvenile criminal offenders,
and efforts to limit courts' jurisdiction in cases of status offense, 20th century.

991.   Bishop, Joan.   VIGOROUS ATTEMPTS TO PROSECUTE: PINKER-
TON MEN ON MONTANA'S RANGE, 1914.   *Montana 1980 30(2): 2-15.*
Montana's livestock industry experienced problems with horse and cattle thieves
well into the 20th century. The influx of homesteaders after 1909 and organized
bands of rustlers and butchers made enforcement difficult. Beginning in 1910,

stockman T. C. Power hired detectives from the Pinkerton National Detective Agency to curb stock loss. Among the most successful was Frank C. Lavigne, employed from 1914 to 1915 to investigate rustling in Teton and Fergus counties. From 1915 to 1925, Lavigne was chief detective for the Montana Livestock Commission. Biographic and bibliographic essay on Lavigne's career and scrapbooks. Based on T. C. Power Papers and Lavigne scrapbooks in Montana Historical Society; 19 illus., 60 notes.   R. C. Myers

992. Bishop, Larry V. and Harvie, Robert A.   LAW, ORDER AND RE-FORM IN THE GALLATIN, 1893-1918. *Montana 1980 30(2): 16-25.* Police-men in Bozeman and sheriffs officers in Gallatin County, Montana, dealt less with frontier violence and more with social reform during 1893 to 1918. Among matters of concern were vagrancy, dogs, traffic control (bicycles and automo-biles), and social problems such as liquor, gambling and prostitution. Often amid partisan political controversy, these law enforcement officials succeeded in fulfill-ing community desires. Based on contemporary newspapers, Bozeman police and Gallatin County sheriff records; 5 illus., 50 notes.   R. C. Myers

993. Blackburn, Bob L.   LAW ENFORCEMENT IN TRANSITION: FROM DECENTRALIZED COUNTY SHERIFFS TO THE HIGHWAY PA-TROL. *Chronicles of Oklahoma 1978 56(2): 194-207.* The 1930's witnessed a flurry of highly publicized crimes in Oklahoma as George "Machine Gun" Kel-ley, Charles "Pretty Boy" Floyd, and Bonnie Parker and Clyde Barrow moved throughout the state. The inability of sheriffs to pursue criminals beyond county borders created a pressure for a new highway patrol which could operate any-where in Oklahoma and simultaneously reduce traffic accidents by enforcing highway safety legislation. By 1937 an effective highway patrol had been estab-lished. Based on state documents and newspapers; 2 photos, map, 29 notes.
                                                              M. L. Tate

994. Block, Alan A.   THE ORGANIZED CRIME CONTROL ACT, 1970: HISTORICAL ISSUES AND PUBLIC POLICY. *Public Hist. 1980 2(2): 39-59.* The Organized Crime Control Act (US, 1970) and all federal efforts have failed to eliminate organized crime because of their Cold War action-before-definition mentality and their concept of organized crime as simply an Italian-Sicilian monolith.

995. Bohmer, Carol.   JUDICIAL ATTITUDES TOWARD RAPE VIC-TIMS. *Judicature 1974 57(7): 303-307.*

996. Brasseaux, Carl A.   THE ADMINISTRATION OF SLAVE REGULA-TIONS IN FRENCH LOUISIANA, 1724-1766. *Louisiana Hist. 1980 21(2): 139-158.* The first slaveholders in colonial Louisiana nominally accepted the French government's Black Code, but they frequently ignored it with impunity. For example, floggings, though prohibited in the code, were accepted as part of the masters' paternal responsibilities. French officials generally used the code in the interests of slaveholders, not to protect slaves. Lessees, who were much harsher than masters in their treatment of slaves, were often brought to court by masters who seemed more concerned about the value of their leased property than about their slaves' welfare. By the 1750's the slaveholding class had gained control over making and administering regulations for blacks, and they further

curtailed slaves' legal protection under the law. Based on documents in the Archives Nationales, Archives des Colonies, Paris; 91 notes.

D. B. Touchstone

997. Brintnall, Michael A. FEDERAL INFLUENCE AND URBAN POLICY ENTREPRENEURSHIP IN THE LOCAL PROSECUTION OF ECONOMIC CRIME. *Policy Studies J. 1979 7(3): 577-591.* Assesses programs instituted by local government prosecutors to deal with white-collar crime and consumer fraud, 1970's, focusing on sources, character, and consequences of this type of policy entrepreneurship and assessing the character of federal influence.

998. Brintnall, Michael A. POLICE AND WHITE COLLAR CRIME. *Policy Studies J. 1978 7(Special issue): 431-435.* While local law enforcement is generally not involved in the investigation of white-collar crime, in those instances where local prosecutors have made committments to this problem, local officials are called in, with good results, indicating future possibilities for their inclusion, 1970's.

999. Caldeira, Gregory A. THE UNITED STATES SUPREME COURT AND CRIMINAL CASES, 1935-1976: ALTERNATIVE MODELS OF AGENDA BUILDING. *British J. of Pol. Sci. [Great Britain] 1981 11(4): 449-470.* Discusses how the US Supreme Court decided what sort of issues should be brought before it in the field of criminal law.

1000. Callan, Sam W. AN EXPERIENCE IN JUSTICE WITHOUT PLEA NEGOTIATION. *Law and Soc. Rev. 1979 13(2): 327-347.* The reasons for the termination of plea negotiation in El Paso County, Texas, are explained. The statistical consequences of doing so are discussed.　　　　　　　　　　J

1001. Cameron, Diane Maher. HISTORICAL PERSPECTIVE ON URBAN POLICE. *J. of Urban Hist. 1978 5(1): 125-132.* Until the last half dozen years, the police were an almost unexamined area of history. This has now begun to change with such books as George L. Mosse, ed., *Police Forces in History* with its cross-national comparisons and James F. Richardson, *Urban Police in the United States* with its interurban comparisons. Perhaps the chief value to both books is that they place the police in social, historical, and political context rather than treating it as a isolated topic. 12 notes.　　　　　T. W. Smith

1002. Carter, Lief H. FLEXIBILITY AND UNIFORMITY IN CRIMINAL JUSTICE. *Policy Studies J. 1974 3(1): 18-25.*

1003. Carter, Marshall. LAW ENFORCEMENT AND FEDERALISM: BORDERING ON TROUBLE. *Policy Studies J. 1978 7(Special issue): 413-418.* Examines conflict between local jurisdiction of law enforcement and the incursion of federalism in the context of the international border between El Paso, Texas, and Ciudad Juarez, Mexico, 1970's.

1004. Castanien, Pliny. SAN DIEGO POLICE: A LOOK BACK. *J. of San Diego Hist. 1980 26(1): 21-52.* Pictorial history of the San Diego police since 1889, when the first city police force was formed.

1005. Church, Thomas W., Jr. PLEA BARGAINS, CONCESSIONS AND THE COURTS: ANALYSIS OF A QUASI-EXPERIMENT. *Law and Soc. Rev. 1976 10(3): 377-401.* Examines the effects of elimination of plea bargaining for serious felonies. The data show a decline in the role of prosecuting attorneys in sentence application and a corresponding increase in the dockets of local judges. Judicial decisionmaking replaced that of prosecuting attorneys in the sentencing of convicted felons. H. R. Mahood

1006. Churchill, Mae. CARTER'S BORN-AGAIN WAR ON CRIME. *Social Policy 1978 9(3): 40-45.* Discusses the Carter Administration's attempt to revive the 10-year war on crime, and concludes that the Law Enforcement Assistance Administration (LEAA) has been a failure and should be discontinued.

1007. Cloninger, Dale O. and Sartorius, Lester C. CRIME RATES, CLEARANCE RATES AND ENFORCEMENT EFFORT: THE CASE OF HOUSTON, TEXAS. *Am. J. of Econ. and Sociol. 1979 38(4): 389-402.* Two time series relationships with respect to police and criminal activities are analyzed. These relationships are: 1. That between police input and police output where the latter was measured by arrest and convictions rates and the former by expenditures and number of officers and, 2. The hypothetical one between the probability of arrest (the clearance ratio; i.e., the proportion of reported crimes for which arrests were made) and crime rates. Theoretically, an increase in expenditures for police effort would cause an increase in the clearance rate and a concomitant reduction in the crime rate. The results of this study showed little or no response in clearance and crime rates to small changes in police expenditures. However, there was evidence that large changes in police effort did produce some response in both clearance and crime rates. The implication of these findings was that the marginal product of police input was small. 6 tables, 24 notes. J

1008. Cloninger, Dale O. DETERRENCE EFFECT OF LAW ENFORCEMENT. *Am. J. of Econ. and Sociol. 1975 34(3): 323-336.* Six attempts to measure the deterrence effect of law enforcement on certain criminal activities, as well as one by the author, have produced no clear, unequivocal evidence to support the belief that increased public expenditures on law enforcement have a deterrent effect on such activity. Yet the effect may exist. Further research into the measurement of the variables crime and enforcement and upon the nature of the relationship between them must be carried on before definite conclusions can be reached about the existence of the deterrence effect. J

1009. Clotfelter, Charles T. PUBLIC SERVICES, PRIVATE SUBSTITUTES, AND THE DEMAND FOR PROTECTION AGAINST CRIME. *Am. Econ. Rev. 1977 67(5): 867-877.* Analyzes private substitutes for public services and applies this analysis to protection against crime, 1960's-73.

1010. Cloyd, Jerald W. PROSECUTION'S POWER, PROCEDURAL RIGHTS, AND PLEADING GUILTY: THE PROBLEM OF COERCION IN PLEA BARGAINING DRUG CASES. *Social Problems 1979 26(40): 452-466.* Provides a portion of a transcript of the plea negotiations of a defendant charged with attempting to sell drugs, and discusses briefly some general problems in plea bargaining, the specific issue in plea bargaining drug cases, and common pressures on typical parties to such plea bargaining since the reorganization of federal drug enforcement agencies in 1973.

1011. Cook, Philip J. and Blose, James. STATE PROGRAMS FOR SCREENING HANDGUN BUYERS. *Ann. of the Am. Acad. of Pol. and Social Sci. 1981 (455): 80-91.* Almost half the states require that buyers be screened by the police to prevent felons, fugitives, ex-mental patients, drug addicts, and so forth from obtaining handguns. These state systems operate within the federal framework created by the Gun Control Act of 1968, which requires that most all interstate transactions in firearms be handled by federally licensed dealers or manufacturers. The states' main problems are: 1) weak federal regulation of licensees, 2) incomplete state criminal history files, and 3) the difficulty of regulating private transactions in used handguns.   J/S

1012. Craig, R. Stephen. CAMERAS IN COURTROOMS IN FLORIDA. *Journalism Q. 1979 56(4): 703-710.* In July 1977 the Florida Supreme Court ordered a one-year pilot program to study the effects of coverage of trials by electronic newsgathering devices. All state judicial proceedings were opened to such coverage, subject to Court guidelines. Two murder trials *(Zamora* and *Herman)* received full electronic coverage and were the object of much local and national interest. After evaluating the results of the experiment, the Court ordered that the privileges accorded the electronic media be made permanent. Although the physical disruption of proceedings caused by the electronic equipment is minimal, the more subtle influences of the electronic media arouse concern. Based on judicial documents and news reports; 53 notes.
                                                                J. S. Coleman

1013. Cressey, Donald R. DOING JUSTICE: THE RULE OF LAW INCLUDES MORE THAN THE STATUTES. *Center Mag. 1977 10(1): 21-28.* Discusses the legislative branch's pressure on judges and prosecuting lawyers to apply stricter criminal sentencing in the 1970's; defends the practice of plea bargaining and other examples of judicial flexibility in maintaining the spirit of the law.

1014. Culver, John H. TELEVISION AND THE POLICE. *Policy Studies J. 1979 7(special issue): 500-504.* Popular television programs overemphasize efficiency and underemphasize obstacles and frustrations of law enforcement, lending false expectations to the public (who demand greater though unrealistic results) as well as to the police (who feel the need to live up to television fantasy).

1015. DaCosta Nunes, Ralph. PUBLIC OPINION, CRIME AND RACE: A CONGRESSIONAL RESPONSE TO LAW AND ORDER IN AMERICA. *Pol. Studies [Great Britain] 1980 28(3): 420-430.* Examines congressional party voting on law and order issues, 1965-73, when the problem was very important for the electorate and associated in the public mind with race. Republicans generally supported hard anticrime legislation, while Democrats favored softer approaches. The influence of black constituents was more complex: it had no effect on Republicans, while Democrats were softer in nonblack districts, and harder as the percentage of blacks increased. In predominantly black districts, however, Democratic support for hard measures was weakest. Congressional voting figures and public opinion polls; 2 tables, 3 fig., 13 notes.
                                                                D. J. Nicholls

1016.   Dalecki, Kenneth.   THE BURGLAR'S BILL.   *Washington Monthly 1976 8(3): 19-22.* Discusses the implications of the proposed Criminal Reform Act for federal government criminal law, including possible legislative compromise on the bill in the Senate, 1975-76.

1017.   Daniels, Richard S.   BLIND TIGERS AND BLIND JUSTICE: THE ARKANSAS RAID ON ISLAND 37, TENNESSEE.   *Arkansas Hist. Q. 1979 38(3): 259-270.* A raid on illegal "blind tigers" (bootleg whiskey outlets) on Island 37 in the Mississippi River by Arkansas men on 31 July 1915 resulted in the death of Sheriff Sam Mauldin. Andy Crum, the ringleader of the "blind tiger" owners was captured and eventually shot by a mob who feared he would be turned over to the over-lenient Tennessee courts. Includes some comparison with lynchings in other parts of the South. Mainly newspaper sources; map, 36 notes.
G. R. Schroeder

1018.   Denno, Deborah.   PSYCHOLOGICAL FACTORS FOR THE BLACK DEFENDANT IN A JURY TRIAL.   *J. of Black Studies 1981 11(3): 313-326.* The *voire dire* process of jury selection and the underrepresentation of Negroes among lawyers and judges makes difficult fair trials for black defendants. Prosecutors try to exclude blacks from juries since black jurors (when they are not ignored or overridden) tend to empathize with underdogs. Biblio.
R. G. Sherer

1019.   Dill, Forrest.   CRIMINAL JUSTICE: THE LOCAL TRADITION. *New York Affairs 1978 5(2): 198-205.* Examines the expenditures of New York metropolitan region local and state governments for criminal justice, assessing the impact of increased state financing on the quality and nature of law enforcement, 1961-77.

1020.   Dill, Forrest.   DISCRETION, EXCHANGE AND SOCIAL CONTROL: BAIL BONDSMEN IN CRIMINAL COURTS.   *Law and Soc. R. 1975 9(4): 639-674.* Analyzes the role of local bondsmen in the criminal courts of two western cities, based on the author's personal observations. According to this study, bail bondsmen: 1) facilitate pretrial release of large numbers of arrested persons, 2) help defendants through complexities of the court system, and 3) aid officials in dealing selectively with difficult cases—refusing bail at times in order to tacitly carry out official wishes.
H. R. Mahood

1021.   Doig, Jameson W.   POLICE POLICY AND POLICE BEHAVIOR: PATTERNS OF DIVERGENCE.   *Policy Studies J. 1978 7(special issue): 436-441.* Ambiguous policy, low visibility of field behavior, police culture, legal restrictions, and inappropriate administrative responses in the use of quantitative measures, and failure to structure police discretion through guidelines and training all contribute to police administration's lack of control of officers' field behavior.

1022.   Donner, Frank.   HOW J. EDGAR HOOVER CREATED HIS INTELLIGENCE POWERS.   *Civil Liberties Rev. 1977 3(6): 34-51.* Discusses the evolution of the intelligence operations and powers of the Federal Bureau of Investigation between 1934 (when the Bureau investigated Nazism in the United States) and 1976.

1023. Dorffi, Christine. SAN FRANCISCO'S HIRED GUNS. *Reason 1979 11(4): 26-29, 33.* Describes the "patrol special" officers of San Francisco, private police regulated by the Police Commission, and provides a history of private policing in San Francisco since the Gold Rush.

1024. Douthit, Nathan. AUGUST VOLLMER, BERKELEY'S FIRST CHIEF OF POLICE, AND THE EMERGENCE OF POLICE PROFESSION-ALISM. *California Hist. Q. 1975 54(2): 101-124.* A study of the career and contributions of August Vollmer (1876-1955), chief of police of Berkeley 1905-32. A progressive who believed that police work could be made more scientific and less vulnerable to political corruption, Vollmer pioneered in use of bicycles, automobiles, call boxes and radios, and attempted to recruit better educated officers, including college graduates. Vollmer wrote books and articles about police professionalism, served as a consultant for other cities, and held offices in police chiefs' associations. During his tenure in Berkeley the city's crime rate remained low, with Berkeley achieving a reputation as a leader in police innovation. In later years Vollmer served as a professor of police administration at the University of California and helped organize the first training program for police officers on the college level. Based on unpublished manuscript materials and other primary sources, and secondary books; illus., 13 photos, 95 notes.

A. Hoffman

1025. Dubnoff, Caren. PRETRIAL PUBLICITY AND DUE PROCESS IN CRIMINAL PROCEEDINGS. *Pol. Sci. Q. 1977 92(1): 89-108.* Examines the roles of the Supreme Court and state appellate courts in defining and upholding the constitutional right to an impartial criminal trial in the face of prejudicial pretrial publicity. Concludes that the Supreme Court refusal to declare national standards has led to widespread denial of judicial relief by most state courts.

J

1026. Ely, James W., Jr. A NEW LOOK AT AN OLD WRIT. *Rev. in Am. Hist. 1981 9(3): 319-323.* Review essay of William F. Duker's *A Constitutional History of Habeas Corpus* (1980).

1027. Fagan, Ronald W., Jr. and Mauss, Armand L. PADDING THE RE-VOLVING DOOR: AN INITIAL ASSESSMENT OF THE UNIFORM AL-COHOLISM AND INTOXICATION TREATMENT ACT IN PRACTICE. *Social Problems 1978 26(2): 232-247.* Discusses the adoption of the act of 1971 in the Seattle area, asserting that although moves toward the decriminalization of public drunkenness have occurred, drunkenness is as prevalent as it was in 1971.

1028. Fairchild, Erika S. ORGANIZATIONAL STRUCTURE AND CON-TROL OF DISCRETION IN POLICE OPERATIONS. *Policy Studies J. 1978 7(special issue): 442-449.* Three models of organizational structure—administrative policymaking by department officials, community pressure, and changes in officer decisionmaking capacity—are examined as they pertain to increasing control of discretion in police operations.

1029. Farrell, Ronald A. and Swigert, Victoria Lynn. PRIOR OFFENSE RECORD AS A SELF-FULFILLING PROPHECY. *Law and Soc. Rev. 1978 12(3): 437-453.* Explorations of differential justice suggest that apparent relationships between class, race, and legal treatment may be explained by the more extensive conviction histories found among lower class and minority populations. But these findings have emerged without adequate exploration of the antecedents of a defendant's criminal record. This article examines the determinants of accumulated criminal histories, viewing the conviction awarded a defendant as the first stage in the construction of a prior offense record. Path analytic techniques were applied to data drawn from a sample of persons arrested for murder in order to examine the nature of relationships among the demographic characteristics of defendants, their prior offense records, access to legal resources, and ultimate dispositions. Patterns evident from the analysis suggest that the operation of the criminal record in the legal system constitutes a continual cycle in the confirmation of criminality. Prior record, itself partly a product of discretionary treatment, becomes a salient factor in the accumulation of additional convictions not only through its direct effect but also through its influence on access to private counsel and bail, which in turn significantly affect outcome.   J

1030. Feuillan, Jacques. EVERY MAN'S EVIDENCE VERSUS A TESTI-MONIAL PRIVILEGE FOR SURVEY RESEARCHERS. *Public Opinion Q. 1976 40(1): 39-50.* The law of evidence in the United States does not generally favor the withholding from the courts of information relating to the commission of crime, and the courts are able to use their contempt powers to try to compel testimony and the production of records. There are few exceptions, but, because social science researchers have a scientific need for confidential access to information which is sought for the public good, they have a legitimate claim to have their promises of confidentiality recognized in law. The professional associations of the social sciences should seek clarifications in the law through legislation, and possibly begin by promulgating and promoting model statutory language.   J

1031. Friedman, Lawrence M. THE DEVELOPMENT OF AMERICAN CRIMINAL LAW. Hawes, Joseph M., ed. *Law and Order in American History* (Port Washington, N.Y.: Kennikat Pr., 1979): 6-24. Traces the development of American criminal law from 1776 to 1900 from the author's *A History of American Law* (New York: Simon and Schuster, 1973), and focuses on the growth and change of criminal statutes.

1032. Friedman, Lawrence M. THE LONG ARM OF THE LAW. *Rev. in Am. Hist. 1978 6(2): 223-228.* Review article prompted by Wilbur R. Miller's *Cops and Bobbies: Police Authority in New York and London, 1830-1870* (Chicago: U. of Chicago Pr., 1977).

1033. Friedman, Lawrence M. PLEA BARGAINING IN HISTORICAL PERSPECTIVE. *Law and Soc. Rev. 1979 13(2): 247-259.* This paper, using mostly data drawn from a study of the criminal work of the Superior Court of Alameda County, California, from 1880 on, explores the history of plea bargaining. Plea bargaining, it turns out, was used in Alameda County from at least 1880, though it was by no means as common in the late 19th century as it is today. There is also ample evidence of "implicit plea bargaining," that is, pleading guilty in expectation of a lighter sentence. The data from this study suggest that plea bargaining cannot be explained simply as a reaction to crowded court conditions. It is connected with structural and social changes in criminal justice, in particular, the rise of professional police and prosecutors.   J

1034.   Galliher, John F.; McCartney, James L.; and Baum, Barbara E.   NE-
BRASKA'S MARIJUANA LAW: A CASE OF UNEXPECTED LEGISLA-
TIVE INNOVATION.   *Law & Soc. R. 1974 8(3): 441-455.* Analyzes the
reasons for the passage in Nebraska in 1969 of a liberal marijuana law.   S

1035.   Galliher, John F. and Basilick, Linda.   UTAH'S LIBERAL DRUG
LAWS: STRUCTURAL FOUNDATIONS AND TRIGGERING EVENTS.
Social Problems 1979 26(3): 284-297. Describes the passage in 1969 and 1971 of
Utah bills reducing possession of marijuana to a misdemeanor and dropping the
mandatory minimum penalties for all drug offenses, and notes how such innovative legislation was especially unexpected in a state whose Mormon faithful
cherish the family and oppose all drugs.

1036.   Gaskins, Richard.   CHANGES IN THE CRIMINAL LAW IN EIGH-
TEENTH-CENTURY CONNECTICUT.   *Am. J. of Legal Hist. 1981 25(4):
309-342.* In early colonial Connecticut moral petty offenses such as swearing,
drunkenness, fornication, breaking the Sabbath, and gambling dominated the
criminal prosecutions. A major change occurred during 1700-50, when personal
and property offenses, such as theft, assumed prominence. Justice Whitman's
record book for Farmingham, Hartford County, 1763-69, reveals that not only
were personal and property crimes more prevalent, but also that civil causes
relating to debt increased significantly. The discussion of the problem of catego-
rizing offenses concludes with an explanation of how the proceedings before the
Superior Courts 1750-70 constituted a definite concern for the preservation of the
economic order. In this context the American Revolution brought no significant
changes. Statutory legislation on property crimes increased unabated with a
continuing desire for the regulation of social behavior.   Based on court records
and secondary sources; 146 notes.   L. A. Knafla

1037.   Gibson, James L.   RACE AS DETERMINANT OF CRIMINAL SEN-
TENCES: A METHODOLOGICAL CRITIQUE AND A CASE STUDY.
Law and Soc. Rev. 1978 12(3): 455-478. In this article I argue that several
conceptual and methodological deficiencies have plagued research on racial discrimination. Discrimination is usually conceptualized as a function of societal or
institutional forces rather than as an attribute of individual decisionmakers,
resulting in research designs that analyze decisions of courts, rather than those
of individual judges. However, a finding of no discrimination in aggregate court
data does not preclude the possibility that individual judges discriminate against
or in favor of minorities. Thus the selection of the unit of analysis, and other
methodological choices, can significantly affect substantive conclusions. Finally,
research has largely been concerned with description, rather than explanation,
and has therefore failed to illuminate the decisional processes that produce discrimination. Each of these critiques is substantiated with data from the Fulton
County (Georgia) Superior Court. My findings suggest three patterns of sentencing among judges: pro-black, anti-black, and nondiscriminatory. Anti-black
judges are strongly tied to traditional southern culture, concerned about crime,
prejudiced against blacks, and relatively punitive in their sentencing philosophies.
In addition, they tend to rely more heavily on the defendant's attitude and prior
record in making their sentencing decisions. Thus, discrimination seems to flow
from both the attitudinal predispositions of the judges and the process they
employ to make decisions.   J

1038. Glazer, Nathan. SHOULD JUDGES ADMINISTER SOCIAL SER-
VICES? *Public Interest 1978 50: 64-80.* In recent years, the role of judges in
the administration of schools, mental hospitals, prisons, and other institutions has
increased considerably. The school desegregation order is the model for the court
decisions which have led to this judicial involvement in social services. An out-
standing example of a judge dealing with social policy administration is Frank
M. Johnson, who issued sweeping orders for the restructuring of Alabama's
mental hospitals and prisons. It is extremely difficult to determine the impact of
this judicial intervention on the ends of social policy, but it is possible to trace
its effect on procedure and personnel: the responsibility, range of discretion, and
authority of administrators and service workers has been reduced along with the
importance of clinical considerations. Greater weight has been given to the research of social scientists and more power has gone to the legal and theoretical
professions at the expense of those who directly deal with the clients of the
services.   S. Harrow

1039. Goldberg-Ambrose, Carole E. CRIMINAL LAW CODE. *Center
Mag. 1981 14(3): 56-64.* Reviews campaigns to codify criminal law in Congress
during 1966-80, and discusses the fate of S.1722, a bill introduced by Edward
Kennedy in 1979, and HR.6915, drafted by the Subcommittee on Criminal Justice of the House Judiciary Committee in 1980.

1040. Goldman, Sheldon. CRIMINAL JUSTICE IN THE FEDERAL
COURTS. *Current Hist. 1976 70(417): 257-260, 271.* The federal courts' responsibilities for handling violators of federal crimes and for overseeing the
criminal justice standards of the states (particularly through the habeas corpus
process) have increased five times during 1960-75; this has resulted in delay, and
affects the quality of justice.

1041. Gottheil, Diane L. THE PARTICIPATION OF WOMEN AND MI-
NORITIES AND PRETRIAL DIVERSION PROGRAMS. *Peace and
Change 1980 6(3): 49-58.* Pretrial diversion programs divert "eligible individuals
out of the [criminal justice] system to provide them with counseling and other
appropriate human services," based on the Champaign County Adult Diversion
Program (ADP) in Urbana, Illinois; 1975-77.

1042. Graber, Doris A. THE MEDIA AND THE POLICE. *Policy Studies
J. 1978 7(special issue): 493-499.* Analysis of story content of six daily newspapers
and five television stations, 1976-77, shows reports about police to have been
moderate in both mention and display with few pertaining to evaluation of police
services.

1043. Gray, Charles M.; Gray, Virginia; and Williams, Bruce. FEDERAL-
ISM, POLICY, AND INNOVATION IN CORRECTIONS. *Policy Studies
Rev. 1981 1(2): 288-297.* Over the past two decades, the trend has been toward
nationalizing corrections policy, with less interstate variation and more federal
standards; it may be expected that there will be a hiatus in state corrections
reform as a result of substantial reductions in the block grants issued by the Law
Enforcement Assistance Administration.

1044. Greenberg, Douglas. THE EFFECTIVENESS OF LAW ENFORCE-
MENT IN EIGHTEENTH-CENTURY NEW YORK. *Am. J. of Legal Hist.
1975 19(3): 173-207.* Throughout the century New York suffered a failure of law
enforcement institutions. Considerable hazards and meager rewards made it
difficult to fill police positions with qualified people. The jails were decrepit, the
juries inadequate, and judges "an ignorant lot . . . often anxious to abuse the
power which such office afforded them." These inadequacies varied widely. Enforcement was more effective in dealing with theft than with other serious crimes,
in prosecuting slaves rather than the English or Dutch, in Suffolk County than
elsewhere, and in the first half of the 18th century than in the latter decades,
especially the crime-ridden 1760's and 1770's. Weakness in law enforcement
contributed to disrespect for government and instability of life in the colony. 68
notes.
                                                                T. Simmerman

1045. Gruhl, John; Spohn, Cassia; and Welch, Susan. WOMEN AS POLI-
CYMAKERS: THE CASE OF TRIAL JUDGES. *Am. J. of Pol. Sci. 1981
25(2): 308-322.* Previous research analyzing differences between men and women
political elites has focused primarily on attitudinal differences, recruitment patterns, or background characteristics. In contrast, this research examines convicting and sentencing behavior of judges in over 30,000 felony cases. Women
generally did not convict and sentence defendants differently than men. However,
female judges were considerably more likely to sentence female defendants to
prison than male judges were.
                                                                J

1046. Gustin, Anton C. A POLICE OFFICER REACTS. *J. of Social Issues
1975 31(1): 211-215.* Questions are raised about articles in this issue, specifically
about the use of questionnaires in research on the police, the difficulties and
shortcomings of survey research, a tendency to ignore the effects of training
programs on the street experience. Training in race relations underestimates both
minority prejudice against the police and some inherent conflicts between blacks
and whites. In the question of police killings, the extreme difficulty of making
split-second decisions to protect one's own life in a society that is positive about
handguns needs to be considered as does the fact that one of the reasons police
kill more than they are killed is simply their technical superiority in the use of
guns. Police-community relations should deemphasize "show-biz" and turn to
social advocacy by police jointly with community to solve the latter's problems.
                                                                J

1047. Gutman, Jeremiah S. THE ABUSES OF POLICE RECORDS.
Center Mag. 1982 15(5): 56-63. Examines "the conflict and tension between the
right of access" by the press and the public to arrest records and the rights of
the subjects of the records.

1048. Hadsell, Richard M. and Coffey, William E. FROM LAW AND OR-
DER TO CLASS WARFARE: BALDWIN-FELTS DETECTIVES IN THE
SOUTHERN WEST VIRGINIA COAL FIELDS. *West Virginia Hist. 1979
40(3): 268-286.* William G. Baldwin and Thomas L. Felts formed Baldwin-Felts
Detectives in the 1890's and for 30 years provided a private police and guard
service for West Virginia coal mines. Their agents infiltrated unions, evicted
undesirables, guarded nonstrikers, and kept order on mine property. Their anti-
union activities became paramount and many were killed in gun battles or am-

bushes. By the 1930's they were outmoded and even illegal. Based on Justus Collins papers and other primary sources; 72 notes.   J. H. Broussard

1049. Hagan, John. THE CORPORATE ADVANTAGE: A STUDY OF THE INVOLVEMENT OF CORPORATE AND INDIVIDUAL VICTIMS IN A CRIMINAL JUSTICE SYSTEM. *Social Forces 1982 60(4): 993-1022.* The legal conceptualization of corporate entities as juristic persons has both obscured and enhanced their influence in the criminal justice process. Consequences of this influence include greater success of corporate than individual actors in getting individual offenders convicted, greater formal equality in the treatment of individuals prosecuted for crimes against corporate than individual victims, and greater satisfaction of corporate than individual victims with their experiences in the criminal justice system. An increase in formal equality may accompany higher rates of conviction for individuals accused of crimes against "juristic persons," and may emphasize the important advantages a formal rational system of criminal law can provide these corporate entities.   J/S

1050. Hagan, John. EXTRA-LEGAL ATTRIBUTES AND CRIMINAL SENTENCING: AN ASSESSMENT OF A SOCIOLOGICAL VIEWPOINT. *Law & Soc. R. 1974 8(3): 357-383.* Reviews the literature on discrimination against defendants in sentencing by courts.   S

1051. Hagan, John and Bernstein, Ilene Nagel. THE SENTENCE BARGAINING OF UPPERWORLD AND UNDERWORLD CRIME IN TEN FEDERAL DISTRICT COURTS. *Law and Soc. Rev. 1979 13(2): 467-478.* This paper explores the use of different types of sentence bargaining tactics in ten federal district courts. We distinguish between proactive and reactive prosecutorial orientation, and hypothesize that proactive prosecution of upperworld crime is associated with more explicit sentence bargaining than is the reactive prosecution of underworld crime. We present evidence for and explanations of this relationship.   J

1052. Haller, Mark H. PLEA BARGAINING: THE NINETEENTH CENTURY CONTEXT. *Law and Soc. Rev. 1979 13(2): 273-279.* Plea bargaining apparently arose independently in a number of urban criminal courts in the nineteenth century. These simultaneous developments were presumably related to a number of broad structural changes that characterized American criminal justice at the time. Chief among them were the creation of urban police departments for the arrest of criminals and the development of a prison system for punishment or rehabilitation. Other developments included the reduced role of the victim, the relative independence of criminal justice from legal norms, and the corruption and political manipulation of the criminal justice system. The paper explores ways that such developments may have provided the context for the institutionalization of plea bargaining as a method of case disposition.   J

1053. Halpern, Stephen C. POLICE EMPLOYEE ORGANIZATIONS AND ACCOUNTABILITY PROCEDURES IN THREE CITIES: SOME REFLECTIONS ON POLICE POLICY-MAKING. *Law & Soc. R. 1974 8(4): 561-582.* Examines the impact of police employee organizations in Buffalo, Philadelphia, and Baltimore on the regulation of police through internal review procedures and civilian review boards, 1958-74.   S

1054.   Hardy, David T.   GUN CONTROL: ARM YOURSELF WITH EVI-
DENCE.   *Reason 1982 14(7): 37-41.* Discusses gun-control legislation in the
United States from 1813 to 1981; shows that prohibition of handguns has not led
to a decrease in the rate of violent crime.

1055.   Harring, Sidney L.   THE POLICE INSTITUTION AS A CLASS
QUESTION: MILWAUKEE SOCIALISTS AND THE POLICE, 1900-1915.
Sci. & Soc. 1982 46(2): 197-221. The role of Milwaukee police in managing the
late 19th-century labor crises of that city shows that the roots of police professionalism lie in the need of a ruling bourgeois to isolate public institutions from
working-class power. In opposition to a police force operating as a class institution enforcing class law, the Milwaukee Social Democratic Party offered a real
alternative for the working class.   Milwaukee Municipal Reference Bureau.
L. V. Eid

1056.   Hartog, Hendrik.   THE PUBLIC LAW OF A COUNTY COURT:
JUDICIAL GOVERNMENT IN EIGHTEENTH-CENTURY MASSACHU-
SETTS.   *Am. J. of Legal Hist. 1976 20(4): 282-329.* The Court of General
Sessions—or sessions court—was the mainstay of conserving the peace, punishing
offenders, and administering local government in county life. Examines the
records of the Middlesex County, Massachusetts, Court of General Sessions of
the Peace, 1728-1803. Analyzes the Court's administration and adjudication of
liquor licensing, poor relief, fornication, and road building and repair; and the
extent to which by 1803 it realized two basic premises of modern government:
"the sovereignty of a centralized system of state authority in which counties and
other units of local government are merely subordinated entities, and the need
for a strict differentiation between judicial and administrative action." Reveals
how in the second half of the 18th century a dramatic distinction between criminal prosecution and administrative regulation was made. Local criminal practice
was integrated into a state-wide system of criminal justice, and the justices of the
peace devolved to "limited administrators of county affairs." Based on manuscript and printed sources; table of criminal trials, 145 notes.   L. A. Knafla

1057.   Haskins, George L.   ECCLESIASTICAL ANTECEDENTS OF
CRIMINAL PUNISHMENT IN EARLY MASSACHUSETTS.   *Massachu-
setts Hist. Soc. Pro. 1957-60 72: 21-35.* Provides the historical background of
ecclesiastical law in colonial Massachusetts dating to the early 17th century in
England, whose legal statutes had roots in Roman law.

1058.   Hayes, Frederick O'R.   PATRICK MURPHY—ON POLICE COR-
RUPTION.   *New York Affairs 1974 2(1): 88-111.* "Patrick Murphy was Police
Commissioner of the City of New York from October, 1970 until May, 1973."
J

1059.   Heinz, Anne M. and Kerstetter, Wayne A.   PRETRIAL SETTLE-
MENT CONFERENCE: EVALUATION OF A REFORM IN PLEA BAR-
GAINING.   *Law and Soc. Rev. 1979 13(2): 349-366.* A field experiment in
Dade County, Florida, evaluated the use of a pretrial settlement conference as a
means of restructuring plea negotiations. All negotiations took place in front of
a judge and victim, defendant, and arresting police officer were invited to attend.
The conferences were brief but generally reached at least an outline of a settle-

ment. They usually included at least one lay party although lay attendance rates were quite low. The change in the structure reduced the time involved in processing cases by lowering the information and decisionmaking costs to the judges and attorneys. No significant changes were observed in the settlement rate or in the imposition of criminal sanctions. There was some evidence that police and victims who attended the sessions obtained more information and developed more positive attitudes about the way their cases were handled.   J

1060. Helmer, William J. THE DEPRESSION DESPERADOS: A STUDY IN MODERN MYTH-MAKING. *Mankind 1975 5(2): 40-46.* Criminals such as John Dillinger spurred the Justice Department and the Federal Bureau of Investigation to modernize and coordinate the efforts of law enforcement agencies in 1933-34.

1061. Henderson, Thomas A. THE RELATIVE EFFECTS OF COMMUNITY COMPLEXITY AND OF SHERIFFS UPON THE PROFESSIONALISM OF SHERIFF DEPARTMENTS. *Am. J. of Pol. Sci. 1975 19(1): 107-132.* "This study examines the relative importance of environmental factors and characteristics of the chief law enforcement officer in explaining professionalism in the organization of sheriff departments. The research population consisted of the sheriff departments of Florida. Path analysis was employed to assess the interrelationship of each of the independent variables and the dependent variable. Path analysis was useful as it permitted a refinement of our understanding of the interrelationship of the variables. Environmental variables were the most important components; but sheriff characteristics were significant factors as well. The results raise questions about the meaning of police professionalism, popular control of law enforcement, and our conceptualization of the policy process."   J

1062. Heumann, Milton and Loftin, Colin. MANDATORY SENTENCING AND THE ABOLITION OF PLEA BARGAINING: THE MICHIGAN FELONY FIREARM STATUTE. *Law and Soc. Rev. 1979 13(2): 393-430.* Increasing concern about the substantial discretion accorded prosecutors in plea negotiations and judges in sentencing decisions has led to a number of proposals to curtail both. In this paper, we assess the consequences of an attempt, simultaneously, to abolish plea bargaining and introduce mandatory sentencing. The Wayne County (Detroit) Prosecutor prohibited his subordinates from plea bargaining in any case in which a recently enacted state statute warranted a mandatory sentence. This statute imposed an additional two-year prison term if a defendant possessed a firearm while committing a felony. Using qualitative data collected from interviews with judges, prosecutors, and defense attorneys, and quantitative disposition data for the six-month periods before and after the law went into effect, we describe the effects of the new statute on dispositions in Detroit. Though there is some evidence that the law and the prohibition on plea barbaining may have selectively increased severity of sentences for certain classes of defendants, for the most part disposition patterns did not appear to have been altered dramatically. In many serious cases, sentences for the primary felony were adjusted downward to take into account the additional two-year penalty; in "equity" cases, in which defendants had not previously received prison time, other mechanisms, such as abbreviated bench trials, were often employed to circumvent the mandatory sentencing provision.   J

1063.   Higginbotham, Don and Price, William S., Jr.   WAS IT MURDER FOR A WHITE MAN TO KILL A SLAVE? CHIEF JUSTICE MARTIN HOWARD CONDEMNS THE PECULIAR INSTITUTION IN NORTH CAROLINA.   *William and Mary Q. 1979 36(4): 593-601.* In 1771, Martin Howard, Chief Justice of the North Carolina Superior Court, in a grand jury charge, denounced slavery. Though Howard was earlier a controversial figure in defending the Stamp Act, he was highly regarded by all factions in North Carolina. Howard did not ask for abolition, but he struck at the hypocrisy of North Carolinians in their quest for political freedom from England while denying the humanity of Negroes. He considered cruelty bad policy. Except for the fruits of his labor, a slave has all other rights of a human being. Howard's plea undoubtedly influenced the subsequent adoption of laws (1774 and 1791) in making it a crime for a white man to murder a Negro. Notes deal primarily with other legal development; 17 notes.   H. M. Ward

1064.   Hindus, Michael Stephen.   THE CONTOURS OF CRIME AND JUSTICE IN MASSACHUSETTS AND SOUTH CAROLINA, 1767-1878. *Am. J. of Legal Hist. 1977 21(3): 212-237.* Criminal law "catalogs in great detail what behavior is so strongly proscribed that society's general resources will be employed to punish and prevent it; . . . . the criminal prosecution exists at a critical junction between law and society, between values (embodied into law) and behavior. The study of crime and justice in history is critical to understand the relationship between law, values and behavior, and serves as an important indicator of the role of formal, legal authority in society." Examines the criminal prosecutions in the court records of two diverse jurisdictions—Massachusetts and South Carolina—to interpret the correlation between crime and the social and economic bases of society. Discusses conceptual and methodological problems and details the evidence. Differences in prosecution are attributable to criminal procedure. The results are illustrative not only of crime and differing social values, but also of "controlling conceptions of criminal law and public justice." Based on the author's dissertation (Berkeley, 1975); 30 notes.   L. A. Knafla

1065.   Humphrey, Theodore C.   THE FRONTIER LAWMAN AS FOLK HERO: THE SEARCH FOR BILL TILGHMAN: PART I.   *J. of the Folklore Inst. 1980 17(2-3): 125-134.* The frontier lawman, although thriving in popular culture as fictional and film westerns, never seems to have developed into a distinctive folktype. William Matthew "Bill" Tilghman, Jr. (1854-1924), famous Oklahoma and Dodge City lawman, is a perfect example. His enduring regional fame derives largely from a film he made in 1915, *The Passing of the Oklahoma Outlaw,* and from a few key books written by his friends and associates. Tilghman made numerous speaking tours accompanying his film, and may have been a sort of sagaman. Yet neither the film nor the books, Fred Sutton's *Hand's Up!* (1927) and Evett D. Nix's *Oklahombres* (1929), managed to foster a living oral tradition. Fieldwork may eventually indicate otherwise. 13 notes. Article to be continued.
                                                                      C. D. Geist

1066.   Jackson, Pamela Irving and Carroll, Leo.   RACE AND THE WAR ON CRIME: THE SOCIOPOLITICAL DETERMINANTS OF MUNICIPAL POLICE EXPENDITURES IN 90 NON-SOUTHERN U.S. CITIES. *Am. Sociol. Rev. 1981 46(3): 290-305.* Uses the racial composition of the city, the level of black mobilization, and the frequency of riots in the 1960's as independent predictors of municipal policing expenditures in 1971. Tests the interdependence of the police expenditure function with the crime and total city revenue functions. Racial composition and the level of black mobilization were significant predictors of municipal policing expenditures. Race-related variables appear to have had a greater effect on police capital expenditures than on expenditures for salaries and operations.   J/S

1067.   Johnson, Dorothy M.   SOME LAWMEN I HAVE KNOWN.   *Montana, the Mag. of Western Hist. 1975 25(1): 55-63.* Anecdotes about city police and US Marshals in Whitefish, Montana; New York City; and Springfield, Illinois (1917-1950). Illus.   S. R. Davison

1068.   Jones, Edward D., III.   THE DISTRICT OF COLUMBIA'S "FIRE-ARMS CONTROL REGULATIONS ACT OF 1975": THE TOUGHEST HANDGUN CONTROL LAW IN THE UNITED STATES—OR IS IT? *Ann. of the Am. Acad. of Pol. and Social Sci. 1981 (455): 138-149.* The District of Columbia's Firearms Control Regulations Act (1975) had two legislative objectives: to reduce the potential of firearms-related crimes and to monitor more effectively firearms' trafficking. In July 1980, the US Conference of Mayors reported that the act significantly reduced firearm and handgun crime. This report met largely with opposition. The author relates the provisions and legislative history of the Firearms Control Regulations Act, analyzes the deficiencies in the Conference of Mayors' research methods and assumptions, and discusses any beneficial effects and weaknesses of the act.   J/S

1069.   Jordan, Laylon Wayne.   POLICE AND POLITICS: CHARLESTON IN THE GILDED AGE, 1880-1900.   *South Carolina Hist. Mag. 1980 81(1): 35-50.* Examines the effectiveness of the Charleston, South Carolina, police, police corruption, and the social composition of police officers, and concludes that the public seems to have been satisfied with police protection.

1070.   Juris, Hervey A. and Duncan, Robert B.   EDUCATION INCENTIVE PLANS FOR THE POLICE: AN EVALUATION OF RECOMMENDATIONS BY THE NATIONAL ADVISORY COMMISSION ON CRIMINAL JUSTICE STANDARDS AND GOALS.   *Urban Affairs Q. 1974 10(2): 197-211.* Reviews progress towards the commission goal of having policemen hold advanced degrees or equivalents by 1982. An Illinois survey concludes that police participate in college courses when time, cash incentives, and promotional opportunities are available. The role of self-development needs and the effect of supervisory climate are still undetermined. 3 tables, notes, biblio.   P. J. Woehrmann

1071.   Kamisar, Yale.   MONDALE ON *MAPP*.   *Civil Liberties Rev. 1977 3(6): 62-64.* Discusses the significance of the Supreme Court decision in *Mapp* v. *Ohio* (US, 1961) on criminal procedure, Walter Mondale's defense of the *Mapp* decision, and the possibility of judicial reversal of this decision.

1072.   Katz, Jack.   LEGALITY AND EQUALITY: PLEA BARGAINING IN THE PROSECUTION OF WHITE-COLLAR AND COMMON CRIMES. *Law and Soc. Rev. 1979 13(2): 431-459.* On the basis of a case study of a U.S. Attorney's office, I sketch differences in the prosecution of white-collar and common crime in order to draw out implications for equality in current proposals to reform plea bargaining. The extent to which the powers of investigation and

prosecution are empirically distinct differs with the two categories of crime. Because of greater social distance between prosecutor and investigator in the enforcement of laws against common crimes, formal records give a misleading impression that legitimate prosecutorial power is being bargained away. Because there is relatively little social distance between the prosecutorial and investigative functions in the prosecution of white-collar crime, the formal record greatly underrepresents the exercise of the power not to prosecute. Reforms that would make bargaining over formal dispositions more consistent with legality or "due" process appear likely to discourage lenience in the prosecution of common crimes while leaving largely unaffected the low visibility exercise of the power not to prosecute white-collar crime.
                                                                              J

1073. Kerp, Thomas Bland. WERE THE LINCOLN CONSPIRATORS DEALT JUSTICE? *Lincoln Herald 1978 80(1): 38-46.* The eight Abraham Lincoln assassination alleged conspirators, especially Edwin Spangler, Dr. Samuel Mudd, and Samuel Arnold, were deprived of due process of law. In 1866 Federal judge Willard Hull decided in *United States v. Commandant of Fort Delaware* that because the Civil War had ended, civilians could not be tried before a military commission, and he ordered the civilians in question released. This established a precedent that should have applied in the cases of Arnold, Mudd, and Spangler, who were imprisoned on the Dry Tortugas, Florida. Instead, another judicial decision, *Ex parte Mudd et al.* (1868), deprived the three civilians of their constitutional right of due process. 9 photos, 35 notes.
                                                                T. P. Linkfield

1074. Killenberg, George M. *BRANZBURG* REVISITED: THE STRUGGLE TO DEFINE NEWSMAN'S PRIVILEGE GOES ON. *Journalism Q. 1978 55(4): 703-710.* In *Branzburg* v. *Hayes* (US, 1972), the Supreme Court ruled 5-4 that journalists must respond to grand jury subpoenas and answer questions relevant to criminal investigations. Since then, rulings from federal and state courts regarding journalists' withholding of confidential information in court have conflicted with each other, in light of the vagueness and diversity of views expressed in the Supreme Court's majority and dissenting opinions. The pattern of rulings indicates, however, that no court is likely to recognize the withholding of information as a journalist's unqualified right under the First Amendment. 48 notes.
                                                            R. P. Sindermann, Jr.

1075. King, Willard L. THE CASE THAT MADE LINCOLN. *Lincoln Herald 1981 84[i.e., 83](3[i.e., 4]): 786-790.* Discusses Abraham Lincoln's defense of Henry B. Truett, who was tried in 1838 for the murder of Dr. J. M. Early; Lincoln successfully defended Truett, even though Lincoln had been admitted to the bar only the year before.

1076. Kobler, Arthur L. FIGURES (AND PERHAPS SOME FACTS) ON POLICE KILLINGS OF CIVILIANS IN THE UNITED STATES, 1965-1969. *J. of Social Issues 1975 31(1): 185-191.* Official reports for a 20-year period show that the police killed about five civilians for every officer killed. A study of newspaper reports from 1965-1969 shows that about half of the police and of their victims were young male minorities in urban areas. About a third of the civilians killed were committing misdemeanors when stopped; they tended to have weapons and to use them. The police who killed civilians tended to be on duty, in uniform, and reported that they killed the civilians to defend themselves or to prevent escape.　　　　　　　　　　　　　　　　　　　　　　　　　　　J

1077.　Kobler, Arthur L.　POLICE HOMICIDE IN A DEMOCRACY. *J. of Social Issues 1975 31(1): 163-184.* Although many more people are killed by police than kill police, many of the former instances do not appear justified. Laws limiting the use of deadly force sometimes permit its use against anyone fleeing police custody. Although police regulations are more limiting than the law, there is little indication that departmental rules are enforced stringently. Prosecutors also appear to be extremely reluctant to prosecute police who have killed citizens. In short, the system appears to function to protect police officers who have killed citizens.　　　　　　　　　　　　　　　　　　　　J

1078.　Kocolowski, Gary P.　EXPANDING POLICE SERVICES IN LATE-NINETEENTH-CENTURY CINCINNATI. *Cincinnati Hist. Soc. Bull. 1973 31(2): 115-126.* Between 1875 and 1900 the police of Cincinnati performed many services, including aid to victims of natural disaster, ambulance services, care for the needy, and locating lost and runaway children. The period 1884-94 was difficult because of unrest, too few officers, and politics. Based on local police reports, manuals, and regulations; 7 photos, 34 notes.　　　H. S. Marks

1079.　Kotecha, Kanti C. and Walker, James L.　POLICE VIGILANTES. *Society 1976 13(3): 48-52.* Considers police violence and vigilantism in the 1970's aimed at circumventing the judicial process in protecting the established order.

1080.　Kovler, Peter.　THE SAGA OF SON OF S. 1: HOW THE CRIMINAL CODE REFORM BILL PASSED THE SENATE. *Civil Liberties Rev. 1979 5(4): 10-18.* Traces the political events since the 1950's, leading to the passing of the Criminal Code Reform Act (US, 1978) by the US Senate.

1081.　Krajewski, Krzystof.　INSTYTUCJA "PLEA BARGAINING" W AMERYKAŃSKIM PROCESIE KARNYM [Plea bargaining in the American penal process]. *Państwo i Prawo [Poland] 1980 35(6): 95-105.* Plea bargaining, one of the most controversial institutions in the US penal process, can be divided into four sections: bargaining concerning the charge, the sentence, concurrent charges, and dropped charges. Several relevant court cases are discussed: Scott v. US; Brady v. US; Euziere v. US; US v. Frontero; US v. Jackson; Garrity v. New Jersey; North Carolina v. Alford. American and Polish law journals and other secondary sources; 25 notes.　　　　　　　　　　　　　　　I. Lukes

1082.　Kramer, Daniel C. and Riga, Robert.　THE NEW YORK COURT OF APPEALS AND THE UNITED STATES SUPREME COURT, 1960-76. *Publius 1978 8(4): 75-111.* Enumerates eight ways " . . . in which a state court can bridle Supreme Court liberalism or spurn Supreme Court conservativism . . ." Examines decisions of the New York Court of Appeals in the constitutional areas of obscenity, search and seizure, right to assigned counsel, and the Miranda warnings. Shows the complexity of the relationship existing between the US Supreme Court and a state court, and the dangers inherent in oversimplifying, while indicating the interdependence of the two. Discusses the composition and philosophy of the individual judges on the New York Court of Appeals. Concludes that scholars should be more precise in describing the relationship between a state court and the US Supreme Court in human rights cases. 172 notes.　　　　　　　　　　　　　　　　　　　　　　　　　　　R. S. Barnard

1083.   Kreps, Gary A.   CHANGE IN CRISIS-RELEVANT ORGANIZA-
TIONS: POLICE DEPARTMENTS AND CIVIL DISTURBANCES.   *Am.
Behavioral Scientist 1973 16(3): 356-367.* Discusses the way police departments
have responded to civil disturbances in the cities during the 1960's and 70's.
S

1084.   Kress, Jack M.   THE ACCUSED VERSUS SOCIETY: A DILEMMA
OF CONFLICTING RIGHTS.   *Current Hist. 1976 71(418): 10-13, 35.* Examines the police stage and the court stage of the criminal justice system and the
need to protect criminal defendants with the due process of the law as well as to
protect society from dangerous individuals.

1085.   Kress, Jack M.   PROGRESS AND PROSECUTION.   *Ann. of the
Am. Acad. of Pol. and Social Sci. 1976 (423): 99-116.* Possessing awesome and
almost unlimited discretionary powers, the district attorney is the most important
figure in America's modern system of criminal justice administration. These
powers stem primarily from the unique fact that the public prosecutor exists in
a system which was initially premised on a common law concept of private
prosecution. The discretion involved in charging and plea-bargaining decisions
exemplifies the power granted a civil law official to administer a common law
jurisprudence. The value of a return to private prosecution as a control upon
unfettered prosecutorial discretion is explored, as well as the suggestion of increased internal guidelines for the exercise of the prosecution function.   J

1086.   LaFree, Gary D.   THE EFFECT OF SEXUAL STRATIFICATION
BY RACE ON OFFICIAL REACTIONS TO RAPE.   *Am. Sociol. Rev. 1980
45(5): 842-854.* Collins argues that sexual access, like other valuable commodi-
ties, is distributed according to relative power within a sexual stratification system. He predicts more serious official reactions to violations of the sexual
stratification system in which men from less powerful groups sexually assault
women from more powerful groups. Race continues to be an obvious correlate
of stratified sexual access in America. But empirical studies have not assessed the
cumulative effect of racial composition of victim-suspect dyads on processing
outcomes in sexual assault cases. The present study examined the effect of race
composition on processing decisions—from case report to final disposition—for
881 sexual assaults in a large, midwestern city. Step-wise multiple regression
analysis showed that, compared to other defendants, black men who assaulted
white women received 1) more serious charges and 2) longer sentences, and were
more likely to 3) have their cases filed as felonies, 4) receive executed sentences,
and 5) be incarcerated in the state penitentiary. At the same time, black men who
assaulted white women were no more likely than other suspects to be arrested or
found guilty. The implications of the results for a sexual stratification theory of
official reactions to sexual assault are discussed.   J

1087.   Langbein, John H.   UNDERSTANDING THE SHORT HISTORY
OF PLEA BARGAINING.   *Law and Soc. Rev. 1979 13(2): 261-272.* As late
as the 18th century, ordinary jury trial at common law was a judge-dominated,
lawyer-free procedure conducted so rapidly that plea bargaining was unnecessary.
Thereafter, the rise of adversary procedure and the law of evidence injected vast
complexity into jury trial and made it unworkable as a routine dispositive procedure. A variety of factors, some quite fortuitous, inclined 19th-century common

law procedure to channel the mounting caseload into nontrial plea bargaining procedure rather than to refine its trial procedure as contemporary Continental legal systems were doing. 12 notes, biblio.   J

1088. Lazerson, Marvin and Brenzel, Barbara. JUVENILES, INCARCERA-TION, AND COMPULSORY LOVE. *Rev. in Am. Hist. 1978 6(1): 87-94.* Review article prompted by Steven L. Schlossman's *Love & the American Delinquent: The Theory and Practice of "Progressive" Juvenile Justice, 1825-1920* (Chicago: U. of Chicago Pr., 1977).

1089. Lee, R. Alton. "NEW DEALERS, FAIR DEALERS, MISDEALERS, AND HISS DEALERS": KARL MUNDT AND THE INTERNAL SECU-RITY ACT OF 1950. *South Dakota Hist. 1980 10(4): 277-290.* Senator Karl Mundt (1900-74) of South Dakota contributed more to the enactment of the Internal Security Act (US, 1950), popularly called the McCarran Act, than has been credited to him. In 1947 Mundt was the first congressman to call for the registration of Communists and members of front organizations. Hearings on this proposal, labeled the Mundt-Nixon bill, were held in 1948. In 1949 Mundt suggested that a Subversive Activities Control Board should be part of any internal security legislation. Due to Mundt's persistence and organization, the Internal Security Act, which included his proposals, was passed in 1950. Based on the Karl Mundt Papers at the Karl E. Mundt Library, Dakota State College, Madison, South Dakota, and other primary sources; illus., 2 photos, 30 notes.
                                                                           P. L. McLaughlin

1090. Lefkowitz, Joel. PSYCHOLOGICAL ATTRIBUTES OF POLICE-MEN: A REVIEW OF RESEARCH AND OPINION. *J. of Social Issues 1975 3(1): 3-26.* This review focuses primarily on personality characteristics of police-men. The data substantiate, with some qualifications, the existence of a nonpatho-logical "modal police personality." Methodological weaknesses prevent, however, an assessment of the relative developmental contributions of predispos-ing self-selection effects, socioeconomic class determinants, organizational selec-tion and selective attrition, occupational socialization, and role-specific behaviors.   J

1091. Levine, James P. THE IMPACT OF "GIDEON": THE PERFOR-MANCE OF PUBLIC AND PRIVATE CRIMINAL DEFENSE LAWYERS. *Polity 1975 8(2): 215-240.* Has the assurance of a lawyer for criminal defendants really mattered? Is not the sophisticated response that legal aid lawyers have neither the experience nor the time and resources and commitment to give mean-ingful help to their clients? Professor Levine reports a study comparing the performance of private criminal lawyers and Legal Aid Society lawyers in Brook-lyn, New York, notes various earlier findings, and proposes certain actions to make the right to counsel more truly effective. But the performance of the legal aid lawyers turns out to be far from inept, token representation. They are surpris-ingly conscientious and effective advocates. However, their clients lack confi-dence in them, so prefer to plea bargain, rather than go to trial. This client perception is a key difference between private and legal aid attorneys.   J

1092. Lewis, Anthony.   THE PRESS AND SOCIETY: THE FARBER CASE.   *Massachusetts Hist. Soc. Pro. 1978 90: 89-99.* The jailing in 1975 of Myron Farber of *The New York Times* for refusing to reveal the identity of his sources as a journalist raises many questions concerning the meaning of freedom of the press. The many aspects of this case are discussed in light of current judicial opinion and the author's own values. Based on an analysis of several court cases concerning related issues, and written and spoken opinions of judges and others.
G. W. R. Ward

1093. Lewis, John D., Jr.   AMERICAN GESTAPO: HOW THE BATF IS RIDING ROUGHSHOD OVER CIVIL LIBERTIES.   *Reason 1980 11(12): 24-28, 44.* The federal Bureau of Alcohol, Tobacco, and Firearms (BATF), faced with less to enforce after moonshining declined in the 1970's, has stepped up its violations of the civil liberties and the Second Amendment rights of legal firearms owners and dealers through paramilitary-style raids, unjustified confiscations of legal firearms, entrapment, and use of untrustworthy informants.

1094. Liebman, Robert and Polen, Michael.   PERSPECTIVES IN POLICING IN NINETEENTH-CENTURY AMERICA.   *Social Sci. Hist. 1978 2(3): 346-360.* Records changes in the character of American policing during the 100 years starting around 1820. Reveals three main perspectives on the rise and reform of urban police: social disorganization, political process, and class conflict. Examines the redistribution of policing actions and describes some political conflicts during the expansion of industrial capitalism. 39 notes.   G. E. Pergl

1095. Lindgren, James.   ORGANIZATIONAL AND OTHER CONSTRAINTS OF CONTROLLING THE USE OF DEADLY FORCE BY POLICE.   *Ann. of the Am. Acad. of Pol. and Social Sci. 1981 (455): 110-119.* Examines the structures of police departments, widespread ownership of firearms, and other factors limiting the regulation of the use of firearms by police; 1968-78.   J/S

1096. Loftin, Colin and McDowall, David.   "ONE WITH A GUN GETS YOU TWO": MANDATORY SENTENCING AND FIREARMS VIOLENCE IN DETROIT.   *Ann. of the Am. Acad. of Pol. and Social Sci. 1981 (455): 150-167.* Mandatory sentences for crimes committed with a gun are a popular policy because they promise a reduction in gun violence at a relatively low cost. In this article we present some results of a study of the implementation of such a law in Detroit, Michigan. Although the law required a two-year mandatory sentence for felonies committed with a gun and the prosecutor followed a strict policy of not reducing the gun law charge, there was little change in the certainty or severity of sentences that could be attributed to the effects of the gun law. Serious violent crimes follow patterns over time that lead us to conclude that the gun law did not significantly alter the number or type of serious crimes in Detroit.   J/S

1097. Loh, Wallace D.   Q: WHAT HAS REFORM OF RAPE LEGISLATION WROUGHT? A: TRUTH IN CRIMINAL LABELLING.   *J. of Social Issues 1981 37(4): 28-52.* Compares the impact of common law and reform rape legislation of prosecution, based on an analysis of 445 forcible and statutory rape cases in King County, Washington. The main impact of the statutory reform has been a symbolic and educative one for society at large, rather than an instrumental one for law enforcement.   J/S

1098. Longbein, John H. TORTURE AND PLEA BARGAINING. *Public Interest 1980 58: 43-61.* There are parallels between the law of plea bargaining and the medieval law of torture. Today, in major American cities, between 95 and 99% of felony convictions are made by plea bargaining, thereby evading trials. Criminal defendants are coerced into plea bargaining by making it costly for an accused person to claim his or her right to a constitutionally guaranteed trial. Because defendants are routinely threatened with increased punishments if they go to trial and are thereafter convicted, they must often opt for a plea bargained lesser sentence. Finds parallels between the coercion in plea bargaining and the use of medieval torture to elicit confessions. The greatest pressure to plea bargain is done by prosecutors with the weakest cases, thereby increasing the probability that innocent persons will confess to crimes they did not commit. Popular cynicism toward the criminal justice system in part results from lack of adjudication in open trial to establish the facts about crime and guilt when plea bargaining is used. Plea bargaining requires prosecutors to usurp determinative and sentencing functions more appropriately left to juries and judges. Proposes the adoption of a nonadversorial criminal justice system such as Germany's as a solution which guarantees the accused a trial which examines evidence and where there is no plea bargaining.   J. M. Herrick

1099. Lyons, Grant. LOUISIANA AND THE LIVINGSTON CRIMINAL CODES. *Louisiana Hist. 1974 15(3): 243-272.* Discusses the life and career of Edward Livingston, the man largely responsible for the writing and passage of a set of liberal laws, Louisiana's system of criminal law, 1822.

1100. Mackey, James and Ahlgren, Andrew. A PICTORIAL MEASURE OF ADOLESCENT PERCEPTIONS OF THE POLICE. *Social Educ. 1980 44(3): 224-227, 248.* Discusses the methodology and results of a Comprehension of Police Outlook and the Perception of Law Officers test which measures the attitudes of adolescents toward police by responding to pictures of police in action; late 1970's.

1101. Maestro, Marcello. BENJAMIN FRANKLIN AND THE PENAL LAWS. *J. of the Hist. of Ideas 1975 36(3): 551-562.* Surveys Benjamin Franklin's writings (1747-89) on criminal law, from "The Speech of Polly Baker" through the 1780's, when he was much influenced by Gaetano Filangieri. Examines the "Letter to Benjamin Vaughan," Franklin's "most important writing on the subject of penal legislation." Based on primary and secondary works; 30 notes.   D. B. Marti

1102. Mangione, Thomas W. and Fowler, Floyd J., Jr. ENFORCING THE GAMBLING LAWS. *J. of Social Issues 1979 35(3): 115-128.* A great deal of controversy surrounds the writing and enforcement of antigambling laws. In large part, this is due to a lack of consensus among citizens, police departments, and prosecutors in defining the objectives of antigambling laws and the methods of enforcing them. It is suggested that since standards of appropriate behavior vary from place to place, the wishes of the local citizens should be the primary guide in determining enforcement effort priorities. The authors differentiate the four main targets of enforcement efforts and conclude that only two—public social gambling and commercial gambling—can be substantially affected by local police. Finally, specific suggestions about how police and prosecutors can cooperate in enforcing local antigambling laws are made.   J

1103.   Marohn, Richard C.   THE ARMING OF THE CHICAGO POLICE IN THE NINETEENTH CENTURY.   *Chicago Hist. 1982 11(1): 40-49.* Economic conditions after the Panic of 1873 had resulted in unrest and riots; for this reason, and because military service during the Civil War had familiarized many men with firearms, police officers in Chicago, Illinois, without any official policy guidelines, began carrying guns; 1863-1910.

1104.   Marx, Gary T.   UNDERCOVER COPS: CREATIVE POLICING OR CONSTITUTIONAL THREAT?   *Civil Liberties Rev. 1977 4(2): 34-44.* Explores the necessity of restriction and close regulation of undercover police activities to avoid violation of constitutional rights, 1970's.

1105.   Marx, Gary T. and Archer, Dane.   COMMUNITY SELF-DEFENSE. *Society 1976 13(3): 38-43.* Discusses vigilantism and citizen involvement in law enforcement since 1965.

1106.   Marx, Gary T.   IRONIES OF SOCIAL CONTROL: AUTHORITIES AS CONTRIBUTORS TO DEVIANCE THROUGH ESCALATION, NON-ENFORCEMENT AND COVERT FACILITATION.   *Social Problems 1981 28(3): 221-246.* Analyzes the nature and sources of three types of interdependence between modern American police agencies and criminals, each involving the possibility of deviance amplification and illustrating that, ironically, authorities often contribute to the deviant behavior they set out to control.

1107.   Mather, Lynn M.   COMMENTS ON THE HISTORY OF PLEA BARGAINING.   *Law and Soc. Rev. 1979 13(2): 281-285.* Discusses changes in criminal law. By the end of the 19th century, punishment was meted out to fit the individual instead of being handed down to fit the crime. Plea bargaining consequently became an important part of the legal system. The criminal case load increased in the 20th century in part because many acts formerly regulated by social custom were legislatively defined as crimes.   S

1108.   McFeeley, Neil D.   A CHANGE OF DIRECTION: HABEAS CORPUS FROM WARREN TO BURGER.   *Western Pol. Q. 1979 32(2): 174-188.* Studies some differences between the Supreme Court of the United States under Chief Justice Warren and that Court today. The Warren Court was primarily concerned with individual liberty while the Burger Court is more concerned with the institutional consequences of its decisions. The paper explores the Burger Court's decisions on cases in the areas of civil rights, voting rights, individual freedoms and criminal justice and then compares the two Courts' decisions on the writ of habeas corpus. The Warren Court utilized that writ to protect the due process rights of state defendants while the Burger Court has retracted the scope of the writ. The recent decisions in *Stone* v. *Powell* and *Wolff* v. *Rice* indicate the Burger Court's primary concern with institutional relationships in derogation of protection of individual liberties.   J

1109. McIver, John P. THE RELATIONSHIP BETWEEN METROPOLITAN POLICE INDUSTRY STRUCTURE AND INTERAGENCY ASSISTANCE: A PRELIMINARY ASSESSMENT. *Policy Studies J. 1978 7(special issue): 406-412.* While reformers claim that fragmentation of metropolitan areas and multiplicity of police services result in reduced quality of police service for residents, studies show that informal cooperative arrangements occur in such areas and in fact improve overall police service.

1110. Mehay, Stephen L. INTERGOVERNMENTAL CONTRACTING FOR MUNICIPAL POLICE SERVICE: AN EMPIRICAL ANALYSIS. *Land Econ. 1979 55(1): 59-72.* Investigates the cost and quality of police service provided communities during 1971-72 in Los Angeles County, California, via the Lakewood Plan. Discusses problems of measuring quality of police service and constructs a regression model to compare service in contract and noncontract communities. Finds that contract cities have lower police cost and apparently less effective service. These conclusions are tentative and numerous other variables need further investigation. Based on state and federal statistics; 3 tables, 17 notes.
E. S. Johnson

1111. Meyer, Marshall W. POLICE SHOOTINGS AT MINORITIES: THE CASE OF LOS ANGELES. *Ann. of the Am. Acad.of Pol. and Social Sci. 1980 (452): 98-110.* Presents data on the involvement of minorities in Los Angeles (California) Police Department shootings, 1974-79. Shootings involving black suspects differed in number, in circumstances, and on some occasions, in outcomes of the shooting review process from shootings involving Hispanics and whites. Few differences appeared between shooting incidents involving Hispanics and shootings involving whites.
J

1112. Miller, W. R. POLICE AUTHORITY IN LONDON AND NEW YORK CITY, 1830-1870. *J. of Social Hist. 1976 8(2): 81-101.* "The London policeman represented the 'public good' as defined by the governing classes' concern to maintain an unequal social order with a minimum of violence and oppression. The result was impersonal authority. The New York policeman represented a 'self-governing people' as a product of that self-government's conceptions of power and the ethnic conflicts which divided that people. The result was personal authority." 95 notes.
L. Ziewacz

1113. Milton, Catherine Higgs et al. "IF I WERE CHIEF OF POLICE OF GOTHAM CITY . . ." *Civil Liberties R. 1975 2(2): 8-38.* Civil libertarians have few kind words for most police practices and fewer still for the entire criminal justice system. But as outsiders and critics, they seldom can do more than push for tactical reforms to try to alleviate the grossest of the injustices. If only they had power, ah, what they would do. . . . Well, what would they do? To find out, *The Civil Liberties Review* invited a number of civil liberties activists—social reformers, political figures, radicals, bleeding-heart liberals, and freedom-loving humorists—to put their money where their civil liberties mouths are. We asked them to assume the role of chief of police of Gotham City, the mythical metropolis that is afflicted with all the urban ills endemic in Chicago, Los Angeles, New York, Boston, Detroit, Washington. We asked them to tell us how they would protect and extend the civil liberties of all citizens while combatting the plague of crime in Gotham. And we offered them, in addition to the job of chief, some power to effect changes in legislation. The answers the chiefs gave us are their own opinions; they don't necessarily reflect the policies of the organizations with which they are affiliated. The drawings are by Isadore Seltzer.   J

1114.   Monkkonen, Eric H.   MUNICIPAL REPORTS AS AN INDICATOR SOURCE: THE NINETEENTH CENTURY POLICE.   *Hist. Methods 1979 12(2): 57-65.* These reports indicate the changing function of the police from social service activities to being crime-control agents. They are also examples of urban bureaucratic behavior. And yet they provide a valuable bridge connecting the various parts of the urban structure. Covers 1880-1903. 4 fig., 13 notes.
D. K. Pickens

1115.   Monkkonen, Eric H.   TOWARD A DYNAMIC THEORY OF CRIME AND THE POLICE: A CRIMINAL JUSTICE SYSTEM PERSPEC- TIVE.   *Hist. Methods Newsletter 1977 10(4): 157-165.* Reviews the major ap- proaches to the history of urban police. The approach is bureaucratic. During the 19th century symbolic order increased with the increased visibility of the police. Actual arrest decreased. Tramps and other elements of the "dangerous class" need to be more closely studied to understand this process. Attempts to link criminal statistics to the behavior and structure of criminal justice institutions. Table, 3 fig., 16 notes.   D. K. Pickens

1116.   Moore, Dhoruba.   STRATEGIES OF REPRESSION AGAINST THE BLACK MOVEMENT.   *Black Scholar 1981 12(3): 10-16.* Describes the federal government's moves against black nationalism, focusing on Operation Cointelpro of the Federal Bureau of Investigation, 1968-71, and its Operation Newkill that began in 1971.

1117.   Moore, Mark H.   KEEPING HANDGUNS FROM CRIMINAL OF- FENDERS.   *Ann. of the Am. Acad. of Pol. and Social Sci. 1981 (455): 92-109.* Current federal law seeks to discriminate between safe and unsafe gun owners— allowing the former and prohibiting the latter from owning guns. Nonetheless gun offenders have acquired guns from many different sources: purchases from licensed dealers, private transfers, thefts, and black markets. Among these, legiti- mate purchases were most important in supplying assaulters, and thefts were the most important in supplying armed robbers. The black market was populated primarily by small-scale, impermanent enterprises, rather than durable firms.
J/S

1118.   Morgan, David R. and Swanson, Cheryl.   ANALYZING POLICE POLICIES: THE IMPACT OF ENVIRONMENT, POLITICS, AND CRIME. *Urban Affairs Q. 1976 11(4): 489-510.* Uses data collected by the Kansas City Chief of Police (1972), the *Municipal Year Book* (1970,1971), and 1970 census data to argue that while specific city characteristics influence four police policy factors considered indicative of innovation, the strength of the influence varies from indicator to indicator. For indicators involving recruitment and technology, demographic factors were more influential than political and crime factors. But demography had less impact than either of the latter two on indicators involving manpower expenditure and community relations factors. Neither the extent of governmental reform nor the degree of police professionalism explained adoption of innovative police policies. Primary and secondary sources; 6 tables, 3 figs., 8 notes, biblio.   L. N. Beecher

1119. Moulds, Elizabeth F. CHIVALRY AND PATERNALISM: DISPARITIES OF TREATMENT IN THE CRIMINAL JUSTICE SYSTEM. *Western Pol. Q. 1978 31(3): 416-430.* Examines the hypothesis that an identifiable factor exists within the criminal justice system which usually results in less harsh handling of female defendants than of male defendants. This factor, often referred to as the "chivalry factor," appears to be related to a more general political and social pattern of paternalistic treatment of women. The analysis focuses on disparities in the sentencing of male and female defendants. The data are drawn from a nationwide study of sentencing done in the early 1960's and from California Bureau of Criminal Statistics records for the period 1970-74. A pattern of less harsh sentencing of women is pervasive; and in the case of the California data, the pattern exists regardless of race, type of crime, or prior record. J

1120. Mulkey, Michael A. THE ROLE OF PROSECUTION AND DEFENSE IN PLEA BARGAINING. *Policy Studies J. 1974 3(1): 54-60.*

1121. Murphy, Patrick V. THE DEVELOPMENT OF THE URBAN POLICE. *Current Hist. 1976 70(417): 245-248, 272.* Glances at the history of policing in metropolitan areas since the first police department was founded in New York in 1854, and concentrates on the role of this branch of the criminal justice system and efforts to reform it in the 1960's.

1122. Nagel, Stuart and Neef, Marian. IMPROVING THE CRIMINAL JUSTICE PROCESS. *Current Hist. 1976 71(418): 6-9, 32.* Studies "pretrial release, legal counsel for the poor, plea bargaining, delay in the court, judicial selection, the jury system, and allocating scarce criminal justice system resources."

1123. Nelson, Robert A. and Sheley, Joseph F. CURRENT BIA INFLUENCE ON INDIAN SELF-DETERMINATION: A CRIMINAL JUSTICE PLANNING ILLUSTRATION. *Social Sci. J. 1982 19(3): 73-85.* Traces the federal government's domination of American Indians until 1970 when, during the administration of Richard Nixon, Congress passed the Indian Self-Determination and Educational Assistance Act (US, 1975); and discusses the continued domination by the Bureau of Indian Affairs (BIA), citing the BIA's reservation crime control programs.

1124. Orman, John M. and Rudoni, Dorothy. EXERCISE OF THE PRESIDENT'S DISCRETIONARY POWER IN CRIMINAL JUSTICE POLICY. *Presidential Studies Q. 1979 9(4): 415-427.* The discretionary power of the president in the administration of criminal justice has symbolic as well as practical importance. Whether the dominant theme is, as in 1968, law and order, or whether it is, as it has been since Watergate, trust in government, the social environment reflects the political, and expectations of justice for all have ramifications beyond the narrowly legal. Accordingly, the president's discretionary power should be depoliticized, so that the president will base his discretionary decisions on more theoretical and impact-oriented grounds. Democracy will benefit. 47 notes. S

1125. Ostrom, Elinor; Parks, Roger B.; and Whitaker, Gordon. DEFINING AND MEASURING STRUCTURAL VARIATIONS IN INTERORGANIZATIONAL ARRANGEMENTS. *Publius 1974 4(4): 87-108.* Analyzing the functioning of governmental agencies requires the conceptualization of intergovernmental arrangements, so that empirical examination can measure the agencies' effectiveness. Examines the structure of intergovernmental arrangements among police agencies in Cumberland County, North Carolina, sets up a matrix of police services, defines six structural measures, (fragmentation, multiplication, duplication, independence, coordination, and dominance), and demonstrates the use of these measures for empirical public policy analysis. Based on the police structure of Cumberland County and secondary sources; map, 5 tables, 17 notes.

J. B. Street

1126. Ostrom, Elinor and Whitaker, Gordon. DOES LOCAL COMMUNITY CONTROL OF POLICE MAKE A DIFFERENCE? SOME PRELIMINARY FINDINGS. *Am. J. of Pol. Sci. 1973 17(1): 48-76.* Using a comparative research design, this study examines the consequences of organizing neighborhood patrol functions on a large scale by a city-wide police force or on a small scale by local communities. The research was conducted in three small independent communities adjacent to Indianapolis, and three matched neighborhoods within the city. The findings indicate a consistent pattern of higher levels of police performance in the independent communities when compared to the Indianapolis neighborhoods. The findings strongly suggest that in the area studied, small police forces under local community control are more effective than a large, city-wide controlled police department in meeting citizen demands for neighborhood police protection. Further studies have been initiated to ascertain if the patterns found in this metropolitan area are also present in other areas. J

1127. Ostrom, Elinor. ON RIGHTEOUSNESS, EVIDENCE, AND REFORM: THE POLICE STORY. *Urban Affairs Q. 1975 10(4): 464-486.* Many recent conclusions regarding police effectiveness made in nationally influential literature have been compromised by local studies with contrary conclusions representing more methodologically sound research. Includes for criticism the *Task Force Report: The Police* (1967) of the President's Commission on Law Enforcement and Administration of Justice. Notes, biblio. P. J. Woehrmann

1128. Palmer, Edward. BLACK POLICE IN AMERICA. *Black Scholar 1973 5(2): 19-27.* The author, a one-time policeman, and cofounder of the Afro-American's Patrolman's League in Chicago, delves into the complex process through which blacks must pass to become policemen and exposes the dynamics operating in the police department to use black police against black people.

M. T. Wilson

1129. Palmer, Stanley H. COPS AND GUNS: ARMING THE AMERICAN POLICE. *Hist. Today (Great Britain) 1978 28(6): 382-389.* Traces the history of criminal violence and law enforcement in Boston, New York, and Chicago, 19th century.

1130. Parkhomenko, V. K. OPERATSIIA "KOINTELPRO" [Operation Cointelpro]. *Voprosy Istorii [USSR] 1979 (10): 67-79.* Tells about the secret war waged by the Federal Bureau of Investigation against the dissidents in the U.S.A.

Shows the scope of the campaign of persecution launched against the democratic and Left movements in the U.S.A. in the period from the 1950's to the early 1970's, describes the methods employed by the FBI in combating political opponents (counter-intelligence, frame-ups, forgeries) and cites factual material illustrating the violation of the constitutional rights of American citizens. In a number of instances U.S. government officials acted as direct accomplices in the secret operations planned by the FBI in its unlawful war against the dissidents.　　J

1131. Parrish, Michael E.　COLD WAR JUSTICE: THE SUPREME COURT AND THE ROSENBERGS. *Am. Hist. Rev. 1977 82(4): 805-842.* In 1953, at the peak of the Cold War, Julius and Ethel Rosenberg were executed by the United States for conspiring to give atomic secrets to the Soviet Union. This reinterpretation of the celebrated "atom spy" case focuses upon the Rosenbergs' many efforts to secure a new trial through appeals to the Supreme Court of the United States. In addition to analyzing the Constitutional and statutory issues raised by the Rosenberg case, this article also explores the conflicts generated by the litigation among members of the Court, including Chief Justice Vinson, Justices Frankfurter, Jackson, and Douglas.　　A

1132. Perrucci, Robert; Anderson, Robert M.; Schendel, Dan E.; and Tracht-man, Leon E.　WHISTLE-BLOWING: PROFESSIONALS' RESISTANCE TO ORGANIZATIONAL AUTHORITY. *Social Problems 1980 28(2): 149-164.* Examines the preconditions for and process of "whistle-blowing," an act of defiance by which a dissatisfied individual or individuals in an organization goes outside that group in order to call to the public's attention unethical or illegal practices of the employer; and illustrates this method of protest with an incident involving the San Francisco Bay Area Rapid Transit District in 1973.

1133. Pfaff, Daniel W.　THE PRESS AND THE SCOTTSBORO RAPE CASES, 1931-32. *Journalism Hist. 1974 1(3): 72-76.* Studies newspaper reporting of trials involving the sentencing of eight Negro youths to death on rape charges in Scottsboro, Alabama, in 1931.

1134. Philips, Verne D. J.　THE AMERICAN MILITARY COURT OF INQUIRY. *Military Hist. of Texas and the Southwest 1978 14(1): 45-52.* Inherited from the British military system during the American Revolution, military courts of inquiry were employed 1776-1880 to investigate questionable conduct of officers and to air grievances between lower and upper officers.

1135. Pierce, Glenn L. and Bowers, William J.　THE BARTLEY-FOX GUN LAW'S SHORT-TERM IMPACT ON CRIME IN BOSTON. *Ann. of the Am. Acad. of Pol. and Social Sci. 1981 (455): 120-137.* Examines the effects of the Bartley-Fox Amendment of 1975, which made the illicit carrying of a firearm punishable with a one-year mandatory prison term. The law substantially reduced the incidence of gun assaults, but produced a more than offsetting increase in nongun armed assaults. It resulted in a reduction in gun robberies, accompanied by a less than corresponding increase in nongun armed robberies. It reduced gun homicides with no increase in nongun homicides. Publicity about the law's intent rather than the punishments was responsible for the reductions in gun-related crimes; 1974-76.　　J/S

1136. Powers, Jacob Mathews. MONTANA EPISODES: TRACKING CON MURPHY. *Montana 1980 30(4): 52-56.* Reprints segments of Jacob Powers's diary detailing the pursuit and capture of outlaw Con Murphy (Jack Redmond). Murphy committed many crimes in the central Montana area during the early 1880's, including robbing the Helena-Fort Benton stagecoach, for which Powers was superintendent. After Murphy's capture and return to Helena, a vigilante mob removed him from jail and hanged him. Covers 1884-85. Based on Powers's diary in his daughter's possession; illus., map.		R. C. Myers

1137. Powers, Richard Gid. J. EDGAR HOOVER AND THE DETECTIVE HERO. *J. of Popular Culture 1975 9(2): 257-278.* A preliminary study of J. Edgar Hoover as one of the most successful practitioners of popular politics, and how he mythologized himself and the Federal Bureau of Investigation. The Bureau was founded in 1908, the result of a political controversy, and gave Theodore Roosevelt a means of appearing as the symbol of law and order. The Bureau's enforcement of the Mann Act (1910), the slacker raids against draft dodgers (1918), and the Red scare raids (1919-20) were early examples of how it mobilized the law in a "pageant of popular politics." After the Teapot Dome scandal and an initial period of rehabilitation, Hoover led the Bureau back into public prominence in 1933 with spectacular cases like the Lindbergh case and the Kansas City Massacre. In the process of making himself the national symbol of law enforcement, Hoover adopted the guise of the detective hero in detective stories and compared the exploits of the detective hero to the FBI agent's routine day. Hoover successfully infiltrated popular culture fields such as the comics, radio, television, films, pulp magazines, cereal boxes, and bubble gum cards. 28 notes.		J. D. Falk

1138. Prettyman, E. Barrett, Jr. *FIKES* V. *ALABAMA:* THE UNCONSTI-TUTIONAL CONVICTION OF "BABY." *Supreme Court Hist. Soc. Y. 1978: 68-76.* In *Fikes* v. *Alabama,* the Supreme Court in 1957 reversed William Earl Fikes's burglary conviction on the grounds that his confession of the 1953 burglary in Selma, Alabama, was obtained unconstitutionally; in 1975 Fikes was released from prison after serving 22 years on a rape conviction to which he had also confessed.

1139. Quarantelli, E. L.; Ponting, J. Rick; and Fitzpatrick, John. POLICE DEPARTMENT PERCEPTIONS OF THE OCCURRENCE OF CIVIL DIS-TURBANCES. *Sociol. and Social Res. 1974 59(1): 30-38.* "A study of police department perceptions of four different civil disturbances in American cities, through interviews with key organizational personnel, yields five general proposi-tions about organizational perceptions of riot participants and dynamics. In general, social control agencies saw specific events and particular types of people rather than sequential happenings and social conditions as being responsible for the occurrence of the disturbances, although they did not perceive the disorders as being organized or planned."		J

1140. Reasons, Charles E. and Wirth, Bernard A. POLICE COMMUNITY RELATIONS UNITS: A NATIONAL SURVEY. *J. of Social Issues 1975 31(1): 27-34.* A national survey of Police-Community Relations Units was made to analyze their size, emergence, purpose, structure and recruitment procedures, internal and external support, handling of complaints and evaluation, rapport and dress, and extent of racial integration. While these units appear to be leaders in certain areas, problems of internal support and substantive external change are noted. The survival of Police-Community Relations Units may necessitate their stopping short of promoting the kind of substantive change necessary to alleviate conflict.   J

1141. Reddy, W. Brendan and Lansky, Leonard M. NOTHING BUT THE FACTS—AND SOME OBSERVATIONS ON NORMS AND VALUES: THE HISTORY OF A CONSULTATION WITH A METROPOLITAN POLICE DIVISION. *J. of Social Issues 1975 31(1): 123-138.* The paper describes a case study of an initial intervention in a large municipal police division. A community group/police confrontation led to the development of an 80-hour community relations training program for 39 police recruits. The program, designed and conducted by a biracial staff, followed an experience-based learning format in sharp contrast to the quasi-military traditional learning format of the police division. Focus is placed on the value and norm conflicts between change agent and the power structure of the urban police system.   J

1142. Reiner, Robert. FUZZY THOUGHTS: THE POLICE AND LAW-AND-ORDER POLITICS. *Sociol. Rev. [Great Britain] 1980 28(2): 377-413.* Compares the politicization of the police in Great Britain and the United States during the 60's and 70's.

1143. Rhodes, Robert P. ELECTRONIC SURVEILLANCE, ORGA-NIZED CRIME, AND CIVIL LIBERTIES. *Policy Studies J. 1978 7(special issue): 419-424.* Examines major public policy issues raised by the use of wiretapping and informants in the control of organized crime juxtaposing rights to privacy, political liberty, and due process with the need to control crime, concluding in favor of civil liberties but with note given to the effectiveness of such modes in crime control, 1969-78.

1144. Richardson, James F. POLICE HISTORY: THE SEARCH FOR LE-GITIMACY. *J. of Urban Hist. 1980 6(2): 231-246.* Reviews 15 recent works in police history and contemporary police administration to examine the legitimacy of police in American society. Police in the modern sense did not exist before the second quarter of the 19th century. Their establishment and growth were directly linked to industrialization and urbanization. Because their power challenges traditional standards of liberty, police have a necessary but suspect place in a libertarian democracy.   T. W. Smith

1145. Riggs, Connie. LAW AND THE BARNLOT. *Indiana Hist. Bull. 1973 50(8): 89-91.* Horse Thief Detecting Associations flourished in Indiana from 1844 into the 20th century, and claimed more than 15,500 members in 1924. Associations secured state charters and pledged protection to all members. While on duty, a member had constabulary power. In time the associations became more social and turned to other problems. They lobbied for highway speed laws and trespassing laws, and even made arrests for intoxication. Protests against these and other activities led to rapid decline of the associations. By 1930 only a few scattered groups remained.   J. F. Paul

1146.   Rodgers, Harrell R., Jr.   LAW AS AN INSTRUMENT OF PUBLIC POLICY. *Am. J. of Pol. Sci. 1973 17(3): 638-647.* Reviews three books concerned with the social policymaking role of the courts: Kenneth M. Dolbeare and Phillip E. Hammond's *The School Prayer Decisions: From Court Policy to Local Practice* (Chicago: U. of Chicago Press, 1971), Neal A. Milner's *The Court and Local Law Enforcement: The Impact of Miranda* (Beverly Hills, California: Sage Publications, 1971), and Frederick M. Wirt's *Politics of Southern Equality: Law and Social Change in a Mississippi County* (Chicago: Aldine, 1970). Court decisions will not be respected or obeyed unless local peoples and/or officials consider them valid and precise. Too little is known of the social effects of court decisions. Fig., 19 notes.   V. L. Human

1147.   Rooks, James E., Jr.   "THE GREAT AND INESTIMABLE PRIVILEGE": THE AMERICAN CRIMINAL JURY. *Current Hist. 1976 70(417): 261-264, 274.* Discusses the constitutional basis for juries (5th, 6th, 7th Constitutional Amendments), the nature of juries, and the 7.4% of crimes that have gone to jury trial since 1945.

1148.   Roper, Robert T.   THE GAG ORDER: ASPHYXIATING THE FIRST AMENDMENT. *Western Pol. Q. 1981 34(3): 372-388.* Discusses the historic US Supreme Court decision that prohibits the enforcement of Gag Orders except as a last resort, then tests some of the Court's assumptions in that decision through a quasi-experimental research design. After considering and rejecting various research approaches used by others to study jury decisionmaking, jury-simulation was determined to be the most effective way to test these hypotheses. The findings indicate that where conventional safeguards are ineffective at precluding any impact of pretrial publicity, the prejudicial effect that most people anticipate of low-level pretrial publicity does not materialize.   J/S

1149.   Rubinstein, Michael L. and White, Teresa J.   ALASKA'S BAN ON PLEA BARGAINING. *Law and Soc. Rev. 1979 13(2): 367-383.* Plea bargaining was banned by Alaska's Attorney General in August of 1975. The ban extended to all crimes, and forbade both charge and sentence negotiations. Its effects, evaluated by the Alaska Judicial Council in a two-year study, were to increase some sentences, increase trials modestly, and—surprisingly—increase the productivity of the criminal justice system. Explicit plea bargaining appears to have been substantially reduced, without any noticeable commensurate increase in implicit bargaining. The Alaska experience strongly suggests the need to reexamine contemporary thinking about plea bargaining.   J

1150.   Ruchelman, Leonard.   POLICE POLICY. *Policy Studies J. 1974 3(1): 48-53.* Discusses formulation of metropolitan area police policy on law enforcement, how it is carried out, and how effective it is in terms of productivity.
                                                                                S

1151.   Rudoni, Dorothy; Baker, Ralph; and Meyer, Fred A., Jr.   POLICE PROFESSIONALISM: EMERGING TRENDS. *Policy Studies J. 1978 7(special issue): 454-460.* Examines ambiguities of the rise of professionalism in the training of police officers, identifies models of professionalism, and discusses the symbolic use of the term by police.

1152. Russell, Francis. SACCO AND VANZETTI: WAS THE TRIAL FAIR? *Modern Age 1975 19(1): 30-41.* Reviews events surrounding the famous Sacco-Vanzetti trial in 1921, concluding that it was fairer and more decorous than most court cases and relatively free from bias and prejudice. Based on primary and secondary sources; 27 notes. M. L. Lifka

1153. Ryan, John Paul and Alfini, James J. TRIAL JUDGES' PARTICIPA-TION IN PLEA BARGAINING: AN EMPIRICAL PERSPECTIVE. *Law and Soc. Rev. 1979 13(2): 479-507.* The trial judge's role in plea bargaining is examined, using national survey data supplemented by observations and inter-views. We analyze the frequency with which judges participate in plea discussions and the organizational, social, and legal contexts that affect the judicial role. Our data suggest the trial judge is often an important or crucial actor in the construc-tion of plea agreements, a finding that contradicts much of the legal and social science literature. Several variables directly influence what role a judge will adopt, including self-perceived skill at negotiating and whether the state has a court rule or case law prohibiting or discouraging judicial participation. Future research should focus upon the impact of judicial participation in plea bargaining. J

1154. St. Clair, Diane. BIBLIOGRAPHY ON REPRESSION. *Black Scholar 1981 12(1): 85-90.* Lists publications, films, and tapes from 1963 dealing with organized US surveillance of covert activities and radical groups, and lists current magazines and organizations that provide information on intelligence agencies and political repression.

1155. Sanborn, Dorothy Wilkins. LAW ENFORCEMENT IN WINDHAM COUNTY, VERMONT: HOW SHERIFF WILKINS KEPT THE PEACE. *Vermont Hist. 1976 44(4): 228-235.* Artemas Ward Johnson Wilkins was born in Weston, Vermont, and moved to Londonderry in 1866. There Wilkins married in 1873 after five years' apprenticeship to a gravestone cutter. He worked in Wardsboro until he started a monument business in Putney in the 1880's. He also sold insurance, real estate and horses. His granddaughter recounts family stories of Wilkins' capturing robbers and murders when he was sheriff, 1900-04. He was choleric, accident prone, and profane; but he scarcely ever used any weapon on a suspect except his voice and presence. 2 photos. T. D. S. Bassett

1156. Scharf, Paul. DEADLY FORCE: THE MORAL REASONING AND EDUCATION OF POLICE OFFICERS FACED WITH THE OPTION OF LETHAL LEGAL VIOLENCE. *Policy Studies J. 1978 7(special issue): 450-453.* Compiles police response to hypothetical "shooting" situations, noting the moral reasoning of respondents in identifying legitimate deadly force by police.

1157. Schlossman, Steven and Wallach, Stephanie. THE CRIME OF PRECOCIOUS SEXUALITY: FEMALE JUVENILE DELINQUENCY IN THE PROGRESSIVE ERA. *Harvard Educ. Rev. 1978 48(1): 65-94.* Examines sex discrimination in juvenile justice under Progressivism; some assumptions on correctional policies from that era are still present.

1158. Senkewicz, Robert M. THE INFLATION OF AN OVERDONE BUSINESS: THE ECONOMIC ORIGINS OF SAN FRANCISCO VIGI-LANTES. *Pacific Hist. 1979 23(3): 63-75.* Examines what lay behind the organization of the San Francisco vigilantes during 1849-56. Contrary to the vigilantes' own version of what happened, there is considerable evidence to indicate that financial self-interest on the part of the importer-merchants faced with an overstock of merchandise was the dominant motivation. Their acts of violence against any who opposed them hardly supported their claims of a primary interest in the establishment of law and order. Primary sources; 28 notes.

R. V. Ritter

1159. Sharwell, George R. A SURVEY OF JUDGES' OPINIONS. *Public Welfare 1978 36(4): 26-29.* Discusses the results of a questionnaire sent to 100 juvenile and family court judges throughout the United States asking, "How are child abuse and neglect proved?"; of the 89 judges who responded 80% agreed in the substance of their response regarding the proof of child abuse in court; 1978.

1160. Sherman, Lawrence W. PERSPECTIVES ON POLICE AND VIOLENCE. *Ann. of the Am. Acad. of Pol. and Social Sci. 1980 (452): 1-12.* Police and violence are central to our conception of government, yet they form a troublesome paradox: in their efforts to stop violence, police must often be violent themselves. J/S

1161. Shotland, R. Lance. SPONTANEOUS VIGILANTES. *Society 1976 13(3): 30-32.* Discusses the phenomenon in the 1970's in which citizens have apprehended suspected criminals and meted out instant punishment at the scene of a crime, bypassing the judicial process.

1162. Sims, Robert C. IDAHO'S CRIMINAL SYNDICALISM ACT: ONE STATE'S RESPONSE TO RADICAL LABOR. *Labor Hist. 1974 15(4): 511-527.* Analyzes Idaho's criminal syndicalism acts which were part of the campaign against the Industrial Workers of the World (I.W.W.). The act was passed as a result of pressure from lumber and mining interests in 1917, and it was vigorously enforced from 1918 to 1920. During the 1920's there were attempts to revive the law, but opposition from organized labor helped make the law a dead issue. The I.W.W. was effectively suppressed through its use. Based upon Idaho statutes, the Moses Alexander Papers, and the *Idaho Statesman*. 50 notes. L. L. Athey

1163. Singer, Henry A. POLICE ACTION-COMMUNITY ACTION. *J. of Social Issues 1975 31(1): 99-106.* An experimental model was used in two cities in Connecticut to bring about improved police-community relations. Participants in the program were 300 police officers up through the grade of captain and 150 civilians representing militant, conservative, and community organizations. Questionnaires given to the police before and after the six-week program indicated dramatic favorable change in the policeman's attitudes toward himself, youth, and Puerto Ricans. However, attitudes toward blacks did not improve and in some cases regressed. J

1164. Skogan, Wesley G. GROUPS IN THE POLICY PROCESS: THE POLICE AND URBAN CRIME. *Policy Studies J. 1975 3(4): 354-359.* Examines the validity of describing urban policy-making in group terms. S

1165. Skolnick, Jerome H. THE DILEMMAS OF REGULATING CASINO GAMBLING. *J. of Social Issues 1979 35(3): 129-143.* One of the major reasons for the reluctance to legalize many of the popular forms of gambling is the belief that these forms are particularly difficult to control honestly. It is generally believed that organized crime has been able to undermine regulatory mechanisms. This paper reports on the difficulties and successes of the Nevada Gambling Control Board's efforts to deal with a sophisticated and complex form of gambling organization and compares and contrasts that regulation with the regulation of casino gambling in England. J

1166. Sloan, Stephen. SIMULATING TERRORISM: FROM OPERATIONAL TECHNIQUES TO QUESTIONS OF POLICY. *Int. Studies Notes 1978 5(4): 3-8.* Discusses a training technique developed at the University of Oklahoma, with cooperation of police and military organizations, to handle terrorism; 1970's.

1167. Smith, Damu. THE UPSURGE OF POLICE REPRESSION: AN ANALYSIS. *Black Scholar 1981 12(1): 35-57.* Describes police violence against Negroes since the industrialization of American cities in the 1830's, with its attendant rise in class conflict, and the legal strictures against blacks since the 19th century, focusing on police violence and repression since 1970.

1168. Smith, Dennis. REFORMING THE POLICE: ORGANIZATIONAL STRATEGIES FOR THE URBAN CRISIS. Hawes, Joseph M., ed. *Law and Order in American History* (Port Washington, N.Y.: Kennikat Pr., 1979): 112-135. Discusses various proposals for police reform, noting that most fail because they do not address all aspects of police organization, and suggests that local control of police for better police-community relations, particularly minorities, and decentralization, may improve police effectiveness and citizen confidence which was destroyed in the urban violence of the late 1960's and early 1970's.

1169. Smith, Paul E. and Hawkins, Richard O. VICTIMIZATION, TYPES OF CITIZEN-POLICE CONTACTS, AND ATTITUDES TOWARD THE POLICE. *Law and Soc. R. 1973 8(1): 135-152.* Discusses why some citizens in Seattle, Washington, held negative attitudes toward the police in 1968. S

1170. Songer, Donald R. CONSENSUAL AND NONCONSENSUAL DECISIONS IN UNANIMOUS OPINIONS OF THE UNITED STATES COURTS OF APPEALS. *Am. J. of Pol. Sci. 1982 26(2): 225-239.* Contrary to the widespread expectation that most unanimous decisions were truly consensual decisions whose outcomes were determined by precedent or other institutional/role restraints, a substantial proportion of the outcomes in unanimous decisions was found to reflect the ideological preferences of the panel majority. Criminal appeals and the unanimous reversals of decisions in cases raising economic issues were the types of cases in which unanimous decisions were most likely to be consistent with the ideology of the court majority. J/S

1171. Spindel, Donna J. THE ADMINISTRATION OF CRIMINAL JUSTICE IN NORTH CAROLINA, 1720-1740. *Am. J. of Legal Hist. 1981 25(2): 141-162.* An exploration into the administration of criminal justice in North Carolina, 1720-1740. The study considers the personnel of the judicial system in terms of social status, experience and training, the meaning of indictments; the demographic structure of crime; and the social status of defendants. The results of a computer analysis of the court records are assessed. Assault was the major crime prosecuted in the colony. Economic growth was reflected in an increase of property offences and in a reorganization of the criminal justice system to accommodate the rapidly increasing business of the courts. Based on the files and dockets of the General Court and the minutes of the precinct courts; 85 notes, 5 tables.										L. A. Knafla

1172. Spindel, Donna J. LAW AND DISORDER: THE NORTH CAROLINA STAMP ACT CRISIS. *North Carolina Hist. Rev. 1980 57(1): 1-16.* The lack of firm police action by the North Carolina colonial government against those demonstrating their opposition to the Stamp Act in 1766 suggests that weak law enforcement encouraged anti-British activity during the pre-Revolutionary period. Governor William Tryon could not enforce the Stamp Act regulations in the Wilmington, North Carolina area owing to several acts of civil disobedience, including disruption of his inauguration. Law enforcement officers often supported these disturbances themselves or lacked the means to quell them. The precedent for future opposition to the law may have been set. Based on colonial manuscript and published records, and colonial newspapers; 8 illus., map, 68 notes.										T. L. Savitt

1173. Spitzer, Stephen and Scull, Andrew T. PRIVATIZATION AND CAPITALIST DEVELOPMENT: THE CASE OF THE PRIVATE POLICE. *Social Problems 1977 25(1): 18-29.* The emergence and transformation of profit-oriented police services is indicative of a larger movement toward extension of capitalist control over the labor process and rationalization of productive activity, 1960-76.

1174. Stanley, David T. HIGHER EDUCATION FOR POLICE OFFICERS: A LOOK AT FEDERAL POLICIES. *State Government 1979 52(1): 35-42.* While it can be shown that federal programs funding higher education for police officers are responsible for a higher level of educational attainment among police forces, it cannot be shown that better performance has resulted from the programs; 1968-79.

1175. Stern, Philip. HOW TO BRIBE JUDGES, FIX PRICES, & DELAY THE INEVITABLE. *Washington Monthly 1980 12(4): 34-38, 40.* Discusses the American Bar Association-backed power of lawyers in the United States, and the significance of the Bar's admission that the middle 70% of the population is inadequately served by the legal profession, and that 90% of lawyers serve only 10% of the population; gives examples of violations, questionable practices, and kickbacks; 1958-80.

1176. Stinson, Steven A. THE FEDERAL BUREAU OF INVESTIGATION: ITS HISTORY, ORGANIZATION, FUNCTIONS AND PUBLICATIONS. *Government Publ. Rev. 1979 6(3): 213-240.* Overview of federal investigative activities since 1790, leading up to the present-day Federal Bureau of Investigation; includes FBI functions, activities, major publications, and the continual controversy over FBI activities.

1177. Stotland, Ezra and Guppy, William. COMMUNITY RELATIONS TRAINING IN THE SEATTLE POLICE ACADEMY. *J. of Social Issues 1975 31(3): 139-144.* Community relations training by social and behavioral scientists was incorporated into the Seattle Police Academy during the 1960s. Initially all of the training was of the stand-up-and-lecture type. But in the late sixties, role playing of difficult interracial and other police situations was conducted. The role-playing procedures and situations were planned and carried out in a collaborative effort between the police and the role-playing experts from the behavioral science community. J

1178. Swanson, Cheryl. THE INFLUENCE OF ORGANIZATION AND ENVIRONMENT ON ARREST POLICIES IN MAJOR U.S. CITIES. *Policy Studies J. 1979 7(special issue): 390-397.* Examination of factors influencing discretionary decisionmaking by police indicates that criminal activity, citizen's preferences, and values of the community rank highest.

1179. Swart, Stanley L. EARLY EFFORTS AT STATE-LEVEL LAW ENFORCEMENT: THE FAILURE OF OHIO'S SUPERVISION OF LOCAL POLICE AUTHORITIES, 1902-1925. *Ohio Hist. 1981 90(2): 141-157.* Discusses the modern concept of "police" authorities and the gradual imposition of a statewide system by central government upon the municipal authorities. Although the initial attempt at state supervision is viewed as a failure, the concept of a strong state executive empowered to supervise local law enforcement agencies —as reflected in the ideology of the Progressive and Police Reform movements, and supported by the actions of the Ohio Supreme Court, the Ohio General Assembly, and Ohio Governors Vic Donahey and James M. Cox—survived such unpopular measures as the Prohibition statutes. Primary sources; illus., 2 tables, 43 notes. L. A. Russell

1180. Talarico, Susette M. and Swanson, Charles R., Jr. STYLES OF POLICING: A PRELIMINARY MAPPING. *Policy Studies J. 1978 7(special issue): 398-405.* Examination of links between individual and departmental styles of policing finds that departmental style is dominant though individual styles, highly influenced by an immediate supervisor, are also common.

1181. Taylor, Jesse. BLOODY SUMMER. *Southern Exposure 1981 9(1): 99-103.* Discusses South Carolina's Bloody Summer of '75 which began when five unarmed black men were shot and killed by white policemen in isolated incidents followed by protests and boycotts led half-heartedly by the NAACP and actively by the Black Star Organization, a local group of black workers and activists.

1182. Teahan, John E. A LONGITUDINAL STUDY OF ATTITUDE SHIFTS AMONG BLACK AND WHITE POLICE OFFICERS. *J. of Social Issues 1975 31(1): 47-56.* Radical increases in racial animosity between white and black officers were found from the time of entering the academy until eighteen months later. All officers seemed to become more hedonistic, impersonal, and detached, and to develop feelings of hostility toward authority figures. As black officers progressed through the academy and on into regular police work, they became increasingly negative toward whites and disillusioned with the department; they began to shift in the direction of a greater sense of black unity and polarity against whites. While blacks saw greater preference being given to whites, white officers perceived the converse with the result that they became also more ethnocentric and polarized. Little evidence was found to indicate that a police experience molds men to feel a greater sense of social concern, or that it motivates them to improve relationships between races. J

1183. Teahan, John E. ROLE PLAYING AND GROUP EXPERIENCE TO FACILITATE ATTITUDE AND VALUE CHANGES AMONG BLACK AND WHITE POLICE OFFICERS. *J. of Social Issues 1975 31(1): 35-45.* White and black police officers were seen in weekly sessions involving role playing and interpersonal feedback during academy training, the purpose being to improve communication and relationships between black and white officers. Contrary to expectation, white officers became both more sensitized to the presence of black-white problems and more prejudiced toward blacks, whereas black officers who attended became more positive toward whites. It was felt that results were due in part to a perception by white officers that the program was initiated for the benefit of blacks rather than for all.   J

1184. Theoharis, Athan G. THE TRUMAN ADMINISTRATION AND THE DECLINE OF CIVIL LIBERTIES: THE FBI'S SUCCESS IN SECURING AUTHORIZATION FOR A PREVENTIVE DETENTION PROGRAM. *J. of Am. Hist. 1978 64(4): 1010-1030.* Uses the history of the Federal Bureau of Investigation's preventive detention program to demonstrate the possible lack of effective executive control over internal security policy during the Cold War. Top level bureaucrats in the FBI and the Justice Department may have made policy decisions regarding the compilation and use of lists of suspected subversives without informing the President. The FBI's desire for written authorization from the Justice Department to ignore the restrictions of the Internal Security Act of 1950 may have been pursued without President Truman's knowledge. Bureaucrats, operating in a vacuum, may have made national security decisions without regard to their constitutionality or to the need for high-level authorization. 31 notes.   T. P. Linkfield

1185. Theoharis, Athan G. FBI SURVEILLANCE DURING THE COLD WAR YEARS: A CONSTITUTIONAL CRISIS. *Public Hist. 1981 3(1): 4-14.* Describes Federal Bureau of Investigation surveillance of supposed dissident political activities from 1940 to 1980, but focuses on the Cold War years, confirming a distinct pattern of indifference to the law and to the constitutional system of checks and balances, though full public knowledge of these activities did not exist until the 1970's.

1186. Theoharis, Athan G. THE FBI'S STRETCHING OF PRESIDENTIAL DIRECTIVES, 1936-1953. *Pol. Sci. Q. 1976-77 91(4): 631-647.* Details the history of presidential directives issued between 1936 and 1953 bearing on the FBI's authority to investigate dissident political activities. He concludes that because presidential supervision of the FBI was inadequate, the FBI was able to self-define the scope of its authority.   J

1187. Thomson, Randall J. and Zingraff, Matthew T. DETECTING SENTENCING DISPARITY: SOME PROBLEMS AND EVIDENCE. *Am. J. of Sociol. 1981 86(4): 869-880.* Focuses on methodological and conceptual problems associated with research on criminal sentencing disparity, identifies five contextual factors that may affect the disparity, and presents an empirical analysis of racial disparity as an argument for 1969, 1973, and 1977.

1188. Thomson, Rebecca W. THE FEDERAL DISTRICT COURT IN WY-OMING, 1890-1982. *Ann. of Wyoming 1982 54(1): 10-25.* Since creation of the US District Court for the District of Wyoming in 1890, only four judges have filled the position. John A. Riner occupied the judgeship during 1890-1923, a time that still resembled the chaotic territorial days but that also included new problems in labor radicalism, oil industry expansion, and prohibition enforcement. His successor, Thomas Blake Kennedy had gained fame as defense attorney for gunfighter Tom Horn, and, as federal district judge, he would take another unpopular stand in the Teapot Dome Case. Ewing T. Kerr was appointed to the position in 1955 and handled important environmental litigation. Since 1975, Clarence A. Brimmer, Jr., has presided over the court. Based on manuscript collections and newspapers; 8 photos, 53 notes.   M. L. Tate

1189. Thornburgh, Richard L. THE FEDERAL ROLE IN CRIMINAL LAW ENFORCEMENT. *Current Hist. 1976 70(417): 249-252, 273.* Traces the federal government's crime control efforts, particularly through the Justice Department, since 1789, focusing on the department's dramatic expansion in the 1930's.

1190. Towne, Susan C. THE HISTORICAL ORIGINS OF BENCH TRIAL FOR SERIOUS CRIME. *Am. J. of Legal Hist. 1982 26(2): 123-159.* Allowing a criminal defendant the opportunity to demand trial by judge alone was a unique common law practice that developed in 17th-century America. The author traces the origins of this practice in the 16th century, and its reemergence in a number of states in the 19th and 20th centuries. The analysis is made from the court records of colonial Massachusetts, Connecticut, New Hampshire, and Maryland, with reference to the records of New York, Arkansas, Louisiana, Iowa, and Illinois. The enactment of trial by bench legislation in the first half of the 20th century paralleled the development of plea bargaining, a practice which arose in response to the growing inefficiency of trial by jury. Based on court records and statutes of the states; 186 notes.   L. A. Knafla

1191. Uhlman, Thomas M. and Walker, N. Darlene. A PLEA IS NO BARGAIN: THE IMPACT OF CASE DISPOSITION ON SENTENCING. *Social Sci. Q. 1979 60(2): 218-234.* A study of 29,295 criminal case histories, in an unspecified American city, designed to determine the effects on length and severity of sentences of plea bargaining. Analysis of this data reveals that the distinctions between plea and trial dispositions of cases are virtually nil. In both severity of sentencing and sentencing on the most serious charge, no fundamental difference was uncovered. These results raise serious questions for a judicial system in which plea bargaining is resorted to with ever-increasing frequency. Covers ca. 1968-74. 3 tables, 13 notes, ref.   V. L. Human

1192. Ulmer, S. Sidney. SOCIAL BACKGROUND AS AN INDICATOR TO THE VOTES OF SUPREME COURT JUSTICES IN CRIMINAL CASES: 1947-1956 TERMS. *Am. J. of Pol. Sci. 1973 17(3): 622-630.* Considers the role of social background as an influencing factor in Supreme Court criminal decisions. 12 social background variables were selected which explained over 91 percent of all decisions during the period 1947-56. Researchers who have reached opposite conclusions probably erred in variable selection, had different objectives, or worked with different courts. Nevertheless, the justices' decisionmaking process is complicated; an intimate knowledge of the social backgrounds of justices probably will never permit precise prediction of decisions. 3 tables, 14 notes.

V. L. Human

1193. Unnever, James D.; Frazier, Charles E.; and Henretta, John C. RACE DIFFERENCES IN CRIMINAL SENTENCING. *Sociol. Q. 1980 21(2): 197-206.* Analyzes prior studies on race differences in criminal sentencing, corrects some procedural difficulties, surveys a Florida sample from 1972-75, and concludes that race remains a substantial factor in sentencing outcomes.

1194. Unsigned. CRIMINAL JUSTICE REFORM: A CASE HISTORY. *Urban R. 1973 6(3): 34-37.*

1195. Voss, Frederick S. and Barber, James G. PINKERTON BROUGHT LAW AND ORDER—19TH-CENTURY STYLE. *Smithsonian 1981 12(5): 60-68.* Recounts the first 50 years of Allan Pinkerton's National Detective Agency, founded in 1850 and one of the first of its kind in the country, which played a part in tracking almost every notable bandit of the time and whose methods presaged many modern police techniques.

1196. Waldinger, Robert J. SLEEP OF REASON: JOHN P. GRAY AND THE CHALLENGE OF MORAL INSANITY. *J. of the Hist. of Medicine and Allied Sci. 1979 34(2): 163-179.* John P. Gray, psychiatrist and superintendent of the New York State Lunatic Asylum at Utica from 1854 to 1886, was spokesman for the conservatives who were opposed to the doctrine of moral insanity. He delivered expert testimony for the prosecution at the trials of Lewis Payne, who conspired to kill Lincoln, and Charles J. Guiteau, who shot President Garfield. Religion was the keystone of his philosophical attack on the doctrine of moral insanity. The theoretical underpinning of Gray's psychology included a peculiar blend of idealism and materialism that did not fall within any one philosophical system. He forced others to confront the theological, psychological, and political implications of the new theory of emotional breakdown. 53 notes.

M. Kaufman

1197. Waldrep, Christopher. EGALITARIANISM IN THE OLIGARCHY: THE GRAND JURY AND CRIMINAL JUSTICE IN LIVINGSTON COUNTY, 1799-1808. *Filson Club Hist. Q. 1981 55(3): 253-267.* The grand jury was a democratic element in an otherwise elite-dominated judicial system in Livingston County, Kentucky, during the years of the Jefferson administration. While jury members were generally more affluent than the average citizen in the county, they also came from the ranks of small farmers and artisans. Particularly in matters of public morality, the grand jury refused to exempt the elite from community standards of behavior. Based on unpublished Livingston County public records; 5 tables, 40 notes.

G. B. McKinney

1198. Walker, Samuel. COUNTING COPS AND CRIME. *Rev. in Am. Hist. 1982 10(2): 212-217.* Reviews Eric H. Monkkonen's *Police in Urban America, 1860-1920* (1981), which identifies behavioral changes of the police and the impact of the police institution on society.

1199. Walker, Samuel. THE RISE AND FALL OF THE POLICEWO-
MEN'S MOVEMENT, 1905-1975. Hawes, Joseph M., ed. *Law and Order in
American History* (Port Washington, N.Y.: Kennikat Pr., 1979): 101-111. Traces
efforts to include women on police forces to 1905 when the first known woman
to have full police powers was hired by the Portland, Oregon, police department,
until 1975 when women were still being hired mostly as clerical workers or in
juvenile divisions.

1200. Waller, Carolyn. LEGAL REPORTER. *Migration Today 1982 10(1):
30-33.* The Immigration and Naturalization Service "has neither the legal, financial, nor manpower resources to effectively control illegal immigration."

1201. Wasby, Stephen L. POLICE TRAINING ABOUT CRIMINAL PRO-
CEDURE: INFREQUENT AND INADEQUATE. *Policy Studies J. 1978
7(Special issue): 461-468.* Using the cases of small town police officers in southern
Illinois and western Massachusetts, examines the importance of including criminal procedure in police training, and identifies certain factors limiting the effectiveness of such training.

1202. Watson, Alan D. THE APPOINTMENT OF SHERIFFS IN COLO-
NIAL NORTH CAROLINA: A REEXAMINATION. *North Carolina Hist.
Rev. 1976 53(4): 385-398.* Challenges several of historian Julian Boyd's interpretations made 50 years ago regarding the appointment of sheriffs in colonial North
Carolina. Revises Boyd's conclusions, using quantitative evidence from 14 counties, on the number of sheriffs who were justices of the peace at the time of
appointment, the frequency of self-recommendation of justices for the office, the
commonness of county court recommendation of justices for sheriff, and the
frequency of governors' use of independent judgment in appointing sheriffs.
Based on MS. and published county records and on secondary sources; 6 tables,
45 notes.   T. L. Savitt

1203. Watts, Eugene J. BLACK AND BLUE: AFRO-AMERICAN PO-
LICE OFFICERS IN TWENTIETH-CENTURY ST. LOUIS. *J. of Urban
Hist. 1981 7(2): 131-168.* Describes the gradual integration of the St. Louis police
and finds that pressure from black politicians and groups on public officials and
police administrators was the major cause of integration. Other factors such as
the professionalization of the police and more militant forms of protest were
found to be of less importance. 2 tables, 57 notes.   T. W. Smith

1204. Watts, Eugene J. PATTERNS OF PROMOTION: THE ST. LOUIS
POLICE DEPARTMENT, 1899-1975. *Social Sci. Hist. 1982 6(2): 233-258.*
Major determinants for bureaucratic promotions include seniority, merit, and
social background. This case study examines promotion among a sample of 1,954
men on the St. Louis Police Department to assess the relative importance of each
factor. Seniority was a critical factor, but merit also played a significant role.
There is little evidence that preservice social background had a major effect on
promotion. Basic promotion patterns remained surprisingly stable through the
study. Based on the personnel files of the St. Louis Police Department; 13 notes,
9 tables, biblio.   L. K. Blaser

1205. Watts, Eugene J. POLICE PRIORITIES IN TWENTIETH CEN-
TURY ST. LOUIS. _J. of Social Hist. 1981 14(4): 649-673._ Crime statistics are
often more a function of police policy than of the actual amount of crime. This
study of order maintenance arrests in St. Louis, Missouri, from 1900 to 1970
demonstrates how police behavior influences arrests in this area. This perspective
focuses attention on the police themselves, rather than the amount of crime,
providing a basis for testing organizational change with behavioral data as well
as a means for examining the ongoing interaction between the police and the
public. Careful use of arrest data, when informed by this theory, can shed significant light on simultaneous police activities and their relationship to police alloca-
tion of resources, general enforcement policy, and institutional dynamics. 3
tables, 8 fig., 27 notes.   J. Powell

1206. Waxfield, Michael G.; Lewis, Dan A.; and Szoc, Ron. PRODUCING
OFFICIAL CRIMES: VERIFIED CRIME REPORTS AS MEASURES OF
POLICE OUTPUT. _Social Sci. 1980 61(2): 221-236._ Analyzes official crime
data as measures of capability, productivity, and performance of police units.
Police records are used to compare 1) crime-related requests and actual police
arrests, 2) frequency of demands for police services and service records, and
3) distribution of police services by areas. Analysis of the Chicago Police Department data for January-July 1976 suggests, among other conclusions, that police
decisions to classify events as crimes are more uniform throughout the city for
more serious crimes than for lesser ones. Based on police and crime data of the
Chicago Police Department; 3 tables, 25 citations.   M. Mtewa

1207. Wenger, Dennis. THE RELUCTANT ARMY: THE FUNCTION-
ING OF POLICE DEPARTMENTS DURING CIVIL DISTURBANCES.
Am. Behavioral Scientist 1973 16(3): 326-342. Discusses the way police depart-
ments have responded to civil disturbances in the cities during the 1960's and 70's.
                                                                          S

1208. White, Frank W. CAMERAS IN THE COURTROOM: A U.S. SUR-
VEY. _Journalism Monographs 1979 (60): 3-41._ Improper and sensationalistic
use of photographic equipment in noted criminal trials led to American Bar
Association Canon 35 discouraging the use of cameras in court in 1937 (amended
to include television, 1952-63), but their gradual inclusion in state courts during
1956-63 (with the judge's permission) resulted in the formation of policies lacking
uniformity.

1209. White, G. Edward. TAKING A FLYER: LEONARD LEVY ON
THE NIXON COURT. _Rev. in Am. Hist. 1975 3(3): 394-398._ Review article
prompted by Leonard W. Levy's _Against the Law: The Nixon Court and Criminal Justice_ (New York: Harper & Row, 1974). Compares the book with earlier
works by Levy; notes the book's provocative and personal nature, summarizes its
portraits of the Supreme Court justices, and assesses the book's major thesis that
the Nixon appointees' control of the Supreme Court in the area of criminal justice
began to significantly change constitutional law.

1210. Wilber, Leon A. DEVELOPMENT OF CRIMINAL LAW IN THE
SUPREME COURT, 1966 TO 1971. _Southern Q. 1973 11(2): 121-145._ Examines Supreme Court cases 1966-71 which pertain to the fifth, sixth, eighth, and

14th amendments to the Constitution. Discusses such issues as the right to a speedy trial, the right to be confronted by an accuser, the right of testimony, freedom from cruel and unusual punishment, due process of law, and equal protection under the law. 60 notes. R. W. Dubay

1211. Wilkinson, S. H. GUN LAWS IN THE USA. *Contemporary Rev. [Great Britain] 1981 239(1390): 246-251.* Examines current concern about gun laws in the United States and the influence of the National Rifle Association on attempts at reform.

1212. Williams, David. THE BUREAU OF INVESTIGATION AND ITS CRITICS, 1919-1921: THE ORIGINS OF FEDERAL POLITICAL SUR-VEILLANCE. *J. of Am. Hist. 1981 68(3): 560-579.* Federal Bureau of Investigation surveillance of political dissent originated with American involvement in World War I, not with the Cold War. Investigations by J. Edgar Hoover, chief of the General Intelligence Division during the Red Scare, were systematic and pervasive and revealed the extreme antiradicalism in the bureau. Hoover learned that Congress and the president would tolerate the bureau's antiradical activities as long as they remained secret. Based in part on FBI files secured through the Freedom of Information Act; 49 notes. T. P. Linkfield

1213. Williams, David. SOWING THE WIND: THE DEPORTATION RAIDS OF 1920 IN NEW HAMPSHIRE. *Hist. New Hampshire 1979 34(1): 1-31.* During 1900-20, the population of eastern Europeans in New Hampshire grew to almost 10% of the state's foreign-born. On 2 January 1920, the US Justice Department arrested 260 New Hampshire residents as part of the nationwide "Palmer raids" directed against radicals. Removal of constitutional safeguards and denial of due process led to ill-treatment of the arrested, until critics of the arrests, and Judge Weston Anderson, originally from New Hampshire, brought about the release of the arrested. Based on Justice Department records and other primary and secondary sources. 60 notes. D. F. Chard

1214. Williams, David. "THEY NEVER STOPPED WATCHING US": FBI POLITICAL SURVEILLANCE, 1924-1936. *UCLA Hist. J. 1981 2: 5-28.* Demonstrates that during 1924-36 Federal Bureau of Investigation Director J. Edgar Hoover violated a restriction on surveillance activities imposed by Attorney General Harlan Fiske Stone. Although Hoover officially declared that the FBI was not interested in political opinions protected by law, he continued to direct political surveillance activities until 1936, when President Franklin Roosevelt approved an expansion of the FBI's function. Hoover justified surveillance in the name of national security. The American Civil Liberties Union, Trade Union Education League, and mass political demonstrations attracted Hoover's attention. Only a vigilant Congress can prevent such constitutional abuses, by adopting an FBI charter prohibiting such surveillance and holding the agency accountable for its actions. Primary and secondary sources; 53 notes. A. Hoffman

1215. Williams, Nudie E. BLACK MEN WHO WORE THE "STAR." *Chronicles of Oklahoma 1981 59(1): 83-90.* Recounts the exploits of three black Oklahoma deputy marshals during the late territorial period. Bass Reeves was born a slave, who, although illiterate, possessed the remarkable memory and indomitable courage that enabled him to capture outlaws and make the charges stick. Zeke Miller effectively enforced the law without utilizing violence and later became a fulltime businessman. Grant Johnson was a Creek freedman, born in Texas, who helped arrest Chitto Harjo in 1898 to end a brief Creek rebellion. The list of Oklahoma black deputy marshals is incomplete due to poor territorial record keeping, but during the entire period no black was ever appointed a US marshal. Based on secondary sources and interviews; 3 photos, 26 notes.

M. L. Tate

1216.   Wilson, James Q.   BUGGINGS, BREAK-INS AND THE FBI. *Commentary 1978 65(6): 52-58.* Traces the history of FBI wiretaps and break-ins during the last 35 years. Supreme Court decisions in 1967 and 1972 tightened restrictions on their use, particularly the case of surreptitious entry. Indictment in 1978 of three former FBI officials for having authorized searches against a domestic group, which the Court forbade, underlines the difficulties in gathering intelligence on potentially dangerous organizations.   J. Tull

1217.   Wilson, James Q.   THE CHANGING FBI: THE ROAD TO AB-SCAM.   *Public Interest 1980 (59): 3-14.* The Federal Bureau of Investigation (FBI) has not launched a vendetta against Congress with Operation Abscam. Changing priorities of the FBI during the 1970's because of congressional pressure led to emphasis on white-collar and organized crime rather than on domestic security cases. Investigation of Congress itself is a logical outgrowth of the FBI's increasing undercover investigation of white-collar crime.   J. M. Herrick

1218.   Wilson, James Q. and Boland, Barbara.   THE EFFECT OF THE PO-LICE ON CRIME.   *Law and Soc. Rev. 1978 12(3): 367-390.* The effect of police practices on the rate of robbery in 35 large American cities is estimated by a set of simultaneous equations. The measures of police resources (patrol units on the street) and police activity on the street (moving citations issued) are more precise than anything thus far available in studies of this kind and permit the use of identification restrictions that allow stronger inferences about the causal effect of arrests on crime rates than has heretofore been possible. Police resources and police activity independently affect the robbery rate after controlling for various socioeconomic factors. The political arrangements that lead to the use of aggressive patrol strategies are discussed and their effect estimated. The implications for, and limitations upon, policy are also discussed.   J

1219.   Wright, Bruce McM.   IN PURSUIT OF JUSTICE: BANGS AND WHIMPERS: BLACK YOUTH AND THE COURTS.   *Freedomways 1975 15(3): 178-187.* Points out unfair treatment of Negroes at all stages of law enforcement.   S

1220.   Wrightsman, Lawrence S.   THE AMERICAN TRIAL JURY ON TRIAL: EMPIRICAL EVIDENCE AND PROCEDURAL MODIFICA-TIONS.   *J. of Social Issues 1978 34(4): 137-164.* The trial jury is one of the most long-lasting and revered of American institutions. Yet recently it has been the recipient of criticism. These attacks have questioned the validity of the assumptions made by the legal system regarding the jury process. Specifically, these assumptions deal with the composition of the venire, the effectiveness of the *voir dire* process, the ability of jurors to disregard pretrial publicity and inadmissable evidence, the capacities of jurors to reconstruct the trial presentation from memory, and the ability of the jury as a deliberative body to act in a rational, evidence-oriented manner. Empirical evidence is presented with respect to each of these assumptions, and suggested reforms are generated whenever the evidence conflicts with the assumptions. J

1221. Wunder, John. AMERICAN LAW AND ORDER COMES TO MISSISSIPPI TERRITORY: THE MAKING OF SARGENT'S CODE, 1798-1800. *J. of Mississippi Hist. 1976 38(2): 131-155.* Describes the development of the "first American codified laws" for the Mississippi Territory under Governor Winthrop Sargent (1798-1800), a staunch Federalist. His unpopular code dealt with such topics as courts, counties, a militia, crime, public morality, aliens, internal security, slaves, and Indians. After the Jeffersonian triumph of 1800 and the establishment of a territorial assembly in Mississippi Territory, Sargent was removed from office and his code was "constructively abolished." Based on published primary and secondary sources; 69 notes. J. W. Hillje

1222. Zeisel, Hans. THE FBI'S BIASED SAMPLING: A STATISTICAL DETECTIVE STORY. *Sci. and Public Affairs 1973 29(1): 38-42.* Because of biased statistics-keeping methods, 1967-73, which tend to blame the courts for high criminal recidivism, the Federal Bureau of Investigation should relinquish its statistics keeping to an independent agency in the Justice Department.

1223. —. [ON IMPROVING POLICE-COMMUNITY RELATIONS]. *J. of Social Issues 1975 31(1): 57-98.*
Kelly, Rita Mae. GENERALIZATIONS FROM AN *OEO* EXPERIMENT IN WASHINGTON, D.C., *pp. 57-86.* Based on an evaluation of an OEO police-community relations experiment, a new conceptual framework is proposed, defining police-community relations as a power relationship with three interrelated dimensions (efficiency, responsiveness, and representativeness) which are related to a behavioral model of personality development and characteristics. Data analyzed within a modified pretest, posttest control group design for police and citizens assess the merits of inservice training versus racial representativeness in improving police responsiveness to ghetto defiinitions of police roles, functions, and accountability to the community. Key conclusions are: (a) in-service training is not always an appropriate means, (b) citizens must be involved, and (c) training of citizens to assume responsibility in law enforcement and police-community relations must begin.
Shellow, Robert. EVALUATING AN EVALUATION, *pp. 87-94.*
Kelly, Rita Mae. COMMENTS ON A VIEW FROM MANAGEMENT, *pp. 95-98.* J

1224. —. THE POLICE DEPARTMENTS OF STATEN ISLAND. *Staten Island Historian 1973 31(14): 113-124.* Describes the police of Staten Island, 1780-1898. County records, newspapers, histories, and photograph collections were used to study individual policemen, uniforms, locations of precinct houses, important cases, and growth. Includes a partial roster of policemen 1870-97. Compiled by the Museum Studies class, Susan E. Wagner High School, Staten Island. 16 illus., biblio. D. Ricciard-O'Beirne

8

PUNISHMENT, REHABILITATION, AND THE PRISONS

1225. Adler, Susan Seidner. BRIBING DELINQUENTS TO BE GOOD. *Commentary 1981 72(4): 55-61.* Examines the system of dealing with juvenile delinquency in New York, especially the treatment of PINS (Persons in Need of Supervision) and those classified DN (dependent-neglected); rehabilitation efforts only reinforce antisocial behavior.

1226. Anderson, David C. CRIME AND PENITENCE. *Working Papers Mag. 1981 8(6): 53-56.* Reviews Francis A. Allen's *The Decline of the Rehabilitative Ideal: Penal Policy and Social Purpose* (1981), which addresses the debate between law and order supporters and prison reformers over prison rehabilitation; despite the flaws in the "rehabilitative ideal" it should remain, but with some changes.

1227. Avrich, Paul. PRISON LETTERS OF RICARDO FLORES MAGON TO LILLY SARNOFF. *Int. Rev. of Social Hist. [Netherlands] 1977 22(3): 379-422.* Ricardo Flores Magón (1874-1922), the foremost Mexican anarchist of the 20th century, spent the last 19 years of his life in the United States. During half of that time he was imprisoned and he died at Leavenworth Penitentiary. While there he began his long correspondence with Lilly Sarnoff (b. 1899), a young New York anarchist and member of the defense committee working for his release. From the files of the International Institute of Social History in Amsterdam, 21 letters of Magón to Sarnoff, covering the period from October 1920 to November 1922, are reprinted here in their original form. Written in English, these letters reveal the horrors of prison life, his attitudes toward the Bolshevik Revolution, and a florid style characteristic of an age of romantic revolutionism.   G. P. Blum

1228. Axilbund, Melvin T. AMERICAN PRISONS AND JAILS. *Current Hist. 1976 70(417): 265-268, 277.* Surveys the demographic composition of prisoners, the educational and social conditions in prisons, and the costs of the criminal justice system in 1974.

1229. Basile, Leon, ed. HARRY STANLEY'S MESS BOOK: OFFENSES AND PUNISHMENTS ABOARD THE ETHAN ALLEN. *Civil War Hist. 1977 23(1): 69-79.* While serving as Master at Arms aboard the bark *Ethan Allen* from August 1863 through April 1865, Tufton K. Stanley kept a mess book which includes a rare Record of Punishment section. He notes the same offenders repeatedly and chronicles much insubordination among sailors. Some major offenses, such as desertion, are treated more lightly than seemingly minor affairs such as abusive language. In his comments to the record, Stanley exhibits compassion, disdain for his duty, and a low opinion of his superiors. He provides insights into a little known aspect of Civil War sailor life. Reprints the mess book's entries. Primary and secondary sources; 6 notes.   R. E. Stack

1230. Bauer, Anne. THE CHARLESTOWN STATE PRISON. *Hist. J. of Western Massachusetts 1973 2(2): 22-29.* The institution's early years were unsatisfactory; escapes, homosexuality, and overcrowding were three main problems. The Boston Prison Discipline Society, however, emphasized the ideas of penal reformers of the time and was able to transform the prison's image. The society claimed that no other prison had superior moral or religious instruction. In the 1840's prisoners had their own gardens. As the buildings grew older and reform interests were drawn elsewhere, conditions deteriorated. In the 1870's a new prison was built. Based on contemporary and secondary sources; 3 illus., 17 notes.
                                                            S. S. Sprague

1231. Bayliss, Garland E. THE ARKANSAS STATE PENITENTIARY UNDER DEMOCRATIC CONTROL, 1874-1896. *Arkansas Hist. Q. 1975 34(3): 195-213.* Between 1874 and 1896 the state penitentiary in Little Rock was leased out to private individuals and nominally supervised by state government representatives. In effect, this system resulted in the use of prisoners, a majority of whom were black, for labor in private and public works. Initiated during the Reconstruction Republican government, convict-lease was continued by Democratic administrations throughout the rest of the century, despite well-publicized abuse of prisoners. Based on newspaper accounts, published documents, manuscript records, and secondary works; 2 illus., 32 notes.   T. L. Savitt

1232. Bedau, Hugo Adam. THE PROBLEM OF CAPITAL PUNISHMENT. *Current Hist. 1976 71(418): 14-18, 34.* Touches on the history of the controversy over the death penalty since the initial organized protests to it in the 1780's, the legal status of capital punishment in the states 1846-1972, the Supreme Court decision *Furman* v. *Georgia* (US, 1972) which called it cruel and unusual punishment, and alternatives to it.

1233. Benjamin, Gerald and Rappaport, Stephen P. ATTICA AND PRISON REFORM. *Pro. of the Acad. of Pol. Sci. 1974 31(3): 200-213.* Examines the prison riots which occurred at New York's Attica State Prison in 1971, and the effect which they had on prison reform within the state.   S

1234. Bennett, Edward W. THE REASONS FOR MICHIGAN'S ABOLITION OF CAPITAL PUNISHMENT. *Michigan Hist. 1978 62(4): 42-55.* Reasons for the abolition of capital punishment in Michigan in 1846 stem from the reform tradition of Puritanism; 1843-46.

1235. Bergeron, Arthur W., Jr., ed. PRISON LIFE AT CAMP PRATT. *Louisiana Hist. 1973 14(4): 386-391.* Excerpts from the published memoirs of George C. Harding describing his six weeks as a prisoner of war in Camp Pratt in New Iberia, Louisiana, 1862.

1236. Berk, Richard A.; Rauma, David; Messinger, Sheldon L.; and Cooley, Thomas F. THE TEST OF THE STABILITY OF PUNISHMENT HYPOTHESIS: THE CASE OF CALIFORNIA, 1851-1970. *Am. Sociol. Rev. 1981 46(6): 805-829.* Many scholars, influenced by Emile Durkheim, have claimed that, for a given society over time and in the absence of major societal upheavals, the proportion of people subjected to punishment by the state closely approximates a constant. Data from California for the period from the opening of the prison system in 1851 to 1970 yields no evidence for the Stability of Punishment hypothesis.   J

1237. Berkson, Larry C. CRUEL AND UNUSUAL PUNISHMENT: THE PARAMETERS OF THE EIGHTH AMENDMENT. *Policy Studies J. 1975 4(2): 131-136.* Distinguishes between corporeal and incorporeal punishment and shows how the Eighth Amendment has been interpreted in the courts to limit the use of either.

1238. Bethell, Tom. CRIMINALS BELONG IN JAIL. *Washington Monthly 1976 7(11): 5-21.* Discusses the consequences, particularly in Washington, D.C., of the Bail Reform Act (1965) which has permitted many accused of violent crime to be released on their own recognizance.

1239. Binder, Guyora. PENAL REFORM AND PROGRESSIVE IDEOLOGY. *Rev. in Am. Hist. 1981 9(2): 224-232.* Review essay of David J. Rothman's *Conscience and Convenience: The Asylum and its Alternatives in Progressive America* (1980), in which "Rothman examines the development of a series of related responses to social deviance arising in early twentieth century America: probation, parole, the juvenile court, the therapeutic mental hospital, and outpatient mental health care."

1240. Black Horse, Francis D. PRISON AND NATIVE PEOPLE. *Indian Hist. 1975 8(1): 54-56.* All native Americans are under pressure to enter the mainstream of dominant white culture, especially those Indians currently in prison. Calls on American Indians to resist assimilation and to remember the plight of their fellows in prison.   E. D. Johnson

1241. Boesche, Roger. THE PRISON: TOCQUEVILLE'S MODEL FOR DESPOTISM. *Western Pol. Q. 1980 33(4): 550-563.* Alexis de Tocqueville's idea of political despotism becomes clearer when we compare it to Tocqueville's long ignored writings on Pennsylvania's prison system, a system he labeled "the most complete despotism." Tocqueville suggests that by using the terror created by this system, especially the despair generated by solitary confinement, the prison often succeeded in reshaping the prisoner's mind and reforming his very "instincts." In a strikingly parallel fashion, Tocqueville chooses the same characteristics to depict the emerging political despotism. The new despotism will rely on isolation, equality, an obsession with the private production and consumption of goods, the eclipse of public life, and the loss of a meaningful future—all of which will render men passive, dominated by a centralized government and a suffocating majority opinion.   J/S

1242. Breeden, James O. ANDERSONVILLE—A SOUTHERN SURGEON'S STORY. *Bull. of the Hist. of Medicine 1973 47(4): 317-343.* Examines the report of Dr. Joseph Jones, a Southerner, entitled "Investigations upon the

Diseases of the Federal Prisoners Confined to Camp Sumpter, Andersonville, Ga." S

1243. Brenzel, Barbara. LANCASTER INDUSTRIAL SCHOOL FOR GIRLS: A SOCIAL PORTRAIT OF A NINETEENTH CENTURY RE-FORM SCHOOL FOR GIRLS. *Feminist Studies 1975 3(1/2): 40-53.* The mid-19th-century conviction that changes in environment could encourage rehabilitation influenced early efforts to reform children. In 1856 the first reform school for girls was established in Lancaster, Massachusetts. It included girls who were merely poor, not actually delinquent. The majority of the girls were adolescents, between 12 and 16, with no mother at home. The school served to protect them from the possibilities of promiscuity and the life of vice which tempted the poverty stricken young woman on her own. The school provided some minimal education and attempted Protestant religious training, but was in the main a shelter for girls, rather than an educational or vocational center. Based on primary and secondary sources; 29 notes. S. R. Herstein

1244. Brenzel, Barbara. DOMESTICATION AS REFORM: A STUDY OF THE SOCIALIZATION OF WAYWARD GIRLS, 1856-1905. *Harvard Educ. Rev. 1980 50(2): 196-213.* Fear and benevolence motivated the juvenile reform policies undertaken at the State Industrial School for Girls in Lancaster, Massachusetts.

1245. Bronstein, Alvin J. REFORM WITHOUT CHANGE: THE FUTURE OF PRISONERS' RIGHTS. *Civil Liberties Rev. 1977 4(3): 27-45.* Surveys recent achievements in prisoners' rights, and the Bill of Rights' effect on those confined to penal institutions in the 1970's.

1246. Brown, Elizabeth Gaspar. THE WAUKESHA COUNTY JAIL: BUILDING, ADMINISTRATION, INMATES, 1901-1904. *Am. J. of Legal Hist. 1979 23(3): 236-264.* A review of the building and running of a county jail, and the inmates who were admitted to it, in Waukesha County, Wisconsin. The prison was first built in 1846 and rebuilt at later dates. Records are decidedly fragmentary, and comparative records from other counties wholly lacking. Vagrancy and drunkenness were the most common causes of internment. White males made up most of the offenders. Literacy of inmates was limited; occupations were numerous and varied. No evidence can be found to suggest that justice was unfair, except that a choice of fine or imprisonment favored the moneyed element. Felonious crimes were few. 5 tables, 18 notes. V. L. Human

1247. Brummett, Barry. GARY GILMORE, POWER, AND THE RHETO-RIC OF SYMBOLIC FORMS. *Western J. of Speech Communication 1979 43(1): 4-13.* Discusses the rhetorical appeal of the Gary Gilmore case, which marked the first death sentence carried out in the United States in 10 years, on 19 January 1977, as a symbolic triumph in the public eye of the powerless over the powerful.

1248. Burlingame, Merrill G. MONTANA'S RIGHTEOUS HANGMEN: A RECONSIDERATION. *Montana 1978 28(4): 36-49.* Examines the composition and motivation of the Montana vigilantes who operated from 23 December 1863 to 2 February 1864. They acted in extralegal fashion, hanging 21 men and banishing untold others. Reviews historic events and available literature and disproves four classic theories. The Montana vigilantes were not a small group of conniving men who took law forcibly into their own hands; at least 2,500 men were involved directly or indirectly. Vigilantism was not a Unionist vs. Confederate movement; it was one of the few unifying factors in this distressing division of Montana politics. The movement was not uniquely Masonic in origin; Masons assumed a prominent but not predominant role. Masonic-Roman Catholic animosity did not exist in the vigilante movement; membership lists indicate cooperative activity by both groups. Secondary sources and original manuscripts in Montana Historical Society, Helena; 18 illus., 39 notes.   R. C. Myers

1249. Caruso, Samuel T. AFTER PEARL HARBOR: ARIZONA'S RESPONSE TO THE GILA RIVER RELOCATION CENTER. *J. of Arizona Hist. 1973 14(4): 335-346.* Sixteen thousand Japanese Americans were imprisoned 1942-45 at Sacaton, a barbed-wire city better known as the Gila River Relocation Center, in south central Arizona. Whites reacted to them as they had to their Apache predecessors—open hostility drowning out sympathetic understanding and concern. Whatever the racial slurs, the restrictive legislation, and other degradations they suffered, the Japanese produced millions of tons of vegetables and performed much labor on state roads. 2 illus., 46 notes.
                                                                    D. L. Smith

1250. Chan, Loren B. EXAMPLE FOR THE NATION: NEVADA'S EXECUTION OF GEE JON. *Nevada Hist. Soc. Q. 1975 18(2): 90-106.* Discusses the case of Gee Jon and Hughie Sing who were found guilty by a jury of murdering a Chinese laundryman at Mina, Nevada, in 1921. As a result of legal maneuverings and appeals to public opinion to save the pair from execution, intense debate in Nevada ensued on racial questions and the issue of capital punishment. Gee Jon was finally executed in 1924. Based on state documents and newspapers; 2 photos, 3 reproductions, 86 notes.   H. T. Lovin

1251. Chase, Edward. *PINS* [PERSONS IN NEED OF SUPERVISION]: THE INVISIBLE TRAGEDY. *New York Affairs 1974 1(4): 48-61.* "Ten thousand New York children are victimized every year under a provision of the Family Court Act. Guilty of no criminal behavior, they are nevertheless held in detention homes, summoned to court and sentenced to state training schools."
                                                                              J

1252. Chu, Judy. PRISONS AND THE ASIAN-AMERICAN: FROM THE INSIDE AND OUTSIDE. *Amerasia J. 1974 2(2): 59-70.* Comments on the position of Asian Americans in prison and the formation of protest groups.
                                                                    M. R. Underdown

1253. Clarke, Stevens H. and Koch, Gary G. THE INFLUENCE OF INCOME AND OTHER FACTORS ON WHETHER CRIMINAL DEFENDANTS GO TO PRISON. *Law and Soc. Rev. 1976 11(1): 57-92.* Investigates 798 burglary and larceny defendants in Charlotte, North Carolina. Such variables as income, age, race, and employment were measured as having influence on sentencing. Severity of offense, prior arrest record, and strength of case also are analyzed. Race, age and employment had little or no impact on sentence.
                                                                    H. R. Mahood

1254.   Cleary, Ann.   LIFE AND DEATH AT ANDERSONVILLE PRISON. *Hist. J. of Western Massachusetts 1973 2(1): 27-42.* Andersonville, Georgia, located in the hungry South and far from sources of supply, overcrowded to 380 percent of capacity, simply could not support its prison population. Inadequate water supply, overcrowding, reduction in food rations, and unsanitary conditions led to an extremely high mortality rate. Some prisoners played cards and chess, swapping items on "Broadway," while others became craftsmen, prayed, or attempted to escape. Based on memoirs and secondary sources; map, 3 illus., 39 notes.   S. S. Sprague

1255.   Cobb, Charles E.   "BEHAVIOR MODIFICATION" IN THE PRISON SYSTEM. *Black Scholar 1974 5(8): 41-44.* Statement by the author to be delivered before a congressional subcommittee. Gives the views of the Commission for Racial Justice of the United Church of Christ on the proposed Center for Correctional Research.   M. M. McCarthy

1256.   Conley, John A.   BEYOND LEGISLATIVE ACTS: PENAL RE-FORM, PUBLIC POLICY, AND SYMBOLIC JUSTICE. *Public Hist. 1981 3(1): 26-39.* Focuses on prison reform in Oklahoma from 1910, when it con-structed its penitentiary, to 1967, when it created a statewide corrections depart-ment.

1257.   Conley, John A.   PRISONS, PRODUCTION, AND PROFIT: RE-CONSIDERING THE IMPORTANCE OF PRISON INDUSTRIES.   *J. of Social Hist. 1980 14(2): 257-275.* Analysis of Oklahoma prisons suggests that historians of 19th- and early 20th-century prison development have ignored the role of prison industries run for profit. The usual emphasis on a struggle over punishment or reform, or between the solitary or congregate system of prison industries as modes of rehabilitation gives inadequate attention to the centrality of prison industries. Information on adjoining states and on the New York prison system buttresses the argument. 48 notes.   C. M. Hough

1258.   Conley, John A.   REVISING CONCEPTIONS ABOUT THE ORIGIN OF PRISONS: THE IMPORTANCE OF ECONOMIC CONSIDER-ATIONS.   *Social Sci. Q. 1981 62(2): 247-258.* Focuses on the origin of the prison in Oklahoma in the late 19th century, showing that, in addition to other complex forces, economic considerations played a significant role in its establishment.

1259.   Coulter, E. Merton.   HANGING AS A SOCIO-PENAL INSTITU-TION IN GEORGIA AND ELSEWHERE. *Georgia Hist. Q. 1973 57(1): 17-55.* Hanging was the only penal institution colonial Georgians brought with them from England. It remained the principal form of capital punishment until 1924. Capital offenses at various times included rape, horse-stealing, counterfeit-ing, perjury, dueling, and murder. Describes several executions. 3 illus., 81 notes.
D. L. Smith

1260.   Crane, Sophie and Crane, Paul.   HISTORIC JAILS OF TENNESSEE. *Tennessee Hist. Q. 1980 39(1): 3-10.* A description of the six of Tennessee's 95 county jails listed in the National Register of Historic Places. These are the jails of Bedford, Franklin, Grundy, Hancock, Lawrence, and Scott Counties. Three (Bedford, Hancock, and Scott) are still in use. They are "a grim reminder of the past and a witness to the yet unsolved problem of how to protect society without completely dehumanizing the criminal and those who guard him." 6 photos.

1261. Dean, David and Dean, Martha. "MOMA WENT TO CONGRESS AND THEN TO JAIL." *Am. Hist. Illus. 1977 12(7): 37-43.* In November 1922, 40-year-old Winnifred Mason Huck was elected to the unexpired congressional term of her late father, Billy Mason of Chicago. She was the third woman and the first mother elected to Congress. During her four-month term and subsequent defeat, she was vocal, received much publicity, and enjoyed herself. She started a syndicated column, "Talks to Mothers of Flappers." She later wrote 25 articles on prison life and the problems ex-convicts have finding employment. This series was based on her serving a month in an Ohio prison (with the cooperation of Governor Vic Donahey) and performing ex-con jobs for two months under her prison name "Elizabeth Sprague." She died in 1936 after a five-year bout with stomach cancer. Based on her scrapbooks of pictures and clippings, contemporary newspapers, and magazine articles; 8 illus.   D. Dodd

1262. DelCastillo, Adelaida R.   STERILIZATION: AN OVERVIEW. Mora, Magdalena and DelCastillo, Adelaida R., ed. *Mexican Women in the United States: Struggles Past and Present* (Los Angeles: U. of California Chicano Studies Res. Center, 1980): 65-70. Discusses the predominantly punitive rationale underlying the advocacy of sterilization in the United States, especially involving Mexican women. The first sterilization bill was passed in the United States in 1907. More recently, legislators, judges, and doctors have advocated and mandated forced sterilization for other than eugenic purposes. The poor and ethnic minorities, by extension, have come to be seen as social misfits and an economic drain on the state. Their sterilization has been advocated even though it violates a number of juridical precedents, laws, and constitutional rights that protect the fundamentals of privacy and procreation. 40 notes.   J. Powell

1263. Delgado, James P.   GOLD RUSH JAIL: THE PRISON SHIP *EUPHEMIA.* *California History 1981 60(2): 134-141.* Describes the use of the brig *Euphemia* as a prison for San Francisco in the gold rush era. Finding no suitable facility and building materials costly, the San Francisco Town Council purchased the *Euphemia* in October 1849 and had it refitted as a prison ship. At that time many ships in the harbor were being converted to warehouses, hotels, and offices. Prisoners worked on a chain-gang and were locked in cells in the *Euphemia* at night. Complaints soon arose of unsanitary conditions and overcrowding. Use of the ship as a prison ended in mid-1851 with completion of a more permanent jail. The *Euphemia* settled into the mud, not to be rediscovered until 1921 when it was found during construction of a new bank building. Photos, 27 notes.
                                                                      A. Hoffman

1264. Dershowitz, Alan M.   CRIMINAL SENTENCING IN THE UNITED STATES: AN HISTORICAL AND CONCEPTUAL OVERVIEW.   *Ann. of the Am. Acad. of Pol. and Social Sci. 1976 (423): 117-132.* The criminal sentence seeks to reduce the frequency and severity of crimes by employing the following mechanisms: (a) isolating the convicted criminal from the rest of the population, so that he is unable to commit crimes during the period of his enforced isolation; (b) punishing the convicted prisoner, so that he—and others contemplating crime —will be deterred by the prospect of a painful response if convicted; (c) rehabilitating the convicted criminal, so that his desire or need to commit future crimes will be diminished. During different periods of our history, the power to determine the duration of a convicted criminal's sentence has been allocated to different agencies: first to the legislature; then to the judiciary; and now—under indeterminate sentencing—to the parole board. The locus of sentencing authority has a considerable effect on such factors as the length of sentences, the degree of discretion, and the disparity among sentences. The century-long trend in the direction of indeterminancy seems to be ending. It is likely that the coming decades will witness a return to more legislatively-fixed sentences.   J

1265.   DeWolf, L. Harold.   THE DEATH PENALTY: CRUEL, UNUSUAL, UNETHICAL, AND FUTILE.   *Religion in Life 1973 42(1): 37-41.*

1266.   Diamond, Arlyn.   A LEGACY.   *Massachusetts R. 1975 16(3): 588-591.* Calls Michael and Robert Meeropol's *We Are Your Sons: The Legacy of Ethel and Julius Rosenberg, Written by Their Children* (Boston: Houghton Mifflin Co., 1975) a good work that incorporates prison letters to the sons and an account of how the youngsters adjusted to a life without parents. The book is more a social history of American radicalism than a psychological study. Based on primary and secondary sources; 4 notes.   M. J. Barach

1267.   Downs, George and Rocke, David.   BUREAUCRACY AND JUVENILE CORRECTIONS IN THE STATES.   *Policy Studies J. 1979 7(4): 721-727.* Studies the connection between bureaucratic and administrative variables in juvenile corrections, concluding that connections are extensive and complex, both having much impact on policymaking, 1979.

1268.   Dressner, Richard B. and Altschuler, Glenn C.   SENTIMENT AND STATISTICS IN THE PROGRESSIVE ERA: THE DEBATE ON CAPITAL PUNISHMENT IN NEW YORK.   *New York Hist. 1975 56(2): 191-209.* Reviews the arguments for and against capital punishment during the Progressive era, emphasizing those expressed during the Constitutional Convention of New York State in 1915. 3 illus., 43 notes.   R. N. Lokken

1269.   Dunbar, Tony.   IMPRESSIONS OF PARCHMAN PRISON.   *New South 1973 28(3): 37-39.* Despite reforms, Mississippi's Parchman Prison Farm remains a travesty of criminal justice.   S

1270.   Ehrlich, Isaac.   CAPITAL PUNISHMENT AND DETERRENCE: SOME FURTHER THOUGHTS AND ADDITIONAL EVIDENCE.   *J. of Pol. Econ. 1977 85(4): 741-788.* Investigation of the deterrent effect of capital punishment has implications far beyond the propriety of execution as punishment since it concerns the general question of offenders' responsiveness to incentives. This study challenges popular allegations by earlier researchers denying the deterrence hypothesis. The empirical analysis based on cross-sectional data from the United States corroborates my earlier analysis of the time series. Findings indicate a substantial deterrent effect of punishment on murder and related violent crimes and support the economic and econometric models used in investigations of other crimes. Distinctions between classes of executing and nonexecuting states are also examined in light of theory and evidence.   J

1271.   Ehrlich, Isaac.   THE DETERRENT EFFECT OF CAPITAL PUN-
ISHMENT: A QUESTION OF LIFE AND DEATH.   *Am. Econ. R. 1975
65(3): 397-417.* Discerns no simple correlation between the murder rate and the
legal status, or even effective use, of capital punishment. Provides no conclusive
evidence for or against the existence of a deterrent effect. Analysis assumes
offender responsiveness to incentives.   D. K. Pickens

1272.   Ellis, Desmond; Grasmick, Harold G.; and Gilman, Bernard.   VIO-
LENCE IN PRISONS: A SOCIOLOGICAL ANALYSIS.   *Am. J. of Sociol.
1974 80(1): 16-43.* "In this study an attempt was made to construct and then test
a causal model of reported aggressive transgressions in 29 felon and 26 misdemeanant prisons and among 278 felon inmates. We found, first, that of the seven
independent variables included in the model, only three—the percentage incarcerated for violent offenses, percentage incarcerated for one year or more, and
parole referral date—appear in both felon and misdemeanant cases. Second, only
age and visits are related to aggressive transgressions at both aggregate (prison)
and individual (inmate) levels. Third, a larger proportion of all possible relationships between variables were supported by the data in felon prisons. The study
concludes with a discussion of the implications of our findings for the functional-
ist-diffusionist debate and for social policy."   J

1273.   Faia, Michael A.   WILLFUL, DELIBERATE, PREMEDITATED
AND IRRATIONAL: REFLECTIONS ON THE FUTILITY OF EXECU-
TIONS.   *State Government 1982 55(1): 14-21.* Covers 1907-81.

1274.   Fairchild, Erika S.   NEW PERSPECTIVES ON CORRECTIONS
POLICY.   *Policy Studies J. 1974 3(1): 74-82.*

1275.   Feinman, Clarice.   AN AFRO-AMERICAN EXPERIENCE: THE
WOMEN IN NEW YORK CITY'S JAIL.   *Afro-Am. in New York Life and
Hist. 1977 1(2): 201-210.* Discusses the House of Detention for Women and its
successor, the New York City Correctional Institution for Women, 1932-75,
where because of a mainly black staff, problems of race relations do not exist for
Negroes there.

1276.   Finger, Bill.   WHAT YOU CAN DO: INTERVIEW WITH JOE IN-
GLE.   *Southern Exposure 1978 6(4): 88-93.* Joe Ingle, director of the Southern
Coalition on Jails and Prisons, emphasizes his role and that of his group in their
work of supporting alternatives to imprisonment and on the abolition of the death
penalty. The group encourages ordinary citizens to visit prisoners, establish
friendships, and then create outside structures in which both parties can work
together for reform. One of the group's main goals is to work through the
legislative process to bring about an end to prison construction.   N. Lederer

1277.   Flynn, Edith Elisabeth.   FROM CONFLICT THEORY TO CON-
FLICT RESOLUTION: CONTROLLING COLLECTIVE VIOLENCE IN
PRISONS.   *Am. Behavioral Scientist 1980 23(5): 745-776.* Argues that sociological theory, effectively applied to the prison system of the 1960's and 1970's, could
alleviate much of the violence and inefficiency of the present system.

1278.   Foster, Samuel C.   "WE ARE PRISONERS OF WAR": A TEXAN'S ACCOUNT OF THE CAPTURE OF FORT HINDMAN. *Civil War Times Illus. 1977 16(2): 24-33.* Excerpts from Captain Samuel F. Foster's diary during 8-12 January 1863 describe the federal gunboat attack on Fort Hindman, Arkansas Post. This was Captain Foster's first war experience. Also describes Foster's life in prison. Illus.   E. P. Stickney

1279.   Franklin, H. Bruce.   THE LITERATURE OF THE AMERICAN PRISON. *Massachusetts Rev. 1977 18(1): 51-78.* Hundreds of books by American convicts and ex-convicts have been published in the last 20 years. This constitutes an unprecedented phenomenon; a vast body of literature which is coherent in itself. Dating from Malcolm X, it includes Eldridge Cleaver, Bobby Seale, Hurricane Carter, and Etheridge Knight. The authors are divided into two camps, the political activist thrust into prison and the common criminal thrust into political activism. The literature aptly describes life in prison and the authors' thoughts thereon. Based on primary (government documents and prisoners' works) and secondary sources; 25 notes.   E. R. Campbell

1280.   Freedman, Estelle B.   THEIR SISTERS' KEEPERS: AN HISTORICAL PERSPECTIVE ON FEMALE CORRECTIONAL INSTITUTIONS IN THE UNITED STATES: 1870-1900. *Feminist Studies 1974 2(1): 77-95.* The attack of 19th-century women prison reformers on the patriarchal prison system and the substitution of a matriarchal one was a "necessary intermediate route to sexual equality." In the 1820's a number of American women began efforts to reform the prisons and several states enacted reforms such as hiring female matrons and providing separate quarters for women. The post-Civil War women's prison reform movement grew out of four factors: 1) the increase in female prison population, 2) women's Civil War social service experience, 3) the charities organization movement and prison reform movement, and 4) an "embryonic feminist analysis of women's place in American society" which led to a separatist approach to female correction. Reformers argued for female superiority in correctional work and structured their reformatory programs on the traditional female virtues of domesticity and purity, which contradicted the concept of equal rights and limited their work to traditional women's roles. Today's reintegration of the correctional system should aim at equal rights, the integration of the "achievements of women's reforms into co-educational institutions" and the end to the "treatment of women as morally superior domestics." 70 notes.   J. D. Falk

1281.   French, Laurence.   AN ASSESSMENT OF THE BLACK FEMALE PRISONER IN THE SOUTH. *Signs: J. of Women in Culture and Soc. 1977 3(2): 483-488.* Black women are overrepresented in North Carolina prisons. This social profile portrays North Carolina's serious male and female offenders as being black, poorly educated, and marginally employable. Differences between the male and female samples include a higher proportion of blacks with poorer educational and occupational backgrounds in the female sample, and a greater proportion of black female offenders institutionalized for victimless crimes, notably drug-related offenses, 1970's. Based on prison and government records; 5 tables, 7 notes.   J. K. Gammage

1282. Gallagher, Kevin J.   INMATES OF THE CITY ALMSHOUSE, POUGHKEEPSIE, NEW YORK.   *J. of the Afro-American Hist. and Geneal. Soc. 1981 2(1): 11-14.* Abstracted from *Records of Inmates—City Alms House, under Act Chapter 140, Laws of 1875,* lists the name, age, marital status, birthplace, and date of first entry to the almshouse, of black inmates.

1283. Gardner, Martin R.   MORMONISM AND CAPITAL PUNISHMENT: A DOCTRINAL PERSPECTIVE, PAST AND PRESENT.   *Dialogue 1979 12(1): 9-26.* Early Mormon leaders such as Joseph Smith, Brigham Young, Jedediah M. Grant, and Heber C. Kimball taught that, according to scripture, some crimes are so heinous that only the spilling of the perpetrator's blood can achieve atonement for his soul. The option of execution by firing squad—the shedding of blood—is peculiar to Utah in the United States due to the Mormons' influence on state laws. Decapitation was another option in the Territory of Utah during 1852-76, as was hanging, which persists. Although elements of utilitarianism appeared in some early Mormon arguments for capital punishment as a deterrent to crime, retribution and atonement were emphasized. In the 20th century there are few references to the blood atonement doctrine. Recently Elder Bruce R. McConkie wrote that there has never been a doctriine of blood atonement in the Church of Latter-Day Saints. 46 notes, ref.   S

1284. Gerber, David A.   LYNCHING AND LAW AND ORDER: ORIGINS AND PASSAGE OF THE OHIO ANTI-LYNCHING LAW OF 1894.   *Ohio Hist. 1974 83(1): 33-50.* Harry C. Smith and Albion W. Tourgée attempted to legislate lynching out of existence. Tourgée wanted to fine communities in which outrages occurred. An 1896 compromise resulted in legislation that became a model for other states. Primary and secondary sources; 3 illus., 43 notes.
S. S. Sprague

1285. Gibney, Abbott M.   "YOUR AFFECTIONATE SON": THE CIVIL WAR LETTERS OF FRANK E. LANSING.   *Michigan Hist. 1974 58(1): 25-53.* Frank E. Lansing, who served in both the eastern and western theaters with the 20th Michigan Infantry and who was imprisoned at Andersonville for seven months in 1864, was a keen-eyed and objective observer of military life. In approximately 40 letters written to his family during 1862-65, Lansing provided a clear and inclusive view of all phases of his army career. Based upon Lansing's letters and secondary sources; 7 illus., map, 44 notes.   D. W. Johnson

1286. Glidden, William B.   INTERNMENT CAMPS IN AMERICA, 1917-1920.   *Military Affairs 1973 37(4): 137-141.* About 6,000 enemy aliens were interned in the United States during World War I in camps at Fort Douglas (Utah), Fort Oglethorpe (Georgia), Fort McPherson (Georgia), and Hot Springs (North Carolina). All camps came to be operated by the Army. Although the treatment was good, the internees were not allowed much communication with the outside. This worked a hardship on those with families and also induced some mental problems. As the war continued the order and morale of the camps deteriorated; nevertheless, only about 500 of the civilian internees chose to return to Germany before the camps closed in April 1920. Based on Army records; 17 notes.   K. J. Bauer

1287. Greenberg, David F. THE INCAPACITATIVE EFFECT OF IM-PRISONMENT: SOME ESTIMATES. *Law and Soc. R. 1975 9(4): 541-580.* Discusses through the use of quantitative data the predictability of parolees returning to crime after being paroled. Finds a rather low rate of parolees return-ing to crime, although many were imprisoned again because of technical viola-tions of parole. The parole system has two serious flaws: it is not accurate in predicting the best parole risks and it does not prevent some parolees from returning to crime.   H. R. Mahood

1288. Greene, William Robert. EARLY DEVELOPMENT OF THE ILLI-NOIS STATE PENITENTIARY SYSTEM. *J. of the Illinois State Hist. Soc. 1977 70(3): 185-195.* Illinois officials, responding to the national penal reform movement, established the first state penitentiary at Alton in 1831. Previously, there were only county jails and military prisons. The prison was moved to Joliet in 1860. Until 1867, the penitentiary was operated under a system whereby the building and convicts were leased. A modified contract system for prison labor prevailed until prohibited by law in 1903. 4 illus., 87 notes.   J

1289. Gross, Harriet. JANE KENNEDY: MAKING HISTORY THROUGH MORAL PROTEST. *Frontiers 1977 2(2): 73-81.* Jane Kennedy describes her career as a political activist since 1964, including her involvement in the civil rights movement, the anti-Vietnam War movement, and her two prison terms; part of a special issue on women's oral history.

1290. Guenther, Anthony L. and Guenther, Mary Quinn. SCREWS VS. THUGS. *Society 1974 11(5): 42-50.* Despite the theoretical rehabilitation goals of prisons, the strongest influence on the prisoner is the correctional officer and his preoccupation with the custodial function and problems of his job.   S

1291. Guerrero, Gene. SCIENTIFIC PENOLOGY COMES TO GEORGIA. *Southern Exposure 1978 6(4): 42-47.* Beginning in the early 1970's with the gubernatorial administration of Jimmy Carter, systematic reform efforts aimed at ending Georgia's abysmal prison conditions began in earnest. Work release programs were introduced, along with the professionalization of the cor-rectional staff and innovative educational efforts. Over the years, however, the greatest emphasis has been placed on methods by which the personalities of rebellious prisoners can be modified in order to make them more responsive to incarceration. Various innovations have been introduced and discarded at consid-erable expense, while basic educational programs have been neglected.
                                                                                N. Lederer

1292. Haas, Kenneth C. THE "NEW FEDERALISM" AND PRISONERS' RIGHTS: STATE SUPREME COURTS IN COMPARATIVE PERSPEC-TIVE. *Western Pol. Q. 1981 34(4): 552-571.* Utilizes a comparative perspective to evaluate the strength and breadth of the "new federalism"—the willingness of some state supreme courts to take a more expansive approach than that adopted by the federal courts in the protection of individual liberties. A textual analysis of state supreme court decisions in the area of corrections law from 1969 to 1980 reveals that these courts have proved to be unsympathetic toward prisoners' efforts to seek judicial redress of their grievances. It thus appears that the spirit of state court activism which has been evident in many other areas of law has bypassed an entire class of litigants. The article concludes with some predictions concerning the future of the new federalism and the prisoners' rights movement.

J

1293. Haffner, Gerald O., ed.   A BRITISH PRISONER OF WAR IN THE AMERICAN REVOLUTION: THE EXPERIENCES OF JACOB SCHIEFFELIN FROM VINCENNES TO WILLIAMSBURG, 1779-1780. *Virginia Mag. of Hist. and Biog. 1978 86(1): 17-25.* When George Rogers Clark captured Vincennes, Indiana, in February 1779, British Lieutenant Jacob Schieffelin was captured and sent to prison in Virginia. His often harsh treatment resulted from the hope of Virginia officials that British authorities would change their handling of American prisoners of war. Edited from the original published version of Schieffelin's journal found in Rivington's New York *Royal Gazette.*

R. F. Oaks

1294. Hagerman, Robert L.   A DOLEFUL TRAGEDY: OR HOW NOT TO ESCAPE FROM WINDSOR PRISON.   *New-England Galaxy 1978 19(4): 38-42.* Recounts the suspected escape of Joseph Burnham from Windsor State Prison in Vermont despite his reported death on 15 October 1826. A legislative investigating commission on 28 October 1829 laid to rest rumors of Burnham using poison to simulate death and reports of his being seen in New York City after 15 October 1826.

P. C. Marshall

1295. Hahn, Nicolas Fischer.   FEMALE STATE PRISONERS IN TENNESSEE: 1831-1979.   *Tennessee Hist. Q. 1980 39(4): 485-497.* In Tennessee, an independent prison for women was established only gradually, over nearly 100 years. During the Civil War, the sexes were mixed together in the state's penitentiary. Beginning ca. 1880, the separation process occurred in five steps. First, female prisoners were isolated in one part of the penitentiary. Second, in the 1890's, a separate wing was built for them. At the turn of the century women were removed to a separate building. Fourth, in 1930, a cell-house was constructed apart from the main penitentiary but still on the main grounds and administratively dependent. Finally, in 1965, female prisoners were provided with a new and entirely autonomous prison. Primary sources; 45 notes.

J. Powell

1296. Hawes, Joseph M.   PRISONS IN EARLY NINETEENTH-CENTURY AMERICA: THE PROCESS OF CONVICT REFORMATION. Hawes, Joseph M., ed. *Law and Order in American History* (Port Washington, N.Y.: Kennikat Pr., 1979): 37-52. Compares the ideas of the founders of the Auburn, New York, and Pennsylvania prison systems from 1787 to 1845; Pennsylvania prisons, with Quaker influence, "preferred a noncoercive, practically passive, approach to reform and religion," while the supporters of the Auburn believed that "religion and reform were active human pursuits."

1297. Heale, M. J.   THE FORMATIVE YEARS OF THE NEW YORK PRISON ASSOCIATION, 1844-1862.   *New-York Hist. Soc. Q. 1975 59(4): 320-347.* Presented as a "Case Study in Antebellum Reform," indicates that the Prison Association was not easy to stereotype as an American reform movement. Formed largely as a reaction against the severity of the prison system identified with Sing Sing and Auburn after the 1820's, it began as an attempt to introduce rehabilitation of the prisoner. To do this conditions would have to be improved, discipline ameliorated, and help afforded ex-prisoners. The association recognized that society was responsible in part for the condition of law-breakers. It was one of the first groups to use statistical analysis and probably made its greatest contribution in improving prison conditions and pioneering methods of assistance to the ex-convict. Since it included members of all political parties, religious groups, and social levels (although the wealthy noticeably dominated) the association did not conform to the usual interpretation of a reform group. In addition, it was important as the predecessor of the Correctional Association of New York. Based on Prison Association minutes and reports; 5 illus., 39 notes.

C. L. Grant

1298. Hinds, Lennox S. THE DEATH PENALTY: CONTINUING THREAT TO AMERICA'S POOR. *Freedomways 1976 16(1): 39-43.* The death penalty as a deterrent to crime is not viable; it is a blatant form of discrimination against black, brown, and red minorities as well as the poor in the United States.

1299. Hirsch, Andrew von. GIVING CRIMINALS THEIR JUST DESERTS. *Civil Liberties R. 1976 3(1): 23-35.* Discusses reasonable and effective means of punishing criminals. Too often prisons and rehabilitation programs fail to prevent recurrent crime. Evaluates James Q. Wilson's suggestions in his book, *Thinking About Crime.* Advocates use of the commensurate-deserts principle in prison sentencing.   S

1300. Hoffa, James R. CRIMINAL JUSTICE FROM THE INSIDE. *Judicature 1973 56(10): 422-426.* Reform of prison conditions is needed.   S

1301. Hougen, Harvey R. THE IMPACT OF POLITICS AND PRISON INDUSTRY ON THE GENERAL MANAGEMENT OF THE KANSAS STATE PENITENTIARY, 1883-1909. *Kansas Hist. Q. 1977 43(3): 297-318.* Examines the Kansas State Penitentiary at Lansing during 1883-1909, when the office of warden was generally used to reward political allies of the governor, and the prison usually turned a profit thanks to prison industry and mining. Authorities allowed the institution to become overcrowded by taking in Oklahoma convicts for a fee, permitted various brutal forms of corporal punishment, and imposed 24-hour silence. Former prisoners reported that sodomy was rife in the prison coal mine, due to lack of supervision. In 1908, at the insistence of Oklahoma reformer Kate Barnard, a joint Kansas-Oklahoma committee investigated Lansing, prompting needed changes. Lansing was worse than some other American facilities, but much better than many. Based mainly on contemporary government documents; 7 illus., 47 notes. L. W. Van Wyk

1302. Hougen, Harvey R. KATE BARNARD AND THE KANSAS PENITENTIARY SCANDAL, 1908-1909. *J. of the West 1978 17(1): 9-18.* Spurred by reports of inhuman treatment in the Kansas State Penitentiary, Kate Barnard, Commissioner of Charities and Corrections for the state of Oklahoma, visited the Lansing institution to check on the welfare of Oklahoma citizens imprisoned there, found the conditions appalling, and launched a campaign which brought about much needed prison reform, 1908-09.

1303.   Huston, Terry L.   PRISONS: A MARXIST POSITION.   *Monthly R. 1973 25(6): 29-33.* Attacks the injustices of prison systems in capitalist society.
S

1304.   Iiyama, Patty.   AMERICAN CONCENTRATION CAMPS: RACISM AND JAPANESE-AMERICANS DURING WORLD WAR II.   *Internat. Socialist R. 1973 34(4): 24-33.*

1305.   Jacob, Herbert and Eisenstein, James.   SENTENCES AND OTHER SANCTIONS IN THE CRIMINAL COURTS OF BALTIMORE, CHICAGO, AND DETROIT.   *Pol. Sci. Q. 1975/76 90(4): 617-635.* Most persons accused of felonies in Baltimore, Chicago, and Detroit are not convicted, but nevertheless suffer significant punishment. Although convictions and prison sentences are the result of complex patterns, length of sentence seems to be much more the result of the seriousness of the original charge than of the identity of the judge or race of the defendant.
J

1306.   Jacobs, James B.   AMERICAN PRISONS: THE FRUSTRATION OF INCHING TOWARD REFORM.   *Rev. in Am. Hist. 1978 6(2): 184-189.* Review article prompted by Blake McKelvey's *American Prisons: A History of Good Intentions* (Montclair, N.J.: Patterson Smith, 1977); covers 19th-20th centuries.

1307.   Jacobs, James B.   THE POLITICS OF CORRECTIONS: TOWN/PRISON RELATIONS AS A DETERMINANT OF REFORM.   *Social Service Rev. 1976 50(4): 623-631.* Illinois's minimum-security state prison, Vienna Correctional Center (VCC), is highly successful; the small-town atmosphere and close staff-felon relationships within the prison, combined with active participation in the economic, social, and political interests of the local community, result in both significant penal reform, and economic revival in the life of the community.

1308.   Jensen, Gary F. and Jones, Dorothy.   PERSPECTIVES ON INMATE CULTURE: A STUDY OF WOMEN IN PRISON.   *Social Forces 1976 54(3): 590-603.* This study explores a range of issues bearing on prisonization research based on male populations but does so using cross-sectional questionnaire data gathered from 172 female felons and misdemeanants incarcerated in a prison for women in Raleigh, N. C. The analysis tackles three major issues: (1) the relation of traditional situational variables (career phase and group contact) to inmate perspectives, (2) the relative impact of situational and non-institutional characteristics on inmate perspectives, and (3) variation in traditional patterns among different categories of inmates. In general, we found that the patterns involving career phase and group contact were similar to those found in Wheeler's early research among males and similar to one recent analysis of females. Moreover, of all situational variables examined the traditional situational variables were the most strongly related to inmate perspectives. Several of the background variables examined were, however, more strongly related than the situational variables. On the other hand, the relationship between career phase and subscription to the inmate code was quite variable among different categories of inmates. The variation noted appears relevant for reconciling divergent findings in prisonization research among female inmates.
J

1309. Johnson, Joyce. THE GRIM CORRIDORS OF ALCATRAZ AS A TOURIST ATTRACTION. *Smithsonian 1975 6(7): 105-111.* Traces the history of Alcatraz Island in San Francisco Bay: its use as a prison during 1859-1962, its occupation by Indians in 1969-70, and its status as part of the National Park Service since 1973.

1310. Johnson, Robert C. THE POLITICAL ECONOMY OF CRIMINAL OPPRESSION. *Black Scholar 1977 8(6): 14-22.* Examines the political economy of the prison system as it operates on blacks in America; examines racism, capitalism, and economic inequalities as causes of the disproportionate percentage of blacks in prisons, 1960-76.

1311. Johnson, Roberta Ann. THE PRISON BIRTH OF BLACK POWER. *J. of Black Studies 1975 5(4): 395-414.* Blacks in prisons and blacks in ghettos share many similarities. Both groups are at the mercy of the whites in power, both lack political power, and both have been systematically stripped of their dignity. The same racism existing in the ghetto exists in the prison. Because of the similarities between the ghetto and the prison, the ideas of black power appeal to both groups and serve to politicize both groups. 18 notes, biblio.
K. Butcher

1312. Jordan, Fania Davis. THE SAN QUENTIN SIX: A CASE OF VENGEANCE. *Black Scholar 1974 5(6): 44-51.* Relates details of the legal struggles of the San Quentin Six. Gives brief biographies of the Six; Fleeta Drumgo, David Johnson, Luis Talamantez, Willie Tate, Johnny Larry Spain, and Hugo Pinell.
M. M. McCarthy

1313. Jupiter, Clare. LOST LIVES? A PROFILE OF DEATH ROW. *Southern Exposure 1978 6(4): 76-79.* Most condemned prisoners at the present time are imprisoned on Southern death rows. The historical southern propensity toward lynching appears to be an important factor in the popularity in the South for the death penalty. Most condemned prisoners are black as were most victims of lynchings. Crimes committed by blacks against whites in the South are punished more harshly than crimes committed by whites against anybody. Racial discrimination plays a role in this fact as does the reality that most accused blacks are poor and cannot afford decent legal representation. Illustrated by charts.
N. Lederer

1314. Katz, Ellis. PRISONER'S RIGHTS, STATE'S RIGHTS, AND THE BAYH-KASTENMEIER "INSTITUTIONS BILL." *Publius 1978 8(1): 179-198.* In *Monroe* v. *Pape* (US, 1961), the US Supreme Court resurrected an 1871 civil rights act (42 U.S.C.A. 1983) enabling institutionalized persons to seek relief in federal courts for violations of their rights. In *Holt* v. *Sarver* (US, 1970), District Court Judge J. Smith Henley issued the first of a number of recent injunctions requiring that specific steps be taken to improve conditions at specific institutions. However, in *Solomon* v. *Mattson* (US, 1976), the authority of the US Attorney General to initiate prisoners' rights lawsuits without mandate from Congress was denied, whence the 1977 introduction by Senator Birch Bayh (Dem.-Indiana) and Representative Robert W. Kastenmeier (Dem.-Wisc.) of a bill to provide the Attorney General with such a mandate. Questions this approach, both in its tendency to perpetuate an adversary model in prison reform efforts, and in its tendency to undermine the state-federal balance in this area. 14 notes.　　　　　　　　　　　　　　　　　　　　　　　L. W. Van Wyk

1315.　Keller, Charles.　PRISON REFORM AND INDIANS.　*Indian Hist. 1976 9(1): 34-38.* Discusses similarities between imprisonment of convicted criminals and confining American Indians on reservations in the 19th century. The prison reform movement and the program to convert the Indians into farmers and craftsmen were both economic rather than humanitarian, designed to increase the labor force rather than to improve the welfare of the prisoner or Indian. 14 ref.
　　　　　　　　　　　　　　　　　　　　　　　　　　　E. D. Johnson

1316.　King, David R.　THE BRUTALIZATION EFFECT: EXECUTION PUBLICITY AND THE INCIDENCE OF HOMICIDE IN SOUTH CAROLINA.　*Social Forces 1978 57(2): 683-687.* In this note we report the results of a study of the effects of execution publicity on the incidence of homicide in a single State, South Carolina. The basic purpose is to see whether the data are consistent with the brutalization hypothesis; the use of the death penalty as a punishment by the state deadens people's respect for life and thus increases the incidence of homicide.　　　　　　　　　　　　　　　　　　　　J

1317.　Koppes, Clayton R.　THE INDUSTRIAL WORKERS OF THE WORLD AND COUNTY-JAIL REFORM IN KANSAS, 1915-1920.　*Kansas Hist. Q. 1975 41(1): 63-86.* A nationwide effort to jail the leaders of the Industrial Workers of the World (IWW) during World War I led to the arrest of 26 men in Kansas. They were held for two years before being brought to trial. The county jails in which they were held pending trial were antiquated pestholes. The campaign to bring about their modernization, led by the IWW, is described in detail. Based on manuscripts in the National Archives, Library of Congress, Kansas State Historical Society, and Federal Records Center, Kansas City, Missouri, and other primary and secondary sources; 4 photos, 67 notes.　　　　W. F. Zornow

1318.　Krammer, Arnold P.　GERMAN PRISONERS OF WAR IN THE UNITED STATES.　*Military Affairs 1976 40(2): 68-73.* Discusses the problems involved in establishing and administering camps for German POW's. Two fundamental principles affected their treatment: the humanitarian intent of the Geneva Convention, and the fact that enemy nations held American soldiers. At the beginning of the war, the government's inefficient division of responsibility led to unpreparedness, but problems were soon worked out and prisoners were working in a variety of tasks. Some complications arose around the ire of American labor unions, the special position of Italy, and political leadership in the camps. The program's success was partly responsible for the healthy postwar reconstruction of American-German relations. Based on primary and secondary sources; 41 notes.　　　　　　　　　　　　　　　　　　　A. M. Osur

1319.　Kremer, Gary R. and Gage, Thomas E.　THE PRISON AGAINST THE TOWN: JEFFERSON CITY AND THE PENITENTIARY IN THE 19TH CENTURY.　*Missouri Hist. Rev. 1980 74(4): 414-432.* Penitentiaries, the purveyors of order, often became transmitters of disorder, chaos, and anxiety. Before 1853 Missouri leased its prison to private persons who employed the convicts outside its walls. Residents of Jefferson City feared escapees and resented the competition of cheap labor. After 1853 the state built factories within the prison walls. This reduced the number of escapes, but the prison still remained a disquieting element by producing goods to compete in the market. Based on records of the Missouri legislature, reports of the Board of Inspectors of the Missouri State Penitentiary, newspapers, and secondary sources; illus., 47 notes. W. F. Zornow

1320. Kroll, Michael A. THE PRISON EXPERIMENT: A CIRCULAR HISTORY. *Southern Exposure 1978 6(4): 6-11.* The history of imprisonment in America can be divided into five distinct eras: Early American Prison (1790-1830); Penitentiary System (1830-1870); Reformatory System (1870-1900); Industrial System (1900-1935); Rehabilitative System (1935-?). Today a growing percentage of public opinion supported by many professional penologists feels that rehabilitation should be replaced by a harsher, more punitive system in which prisoners receive their "just desserts." N. Lederer

1321. Kronstadt, Sylvia. THE PRISON GUARDS: AN UNHAPPY LOT. *New York Affairs 1974 2(2): 60-77.* "Poorly selected, poorly trained and poorly led, New York City's correction officers serve out their two decades of tension, boredom and demoralization awaiting retirement. Their state is yet another failure of the 'criminal injustice' system." J

1322. Lamott, Kenneth. IS PRISON OBSOLETE? *Horizon 1975 17(3): 40-47.* Asks whether the historic (particularly 19th-century) purposes of prisons —vengeance, deterrence, and reform—are an effective means of social reform in the 20th century. S

1323. Largey, Gale. THE HANGING. *Society 1981 18(6): 73-75.* Provides photographs that give a glimpse of the emotional force surrounding the public display of a local hanging on 27 June 1898 in the rural community of Mansfield, Pennsylvania; witnessing the hanging had a brutalizing rather than a deterring effect.

1324. Longaker, Richard. EMERGENCY DETENTION: THE GENERATION GAP, 1950-1971. *Western Pol. Q. 1974 27(3): 395-408.* The Emergency Detention Act, Title II of the McCarran Internal Security Act (1950-71), provided for potential incarceration of Communists and political saboteurs in detention camps. S

1325. Mackey, Philip English. AN ALL-STAR DEBATE ON CAPITAL PUNISHMENT, BOSTON, 1854. *Essex Inst. Hist. Collections 1974 110(3): 181-199.* Examines the Massachusetts movement to abolish capital punishment and the open hearings which debated the topic. S

1326. Mackey, Philip English. EDWARD LIVINGSTON AND THE ORIGINS OF THE MOVEMENT TO ABOLISH CAPITAL PUNISHMENT IN AMERICA. *Louisiana Hist. 1976 16(2): 145-166.* Presents a biographical sketch of Edward Livingston (1764-1836), emphasizing his legal reform efforts in Louisiana and elsewhere, and especially his opposition to capital punishment. Traces early efforts to ban capital punishment in other states. Primary and secondary sources; photo, 33 notes. R. L. Woodward

1327. Mackey, Philip English. "THE RESULT MAY BE GLORIOUS"—ANTI-GALLOWS MOVEMENT IN RHODE ISLAND, 1838-1852. *Rhode Island Hist. 1974 33(1): 19-30.* Traces the history of the movement to abolish capital punishment and assesses the role of various factors in ending hanging in 1852. Based on records in the Rhode Island State Archives, Providence, published documents and reports, newspapers, periodicals, pamphlets, and secondary accounts.					P. J. Coleman

1328. Maestro, Marcello. A PIONEER FOR THE ABOLITION OF CAPITAL PUNISHMENT: CESARE BECCARIA. *J. of the Hist. of Ideas 1973 34(3): 463-468.* Explains the arguments in and influence of Cesare Becarria's *Dei delitti e delle pene* (1764). Beccaria's general examination of crime and punishment included a "daring chapter" which found capital punishment without basis in natural right, less efficient than imprisonment as a deterrent to crime, and an unwholesome example of barbarism. Beccaria's book was published in London and was widely distributed in North America. Quoted by John Adams, Thomas Jefferson, and Benjamin Rush, it exerted influence on early American penal reform. Primary and secondary sources; 9 notes.					D. B. Marti

1329. Magee, Doug. BARELY LIVING: INTERVIEWS FROM DEATH ROW. *Southern Exposure 1980 8(4): 56-66.* Reprints two interviews with prisoners on death row, Doug McCray and Jimmy Lee Gray, who were found guilty of murder.

1330. Mancini, Matthew J. RACE, ECONOMICS, AND THE ABANDONMENT OF CONVICT LEASING. *J. of Negro Hist. 1978 63(4): 339-352.* Analyzes the convict lease system in Georgia as a component of that larger web of law and custom which effectively insured the South's racial hierarchy. Only when the system lost its profitability to the lessees was it finally abandoned. Covers 1868-1909. Based upon records in the Georgia Department of Archives and History; table, 2 fig., 41 notes.					N. G. Sapper

1331. Martinson, Robert. WHAT WORKS?—QUESTIONS AND ANSWERS ABOUT PRISON REFORM. *Public Interest 1974 (35): 22-54.* Surveys over 200 studies on prison reform, and concludes that "with few and isolated exceptions, the rehabilitation efforts that have been reported so far have had no appreciable effect on recidivism." Calls for "a more fullhearted commitment to the strategy of treatment," including more extensive educational programs, supervision, and personal counselling. 6 notes, biblio.					D. D. Cameron / S

1332. Mattick, Hans. THE PROSAIC SOURCES OF PRISON VIOLENCE. *Public Welfare 1973 31(4): 54-60.*

1333. Mazet, Horace S. FROM REVOLUTIONARY WAR HERO TO VERMONT PRISONER. *Am. Hist. Illus. 1982 16(10): 10-11, 46-47.* Discusses the heroism of William Barton during the American Revolution, when he captured British General Richard Prescott in order to exchange him for the release of General Charles Lee of the Continental Army in 1777, and Barton's subsequent imprisonment from 1812 to 1825 for refusing to pay damages to Jonathan Allyn in a civil suit over some land; Barton died in 1831.

1334. Mazunan, George T. and Walker, Nancy. RESTRICTED AREAS: GERMAN PRISONER-OF-WAR CAMPS IN WESTERN NEW YORK, 1944-1946. *New York Hist. 1978 59(1): 55-72.* Discusses the organization and administration of prisoner-of-war camps in western New York, from Naples to Fredonia, where 4,500 Germans were encamped during 1944-46. Because of the shortage of civilian labor during World War II, German prisoners were employed in the region's agricultural and food processing industries. Describes the conditions of such prison labor. 7 illus., 37 notes.   R. N. Lokken

1335. McGuirl, Marlene C. "THE FORGOTTEN POPULATION": WOMEN IN PRISON. *Q. J. of the Lib. of Congress 1975 32(4): 338-345.* Analysis shows that women have been convicted of crimes of a primarily economic nature, that 80 percent of the imprisoned females have children, that 30 percent of women in prison were on public welfare, and that women as a group received lighter or shorter sentences than men, although indeterminate sentences may lead to a longer period of detainment. 49 notes.   E. P. Stickney

1336. McLaughlin, Florence C. DIARY OF SALISBURY PRISON BY JAMES W. EBERHART. *Western Pennsylvania Hist. Mag. 1973 56(3): 211-251.* The prison life of a Union sergeant in this Confederate prison in North Carolina.   S

1337. Meltsner, Michael. A DEATHWATCHER'S JOURNAL. *Working Papers for a New Soc. 1977 5(2): 38-45.* Discusses the faltering legal and political battles against the death penalty which, after a 10-year moratorium on its use, was revived as a national issue with the execution of Gary Mark Gilmore in January 1977.

1338. Miller, Marc. THE NUMBERS GAME: A *SOUTHERN EXPOSURE* SPECIAL REPORT. *Southern Exposure 1978 6(4): 25-29.* Statistics indicate that Southern prisons incarcerate a greater proportion of their citizens than do states in other regions of the country. Prison systems in the South are racist; prisoners are unskilled and uneducated; prison conditions in the South are worse than elsewhere. Southern prison systems are engaging in massive construction programs designed to alleviate overcrowding in their prisons, while they neglect appropriations to provide adequate pay for correctional officials and rehabilitative programs for inmates. Illustrated by six charts. Based on data from State documents.   N. Lederer

1339. Mills, Michael and Morris, Norval. PRISONERS AS LABORATORY ANIMALS. *Society 1974 11(5): 60-66.* Studies the use of prisoners in medical and quasimedical research, the nature of the tests, why prisoners volunteer, and recommendations to improve the conditions of experimentation.   S

1340. Mitson, Betty E. LOOKING BACK IN ANGUISH: ORAL HISTORY AND JAPANESE-AMERICAN EVACUATION. *Oral Hist. R. 1974: 24-51.* Discusses West Coast oral history projects on the evacuation and incarceration of Japanese Americans during World War II with details from the taped experiences of Togo Tanaka and Karl and Elaine Yoneda. Illus., 53 notes.   D. A. Yanchisin

1341.   Moore, William Haas.   PRISONERS IN THE PROMISED LAND: THE MOLOKANS IN WORLD WAR I.   *J. of Arizona Hist. 1973 14(4): 281-302.* The Molokans, a Russian religious sect, left Russia because they opposed military service and war itself. They came to the United States and settled in the Phoenix, Arizona, area. Though originally the United States had no draft law, the federal draft law of 1917 posed some difficulties. Since they were emigrés, the Molokans had to register as such, but no amount of explanation convinced them that registration was not equivalent to a draft. Though the state had many draft dodgers and Spanish-speaking Mexican nationals who were unaware of the registration requirement, an example was made of the Molokans and those who refused to register were jailed. Twenty-eight of the 34 jailed were released 10 months later upon agreement to register. On a technicality, the other six were regarded as deserters and transferred to a guardhouse on a military post in the state, but were released in 1919 as part of an amnesty program for religious conscientious objectors. 68 notes.   D. L. Smith

1342.   Morash, Merry A. and Anderson, Etta A.   LIBERAL THINKING ON REHABILITATION: A WORK-ABLE SOLUTION TO CRIME.   *Social Problems 1978 25(5): 556-563.* Examines contemporary American liberals' attitudes about work as a rehabilitative measure. These ideas have shaped correctional philosophy, programs, and the fate of offenders. Engaging offenders in work actually has been of limited benefit to them and has not reduced recidivism. But ideology is a powerful influence on social action and the ideology of work as rehabilitative remains. Instead, "it appears that correctional organizations and social institutions in general keep offenders out of the labor force, support labor and industry interests, and maintain existing class arrangements." Primary and secondary sources; 6 notes; ref.   A. M. Osur

1343.   Moulder, Rebecca Hunt.   CONVICTS AS CAPITAL: THOMAS O'-CONNOR AND THE LEASES OF THE TENNESSEE PENITENTIARY SYSTEM, 1871-1883.   *East Tennessee Hist. Soc. Publ. 1976 48: 40-70.* Thomas O'Connor, gambler, lieutenant in the Civil War who claimed the postwar title of major, entrepreneur, and Democratic standard bearer, became involved in the Tennessee convict lease system. His operation of the system not only became involved in politics but also became a focus of corruption, undermining a good idea gone bad. The convict details went from work in the coal mines to operations on the railroads. They were always compounded by brutality and Reconstruction mismanagement. Based on secondary sources, original documents, and state reports; 71 notes.   D. A. Yanchisin

1344.   Neal, Harry E.   REBELS, ROPES, AND REPRIEVES.   *Civil War Times Illus. 1976 14(10): 30-35.* Discusses the threats exchanged between Union and Confederate prisoner of war camps over the threatened hanging of two Union officers, John M. Flinn and Henry W. Sawyer, 1863.

1345.   Neier, Aryeh.   SEX AND CONFINEMENT.   *Civil Liberties Rev. 1978 5(2): 6-16.* The lack of opportunity for private sexual contact in US prisons, mental hospitals, institutions for the retarded, homes for the elderly, and juvenile institutions causes the encounters that do occur to be degrading and sometimes brutal.

1346. Northan, Irene. THE GREAT ESCAPERS: AMERICAN PRISON-ERS IN MILL PRISON. *New-England Galaxy 1976 18(2): 57-64.* Describes the plight of American prisoners at Mill Prison, Millbay, England, during the American Revolution, 1777-82. Their ingenious methods to escape from this jail are carefully illustrated. P. C. Marshall

1347. Novak, Michael. TOM WICKER'S ATTICA. *Commentary 1975 59(5): 49-56.* Reviews Tom Wicker's *A Time to Die* (New York: Quadrangle 1975) in the context of Wicker's perspective as a Southerner at the Attica prison riots. S

1348. Ohlin, Lloyd E.; Coates, Robert B.; and Miller, Alden D. RADICAL CORRECTIONAL REFORM: A CASE STUDY OF THE MASSACHU-SETTS YOUTH CORRECTIONAL SYSTEM. *Harvard Educ. R. 1974 44(1): 74-111.*

1349. Okihiro, Gary Y. TULE LAKE UNDER MARTIAL LAW: A STUDY IN JAPANESE RESISTANCE. *J. of Ethnic Studies 1977 5(3): 71-85.* Examines the "orthodox interpretation" of the wartime internment of American Japanese, and the simplistic categorizations of Issei, Kibei, and Nisei found at the base of most treatments of the topic. Also attacks the "myth of the model minority" relative to Japanese Americans, especially as seen in *The Spoilage* by Thomas and Nishimoto. Analyzes the period of military rule by the Army at the Tule Lake Camp for "segregees" or "disloyals" during November 1943-January 1944, with the arrest and detention of the democratically elected representative body for the internees, the *Daihyo Sha Kai,* and the substitution of Army-named "block managers" for maintaining order. The authorities manipulated the famous "Status Quo" ballot of 11 January 1944, but the basic unity of purpose among factions of the internees did not waver; various groupings among the prisoners simply held different approaches to the same goal, that of gaining respect for their basic human rights and bringing reforms into camp administration. Primary sources; 44 notes. G. J. Bobango

1350. Olson, Gordon L., ed. "I FELT LIKE I MUST BE ENTERING . . . ANOTHER WORLD": THE ANONYMOUS MEMOIRS OF AN EARLY INMATE OF THE WYOMING PENITENTIARY. *Ann. of Wyoming 1975 47(2): 152-190.* This inside story of a convict who spent much of the period 1904-20 in the state penitentiary is a tale of the dungeon, mutilations, suicides, and escape attempts. Illus., 29 notes. S. S. Sprague

1351. Overton, Albert G. and Loose, J. W. W. PRISONER-OF-WAR BAR-RACKS IN LANCASTER USED DURING THE REVOLUTIONARY WAR. *J. of the Lancaster County Hist. Soc. 1981 84(3): 131-134.* Reprints a copy of the floorplan of the prisoner-of-war barracks where British and Hessian prisoners were held in Lancaster, drawn in 1777 by Judge William Augustus Atlee; the barracks collapsed in 1784.

1352. Parker, George Claflin. "I FEEL . . . JUST LIKE WRITING YOU A LETTER." *Civil War Times Illus. 1977 16(1): 12-21.* George Claflin Parker of the 21st Massachusetts Volunteer Infantry shared his experiences during the Second Battle of Bull Run in 1862 in letters to his mother-in-law. He was briefly confined in Libby Prison, Richmond. He tells of his experiences as an exchanged prisoner in Alexandria, Virginia. Illus. E. P. Stickney

1353. Pederson, William D.   INMATE MOVEMENTS AND PRISON UPRISINGS: A COMPARATIVE STUDY.   *Social Sci. Q. 1978 59(3): 509-524.* Fifteen "criminal" and political uprisings from five inmate movements in American, Soviet, and German prisons are compared.   J

1354. Peterson, Andrew A.   DETERRING STRIKES BY PUBLIC EMPLOYEES: NEW YORK'S TWO-FOR-ONE SALARY PENALTY AND THE 1979 PRISON GUARD STRIKE.   *Industrial and Labor Relations Rev. 1981 34(4): 545-562.* Focuses on the Taylor Law's requirement that New York State strikers lose two days' salary for each day they are on strike. Particular emphasis is placed on the litigation that occurred in the aftermath of the statewide strike by prison guards in 1979, when the guards' union challenged several aspects of the two-for-one penalty. The author concludes that the act's current provision governing payment of the penalty imposes a major hardship on participants in a long strike, and he recommends the act be amended in a way that he believes will not undermine the deterrent purposes of the penalty.   J/S

1355. Pierce, Virgil Caleb.   UTAH'S FIRST CONVICT LABOR CAMP. *Utah Hist. Q. 1974 42(3): 245-257.* A convict labor law was passed in Utah in 1911 to make extensive use of prisoners on state road projects. The first camp was established near Willard, Box Elder County. It proved successful, and saved the state much money. After 1920 the use of convict labor declined; by the 1930's it was nearly unknown. "Opposition to convict labor came because of the competition it brought to wage laborers." Convict labor served as an important step in the development of an effective prison vocational training program in Utah. Illus., 42 notes.   E. P. Stickney

1356. Plattner, Marc F.   THE REHABILITATION OF PUNISHMENT. *Public Interest 1976 (44): 104-114.* From 1870-1960's American penology subscribed to the ideals of rehabilitation and indeterminate sentences. In the 1970's there has been a turning away from rehabilitation and a return to determinate sentencing. The sources of this change developed in the 1960's with the New Left attack on American society. Convicts were considered rebels and their rehabilitation a means of remodeling them to an unjust society. This view was forcibly stated in Jessica Mitford's *Kind and Unusual Punishment*, 1973. Some American liberals also joined the attack because of their concern for civil liberties and the rights of individuals. Two recent books which address these issues are *Doing Justice*, the report of the predominantly liberal Committee for the Study of Incarceration, written by Andrew Von Hirsch, and *Punishing Criminals*, by the conservative social scientist, Ernest van den Haag. Von Hirsch, from a civil libertarian point of view, gives precedence to justice over utilitarian considerations. While punishment should be used sparingly, he wants a return to the concept of "desert," with punishment being proportional to the seriousness of the crime. Van den Haag stresses the importance of defending the social order over doing justice to the individual, and calls for the preventive confinement of dangerous offenders beyond the terms of punishment deserved by their crimes.
                                                                    S. Harrow

1357. Pluth, Edward J.   PRISONER OF WAR EMPLOYMENT IN MINNESOTA DURING WORLD WAR II.   *Minnesota Hist. 1975 44(8): 290-303.* The employment of prisoners of war, mainly Germans, in Minnesota agriculture, logging, and factory operations during 1943-45 was of considerable economic importance to the state. The prisoners made a valuable contribution in crop harvesting and canning, less so in logging and factory work. Community resistance to housing prisoners of war in or near populated areas was less than expected. The opposition of labor unions to the use of prisoner labor, especially in the lumbering industry, did not prevent the employment of such labor. Based on primary research and oral interviews.   N. Lederer

1358. Pollack, Harriet and Smith, Alexander B. COURTS AS A VEHICLE FOR PRISON REFORM. *Judicature 1973 56(10): 412-418.*

1359. Pritchett, Merrill R. and Shea, William L. THE AFRIKA KORPS IN ARKANSAS, 1943-1946. *Arkansas Hist. Q. 1978 37(1): 3-22.* Approximately 23,000 German prisoners of war, most from Erwin Rommel's Afrika Korps, were quartered in Camp Chaffee, Camp Robinson, and Camp Dermott in Arkansas. Discusses facilities, treatment of prisoners, spare time activities such as sports, music, drama and education, escape attempts, and especially the prisoners' value as agricultural laborers. Primary sources; 2 illus., map, diagram, 32 notes.
                                                                G. R. Schroeder

1360. Radelet, Michael L. RACIAL CHARACTERISTICS AND THE IMPOSITION OF THE DEATH PENALTY. *Am. Sociol. Rev. 1981 46(6): 918-927.* Questions whether death penalty statutes passed after the 1972 Supreme Court decision in Furman v. Georgia successfully eliminate racial disparities in capital cases. Over 600 homicide indictments in 20 Florida counties, 1976-77 were examined, focusing on homicides between strangers. When controlling for race of the victim, the data do not clearly support the hypothesis that race of the defendant is strongly associated with the probability of a first degree murder indictment or the imposition of the death penalty.   J

1361. Rector, Milton G. IMPRISONMENT IN AMERICA. *Crisis 1979 86(5): 166-168.* The United States leads the Western world in the number of people it imprisons. This reflects the public's fear of crime. Overflowing prisons have resulted in a nationwide building program at very high construction and operational costs. The nation needs to review its sentencing policies and put the emphasis on helping the victim and society, not on punishing ourselves.
                                                                A. G. Belles

1362. Riggs, Connie. THE HUMAN SQUIRREL CAGE. *Indiana Hist. Bull. 1975 52(10): 123-126.* Describes the history, design, and operation of the Montgomery County Jail in Crawfordsville, Indiana, 1883-1973, with remarks on its preservation.   S

1363. Risjord, Norman K. EARLY VIRGINIA: A PRISON WITH OPPORTUNITY. *Virginia Cavalcade 1974 24(2): 62-69.* Many prisoners convicted of political crimes abroad and sent to Yorktown in 1716 readily established themselves as productive citizens in the colony—prominent among them, George and Francis Hume, who provide an early version of the classic American success story.   S

1364. Robinson, James W. and Jensen, Walter, Jr. BREAKING DOWN THE "WALLS OF SILENCE." *Arbitration J. 1974 29(4): 225-246.* Examines the possibility of meaningful prison grievance procedures in the context of legal requirements and institutional needs. S

1365. Rothman, David J. SOCIAL CONTROL: THE USES AND ABUSES OF THE CONCEPT IN THE HISTORY OF INCARCERATION. *Rice U. Studies 1981 67(1): 9-20.* Discusses the meaning of social control, which in 19th- and early 20th-century Great Britain and America was tantamount to a striving after a collective harmony and cohesion in society, based on the notions of human perfectability and progress: a concept that rejected the data of actual prison abuses for the mere rhetoric of humanitarianism; discussion, pp. 75-78.

1366. Schaich, Warren L. and Hope, Diane S. THE PRISON LETTERS OF MARTIN SOSTRE: DOCUMENTS OF RESISTANCE. *J. of Black Studies 1977 7(3): 281-300.* In 1968 Martin Sostre, owner of an Afro-Asian bookstore in Buffalo, New York and a black activist, was convicted of a narcotics offense. He was jailed until 1975 and spent much of this time in solitary confinement. His prison letters reveal how Sostre's dialogue with himself helped him to maintain his resistance both to political authority and to various "postures of victimage" such as cooperation with prison officials, withdrawal into religion or spiritualism, and acceptance of a rigid ideological viewpoint. In the end, Sostre's philosophy was "a strange blending of Marxism, Black Nationalism, yoga, Feminism, spiritualism, and anarchism." Primary and secondary sources; 16 notes, biblio.

D. C. Neal

1367. Schlossman, Steven. END OF INNOCENCE: SCIENCE AND THE TRANSFORMATION OF PROGRESSIVE JUVENILE JUSTICE, 1899-1917. *Hist. of Educ. [Great Britain] 1978 7(3): 207-218.* Examines the educational function of juvenile corrective education as envisioned by American educationalists and jurists in this period. The juvenile court system fostered a philosophy based on the belief that a probationary officer dealing with the young offender at home was most likely to reeducate him. The belief was gradually proved wanting in many ways, and was abandoned by the 1920's. 56 notes.

S

1368. Shakur, Assata (Joanne Chesimard). WOMEN IN PRISON: HOW WE ARE. *Black Scholar 1978 9(7): 8-15.* The author recounts her experiences in New York's Riker's Island Correctional Institution for Women, focusing on treatment, drugs, and backgrounds of the mainly black prison population.

1369. Shedd, Jeffrey. MAKING GOOD(S) BEHIND BARS. *Reason 1982 13(11): 23-32.* Discusses the operation of convict-run businesses in US prisons, focusing on the Maine State Prison in the late 1970's.

1370. Shelden, Randall G. FROM SLAVE TO CASTE SOCIETY: PENAL CHANGES IN TENNESSEE, 1830-1915. *Tennessee Hist. Q. 1979 38(4): 462-478.* In 1831, Tennessee opened its first state prison with an inmate population predominantly white. With the end of slavery, prison became a kind of substitute for servitude. Blacks came to predominate as inmates, and concomitantly convicts began to be leased out as cheap labor. Similarly, urban working-class children were often placed in training schools to control them and to exploit their labor. Based on the author's unpublished PhD dissertation; 63 notes.

1371. Silliman, Lee. 1870: TO THE HANGMAN'S TREE: HELENA'S LAST VIGILANTE EXECUTION. *Montana 1978 28(4): 50-57.* Vigilantes hanged George Wilson and Arthur Compton in Helena, Montana, on 30 April 1870. They were executed for the robbery and beating of an elderly man named George Lenharth. Even though the machinery for administering official justice existed, public outrage and tradition combined to overwhelm the law for the last time in Helena. It was a final convulsive action on the part of citizens who were unconvinced that legal justice deterred violent crime. Discusses the specific incident and the history of vigilante activities in Helena. Based on contemporary newspapers, secondary works, and original materials in the Montana Historical Society, Helena; 6 illus., 10 notes.   R. C. Myers

1372. Sims, Robert C. THE JAPANESE AMERICAN EXPERIENCE IN IDAHO. *Idaho Yesterdays 1978 22(1): 2-10.* About 1900 the Japanese came into Idaho to work on the railroads. They stayed to work in agriculture, despite state and federal discriminatory laws. A new dimension of Japanese American settlement occurred when a World War II relocation camp was set up near Hunt, Idaho. Few people stayed in the area after the war. Their experiences had been too unpleasant. Primary sources; 2 illus., 57 notes.   B. J. Paul

1373. Spencer, Ralph. PRISONERS OF WAR IN CHEYENNE COUNTY, 1943-1946. *Nebraska Hist. 1982 63(3): 438-448.* Around 12,000 prisoners were located in some 20 camps in Nebraska. The article examines the treatment of German and Italian prisoners in the various camps located in Cheyenne County during World War II. Based on interviews, newspapers, and records in the National Archives.   R. Lowitt

1374. Spidle, Jake W. AXIS INVASION OF THE AMERICAN WEST: POWS IN NEW MEXICO, 1942-1946. *New Mexico Hist. R. 1974 49(2): 93-122.* During World War II a prisoner of war camp was built 14 miles southeast of Roswell, New Mexico. Some of the more than 425,000 enemy captives were placed in this camp. American historians have written very little about the prisoner of war camps because little information is available. Rommel's men predominated in the prisoners held in the New Mexico camp. 147 notes.
                                                                    J. H. Krenkel

1375. Strange, Heather and McCrory, Joseph. BULLS AND BEARS ON THE CELL BLOCK. *Society 1974 11(5): 51-59.* Prisoner market systems, a common element in today's rehabilitation programs, can counteract sterility and repetition in prison life.   S

1376. Sunseri, Alvin R., ed. TRANSIENT PRISONER: THE REMINIS-CENCES OF WILLIAM H. GILBERT. *J. of the Illinois State Hist. Soc. 1981 74(1): 41-50.* Memoir and poem composed shortly before William H. Gilbert's death in 1905. Gilbert enlisted with the Chicago Zouaves (Company A) of the 19th Illinois Infantry in 1861 and served for two years before being taken prisoner at the battle of Chickamauga on 20 September 1863. He spent 17 months in prisons at Atlanta, Libby, Pemberton, Andersonville, Charleston, and Florence. On 22 February 1865, while being transferred to Raleigh, he escaped. In all the prisons, the quality of the food was poor and the officers and guards were sadistic. 6 illus., 19 notes.   A. W. Novitsky

1377. Switzer, Walter E. CAPITAL PUNISHMENT. *Pacific Hist. 1979 23(4): 45-80.* On 18 February 1972 the California Supreme Court seemingly brought to an end a judicial and political struggle to prohibit capital punishment in California, a situation that had been building in intensity since the execution of Caryl Chessman in 1960. It declared that the California Constitution prohibited capital punishment. Nine months later California voters negated the decision by approving a constitutional amendment that expressly allowed the death penalty. Examines the events and judicial actions leading up to these two occurrences. Based on federal and state cases and secondary sources; 212 notes, biblio.
H. M. Parker, Jr.

1378. Velez-I., Carlos G. SE ME ACABÓ LA CANCIÓN: AN ETHNOGRAPHY OF NON-CONSENTING STERILIZATIONS AMONG MEXICAN WOMEN IN LOS ANGELES. Mora, Magdalena and DelCastillo, Adelaida R., ed. *Mexican Women in the United States: Struggles Past and Present* (Los Angeles: U. of California Chicano Studies Res. Center, 1980): 71-91. Analyzes the involuntary sterilization of 10 Mexican women. Sterilizations result in the total disruption of the victim's social and psychological well-being. Mainly secondary sources; 17 notes, biblio.
J. Powell

1379. Vodicka, John. PRISON PLANTATION: THE STORY OF ANGOLA. *Southern Exposure 1978 6(4): 32-38.* The Louisiana State Prison at Angola was founded in 1900 to replace the harsh and brutal convict lease system. It has been through the years an establishment run primarily as an agricultural business enterprise worked predominantly by black prisoners. Its history has been characterized by abysmal conditions and punitive treatment of prisoners with sporadic and short-lasting efforts at reform. Although the abuse of convict guards has been eliminated from the prison and new facilities have been constructed, Angola remains today in treatment and attitude toward convicts much as it did in 1931.
N. Lederer

1380. von Hirsch, Andrew. THE AIMS OF IMPRISONMENT. *Current Hist. 1976 71(418): 1-5, 33.* Discusses practices of and rationales for imprisonment and examines three alternative models: "a model that relies on isolating offenders from society; one that is based on general deterrence; and finally, one that employs the moral notion of 'just deserts'."

1381. Weiss, David. SONGS FROM THE YARD: SING SING'S LOST POET. *Am. Heritage 1979 30(6): 18-21.* Discusses the poetry of John T. Connors, an inmate at New York's Sing Sing Prison from 1878 to 1888, and examines six of his harshly humorous poems written about prison life.

1382. Wik, Esther I. THE JAILKEEPER AT SALEM IN 1692. *Essex Inst. Hist. Collections 1975 111(3): 221-227.* Biography of William Dounton, a carpenter in Salem who also functioned as the jailkeeper in Salem, 1692, during the witch trials.

1383. Wilkins, William D. FORGOTTEN IN THE BLACK HOLE: A DIARY FROM LIBBY PRISON. *Civil War Times Illus. 1976 15(3): 36-44.* Discusses conditions in Libby Prison (in Richmond, Virginia), through a diary kept by a federal prisoner of war, William D. Wilkins, 1862.

1384. Williams, Randall. THE LEGACY OF LEGALIZED MURDER. *Southern Exposure 1978 6(4): 70-73.* Despite recent agitation against the death penalty and Supreme Court decisions restricting its application, the population on death row in various states continues to grow. Execution by lethal injection seems to be gaining in popularity among legislators as a "more humane" method of execution as opposed to electrocution and death by hanging. The public growing desperation in regard to crime prevention is a major factor in the rising popularity of administering the death penalty. Reformers emphasize that persons convicted of capital crimes can be successfully rehabilitated and that the death penalty does not deter murder but their claims are increasingly discarded in favor of greater punitive action. N. Lederer

1385. Williams, Walter L., ed. A CONFEDERATE VIEW OF PRISON LIFE: A VIRGINIAN IN FORT DELAWARE, 1863. *Delaware Hist. 1979 18(4): 226-235.* Based on the unpublished diary of Joseph Edward Purvis, Fort Delaware prison was a scene of sickness and death, of monotony and rumors, but also a place of religion among the prisoners who sought solace from their daily torments. The diary describes the daily routine of the prisoners and recounts tales of illness, religious interest, and despair. Purvis survived his prison experience. 10 notes. R. M. Miller

1386. Wilson, James Q. "WHAT WORKS?" REVISITED: NEW FINDINGS ON CRIMINAL REHABILITATION. *Public Interest 1980 (61): 3-17.* Examines evaluative studies of rehabilitative efforts aimed at criminal offenders. Most studies have shown little if any beneficial effects of rehabilitation. Likewise, many studies of the effectiveness of psychotherapy show negative or neutral outcomes. There is some evidence, however, that intelligent, motivated persons benefit both from psychotherapy and rehabilitation. Analyzes Charles A. Murray's and Louis A. Cox, Jr.'s *Beyond Probation* (1979), on chronic delinquents in Chicago who were placed in a variety of rehabilitative and deterrent settings; they found that strictness of supervision produced the greatest reduction in arrest rates. Secondary sources; 5 notes. J. M. Herrick

1387. Winfree, L. Thomas and Griffiths, C. Taylor. AN EXAMINATION OF FACTORS RELATED TO THE PAROLE SURVIVAL OF AMERICAN INDIANS. *Plains Anthropologist 1975 20(70, Part 1): 311-319.* This paper examines the parole survival of American Indians and non-American Indians released from a Western state prison. In order to determine whether the parole outcome exists independent of the ethnicity of the parolee, six pre-prison, prison and post-prison experiences were statistically associated with the parole outcome. The analysis reveals that the parole survival of the offender is in large part independent of ethnicity. Since the objective measures, or the experiences of the offenders, fail to explain the differences in the parole survival rates, the research suggests that attention should be focused on the activities of judges, parole boards and the parole officers in the field, for they have a great deal of discretion in the determination of parole survival. J

1388. Wolfgang, Marvin E. and Riedel, Marc. RACE, JUDICIAL DISCRETION, AND THE DEATH PENALTY. *Ann. of the Am. Acad. of Pol. and Social Sci. 1973 (407): 119-133.* "The record of executions in the United States has long shown that black defendants are disproportionately subjected to this sanction. But racial differentials in the use of the death penalty may not alone reveal the existence of racial discrimination. The Supreme Court in the *Furman* decision ruled that the death penalty is unconstitutional because it is a 'cruel and unusual' punishment. Some allusions to racial discrimination appeared in the opinions, but more evidence seems called for. Some earlier studies of racial differentials in sentencing are reviewed, followed by a summary of the research procedure and conclusions from an elaborate study of sentencing for rape in states where that offense has been a capital crime. Strong statistically significant differences in the proportions of blacks sentenced to death, compared to whites, when a variety of nonracial aggravating circumstances are considered, permit the conclusion that the sentencing differentials are the product of racial discrimination."

J

1389. Wollenberg, Charles. SCHOOLS BEHIND BARBED WIRE. *California Hist. Q. 1976 55(3): 210-217.* A brief survey of the public school system set up by the War Relocation Authority for the children of Japanese Americans sent to the relocation centers in World War II. Of 110,000 evacuees, 25,000 were school age children. The public schools sought to teach American ideals within the hypocritical framework of prison camps. Supplies, equipment, books, and teachers were characterized as second-rate. Yet school life offered continuity amid the shattering effect of relocation. The traditional emphasis on education continued through the war years. Despite imprisonment because of race and shortcomings in the schools, most Nisei remained committed to the ideals of assimilation and education. Based on contemporary and secondary published works; photos, 24 notes.   A. Hoffman

1390. Wynne, John M., Jr. UNIONS AND BARGAINING AMONG EMPLOYEES OF STATE PRISONS. *Monthly Labor Rev. 1978 101(3): 10-16.* Unionization of employees during the 1970's in state prisons has improved employee economic benefits and working conditions through collective bargaining and lobbying, but gains for employees have not necessarily improved the penal institutions (because of resultant conflict and restrictions on prison authorities).

1391. Zavoral, Nolan. ALWAYS THE SPECTRE OF PRISON: BRINGING THE PRIVATE HELLS OF FORMER INMATES TO WISCONSIN COMMUNITIES. *Arts in Soc. 1975 12(1): 66-73.* Interviews four ex-convicts who toured Wisconsin in a play about prisons, *Halfway to Somewhere*, during 1973-74.   S

1392. Zeigler, Herb. PRISON: WHAT'S IT ALL ABOUT? *Society 1974 11(5): 67-69.* An inmate of Folsom State Prison reports on the failings of the California Department of Corrections.   S

1393. Zimmer, Lynn and Jacobs, James B. CHALLENGING THE TAYLOR LAW: PRISON GUARDS ON STRIKE. *Industrial and Labor Relations Rev. 1981 34(4): 531-544.* In analyzing the 1979 strike by nearly all of the prison guards in New York, focuses on the social organization of the prison environment and the guards' changing occupational role as critical causes of the New York State prison guard strike. Collective bargaining is not well suited to resolving those problems, and in fact the bargaining system may have aggravated them. It was the state's use of National Guard troops and the application of Taylor Law sanctions, rather than any bargaining strategy by either party, that brought the guards back to work.   J/S

1394.   Zumbrunnen, Wanita A.   THE WHITE PALACE OF THE WEST. *Palimpsest 1978 59(3): 88-97.* Details the planning, construction, and early history of the Anamosa Reformatory of Iowa. Most responsible for the choice of the prison location was State Senator John McKean of Anamosa. The prison has been in constant use since 1874 and was nicknamed "the white palace of the West" because of its locally quarried, cut-stone walls. Based on archival and published sources; 4 photos, note.   T. M. Heskin

1395.   —.   THE FAITH OF CALIFORNIA'S JEWISH PRISONERS—1922. *Western States Jewish Hist. Q. 1982 14(3): 245-247.* William R. Blumenthal, secretary of the Jewish Committee for Personal Service in the State Institutions, initiated a social service program for Jews in state prisons, including Folsom Prison. Blumenthal, and other participants, held religious services in the prisons, visited the families of prisoners, and helped settle their business matters. The prisoners were encouraged by these charities to overcome the circumstances that caused their temporary social failures. Reprinted from *Emanu-El,* San Francisco, 13 October 1922.   B. S. Porter

1396.   —.   [MAY 1970 RIOT].   *Richmond County Hist. 1975 7(2): 103-119.* Smith, John M., Jr.   THE RIOT OF MAY 1970: A HUMANISTIC PERSPEC-TIVE,   *pp. 103-115.* Discusses an 11 May 1970 race riot ostensibly set off by the death of a black juvenile inmate in the Augusta county jail purportedly because of police brutality. 19 notes.
Walker, Ralph.   REACTION,   *pp. 117-118.*
Washington, I. E.   REACTION,   *p. 119.*

SUBJECT INDEX

Subject Profile Index (ABC-SPIndex) carries both generic and specific index terms. Begin a search at the general term but also look under more specific or related terms.

Each string of index descriptors is intended to present a profile of a given article; however, no particular relationship between any two terms in the profile is implied. Terms within the profile are listed alphabetically after the leading term. The variety of punctuation and capitalization reflects production methods and has no intrinsic meaning; e.g., there is no difference in meaning between "History, study of" and "History (study of)."

Cities, towns, and counties are listed following their respective states or provinces; e.g., "Ohio (Columbus)." Terms beginning with an arabic numeral are listed after the letter Z. The chronology of the bibliographic entry follows the subject index descriptors. In the chronology, "c" stands for "century"; e.g., "19c" means "19th century."

Note that "United States" is not used as a leading index term; if no country is mentioned, the index entry refers to the United States alone. When an entry refers to both Canada and the United States, both "Canada" and "USA" appear in the string of index descriptors, but "USA" is not a leading term. When an entry refers to any other country and the United States, only the other country is indexed.

The last number in the index string, in italics, refers to the bibliographic entry number.

A

Abbe, Charles E. Florida. Grismer, Karl H. Murder. Sara Sota Vigilance Committee. Trials. 1884-86. *375*

Abolition Movement. Brown, John. Harpers Ferry raid. North Carolina. Sectional Conflict. State Politics. 1840-60. *554*

—. Democratic Party. New York (Utica). Proslavery Sentiments. Riots. 1835. *583*

—. Illinois (Alton). Lovejoy, Elijah P. (murder). Missouri (St. Louis). St. Louis *Observer* (newspaper). Violence. 1833-37. *299*

—. Pennsylvania Hall (burning). Pennsylvania (Philadelphia). Riots. Women. 1833-37. *514*

Acculturation. Alcoholism. Indians. Murder. Navajo Indians. 1956-65. *369*

—. Cuban Americans. Drug abuse. Immigration. Social Customs. Values. Youth. 1950-80. *912*

Adolescence. Attitudes. Police. 1970's. *1100*

—. Conformity. Educational pressure, parental. Marijuana use. 1969-71. *951*

Adolescents. Behavior. Graffiti. New York City. Subways. 1969-82. *464*

—. Drug abuse. Marijuana. New York. 1953-73. *886*

Adultery. Capital Punishment. Connecticut (Hartford). Johnson, Elizabeth (trial). Newton, Thomas. Witchcraft (supposed). 1648-92. *874*

Advertising. Circus. Rat sheets. 1870-1910. *506*

Africa. Barry, Marion. City Government. District of Columbia. Negroes. *Washington Post* (newspaper). 1979. *748*

Age. Punishment. 1970's. *22*

Aged. Crime, fear of. Social Problems. 1970-80. *282*

—. Crime waves. Ideology. Mass Media. New York City. 1976. *73*

—. Crisis, rhetoric of. Public Opinion. 1971-75. *47*

Aggression, verbal. Boys. Communications Behavior. Films. Juvenile Delinquency. Violence. 1970's. *226*

Agnew, Spiro T. Ethics. Morality, public. Political Corruption. Watergate Scandal. 1960's-70's. *773*

Agricultural Labor. Farmers. Industrial Workers of the World. Labor Disputes. Ranchers. Washington (Yakima Valley). 1910-36. *584*

Agriculture. Convict Labor. Louisiana State Prison (Angola). Prisons. Working Conditions. 1900-78. *1379*

—. Idaho. Internment. Japanese Americans. Railroads. World War II. 1900-45. *1372*

Airplanes. Economic Conditions. Hijacking. 1961-76. *134*

Alabama. Arrests. Burr, Aaron. Documents. Perkins, Nicholas. 1807. *785*

—. Capital Punishment. Harris, Johnny (interview). Judicial Process. Prisons. Racism. 1979. *377*

—. Ethics. Law. Political Corruption. State Politics. 1970's. *656*

—. Military. Racism. Randolph, Ryland. Reconstruction. Trials. Tuscaloosa *Independent Monitor*. 1868. *316*

—. NAACP. Norris, Clarence. Pardon request. Scottsboro Case. 1931-76. *373*

Alabama (Birmingham). Anti-Communist Movements. Floggings. Gelders, Joseph. Giles, G. C. Letters. Police. 1936. *353*

—. Baxley, William. Bombings. Chambliss, Robert. Murder. State Government. Trials. 1963-78. *384*

—. Gelders, Joseph. Labor Unions and Organizations. Violence. 1930's. *352*

Alabama (Butler County). Lynching. Negroes. 1895. *315*

Alabama (Eutaw). Politics. Reconstruction. Riots. Terrorism. 1870. *550*

Alabama (Mobile). Donal, Michael Lee. Lynching. 1981. *342*

Alabama (Perry County). Frontier and Pioneer Life. 1820-32. *106*

Alabama (Scottsboro). Historiography. Myths and Symbols. Racism. Trials. 1931-80. *266*

Alabama (Selma). Constitutional Law. *Fikes* v. *Alabama* (US, 1957). Fikes, William Earl. Supreme Court. 1948-75. *1138*

Anti-Catholicism. Anti-Irish sentiments. Cheverus, Jean Louis Lefebvre de. Lyon, Marcus (murder). Massachusetts (Northampton). Trials. 1805-06. *312*
—. Arson. Mary Edmond St. George, Sister. Massachusetts (Boston; Charlestown). Riots. Sex roles. Ursuline Convent. 1834. *563*
—. Carmelites, Discalced. Maryland (Baltimore). Nativism. Riots. 1830-60. *575*
—. Massachusetts (Charlestown). Riots. Ursulines. 1834. *593*
Anti-Communist Movements. Alabama (Birmingham). Floggings. Gelders, Joseph. Giles, G. C. Letters. Police. 1936. *353*
—. Alien Anarchist Act (US, 1918). Congress. Law Enforcement. Leftism. Post, Louis F. 1919-20. *642*
—. Caute, David (review article). Communist Party. Law Enforcement. Liberalism. National Security. USSR. 1945-54. *709*
—. Committee of State Security (KGB). Espionage. Hiss, Alger. Oswald, Lee Harvey. USSR. 1938-78. *139*
—. Emergency detention. McCarran Internal Security Act (1950). 1950-71. *1324*
—. Internal Security Act (US, 1950). Mundt, Karl. 1947-50. *1089*
—. Louisiana (New Orleans). School Integration. Senate Internal Security Subcommittee. Southern Conference Educational Fund Inc. Williams, Aubrey W. 1954. *774*
Anti-Gallows Movement. Capital punishment. Law Reform. Rhode Island. 1838-52. *1327*
Anti-Irish sentiments. Anti-Catholicism. Cheverus, Jean Louis Lefebvre de. Lyon, Marcus (murder). Massachusetts (Northampton). Trials. 1805-06. *312*
Anti-lynching law of 1894. Law Reform. Ohio. Smith, Harry C. Tourgée, Albion W. 1890-96. *1284*
Antinomian controversy. Hutchinson, Anne (criminal trial). Massachusetts (Boston). Puritans. Winthrop, John. 1634-38. *747*
Antique swindle. Military antiques, fraudulent. 1970-76. *459*
Anti-Radicals. Ashburn, George W. (murder). Georgia. Reconstruction. Trials. 1868. *317*
Anti-Saloon League. New Mexico. Prohibition. 1910-17. *828*
Anti-Semitism. Juvenile Delinquency. New York (Long Island). 1980-81. *493*
Antitrust. Justice Department (Antitrust Division). Price fixing. 1963-73. *472*
—. Law Enforcement. Public Opinion. 1890's-1970's. *160*
Anti-Vietnam War movement. Civil rights. Kennedy, Jane. Oral history. Political Protest. Women. 1964-77. *1289*
Appalachia. Cherokee Indians, Eastern. Indians. Violence. 1970's. *80*
Appellate courts. Attitudes. Evidence. *Mapp* v. *Ohio* (US, 1961). *Miranda* v. *Arizona* (US, 1966). Police. 1961-78. *982*
—. Constitutional Law. New York. Supreme Court. 1960-76. *1082*
—. Court opinions. 1931-72. *1170*
—. Decisionmaking. Judicial Process. 1965-75. *8*
Applegate, Jesse. Judicial process. Overland Journeys to the Pacific. 1840's-60's. *138*
Arab-Israeli conflict. Assassination. Kennedy, Robert F. Psychoanalysis. Sirhan, Sirhan B. 1948-68. *780*
Arapaho Indians. Cheyenne Indians. Dawes Act (US, 1887). Fraud. Indians (agencies). Land allotment. Oklahoma. 1910's. *458*

Archbald, Robert Wodrow. Commerce Court (US). Conflicts of interest. Congress. Impeachment. Pennsylvania. 1912-13. *743*
Architecture. American Revolution. Atlee, William Augustus. Barracks. Pennsylvania (Lancaster). Prisoners of War. 1777. *1351*
Archives. Documents. Historiography. Photographs. Theft. 1950's-78. *503*
Arizona. Anecdotes. Outlaws. 1880-1900. *46*
—. Bai-a-lil-le (medicine man). Courts. Fort Huachuca. Indian Rights Association. Navajo Indians. Utah, southeastern. 1906-09. *590*
—. Ballads. Capital Punishment. "Corrido de los Hermanos" (ballad). Hernández, Federico. Hernández, Manuel. 1934. *414*
—. Cameron, Ralph Henry. Senate. 1920-27. *728*
—. Conscription, military. Indians. Papago Indians. Pia Machita (leader). Political Protest. 1930-41. *673*
—. Dake, Crawley P. Law enforcement. 1878-81. *981*
—. Fraud. Government. Law. Real estate. Tombstone Townsite Co. 1880's. *500*
—. Gila River Relocation Center. Japanese Americans. Race Relations. World War II (concentration camps, public opinion). 1942-45. *1249*
—. Ku Klux Klan. 1921-25. *1*
—. Law. Mormons. Polygamy. 1880's. *816*
—. Myths and Symbols. Outlaws. Ringo, John. Texas. 1864-82. *33*
Arizona (Phoenix). Draft (refusal). Immigration. Molokans. World War I (conscientious objectors). 1917-19. *1341*
—. Lynching. 1879. *448*
Arizona (St. Michael's). Day, Samuel Edward, Jr. Dugan, Frank. Law Enforcement. Murder. Navajo Indians. 1920's. *430*
Arizona (Shivwits Plateau). Dunn, William. Grand Canyon expedition. Howland brothers. Paiute Indians. 1869. *297*
—. Dunn, William. Howland brothers. Indian Wars. Murder. Paiute Indians. Walapai Indians. 1866-69. *323*
Arizona (Solomonville). Juries (fixed). McIntosh, Otis. Murder. 1902. *45*
Arizona (Tombstone). Elder, Kate. Gunfights. O.K. Corral. 1870's-80's. *301*
Arizona (Tucson). Drachman, Mose (memoirs). Gambling. 1880-93. *847*
Arkansas. Civil War (personal narratives). Fort Hindman (battle). Foster, Samuel F. Prisoners of War. 1863. *1278*
—. Germany. Prisoners of war. World War II. 1943-46. *1359*
Arkansas (Elaine). Farmers, tenant. Race Relations. Sharecroppers. Violence. 1919. *442*
Arkansas State Penitentiary. Convict lease system. Democratic administrations. Prisoners, abuse of. 1874-96. *1231*
Armies. American Federation of Labor. Police. Streetcars. Strikes. Tennessee (Knoxville). 1919-20. *516*
—. Drugs. Mexico. New Mexico (Columbus). Pershing, John J. Prostitution. Punitive expeditions. Venereal disease. 1916-17. *932*
Arnold, Benedict. American Revolution. Public Opinion. Treason. 1775-83. *772*
Arnold, Philip. Fraud. Mines. Ralston, William Chapman. Slack, John. Utah. 1872. *465*
Arrest rates. Alcoholism. California (Los Angeles). Urbanization. 1898-1970. *907*
—. Boarding schools. Indians. Rule-breaking. 1976. *122*
Arrests. Alabama. Burr, Aaron. Documents. Perkins, Nicholas. 1807. *785*

—. Behavior. Missouri (St. Louis). Organizations. Police. Statistics. 1900-70. *1205*

—. Cities. Law Enforcement. Public places. 1860-1980. *176*

—. Men. Police. Women. 1972. *207*

—. Men. Statistics. Women. 1965-77. *252*

Arrests, false. Drug Abuse. Lawrence, Paul. Police. Vermont (St. Albans). 1967-74. *869*

Arson. Anti-Catholicism. Mary Edmond St. George, Sister. Massachusetts (Boston; Charlestown). Riots. Sex roles. Ursuline Convent. 1834. *563*

—. New York (Albany). Slavery. 1793-99. *469*

—. Preservation. 1975-81. *501*

Artifacts, pre-Columbian. Law. Mexico. National Stolen Property Act (US, 1976). *United States* v. *McClain* (US, 1973). 1973-77. *499*

Arts. Europe. Popular Culture. USA. Violence. 20c. *264*

Ashburn, George W. (murder). Anti-Radicals. Georgia. Reconstruction. Trials. 1868. *317*

Asian Americans. Prisons. Protest groups, formation of. 1974. *1252*

Assassination. Arab-Israeli conflict. Kennedy, Robert F. Psychoanalysis. Sirhan, Sirhan B. 1948-68. *780*

—. Attitudes. Black Nationalism. Malcolm X. Political commentary. 1965. *776*

—. Booth, John Wilkes. Diaries. *Lincoln Conspiracy* (book, film). Stanton, Edwin M. 1865. 1977. *689*

—. Booth, John Wilkes. District of Columbia. Lincoln, Abraham. Sawyer, Frederick A. (eyewitness account). 1865. *765*

—. Booth, John Wilkes. Fiction. Lincoln, Abraham. 1865-1979. *699*

—. Booth, John Wilkes. Firearms. Lincoln, Abraham. Weapons. 1865. *649*

—. Booth, John Wilkes. Identification. Lincoln, Abraham. Tattoos. Virginia (Bowling Green area). 1865. *698*

—. Booth, John Wilkes. Lincoln, Abraham. 1865. *615*

—. Caldwell, Thomas S. Harris, A. H. Louisiana (Franklin Parish). State Politics. 1873. *405*

—. Capital Punishment. Garfield, James A. Guiteau, Charles. Trials. 1881-82. *789*

—. Cermak, Anton. Florida (Miami). Roosevelt, Franklin D. Zangara, Giuseppe. 1933. *658*

—. Colby, Thomas. Colfax County War. Land. Maxwell Grant. New Mexico. 1875-1900. *398*

—. Committee of State Security (KGB). Epstein, Edward J. Kennedy, John F. McMillan, Priscilla Johnson. Oswald, Lee Harvey (review article). 1960-78. *718*

—. Conspiracies. Lincoln, Abraham. Risvold, Floyd (review article). Trials. Weichmann, Louis J. (account). 1864-66. *792*

—. Conspiracy. Due process. Lincoln, Abraham. 1865-68. *1073*

—. Conspiracy. Lincoln, Abraham. Mental Illness (alleged). Trials. Weichmann, Louis J. 1865. 1895. *556*

—. Conspiracy theory. Historiography. Lincoln, Abraham (assassination). Public opinion. Trials. 1865-67. *793*

—. Conspiracy theory. Kennedy, John F. Warren Commission. 1960's-79. *736*

—. Criminal investigations. District of Columbia. Lincoln, Abraham. Police. Richards, A. C. Trials. 1865-69. *758*

—. Criminal investigations. Historiography. Lincoln, Abraham. Stanton, Edwin M. Trials. 1865-1980. *631*

—. Florida (Dry Tortugas). Fort Jefferson. Johnson, Andrew. Lincoln, Abraham. Mudd, Samuel A. (pardon). 1865-96. *759*

—. Garfield, James A. Guiteau, Charles. Mental Illness. 1860's-82. *752*

—. Goebel, William Justus. Governors. Powers, Caleb. 1856-99. 1910-20. *651*

—. Gray, John P. Moral insanity. New York State Lunatic Asylum. Psychiatry. Religion. Trials. 1854-86. *1196*

—. Gun control. Presidency. Public opinion. Sociopaths. 1950's-70's. *801*

—. Hennessy, David. Italian Americans. Louisiana (New Orleans). Nativism. *State of Louisiana* v. *Natali et al.* (1891). Vigilantism. 1890-91. *302*

—. Hill, Marvin S. Illinois (Carthage). Mormons. Oaks, Dallin H. Smith, Joseph. Trials (review article). 1844. 1977. *345*

—. Kennedy, John F. 1960's. *712*

—. Lincoln, Abraham. Surratt, Mary. Trials. Weichmann, Louis J. Witnesses. 1865. *681*

—. Mass Media. Political change. Presidents. 1950-80. *782*

—. Presidency. Secret Service. 1804-1981. *720*

—. Psychology. 1835-1975. *648*

Assassination, attempted. Florida (Miami). Roosevelt, Franklin D. Zangara, Giuseppe. 1933. *771*

—. Jackson, Andrew. Lawrence, Richard. 1835. *636*

—. Jackson, Andrew. Lawrence, Richard. Politics. 1835. *768*

—. Jackson, Andrew. Lawrence, Richard. Wilde, Richard Henry (letter). 1834-35. *791*

Assassination (theories). Sirhan, Sirhan B. 1967-75. *627*

Assault. Courts. Criminal law. Economic growth. North Carolina. 1720-40. *1171*

—. Criminal justice system. Negroes. Rape. Robberies. 1960's-70's. *108*

Assimilation. Feinberg, Siegmund. Jews. Schwartz, Benedict. Texas. 1857. *358*

—. Indian-White Relations. Prisons. 1975. *1240*

Assiniboine Indians. Cypress Hills Massacre. Indians. Law. Liquor trade. 1873. *335*

Association of Southern Women for the Prevention of Lynching. Ames, Jessie Daniel. Lynching. South. Women. 1928-42. *381*

Atlantic Ocean. Pirates. Social Organization. 1716-26. *204*

Atlee, William Augustus. American Revolution. Architecture. Barracks. Pennsylvania (Lancaster). Prisoners of War. 1777. *1351*

Atomic Energy Commission. Espionage. Federal Bureau of Investigation. Greenglass, David. Nuclear Arms. Rosenberg case. Trials. 1942-74. *738*

—. Greenglass, David. Nuclear Science and Technology. Rosenberg case. Secrecy. Trials. 1945-51. *613*

Atomic power plants. Terrorism. 1974. *489*

Attica State Prison. New York. Prison reform. Riots. 1971. *1233*

—. New York. Prison riots. Wicker, Tom (review article). 1970's. *1347*

Attitude shifts. Police. Racial animosity, increases in. 1970's. *1182*

Attitudes. Adolescence. Police. 1970's. *1100*

—. Appellate courts. Evidence. *Mapp* v. *Ohio* (US, 1961). *Miranda* v. *Arizona* (US, 1966). Police. 1961-78. *982*

—. Assassination. Black Nationalism. Malcolm X. Political commentary. 1965. *776*

—. Barrios. California, southern. Civil Rights. Mexican Americans. Police. Social Conditions. 1975. *171*

—. Bristow, Edward. Connelly, Mark. Davidson, Sue. Gorham, Deborah. Great Britain. Prostitution (review article). Rosen, Ruth. Women. 1864-1920. *960*

—. Brownmiller, Susan (review article). Feminism. Rape. 1976. *416*
—. California. Civil liberties. Civil liberties. Mexican Americans. Police. Whites. 1971-80. *172*
—. California (San Francisco). Law enforcement. Prostitution. 1880-1934. *936*
—. Capital Punishment. Pennsylvania (Mansfield). Photographs. 1898. *1323*
—. Court records. Law Enforcement. New England. Sodomy. 1630-80. *911*
—. Discrimination. Drug control. Legislation. Police. 1914-76. *920*
—. Films. Heroes. Psychopaths. 1947-76. *59*
—. Friends, Society of. New York (Auburn). Pennsylvania. Prisons. Reform. Religion. 1787-1845. *1296*
—. Gambling. Law. Nevada. 1931. *849*
—. Homosexuals. Sex roles. 1969-80. *877*
—. Howard, Martin. Law. Murder. North Carolina. Slavery. 1765-91. *1063*
—. Impeachment. Johnson, Andrew. Letters. Republican Party. Ross, Edmund. 1867-68. *626*
—. Individualism. Literature. Murder. Trials. 1920-29. *304*
—. Labor. Liberals. Rehabilitation. 1950's-78. *1342*
—. Police. Violence. 1978. *1156*
—. Rape. 1970's. *407*
—. Rape. Sociology. 1970's. *321*
—. Rape. Women's movement. 1970's. *305*
—. Violence. 1981. *225*
Attitudes (review article). City Life. Maxfield, Michael G. Merry, Sally Engle. Skogan, Wesley G. 1981. *231*
Audiences. Films. Pornography. 1960's-70's. *929*
Authority. Bay Area Rapid Transit District. California (San Francisco Bay area). Exposés. Organizations. Professionals. 1973-80. *1132*
—. Great Britain (London). New York City. Police. Social order. 1830-70. *1112*
Authors. Hammett, Dashiell. 20c. *18*
—. Literature. Negroes. Political activism. Prisons. 1950's-77. *1279*
Autobiography and Memoirs. Brinkerhoff, Roeliff. Lincoln, Abraham (assassination). 1865. *737*
Avery, William Waightstill. Code of honor. Flemming, Samuel (death). Juries. Murder. North Carolina (Morganton). Upper Classes. 1851. *332*

B

Bahamas (Nassau). *Creole* affair. Great Britain. Mutinies. Slave Revolts. 1841. *557*
Bai-a-lil-le (medicine man). Arizona. Courts. Fort Huachuca. Indian Rights Association. Navajo Indians. Utah, southeastern. 1906-09. *590*
Bail bonds. California (San Francisco). City Government. McDonough, Peter P. Vice. 1896-1937. *618*
Bail bondsmen. Courts, criminal. Social control. 1975. *1020*
Bail Reform Act (1965). District of Columbia. Violence. 1976. *1238*
Baker, Ella Jo (interview). Civil Rights Organizations. Hamer, Fannie Lou (interview). Mississippi. Murder. Students. 1964. *609*
Baker, Howard. Presidency. Watergate Scandal. 1972-73. *753*
Baker, James. Murder. Park, Hugh. Washington (Shaw Island). 1885. *343*

Baker, Newton D. Liquor. Military training. Prostitution. Texas (El Paso). War Department. World War I. 1917-18. *834*
Baldwin-Felts Detectives. Coal Mines and Mining. Law Enforcement. West Virginia (southern). 1890's-1935. *1048*
Ballad of the Braswell Boys. Braswell brothers. Capital Punishment. Folk Songs. Tennessee (Putnam County). 1875-78. *350*
Ballads. Arizona. Capital Punishment. "Corrido de los Hermanos" (ballad). Hernández, Federico. Hernández, Manuel. 1934. *414*
Bank robberies. Grand National Bank. Missouri (St. Louis). Vandeventer Securities Co. 1930. *348*
Banking. Western States. 1864-1932. *456*
Banks, savings (review article). Olmstead, Alan L. Osthaus, Carl R. 1819-70's. *495*
Baptists. Fox, George. Friends, Society of. Olney, Thomas, Jr. Politics. Rhode Island. 1672-73. *83*
Barbiturates. Amphetamines. Drug Abuse. 1903-65. *880*
Bargaining. Communications Behavior. Dean, John (resignation). Executive Behavior. Watergate Scandal. 1973. *775*
Barkley, Alben. Gambling, pari-mutuel. Kentucky. Louisville Churchmen's Federation. Progressivism. 1917-27. *934*
Barnard, Kate. Kansas State Penitentiary. Oklahoma. Prisons. Reform. 1908-09. *1302*
—. Kansas State Penitentiary. Political Corruption. Prisons. Reform. Working Conditions. 1883-1909. *1301*
Barnes, William, Jr. Bossism. Lawsuits. New York. Republican Party. Roosevelt, Theodore. 1915. *629*
Barracks. American Revolution. Architecture. Atlee, William Augustus. Pennsylvania (Lancaster). Prisoners of War. 1777. *1351*
Barrios. Attitudes. California, southern. Civil Rights. Mexican Americans. Police. Social Conditions. 1975. *171*
Barry, Marion. Africa. City Government. District of Columbia. Negroes. *Washington Post* (newspaper). 1979. *748*
Barry, Marion (interview). Civil Rights Organizations. Lewis, John (interview). Nonviolence. Sit-ins. Tennessee (Nashville). 1960. *610*
Bass, Sam. Billy the Kid. Floyd, Charles Arthur "Pretty Boy". Folklore. Heroes. James, Jesse. Outlaws. 1860-1934. *169*
Bath Consolidated School. Kehoe, Andrew. Michigan. Murder. 1927. *394*
Baxley, William. Alabama (Birmingham). Bombings. Chambliss, Robert. Murder. State Government. Trials. 1963-78. *384*
Bay Area Rapid Transit District. Authority. California (San Francisco Bay area). Exposés. Organizations. Professionals. 1973-80. *1132*
Beatty, James H. Coxey, Jacob S. Idaho. Political Protest. Trials. 1894. *602*
Becarria, Cesare. Capital punishment. Italy. Penal reform. USA. 1764-97. *1328*
Behavior. Adolescents. Graffiti. New York City. Subways. 1969-82. *464*
—. Arrests. Missouri (St. Louis). Organizations. Police. Statistics. 1900-70. *1205*
—. Bomb threats. Mass media. Terrorism. 1966-80. *158*
—. Civil disturbances, control of. National Guard. 1975. *518*
—. Drugs. High schools. Puerto Rico. Youth. 1970-80. *927*
—. Great Britain. News. Suicide. Werther effect. 1947-68. *915*
—. Police. 1978. *1021*

Behavior, antisocial. Drug Abuse. 1975. *955*
Behavior modification. Center for Correctional Research. Prison system. United Church of Christ (Commission for Racial Justice). 1974. *1255*
Behavioral differences. Defendants (sex of). Judges, male and female. Rape. 1968. *363*
Behaviorism. Civil disturbances. Riots. 1955-75. *542*
Belcher, Jonathan. Colonial government. Dunk, George Montagu. Land ownership. Law Enforcement. Morris, Robert Hunter. New Jersey. Riots. 1748-53. *545*
Belgium (Brussels). International Tribunal on Crimes Against Women. Women. 1976. *217*
Bell, William H. Diaries. Law Enforcement. New York City. 1850-51. *272*
Bench trials. Trials. 1607-1950. *1190*
Berkowitz, David ("Son of Sam"). Folklore. Murder. New York City. Reporters and Reporting. 1977. *443*
Bernstein, Carl. Journalism (magnified role). Politics and Media. Watergate scandal. Woodward, Bob. 1972-74. *667*
Betenson, Lula Parker (interview). Cassidy, Butch (Robert Leroy Parker). Outlaws. 1905-25. 1975. *309*
Bibliographies. Detective fiction. Fiction. Literary criticism. 1840's-1970's. *159*
—. Fiction. Nonfiction. Sacco-Vanzetti Case. 1920-27. *310*
—. Indians. 1945-79. *157*
—. Political repression. 1963-81. *1154*
—. Riots. 1700-1850. *540*
—. Violence. Women, battered. 1970's. *453*
Big Sleep (film). Bogart, Humphrey. Kinesics. *Maltese Falcon* (film). 1941-46. *270*
Bill of Rights. Civil Rights. Prisons. 1970's. *1245*
Billy the Kid. Bass, Sam. Floyd, Charles Arthur "Pretty Boy". Folklore. Heroes. James, Jesse. Outlaws. 1860-1934. *169*
Birth cohort. Juvenile delinquents. Methodology. Pennsylvania (Philadelphia). 1964-73. *279*
Birth control. Law. Medicine and State. Public Policy. 19c. *868*
Bittman, William. Criminal prosecution (avoidance). Lawyers. O'Brien, Paul. Watergate Scandal. 1972-73. *756*
Black Liberation Army. Boudin, Kathy. Leftism. Terrorism. Weather Underground. 1967-81. *659*
Black Nationalism. Assassination. Attitudes. Malcolm X. Political commentary. 1965. *776*
—. Federal Bureau of Investigation. Operation Cointelpro. Operation Newkill. 1968-71. *1116*
Black Power. Ghettos. Prisons. 1970's. *1311*
Black Star Organization. NAACP. Police. Race Relations. South Carolina. Violence. 1975. *1181*
Blackburn, Gideon. Cherokee Indians. Indians. Missions and Missionaries. Presbyterian Church. Schools. Whiskey. 1809-10. *164*
Blackmail. Illinois (Chicago). Kefauver, Estes. Korshak, Sidney R. Organized Crime. Senate Committee to Investigate Organized Crime. 1950-76. *178*
Blackouts. Looting. New York City. Poverty. 1977. *521*
Blocker, Jack S., Jr. Bordin, Ruth. Epstein, Barbara Leslie. Temperance Movements (review article). Tyrrell, Ian R. 19c. *842*
Blumenthal, William R. California. Jewish Committee for Personal Service in the State Institutions. Prisons. Social Work. 1922. *1395*

Boarding schools. Arrest rates. Indians. Rule-breaking. 1976. *122*
Body-snatching. Boyd, Ben. Kinealy, James. Lincoln, Abraham. 1874-88. *486*
—. Illinois (Springfield). Lincoln, Abraham. Mullen, Terrance. 1876. *131*
Bogart, Humphrey. *Big Sleep* (film). Kinesics. *Maltese Falcon* (film). 1941-46. *270*
Bomb threats. Behavior. Mass media. Terrorism. 1966-80. *158*
Bombing attack. Civil rights. Informers. Jewish Defense League. Legal defenses. Seigel, Sheldon. 1972-73. *322*
Bombing, concealment of. Cambodia. Impeachment (proposed). Nixon, Richard M. Vietnam War (extension of). 1969-74. *653*
Bombings. Alabama (Birmingham). Baxley, William. Chambliss, Robert. Murder. State Government. Trials. 1963-78. *384*
—. California (San Francisco). Mooney, Tom. San Quentin Prison. Socialist Party. Trials. 1916-42. *154*
Bonnie, Richard J. Drug Abuse (review article). Law enforcement. Musto, David F. Whitebread, Charles H., II. 1860's-1974. *921*
Books (editions). Forgeries. Illinois (Chicago). Libraries. Publishers and Publishing. Wise, Thomas. Wrenn, John. 1890-1930. *474*
Booth, John Wilkes. Assassination. Diaries. *Lincoln Conspiracy* (book, film). Stanton, Edwin M. 1865. 1977. *689*
—. Assassination. District of Columbia. Lincoln, Abraham. Sawyer, Frederick A. (eyewitness account). 1865. *765*
—. Assassination. Fiction. Lincoln, Abraham. 1865-1979. *699*
—. Assassination. Firearms. Lincoln, Abraham. Weapons. 1865. *649*
—. Assassination. Identification. Lincoln, Abraham. Tattoos. Virginia (Bowling Green area). 1865. *698*
—. Assassination. Lincoln, Abraham. 1865. *615*
—. Clarke, Asia Booth. Letters. 1852-74. *697*
—. Conspiracy. Eisenschiml, Otto. Kidnapping. Lincoln, Abraham. Research. War Department. 1865. ca 1930-80. *690*
—. Corbett, Thomas H. Lincoln, Abraham. 1832-1908. *364*
—. Oil Industry and Trade. Pennsylvania (northwestern). ca 1858-65. *744*
Bootlegging. Depressions. Florida (Hernando County). Law enforcement. Liquor. Prohibition. 1929-33. *837*
Borden, Lizzie. Massachusetts. Murder. Trials. 1890-1927. *355*
Border policy. Aliens, illegal. Economic Conditions. Mexico. USA. 1952-75. *824*
Bordin, Ruth. Blocker, Jack S., Jr. Epstein, Barbara Leslie. Temperance Movements (review article). Tyrrell, Ian R. 19c. *842*
Bossism. Barnes, William, Jr. Lawsuits. New York. Republican Party. Roosevelt, Theodore. 1915. *629*
—. City Government. Kenny, John V. New Jersey (Jersey City). 1949-72. *731*
—. DeSapio, Carmine. New York. Tammany Hall. 1950's-60's. *657*
Boston Prison Discipline Society. Charlestown state prison. Massachusetts. Penal reformers. 1804-78. *1230*
Boudin, Kathy. Black Liberation Army. Leftism. Terrorism. Weather Underground. 1967-81. *659*
Boundaries. Federalism. Law Enforcement (local). Mexico (Juarez). Texas (El Paso). 1970's. *1003*

Boutwell, George S. House of Representatives. Impeachment. Johnson, Andrew. 1865-68. *662*

Bowden, Joan. Comprehensive Employment and Training Act (US, 1973). Corruption. New Jersey (Atlantic County). 1980-81. *466*

Bowers, J. Milton. California (San Francisco). Converts. Jews. Levy, Cecilia Benhayon. Murder. 1885-89. *424*

Boyd, Ben. Body-snatching. Kinealy, James. Lincoln, Abraham. 1874-88. *486*

Boys. Aggression, verbal. Communications Behavior. Films. Juvenile Delinquency. Violence. 1970's. *226*

Brady, Mathew B. Daguerreotypes (engravings from). Phrenological analysis. Simpson, Marmaduke B. 1846. *255*

Brandenburg v. *Ohio* (US, 1969). Freedom of Speech. Political Speeches. 1969-80. *939*

Branzburg v. *Hayes* (US, 1972). Confidentiality. Constitutional Amendments (1st). Courts. Criminal investigations. Reporters and Reporting. 1972-78. *1074*

Braswell brothers. *Ballad of the Braswell Boys.* Capital Punishment. Folk Songs. Tennessee (Putnam County). 1875-78. *350*

Breckinridge, W. C. P. Democratic Party. House of Representatives. Morality. Political scandals. Pollard, Madeline. Sex. 1884-1904. *888*

Brenham fire. Military Occupation. Reconstruction. Sheridan, Philip A. Texas. 1865-70. *485*

Brewer, John. Hanawalt, Barbara A. Hindus, Michael S. Koehler, Lyle. Northeastern or North Atlantic States. South Carolina. Styles, John. 17c-1878. *113*

Bright, Jesse D. Civil War. Indiana. Senate. Treason. 1861-62. *655*

Brimmer, Clarence A., Jr. District Courts. Kennedy, Thomas Blake. Kerr, Ewing T. Riner, John A. Wyoming. 1890-1982. *1188*

Brinkerhoff, Roeliff. Autobiography and Memoirs. Lincoln, Abraham (assassination). 1865. *737*

Bristow, Edward. Attitudes. Connelly, Mark. Davidson, Sue. Gorham, Deborah. Great Britain. Prostitution (review article). Rosen, Ruth. Women. 1864-1920. *960*

British North America. Constitutional Law. Great Britain. Impeachment. 1680's-1773. *702*

—. Corruption. Europe. National Self-image. 1650-1776. *130*

Brooklyn *Eagle*. Civil War. Gold. Hoaxes. Howard, Joseph. Prices. Stock Exchange. 1864. *504*

Brooks, Preston S. Civil War (antecedents). Congress. Republican Party. Sumner, Charles. Violence. 1856. *683*

Brotherhood of Timber Workers. Emerson, Arthur L. Industrial Workers of the World. Labor Disputes. Louisiana, western. Lumber and Lumbering. Texas, eastern. 1900-16. *535*

Brown, Henry. Kansas (Caldwell). Law Enforcement. Lynching. Medicine Valley Bank. Murder. Robberies, attempted. 1881-84. *306*

Brown, John. Abolition Movement. Harpers Ferry raid. North Carolina. Sectional Conflict. State Politics. 1840-60. *554*

—. Buchanan, James. Harpers Ferry raid. Letters. West Virginia. Wise, Henry Alexander. 1859. *607*

—. Civil War (antecedents). Harpers Ferry raid. North Carolina. Slavery. Social Psychology. 1859-60. *513*

—. Civil War (antecedents). Harpers Ferry Raid. West Virginia. 1859. *562*

—. Harpers Ferry raid. Terrorism. West Virginia. 1859. *548*

Brown, Richard Maxwell (review article). Vigilantes. Violence. 1736-1960's. 1975. *337*

Brownmiller, Susan (review article). Attitudes. Feminism. Rape. 1976. *416*

—. Men. Negroes. Racism. Rape. 1975. *319*

—. Rape. 1300-1975. *412*

Bruce, Dickson D., Jr. Cities. Johnson, David R. Lane, Roger. Police. 19c. *71*

Brutalization hypothesis. Capital Punishment. Life, respect for. Murder. Publicity. South Carolina. 1950-63. *1316*

Buchanan, James. Brown, John. Harpers Ferry raid. Letters. West Virginia. Wise, Henry Alexander. 1859. *607*

Buck's Stove and Range Co. American Federation of Labor. Courts. Criminal conspiracy (doctrine). Labor Law. 1907-11. *700*

Budgets. Institutions. Law Enforcement. Models. Republican Party. 1935-79. *35*

Bull Run (2d battle). Civil War (personal narratives). Libby Prison. Parker, George Claflin. Prisoners of War. Virginia (Alexandria, Richmond). 1862. *1352*

Bureau of Alcohol, Tobacco, and Firearms. Civil Rights (violations). Constitutional Amendments (2nd). 1970-80. *1093*

Bureau of Indian Affairs. Burleigh, Walter M. Indian agents. Taliaferro, Lawrence. 1819-77. *786*

—. Criminal law. Federal Programs. Indian Self-Determination and Educational Assistance Act (US, 1975). 1970-82. *1123*

Bureaucracies. Federal Government. Misconduct in office. Public Employees. 1970's. *677*

—. Juvenile Delinquency. Public Policy. State Government. 1979. *1267*

Bureaucratization. Alberta. Indians. Sentencing. Urbanization. 1973. *99*

Burger, Warren E. Civil Rights. Habeas corpus. Institutions. Supreme Court. Warren, Earl. 1954-77. *1108*

Burleigh, Walter M. Bureau of Indian Affairs. Indian agents. Taliaferro, Lawrence. 1819-77. *786*

Burnham, Joseph. Escapes (supposed). Legislative Investigations. Vermont. Windsor State Prison. 1826-32. *1294*

Burr, Aaron. Alabama. Arrests. Documents. Perkins, Nicholas. 1807. *785*

—. Conspiracies. Treason (alleged). Trials. Wilkinson, James. 1783-1836. *694*

—. Old Southwest. Treason. Trials. 1782-1836. *788*

Burrow, Reuben Huston. Florida. Jackson, Thomas. Private detectives. Railroads. Robberies. 1885-90. *403*

Business. Cities. Communist Party. Government. Negroes. Riots. 1960's. *569*

—. City Politics. Louisiana (New Orleans). Prostitution. Social Reform. Voting and Voting Behavior. 1851-58. *950*

—. Economic Conditions. Morality. Nixon, Richard M. Political support. Watergate scandal. 1969-74. *647*

—. Government. Political Corruption. 17c-1976. *634*

—. Maine State Prison. Prisons. 1978-82. *1369*

—. Organized Crime. 20c. *246*

—. Police. Riot control. Tear gas. Technology. War Department (Chemical Warfare Section). World War I. 1914-23. *559*

—. Violence. 1973-80. *327*

Business community. Ethics. Mormons. Theology. Watergate scandal. 1974. *808*

Butler, Pierce M. Cherokee Indians. Foreman, James. Indian Territory. Murder. Political factionalism. Watie, Stand. 1830-42. *486*

Butler, Smedley D. Law Enforcement. Pennsylvania (Philadelphia). Prohibition. 1924-25. *980*

C

Cain, James M. California (Los Angeles). Depressions. Novels. 1925-45. *72*

Caldwell, Thomas S. Assassination. Harris, A. H. Louisiana (Franklin Parish). State Politics. 1873. *405*

California. Attitudes. Civil liberties. Civil liberties. Mexican Americans. Police. Whites. 1971-80. *172*

—. Blumenthal, William R. Jewish Committee for Personal Service in the State Institutions. Prisons. Social Work. 1922. *1395*

—. Capital punishment. Courts. Elections. 1954-72. *1377*

—. Chandler, Raymond. Fiction. Hammett, Dashiell. Macdonald, Ross. Queen, Ellery. Villains. 1920-79. *189*

—. Chinese. Economic Structure. Family. Prostitution. Women. 1849-1925. *873*

—. Corrections, Department of. Folsom State Prison. Prisons. 1973-74. *1392*

—. Drug Abuse. Great Britain. Hallucinogens. Intellectuals. LSD. Mullendore, William C. 1930-70. *956*

—. Drug abuse. Medical care. Prescriptions. San Francisco Polydrug Project. Women. 1969-79. *841*

—. Durkheim, Emile. Punishment. Social Theory. 1851-1970. *1236*

—. Frank, Leo. Georgia. Jews. Progressivism. Trials. 1913-15. *341*

—. Gold Rushes. Mexican Americans. Murieta, Joaquin. Outlaws. ca 1848-53. *422*

—. Law Enforcement. Prohibition. Thompson, David (account). Winemaking. 1930. *953*

—. Rural-Urban Studies. Social Conditions. Violence. 1955-75. *330*

—. San Quentin Six. Trials. 1974. *1312*

California (Alameda County). Courts. Plea bargaining. Sentencing. 1880-1970's. *1033*

California (Alcatraz Island). Historical Sites and Parks. Indians (government relations). National Park Service. Prisons. 1859-1975. *1309*

California (Anaheim). City Government. Ku Klux Klan. Political Participation. ca 1923-25. *166*

California (Berkeley). Colleges and Universities. Police professionalism. Vollmer, August. 1905-55. *1024*

California (East Los Angeles). Gangs. Machismo (concept). Mexican Americans. Values. Violence. ca 1965-78. *328*

California (Los Angeles). Alcoholism. Arrest rates. Urbanization. 1898-1970. *907*

—. Cain, James M. Depressions. Novels. 1925-45. *72*

—. Chandler, Raymond. Migration, Internal. Novels (detective). Social Change. ca 1930-80. *244*

—. Immigration and Naturalization Service. Industrial Relations. International Ladies' Garment Workers' Union. Lilli Diamond Originals. Mexican Americans. Raids. 1976-77. *957*

—. Mass media. Political Protest. Violence. Women. 1977. *366*

—. Mayors. Recall. Shaw, Frank L. 1933-38. *796*

—. Mexican Americans. Sterilization. Women. 1970-78. *1378*

—. Minorities. Police. Shootings. 1974-79. *1111*

California (Los Angeles County). Drug abuse. Law Enforcement. Rehabilitation. Statistics. 1969-79. *899*

—. Juvenile delinquents. Police labeling. Recidivism. 1974. *129*

—. Law Enforcement. 1850-56. *280*

California (Los Angeles, Orange counties). Community work. Drunk driving cases. Voluntary Action Centers. 1976. *969*

California (North Richmond, Richmond). Juvenile Delinquency. Negroes. Neighborhoods. Riots. 1968. *561*

California (Oakland, San Francisco). Labor. Louisiana (New Orleans). Michigan (Detroit). Police. Racism. 1971-81. *284*

California (Oxnard). Drug abuse programs. Mexican Americans. 1972-73. *810*

California (Rincon). Goldsmith, Simon. Jews. Kallman, George. Murder. 1875-1903. *423*

California (Sacramento). Courts. Land grants. Militia. Riots. Squatters. Sutter, John Augustus. 1850. *523*

California (San Diego). Housing. Ohio (Cleveland). 1970. *214*

—. Photographs. Police. 1889-1980. *1004*

California (San Francisco). Attitudes. Law enforcement. Prostitution. 1880-1934. *936*

—. Bail bonds. City Government. McDonough, Peter P. Vice. 1896-1937. *618*

—. Bombings. Mooney, Tom. San Quentin Prison. Socialist Party. Trials. 1916-42. *154*

—. Bowers, J. Milton. Converts. Jews. Levy, Cecilia Benhayon. Murder. 1885-89. *424*

—. City Government. Courts. Homosexuals. Police. Riots. 1979. *525*

—. City Government. Progressivism. Prostitution. Social Reform. 1910-14. *937*

—. *Euphemia* (vessel). Prison ships. 1849-1921. *1263*

—. Imports. Merchants. Self-interest. Vigilantism. 1849-56. *1158*

—. Police, private. 1850's-1979. *1023*

California (San Francisco Bay area). Authority. Bay Area Rapid Transit District. Exposés. Organizations. Professionals. 1973-80. *1132*

—. Prostitution. Youth. 1981. *940*

California (San Joaquin County). Social Conditions. Values. 1890-1970. *98*

California, southern. Attitudes. Barrios. Civil Rights. Mexican Americans. Police. Social Conditions. 1975. *171*

—. Immigration. Mexico. Operation Wetback. Texas. 1950-74. *930*

California (Watsonville). Depressions. Filipino Americans. Racism. Riots. Violence. 1926-30. *527*

California (Wheatland). Industrial Workers of the World. Migrant Labor. State Government. Strikes. Trials. 1913-17. *522*

Calomiris, Angela. Documentaries. Federal Bureau of Investigation. New York City Photo League. Photography, Journalistic. 1930-51. *988*

Cambodia. Bombing, concealment of. Impeachment (proposed). Nixon, Richard M. Vietnam War (extension of). 1969-74. *653*

Cameras. Florida. Herman, Mark. Mass Media. Supreme courts, state. Trials. Zamora, Ronney. 1977-79. *1012*

Cameron, Ralph Henry. Arizona. Senate. 1920-27. *728*

Cameron, William Evelyn. Conservation of Natural Resources. Fishing. Oysters. State Government. Virginia. 1882-85. *479*

Camp Pratt. Harding, George C. (memoirs). Louisiana (New Iberia). Prisoners of war. 1862. *1235*

Campaign Finance. Connally, John. Watergate scandal. 1973. *692*

—. Nixon, Richard M. Political parties. Watergate scandal. 1968-74. *716*

Canada. Civil rights. Law. Mexico. USA. Violence. 18c-1974. *534*

—. Obscenity. Pornography. President's Commission on Obscenity and Pornography. 1970-75. *931*

Censorship campaigns. Cities. Freedom of the Press. Obscenity law. Supreme Court decisions. 1957-75. *928*

Center for Correctional Research. Behavior modification. Prison system. United Church of Christ (Commission for Racial Justice). 1974. *1255*

Central Intelligence Agency. Cubans. Federal Bureau of Investigation (New Orleans). Oswald, Lee Harvey. 1963. *727*

Cermak, Anton. Assassination. Florida (Miami). Roosevelt, Franklin D. Zangara, Giuseppe. 1933. *658*

Chambers, Whittaker. Communist Party. Espionage. Hiss, Alger. Research. Treason. Weinstein, Allen (review article). 1920's-78. *708*

—. Communist Party. Espionage. Hiss, Alger. Trials. 1934-49. *707*

—. Courts. Hiss, Alger. House Committee on Un-American Activities. Innocence, presumption of. Nixon, Richard M. 1948-76. *732*

—. Espionage. Hiss, Alger. Perjury. Weinstein, Allen (review article). 1930's-50. 1978. *717*

—. Espionage. Hiss, Alger. Perjury. Weinstein, Allen (review article). 1936-50. 1978. *705*

—. Hiss, Alger. House Committee on Un-American Activities. Lawsuits. Libel. Marbury, William L. (account). Perjury. 1922-51. *735*

Chambliss, Robert. Alabama (Birmingham). Baxley, William. Bombings. Murder. State Government. Trials. 1963-78. *384*

Chandler, Raymond. California. Fiction. Hammett, Dashiell. Macdonald, Ross. Queen, Ellery. Villains. 1920-79. *189*

—. California (Los Angeles). Migration, Internal. Novels (detective). Social Change. ca 1930-80. *244*

Charles I. Friends, Society of. Massachusetts Bay Colony. Persecution. 1661. *34*

Charlestown state prison. Boston Prison Discipline Society. Massachusetts. Penal reformers. 1804-78. *1230*

Chase, Samuel. Fries, John. Pennsylvania. Treason (alleged). *United States* v. *John Fries* (US, 1800). 1799-1805. *665*

Cheatham, Mel. Capital Punishment. Mississippi (Grenada County). Murder. Race Relations. Tillman, James. Trials. 1889-90. *400*

Cherokee Indians. Blackburn, Gideon. Indians. Missions and Missionaries. Presbyterian Church. Schools. Whiskey. 1809-10. *164*

—. Butler, Pierce M. Foreman, James. Indian Territory. Murder. Political factionalism. Watie, Stand. 1830-42. *449*

—. Foreman, James. Politics. South. Walker, John, Jr. (assassination). 1820's-30's. *723*

Cherokee Indians, Eastern. Appalachia. Indians. Violence. 1970's. *80*

Cheverus, Jean Louis Lefebvre de. Anti-Catholicism. Anti-Irish sentiments. Lyon, Marcus (murder). Massachusetts (Northampton). Trials. 1805-06. *312*

Cheyenne Indians. Arapaho Indians. Dawes Act (US, 1887). Fraud. Indians (agencies). Land allotment. Oklahoma. 1910's. *458*

Chicopee News. Massachusetts, western. Massachusetts (Westfield). Newspapers. Prostitution. 1911. *952*

Child abuse. Criminal Law. Family courts. Juvenile Courts. 1978. *1159*

—. Family. 1978. *451*

—. Government. Law. 1973-74. *385*

—. Law. 1970's. *339*

—. New York City. Society for the Prevention of Cruelty to Children. 1820's-80's. *420*

Children. Civil Rights. Courts. Whites. 1955-80. *281*

—. Education. New York House of Refuge. Reformatories. 1800-30. *222*

Children (noncriminal). Detention homes. Family Court Act: Persons in Need of Supervision provision (New York). New York. -1974. *1251*

Chinatowns. Tourist business. Vice. 1865-1920. *896*

Chinese. California. Economic Structure. Family. Prostitution. Women. 1849-1925. *873*

Chinese Americans. Capital punishment. Jon, Gee. Nevada (Mina). Sing, Hughie. 1921-24. *1250*

—. Discrimination, Employment. Negroes. Vice industry. 1880-1940. *895*

—. Health. 1960-80. *192*

Chloral hydrate. Cities. "Mickey Finn" (potion). Vice areas. 1850's-1910's. *351*

Christianity (converts). Idaho. Murderers. Orchard, Harry. 1899-1906. *386*

Christie, Ned (Cherokee Indian). Indians (government relations). Justice, concept of. Law and order. 1884-92. *370*

Circus. Advertising. Rat sheets. 1870-1910. *506*

Cities *See also* Metropolitan areas.

—. Arrests. Law Enforcement. Public places. 1860-1980. *176*

—. Bruce, Dickson D., Jr. Johnson, David R. Lane, Roger. Police. 19c. *71*

—. Business. Communist Party. Government. Negroes. Riots. 1960's. *569*

—. Capitalism. Economic Growth. 1950-71. *117*

—. Censorship campaigns. Freedom of the Press. Obscenity law. Supreme Court decisions. 1957-75. *928*

—. Chloral hydrate. "Mickey Finn" (potion). Vice areas. 1850's-1910's. *351*

—. Civil disturbances. Police departments. 1960's-70's. *1083*

—. Civil disturbances. Police departments, functioning of. 1960's-70's. *1207*

—. Civilian review boards. Employee organizations. Police, regulation of. 1958-74. *1053*

—. Consumers. Fraud. Local government. Public Policy. White-collar crime. 1970's. *997*

—. Contagion. Diffusion. Negroes. Police. Riots. 1966-67. *578*

—. Courts. Police. Social Conditions. 1960-75. *146*

—. Crime rates. 1951-70. *121*

—. Crime rates. Crowding. Methodology. ca 1960-75. *287*

—. Crime statistics. Federal Bureau of Investigation. 1974. *241*

—. Crime statistics. Population. 1970's. *85*

—. Criminal justice system (review article). 1970's. *51*

—. Criminology. Police. Statistics. 1840-1977. *1115*

—. Firearms. Police. Violence. 19c. *1129*

—. Folklore. Women. 1976-78. *433*

—. Illinois (Chicago). Loansharking. New York City. 1870's-1960's. *293*

—. Indians. Law. Migration, Internal. Washington (Seattle). 1970's. *39*

—. Law and Society. Police. Public Policy. Robberies. 1970's. *1218*

—. Methodology. Police. Public Records. 1880-1903. 1979. *1114*

—. Monkkonen, Eric H. Police (review article). 1860-1920. *1198*

—. Mosse, George L. Police (review article). Richardson, James F. 19c-20c. *1001*

—. Belcher, Jonathan. Dunk, George Montagu. Land ownership. Law Enforcement. Morris, Robert Hunter. New Jersey. Riots. 1748-53. *545*

—. Partridge, Alexander (execution). Rhode Island. 1652. *257*

Colonization. Government, Resistance to. Indian Wars. Wounded Knee (massacre, occupation). 1805-1980. *587*

Colorado. Drug Abuse. Law. 1870's-90's. *964*

—. Law Enforcement. National Guard. Strikes. 1860-1970. *589*

Colorado (Denver). Prohibition. Wickersham Committee (1931). 1907-33. *866*

Colorado Fuel and Iron Company. Coal Mines and Mining. Ludlow Massacre. National Guard. Strikes. 1913-14. *533*

Colorado, southeastern. Coe, William. New Mexico, northeastern. Outlaws. Robbers' Roost (hideout). ca 1867-68. *260*

Colored Protective Association. Civil Rights. NAACP. Negroes. Pennsylvania (Philadelphia). Riots. 1918. *539*

Colson, Charles. International Telephone and Telegraph Corporation. Watergate Scandal. 1972-73. *713*

Columbians, Inc. Georgia (Atlanta). Patriotism. Racism. 1946-47. *60*

Columbus *Enquirer-Sun* (newspaper). Georgia. Harris, Julian LaRose. Ku Klux Klan. Racism. 1920's. *230*

—. Georgia. Harris, Julian LaRose. Ku Klux Klan (opposition to). Press. 1920's. *184*

Comancheros. Cattle. Hittson, John. Indians. New Mexico. Ranchers. Rustling. 1872-73. *564*

Combahee River Collective. Feminism. Massachusetts (Boston). Murder. Negroes. Pamphlets. Self-defense. 1979. *454*

Commensurate-deserts principle. Sentencing. Wilson, James Q. (review article). 1940's-76. *1299*

Commerce Court (US). Archbald, Robert Wodrow. Conflicts of interest. Congress. Impeachment. Pennsylvania. 1912-13. *743*

Committee for Boston. Massachusetts (Boston). Racism. Violence. White, Kevin H. 1976. *507*

Committee of Fifteen. Local Politics. New York City. Tammany Hall. Vice reform. 1900-01. *671*

Committee of State Security (KGB). Anti-Communist Movements. Espionage. Hiss, Alger. Oswald, Lee Harvey. USSR. 1938-78. *139*

—. Assassination. Epstein, Edward J. Kennedy, John F. McMillan, Priscilla Johnson. Oswald, Lee Harvey (review article). 1960-78. *718*

Communications. Drug abuse. Students (college and university). 1973. *865*

Communications Behavior. Aggression, verbal. Boys. Films. Juvenile Delinquency. Violence. 1970's. *226*

—. Bargaining. Dean, John (resignation). Executive Behavior. Watergate Scandal. 1973. *775*

Communism. Courts. Hiss, Alger. Treason. 1948-51. *283*

—. Demonstrations. Georgia Insurrection Law. *Herndon* v. *Lowry* (US, 1937). International Labor Defense. Martin, Charles H. (review article). 1932-37. *666*

—. Espionage. Meeropol, Michael. Meeropol, Robert. Radicals and Radicalism. Rosenberg Case (review article). 1940's-70's. *1266*

—. Films. Hiss, Alger. Reed, John. 20c. *729*

Communist Countries. Capitalism. Rape. 1978. *320*

Communist Party. Anti-Communist Movements. Caute, David (review article). Law Enforcement. Liberalism. National Security. USSR. 1945-54. *709*

—. Business. Cities. Government. Negroes. Riots. 1960's. *569*

—. Chambers, Whittaker. Espionage. Hiss, Alger. Research. Treason. Weinstein, Allen (review article). 1920's-78. *708*

—. Chambers, Whittaker. Espionage. Hiss, Alger. Trials. 1934-49. *707*

—. Civil Rights. Press. Senate Internal Security Subcommittee. Supreme Court. 1955-59. *719*

—. Espionage. House Committee on Un-American Activities. Legislation. Radicals and Radicalism. 1946-50's. *611*

—. Georgia (Atlanta). Herndon, Angelo. International Labor Defense. Negroes. 1932-37. *739*

Communist Workers Party. Civil rights movement. Community Relations Service. Intelligence Service. North Carolina (Greensboro). 1964-79. *30*

—. Demonstrations. Ku Klux Klan. Murder. Nazism. North Carolina (Greensboro). Trials. 1979-80. *354*

—. Ku Klux Klan. Law Enforcement. Murder. National Socialist White People's Party. North Carolina (Greensboro). Trials. 1979-80. *392*

—. Ku Klux Klan. North Carolina (Greensboro). Social Classes. Violence. 1979. *530*

Community control. Indiana (Indianapolis environs). Police. 1973. *1126*

Community Relations Service. Civil rights movement. Communist Workers Party. Intelligence Service. North Carolina (Greensboro). 1964-79. *30*

Community relations training. Metropolitan Areas. Police. 1967-74. *1141*

—. Police academy. Washington (Seattle). 1960's. *1177*

Community solidarity. Erickson, Kai T. (theory). Inverarity, James M. Justice, repressive. Louisiana. Lynching. Populism. 1889-96. 1976. *452*

Community standards. *Miller* v. *California* (US, 1973). Obscenity (definitions). 1973. *878*

Community work. California (Los Angeles, Orange counties). Drunk driving cases. Voluntary Action Centers. 1976. *969*

Compensation programs. State Government. Victims. Violence. 1950-70's. *378*

Comprehensive Employment and Training Act (US, 1973). Bowden, Joan. Corruption. New Jersey (Atlantic County). 1980-81. *466*

Compton, Arthur. Hangings. Montana (Helena). Vigilantes. Wilson, George. 1870. *1371*

Computers. Criminology. Information Storage and Retrieval Systems. 1980. *155*

Concealed weapons permits. Firearms. Washington (Seattle). 1960's-72. *390*

Concentration Camps. Japanese Americans. Public schools. World War II. 1942-45. *1389*

—. Japanese Americans. Racism. World War II. 1940-45. *1304*

Confederate Army. Daily Life. Delaware. Fort Delaware. Prisoners of War. Purvis, Joseph Edward. 1863. *1385*

Confederate States of America. Capital Punishment. Texas (Gainesville). Trials. Unionists. 1862. *597*

Confidentiality. *Branzburg* v. *Hayes* (US, 1972). Constitutional Amendments (1st). Courts. Criminal investigations. Reporters and Reporting. 1972-78. *1074*

Conflict and Conflict Resolution. Prisons. Violence. 1960-80. *1277*

Cubans. Central Intelligence Agency. Federal Bureau of Investigation. Louisiana (New Orleans). Oswald, Lee Harvey. 1963. *727*

Cullen, James. Lynching. Maine (Aroostook County). Murder. 1873. *404*

Curtis, Lynn A. Crime, causes of. Unemployment. 1970's. *275*

Cypress Hills Massacre. Assiniboine Indians. Indians. Law. Liquor trade. 1873. *335*

D

Daguerreotypes (engravings from). Brady, Mathew B. Phrenological analysis. Simpson, Marmaduke B. 1846. *255*

Daily Life. Confederate Army. Delaware. Fort Delaware. Prisoners of War. Purvis, Joseph Edward. 1863. *1385*

Dake, Crawley P. Arizona. Law enforcement. 1878-81. *981*

"Dangerous" people. Criminal Law. Social Problems. 1776-1976. *174*

Dark Tobacco District Planters Protective Association of Kentucky and Tennessee. Kentucky. Marketing. Tennessee (Robertson County). Tobacco. 1904-13. *544*

Davidson, Sue. Attitudes. Bristow, Edward. Connelly, Mark. Gorham, Deborah. Great Britain. Prostitution (review article). Rosen, Ruth. Women. 1864-1920. *960*

Dawes Act (US, 1887). Arapaho Indians. Cheyenne Indians. Fraud. Indians (agencies). Land allotment. Oklahoma. 1910's. *458*

Day, Samuel Edward, Jr. Arizona (St. Michael's). Dugan, Frank. Law Enforcement. Murder. Navajo Indians. 1920's. *430*

De Mau Mau, organization. Illinois (Chicago). Murder. Negroes. Veterans. Vietnam War. 1968-73. *435*

De Tocqueville, Alexis. Marx, Karl. Nixon, Richard M. Political Theory. Watergate Scandal. Weber, Max. 1972. *804*

Dean, John (resignation). Bargaining. Communications Behavior. Executive Behavior. Watergate Scandal. 1973. *775*

Deane, Silas. American Revolution. Diplomacy. France. Lee, Arthur. Military Aid. Politics. 1773-89. *630*

Death and Dying. Discovery and Exploration. Lewis, Meriwether. Suicide. 1774-1809. *890*

Debt. Coleman, Peter J. (review article). Credit. 1607-1900. 1974. *467*

Decisionmaking. Appellate Courts. Judicial Process. 1965-75. *8*

—. City Government. Police. 1978. *1178*

—. Constitutional Amendments (1st). Gag Orders. Juries. 1931-80. *1148*

Defendants, pro se. Morality. Politics. Social issues. Trials. 1960's-70's. *817*

Defendants (sex of). Behavioral differences. Judges, male and female. Rape. 1968. *363*

"The Defenders" (program). Criminal justice system. "Perry Mason" (program). Stereotypes. Television. Trials. 1949-73. *276*

Defense industries. General Electric Company. Pennsylvania (King of Prussia). Political Protest. Rush, Molly. 1980. *586*

Delaware. Confederate Army. Daily Life. Fort Delaware. Prisoners of War. Purvis, Joseph Edward. 1863. *1385*

Democracy. Civil disobedience. 20c. *508*

—. Civil disobedience. Social institutions, reforms in. -1973. *585*

—. Existentialism. Individualism. Political corruption. 20c. *661*

—. National goals. Social Problems. 1973. *31*

—. Political Speeches. Prohibition. Women's organizations. 1920-34. *831*

Democratic administrations. Arkansas State Penitentiary. Convict lease system. Prisoners, abuse of. 1874-96. *1231*

Democratic Party. Abolition Movement. New York (Utica). Proslavery Sentiments. Riots. 1835. *583*

—. Breckinridge, W. C. P. House of Representatives. Morality. Political scandals. Pollard, Madeline. Sex. 1884-1904. *888*

—. Civil War. Conscription, Military (resistance). Pennsylvania. 1861-64. *778*

—. Elections. Illinois (Chicago). Jarecki, Edmund Kasper. Political Corruption. 1922-54. *637*

—. Erie Canal Ring. Governmental Investigations. New York. Political Reform. Tilden, Samuel J. 1868-76. *616*

—. Impeachment. New York. State Politics. Sulzer, William. Tammany Hall. 1912-13. *803*

Democratic Party (convention). Historiography. Illinois (Chicago). Mass media. Public opinion. Violence. 1968. *553*

Democratic society. Marxism. Terrorism. -1973. *115*

Demography. City Politics. Missouri (Kansas City). Police policies, innovative. 1970's. *1118*

Demonstrations. American Civil Liberties Union. Federal Bureau of Investigation. Hoover, J. Edgar. Political surveillance. Trade Union Education League. 1924-36. *1214*

—. Civil rights. King, Martin Luther, Jr. *(Letter from a Birmingham Jail)*. 1963. *566*

—. Civil Rights. Negroes. Oklahoma (Oklahoma City). Restaurants. 1958-64. *543*

—. Communism. Georgia Insurrection Law. *Herndon v. Lowry* (US, 1937). International Labor Defense. Martin, Charles H. (review article). 1932-37. *666*

—. Communist Workers Party. Ku Klux Klan. Murder. Nazism. North Carolina (Greensboro). Trials. 1979-80. *354*

Depressions. Bootlegging. Florida (Hernando County). Law enforcement. Liquor. Prohibition. 1929-33. *837*

—. Cain, James M. California (Los Angeles). Novels. 1925-45. *72*

—. California (Watsonville). Filipino Americans. Racism. Riots. Violence. 1926-30. *527*

—. New Deal. Working class. 1929-39. *229*

Deprogramming. Converts. Sects, Religious. 1970's. *211*

DeSapio, Carmine. Bossism. New York. Tammany Hall. 1950's-60's. *657*

Despotism. Pennsylvania. Political Theory. Prisons. Tocqueville, Alexis de. 1831. *1241*

Detective fiction *See also* Fiction, Novels, Literature.

—. Bibliographies. Fiction. Literary criticism. 1840's-1970's. *159*

—. Gardner, Erle Stanley. 1910-40. *84*

—. National Characteristics. 1900-80. *278*

—. Stein, Gertrude. Women. 1933-36. *135*

Detention homes. Children (noncriminal). Family Court Act: Persons in Need of Supervision provision (New York). New York. -1974. *1251*

Detention, preventive. Civil Rights. Cold War. Federal Bureau of Investigation. National security. Truman, Harry S. (administration). 1945-52. *1184*

Deterrence. Capital punishment. 1940's-70's. *1270*

Detroit River. Michigan. Ontario. Prohibition. Smuggling. 1920's. *851*

Deviant behavior. Criminology. Research. Social Conditions. 1949-80. *237*

—. Drug Abuse. Social Theory. Youth. 1972-79. *966*
—. Law Enforcement. Social control. 1960-80. *1106*
—. Liberalism. Looting. New York City. Political Attitudes. Racism. 1977. *526*
—. Research. Sex. 1940-75. *245*
Diaries. Assassination. Booth, John Wilkes. *Lincoln Conspiracy* (book, film). Stanton, Edwin M. 1865. 1977. *689*
—. Bell, William H. Law Enforcement. New York City. 1850-51. *272*
—. Civil War. Libby Prison. Prisoners of War. Virginia (Richmond). Wilkins, William D. 1862. *1383*
—. Graham, Stephen. North Carolina (Duplin County). Slave Revolts. 1831. *599*
—. Horsmanden, Daniel. New York. Slave Revolts. 1741. *572*
—. Lynching. Montana, central. Murphy, Con (Jack Redmond). Outlaws. Powers, Jacob. 1884-85. *1136*
Dickens, Charles *(Mystery of Edwin Drood)*. John Jasper (fictional character). Pennsylvania (Philadelphia). Trials (mock). 1914. *216*
Diffusion. Cities. Contagion. Negroes. Police. Riots. 1966-67. *578*
Diplomacy. American Revolution. Deane, Silas. France. Lee, Arthur. Military Aid. Politics. 1773-89. *630*
Discovery and Exploration. Death and Dying. Lewis, Meriwether. Suicide. 1774-1809. *890*
Discrimination. Attitudes. Drug control. Legislation. Police. 1914-76. *920*
—. Capital Punishment. Crime prevention. Minorities. Poor. 1972-76. *1298*
—. Capital Punishment. Judicial Process. Lynching. South. 1978. *1313*
—. Civil-Military Relations. Negroes. Race Relations. Texas (Rio Grande City). Violence. Whites. 1899-1900. *311*
—. DuBois, W. E. B. (petition). Georgia. Ingram case. Sentencing. UN. 1947-49. *359*
—. Georgia (Fulton County). Judicial Administration. Methodology. Negroes. Sentencing. 1970's. *1037*
—. Negroes. Politics. Violence. 1960-69. *57*
Discrimination, Employment. Chinese Americans. Negroes. Vice industry. 1880-1940. *895*
Discrimination (review article). Courts. Sentencing. ca 1930's-73. *1050*
Disease. Andersonville Prison. Civil War (prisoners and prisons). Georgia. Jones, Joseph. 1864-65. *1242*
—. Criminal responsibility. Drug Addiction. Legal philosophy. 1960's-70's. *971*
District attorney. Law. Prosecution, private. 1970's. *1085*
District Courts. Brimmer, Clarence A., Jr. Kennedy, Thomas Blake. Kerr, Ewing T. Riner, John A. Wyoming. 1890-1982. *1188*
—. Sentencing. Social Status. White-collar crime. 1974-77. *471*
District of Columbia. Africa. Barry, Marion. City Government. Negroes. *Washington Post* (newspaper). 1979. *748*
—. Assassination. Booth, John Wilkes. Lincoln, Abraham. Sawyer, Frederick A. (eyewitness account). 1865. *765*
—. Assassination. Criminal investigations. Lincoln, Abraham. Police. Richards, A. C. Trials. 1865-69. *758*
—. Bail Reform Act (1965). Violence. 1976. *1238*
—. Civil War. Police. 1861-65. *123*
—. Drunkenness, public. Law Reform. Minnesota (Minneapolis). Police. 1960's-70's. *811*

—. Firearms Control Regulations Act (1975). Gun control. Methodology. US Conference of Mayors (report). 1975-80. *1068*
—. Law enforcement. Massage parlors. Prostitution. 1970's. *945*
—. Lobbying. Politics. Woman's Lobby (organization). 1970's. *32*
—. Police-community relations. Race Relations. 1968-71. *1223*
Documentaries. Calomiris, Angela. Federal Bureau of Investigation. New York City Photo League. Photography, Journalistic. 1930-51. *988*
Documents. Alabama. Arrests. Burr, Aaron. Perkins, Nicholas. 1807. *785*
—. Archives. Historiography. Photographs. Theft. 1950's-78. *503*
Dodge, William H. McGuire, James. Murder. Nebraska (Nebraska City). Trials. 1874-76. *425*
Donal, Michael Lee. Alabama (Mobile). Lynching. 1981. *342*
Dounton, William. Jailkeepers. Massachusetts (Salem). Trials. Witchcraft. 1692. *1382*
Drachman, Mose (memoirs). Arizona (Tucson). Gambling. 1880-93. *847*
Draft (refusal). Arizona (Phoenix). Immigration. Molokans. World War I (conscientious objectors). 1917-19. *1341*
Drama. Editors and Editing. Fraud (alleged). Gosse, Edmund. Stevenson, Robert Louis *(The Hanging Judge)*. Wise, T. J. 1914. *502*
—. James gang. 1880-1900. *101*
Drewry, William S. *(The Southhampton Insurrection)*. Novels. Olmsted, Frederick Law. Slave Revolts. Styron, William *(The Confessions of Nat Turner)*. Turner, Nat. Virginia. 1831. 1967. *517*
Dreyfus, Alfred. Court cases. Hiss, Alger. Justice. 1948-75. *687*
Dropouts. Crime, fear of. Pennsylvania (Philadelphia). Schools. Students. Truancies. 1970. *133*
Drug abuse. 1970's. *830*
—. Acculturation. Cuban Americans. Immigration. Social Customs. Values. Youth. 1950-80. *912*
—. Adolescents. Marijuana. New York. 1953-73. *886*
—. Amphetamines. Barbiturates. 1903-65. *880*
—. Arrests, false. Lawrence, Paul. Police. Vermont (St. Albans). 1967-74. *869*
—. Behavior, antisocial. 1975. *955*
—. California. Great Britain. Hallucinogens. Intellectuals. LSD. Mullendore, William C. 1930-70. *956*
—. California. Medical care. Prescriptions. San Francisco Polydrug Project. Women. 1969-79. *841*
—. California (Los Angeles County). Law Enforcement. Rehabilitation. Statistics. 1969-79. *899*
—. Civil rights. Federal regulation. Law. 1978. *949*
—. Colleges and universities. Educational Policy. 1975. *926*
—. Colorado. Law. 1870's-90's. *964*
—. Communications. Students (college and university). 1973. *865*
—. Congress. Legislation, drug control. 1975. *947*
—. Deviant Behavior. Social Theory. Youth. 1972-79. *966*
—. Economic Conditions. Immigration. Inhalants. Mexican Americans. Social Conditions. Youth. 1930-80. *848*
—. Federal Government. 1975. *909*
—. Federal Government. Nixon, Richard M. (administration). Public Policy. 1971-77. *823*

Frederick House Massacre. Fur Trade. Hudson's Bay Company. Indian-White Relations. Ontario. 1812-13. *383*

Freedom of Speech. *Brandenburg* v. *Ohio* (US, 1969). Political Speeches. 1969-80. *939*

—. Georgia. Obscenity. *Stanley* v. *Georgia* (US, 1969). Supreme Court. 1968-79. *822*

—. Oklahoma. Political Repression. Vigilantes. World War I. 1914-17. *538*

Freedom of the Press. Censorship campaigns. Cities. Obscenity law. Supreme Court decisions. 1957-75. *928*

—. Constitutional Amendments (1st). Government. Libel. Secrecy. 1793-1800. *703*

—. Courts. Farber, Myron. *New York Times* (newspaper). Reporters and Reporting (sources). 1975-79. *1092*

—. Law Enforcement. Mass Media. Terrorism. 1968-78. *11*

Freedom rides. Civil Rights Movement. Collins, Lucretia (reminiscences). Farmer, James (reminiscences). 1961. *537*

French and Indian War. Great Britain. Pennsylvania (Philadelphia). Smuggling. Trade. West Indies. 1754-63. *476*

Friends, Society of. Attitudes. New York (Auburn). Pennsylvania. Prisons. Reform. Religion. 1787-1845. *1296*

—. Baptists. Fox, George. Olney, Thomas, Jr. Politics. Rhode Island. 1672-73. *83*

—. Charles I. Massachusetts Bay Colony. Persecution. 1661. *34*

—. Criminal justice. Peace bonds. Pennsylvania (Philadelphia). 1680-1829. *142*

Fries, John. Chase, Samuel. Pennsylvania. Treason (alleged). *United States* v. *John Fries* (US, 1800). 1799-1805. *665*

Frontier and Pioneer Life. Alabama (Perry County). 1820-32. *106*

—. Historiography. Indiana (Marion County). Violence. 1823-50. *21*

—. Hollon, W. Eugene. Slotkin, Richard. Violence (review article). 18c-19c. 1973-74. *446*

—. Kansas. Law Enforcement. Morality. Prostitution. Towns. 1868-85. *894*

—. Lawman (symbol). Popular culture. Tilghman, Bill. 1874-1924. 1979. *1065*

—. Military Camps and Forts. Prostitution. Western States. 1860's. *829*

—. Preservation. Prisons. Tennessee. ca 1860-1979. *1260*

Fugitive Slave Act (1850). Kentucky (Boone County, Bourbon County). Michigan (Cass County). Slaveholders. 1830-60. *440*

Fugitives. Capital Punishment. Indentured servants. Indians. Murder. Narraganset Indians. Plymouth Colony. 1621-38. *367*

Fur Trade. Frederick House Massacre. Hudson's Bay Company. Indian-White Relations. Ontario. 1812-13. *383*

G

Gabriel's Plot. Rebellions. Slavery. Virginia. 1799-1800. *224*

Gag Orders. Constitutional Amendments (1st). Decisionmaking. Juries. 1931-80. *1148*

Gambling. 1974-75. *885*

—. Arizona (Tucson). Drachman, Mose (memoirs). 1880-93. *847*

—. Attitudes. Law. Nevada. 1931. *849*

—. Casinos. Great Britain. Law Enforcement. Nevada Gambling Control Board. 1960's-70's. *1165*

—. Cockfighting. 1979. *871*

—. Law Enforcement. 1970's. *1102*

—. Legalization. 1974. *879*

—. Legalization. Social problems. 1975. *846*

—. Nevada (Virginia City). Prostitution. 1870. *821*

—. New York City. Organized Crime. 1965-78. *205*

—. Public opinion. Voting and Voting Behavior. 19c-20c. *884*

—. Public Policy. State Government. Taxation. 1970's. *946*

Gambling, legalized. Government revenues. 1960's-73. *900*

Gambling, pari-mutuel. Barkley, Alben. Kentucky. Louisville Churchmen's Federation. Progressivism. 1917-27. *934*

Gangs. California (East Los Angeles). Machismo (concept). Mexican Americans. Values. Violence. ca 1965-78. *328*

Gardner, Erle Stanley. Detective fiction. 1910-40. *84*

Garfield, James A. Assassination. Capital Punishment. Guiteau, Charles. Trials. 1881-82. *789*

—. Assassination. Guiteau, Charles. Mental Illness. 1860's-82. *752*

Gelders, Joseph. Alabama (Birmingham). Anti-Communist Movements. Floggings. Giles, G. C. Letters. Police. 1936. *353*

—. Alabama (Birmingham). Labor Unions and Organizations. Violence. 1930's. *352*

General Electric Company. Defense industries. Pennsylvania (King of Prussia). Political Protest. Rush, Molly. 1980. *586*

Geneva Convention. Prisoners of War (Germans). USA. World War II. 1941-45. *1318*

Genocide. Georgia (Atlanta). Negroes. Racism. 20c. *371*

Geographic Mobility. City Life. Suburbanization. Texas (Dallas). 1956-76. *125*

Georgia. Andersonville Prison. Civil War. 1862-65. *1254*

—. Andersonville Prison. Civil War (prisoners and prisons). Disease. Jones, Joseph. 1864-65. *1242*

—. Anti-Radicals. Ashburn, George W. (murder). Reconstruction. Trials. 1868. *317*

—. California. Frank, Leo. Jews. Progressivism. Trials. 1913-15. *341*

—. Capital punishment. Hangings. 18c-1924. *1259*

—. Columbus *Enquirer-Sun* (newspaper). Harris, Julian LaRose. Ku Klux Klan. Racism. 1920's. *230*

—. Columbus *Enquirer-Sun* (newspaper). Harris, Julian LaRose. Ku Klux Klan (opposition to). Press. 1920's. *184*

—. Convict lease system. Economic Conditions. Racism. 1868-1909. *1330*

—. Discrimination. DuBois, W. E. B. (petition). Ingram case. Sentencing. UN. 1947-49. *359*

—. Freedom of speech. Obscenity. *Stanley* v. *Georgia* (US, 1969). Supreme Court. 1968-79. *822*

—. Prisons. Reform. 1970's. *1291*

Georgia (Atlanta). Columbians, Inc. Patriotism. Racism. 1946-47. *60*

—. Communist Party. Herndon, Angelo. International Labor Defense. Negroes. 1932-37. *739*

—. Crime coverage. Michigan (Detroit). Newspapers. 1974. *44*

—. Genocide. Negroes. Racism. 20c. *371*

Georgia (Augusta). Race riots. 1970. *1396*

Georgia (Baldwin County). Law. Punishment. Slaves. Trials. 1812-26. *234*

Georgia (Carroll, Houston counties). Violence. Whitecapping. 1893. *347*

Georgia (DeKalb, Hancock, Lincoln, and Putnam Counties). Slave code. Trials. 1819-58. *62*

—. Attitudes. Bristow, Edward. Connelly, Mark. Davidson, Sue. Gorham, Deborah. Prostitution (review article). Rosen, Ruth. Women. 1864-1920. *960*
—. Bahamas (Nassau). *Creole* affair. Mutinies. Slave Revolts. 1841. *557*
—. Behavior. News. Suicide. Werther effect. 1947-68. *915*
—. British North America. Constitutional Law. Impeachment. 1680's-1773. *702*
—. California. Drug Abuse. Hallucinogens. Intellectuals. LSD. Mullendore, William C. 1930-70. *956*
—. Capital Punishment. Ecclesiastical law. Massachusetts. Roman Empire. 17c. *1057*
—. Casinos. Gambling. Law Enforcement. Nevada Gambling Control Board. 1960's-70's. *1165*
—. Conscription, Military. Kidnapping. Massachusetts (Boston). Navies. Riots. 1747. *555*
—. Criminal responsibility. Insanity. USA. ca 1268-1954. *202*
—. Drug addiction. Heroin maintenance. USA. 1973-. *839*
—. France. Spain. Swindlers and Swindling. Wilkinson, James. 1787-1813. *498*
—. French and Indian War. Pennsylvania (Philadelphia). Smuggling. Trade. West Indies. 1754-63. *476*
—. Impeachment. Maryland. Pennsylvania. Provincial Legislatures. Virginia. 14c-16c. 1635-85. *701*
—. Industrial Revolution. USA. ca 1775-19c. *136*
—. Judicial Process. Law. Plea bargaining. 18c-20c. *1087*
—. Law (Anglo-American). Religion. Secularization. USA. 1800-1970. *56*
—. Plea bargaining. 17c-20c. *976*
—. Police. Politics. 1964-79. *1142*
—. Prisons. Social control. 1790-1930. *1365*
Great Britain (London). Authority. New York City. Police. Social order. 1830-70. *1112*
—. Miller, Wilbur R. (review article). New York City. Police. 1830-70. 1977. *1032*
Great Britain (Millbay). American Revolution. Mill Prison. Prisoners of War (escapes). USA. 1777-82. *1346*
Great Plains. Alcoholism. Indians. 1802-1971. *902*
Greene, William Cornell. Copper Mines and Mining. Mexico (Sonora; Cananea). Multinational Corporations. Stock manipulations. Taylor, Frederick Winslow. Wadleigh, Atherton B. 1901-07. *482*
Greenglass, David. Atomic Energy Commission. Espionage. Federal Bureau of Investigation. Nuclear Arms. Rosenberg case. Trials. 1942-74. *738*
—. Atomic Energy Commission. Nuclear Science and Technology. Rosenberg case. Secrecy. Trials. 1945-51. *613*
Gribetz, Lewis J. Jews. Law. New York City. Poultry. Walker, James J. 1888-1940. *468*
Grismer, Karl H. Abbe, Charles E. Florida. Murder. Sara Sota Vigilance Committee. Trials. 1884-86. *375*
Group dynamics. Political Attitudes. Watergate scandal. 1972-76. *684*
Gudgell, Mary. Lynching. Murder. Segal, George. Utah (Ogden). 1883-84. *333*
Guiteau, Charles. Assassination. Capital Punishment. Garfield, James A. Trials. 1881-82. *789*
—. Assassination. Garfield, James A. Mental Illness. 1860's-82. *752*
Gun control. Assassination. Presidency. Public opinion. Sociopaths. 1950's-70's. *801*

—. Constitutional Amendments (2nd). Crime control. 1975. *979*
—. Constitutional Amendments (2nd). Murder rates. 1970's. *361*
—. District of Columbia. Firearms Control Regulations Act (1975). Methodology. US Conference of Mayors (report). 1975-80. *1068*
—. Handguns. 1968-77. *1117*
—. Handguns. State Government. 1968-80. *1011*
—. Law. National Rifle Association. 1970's. *1211*
—. Massachusetts (Boston). 1974-76. *1135*
Gunfights. Arizona (Tombstone). Elder, Kate. O.K. Corral. 1870's-80's. *301*

H

Habeas corpus. Burger, Warren E. Civil Rights. Institutions. Supreme Court. Warren, Earl. 1954-77. *1108*
—. Courts, federal. Criminal justice. State Government. 1960-75. *1040*
—. Duker, William F. (review article). 18c-20c. *1026*
Hada, John. Citizenship. Ford, Gerald R. Japanese American Citizens League. Pardons. Tokyo Rose (Iva Toguri d'Aquino). Uyeda, Clifford I. (account). 1973-77. *795*
Haddock, George C. Iowa. Murder. Temperance Movements. 1855-1915. *418*
Hair, William I. Haynes, Robert V. Louisiana (New Orleans). Race Relations. Riots (review article). Texas (Houston). 1900-17. 1970's. *596*
—. Haynes, Robert V. Martin, Charles H. Racism (review article). South. 1900-30's. 1976. *520*
Haiti. Immigration. 1950-80. *813*
Haitians. Federal policy. Refugees. 1970's. *844*
Halfway to Somewhere (play). Ex-convicts (interviews). Prisons. Theater. Wisconsin. 1973-74. *1391*
Hallucinogens. California. Drug Abuse. Great Britain. Intellectuals. LSD. Mullendore, William C. 1930-70. *956*
Halperin, Morton H. Federal Government. Lawsuits. National Security Council. Wiretapping. 1969-71. *102*
Hamer, Fannie Lou (interview). Baker, Ella Jo (interview). Civil Rights Organizations. Mississippi. Murder. Students. 1964. *609*
Hammett, Dashiell. Authors. 20c. *18*
—. California. Chandler, Raymond. Fiction. Macdonald, Ross. Queen, Ellery. Villains. 1920-79. *189*
Hanawalt, Barbara A. Brewer, John. Hindus, Michael S. Koehler, Lyle. Northeastern or North Atlantic States. South Carolina. Styles, John. 17c-1878. *113*
Handguns. Gun Control. 1968-77. *1117*
—. Gun Control. State Government. 1968-80. *1011*
Hangings. Capital punishment. Georgia. 18c-1924. *1259*
—. Compton, Arthur. Montana (Helena). Vigilantes. Wilson, George. 1870. *1371*
—. Hodges, Stephen. Hodges, William. Iowa. Mormons (Danites). Murder. 1845. *349*
Hangings, threatened. Civil War. Flinn, John M. Prisoner of war camps. Sawyer, Henry W. 1863. *1344*
Harding, George C. (memoirs). Camp Pratt. Louisiana (New Iberia). Prisoners of war. 1862. *1235*
Harding, Warren G. (administration). Teapot Dome Scandal. 1923-24. *746*
Harpers Ferry raid. Abolition Movement. Brown, John. North Carolina. Sectional Conflict. State Politics. 1840-60. *554*

I

—. Civil Disobedience. Watergate Scandal. 1939-74. *628*
—. House Judiciary Committee. Impeachment. Nixon, Richard M. Partisanship. 1974. *678*
—. Juvenile justice. Technology. 1967-75. *223*
Illinois. Congress. Employment. Huck, Winnifred Mason. Prisons. 1922-36. *1261*
—. Firearms ownership. Models. Protection. Sports. 1970's. *148*
—. Immigration and Naturalization Service. Mexican Americans. ca 1970-76. *985*
—. Indians. Justice. Murder. Trials. Winnebago Indians. 1820-30. *447*
—. Prisons. State Government. 1831-1903. *1288*
—. Prisons (minimum-security). Reform. Town-prison relations. Vienna Correctional Center. 1971-75. *1307*
Illinois (Alton). Abolition movement. Lovejoy, Elijah P. (murder). Missouri (St. Louis). St. Louis *Observer* (newspaper). Violence. 1833-37. *299*
Illinois (Blue Island, Chicago). Capital Punishment. Murder. Staub, Albert. Swiss Americans. Theft. 1857-58. *346*
Illinois (Carthage). Assassination. Hill, Marvin S. Mormons. Oaks, Dallin H. Smith, Joseph. Trials (review article). 1844. 1977. *345*
Illinois (Charleston). Civil War. Lincoln, Abraham (family). Riots. 1863-64. *511*
Illinois (Chicago). Blackmail. Kefauver, Estes. Korshak, Sidney R. Organized Crime. Senate Committee to Investigate Organized Crime. 1950-76. *178*
—. Books (editions). Forgeries. Libraries. Publishers and Publishing. Wise, Thomas. Wrenn, John. 1890-1930. *474*
—. Capone, Al. 1919-47. *173*
—. Cities. Loansharking. New York City. 1870's-1960's. *293*
—. Citizen complaints. Juvenile Courts. Policing of Juveniles Project. 1968-69. *25*
—. Crime reports. Police. 1976. *1206*
—. De Mau Mau, organization. Murder. Negroes. Veterans. Vietnam War. 1968-73. *435*
—. Democratic Party. Elections. Jarecki, Edmund Kasper. Political Corruption. 1922-54. *637*
—. Democratic Party (convention). Historiography. Mass media. Public opinion. Violence. 1968. *553*
—. Drug Addiction. Medicines, patent. Opium. 1880's-1910. *862*
—. Drunken drivers. Jail sentences. Judicial policy. 1971. *925*
—. Economic conditions. Firearms. Police. 1863-1910. *1103*
—. Extradition. Foreign Relations. Refugees. Rudowitz, Christian Ansoff. Russia. 1908-09. *86*
—. Maryland (Baltimore). Michigan (Detroit). Sentencing. 1975-76. *1305*
—. Militia. Police. Riots. Strikes. Wages. 1877. *601*
—. Progressivism. Prostitution. Social justice. 1910-15. *814*
Illinois (Chicago area). Juvenile Delinquency. Negroes. Suburbs. 1970-80. *558*
—. Suburbs. 1969-73. *28*
Illinois (Hancock County). Mobs. Mormons. Murder. Persecution. Smith, Hyrum. Smith, Joseph. 1844-46. *546*
Illinois, southern. Judicial Process. Massachusetts, western. Police training. 1974-78. *1201*
Illinois (Springfield). Body-snatching. Lincoln, Abraham. Mullen, Terrance. 1876. *131*
Illinois (Urbana). Criminal Justice System. Minorities. Pretrial diversion programs. Women. 1975-77. *1041*

I'm Alone (vessel). Canada. Prohibition. Smuggling. USA. 1921-29. *961*
Immigrants. Industrial Workers of the World. New Jersey (Paterson). Strikes. Textile Industry. Violence. 1913. *588*
Immigration. Acculturation. Cuban Americans. Drug abuse. Social Customs. Values. Youth. 1950-80. *912*
—. Aliens, illegal. Congress. Economic conditions. Public Policy. 1978. *916*
—. Aliens, illegal. Mexican Americans. 1970's. *973*
—. Aliens (illegal). Mexicans. 1975-82. *883*
—. Aliens, illegal. Mexicans. Public Policy (recommendations). 1970's. *860*
—. Arizona (Phoenix). Draft (refusal). Molokans. World War I (conscientious objectors). 1917-19. *1341*
—. California, southern. Mexico. Operation Wetback. Texas. 1950-74. *930*
—. Coppola, Francis Ford. *Godfather* (novel, film). Italian-American life. Puzo, Mario. 1970's. *239*
—. Drug abuse. Economic Conditions. Inhalants. Mexican Americans. Social Conditions. Youth. 1930-80. *848*
—. Haiti. 1950-80. *813*
Immigration and Nationality Act (US, 1952; amended 1978). Constitutionality. Nazism. War criminals. 1978. *650*
Immigration and Naturalization Service. Aliens, illegal. Federal Policy. 1966-76. *941*
—. California (Los Angeles). Industrial Relations. International Ladies' Garment Workers' Union. Lilli Diamond Originals. Mexican Americans. Raids. 1976-77. *957*
—. Federal Policy. Law Enforcement. 1972-82. *1200*
—. Illinois. Mexican Americans. ca 1970-76. *985*
Immigration, illegal. Labor force. Methodology. 1976. *825*
Impeachment. Archbald, Robert Wodrow. Commerce Court (US). Conflicts of interest. Congress. Pennsylvania. 1912-13. *743*
—. Attitudes. Johnson, Andrew. Letters. Republican Party. Ross, Edmund. 1867-68. *626*
—. Boutwell, George S. House of Representatives. Johnson, Andrew. 1865-68. *662*
—. British North America. Constitutional Law. Great Britain. 1680's-1773. *702*
—. Congress. Johnson, Andrew. Reconstruction. 1865-69. *761*
—. Congress. Presidents. 1970's. *696*
—. Democratic Party. New York. State Politics. Sulzer, William. Tammany Hall. 1912-13. *803*
—. Great Britain. Maryland. Pennsylvania. Provincial Legislatures. Virginia. 14c-16c. 1635-85. *701*
—. House Judiciary Committee. Ideology. Nixon, Richard M. Partisanship. 1974. *678*
—. Hubbell, Levi. State Politics. Supreme courts, state. Wisconsin. 1827-76. *685*
—. Johnson, Andrew. 1865-68. *726*
—. Johnson, Andrew. Michigan. 1865-68. *722*
—. Johnson, Andrew. Reconstruction. Trefousse, Hans L. (review article). 1865-68. 1975. *751*
—. Johnson, Andrew. Senate. 1865-1974. *784*
—. Judges. Land claims. Lawless, Luke. Missouri. Peck, James Hawkins. Senate. Trials. 1822-31. *640*
—. Methodology. Nixon, Richard M. Senate. 1974. *798*
—. Politics. Presidents. 1787-1979. *734*

K

Kennedy, John F. Assassination. 1960's. *712*
—. Assassination. Committee of State Security (KGB). Epstein, Edward J. McMillan, Priscilla Johnson. Oswald, Lee Harvey (review article). 1960-78. *718*
—. Assassination. Conspiracy theory. Warren Commission. 1960's-79. *736*
Kennedy, Robert F. Arab-Israeli conflict. Assassination. Psychoanalysis. Sirhan, Sirhan B. 1948-68. *780*
Kennedy, Thomas Blake. Brimmer, Clarence A., Jr. District Courts. Kerr, Ewing T. Riner, John A. Wyoming. 1890-1982. *1188*
Kenny, John V. Bossism. City Government. New Jersey (Jersey City). 1949-72. *731*
Kentucky. Alcoholism. Moonshining. 1900's. *812*
—. Barkley, Alben. Gambling, pari-mutuel. Louisville Churchmen's Federation. Progressivism. 1917-27. *934*
—. Dark Tobacco District Planters Protective Association of Kentucky and Tennessee. Marketing. Tennessee (Robertson County). Tobacco. 1904-13. *544*
—. Feuds. Law. Violence. West Virginia. 1820-1903. *362*
Kentucky (Boone County, Bourbon County). Fugitive Slave Act (1850). Michigan (Cass County). Slaveholders. 1830-60. *440*
Kentucky (Livingston County). Egalitarianism. Elites. Grand jury. Judicial Process. 1799-1808. *1197*
Kerr, Ewing T. Brimmer, Clarence A., Jr. District Courts. Kennedy, Thomas Blake. Riner, John A. Wyoming. 1890-1982. *1188*
Kidnapping. Booth, John Wilkes. Conspiracy. Eisenschiml, Otto. Lincoln, Abraham. Research. War Department. 1865. ca 1930-80. *690*
—. Cannon, Patty. Murder. Slave Trade. 1820's-30's. *382*
—. Conscription, Military. Great Britain. Massachusetts (Boston). Navies. Riots. 1747. *555*
—. Criminal investigations. Hauptmann, Bruno Richard. Lindbergh, Charles A., Jr. New Jersey. 1932-36. *360*
—. Hearst, Patricia. Mass media. Myths and Symbols. National Characteristics. 1974-76. *165*
Kinealy, James. Body-snatching. Boyd, Ben. Lincoln, Abraham. 1874-88. *486*
Kinesics. *Big Sleep* (film). Bogart, Humphrey. *Maltese Falcon* (film). 1941-46. *270*
King, Martin Luther, Jr. Civil rights. Political Protest. 1955-68. *568*
King, Martin Luther, Jr. *(Letter from a Birmingham Jail).* Civil rights. Demonstrations. 1963. *566*
King, William Lyon Mackenzie. Canada. Espionage. Gouzenko, Igor. Hiss, Alger. USA. USSR. White, Harry Dexter. 1945. *619*
Kinsey, Alfred C. Government. Obscenity law. Research, scientific. *United States* v. *31 Photographs* (US, 1957). 1945-60. *943*
Kiowa Indians (chiefs). Indian Wars. Legal status. Sherman, William Tecumseh. Texas. 1871-78. 1963. *193*
Koehler, Lyle. Brewer, John. Hanawalt, Barbara A. Hindus, Michael S. Northeastern or North Atlantic States. South Carolina. Styles, John. 17c-1878. *113*
Korshak, Sidney R. Blackmail. Illinois (Chicago). Kefauver, Estes. Organized Crime. Senate Committee to Investigate Organized Crime. 1950-76. *178*
Ku Klux Klan. 1868-1920's. *40*
—. 1960-81. *243*

—. Arizona. 1921-25. *1*
—. California (Anaheim). City Government. Political Participation. ca 1923-25. *166*
—. Columbus *Enquirer-Sun* (newspaper). Georgia. Harris, Julian LaRose. Racism. 1920's. *230*
—. Communist Workers Party. Demonstrations. Murder. Nazism. North Carolina (Greensboro). Trials. 1979-80. *354*
—. Communist Workers Party. Law Enforcement. Murder. National Socialist White People's Party. North Carolina (Greensboro). Trials. 1979-80. *392*
—. Communist Workers Party. North Carolina (Greensboro). Social Classes. Violence. 1979. *530*
—. Georgia (Macon). Morality. Violence. Yarbrough, C. A. 1919-25. *118*
—. Indiana (Gary, Valparaiso). Nativism. 1920's. *17*
—. Law and order campaign. Patriotism. Reform efforts. Stereotypes. Wisconsin (Madison, Dane County). 1922-27. *90*
—. Local Politics. Nevada. Vigilantism. 1920-29. *256*
—. Louisiana (Shreveport). Morality. 1920-29. *93*
—. Lusk, Virgil. North Carolina (Asheville). Reconstruction. Republican Party. Shotwell, Randolph. Violence. 1869. *163*
—. Mississippi (Meridian). Race Relations. Reconstruction. 1865-71. *441*
—. Negroes. Racism. Reconstruction. South Carolina (up-country). Violence. 1868-71. *249*
—. South. Violence. 1979. *65*
—. Violence. Voluntary Associations. 1871-1977. *124*
Ku Klux Klan (opposition to). Columbus *Enquirer-Sun* (newspaper). Georgia. Harris, Julian LaRose. Press. 1920's. *184*
Kyles, Connie Lynn. Murder. 1977-80. *331*

L

Labor. Aliens, illegal. National Labor Relations Board. *NLRB* v. *Apollo Tire Co.* (US, 1979). *NLRB* v. *Sure-Tan, Inc.* (US, 1978). 1978-79. *959*
—. Attitudes. Liberals. Rehabilitation. 1950's-78. *1342*
—. California (Oakland, San Francisco). Louisiana (New Orleans). Michigan (Detroit). Police. Racism. 1971-81. *284*
—. Fletcher, Benjamin Harrison. Industrial Workers of the World. Longshoremen. Negroes. 1910-33. *777*
—. Negroes. Prisons. Tennessee. 1830-1915. *1370*
Labor Disputes. Agricultural Labor. Farmers. Industrial Workers of the World. Ranchers. Washington (Yakima Valley). 1910-36. *584*
—. Brotherhood of Timber Workers. Emerson, Arthur L. Industrial Workers of the World. Louisiana, western. Lumber and Lumbering. Texas, eastern. 1900-16. *535*
—. Industrial Workers of the World. Ohio (Toledo). Radicals and Radicalism. US Bureau of Investigation. 1918-20. *37*
—. Police. Social Democratic Party. Wisconsin (Milwaukee). Working class. 1900-15. *1055*
Labor force. Immigration, illegal. Methodology. 1976. *825*
Labor Law. American Federation of Labor. Buck's Stove and Range Co. Courts. Criminal conspiracy (doctrine). 1907-11. *700*

—. Criminal syndicalism acts. Idaho. Industrial Workers of the World. State Government. 1917-33. *1162*

Labor, prison. Germans. New York, western. Prisoner of war camps. World War II. 1944-46. *1334*

Labor Reform. Teamsters, International Brotherhood of. 1970's. *14*

Labor Unions and Organizations. Alabama (Birmingham). Gelders, Joseph. Violence. 1930's. *352*

—. Aliens, illegal. Mexico. 1867-1977. *815*

—. Prisons. Public Employees. Working conditions. 1970's. *1390*

Lakewood Plan. City Government. Contracts. Intergovernmental Relations. Police. 1971-72. *1110*

Lambdin, William. Mormons. Rare Books. Smith, Joseph *(Book of Commandments)*. West Virginia (Wheeling). 1830-33. *515*

Lancaster Industrial School for Girls. Girls. Massachusetts. Reform schools. ca 1850-70. *1243*

Land. Assassination. Colby, Thomas. Colfax County War. Maxwell Grant. New Mexico. 1875-1900. *398*

—. Fraud. Indians. Michigan. 1855-1900. *488*

Land allotment. Arapaho Indians. Cheyenne Indians. Dawes Act (US, 1887). Fraud. Indians (agencies). Oklahoma. 1910's. *458*

Land claims. Impeachment. Judges. Lawless, Luke. Missouri. Peck, James Hawkins. Senate. Trials. 1822-31. *640*

Land grants. California (Sacramento). Courts. Militia. Riots. Squatters. Sutter, John Augustus. 1850. *523*

—. New Mexico. Ortiz y Alarid, Gasper. Roque Lovato Grant. 1785-1894. *463*

Land ownership. Belcher, Jonathan. Colonial government. Dunk, George Montagu. Law Enforcement. Morris, Robert Hunter. New Jersey. Riots. 1748-53. *545*

Land Tenure. Connecticut. Fitch, Jeremiah. Hartford riot. Social change. 1700-22. *592*

Lane, Roger. Bruce, Dickson D., Jr. Cities. Johnson, David R. Police. 19c. *71*

—. Law Enforcement. Schneider, John C. Violence (review article). 1830-1900. 1978-81. *175*

Lansing, Frank E. (letters). Civil War. Michigan Infantry, 20th. 1862-65. *1285*

Lansky, Meyer. New York City (Lower East Side). Organized Crime. 1911-80. *81*

Lappeus, James H. City Government. Oregon (Portland). Police. Wilbur, Hiram. 1851-74. *263*

Lattimer Massacre. Coal miners. Martin, James. Pennsylvania. Slovak Americans. Strikes. Trials. 1897-98. *408*

—. Coal miners. Pennsylvania. Slovak Americans. Strikes. 1897. *431*

Lavigne, Frank C. Livestock. Montana Livestock Commission. Pinkerton National Detective Agency. Power, T. C. Rustling. 1910-25. *991*

Law. Alabama. Ethics. Political Corruption. State Politics. 1970's. *656*

—. Alcoholism. Marijuana use. Victimless crime. 1960's-75. *910*

—. Arizona. Fraud. Government. Real estate. Tombstone Townsite Co. 1880's. *500*

—. Arizona. Mormons. Polygamy. 1880's. *816*

—. Artifacts, pre-Columbian. Mexico. National Stolen Property Act (US, 1976). *United States* v. *McClain* (US, 1973). 1973-77. *499*

—. Assiniboine Indians. Cypress Hills Massacre. Indians. Liquor trade. 1873. *335*

—. Attitudes. Gambling. Nevada. 1931. *849*

—. Attitudes. Howard, Martin. Murder. North Carolina. Slavery. 1765-91. *1063*

—. Birth control. Medicine and State. Public Policy. 19c. *868*

—. Canada. Civil rights. Mexico. USA. Violence. 18c-1974. *534*

—. Capital Punishment. Gilmore, Gary. Politics. 1967-77. *1337*

—. Child abuse. 1970's. *339*

—. Child abuse. Government. 1973-74. *385*

—. Cities. Indians. Migration, Internal. Washington (Seattle). 1970's. *39*

—. Civil rights. Drug Abuse. Federal regulation. 1978. *949*

—. Civilians, killing of. Police. 1952-73. *1077*

—. Colorado. Drug Abuse. 1870's-90's. *964*

—. Corporations. Ford Motor Company. 1976-80. *426*

—. Court decisions (review article). Public policy. Social Change. 1973. *1146*

—. Court records (access to). Evidence. Research. Social sciences. 1970's. *1030*

—. District attorney. Prosecution, private. 1970's. *1085*

—. Drug abuse. Medical Ethics. Tardive dyskenesia. 1968-73. *820*

—. Drugs. 1875-1980. *908*

—. Due process. Virginia. 1634-1700. *989*

—. Feuds. Kentucky. Violence. West Virginia. 1820-1903. *362*

—. Florida. Race Relations. Segregation. Social customs. 1865-1977. *236*

—. Georgia (Baldwin County). Punishment. Slaves. Trials. 1812-26. *234*

—. Great Britain. Judicial Process. Plea bargaining. 18c-20c. *1087*

—. Gribetz, Lewis J. Jews. New York City. Poultry. Walker, James J. 1888-1940. *468*

—. Gun Control. National Rifle Association. 1970's. *1211*

—. Juvenile Delinquency (review essay). Youth. 1800-1971. *168*

—. Liability. Slavery. South. 1771-1858. *181*

—. Louisiana. Slavery. 1724-66. *996*

—. Louisiana (New Orleans). Slave revolts. Turner, Nat. 1831. *600*

—. Miscegenation. Wyoming. 1869-1965 *867*

—. Morality. ca 1960-80. *977*

—. Negroes. Racism. Social inequalities. 1800-1974. *55*

—. Pennsylvania. Reporters and Reporting. Walter, Gregory P. Wiretapping. 1957-72. *209*

—. Prostitution. Rape. Social Organization. Women. 20c. *9*

—. Sentencing. 1790-1970's. *1264*

—. *United States* v. *Willie Decoster, Jr.* (1975). 1965-75. *987*

Law and order. Christie, Ned (Cherokee Indian). Indians (government relations). Justice, concept of. 1884-92. *370*

—. Congress. Political Parties. Public opinion. Race. 1965-73. *1015*

—. Murder. Political Commentary. Press. Riots. Smith, Joseph. 1844. *326*

Law and order campaign. Ku Klux Klan. Patriotism. Reform efforts. Stereotypes. Wisconsin (Madison, Dane County). 1922-27. *90*

Law and Society. Carpetbaggers. Congress. Howard, Charley. Lotteries. Louisiana. Morris, John. State Legislatures. 1868-95. *924*

—. Cities. Police. Public Policy. Robberies. 1970's. *1218*

—. Court dispositions. Public Opinion. 1974. *97*

—. Courts (administration). Criminal justice system (models of). 1954-71. *70*

—. Connecticut. Law enforcement. New Jersey. New York. Public Finance. State government. 1961-77. *1019*

—. Executive Power. Intergovernmental Relations. Ohio. Police. State Government. 1902-25. *1179*

Local Government (jurisdiction). Nevada. Prostitution. ca 1850-1974. *948*

Local Government (structure). North Carolina (Cumberland County). Police agencies. Public policy analysis. 1974. *1125*

Local history. Race Relations. Violence. 1800-1920. *541*

Local Politics. Committee of Fifteen. New York City. Tammany Hall. Vice reform. 1900-01. *671*

—. Ku Klux Klan. Nevada. Vigilantism. 1920-29. *256*

Longshoremen. Fletcher, Benjamin Harrison. Industrial Workers of the World. Labor. Negroes. 1910-33. *777*

Looting. Blackouts. New York City. Poverty. 1977. *521*

—. Deviant Behavior. Liberalism. New York City. Political Attitudes. Racism. 1977. *526*

Lotteries. Carpetbaggers. Congress. Howard, Charley. Law and Society. Louisiana. Morris, John. State Legislatures. 1868-95. *924*

Louisiana. Carpetbaggers. Congress. Howard, Charley. Law and Society. Lotteries. Morris, John. State Legislatures. 1868-95. *924*

—. Community solidarity. Erickson, Kai T. (theory). Inverarity, James M. Justice, repressive. Lynching. Populism. 1889-96. 1976. *452*

—. Country Life. Murder. Social Customs. Weapons. 19c-1979. *295*

—. Criminal Law. Livingston, Edward. 1822. *1099*

—. Law. Slavery. 1724-66. *996*

—. Social Classes. Violence. 1960-76. *292*

Louisiana (Franklin Parish). Assassination. Caldwell, Thomas S. Harris, A. H. State Politics. 1873. *405*

Louisiana (New Iberia). Camp Pratt. Harding, George C. (memoirs). Prisoners of war. 1862. *1235*

Louisiana (New Orleans). Anti-Communist Movements. School Integration. Senate Internal Security Subcommittee. Southern Conference Educational Fund Inc. Williams, Aubrey W. 1954. *774*

—. Assassination. Hennessy, David. Italian Americans. Nativism. *State of Louisiana* v. *Natali et al.* (1891). Vigilantism. 1890-91. *302*

—. Business. City Politics. Prostitution. Social Reform. Voting and Voting Behavior. 1851-58. *950*

—. California (Oakland, San Francisco). Labor. Michigan (Detroit). Police. Racism. 1971-81. *284*

—. Central Intelligence Agency. Cubans. Federal Bureau of Investigation. Oswald, Lee Harvey. 1963. *727*

—. Civil War. Race relations. Reconstruction. Riots. 1862-66. *605*

—. Drugs. Smuggling. 1920-30. *958*

—. Hair, William I. Haynes, Robert V. Race Relations. Riots (review article). Texas (Houston). 1900-17. 1970's. *596*

—. Law. Slave revolts. Turner, Nat. 1831. *600*

—. Metropolitan Police Force. Negroes. Politics. Riots. Whites. 1868. *549*

—. Race Relations. Reconstruction. Riots. 1866. *604*

—. Republican Party. 1864-66. *603*

Louisiana (Shreveport). Ku Klux Klan. Morality. 1920-29. *93*

Louisiana State Prison (Angola). Agriculture. Convict Labor. Prisons. Working Conditions. 1900-78. *1379*

Louisiana, western. Brotherhood of Timber Workers. Emerson, Arthur L. Industrial Workers of the World. Labor Disputes. Lumber and Lumbering. Texas, eastern. 1900-16. *535*

Louisville Churchmen's Federation. Barkley, Alben. Gambling, pari-mutuel. Kentucky. Progressivism. 1917-27. *934*

Lovejoy, Elijah P. (murder). Abolition movement. Illinois (Alton). Missouri (St. Louis). St. Louis *Observer* (newspaper). Violence. 1833-37. *299*

LSD. California. Drug Abuse. Great Britain. Hallucinogens. Intellectuals. Mullendore, William C. 1930-70. *956*

Ludlow Massacre. Coal Mines and Mining. Colorado Fuel and Iron Company. National Guard. Strikes. 1913-14. *533*

Lumber and Lumbering. Brotherhood of Timber Workers. Emerson, Arthur L. Industrial Workers of the World. Labor Disputes. Louisiana, western. Texas, eastern. 1900-16. *535*

—. Conservation movement. Federal Policy. Pacific Northwest. Property rights. Public Lands. 1870's-90's. *478*

Lusk, Virgil. Ku Klux Klan. North Carolina (Asheville). Reconstruction. Republican Party. Shotwell, Randolph. Violence. 1869. *163*

Lynching. Alabama (Butler County). Negroes. 1895. *315*

—. Alabama (Mobile). Donal, Michael Lee. 1981. *342*

—. Ames, Jessie Daniel. Association of Southern Women for the Prevention of Lynching. South. Women. 1928-42. *381*

—. Anderson, Hans. Law enforcement. Nevada (Douglas County). Uber, Adam. 1897-98. *324*

—. Arizona (Phoenix). 1879. *448*

—. Brown, Henry. Kansas (Caldwell). Law Enforcement. Medicine Valley Bank. Murder. Robberies, attempted. 1881-84. *306*

—. Capital Punishment. Discrimination. Judicial Process. South. 1978. *1313*

—. Cato, Will. Georgia (Statesboro). Hodges, Henry (family). Murder. Negroes. Reed, Paul. 1904. *388*

—. Community solidarity. Erickson, Kai T. (theory). Inverarity, James M. Justice, repressive. Louisiana. Populism. 1889-96. 1976. *452*

—. Cullen, James. Maine (Aroostook County). Murder. 1873. *404*

—. Diaries. Montana, central. Murphy, Con (Jack Redmond). Outlaws. Powers, Jacob. 1884-85. *1136*

—. Florida (LaBelle). Law Enforcement. Racism. Rider, Herbert A. 1926. *411*

—. Gudgell, Mary. Murder. Segal, George. Utah (Ogden). 1883-84. *333*

—. Indiana (Hangman's Crossing). Outlaws. Railroads. Reno brothers. Vigilantes. 1868. *409*

—. Literature. Negroes. 1853-1960's. *340*

—. NAACP. Negroes. Zangrando, Robert L. (review article). 1909-50. *13*

Lyon, Marcus (murder). Anti-Catholicism. Anti-Irish sentiments. Cheverus, Jean Louis Lefebvre de. Massachusetts (Northampton). Trials. 1805-06. *312*

M

Mabry, Joseph A. Forrest, Nathan Bedford. Houston, Sam. State Politics. Tennessee. Upper Classes. Violence. 1800-80. *427*

Macdonald, Ross. California. Chandler, Raymond. Fiction. Hammett, Dashiell. Queen, Ellery. Villains. 1920-79. *189*

Machismo (concept). California (East Los Angeles). Gangs. Mexican Americans. Values. Violence. ca 1965-78. *328*

MacKenzie, Alexander Slidell. Capital Punishment. Courts Martial and Courts of Inquiry. Mutinies (suspected). Navies. *Somers* (vessel). 1841-43. *179*

Mafia. Italian Americans. Stereotypes. 1870's-1920's. *120*

—. Violence. 20c. *191*

Mafia (term). Italian Americans. Kefauver, Estes. Monopolies. Organized Crime. Senate Special Committee to Investigate Interstate Crime. 1890-1951. *177*

Magón, Ricardo Flores. Anarchism and Anarchists. Leavenworth Penitentiary. Letters. Mexico. Sarnoff, Lilly. 1920-22. *1227*

Mailer, Norman *(Executioner's Song).* Capital Punishment. Gilmore, Gary. 1970's. *296*

Maine (Aroostook County). Cullen, James. Lynching. Murder. 1873. *404*

Maine State Prison. Business. Prisons. 1978-82. *1369*

Malcolm X. Assassination. Attitudes. Black Nationalism. Political commentary. 1965. *776*

Maltese Falcon (film). *Big Sleep* (film). Bogart, Humphrey. Kinesics. 1941-46. *270*

Mansfield, Mike. Crime compensation programs. Legislation. McClellan, John. 1963-73. *27*

Manson, Charles. Morality. Murder. Polanski, Roman. Politics. Tate, Sharon. 1969-77. *318*

Mapp v. *Ohio* (US, 1961). Appellate courts. Attitudes. Evidence. *Miranda* v. *Arizona* (US, 1966). Police. 1961-78. *982*

—. Criminal procedure. Mondale, Walter. Supreme Court. 1961-76. *1071*

Marbury, William L. (account). Chambers, Whittaker. Hiss, Alger. House Committee on Un-American Activities. Lawsuits. Libel. Perjury. 1922-51. *735*

Marijuana. Adolescents. Drug abuse. New York. 1953-73. *886*

—. Juvenile Delinquency. 1978. *954*

—. Law Reform. Political Attitudes. 1973. *5*

Marijuana law. Legislative innovation. Nebraska. 1943-70. *1034*

Marijuana use. Adolescence. Conformity. Educational pressure, parental. 1969-71. *951*

—. Alcoholism. Law. Victimless crime. 1960's-75. *910*

Market systems. Prison life. Rehabilitation. 1973. *1375*

Marketing. Dark Tobacco District Planters Protective Association of Kentucky and Tennessee. Kentucky. Tennessee (Robertson County). Tobacco. 1904-13. *544*

Marriage. Employment. Women. 1960-74. *10*

Martial law. Internment. Japanese Americans. Tule Lake Camp. World War II. 1941-44. *1349*

Martin, Charles H. Hair, William I. Haynes, Robert V. Racism (review article). South. 1900-30's. 1976. *520*

Martin, Charles H. (review article). Communism. Demonstrations. Georgia Insurrection Law. *Herndon* v. *Lowry* (US, 1937). International Labor Defense. 1932-37. *666*

Martin, James. Coal miners. Lattimer Massacre. Pennsylvania. Slovak Americans. Strikes. Trials. 1897-98. *408*

Marx, Karl. De Tocqueville, Alexis. Nixon, Richard M. Political Theory. Watergate Scandal. Weber, Max. 1972. *804*

Marxism. Capitalism. Prison system, injustices. 18c-1973. *1303*

—. Criminology. Social Theory. 1969-74. *286*

—. Democratic society. Terrorism. -1973. *115*

—. Railroads. Strikes. Workingmen's Party. 1877. *536*

Mary Edmond St. George, Sister. Anti-Catholicism. Arson. Massachusetts (Boston; Charlestown). Riots. Sex roles. Ursuline Convent. 1834. *563*

Maryland. Great Britain. Impeachment. Pennsylvania. Provincial Legislatures. Virginia. 14c-16c. 1635-85. *701*

Maryland (Baltimore). Anti-Catholicism. Carmelites, Discalced. Nativism. Riots. 1830-60. *575*

—. Illinois (Chicago). Michigan (Detroit). Sentencing. 1975-76. *1305*

Mass Media. Aged. Crime waves. Ideology. New York City. 1976. *73*

—. Assassination. Political change. Presidents. 1950-80. *782*

—. Behavior. Bomb threats. Terrorism. 1966-80. *158*

—. California (Los Angeles). Political Protest. Violence. Women. 1977. *366*

—. Cameras. Florida. Herman, Mark. Supreme courts, state. Trials. Zamora, Ronney. 1977-79. *1012*

—. Corporations. Watergate scandal. 1973-74. *800*

—. Democratic Party (convention). Historiography. Illinois (Chicago). Public opinion. Violence. 1968. *553*

—. Elections (congressional). Political news. Watergate scandal. 1973-74. *621*

—. Freedom of the Press. Law Enforcement. Terrorism. 1968-78. *11*

—. Hearst, Patricia. Kidnapping. Myths and Symbols. National Characteristics. 1974-76. *165*

—. Myths and Symbols. Popular culture. Violence. ca 1700-1975. *38*

—. Police. Public Opinion. Statistics. 1978. *232*

—. Police. Terrorism. 1970's. *6*

Massachusetts. Borden, Lizzie. Murder. Trials. 1890-1927. *355*

—. Boston Prison Discipline Society. Charlestown state prison. Penal reformers. 1804-78. *1230*

—. Capital Punishment. Ecclesiastical law. Great Britain. Roman Empire. 17c. *1057*

—. Constitutional Amendments (4th). Legislation. Police. Privacy. Searches. Supreme Court. 1974. *978*

—. Courts. Justice, discretionary. Puritans. 1630-48. *140*

—. Criminal law. Justice. Prosecutions. Social Organization. South Carolina. 1767-1878. *1064*

—. Feuerlicht, Roberta Strauss. Murder. Trials. Vanzetti, Bartolomeo. 1920. *329*

—. Girls. Lancaster Industrial School for Girls. Reform schools. ca 1850-70. *1243*

—. Godfrey, John. Social Conditions. Trials. Witchcraft. 1634-75. *660*

—. Social control. 1693-1769. *75*

Massachusetts Bay Colony. Charles I. Friends, Society of. Persecution. 1661. *34*

—. Hutchinson, Anne. Social Organization. Trials. 1637. *806*

Massachusetts (Boston). Antinomian controversy. Hutchinson, Anne (criminal trial). Puritans. Winthrop, John. 1634-38. *747*
—. Capital punishment. Public Opinion (debate). Social Reform. 1836-54. *1325*
—. City Politics. 1880's. *680*
—. Combahee River Collective. Feminism. Murder. Negroes. Pamphlets. Self-defense. 1979. *454*
—. Committee for Boston. Racism. Violence. White, Kevin H. 1976. *507*
—. Conscription, Military. Great Britain. Kidnapping. Navies. Riots. 1747. *555*
—. Gun Control. 1974-76. *1135*
—. Negroes. Statistics. 1830's-60's. *144*
Massachusetts (Boston; Charlestown). Anti-Catholicism. Arson. Mary Edmond St. George, Sister. Riots. Sex roles. Ursuline Convent. 1834. *563*
Massachusetts (Brookfield Township). Spooner, Bathsheba (execution). Spooner, Joshua (murder). 1778. *401*
Massachusetts (Cambridge). Corporal punishment. Eaton, Nathaniel. Harvard University. Puritans. Trials. 1638. *387*
Massachusetts (Cape Ann). Public Records. Witchcraft. 1692. *258*
Massachusetts (Charlestown). Anti-Catholicism. Riots. Ursulines. 1834. *593*
Massachusetts Department of Youth Services. Correctional reform. Juvenile Delinquency. 1969-73. *1348*
Massachusetts (Hampshire County). Courts of Quarter Sessions. Criminal justice system. 1677-1728. *218*
Massachusetts (Lancaster). Girls. Juvenile Delinquency. Social Reform. Socialization. State Industrial School for Girls. 1856-1905. *1244*
Massachusetts (Middlesex County). Court of General Sessions. Judicial Administration. 1728-1803. *1056*
—. Puritans. 17c. *69*
Massachusetts (Northampton). Anti-Catholicism. Anti-Irish sentiments. Cheverus, Jean Louis Lefebvre de. Lyon, Marcus (murder). Trials. 1805-06. *312*
Massachusetts (Salem). Dounton, William. Jailkeepers. Trials. Witchcraft. 1692. *1382*
Massachusetts, western. *Chicopee News.* Massachusetts (Westfield). Newspapers. Prostitution. 1911. *952*
—. Illinois, southern. Judicial Process. Police training. 1974-78. *1201*
Massachusetts (Westfield). *Chicopee News.* Massachusetts, western. Newspapers. Prostitution. 1911. *952*
Massacres. Franklin, Benjamin. Indians. Pamphlets. Paxton Boys. Pennsylvania. 1764. *421*
—. Indians. Militia. Moravians. Ohio (Gnadenhutten). Pennsylvania. 1782. *291*
Massage parlors. District of Columbia. Law enforcement. Prostitution. 1970's. *945*
Mather, Lynn M. Criminal Law. Judicial Administration (review article). Levin, Martin A. Negroes. Rossum, Ralph A. Uhlman, Thomas M. 1960's-70's. *104*
Mauldin, Sam. Crum, Andy. Mississippi River. Murder. Smuggling. Tennessee (Island 37). Whiskey. 1915. *1017*
Maxfield, Michael G. Attitudes (review article). City Life. Merry, Sally Engle. Skogan, Wesley G. 1981. *231*
Maxwell Grant. Assassination. Colby, Thomas. Colfax County War. Land. New Mexico. 1875-1900. *398*
Mayors. California (Los Angeles). Recall. Shaw, Frank L. 1933-38. *796*

McCarran Internal Security Act (1950). Anti-Communist Movements. Emergency detention. 1950-71. *1324*
McClellan, John. Crime compensation programs. Legislation. Mansfield, Mike. 1963-73. *27*
McCray, Doug (interview). Capital Punishment. Gray, Jimmy Lee (interview). Murder. 1970-79. *1329*
McCrea, Jane (murder). American Revolution. Great Britain. Indians. New York. Propaganda. 1777-1850's. *325*
McDonough, Peter P. Bail bonds. California (San Francisco). City Government. Vice. 1896-1937. *618*
McGuire, James. Dodge, William H. Murder. Nebraska (Nebraska City). Trials. 1874-76. *425*
McIntosh, Otis. Arizona (Solomonville). Juries (fixed). Murder. Trials. 1902. *45*
McKean, John. Anamosa Reformatory. Iowa. Prisons. 1872-74. *1394*
McKelvey, Blake (review article). Prisons. Reform. 19c-20c. *1306*
McKenzie, Alexander. Alaska (Nome). Gold. Nativism. Politics. 1898-1901. *473*
McMillan, Priscilla Johnson. Assassination. Committee of State Security (KGB). Epstein, Edward J. Kennedy, John F. Oswald, Lee Harvey (review article). 1960-78. *718*
Medical and quasimedical research. Civil Rights. Prisoners (as volunteers). ca 1965-74. *1339*
Medical care. California. Drug abuse. Prescriptions. San Francisco Polydrug Project. Women. 1969-79. *841*
Medical Ethics. Drug abuse. Law. Tardive dyskenesia. 1968-73. *820*
Medicine and State. Birth control. Law. Public Policy. 19c. *868*
Medicine Valley Bank. Brown, Henry. Kansas (Caldwell). Law Enforcement. Lynching. Murder. Robberies, attempted. 1881-84. *306*
Medicines, patent. Drug Addiction. Illinois (Chicago). Opium. 1880's-1910. *862*
Meeropol, Michael. Communism. Espionage. Meeropol, Robert. Radicals and Radicalism. Rosenberg Case (review article). 1940's-70's. *1266*
Meeropol, Robert. Communism. Espionage. Meeropol, Michael. Radicals and Radicalism. Rosenberg Case (review article). 1940's-70's. *1266*
Mellett, Donald Ring. Canton *Daily News* (newspaper). Corruption. Editors and Editing. Ohio. 1926-27. *406*
Melville, Herman (*Benito Cereno*). Slavery. Symbolism in Literature. Violence. 1799. 1856. *4*
Men. Arrests. Police. Women. 1972. *207*
—. Arrests. Statistics. Women. 1965-77. *252*
—. Brownmiller, Susan (review article). Negroes. Racism. Rape. 1975. *319*
—. Women. 1972-76. *109*
Men, black. Racism. Rape. South. Women, white. 1970's. *303*
Mennonites. Anabaptists. Germany. Switzerland. Taxation. War. 16c-1973. *567*
—. Kansas. Liberty bonds. Pacifism. Vigilantism. World War I. 1918. *560*
Mental Illness. Assassination. Garfield, James A. Guiteau, Charles. 1860's-82. *752*
Mental Illness (alleged). Assassination. Conspiracy. Lincoln, Abraham. Trials. Weichmann, Louis J. 1865. 1895. *556*
—. Mitchell, Martha. Nixon, Richard M. (administration). Press. Watergate scandal. 1972-76. *767*

Mental institutions. Penal reform. Progressivism. Rothman, David J. (review article). ca 1900-15. 1980. *1239*

Merchants. California (San Francisco). Imports. Self-interest. Vigilantism. 1849-56. *1158*

Merrill, Boynton, Jr. (review article). Jefferson, Thomas (nephews). South. Violence. 19c. 1976. *445*

Merry, Sally Engle. Attitudes (review article). City Life. Maxfield, Michael G. Skogan, Wesley G. 1981. *231*

Methadone treatment programs. Heroin addiction. 1940's-73. *852*

—. New York City. Public Policy. 1965-75. *864*

Methodology. Birth cohort. Juvenile delinquents. Pennsylvania (Philadelphia). 1964-73. *279*

—. Cities. Crime rates. Crowding. ca 1960-75. *287*

—. Cities. Police. Public Records. 1880-1903. 1979. *1114*

—. Discrimination. Georgia (Fulton County). Judicial Administration. Negroes. Sentencing. 1970's. *1037*

—. District of Columbia. Firearms Control Regulations Act (1975). Gun control. US Conference of Mayors (report). 1975-80. *1068*

—. Feminism. Liberalism. Pornography. President's Commission on Obscenity and Pornography. Repression. Violence. 1970-80. *845*

—. Immigration, illegal. Labor force. 1976. *825*

—. Impeachment. Nixon, Richard M. Senate. 1974. *798*

—. Legislation. North America. 1784-1979. *100*

—. Police effectiveness. President's Commission on Law Enforcement and Administration of Justice. *Task Force Report: The Police* (1967). 1967-75. *1127*

—. Race. Sentencing. 1969-77. *1187*

Methodology (evaluative). Heroin addiction. Rehabilitation (program efficacy). 1974. *858*

Methodology (subjectivist). Criminologists. 1960's-74. *274*

Metropolitan Areas *See also* Cities.

—. Community relations training. Police. 1967-74. *1141*

—. Income. Inequality. Race. Violence. 1970. *298*

—. Law Enforcement. 1978. *1109*

—. Law enforcement. Police (effectiveness, productivity). 1974. *1150*

—. Literature. Popular Culture (underground). 1840-70. *938*

—. Police. Reform. 1854-1960's. *1121*

Metropolitan Police Force. Louisiana (New Orleans). Negroes. Politics. Riots. Whites. 1868. *549*

Mexican Americans. Aliens (illegal). Economic Conditions. Stereotypes. 1930-76. *903*

—. Aliens, illegal. Immigration. 1970's. *973*

—. Attitudes. Barrios. California, southern. Civil Rights. Police. Social Conditions. 1975. *171*

—. Attitudes. California. Civil liberties. Civil liberties. Police. Whites. 1971-80. *172*

—. California. Gold Rushes. Murieta, Joaquin. Outlaws. ca 1848-53. *422*

—. California (East Los Angeles). Gangs. Machismo (concept). Values. Violence. ca 1965-78. *328*

—. California (Los Angeles). Immigration and Naturalization Service. Industrial Relations. International Ladies' Garment Workers' Union. Lilli Diamond Originals. Raids. 1976-77. *957*

—. California (Los Angeles). Sterilization. Women. 1970-78. *1378*

—. California (Oxnard). Drug abuse programs. 1972-73. *810*

—. Drug abuse. Economic Conditions. Immigration. Inhalants. Social Conditions. Youth. 1930-80. *848*

—. Illinois. Immigration and Naturalization Service. ca 1970-76. *985*

—. Newspapers. Panama Canal (issue). Political Campaigns (presidential). Reagan, Ronald. Treaties. 1976-80. *595*

—. Racism. Sterilization. Women. 20c. *1262*

Mexicans. Aliens (illegal). Immigration. 1975-82. *883*

—. Aliens, illegal. Immigration. Public Policy (recommendations). 1970's. *860*

—. Aliens (illegal). Migrant Labor. Oregon (Hood River Valley). Wages. 1978. *840*

Mexico. Aliens, illegal. Border policy. Economic Conditions. USA. 1952-75. *824*

—. Aliens, illegal. Economic Conditions. 1972-73. *918*

—. Aliens (illegal). Economic Conditions. USA. 1946-65. *857*

—. Aliens, illegal. Labor Unions and Organizations. 1867-1977. *815*

—. Anarchism and Anarchists. Leavenworth Penitentiary. Letters. Magón, Ricardo Flores. Sarnoff, Lilly. 1920-22. *1227*

—. Armies. Drugs. New Mexico (Columbus). Pershing, John J. Prostitution. Punitive expeditions. Venereal disease. 1916-17. *932*

—. Artifacts, pre-Columbian. Law. National Stolen Property Act (US, 1976). *United States* v. *McClain* (US, 1973). 1973-77. *499*

—. California, southern. Immigration. Operation Wetback. Texas. 1950-74. *930*

—. Canada. Civil rights. Law. USA. Violence. 18c-1974. *534*

—. Cattle. Navies. *Rio Bravo* (vessel). Rio Grande. Rustling. Texas. 1840's-79. *487*

—. Conspiracy. Foreign Relations. Revolutionary Movements. Reyes, Bernardo. State Politics. Texas. Trials. 1911-12. *693*

Mexico (Juarez). Boundaries. Federalism. Law Enforcement (local). Texas (El Paso). 1970's. *1003*

Mexico (Sonora; Cananea). Copper Mines and Mining. Greene, William Cornell. Multinational Corporations. Stock manipulations. Taylor, Frederick Winslow. Wadleigh, Atherton B. 1901-07. *482*

Michigan. Bath Consolidated School. Kehoe, Andrew. Murder. 1927. *394*

—. Capital Punishment (abolition). Puritans. Reform. 17c-1846. *1234*

—. Detroit River. Ontario. Prohibition. Smuggling. 1920's. *851*

—. Fraud. Indians. Land. 1855-1900. *488*

—. Impeachment. Johnson, Andrew. 1865-68. *722*

Michigan (Cass County). Fugitive Slave Act (1850). Kentucky (Boone County, Bourbon County). Slaveholders. 1830-60. *440*

Michigan (Detroit). California (Oakland, San Francisco). Labor. Louisiana (New Orleans). Police. Racism. 1971-81. *284*

—. Crime coverage. Georgia (Atlanta). Newspapers. 1974. *44*

—. Criminal justice system. Prisons. Ravitz, Justin C. (interview). 1972-73. *203*

—. Economic Theory. Police. 1926-77. *149*

—. Firearms. Sentencing. 1976-79. *1096*

—. Illinois (Chicago). Maryland (Baltimore). Sentencing. 1975-76. *1305*

Michigan Infantry, 20th. Civil War. Lansing, Frank E. (letters). 1862-65. *1285*

Michigan (Wayne County; Detroit). Courts. Firearms. Plea bargaining. Sentencing. 1970's. *1062*

"Mickey Finn" (potion). Chloral hydrate. Cities. Vice areas. 1850's-1910's. *351*

Middle Classes. Courts. Industrialists. Juvenile Delinquency. Philanthropy. Reform. 1890-99. *199*

—. Drug Abuse. Whites. Youth. 1960-80. *897*

Migrant Labor. Aliens (illegal). Mexicans. Oregon (Hood River Valley). Wages. 1978. *840*

—. California (Wheatland). Industrial Workers of the World. State Government. Strikes. Trials. 1913-17. *522*

Migration, Internal. California (Los Angeles). Chandler, Raymond. Novels (detective). Social Change. ca 1930-80. *244*

—. Cities. Indians. Law. Washington (Seattle). 1970's. *39*

Military. Alabama. Racism. Randolph, Ryland. Reconstruction. Trials. Tuscaloosa *Independent Monitor*. 1868. *316*

—. Civil Disturbances. Executive Power. 1789-1978. *594*

—. New Mexico (Sante Fe). Presidial Company. Prices. 18c. *480*

—. Oklahoma, University of. Police. Simulation and Games. Terrorism. 1970's. *1166*

Military Aid. American Revolution. Deane, Silas. Diplomacy. France. Lee, Arthur. Politics. 1773-89. *630*

Military antiques, fraudulent. Antique swindle. 1970-76. *459*

Military Camps and Forts. Frontier and Pioneer Life. Prostitution. Western States. 1860's. *829*

Military justice system. 1973. *54*

Military Occupation. Brenham fire. Reconstruction. Sheridan, Philip A. Texas. 1865-70. *485*

Military Offenses. Civil War. *Ethan Allen* (vessel). Navies. Stanley, Tufton K. (mess book). 1863-65. *1229*

Military Service (enlistees). American Revolution. Capital Punishment. Connecticut (Hartford, Waterbury). Dunbar, Moses. Great Britain. Treason. 1777. *704*

Military training. Baker, Newton D. Liquor. Prostitution. Texas (El Paso). War Department. World War I. 1917-18. *834*

Militia. California (Sacramento). Courts. Land grants. Riots. Squatters. Sutter, John Augustus. 1850. *523*

—. Illinois (Chicago). Police. Riots. Strikes. Wages. 1877. *601*

—. Indians. Massacres. Moravians. Ohio (Gnadenhutten). Pennsylvania. 1782. *291*

Mill Prison. American Revolution. Great Britain (Millbay). Prisoners of War (escapes). USA. 1777-82. *1346*

Miller v. *California* (US, 1973). Community standards. Obscenity (definitions). 1973. *878*

—. Obscenity. Supreme Court. Values, local-popular. 1973. *923*

Miller, Wilbur R. (review article). Great Britain (London). New York City. Police. 1830-70. 1977. *1032*

Miller, Zeke. Johnson, Grant. Law Enforcement. Negroes. Oklahoma. Reeves, Bass. 1876-1907. *1215*

Mina (Eskimo woman). Eskimos. Hudson Bay. Religion. 1940's-50's. *344*

Mines. Arnold, Philip. Fraud. Ralston, William Chapman. Slack, John. Utah. 1872. *465*

Minnesota. Employment. Germans. Prisoners of war. World War II. 1942-46. *1357*

Minnesota (Minneapolis). District of Columbia. Drunkenness, public. Law Reform. Police. 1960's-70's. *811*

Minnesota (St. Paul). Law Enforcement. 1869-74. *16*

Minorities. California (Los Angeles). Police. Shootings. 1974-79. *1111*

—. Capital Punishment. Crime prevention. Discrimination. Poor. 1972-76. *1298*

—. Cooke, Janet. Hoaxes. Pulitzer Prize. Reporters and Reporting. *Washington Post* (newspaper). 1980. *185*

—. Criminal Justice System. Illinois (Urbana). Pretrial diversion programs. Women. 1975-77. *1041*

Miranda v. *Arizona* (US, 1966). Appellate courts. Attitudes. Evidence. *Mapp* v. *Ohio* (US, 1961). Police. 1961-78. *982*

—. Correctional agencies. Courts. Police. 1974. *150*

Miscegenation. Law. Wyoming. 1869-1965. *867*

Misconduct in office. Bureaucracies. Federal Government. Public Employees. 1970's. *677*

—. Historians. House Judiciary Committee. Impeachment Inquiry. Presidents. Woodward, C. Vann (review article). 1789-1974. *617*

Missions and Missionaries. Blackburn, Gideon. Cherokee Indians. Indians. Presbyterian Church. Schools. Whiskey. 1809-10. *164*

Mississippi. Baker, Ella Jo (interview). Civil Rights Organizations. Hamer, Fannie Lou (interview). Murder. Students. 1964. *609*

—. Juvenile courts. 1916-75. *975*

—. Parchman Prison Farm. Prisons. 1972-73. *1269*

Mississippi (Grenada County). Capital Punishment. Cheatham, Mel. Murder. Race Relations. Tillman, James. Trials. 1889-90. *400*

Mississippi (Meridian). Ku Klux Klan. Race Relations. Reconstruction. 1865-71. *441*

Mississippi River. Crum, Andy. Mauldin, Sam. Murder. Smuggling. Tennessee (Island 37). Whiskey. 1915. *1017*

Mississippi Territory. Law, codified. Sargent, Winthrop. 1798-1800. *1221*

Missouri. Impeachment. Judges. Land claims. Lawless, Luke. Peck, James Hawkins. Senate. Trials. 1822-31. *640*

—. Oklahoma. Outlaws. Social bandit tradition. 1866-96. *437*

Missouri (Jefferson City). Employment. Prisons. 1833-99. *1319*

Missouri (Kansas City). City Politics. Demography. Police policies, innovative. 1970's. *1118*

Missouri (St. Louis). Abolition movement. Illinois (Alton). Lovejoy, Elijah P. (murder). St. Louis *Observer* (newspaper). Violence. 1833-37. *299*

—. Arrests. Behavior. Organizations. Police. Statistics. 1900-70. *1205*

—. Bank robberies. Grand National Bank. Vandeventer Securities Co. 1930. *348*

—. City Politics. Integration. Police. Political Protest. Pressure Groups. Professionalization. 1900-70. *1203*

—. Licensing. Prostitution. 1870-79. *967*

—. Police. Promotions. 1899-1975. *1204*

Mitchell, John (1870-1919). Conflicts of interest. Finance. United Mine Workers of America. 1899-1908. *481*

Mitchell, Martha. Mental Illness (alleged). Nixon, Richard M. (administration). Press. Watergate scandal. 1972-76. *767*

Mitford, Jessica. Penology (review article). Rehabilitation. VandenHaag, Ernest. VonHirsch, Andrew. 1960's-70's. *1356*

Moama Hotel. Hawaii (Honolulu). Murder. Stanford, Jane. 1905. *391*

Mobs. Illinois (Hancock County). Mormons. Murder. Persecution. Smith, Hyrum. Smith, Joseph. 1844-46. *546*

—. Costs. Prisons. 1893-1909. *1258*
—. Freedom of speech. Political Repression. Vigilantes. World War I. 1914-17. *538*
—. Highway patrol. Sheriffs. 1930's. *993*
—. Hollins, Jess. International Labor Defense. NAACP. Race Relations. Rape. Trials. 1931-36. *374*
—. Johnson, Grant. Law Enforcement. Miller, Zeke. Negroes. Reeves, Bass. 1876-1907. *1215*
—. Missouri. Outlaws. Social bandit tradition. 1866-96. *437*
—. Prison industries. Profit. 1909-60. *1257*
—. Prisons. Reform. 1910-67. *1256*
Oklahoma (Cleveland, Pottawatomie counties). Jones Family (group). Sedition. Trials. Working Class Union. World War I. 1917. *745*
Oklahoma (Oklahoma City). Civil Rights. Demonstrations. Negroes. Restaurants. 1958-64. *543*
Oklahoma, University of. Military. Police. Simulation and Games. Terrorism. 1970's. *1166*
Old Southwest. Burr, Aaron. Treason. Trials. 1782-1836. *788*
Olmstead, Alan L. Banks, savings (review article). Osthaus, Carl R. 1819-70's. 1976. *495*
Olmsted, Frederick Law. Drewry, William S. *(The Southhampton Insurrection).* Novels. Slave Revolts. Styron, William *(The Confessions of Nat Turner).* Turner, Nat. Virginia. 1831. 1967. *517*
Olney, Thomas, Jr. Baptists. Fox, George. Friends, Society of. Politics. Rhode Island. 1672-73. *83*
Ontario. Detroit River. Michigan. Prohibition. Smuggling. 1920's. *851*
—. Frederick House Massacre. Fur Trade. Hudson's Bay Company. Indian-White Relations. 1812-13. *383*
Operation Abscam. Congress. Federal Bureau of Investigation. White-collar crime. 1970-80. *1217*
Operation Cointelpro. Black nationalism. Federal Bureau of Investigation. Operation Newkill. 1968-71. *1116*
—. Federal Bureau of Investigation. Internal security. Leftism. 1956-71. *1130*
Operation Newkill. Black nationalism. Federal Bureau of Investigation. Operation Cointelpro. 1968-71. *1116*
Operation Wetback. California, southern. Immigration. Mexico. Texas. 1950-74. *930*
Opium. Drug Addiction. Illinois (Chicago). Medicines, patent. 1880's-1910. *862*
—. Social Problems. 1700-1974. *970*
Oral history. Anti-Vietnam War movement. Civil rights. Kennedy, Jane. Political Protest. Women. 1964-77. *1289*
—. Japanese Americans, incarceration of. Tanaka, Togo. World War II. Yoneda, Elaine. Yoneda, Karl. 1941-45. *1340*
Orchard, Harry. Christianity (converts). Idaho. Murderers. 1899-1906. *386*
Oregon (Hood River Valley). Aliens (illegal). Mexicans. Migrant Labor. Wages. 1978. *840*
Oregon (Portland). City Government. Lappeus, James H. Police. Wilbur, Hiram. 1851-74. *263*
Organizational structure. Police. 1978. *1028*
Organizations. Arrests. Behavior. Missouri (St. Louis). Police. Statistics. 1900-70. *1205*
—. Authority. Bay Area Rapid Transit District. California (San Francisco Bay area). Exposés. Professionals. 1973-80. *1132*

Organized Crime. Blackmail. Illinois (Chicago). Kefauver, Estes. Korshak, Sidney R. Senate Committee to Investigate Organized Crime. 1950-76. *178*
—. Business. Politics. 20c. *246*
—. Civil Rights. Electronic surveillance. 1969-78. *1143*
—. Cold War. Federal Policy. Organized Crime Control Act (US, 1970). 1950-80. *994*
—. Editorials. Florida (Dade County; Miami). Renick, Ralph. Television. WTVJ (station). 1966. *7*
—. Ethnic groups. New York. 1930-50. *29*
—. Gambling. New York City. 1965-78. *205*
—. Italian Americans. Kefauver, Estes. Mafia (term). Monopolies. Senate Special Committee to Investigate Interstate Crime. 1890-1951. *177*
—. Lansky, Meyer. New York City (Lower East Side). 1911-80. *81*
—. Negroes. Puerto Ricans. 1974. *119*
—. Research. 1950-71. *114*
—. Washington (Seattle). 1960-78. *41*
Organized Crime Control Act (US, 1970). Cold War. Federal Policy. Organized Crime. 1950-80. *994*
Ortiz y Alarid, Gasper. Land grants. New Mexico. Roque Lovato Grant. 1785-1894. *463*
Osthaus, Carl R. Banks, savings (review article). Olmstead, Alan L. 1819-70's. 1976. *495*
Oswald, Lee Harvey. Anti-Communist Movements. Committee of State Security (KGB). Espionage. Hiss, Alger. USSR. 1938-78. *139*
—. Central Intelligence Agency. Cubans. Federal Bureau of Investigation. Louisiana (New Orleans). 1963. *727*
Oswald, Lee Harvey (review article). Assassination. Committee of State Security (KGB). Epstein, Edward J. Kennedy, John F. McMillan, Priscilla Johnson. 1960-78. *718*
Outlaws. Anecdotes. Arizona. 1880-1900. *46*
—. Arizona. Myths and Symbols. Ringo, John. Texas. 1864-82. *33*
—. Bass, Sam. Billy the Kid. Floyd, Charles Arthur "Pretty Boy". Folklore. Heroes. James, Jesse. 1860-1934. *169*
—. Betenson, Lula Parker (interview). Cassidy, Butch (Robert Leroy Parker). 1905-25. 1975. *309*
—. California. Gold Rushes. Mexican Americans. Murieta, Joaquin. ca 1848-53. *422*
—. Coe, William. Colorado, southeastern. New Mexico, northeastern. Robbers' Roost (hideout). ca 1867-68. *260*
—. Diaries. Lynching. Montana, central. Murphy, Con (Jack Redmond). Powers, Jacob. 1884-85. *1136*
—. Folklore. James, Frank. James, Jesse. 1860's-1915. *300*
—. Indiana (Hangman's Crossing). Lynching. Railroads. Reno brothers. Vigilantes. 1868. *409*
—. Missouri. Oklahoma. Social bandit tradition. 1866-96. *437*
—. Railroads. Robberies. Western States. 1866-1932. *484*
Overland Journeys to the Pacific. Applegate, Jesse. Judicial process. 1840's-60's. *138*
Owen, Robert. Fraud (alleged). Pennsylvania (New Harmony). Rapp, Frederick. Real Estate. 1825. *455*
Oysters. Cameron, William Evelyn. Conservation of Natural Resources. Fishing. State Government. Virginia. 1882-85. *479*

P

Pacific Northwest. Conservation movement. Federal Policy. Lumber and Lumbering. Property rights. Public Lands. 1870's-90's. *478*
—. Indians. Suicide. 1954-72. *935*
Pacifism. Kansas. Liberty bonds. Mennonites. Vigilantism. World War I. 1918. *560*
Paiute Indians. Arizona (Shivwits Plateau). Dunn, William. Grand Canyon expedition. Howland brothers. 1869. *297*
—. Arizona (Shivwits Plateau). Dunn, William. Howland brothers. Indian Wars. Murder. Walapai Indians. 1866-69. *323*
Palmer raids. Anderson, Weston. Due process. Ethnic Groups. Justice Department. New Hampshire. 1900-20. *1213*
Pamphlets. Combahee River Collective. Feminism. Massachusetts (Boston). Murder. Negroes. Self-defense. 1979. *454*
—. Franklin, Benjamin. Indians. Massacres. Paxton Boys. Pennsylvania. 1764. *421*
Panama Canal (issue). Mexican Americans. Newspapers. Political Campaigns (presidential). Reagan, Ronald. Treaties. 1976-80. *595*
Papago Indians. Arizona. Conscription, military. Indians. Pia Machita (leader). Political Protest. 1930-41. *673*
Parchman Prison Farm. Mississippi. Prisons. 1972-73. *1269*
Pardon request. Alabama. NAACP. Norris, Clarence. Scottsboro Case. 1931-76. *373*
Pardons. Amnesty, conditional. Ford, Gerald R. Justice. Nixon, Richard M. Vietnam War. 1974. *638*
—. Citizenship. Ford, Gerald R. Hada, John. Japanese American Citizens League. Tokyo Rose (Iva Toguri d'Aquino). Uyeda, Clifford I. (account). 1973-77. *795*
Park, Hugh. Baker, James. Murder. Washington (Shaw Island). 1885. *343*
Parker, George Claflin. Bull Run (2d battle). Civil War (personal narratives). Libby Prison. Prisoners of War. Virginia (Alexandria, Richmond). 1862. *1352*
Parole survival. Ethnicity. Indians. Prisons. Western States. 1972. *1387*
Parole system. Imprisonment, effect of. 1975. *1287*
Partisanship. House Judiciary Committee. Ideology. Impeachment. Nixon, Richard M. 1974. *678*
Partridge, Alexander (execution). Colonial Government. Rhode Island. 1652. *257*
Paternalism. Courts. Women. 1960's-74. *1119*
Patriarchy. Incest, father-daughter. Psychotherapy. 1970's. *870*
Patriotism. Columbians, Inc. Georgia (Atlanta). Racism. 1946-47. *60*
—. Ethnic Groups. Montana (Lewistown). Riots. World War I. 1917-18. *608*
—. Ku Klux Klan. Law and order campaign. Reform efforts. Stereotypes. Wisconsin (Madison, Dane County). 1922-27. *90*
Patterson, Malcolm. Carmack, Edward Ward. Cooper, Duncan J. Cooper, Robin. Murder. Prohibition. Tennessee (Nashville). Trials. 1888-1909. *368*
Paul, Alice. Constitutional Amendments (21st). Equal Rights Amendment (proposed). Woman Suffrage. 1907-72. *679*
Paul, Jerry. Civil rights. Little, Joan. Murder (alleged). North Carolina (Beaufort County). Trials. 1974-78. *288*
Paxton Boys. Franklin, Benjamin. Indians. Massacres. Pamphlets. Pennsylvania. 1764. *421*

Payola. Federal regulation. Music. Radio. Television. 1930's-79. *460*
Peace bonds. Criminal justice. Friends, Society of. Pennsylvania (Philadelphia). 1680-1829. *142*
Peck, James Hawkins. Impeachment. Judges. Land claims. Lawless, Luke. Missouri. Senate. Trials. 1822-31. *640*
Penal reform *See also* Prison reform.
—. Becarria, Cesare. Capital punishment. Italy. USA. 1764-97. *1328*
—. Mental institutions. Progressivism. Rothman, David J. (review article). ca 1900-15. 1980. *1239*
Penal reformers. Boston Prison Discipline Society. Charlestown state prison. Massachusetts. 1804-78. *1230*
Pennsylvania. Archbald, Robert Wodrow. Commerce Court (US). Conflicts of interest. Congress. Impeachment. 1912-13. *743*
—. Attitudes. Friends, Society of. New York (Auburn). Prisons. Reform. Religion. 1787-1845. *1296*
—. Chase, Samuel. Fries, John. Treason (alleged). *United States* v. *John Fries* (US, 1800). 1799-1805. *665*
—. Civil War. Conscription, Military (resistance). Democratic Party. 1861-64. *778*
—. Coal miners. Lattimer Massacre. Martin, James. Slovak Americans. Strikes. Trials. 1897-98. *408*
—. Coal miners. Lattimer Massacre. Slovak Americans. Strikes. 1897. *431*
—. Despotism. Political Theory. Prisons. Tocqueville, Alexis de. 1831. *1241*
—. Education. Morality. Wickersham, James P. 1866-81. *3*
—. Franklin, Benjamin. Indians. Massacres. Pamphlets. Paxton Boys. 1764. *421*
—. Great Britain. Impeachment. Maryland. Provincial Legislatures. Virginia. 14c-16c. *701*
—. Indians. Massacres. Militia. Moravians. Ohio (Gnadenhutten). 1782. *291*
—. Law. Reporters and Reporting. Walter, Gregory P. Wiretapping. 1957-72. *209*
Pennsylvania (Cumberland County). Indians (massacred). Stump, Frederick. 1768. *380*
Pennsylvania Hall (burning). Abolition movement. Pennsylvania (Philadelphia). Riots. Women. 1833-37. *514*
Pennsylvania (Harrisburg). Politics. State Legislatures. 1870's. *695*
Pennsylvania (King of Prussia). Defense industries. General Electric Company. Political Protest. Rush, Molly. 1980. *586*
Pennsylvania (Lancaster). American Revolution. Architecture. Atlee, William Augustus. Barracks. Prisoners of War. 1777. *1351*
—. Counterfeiting. Jacobs, William M. Kendig, William L. Revenue Stamps. 1865-1900. *492*
Pennsylvania (Mansfield). Attitudes. Capital Punishment. Photographs. 1898. *1323*
Pennsylvania (New Harmony). Fraud (alleged). Owen, Robert. Rapp, Frederick. Real Estate. 1825. *455*
Pennsylvania (northwestern). Booth, John Wilkes. Oil Industry and Trade. ca 1858-65. *744*
Pennsylvania (Philadelphia). Abolition movement. Pennsylvania Hall (burning). Riots. Women. 1833-37. *514*
—. Birth cohort. Juvenile delinquents. Methodology. 1964-73. *279*
—. Butler, Smedley D. Law Enforcement. Prohibition. 1924-25. *980*
—. Civil Rights. Colored Protective Association. NAACP. Negroes. Riots. 1918. *539*
—. Crime, fear of. Dropouts. Schools. Students. Truancies. 1970. *133*

—. Criminal justice. Friends, Society of. Peace bonds. 1680-1829. *142*
—. Dickens, Charles *(Mystery of Edwin Drood).* John Jasper (fictional character). Trials (mock). 1914. *216*
—. French and Indian War. Great Britain. Smuggling. Trade. West Indies. 1754-63. *476*
—. Negroes. Racism. Riots. Social Classes. 1830-49. *571*
Pennsylvania (Pittsburgh). Credit. Loansharking. Reform. Working Class. 1900-15. *491*
—. Railroads. Strikes. 1877. *528*
Pennsylvania (Whiskey Run). Coal Mines and Mining. Italian Americans. Murder. 1906-41. *314*
Penology (review article). Mitford, Jessica. Rehabilitation. VandenHaag, Ernest. VonHirsch, Andrew. 1960's-70's. *1356*
Periodicals. Antibiotics. Conflicts of interest. Federal regulation. Food and Drug Administration. Pharmaceutical Industry. Welch, Henry. 1959-62. *742*
Perjury. Chambers, Whittaker. Espionage. Hiss, Alger. Weinstein, Allen (review article). 1930's-50. 1978. *717*
—. Chambers, Whittaker. Espionage. Hiss, Alger. Weinstein, Allen (review article). 1936-50. 1978. *705*
—. Chambers, Whittaker. Hiss, Alger. House Committee on Un-American Activities. Lawsuits. Libel. Marbury, William L. (account). 1922-51. *735*
Perjury, possible. Ford, Gerald R. House of Representatives. Watergate Scandal. 1973-75. *632*
Perkins, Nicholas. Alabama. Arrests. Burr, Aaron. Documents. 1807. *785*
"Perry Mason" (program). Criminal justice system. "The Defenders" (program). Stereotypes. Television. Trials. 1949-78. *276*
Persecution. Charles I. Friends, Society of. Massachusetts Bay Colony. 1661. *34*
—. Illinois (Hancock County). Mobs. Mormons. Murder. Smith, Hyrum. Smith, Joseph. 1844-46. *546*
Pershing, John J. Armies. Drugs. Mexico. New Mexico (Columbus). Prostitution. Punitive expeditions. Venereal disease. 1916-17. *932*
Personal narratives. Civil War. Gilbert, William H. Prisoners of War. 1863-65. *1376*
Personality characteristics. Police. 1970's. *1090*
Petersen, Henry. Liddy, Gordon. Political ethics. Watergate Scandal. ca 1970-74. *733*
Peyote. Indians. Nevada. Religion. 1886-1972. *944*
Pharmaceutical Industry. Antibiotics. Conflicts of interest. Federal regulation. Food and Drug Administration. Periodicals. Welch, Henry. 1959-62. *742*
Philanthropy. Courts. Industrialists. Juvenile Delinquency. Middle Classes. Reform. 1890-99. *199*
Philosophy. Negroes. New York (Buffalo). Prisons. Sostre, Martin (letters). 1968-75. *1366*
Philosophy of History. Morality, public. Political Crimes. Watergate scandal. -1974. *799*
Photographs. Archives. Documents. Historiography. Theft. 1950's-78. *503*
—. Attitudes. Capital Punishment. Pennsylvania (Mansfield). 1898. *1323*
—. California (San Diego). Police. 1889-1980. *1004*
Photography, Journalistic. Calomiris, Angela. Documentaries. Federal Bureau of Investigation. New York City Photo League. 1930-51. *988*
—. Public Policy. Television. Trials. 1937-78. *1208*

Phrenological analysis. Brady, Mathew B. Daguerreotypes (engravings from). Simpson, Marmaduke B. 1846. *255*
Physicians. Editors and Editing. Murder. Sheppard, Sam. Trials. 1957-66. *338*
—. Leale, Charles Augustus. Lincoln, Abraham (death). 1865. *762*
Pia Machita (leader). Arizona. Conscription, military. Indians. Papago Indians. Political Protest. 1930-41. *673*
Pinkerton National Detective Agency. Lavigne, Frank C. Livestock. Montana Livestock Commission. Power, T. C. Rustling. 1910-25. *991*
—. Law Enforcement. 1850-1900. *1195*
Pirates. Atlantic Ocean. Social Organization. 1716-26. *204*
Plea bargaining. Alaska. Courts. Sentencing. 1970's. *1149*
—. California (Alameda County). Courts. Sentencing. 1880-1970's. *1033*
—. Coercion. Torture. Trials. ca 15c-1978. *1098*
—. Courts. Drugs. 1973-74. *1010*
—. Courts. Firearms. Michigan (Wayne County; Detroit). Sentencing. 1970's. *1062*
—. Courts. Florida (Dade County). Pretrial settlement conference. Sentencing. 1970's. *1059*
—. Courts. Sentencing. 1950-79. *1081*
—. Courts. Sentencing. 1970's. *1051*
—. Courts. Sentencing. 19c. *1052*
—. Courts. Sentencing. Texas (El Paso County). 1970's. *1000*
—. Courts. White-collar crime. 1970's. *1072*
—. Criminal law. 19c-20c. *1107*
—. Criminal Law. Lawyers (Prosecution and defense). 1968-74. *1120*
—. Great Britain. 17c-20c. *976*
—. Great Britain. Judicial Process. Law. 18c-20c. *1087*
—. Judges. Trials. 1970's. *1153*
—. Legislative branch. Sentencing. 1970's. *1013*
—. Sentencing. Trials. 1968-74. *1191*
Plea bargaining, elimination of. Felonies. Judges. 1970's. *1005*
Plymouth Colony. Capital Punishment. Fugitives. Indentured servants. Indians. Murder. Narraganset Indians. 1621-38. *367*
Poetry. Connors, John T. Humor. New York. Prisons. Sing Sing Prison. 1878-88. *1381*
Polanski, Roman. Manson, Charles. Morality. Murder. Politics. Tate, Sharon. 1969-77. *318*
Police. Adolescence. Attitudes. 1970's. *1100*
—. Alabama (Birmingham). Anti-Communist Movements. Floggings. Gelders, Joseph. Giles, G. C. Letters. 1936. *353*
—. American Federation of Labor. Armies. Streetcars. Strikes. Tennessee (Knoxville). 1919-20. *516*
—. Appellate courts. Attitudes. Evidence. *Mapp v. Ohio* (US, 1961). *Miranda v. Arizona* (US, 1966). 1961-78. *982*
—. Arrests. Behavior. Missouri (St. Louis). Organizations. Statistics. 1900-70. *1205*
—. Arrests. Men. Women. 1972. *207*
—. Arrests, false. Drug Abuse. Lawrence, Paul. Vermont (St. Albans). 1967-78. *869*
—. Assassination. Criminal investigations. District of Columbia. Lincoln, Abraham. Richards, A. C. Trials. 1865-69. *758*
—. Attitude shifts. Racial animosity, increases in. 1970's. *1182*
—. Attitudes. Barrios. California, southern. Civil Rights. Mexican Americans. Social Conditions. 1975. *171*

Political pressure. Crime statistics. Federal Bureau of Investigation (Uniform Crime Reporting Program). 1965-73. *227*
Political prisoners (review article). Germany. USA. 20c. *779*
Political prisoners, transported. Hume, Francis. Hume, George. Social History. Virginia (Yorktown). 1716-60. *1363*
Political Protest. Anti-Vietnam War movement. Civil rights. Kennedy, Jane. Oral history. Women. 1964-77. *1289*
—. Arizona. Conscription, military. Indians. Papago Indians. Pia Machita (leader). 1930-41. *673*
—. Beatty, James H. Coxey, Jacob S. Idaho. Trials. 1894. *602*
—. California (Los Angeles). Mass media. Violence. Women. 1977. *366*
—. City Politics. Integration. Missouri (St. Louis). Police. Pressure Groups. Professionalization. 1900-70. *1203*
—. Civil disobedience. 1956-72. *577*
—. Civil rights. King, Martin Luther, Jr. 1955-68. *568*
—. Defense industries. General Electric Company. Pennsylvania (King of Prussia). Rush, Molly. 1980. *586*
—. Models (nonrecursive). Police. Violence. 1960-70's. *570*
Political Reform. Congress. Watergate scandal (effects). 1972-74. *764*
—. Democratic Party. Erie Canal Ring. Governmental Investigations. New York. Tilden, Samuel J. 1868-76. *616*
Political repression. Bibliographies. 1963-81. *1154*
—. Freedom of speech. Oklahoma. Vigilantes. World War I. 1914-17. *538*
—. Radicals and Radicalism. 1919-22. *509*
Political scandals. Breckinridge, W. C. P. Democratic Party. House of Representatives. Morality. Pollard, Madeline. Sex. 1884-1904. *888*
Political Speeches. *Brandenburg* v. *Ohio* (US, 1969). Freedom of Speech. 1969-80. *939*
—. Democracy. Prohibition. Women's organizations. 1920-34. *831*
Political support. Business. Economic Conditions. Morality. Nixon, Richard M. Watergate scandal. 1969-74. *647*
Political surveillance. American Civil Liberties Union. Demonstrations. Federal Bureau of Investigation. Hoover, J. Edgar. Trade Union Education League. 1924-36. *1214*
Political Systems. Nixon, Richard M. (resignation). 1974. *770*
Political Theory. Consent (issue). Courts. Women. 1980. *396*
—. Criminal justice. Prison reforms. 1974. *206*
—. De Tocqueville, Alexis. Marx, Karl. Nixon, Richard M. Watergate Scandal. Weber, Max. 1972. *804*
—. Despotism. Pennsylvania. Prisons. Tocqueville, Alexis de. 1831. *1241*
Politics. Alabama (Eutaw). Reconstruction. Riots. Terrorism. 1870. *550*
—. Alaska (Nome). Gold. McKenzie, Alexander. Nativism. 1898-1901. *473*
—. American Revolution. Deane, Silas. Diplomacy. France. Lee, Arthur. Military Aid. 1773-89. *630*
—. Assassination, attempted. Jackson, Andrew. Lawrence, Richard. 1835. *768*
—. Baptists. Fox, George. Friends, Society of. Olney, Thomas, Jr. Rhode Island. 1672-73. *83*
—. Business. Organized Crime. 20c. *246*
—. Capital Punishment. Gilmore, Gary. Law. 1967-77. *1337*

—. Cherokee Indians. Foreman, James. South. Walker, John, Jr. (assassination). 1820's-30's. *723*
—. Cities. Race Relations. Riots. Social Conditions. 1967-69. *573*
—. Civil rights movement. Negroes. Riots. Tennessee (Columbia). Truman, Harry S. 1946. *512*
—. Constitutions. Watergate scandal. 1973-74. *622*
—. Crime rates. Law Enforcement Assistance Administration. 1967-74. *269*
—. Criminal Code Reform Act (US, 1978). Senate. 1950's-78. *1080*
—. Defendants, pro se. Morality. Social issues. Trials. 1960's-70's. *817*
—. Discrimination. Negroes. Violence. 1960-69. *57*
—. District of Columbia. Lobbying. Woman's Lobby (organization). 1970's. *32*
—. Employment. Negroes. Texas. Violence. White supremacy. 1900-10. *89*
—. Executive Power. Federal Policy. Justice. Law Enforcement. Social Conditions. 1960-79. *1124*
—. Government. Law (review article). 1940-80. *267*
—. Great Britain. Police. 1964-79. *1142*
—. Impeachment. Presidents. 1787-1979. *734*
—. Louisiana (New Orleans). Metropolitan Police Force. Negroes. Riots. Whites. 1868. *549*
—. Manson, Charles. Morality. Murder. Polanski, Roman. Tate, Sharon. 1969-77. *318*
—. Pennsylvania (Harrisburg). State Legislatures. 1870's. *695*
Politics and Media. Bernstein, Carl. Journalism (magnified role). Watergate scandal. Woodward, Bob. 1972-74. *667*
Politics of cover-up. Nixon, Richard M. Presidency. Watergate (scandal). 1972-73. *769*
Politics, popular. Federal Bureau of Investigation. Hoover, J. Edgar. Law enforcement, symbol of. Popular culture. 1908-60's. *1137*
Pollard, Henry Rives. Capitols. Coleman, William D. Editors and Editing. Shootings. Tyler, Nathaniel. Virginia (Richmond). 1866. *308*
Pollard, Madeline. Breckinridge, W. C. P. Democratic Party. House of Representatives. Morality. Political scandals. Sex. 1884-1904. *888*
Polygamy. Arizona. Law. Mormons. 1880's. *816*
—. Civil disobedience. Clawson, Rudger. Federal government. Mormons. Sharp, John. Utah. 1862-91. *510*
—. Constitutional Law. Morality. Mormons. Religious Liberty. *Reynolds* v. *United States* (US, 1878). Supreme Court. 1862-78. *836*
—. Mormons. Prisons. Utah. 1880's. *818*
Poor. Capital Punishment. Crime prevention. Discrimination. Minorities. 1972-76. *1298*
Poorhouses. Negroes. New York (Poughkeepsie). Public Records. 1282
Popular Culture. Arts. Europe. USA. Violence. 20c. *264*
—. Federal Bureau of Investigation. Hoover, J. Edgar. Law enforcement, symbol of. Politics, popular. 1908-60's. *1137*
—. Films, detective. 1940's-79. *143*
—. Frontier and Pioneer Life. Lawman (symbol). Tilghman, Bill. 1874-1924. 1979. *1065*
—. Literature. 19c-1975. *200*
—. Mass media. Myths and Symbols. Violence. ca 1700-1975. *38*
Popular Culture (underground). Literature. Metropolitan Areas. 1840-70. *938*
Population. Cities. Crime statistics. 1970's. *85*
—. Cities. Social Theory. 1970-79. *248*

—. Civil rights. Legislation. Race Relations.
Riots. Tennessee (Memphis). 1865-66. *574*
—. Property. 1947-77. *43*
Populism. Community solidarity. Erickson, Kai T.
(theory). Inverarity, James M. Justice,
repressive. Louisiana. Lynching. 1889-96.
1976. *452*
Pornography. Audiences. Films. 1960's-70's.
929
—. Censorship. Films, X-rated. Obscenity law.
Supreme Court. 1970's. *922*
—. Censorship. Obscenity. President's Commission
on Obscenity and Pornography. 1970-75. *931*
—. Feminism. Liberalism. Methodology.
President's Commission on Obscenity and
Pornography. Repression. Violence. 1970-80.
845
Post, Louis F. Alien Anarchist Act (US, 1918).
Anti-Communist Movements. Congress. Law
Enforcement. Leftism. 1919-20. *642*
Potawatomi Indians. Alcoholism. American Fur
Company. Indian-White Relations. Iowa
(Council Bluffs). Kansas. Liquor trade.
1837-49. *893*
Poultry. Gribetz, Lewis J. Jews. Law. New York
City. Walker, James J. 1888-1940. *468*
Poverty. Blackouts. Looting. New York City.
1977. *521*
—. Criminal Law. Criminologists. Social reform.
ca 1950-71. *265*
—. Ex-convicts. Unemployment Insurance.
1970-80. *15*
Power, T. C. Lavigne, Frank C. Livestock.
Montana Livestock Commission. Pinkerton
National Detective Agency. Rustling. 1910-25.
991
Powers, Caleb. Assassination. Goebel, William
Justus. Governors. 1856-99. 1910-20. *651*
Powers, Jacob. Diaries. Lynching. Montana,
central. Murphy, Con (Jack Redmond).
Outlaws. 1884-85. *1136*
Preparedness. American Defense Society. Political
Corruption. Republican Party. Wilson,
Woodrow (administration). World War I.
1915-32. *63*
Presbyterian Church. Blackburn, Gideon. Cherokee
Indians. Indians. Missions and Missionaries.
Schools. Whiskey. 1809-10. *164*
Prescott, Richard. American Revolution. 1775-1831.
1333
Prescriptions. California. Drug abuse. Medical
care. San Francisco Polydrug Project. Women.
1969-79. *841*
Preservation. Arson. 1975-81. *501*
—. Frontier and Pioneer Life. Prisons. Tennessee.
ca 1860-1979. *1260*
Presidency. Assassination. Gun control. Public
opinion. Sociopaths. 1950's-70's. *801*
—. Assassination. Secret Service. 1804-1981.
720
—. Baker, Howard. Watergate Scandal. 1972-73.
753
—. Executive privilege. Separation of powers.
Watergate briefs. 1972-73. *644*
—. Nixon, Richard M. Politics of cover-up.
Watergate (scandal). 1972-73. *769*
—. Political corruption. Watergate Scandal.
1972-73. *635*
Presidential directives. Federal Bureau of
Investigation. Political activism. 1936-53.
1186
Presidential power. Kennedy administration. Nixon,
Richard M. (administration). Political
Corruption. Watergate Scandal. 1940's-73.
669
Presidential power (limitations of). Political Ethics.
Watergate scandal. 1972. *691*

Presidents. Assassination. Mass Media. Political
change. 1950-80. *782*
—. Congress. Impeachment. 1970's. *696*
—. Historians. House Judiciary Committee.
Impeachment Inquiry. Misconduct in Office.
Woodward, C. Vann (review article). 1789-1974.
617
—. Impeachment. Politics. 1787-1979. *734*
President's Commission on Law Enforcement and
Administration of Justice. Methodology. Police
effectiveness. *Task Force Report: The Police*
(1967). 1967-75. *1127*
President's Commission on Obscenity and
Pornography. Censorship. Obscenity.
Pornography. 1970-75. *931*
—. Feminism. Liberalism. Methodology.
Pornography. Repression. Violence. 1970-80.
845
Presidial Company. Military. New Mexico (Sante
Fe). Prices. 18c. *480*
Press. Civil Rights. Communist Party. Senate
Internal Security Subcommittee. Supreme Court.
1955-59. *719*
—. Columbus *Enquirer-Sun* (newspaper). Georgia.
Harris, Julian LaRose. Ku Klux Klan
(opposition to). 1920's. *184*
—. House Commerce Committee. Legislative
investigations. Political Corruption. 1957-58.
614
—. Law and order. Murder. Political Commentary.
Riots. Smith, Joseph. 1844. *326*
—. Mental Illness (alleged). Mitchell, Martha.
Nixon, Richard M. (administration). Watergate
scandal. 1972-76. *767*
Pressure Groups. City Politics. Integration.
Missouri (St. Louis). Police. Political Protest.
Professionalization. 1900-70. *1203*
Pretrial diversion programs. Criminal Justice
System. Illinois (Urbana). Minorities. Women.
1975-77. *1041*
Pretrial settlement conference. Courts. Florida
(Dade County). Plea bargaining. Sentencing.
1970's. *1059*
Preventive detention. Alcoholism (drivers).
Highways (safety). Teenagers. 1966-72. *853*
Price fixing. Antitrust. Justice Department
(Antitrust Division). 1963-73. *472*
Prices. Brooklyn *Eagle*. Civil War. Gold. Hoaxes.
Howard, Joseph. Stock Exchange. 1864. *504*
—. Military. New Mexico (Sante Fe). Presidial
Company. 18c. *480*
Prison Association. New York. Reform.
Rehabilitation. 1844-62. *1297*
Prison guards. New York. Public employees.
Strikes. Wages. 1979. *1354*
—. New York. Strikes. 1979. *1393*
—. New York City. Public Employees. 1962-73.
1321
—. Rehabilitation. Social Problems. 1972. *1290*
Prison industries. Oklahoma. Profit. 1909-60.
1257
Prison life. Market systems. Rehabilitation. 1973.
1375
Prison reform *See also* Penal reform.
—. Attica State Prison. New York. Riots. 1971.
1323
—. Civil Rights. Justice Department. Lawsuits.
States' rights. 1961-77. *1314*
—. Courts. 1971-73. *1358*
—. Criminal justice. Hoffa, James R. (personal
narrative). 1967-73. *1300*
—. Equal rights. Integration. Women.
1820's-1900. *1280*
—. Rehabilitation. 1966-72. *1331*
Prison reforms. Criminal justice. Political theory.
1974. *206*
Prison riots. Attica State Prison. New York.
Wicker, Tom (review article). 1970's. *1347*

Prison ships. California (San Francisco). *Euphemia* (vessel). 1849-1921. *1263*

Prison system. Behavior modification. Center for Correctional Research. United Church of Christ (Commission for Racial Justice). 1974. *1255*

—. Economic inequalities. Negroes. Racism. 1960-76. *1310*

Prison system, injustices. Capitalism. Marxism. 18c-1973. *1303*

Prisoner of war camps. Civil War. Flinn, John M. Hangings, threatened. Sawyer, Henry W. 1863. *1344*

—. Germans. Labor, prison. New York, western. World War II. 1944-46. *1334*

—. New Mexico. World War II. 1942-46. *1374*

Prisoners, abuse of. Arkansas State Penitentiary. Convict lease system. Democratic administrations. 1874-96. *1231*

Prisoners (as volunteers). Civil Rights. Medical and quasimedical research. ca 1965-74. *1339*

Prisoners of War. American Revolution. Architecture. Atlee, William Augustus. Barracks. Pennsylvania (Lancaster). 1777. *1351*

—. American Revolution (personal narratives). Great Britain. Indiana. Schieffelin, Jacob. Virginia (Williamsburg). 1779-80. *1293*

—. Arkansas. Civil War (personal narratives). Fort Hindman (battle). Foster, Samuel F. 1863. *1278*

—. Arkansas. Germany. World War II. 1943-46. *1359*

—. Bull Run (2d battle). Civil War (personal narratives). Libby Prison. Parker, George Claflin. Virginia (Alexandria, Richmond). 1862. *1352*

—. Camp Pratt. Harding, George C. (memoirs). Louisiana (New Iberia). 1862. *1235*

—. Civil War. Diaries. Libby Prison. Virginia (Richmond). Wilkins, William D. 1862. *1383*

—. Civil War. Gilbert, William H. Personal narratives. 1863-65. *1376*

—. Confederate Army. Daily Life. Delaware. Fort Delaware. Purvis, Joseph Edward. 1863. *1385*

—. Employment. Germans. Minnesota. World War II. 1942-46. *1357*

—. Nebraska (Cheyenne County). World War II. 1943-46. *1373*

Prisoners of War (escapes). American Revolution. Great Britain (Millbay). Mill Prison. USA. 1777-82. *1346*

Prisoners of War (Germans). Geneva Convention. USA. World War II. 1941-45. *1318*

Prisoners' rights. New Federalism. Supreme courts, state. 1969-80. *1292*

Prisons *see also* names of individual prisons, e.g. Andersonville Prison, Attica State Prison, etc.

—. Agriculture. Convict Labor. Louisiana State Prison (Angola). Working Conditions. 1900-78. *1379*

—. Alabama. Capital Punishment. Harris, Johnny (interview). Judicial Process. Racism. 1979. *377*

—. Anamosa Reformatory. Iowa. McKean, John. 1872-74. *1394*

—. Asian Americans. Protest groups, formation of. 1974. *1252*

—. Assimilation. Indian-White Relations. 1975. *1240*

—. Attitudes. Friends, Society of. New York (Auburn). Pennsylvania. Reform. Religion. 1787-1845. *1296*

—. Authors. Literature. Negroes. Political activism. 1950's-77. *1279*

—. Barnard, Kate. Kansas State Penitentiary. Oklahoma. Reform. 1908-09. *1302*

—. Barnard, Kate. Kansas State Penitentiary. Political Corruption. Reform. Working Conditions. 1883-1909. *1301*

—. Bill of Rights. Civil Rights. 1970's. *1245*

—. Black Power. Ghettos. 1970's. *1311*

—. Blumenthal, William R. California. Jewish Committee for Personal Service in the State Institutions. Social Work. 1922. *1395*

—. Business. Maine State Prison. 1978-82. *1369*

—. California. Corrections, Department of. Folsom State Prison. 1973-74. *1392*

—. California (Alcatraz Island). Historical Sites and Parks. Indians (government relations). National Park Service. 1859-1975. *1309*

—. Capital Punishment. Construction. Ingle, Joe (interview). Legislation. Reform. Southern Coalition on Jails and Prisons. 1978. *1276*

—. Conflict and Conflict Resolution. Violence. 1960-80. *1277*

—. Congress. Employment. Huck, Winnifred Mason. Illinois. 1922-36. *1261*

—. Connors, John T. Humor. New York. Poetry. Sing Sing Prison. 1878-88. *1381*

—. Convicts (personal account). Wyoming. 1904-20. *1350*

—. Costs. Oklahoma. 1893-1909. *1258*

—. County-jail reform. Industrial Workers of the World. Kansas. 1915-20. *1317*

—. Criminal justice system. Michigan (Detroit). Ravitz, Justin C. (interview). 1972-73. *203*

—. Criminal justice system. Social conditions. 1974. *1228*

—. Despotism. Pennsylvania. Political Theory. Tocqueville, Alexis de. 1831. *1241*

—. Economic Policy. Indians (reservations). Reform. 19c. *1315*

—. Employment. Missouri (Jefferson City). 1833-99. *1319*

—. Ethnicity. Indians. Parole survival. Western States. 1972. *1387*

—. Ex-convicts (interviews). *Halfway to Somewhere* (play). Theater. Wisconsin. 1973-74. *1391*

—. Frontier and Pioneer Life. Preservation. Tennessee. ca 1860-1979. *1260*

—. Georgia. Reform. 1970's. *1291*

—. Great Britain. Social control. 1790-1930. *1365*

—. Hospitals. Sex. 1970's. *1345*

—. Illinois. State Government. 1831-1903. *1288*

—. Labor. Negroes. Tennessee. 1830-1915. *1370*

—. Labor Unions and Organizations. Public Employees. Working conditions. 1970's. *1390*

—. McKelvey, Blake (review article). Reform. 19c-20c. *1306*

—. Mississippi. Parchman Prison Farm. 1972-73. *1269*

—. Mormons. Polygamy. Utah. 1880's. *818*

—. Negroes. New York. Riker's Island Correctional Institution for Women. Women. 1978. *1368*

—. Negroes. New York (Buffalo). Philosophy. Sostre, Martin (letters). 1968-75. *1366*

—. Negroes. New York City Correctional Institution for Women. Race relations. Women. 1932-75. *1275*

—. Negroes. North Carolina. Women. 1970's. *1281*

—. Oklahoma. Reform. 1910-67. *1256*

—. Public opinion. 1790-1978. *1320*

—. Rehabilitation reforms. 1974. *1274*

—. Sentencing. 1979. *1361*

—. Social reform. 19c-20c. *1322*

—. Sociology. Violence. 1971. *1272*

—. South. 1978. *1338*

—. Statistics. Wisconsin (Waukesha County). 1901-04. *1246*

—. Tennessee. Women. 1831-1979. *1295*

—. Violence. 1969-73. *1332*

—. Utah (Salt Lake City). 1908-11. *905*
Prostitution (review article). Attitudes. Bristow,
Edward. Connelly, Mark. Davidson, Sue.
Gorham, Deborah. Great Britain. Rosen, Ruth.
Women. 1864-1920. *960*
Protection. Firearms ownership. Illinois. Models.
Sports. 1970's. *148*
Protest groups, formation of. Asian Americans.
Prisons. 1974. *1252*
Provincial Government. North Carolina. Sheriffs,
appointment of. ca 1730-76. *1202*
Provincial Legislatures. Great Britain.·
Impeachment. Maryland. Pennsylvania.
Virginia. 14c-16c. 1635-85. *701*
Psychiatry. Assassination. Gray, John P. Moral
insanity. New York State Lunatic Asylum.
Religion. Trials. 1854-86. *1196*
—. Value sets. 1975. *196*
Psychiatry (uses of). Courts. Juvenile Delinquency.
1920's-73. *105*
Psychoanalysis. Arab-Israeli conflict. Assassination.
Kennedy, Robert F. Sirhan, Sirhan B. 1948-68.
780
Psychoanalytic theory. Criminal motivation.
1916-60's. *74*
Psychology. Assassination. 1835-1975. *648*
Psychopaths. Attitudes. Films. Heroes. 1947-76.
59
Psychotherapy. Incest, father-daughter. Patriarchy.
1970's. *870*
Public Administration. Judges. Social policy.
1970's. *1038*
Public Employees. Bureaucracies. Federal
Government. Misconduct in office. 1970's.
677
—. Labor Unions and Organizations. Prisons.
Working conditions. 1970's. *1390*
—. New York. Prison guards. Strikes. Wages.
1979. *1354*
—. New York City. Prison guards. 1962-73.
1321
Public expenditures. Law enforcement, deterrence
effect of. 1969-71. *1008*
Public Finance. Cities. Police. Race. 1960-71.
1066
—. Connecticut. Law enforcement. Local
Government. New Jersey. New York. State
government. 1961-77. *1019*
Public health. Drug abuse. National Institute of
Mental Health. 1935-75. *826*
Public housing. Ohio (Cleveland). 1970's. *215*
Public Lands. Conservation movement. Federal
Policy. Lumber and Lumbering. Pacific
Northwest. Property rights. 1870's-90's. *478*
Public Opinion. Aged. Crisis, rhetoric of. 1971-75.
47
—. American Revolution. Arnold, Benedict.
Treason. 1775-83. *772*
—. Antitrust. Law Enforcement. 1890's-1970's.
160
—. Assassination. Conspiracy theory.
Historiography. Lincoln, Abraham
(assassination). Trials. 1865-67. *793*
—. Assassination. Gun control. Presidency.
Sociopaths. 1950's-70's. *801*
—. Capital Punishment. Gray, Judd. Morality.
Murder. Snyder, Ruth. Trials. Women.
1925-28. *357*
—. Censorship. Libraries. Obscenity. Supreme
Court decisions. 1973-75. *933*
—. City Politics. Police. South Carolina
(Charleston). 1880-1900. *1069*
—. Congress, Law and order. Political Parties.
Race. 1965-73. *1015*
—. Court dispositions. Law and society. 1974.
97
—. Criminal justice system. 1974. *208*

—. Democratic Party (convention). Historiography.
Illinois (Chicago). Mass media. Violence.
1968. *553*
—. Gambling. Voting and Voting Behavior.
19c-20c. *884*
—. Impeachment (presidential). Watergate scandal.
1973-74. *809*
—. Impeachment, proposed. *New York Times*
(newspaper). Nixon, Richard M. (resignation).
1973. *645*
—. Law enforcement. Violence. 1967-73. *67*
—. Mass Media. Police. Statistics. 1978. *232*
—. News stories, pretrial. 1975. *247*
—. Nixon, Richard M., administration. Political
Corruption. Watergate scandal. 1972-74.
670
—. Police. 1960-75. *151*
—. Police (image of). Washington (Seattle). 1968.
1169
—. Political Corruption. Watergate scandal.
1970-73. *740*
—. Political legitimacy. Social control. Watergate
scandal. 1973-74. *663*
—. Prisons. 1790-1978. *1320*
—. Southwest. 1973-75. *268*
Public Opinion (debate). Capital punishment.
Massachusetts (Boston). Social Reform.
1836-54. *1325*
Public Opinion (surveys). Political Corruption.
1935-73. *668*
Public places. Arrests. Cities. Law Enforcement.
1860-1980. *176*
Public Policy. Aliens, illegal. Congress. Economic
conditions. Immigration. 1978. *916*
—. Birth control. Law. Medicine and State.
19c. *868*
—. Bureaucracies. Juvenile Delinquency. State
Government. 1979. *1267*
—. Cities. Consumers. Fraud. Local government.
White-collar crime. 1970's. *997*
—. Cities. Law and Society. Police. Robberies.
1970's. *1218*
—. Cities. Police. 1970-75. *1164*
—. Court decisions (review article). Law. Social
Change. 1973. *1146*
—. Crime, predatory. Criminal justice system.
1970's. *180*
—. Crime prevention. 1960's-70's. *213*
—. Criminal justice system. Economic conditions.
Social Conditions. 18c-20c. 1970's. *61*
—. Drug abuse. Federal Government. Nixon,
Richard M. (administration). 1971-77. *823*
—. Economics. Heroin addiction. 1972. *972*
—. Gambling. State Government. Taxation.
1970's. *946*
—. Methadone treatment programs. New York
City. 1965-75. *864*
—. Photography, Journalistic. Television. Trials.
1937-78. *1208*
Public policy analysis. Local Government
(structure). North Carolina (Cumberland
County). Police agencies. 1974. *1125*
Public Policy (recommendations). Aliens, illegal.
Immigration. Mexicans. 1970's. *860*
—. Criminal justice system. 1970's. *285*
Public Records. Cities. Methodology. Police.
1880-1903. 1979. *1114*
—. Information access. Police. Privacy. 1982.
1047
—. Massachusetts (Cape Ann). Witchcraft. 1692.
258
—. Negroes. New York (Poughkeepsie).
Poorhouses. 1875. *1282*
Public relations. Entertainment industry. Federal
Bureau of Investigation. Hoover, J. Edgar.
1930's-60's. *201*
Public schools. Concentration Camps. Japanese
Americans. World War II. 1942-45. *1389*

—. Individualism. Law Enforcement. Singer, John (death). Utah (Summit County). 1979. *565*
—. Students. Teachers. 1960-78. *262*
Public services. Private sector. 1960's-73. *1009*
Publicity. Brutalization hypothesis. Capital Punishment. Life, respect for. Murder. South Carolina. 1950-63. *1316*
Publicity, pretrial. Due process. Supreme Court. Trials (criminal). 1951-75. *1025*
Publishers and Publishing. Books (editions). Forgeries. Illinois (Chicago). Libraries. Wise, Thomas. Wrenn, John. 1890-1930. *474*
Puerto Ricans. Negroes. Organized Crime. 1974. *119*
Puerto Rico. Behavior. Drugs. High schools. Youth. 1970-80. *927*
—. Violence. 1940-73. *415*
Pulitzer Prize. Cooke, Janet. Hoaxes. Minorities. Reporters and Reporting. *Washington Post* (newspaper). 1980. *185*
—. Cooke, Janet. Reporters and Reporting. 1980. *186*
Punishment. Age. 1970's. *22*
—. California. Durkheim, Emile. Social Theory. 1851-1970. *1236*
—. Georgia (Baldwin County). Law. Slaves. Trials. 1812-26. *234*
Punishment, cruel and unusual. Constitutional Amendments (8th). Courts. 1927-75. *1237*
Punitive expeditions. Armies. Drugs. Mexico. New Mexico (Columbus). Pershing, John J. Prostitution. Venereal disease. 1916-17. *932*
Puritans. Antinomian controversy. Hutchinson, Anne (criminal trial). Massachusetts (Boston). Winthrop, John. 1634-38. *747*
—. Capital Punishment (abolition). Michigan. Reform. 17c-1846. *1234*
—. Corporal punishment. Eaton, Nathaniel. Harvard University. Massachusetts (Cambridge). Trials. 1638. *387*
—. Courts. Justice, discretionary. Massachusetts. 1630-48. *140*
—. Massachusetts (Middlesex County). 17c. *69*
Purvis, Joseph Edward. Confederate Army. Daily Life. Delaware. Fort Delaware. Prisoners of War. 1863. *1385*
Puzo, Mario. Coppola, Francis Ford. *Godfather* (novel, film). Immigration. Italian-American life. 1970's. *239*

Q

Queen, Ellery. California. Chandler, Raymond. Fiction. Hammett, Dashiell. Macdonald, Ross. Villains. 1920-79. *189*
Quejo (Indian). Indian-White Relations. Nevada. 1890's-1970's. *444*

R

Race. Capital Punishment. Florida. Murder. Supreme Court. 1976-77. *1360*
—. Cities. Police. Public Finance. 1960-71. *1066*
—. Congress. Law and order. Political Parties. Public opinion. 1965-73. *1015*
—. Criminal record. Murder. Sentencing. Social Classes. 1955-77. *1029*
—. Florida. Sentencing. 1920's-78. *1193*
—. Income. Inequality. Metropolitan Areas. Violence. 1970. *298*
—. Judicial Administration. Law Enforcement. Rape. Sentencing. Social Organization. 1970-75. *1086*
—. Methodology. Sentencing. 1969-77. *1187*
—. Nationality. Negroes. 1901-70. *271*

Race (differentials, discrimination). Capital Punishment. Courts (sentencing). Negroes. -1973. *1388*
Race relations. American Revolution. North Carolina. Slave revolts. 1775-1802. *519*
—. Arizona. Gila River Relocation Center. Japanese Americans. World War II (concentration camps, public opinion). 1942-45. *1249*
—. Arkansas (Elaine). Farmers, tenant. Sharecroppers. Violence. 1919. *442*
—. Black Star Organization. NAACP. Police. South Carolina. Violence. 1975. *1181*
—. Capital Punishment. Cheatham, Mel. Mississippi (Grenada County). Murder. Tillman, James. Trials. 1889-90. *400*
—. Cities. Politics. Riots. Social Conditions. 1967-69. *573*
—. City Government. New York City. Riots. Violence. 1960-64. *579*
—. Civil rights. Legislation. Population. Riots. Tennessee (Memphis). 1865-66. *574*
—. Civil War. Louisiana (New Orleans). Reconstruction. Riots. 1862-66. *605*
—. Civil-Military Relations. Discrimination. Negroes. Texas (Rio Grande City). Violence. Whites. 1899-1900. *311*
—. Connecticut. Police-community relations. 1972-73. *1163*
—. Criminal justice system. North Carolina. School Integration. Wilmington Ten (trial). 1971-77. *393*
—. District of Columbia. Police-community relations. 1968-71. *1223*
—. Economic Conditions. Florida (Miami). Riots. Social Conditions. 1973-80. *576*
—. Economic Conditions. Negroes. Social change. Violence. 1960's. *127*
—. Florida. Law. Segregation. Social customs. 1865-1977. *236*
—. Hair, William I. Haynes, Robert V. Louisiana (New Orleans). Riots (review article). Texas (Houston). 1900-17. 1970's. *596*
—. Hollins, Jess. International Labor Defense. NAACP. Oklahoma. Rape. Trials. 1931-36. *374*
—. Infantry, black. Mutinies. Negroes. Texas (Houston). 1917. *547*
—. Ku Klux Klan. Mississippi (Meridian). Reconstruction. 1865-71. *441*
—. Law Enforcement. Reconstruction. Riots. Tennessee (Memphis). 1866. *598*
—. Local history. Violence. 1800-1920. *541*
—. Louisiana (New Orleans). Reconstruction. Riots. 1866. *604*
—. Negroes. New York City Correctional Institution for Women. Prisons. Women. 1932-75. *1275*
—. Police. Role playing. Value changes. 1970's. *1183*
—. Police-community relations. 1972-73. *1140*
—. Police-community relations. Training programs. 1960's-70's. *1046*
Race relations. Georgia (Augusta). 1970. *1396*
Racial animosity, increases in. Attitude shifts. Police. 1970's. *1182*
Racism. Alabama. Capital Punishment. Harris, Johnny (interview). Judicial Process. Prisons. 1979. *377*
—. Alabama. Military. Randolph, Ryland. Reconstruction. Trials. Tuscaloosa *Independent Monitor*. 1868. *316*
—. Alabama (Scottsboro). Historiography. Myths and Symbols. Trials. 1931-80. *266*
—. Brownmiller, Susan (review article). Men. Negroes. Rape. 1975. *319*

—. California (Oakland, San Francisco). Labor. Louisiana (New Orleans). Michigan (Detroit). Police. 1971-81. *284*
—. California (Watsonville). Depressions. Filipino Americans. Riots. Violence. 1926-30. *527*
—. Columbians, Inc. Georgia (Atlanta). Patriotism. 1946-47. *60*
—. Columbus *Enquirer-Sun* (newspaper). Georgia. Harris, Julian LaRose. Ku Klux Klan. 1920's. *230*
—. Committee for Boston. Massachusetts (Boston). Violence. White, Kevin H. 1976. *507*
—. Concentration camps. Japanese Americans. World War II. 1940-45. *1304*
—. Convict lease system. Economic Conditions. Georgia. 1868-1909. *1330*
—. Deviant Behavior. Liberalism. Looting. New York City. Political Attitudes. 1977. *526*
—. Economic inequalities. Negroes. Prison system. 1960-76. *1310*
—. Episcopal Church, Protestant. New York City. Newspapers. Riots. St. Philip's Church. Williams, Peter, Jr. 1830-50. *551*
—. Florida (LaBelle). Law Enforcement. Lynching. Rider, Herbert A. 1926. *411*
—. Genocide. Georgia (Atlanta). Negroes. 20c. *371*
—. Justice, system of. Negroes. 1975. *250*
—. Ku Klux Klan. Negroes. Reconstruction. South Carolina (up-country). Violence. 1868-71. *249*
—. Law. Negroes. Social inequalities. 1800-1974. *55*
—. Men, black. Rape. South. Women, white. 1970's. *303*
—. Mexican Americans. Sterilization. Women. 20c. *1262*
—. Negroes. Pennsylvania (Philadelphia). Riots. Social Classes. 1830-49. *571*
Racism (review article). Hair, William I. Haynes, Robert V. Martin, Charles H. South. 1900-30's. 1976. *520*
Radicals and Radicalism. Communism. Espionage. Meeropol, Michael. Meeropol, Robert. Rosenberg Case (review article). 1940's-70's. *1266*
—. Communist Party. Espionage. House Committee on Un-American Activities. Legislation. 1946-50's. *611*
—. Federal Bureau of Investigation. Hoover, J. Edgar. Surveillance. 1919-21. *1212*
—. Industrial Workers of the World. Labor Disputes. Ohio (Toledo). US Bureau of Investigation. 1918-20. *37*
—. Political repression. 1919-22. *509*
Radio. Federal regulation. Music. Payola. Television. 1930's-79. *460*
Raids. California (Los Angeles). Immigration and Naturalization Service. Industrial Relations. International Ladies' Garment Workers' Union. Lilli Diamond Originals. Mexican Americans. 1976-77. *957*
"Railroad Bill" (ballad). Folk Songs. Negroes. Whites. 1893-1980. *212*
Railroads. Agriculture. Idaho. Internment. Japanese Americans. World War II. 1900-45. *1372*
—. Burrow, Reuben Huston. Florida. Jackson, Thomas. Private detectives. Robberies. 1885-90. *403*
—. Fraud. New York & New Haven Railroad. Schuyler, Robert. Stocks and Bonds. 1844-1902. *490*
—. Government. Strikes. 1877. *532*
—. Indiana (Hangman's Crossing). Lynching. Outlaws. Reno brothers. Vigilantes. 1868. *409*

—. Marxism. Strikes. Workingmen's Party. 1877. *536*
—. Nebraska (Omaha). Robberies. Union Pacific Railroad. 1909. *428*
—. Outlaws. Robberies. Western States. 1866-1932. *484*
—. Pennsylvania (Pittsburgh). Strikes. 1877. *528*
Ralston, William Chapman. Arnold, Philip. Fraud. Mines. Slack, John. Utah. 1872. *465*
Ranchers. Agricultural Labor. Farmers. Industrial Workers of the World. Labor Disputes. Washington (Yakima Valley). 1910-36. *584*
—. Cattle. Comancheros. Hittson, John. Indians. New Mexico. Rustling. 1872-73. *564*
Randolph, Ryland. Alabama. Military. Racism. Reconstruction. Trials. Tuscaloosa *Independent Monitor*. 1868. *316*
Rape. Assault. Criminal justice system. Negroes. Robberies. 1960's-70's. *108*
—. Attitudes. 1970's. *407*
—. Attitudes. Brownmiller, Susan (review article). Feminism. 1976. *416*
—. Attitudes. Sociology. 1970's. *321*
—. Attitudes. Women's movement. 1970's. *305*
—. Behavioral differences. Defendants (sex of). Judges, male and female. 1968. *363*
—. Brownmiller, Susan (review article). 1300-1975. *412*
—. Brownmiller, Susan (review article). Men. Negroes. Racism. 1975. *319*
—. Capital Punishment. Negroes. Newspapers. Reporters and Reporting. Scottsboro Case. Trials. 1931-32. *1133*
—. Capitalism. Communist Countries. 1978. *320*
—. Hollins, Jess. International Labor Defense. NAACP. Oklahoma. Race Relations. Trials. 1931-36. *374*
—. Judicial Administration. Law Enforcement. Race. Sentencing. Social Organization. 1970-75. *1086*
—. Law. Prostitution. Social Organization. Women. 20c. *9*
—. Law (proposed). North Carolina. Research Committee on Sexual Assault. 1975-76. *334*
—. Legislation. Reform. Washington (King County). 1974-81. *1097*
—. Men, black. Racism. South. Women, white. 1970's. *303*
—. Police. 1970-75. *891*
—. Sex roles. Sterilization. Wife beating. Women. 1975-81. *439*
—. Women. 1974-80. *356*
Rape victims. Judges (attitudes). Women. 1974. *995*
Rapp, Frederick. Fraud (alleged). Owen, Robert. Pennsylvania (New Harmony). Real Estate. 1825. *455*
Rare Books. Lambdin, William. Mormons. Smith, Joseph *(Book of Commandments)*. West Virginia (Wheeling). 1830-33. *515*
Rat sheets. Advertising. Circus. 1870-1910. *506*
Ravitz, Justin C. (interview). Criminal justice system. Michigan (Detroit). Prisons. 1972-73. *203*
Reagan, Ronald. Mexican Americans. Newspapers. Panama Canal (issue). Political Campaigns (presidential). Treaties. 1976-80. *595*
Reagan, Ronald (administration). Aliens, illegal. Carter, Jimmy (administration). 1977-81. *872*
—. Task Force on Violent Crime. 1981. *402*
Real estate. Arizona. Fraud. Government. Law. Tombstone Townsite Co. 1880's. *500*
—. Fraud (alleged). Owen, Robert. Pennsylvania (New Harmony). Rapp, Frederick. 1825. *455*

—. Conscription, Military. Great Britain. Kidnapping. Massachusetts (Boston). Navies. 1747. *555*

—. Economic Conditions. Florida (Miami). Race Relations. Social Conditions. 1973-80. *576*

—. Episcopal Church, Protestant. New York City. Newspapers. Racism. St. Philip's Church. Williams, Peter, Jr. 1830-50. *551*

—. Ethnic Groups. Montana (Lewistown). Patriotism. World War I. 1917-18. *608*

—. Florida (Dade County; Liberty City). Negroes. Police. 1979-80. *531*

—. Illinois (Chicago). Militia. Police. Strikes. Wages. 1877. *601*

—. Law and order. Murder. Political Commentary. Press. Smith, Joseph. 1844. *326*

—. Law enforcement. Ohio (Niles). State government. 1924. *524*

—. Law Enforcement. Race Relations. Reconstruction. Tennessee (Memphis). 1866. *598*

—. Louisiana (New Orleans). Metropolitan Police Force. Negroes. Politics. Whites. 1868. *549*

—. Louisiana (New Orleans). Race Relations. Reconstruction. 1866. *604*

—. Negroes. Pennsylvania (Philadelphia). Racism. Social Classes. 1830-49. *571*

—. New York City. Terrorism. 1690-1980. *580*

Riots (participants, dynamics). Cities. Police departments. 1968-74. *1139*

Riots (review article). Hair, William I. Haynes, Robert V. Louisiana (New Orleans). Race Relations. Texas (Houston). 1900-17. 1970's. *596*

Risvold, Floyd (review article). Assassination. Conspiracies. Lincoln, Abraham. Trials. Weichmann, Louis J. (account). 1864-66. *792*

Robberies. Assault. Criminal justice system. Negroes. Rape. 1960's-70's. *108*

—. Burrow, Reuben Huston. Florida. Jackson, Thomas. Private detectives. Railroads. 1885-90. *403*

—. Cities. Law and Society. Police. Public Policy. 1970's. *1218*

—. Nebraska (Omaha). Railroads. Union Pacific Railroad. 1909. *428*

—. Outlaws. Railroads. Western States. 1866-1932. *484*

—. Victims. 1947-77. *461*

Robberies, attempted. Brown, Henry. Kansas (Caldwell). Law Enforcement. Lynching. Medicine Valley Bank. Murder. 1881-84. *306*

Robbers' Roost (hideout). Coe, William. Colorado, southeastern. New Mexico, northeastern. Outlaws. ca 1867-68. *260*

Role playing. Police. Race Relations. Value changes. 1970's. *1183*

Roman Empire. Capital Punishment. Ecclesiastical law. Great Britain. Massachusetts. 17c. *1057*

Roosevelt, Franklin D. Assassination. Cermak, Anton. Florida (Miami). Zangara, Giuseppe. 1933. *658*

—. Assassination, attempted. Florida (Miami). Zangara, Giuseppe. 1933. *771*

—. Civil Rights. Federal Bureau of Investigation. 1936-80. *986*

Roosevelt, Theodore. Barnes, William, Jr. Bossism. Lawsuits. New York. Republican Party. 1915. *629*

Roque Lovato Grant. Land grants. New Mexico. Ortiz y Alarid, Gasper. 1785-1894. *463*

Rosen, Ruth. Attitudes. Bristow, Edward. Connelly, Mark. Davidson, Sue. Gorham, Deborah. Great Britain. Prostitution (review article). Women. 1864-1920. *960*

Rosenberg case. Atomic Energy Commission. Espionage. Federal Bureau of Investigation. Greenglass, David. Nuclear Arms. Trials. 1942-74. *738*

—. Atomic Energy Commission. Greenglass, David. Nuclear Science and Technology. Secrecy. Trials. 1945-51. *613*

—. Cold War. Espionage. Nuclear Arms. Supreme Court. 1953. *1131*

—. Cold War. Espionage. Trials. 1951-53. *686*

Rosenberg Case (review article). Communism. Espionage. Meeropol, Michael. Meeropol, Robert. Radicals and Radicalism. 1940's-70's. *1266*

Ross, Edmund. Attitudes. Impeachment. Johnson, Andrew. Letters. Republican Party. 1867-68. *626*

Ross, Tom. Cattle Raising. Good, Milt. Murder. Rustlers. Texas (Seminole). 1923-29. *399*

Rossum, Ralph A. Criminal Law. Judicial Administration (review article). Levin, Martin A. Mather, Lynn M. Negroes. Uhlman, Thomas M. 1960's-70's. *104*

Rothman, David J. (review article). Mental institutions. Penal reform. Progressivism. ca 1900-15. 1980. *1239*

Rudowitz, Christian Ansoff. Extradition. Foreign Relations. Illinois (Chicago). Refugees. Russia. 1908-09. *86*

Rule-breaking. Arrest rates. Boarding schools. Indians. 1976. *122*

Rural-Urban Studies. California. Social Conditions. Violence. 1955-75. *330*

—. Women. 1962-75. *251*

Rush, Molly. Defense industries. General Electric Company. Pennsylvania (King of Prussia). Political Protest. 1980. *586*

Russell, Francis. Historiography (revisionist). Sacco, Nicola. Tresca, Carlo. Trials. Vanzetti, Bartolomeo. 1920-43. *397*

Russia. Extradition. Foreign Relations. Illinois (Chicago). Refugees. Rudowitz, Christian Ansoff. 1908-09. *86*

Rustlers. Cattle Raising. Good, Milt. Murder. Ross, Tom. Texas (Seminole). 1923-29. *399*

Rustling. Cattle. Comancheros. Hittson, John. Indians. New Mexico. Ranchers. 1872-73. *564*

—. Cattle. Mexico. Navies. *Rio Bravo* (vessel). Rio Grande. Texas. 1840's-79. *487*

—. Lavigne, Frank C. Livestock. Montana Livestock Commission. Pinkerton National Detective Agency. Power, T. C. 1910-25. *991*

S

Sacco, Nicola. Historiography (revisionist). Russell, Francis. Tresca, Carlo. Trials. Vanzetti, Bartolomeo. 1920-43. *397*

Sacco-Vanzetti Case. Bibliographies. Fiction. Nonfiction. 1920-27. *310*

Sacco-Vanzetti trial. Trials. 1920-21. *1152*

St. Louis *Observer* (newspaper). Abolition movement. Illinois (Alton). Lovejoy, Elijah P. (murder). Missouri (St. Louis). Violence. 1833-37. *299*

St. Philip's Church. Episcopal Church, Protestant. New York City. Newspapers. Racism. Riots. Williams, Peter, Jr. 1830-50. *551*

Salisbury Prison. Civil War (prisoners and prisons) (diaries). Eberhart, James W. North Carolina. Virginia. 1864-65. *1336*

San Francisco Polydrug Project. California. Drug abuse. Medical care. Prescriptions. Women. 1969-79. *841*

Social Organization. Atlantic Ocean. Pirates.
1716-26. *204*
—. City Politics. Police. 1820's-1910's. *1094*
—. Criminal law. Justice. Massachusetts.
Prosecutions. South Carolina. 1767-1878.
1064
—. Hutchinson, Anne. Massachusetts Bay Colony.
Trials. 1637. *806*
—. Judicial Administration. Law Enforcement.
Race. Rape. Sentencing. 1970-75. *1086*
—. Law. Prostitution. Rape. Women. 20c.
9
Social policy. American Plan. Council of National
Defense. Federal government. Prostitution.
Venereal disease. Voluntary associations. World
War I. 1917-21. *917*
—. Judges. Public Administration. 1970's. *1038*
Social Problems. Aged. Crime, fear of. 1970-80.
282
—. City Life. Virginia (Hopewell). 1915-18.
52
—. Criminal Law. "Dangerous" people. 1776-1976.
174
—. Democracy. National goals. 1973. *31*
—. Drug abuse. National Commission on
Marihuana and Drug Abuse (Schafer
Commission). 1975. *889*
—. Gambling. Legalization. 1975. *846*
—. Individualism. Law enforcement. 1970-80.
983
—. Opium. 1700-1974. *970*
—. Prison guards. Rehabilitation. 1972. *1290*
—. Wife beating. 1970's. *429*
Social Psychology. Brown, John. Civil War
(antecedents). Harpers Ferry raid. North
Carolina. Slavery. 1859-60. *513*
—. Crime control. 1960's-70's. *147*
Social Reform. Business. City Politics. Louisiana
(New Orleans). Prostitution. Voting and Voting
Behavior. 1851-58. *950*
—. California (San Francisco). City Government.
Progressivism. Prostitution. 1910-14. *937*
—. Capital punishment. Massachusetts (Boston).
Public Opinion (debate). 1836-54. *1325*
—. Criminal code, federal. Law Reform.
1960's-70's. *128*
—. Criminal Law. Criminologists. Poverty. ca
1950-71. *265*
—. Girls. Juvenile Delinquency. Massachusetts
(Lancaster). Socialization. State Industrial
School for Girls. 1856-1905. *1244*
—. Law Enforcement. Montana (Bozeman, Gallatin
counties). 1893-1918. *992*
—. Prisons. 19c-20c. *1322*
—. Prisons (grievance procedures). 1974. *1364*
—. Prostitution. 1870-1920. *855*
Social science, pure and policy. Criminal justice and
education. 1956-73. *145*
Social sciences. Court records (access to). Evidence.
Law. Research. 1970's. *1030*
Social Status. 1934-79. *24*
—. District courts. Sentencing. White-collar crime.
1974-77. *471*
—. Drug abuse. Street status. Youth. 1969-73.
854
Social Theory. California. Durkheim, Emile.
Punishment. 1851-1970. *1236*
—. Cities. Population. 1970-79. *248*
—. Criminology. Marxism. 1969-74. *286*
—. Deviant Behavior. Drug Abuse. Youth.
1972-79. *966*
—. Murder. Verkko, Veli. Women. 1951-79.
438
Social Theory (empirical, normative). Crime, causes
of. Law Reform. 1750-1934. *68*
Social Work. Blumenthal, William R. California.
Jewish Committee for Personal Service in the
State Institutions. Prisons. 1922. *1395*

—. Juvenile delinquency. New York. 1980. *1225*
Socialist Party. Bombings. California (San
Francisco). Mooney, Tom. San Quentin Prison.
Trials. 1916-42. *154*
Socialization. Girls. Juvenile Delinquency.
Massachusetts (Lancaster). Social Reform.
State Industrial School for Girls. 1856-1905.
1244
Society for the Prevention of Cruelty to Children.
Child abuse. New York City. 1820's-80's.
420
Sociology. Attitudes. Rape. 1970's. *321*
—. Prisons. Violence. 1971. *1272*
Sociopaths. Assassination. Gun control. Presidency.
Public opinion. 1950's-70's. *801*
Sodomy. Attitudes. Court records. Law
Enforcement. New England. 1630-80. *911*
Somers (vessel). Capital Punishment. Courts
Martial and Courts of Inquiry. MacKenzie,
Alexander Slidell. Mutinies (suspected). Navies.
1841-43. *179*
Sostre, Martin (letters). Negroes. New York
(Buffalo). Philosophy. Prisons. 1968-75.
1366
South. Ames, Jessie Daniel. Association of Southern
Women for the Prevention of Lynching.
Lynching. Women. 1928-42. *381*
—. Capital Punishment. Discrimination. Judicial
Process. Lynching. 1978. *1313*
—. Cherokee Indians. Foreman, James. Politics.
Walker, John, Jr. (assassination). 1820's-30's.
723
—. Country Life. Murder. Negroes. Religion.
Whites. 1916-20. *436*
—. Courts. Criminal law. Legislatures. Slave
trials. ca 1820-64. *76*
—. Hair, William I. Haynes, Robert V. Martin,
Charles H. Racism (review article). 1900-30's.
1976. *520*
—. Jefferson, Thomas (nephews). Merrill, Boynton,
Jr. (review article). Violence. 19c. 1976.
445
—. Ku Klux Klan. Violence. 1979. *65*
—. Law. Liability. Slavery. 1771-1858. *181*
—. Men, black. Racism. Rape. Women, white.
1970's. *303*
—. Mormons. Violence. 1884-1905. *410*
—. Prisons. 1978. *1338*
South Carolina. Black Star Organization. NAACP.
Police. Race Relations. Violence. 1975. *1181*
—. Brewer, John. Hanawalt, Barbara A. Hindus,
Michael S. Koehler, Lyle. Northeastern or
North Atlantic States. Styles, John. 17c-1878.
113
—. Brutalization hypothesis. Capital Punishment.
Life, respect for. Murder. Publicity. 1950-63.
1316
—. Courts. Criminal prosecution. Negroes.
1800-60. *111*
—. Criminal law. Justice. Massachusetts.
Prosecutions. Social Organization. 1767-1878.
1064
—. Duels. Social Customs. 1812-80. *376*
South Carolina (Charleston). City Politics. Police.
Public Opinion. 1880-1900. *1069*
South Carolina (up-country). Ku Klux Klan.
Negroes. Racism. Reconstruction. Violence.
1868-71. *249*
Southern Coalition on Jails and Prisons. Capital
Punishment. Construction. Ingle, Joe
(interview). Legislation. Prisons. Reform.
1978. *1276*
Southern Conference Educational Fund Inc.
Anti-Communist Movements. Louisiana (New
Orleans). School Integration. Senate Internal
Security Subcommittee. Williams, Aubrey W.
1954. *774*
Southwest. Public Opinion. 1973-75. *268*

—. Behavior. Bomb threats. Mass media. 1966-80. *158*
—. Black Liberation Army. Boudin, Kathy. Leftism. Weather Underground. 1967-81. *659*
—. Brown, John. Harpers Ferry raid. West Virginia. 1859. *548*
—. Civil aviation, international. USA. 1960-76. *457*
—. Democratic society. Marxism. -1973. *115*
—. Freedom of the Press. Law Enforcement. Mass Media. 1968-78. *11*
—. Industrialization. 1945-78. *688*
—. Mass Media. Police. 1970's. *6*
—. Military. Oklahoma, University of. Police. Simulation and Games. 1970's. *1166*
—. New York City. Riots. 1690-1980. *580*
Terrorism (worldwide). -1973. *259*
Texas. Arizona. Myths and Symbols. Outlaws. Ringo, John. 1864-82. *33*
—. Assimilation. Feinberg, Siegmund. Jews. Schwartz, Benedict. 1857. *358*
—. Brenham fire. Military Occupation. Reconstruction. Sheridan, Philip A. 1865-70. *485*
—. California, southern. Immigration. Mexico. Operation Wetback. 1950-74. *930*
—. Cattle. Mexico. Navies. *Rio Bravo* (vessel). Rio Grande. Rustling. 1840's-79. *487*
—. Conspiracy. Foreign Relations. Mexico. Revolutionary Movements. Reyes, Bernardo. State Politics. Trials. 1911-12. *693*
—. Employment. Negroes. Politics. Violence. White supremacy. 1900-10. *89*
—. Indian Wars. Kiowa Indians (chiefs). Legal status. Sherman, William Tecumseh. 1871-78. 1963. *193*
Texas (Austin). Slavery. Vigilantism. 1840-60. *132*
Texas (Dallas). City Life. Geographic Mobility. Suburbanization. 1956-76. *125*
Texas, eastern. Brotherhood of Timber Workers. Emerson, Arthur L. Industrial Workers of the World. Labor Disputes. Louisiana, western. Lumber and Lumbering. 1900-16. *535*
Texas (El Paso). Baker, Newton D. Liquor. Military training. Prostitution. War Department. World War I. 1917-18. *834*
—. Boundaries. Federalism. Law Enforcement (local). Mexico (Juarez). 1970's. *1003*
Texas (El Paso County). Courts. Plea bargaining. Sentencing. 1970's. *1000*
Texas (Gainesville). Capital Punishment. Confederate States of America. Trials. Unionists. 1862. *597*
Texas (Houston). Hair, William I. Haynes, Robert V. Louisiana (New Orleans). Race Relations. Riots (review article). 1900-17. 1970's. *596*
—. Infantry, black. Mutinies. Negroes. Race Relations. 1917. *547*
—. Police. 1960-76. *1007*
Texas (Rio Grande City). Civil-Military Relations. Discrimination. Negroes. Race Relations. Violence. Whites. 1899-1900. *311*
Texas (Seminole). Cattle Raising. Good, Milt. Murder. Ross, Tom. Rustlers. 1923-29. *399*
Textile Industry. Immigrants. Industrial Workers of the World. New Jersey (Paterson). Strikes. Violence. 1913. *588*
Theater. Ex-convicts (interviews). *Halfway to Somewhere* (play). Prisons. Wisconsin. 1973-74. *1391*
Theaters. Prostitution. 19c. *882*
Theft *See also* Robberies.
—. Archives. Documents. Historiography. Photographs. 1950's-78. *503*

—. Capital Punishment. Illinois (Blue Island, Chicago). Murder. Staub, Albert. Swiss Americans. 1857-58. *346*
Theology. Business community. Ethics. Mormons. Watergate scandal. 1974. *808*
—. Capital punishment. Mormons. Utah. 1843-1978. *1283*
Thompson, David (account). California. Law Enforcement. Prohibition. Winemaking. 1930. *953*
Tilden, Samuel J. Democratic Party. Erie Canal Ring. Governmental Investigations. New York. Political Reform. 1868-76. *616*
Tilghman, Bill. Frontier and Pioneer Life. Lawman (symbol). Popular culture. 1874-1924. 1979. *1065*
Tillman, James. Capital Punishment. Cheatham, Mel. Mississippi (Grenada County). Murder. Race Relations. Trials. 1889-90. *400*
Tobacco. Dark Tobacco District Planters Protective Association of Kentucky and Tennessee. Kentucky. Marketing. Tennessee (Robertson County). 1904-13. *544*
Tocqueville, Alexis de. Despotism. Pennsylvania. Political Theory. Prisons. 1831. *1241*
Tokyo Rose (Iva Toguri d'Aquino). Citizenship. Ford, Gerald R. Hada, John. Japanese American Citizens League. Pardons. Uyeda, Clifford I. (account). 1973-77. *795*
Tombstone Townsite Co. Arizona. Fraud. Government. Law. Real estate. 1880's. *500*
Torture. Coercion. Plea bargaining. Trials. ca 15c-1978. *1098*
Tourgée, Albion W. Anti-lynching law of 1894. Law Reform. Ohio. Smith, Harry C. 1890-96. *1284*
Tourist business. Chinatowns. Vice. 1865-1920. *896*
Town-prison relations. Illinois. Prisons (minimum-security). Reform. Vienna Correctional Center. 1971-75. *1307*
Towns. Frontier and Pioneer Life. Kansas. Law Enforcement. Morality. Prostitution. 1868-85. *894*
Trade. French and Indian War. Great Britain. Pennsylvania (Philadelphia). Smuggling. West Indies. 1754-63. *476*
Trade Union Education League. American Civil Liberties Union. Demonstrations. Federal Bureau of Investigation. Hoover, J. Edgar. Political surveillance. 1924-36. *1214*
Training programs. Police-community relations. Race relations. 1960's-70's. *1046*
Trans-Mississippi West. Prostitution. Social Conditions. Women. 1850-1900. *962*
Treason. American Revolution. Arnold, Benedict. Public Opinion. 1775-83. *772*
—. American Revolution. Capital Punishment. Connecticut (Hartford, Waterbury). Dunbar, Moses. Great Britain. Military Service (enlistees). 1777. *704*
—. Bright, Jesse D. Civil War. Indiana. Senate. 1861-62. *655*
—. Burr, Aaron. Old Southwest. Trials. 1782-1836. *788*
—. Chambers, Whittaker. Communist Party. Espionage. Hiss, Alger. Research. Weinstein, Allen (review article). 1920's-78. *708*
—. Communism. Courts. Hiss, Alger. 1948-51. *283*
Treason (alleged). Burr, Aaron. Conspiracies. Trials. Wilkinson, James. 1783-1836. *694*
—. Chase, Samuel. Fries, John. Pennsylvania. *United States* v. *John Fries* (US, 1800). 1799-1805. *665*
Treaties. Mexican Americans. Newspapers. Panama Canal (issue). Political Campaigns (presidential). Reagan, Ronald. 1976-80. *595*

Treblinka (concentration camp). Citizenship. Fedorenko, Feodor. War crimes. World War II. 1942-79. *210*

Trefousse, Hans L. (review article). Impeachment. Johnson, Andrew. Reconstruction. 1865-68. 1975. *751*

Tresca, Carlo. Historiography (revisionist). Russell, Francis. Sacco, Nicola. Trials. Vanzetti, Bartolomeo. 1920-43. *397*

Trials. Abbe, Charles E. Florida. Grismer, Karl H. Murder. Sara Sota Vigilance Committee. 1884-86. *375*

—. Alabama. Military. Racism. Randolph, Ryland. Reconstruction. Tuscaloosa *Independent Monitor.* 1868. *316*

—. Alabama (Birmingham). Baxley, William. Bombings. Chambliss, Robert. Murder. State Government. 1963-78. *384*

—. Alabama (Scottsboro). Historiography. Myths and Symbols. Racism. 1931-80. *266*

—. Anti-Catholicism. Anti-Irish sentiments. Cheverus, Jean Louis Lefebvre de. Lyon, Marcus (murder). Massachusetts (Northampton). 1805-06. *312*

—. Anti-Radicals. Ashburn, George W. (murder). Georgia. Reconstruction. 1868. *317*

—. Arizona (Solomonville). Juries (fixed). McIntosh, Otis. Murder. 1902. *45*

—. Assassination. Capital Punishment. Garfield, James A. Guiteau, Charles. 1881-82. *789*

—. Assassination. Conspiracies. Lincoln, Abraham. Risvold, Floyd (review article). Weichmann, Louis J. (account). 1864-66. *792*

—. Assassination. Conspiracy. Lincoln, Abraham. Mental Illness (alleged). Weichmann, Louis J. 1865. 1895. *556*

—. Assassination. Conspiracy theory. Historiography. Lincoln, Abraham (assassination). Public opinion. 1865-67. *793*

—. Assassination. Criminal investigations. District of Columbia. Lincoln, Abraham. Police. Richards, A. C. 1865-69. *758*

—. Assassination. Criminal investigations. Historiography. Lincoln, Abraham. Stanton, Edwin M. 1865-1980. *631*

—. Assassination. Gray, John P. Moral insanity. New York State Lunatic Asylum. Psychiatry. Religion. 1854-86. *1196*

—. Assassination. Lincoln, Abraham. Surratt, Mary. Weichmann, Louis J. Witnesses. 1865. *681*

—. Atomic Energy Commission. Espionage. Federal Bureau of Investigation. Greenglass, David. Nuclear Arms. Rosenberg case. 1942-74. *738*

—. Atomic Energy Commission. Greenglass, David. Nuclear Science and Technology. Rosenberg case. Secrecy. 1945-51. *613*

—. Attitudes. Individualism. Literature. Murder. 1920-29. *304*

—. Beatty, James H. Coxey, Jacob S. Idaho. Political Protest. 1894. *602*

—. Bench trials. 1607-1950. *1190*

—. Bombings. California (San Francisco). Mooney, Tom. San Quentin Prison. Socialist Party. 1916-42. *154*

—. Borden, Lizzie. Massachusetts. Murder. 1890-1927. *355*

—. Burr, Aaron. Conspiracies. Treason (alleged). Wilkinson, James. 1783-1836. *694*

—. Burr, Aaron. Old Southwest. Treason. 1782-1836. *788*

—. California. Frank, Leo. Georgia. Jews. Progressivism. 1913-15. *341*

—. California. San Quentin Six. 1974. *1312*

—. California (Wheatland). Industrial Workers of the World. Migrant Labor. State Government. Strikes. 1913-17. *522*

—. Cameras. Florida. Herman, Mark. Mass Media. Supreme courts, state. Zamora, Ronney. 1977-79. *1012*

—. Capital Punishment. Cheatham, Mel. Mississippi (Grenada County). Murder. Race Relations. Tillman, James. 1889-90. *400*

—. Capital Punishment. Confederate States of America. Texas (Gainesville). Unionists. 1862. *597*

—. Capital Punishment. Gilmore, Gary. Rhetoric. 1976-77. *1247*

—. Capital Punishment. Gray, Judd. Morality. Murder. Public Opinion. Snyder, Ruth. Women. 1925-28. *357*

—. Capital Punishment. Negroes. Newspapers. Rape. Reporters and Reporting. Scottsboro Case. 1931-32. *1133*

—. Carmack, Edward Ward. Cooper, Duncan J. Cooper, Robin. Murder. Patterson, Malcolm. Prohibition. Tennessee (Nashville). 1888-1909. *368*

—. Chambers, Whittaker. Communist Party. Espionage. Hiss, Alger. 1934-49. *707*

—. Civil rights. Little, Joan. Murder (alleged). North Carolina (Beaufort County). Paul, Jerry. 1974-78. *288*

—. Civil War. Kautz, August V. (reminiscences). Lincoln conspirators. 1865. *654*

—. Coal miners. Lattimer Massacre. Martin, James. Pennsylvania. Slovak Americans. Strikes. 1897-98. *408*

—. Coercion. Plea bargaining. Torture. ca 15c-1978. *1098*

—. Cold War. Espionage. Rosenberg case. 1951-53. *686*

—. Communist Workers Party. Demonstrations. Ku Klux Klan. Murder. Nazism. North Carolina (Greensboro). 1979-80. *354*

—. Communist Workers Party. Ku Klux Klan. Law Enforcement. Murder. National Socialist White People's Party. North Carolina (Greensboro). 1979-80. *392*

—. Conspiracy. Foreign Relations. Mexico. Revolutionary Movements. Reyes, Bernardo. State Politics. Texas. 1911-12. *693*

—. Corporal punishment. Eaton, Nathaniel. Harvard University. Massachusetts (Cambridge). Puritans. 1638. *387*

—. Criminal justice system. "The Defenders" (program). "Perry Mason" (program). Stereotypes. Television. 1949-73. *276*

—. Defendants, pro se. Morality. Politics. Social issues. 1960's-70's. *817*

—. Dodge, William H. McGuire, James. Murder. Nebraska (Nebraska City). 1874-76. *425*

—. Dounton, William. Jailkeepers. Massachusetts (Salem). Witchcraft. 1692. *1382*

—. Editors and Editing. Murder. Physicians. Sheppard, Sam. 1957-66. *338*

—. Feuerlicht, Roberta Strauss. Massachusetts. Murder. Vanzetti, Bartolomeo. 1920. *329*

—. Georgia (Baldwin County). Law. Punishment. Slaves. 1812-26. *234*

—. Georgia (DeKalb, Hancock, Lincoln, and Putnam Counties). Slave code. 1819-58. *62*

—. Godfrey, John. Massachusetts. Social Conditions. Witchcraft. 1634-75. *660*

—. *Herbert Fuller* (vessel). Murder. New England. 19c. *389*

—. Hiss, Alger. Nixon, Richard M. ca 1945-75. *633*

—. Historiography (revisionist). Russell, Francis. Sacco, Nicola. Tresca, Carlo. Vanzetti, Bartolomeo. 1920-43. *397*

—. Hollins, Jess. International Labor Defense. NAACP. Oklahoma. Race Relations. Rape. 1931-36. *374*

AUTHOR INDEX